Excel Models for Business and Operations Management

Second Edition

About the author

Dr Barlow holds degrees in mathematics, computer science, and mechanical engineering. As well as extensive teaching experience – previously at the Universities of Cape Town, South Africa and Wollongong, Australia – he has held various positions in computer consultancy and the petroleum industry. He has published numerous papers in the areas of computer applications and systems management.

Excel Models for Business and Operations Management

Second Edition

John F. Barlow

John Wiley & Sons, Ltd

Other Wiley Editorial Offices

John Wiley & Sons Inc., 111 River Street, Hoboken, NJ 07030, USA

Jossey-Bass, 989 Market Street, San Francisco, CA 94103-1741, USA

Wiley-VCH Verlag GmbH, Boschstr. 12, D-69469 Weinheim, Germany

John Wiley & Sons Australia Ltd, 33 Park Road, Milton, Queensland 4064, Australia

John Wiley & Sons (Asia) Pte Ltd, 2 Clementi Loop #02-01, Jin Xing Distripark, Singapore 129809

John Wiley & Sons Canada Ltd, 22 Worcester Road, Etobicoke, Ontario, Canada M9W 1L1

Wiley also publishes its books in a variety of electronic formats. Some content that appears in print
may not be available in electronic books.

Library of Congress Cataloging-in-Publication Data

Barlow, John F.
      Excel models for business and operations management / John F. Barlow.– 2nd ed.
         p.   cm.
      ISBN-13 978-0-470-01509-4
      ISBN-10 0-470-01509-8
      1. Microsoft Excel (Computer file)   2. Business–Mathematical models–
Computer programs.   3. Business–Decision making–Mathematical models–
Computer programs.   I. Title.

      HF5548.4.M523B37   2005
      658′. 05554—dc22   2005003239

British Library Cataloguing in Publication Data

A catalogue record for this book is available from the British Library

ISBN-13 978-0-470-01509-4
ISBN-10 0-470-01509-8 (PB)

Typeset in 10/12pt Times by TechBooks, New Delhi, India
Printed and bound in Great Britain by Biddles Ltd, King's Lynn,
This book is printed on acid-free paper responsibly manufactured from sustainable forestry
in which at least two trees are planted for each one used for paper production.

To Mary
and 'the Gang of 4'

Contents

Preface   xiii

1   A systems view of business   1

Overview   1
A systems view of business operations   2
A manufacturing business model   3
Finance and cost accounting   3
The marketing function   5
The production function   5
Management decision-making   12
Enterprise resource planning (ERP)   15
References and further reading   16

2   Model-building tools   17

Overview   17
Modelling characteristics   18
Risk and uncertainty in decision-making   20
Linear programming (LP)   21
Using Excel's 'Analysis ToolPak'   26
Statistical methods   27
Decision analysis   34
Simulation   42
Excel functions used in model-building   46
Exercises   49
References and further reading   51

PART 1   BUSINESS MODELS   **53**

3   Financial models   **55**

Overview   55
Financial statements   56
Ratio analysis   56
Net present value (NPV)   59
Investment appraisal   61
Portfolio management   64
Capital budgeting using decision trees   68
Cash flow analysis   69
Investment financing: a simulation model   74
Financial planning   78
Commercial add-in products for Excel   82
Excel functions used in model-building   82
Exercises   86
References and further reading   88

4   Investment analysis models   **89**

Overview   89
Risk preference attitudes   90
Utility theory   91
Portfolio theory: the Markowitz model   94
Portfolio analysis: the efficient frontier   97
Single index model (SIM)   101
The capital asset pricing model (CAPM)   106
Bond valuation   108
Duration and bond volatility   113
The Black–Scholes option pricing model   117
Excel functions used in model-building   120
Exercises   124
References and further reading   126

5   Worksheet applications in cost accounting   **127**

Overview   127
Cost-volume-profit analysis   128
Depreciation   130
Equipment replacement   132
Statistical replacement analysis   136
Simulation model for replacement/repairs   140
Comparison between simulation and statistical results   144
Budgeting   144

Job costing   150
The learning curve   155
Checking the accuracy of learning curves   158
Excel functions used in model-building   160
Exercises   163
References and further reading   166

6   Marketing models   **167**

Overview   167
Organising and presenting data   167
Correlation analysis and linear regression   170
Forecasting – time series and exponential smoothing   174
Forecasting – exponential smoothing   178
Salesforce models   186
Goal programming   190
Excel functions used in model-building   200
Exercises   201
References and further reading   205

7   Purchase order processing: a database application   **206**

Overview   206
Creating a simple macro   207
Purchase order processing   209
Creating the title screen   210
Products and suppliers worksheets   214
Creating the purchase order form   215
Creating the database and its associated macros   219
Macros for transferring data into the database   221
Adding macros to buttons   224
Amending purchase orders   225
Printing purchase orders   230
Protecting the POP database application   232
Excel functions used in model-building   236
Exercises   237
References and further reading   239

PART 2   MODELS FOR OPERATIONS MANAGEMENT   **241**

8   Statistical applications in quality control   **243**

Overview   243
Probability distributions   244
Acceptance sampling   249

Estimation – drawing conclusions from samples   253
Hypothesis testing – checking out a claim!   257
Analysis of variance (ANOVA)   258
Statistical process control   263
Excel functions used in model-building   272
Exercises   275
References and further reading   278

9   Inventory control models   **279**

Overview   279
Glossary of inventory terms   280
Characteristics of inventory models   281
Deterministic models   282
Production order quantity model   284
Inventory models with constraints   291
Probabilistic models   293
Inventory control: a simulation approach   304
Material requirements planning   307
Lot-sizing methods   315
Just-in-time (JIT) approach to inventory management   318
Excel functions used in model-building   318
Exercises   319
References and further reading   323

10 Models for production operations   **324**

Overview   324
Logistics models   325
Other network flow applications   331
Production planning and scheduling   339
Queuing models   353
Excel functions used in model-building   362
Exercises   364
References and further reading   369

11 Project management   **370**

Overview   370
Project management techniques   371
The project network   371
Simulation model for project management   392
Exercises   396
References and further reading   399

Appendix   Excel refresher notes   **400**

Basic Excel commands   400
Drawing charts with ChartWizard   405
Object linking and embedding (OLE)   407

Index   409

Preface

The popularity of spreadsheets in both academia and the business world has increased considerably over the past six years. Microsoft's Office, which includes Excel as a core element, is now one of the most widely used software products around. It is therefore no surprise to see that Office has undergone several revisions since the first edition of this textbook was published. The objective of the new edition, however, remains the same: to help readers develop their own worksheet (Excel's term for a spreadsheet) models.

The book takes a structured view of management decision-making by integrating the activities of a manufacturing organisation. Everyday examples from finance, marketing, and operations management form the basis of the book's 'hands-on' development models. The text is entirely assignment-based and uses Microsoft's Excel software to develop over eighty models. As in the previous edition, the emphasis is on the practical implementation of real-world models rather than traditional theoretical concepts. The book's active learning approach encourages the reader to focus on developing skills in 'how' to build a model while summarising the mathematical logic as to 'why' the model is so constructed.

The book's primary objective is to help the reader 'put theory into practice'. In order to create an effective spreadsheet, a student must understand what variables should be included and what relationship exists between the variables, i.e., the model's formulation. Allowing students to think through the question of 'why' a model is built in a particular way helps to increase analytical skills. If students are encouraged to use their own initiative through groundwork assignments and class discussions, they are better placed to transfer decision-making and problem-solving skills into the workplace.

The book's format is subject-focused following standard business/operations management texts. The mathematical concepts of management science/operations research provide the tools for model building. There are two introductory chapters, the first showing how the book's chapter topics are interrelated while the second chapter explains the main model-building techniques that are used throughout the book. The rest of the book's nine chapters are divided into two main parts, each containing models for business and operations management respectively. End-of-chapter assignments (with answers) allow the student to develop their analytical skills by (i) modifying existing models, and (ii) building new applications.

The text is ideally suited to business studies, finance, accounting, and operations management courses which offer practical computing skills as an integral part of the course syllabus. Models that are developed cover the areas of finance, accounting, marketing and forecasting, statistical quality control, logistics and distribution, production planning, job scheduling and sequencing, inventory control including material requirements planning (MRP), and project management. In addition, a chapter is devoted entirely to the development of an internal database application using Excel's Visual Basic for Applications (VBA) language. This chapter includes a complete listing of the eleven macros used to build the purchase order processing (POP) system.

Formulae templates for all models are provided throughout the text. While it is assumed that the reader is already familiar with Excel's basic concepts, brief refresher notes are included as an appendix. Where Excel's functions are introduced for the first time, a full description for each function is given at the end of the relevant chapter. For readers who want to pursue the mathematical techniques behind specific models in greater depth, a bibliography is provided at the end of each chapter.

There is an accompanying website at http://www.wiley.com/go/barlow2e containing all worksheet models developed throughout the text. The website contains ten workbooks, each workbook file corresponding to a chapter in the book. The workbook files are named as Chapter2, Chapter3, . . . Chapter11. (Note: Chapter 1 does not contain any spreadsheets.) Within each workbook, worksheets represent the figures that appear in that chapter, e.g., Chapter3 contains worksheets Fig. 3.1, Fig. 3.2, Fig 3.3, etc. Solutions to all end-of-chapter exercises are available to adopters of the text on the website.

NEW FOR THE SECOND EDITION

- A new chapter entitled *Investment Analysis Models* has been added. As well as expanding the subject of portfolio theory introduced in Chapter 3, asset pricing models including the capital asset pricing model (CAPM) and single index model (SIM) are covered. Other topics discussed are bond valuation, duration, and the Black–Scholes option pricing model. This new chapter should be of particular interest to both students and practitioners in the area of finance.

- The 'Time Series and Exponential Smoothing' section in Chapter 6 now provides a model for the Holt-Winters' triple-parameter method for multiplicative seasonal effects.

- The 'Production Planning and Scheduling' section in Chapter 10 has been expanded to cover priority job sequencing. A VBA routine is included for Johnson's Rule for sequencing a series of jobs through two facilities.

- All models and Appendix notes have been upgraded to reflect the latest versions of applications software and operating systems, namely Microsoft's Office 2003 and Windows XP.

- New topics such as enterprise resource planning have been introduced where appropriate, and end-of-chapter bibliographies have been updated.

ACKNOWLEDGEMENTS

I am grateful to the reviewers for their many helpful comments and suggestions for improving the book. These views have been incorporated wherever practicable. It is also encouraging to see that other authors find merit in adopting an active learning approach to problem solving, and their important contributions have been recognised in the end-of-chapter bibliographies. I would like to thank editors Sarah Booth, Rachel Goodyear and David Barnard for all their support throughout the book's production. Finally, with a text involving so many formulae, the responsibility for any errors or omissions that remain undetected is mine alone. Feedback on corrections, questions, or ideas is always welcome and will be duly acknowledged.

1

A systems view of business

OVERVIEW

This textbook develops models for various aspects of business and operations management. In order to illustrate how the activities of a typical manufacturing business are interrelated, a systems approach is now presented. The systems approach provides an overall view of an organisation's activities whereby an organisation is separated into identifiable subsystems or departments. All such departments are interdependent and perform specific tasks of work which contribute to the organisation's goals. The simplest model of a business system consists of three basic elements, namely inputs, processes, and outputs (Figure 1.1). Output information is used as a control mechanism – normally called a feedback loop – to correct deviations from planned performance.

For example, consider a bakery. The inputs consist of the raw materials that are used to make bread, namely flour, yeast, and water. The actual process is the baking, performed in an oven in which the ingredients are converted into outputs, i.e., bread. In this case, the process is controlled by monitoring the oven's output, i.e., temperature. A temperature feedback loop thus ensures that the correct baking conditions are maintained.

Outputs can be either finished goods or services. A manufacturing business produces a tangible output such as a car or furniture whereas service-orientated businesses, e.g., a bank or hospital, are more customer focused. Generally, service operations use more labour and less equipment than manufacturing. The word 'throughput' is sometimes used to refer to items that are still in the process stage and have not yet been converted into finished goods.

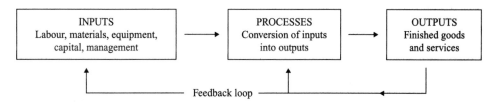

Figure 1.1 Systems view of business.

A SYSTEMS VIEW OF BUSINESS OPERATIONS

In most organisations, departments are formed by grouping similar functions together. While all organisations do not have the same functions, one common approach to functional organisation is to have four main divisions, namely human resources, marketing, finance/accounting and production. Within each of these four divisions, there are further functional subsystems or departments, creating a hierarchical structure as shown in Figure 1.2. In this textbook, the term 'business management' is interpreted in the wider sense of covering all four divisional areas while 'operations management' is concerned specifically with the activities of the production division.

The human resources division deals with the human aspects of an organisation such as labour relations, the work environment, and in-house training. Because personnel activities are people-orientated, the human resources division use computers chiefly as information-retrieval systems, utilising records which are stored in a database. Mathematical applications relating to personnel actions are restricted here to staff planning models in marketing.

The objectives of the marketing division are twofold (i) to identify and (ii) to satisfy customer needs – at a profit to the organisation. In other words, the marketing division not only helps to sell profitably what the production division produces but it also helps to determine what those products should be. Market research is used to identify what consumers actually want, including their preferences and behaviour patterns. The product development department then translates these consumer preferences into general specifications for a new or modified product. At a later stage, the general specifications are refined into detailed product design by the production division. Product development is an example of an interfacing activity requiring input from both marketing and production. Other marketing subsystems which contribute to customer sales are sales forecasting, advertising, salesforce allocation and scheduling, and product pricing.

Because the finance/accounting function focuses on the organisation's economic well-being, accounting activities extend into all business operations. Financial accounting provides economic information for managerial decision-making within the company. Strategic and

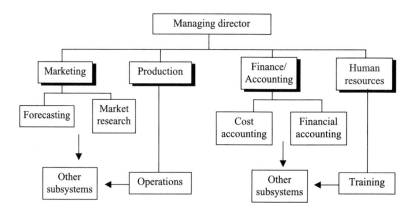

Figure 1.2   Typical functional organisation of a manufacturing business.

operational planning, performance measurement and control, and product costing are common accounting functions that must be performed by management. Another important aspect of managerial control is budgeting. Budgeting is the practical outcome of business planning and is used to ensure that expenditure does not exceed income, i.e., to ensure that the company makes a profit.

The main objective of the production division is to convert raw materials into finished goods. The first step in the manufacturing process is to decide what is to be made and when it is needed. After customer requirements have been established, a product is then designed. This product may be a modification of an existing product or it may be completely new. The resources required to manufacture the product are specified and, where appropriate, the necessary amounts quantified. These resources include raw materials and spare parts, labour, and production facilities.

After the product design and manufacturing processes are determined, the product must be scheduled along with any other products made by the organisation. An effective production schedule is a vital element of production operations. It involves checking production capacity, i.e., is there sufficient labour and materials available, is machine capacity adequate to perform the job, etc.? Having established that there is adequate capacity, the next step is to order the necessary raw materials and parts. Machines and personnel are then scheduled to perform the necessary manufacturing steps. During certain stages of production, the product is examined and compared to its design specifications for performance and quality, i.e., quality control is performed. If the finished product meets all the original design specifications, it is shipped directly to the customer or stored in the warehouse.

A MANUFACTURING BUSINESS MODEL

The interrelationships between the various business functions outlined above can be better understood by examining a model of a manufacturing organisation. The model of Figure 1.3 is not a mathematical model, but a diagram showing the basic data flows between the main subsystems in the organisation. The shaded area contains the key subsystems within the production division.

FINANCE AND COST ACCOUNTING

The two main categories of accounting are financial accounting and management or cost accounting. The terms 'management accounting' and 'cost accounting' are often used interchangeably. Strictly speaking, cost accounting refers to a manufacturing business, and focuses on the costs of raw materials, labour, and overhead expenses incurred in the production of finished goods. Management accounting is a more generic term referring to the managerial functions of organisational planning and control. Performance measurement and control, product costing, and purchasing decisions are common managerial accounting functions that must be performed by a company's management.

The finance function covers both financial accounting and financial management. Financial accounting is concerned primarily with providing information for parties external to the

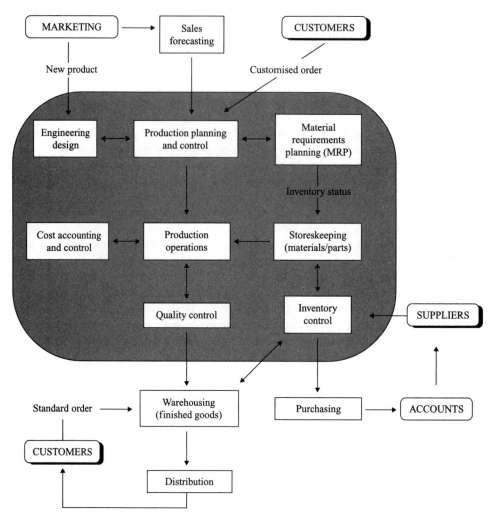

Figure 1.3   Manufacturing business model.

business such as investors, banking institutions and government agencies. If a company wants to borrow money, it must provide the lending institutions with information to show that the company is a sound investment. Likewise, shareholders want to see financial statements indicating how well the company is doing and how much their investment is worth!

The objective of financial management is twofold (i) to ensure that there are sufficient funds available to meet the organisation's financial obligations and (ii) to maximise the returns on invested funds that are not needed to meet current commitments. In order to maximise profit, financial managers must decide whether the benefits accruing from any investment are sufficient to justify the original outlay. Investment situations include capital budgeting decisions relating to expansion plans or new product development, and long-term investments such as government bonds or shares in other companies.

One important aspect of managerial control is budgeting. A budget is a plan – usually expressed in monetary terms – covering a fixed period of time, e.g. one year. It shows the activities that the company intends to undertake in order to achieve its profit goal. While the budget provides projected data, the cost accounting subsystem produces actual data. Variances from set targets are found by comparing actual costs with budgeted or standard costs. For example, a negative or unfavourable variance occurs if actual production uses materials that are more costly than planned. On the other hand, if actual labour hours used in the manufacture of a product are less than budgeted figures, then a positive or favourable variance results.

THE MARKETING FUNCTION

The marketing function utilises a considerable amount of qualitative information which introduces uncertainty into the decision-making process. Qualitative decisions that must be taken by marketing managers include anticipating customer needs, forecasting product sales, and evaluating new sources of competition. Decision-makers often use spreadsheet models as a quantitative tool to obtain answers to various 'what-if' questions. When managers are able to see the immediate effect of changes to sensitive parameters such as sales volume or product price, they are better placed to evaluate feasible alternatives. Because models provide valuable help in performing such sensitive analysis, they are often called decision support systems (DSS).

No organisation can function effectively without a forecast for the goods or services which it provides. A key objective of the marketing division is to produce sales forecasts. Since the projections of sales volumes for future periods often form the basis of organisational objectives, their accuracy is of vital concern. Many statistical models have been developed in an effort to improve forecasting accuracy, including regression-based models, the moving-average method, and exponential smoothing techniques.

Production may be initiated on the basis of either sales forecasts or firm customer orders. Goods that are produced on the basis of a forecasted demand use a product-orientated strategy which involves the continuous production of a standardised product such as glass, paper, cement, and steel. Companies that manufacture the same high-volume standardised product each day are in a position to set standards and maintain a given quality.

Some customer orders are for one-off items which involve the production of customised products, in which case a process-orientated strategy is used. An organisation which uses a process-orientated strategy produces low-volume, high-variety products. The production facilities must have a high degree of flexibility in order to handle the frequent process changes that are required to produce different items. Maintaining standards in such a rapidly changing process environment is much more difficult than in a standardised product-orientated business.

THE PRODUCTION FUNCTION

The main purpose of the production function is to transform raw materials into finished goods. The manufacturing process covers the full life-cycle of a product from its inception to completion. Important decisions must be taken on what items to produce, how to design and manufacture them, which raw materials will be required, and how best to ensure that the products meet specified quality and performance. The following sections summarise the essential production subsystems.

Production Planning and Control

Production planning determines how many items to produce, when to produce them, and what facilities are required to produce them. The amount of production is determined by (i) sales forecasts and (ii) specific customer orders. The timing of production depends on (i) availability of labour and materials required for the job and (ii) estimated times required to perform production operations. The production facilities required to manufacture the item are prescribed by the design specifications.

A key output from production planning is the master production schedule (MPS) which shows how many items must be produced and when they will be produced in order to meet customer demands. Because the MPS is based on customer orders and forecasts provided by the marketing division, it is an important link between marketing and production. It shows when incoming sales orders can be scheduled for production operations and when finished goods can be scheduled for delivery. The MPS also provides important inputs to the material requirements planning (MRP) system, which is discussed below.

Before an MPS can be developed, estimates of the amounts of each resource needed to meet MPS requirements must be calculated. A production schedule is therefore dictated by the resource constraints on materials and labour availability, machine capacity, and the production time pattern. Effective capacity planning will indicate whether a proposed production schedule is feasible or not. Inadequate machine capacity could rule out a proposed schedule, or overtime may be necessary to overcome personnel limitations.

Production control involves the co-ordination of three main activities, namely, (i) dispatching, i.e., scheduling which machines and operators will perform which steps in the manufacturing process for each item (ii) monitoring actual operations, and (iii) taking corrective actions when and where necessary.

Material Requirements Planning (MRP)

In manufacturing situations, there is usually an inventory of components (or raw materials) which are used solely in the production of finished products. Since there is no outside demand for this inventory, there is no sense in stocking it until it is needed in production operations. The two main objectives of material requirements planning (MRP) are (i) to reduce order-processing delays by ensuring that materials and parts are available when required for production operations and (ii) reduce inventories and their associated costs by holding only those components and items that are really needed. MRP thus combines two of the most important activities in the manufacturing process, namely, production scheduling and materials control.

MRP is a system for managing inventories by anticipating their use. It helps to reduce inventory levels by quickly determining how much materials/components to order and when those orders should be placed. MRP is most appropriate where a company manufactures many

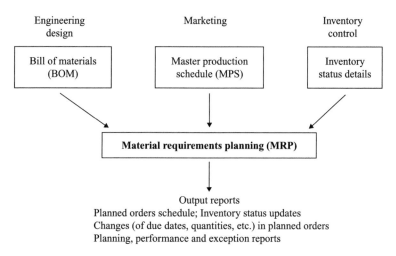

Figure 1.4   Basic input to an MRP system.

products and where product demand is variable. For example, a company may manufacture 100 different items each requiring many components and materials in its assembly. An MRP system must be able to calculate the materials/parts requirements for all 100 items over a fixed period. However, much of the materials and components will be common to many of the items. The MRP system aggregates gross requirements across all the items in order to determine what exactly to order. An MRP system has three major inputs – the master production schedule (MPS), the bill of materials (BOM) and inventory status details – as shown in Figure 1.4.

The master production schedule (MPS) which is discussed in the production planning section above, provides input details of what finished goods are required and when they are needed. The bill of materials (BOM) is a design document listing all of the materials, components, and assemblies/subassemblies needed to make a finished product.

The BOM is developed by the engineering design department and is based on product specifications provided by the marketing division. It not only gives details of a product's components but also shows how it is assembled and how many of each component is required. The primary MRP input from the BOM is the product's structure tree, which depicts the hierarchical levels of subassemblies and components required to make the product, as shown in the bicycle structure tree (Figure 1.5). The structure tree shows three hierarchical levels with bracketed numbers indicating the number of assemblies and components required to make one item on the level above. For example, 50 level-2 spokes are required to make one level-1 wheel assembly, while two wheel assemblies are required in the manufacture of one level-0 bicycle.

The third MRP input, namely inventory status details, gives full and up-to-date information on each inventory item, including quantities on hand, gross requirements, how much has been ordered, safety stock levels, etc. These inventory records also contain details of each component's *lead time*, i.e., the amount of time taken between placing an order and getting the item in stock ready for use. Lead times are a continuous source of uncertainty due to the many activities involved, including timing of order placement, item availability, transportation difficulties, quality control, etc.

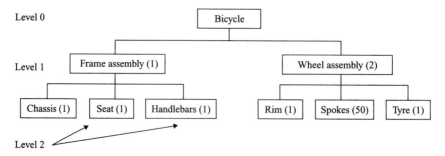

Figure 1.5 BOM product structure tree.

Purchasing

A considerable amount of managerial effort goes into ensuring that the right materials are directed to the right place at the right time and at the right cost. Managing materials in such an effective way is not easy. In a manufacturing environment, materials management involves co-ordinating the activities of three interrelated areas, namely materials purchasing, inventory planning and control, and the delivery/inspection system. The purpose of materials management is to increase the efficiency of production operations by integrating all material acquisition, movement, and storage activities within the company.

Traditionally, the purchasing function was concerned solely with drawing up a list of reliable suppliers and then using a 'lowest cost' criterion to choose the best supplier. However, this narrow view of buying materials at lowest cost represents only one aspect of purchasing management. Nowadays, there is more emphasis on developing a satisfactory supplier-buyer relationship whereby the sharing and exchanging of ideas can benefit both sides. The competitive advantages to be gained from purchasing depend upon both parties working closely together to identify mutual interests. For example, suppliers can use their knowledge of what is available in the market-place to suggest substitute materials that are cheaper or more reliable than those currently being purchased by an organisation.

The importance of having a mutual understanding between suppliers and purchasers is highlighted in the popular 'just-in-time' (JIT) approach to materials purchasing. The JIT philosophy of purchasing items from suppliers just when they are required, reduces – and in some cases eliminates – inventories. Most companies appreciate that capital can be wastefully tied up in inventories which sit around gathering dust. The JIT approach is seen as a way to eliminate such waste by synchronising manufacturing processes and reducing inventory holding costs. However, for JIT to be successful, purchasing management must have confidence that their suppliers can deliver materials in the required amount and at the right time. Any delay in the supply would cause serious production problems – hence the need for a mutual value-added relationship!

The activities of receiving, inspecting, and storing materials are other important aspects of purchasing management and also form part of the logistics function which is discussed below. If materials or goods arrive late, production operations may be halted or sales lost. The problem of late deliveries must be properly addressed in order to avoid friction between supplier and purchaser. Does the problem lie with the supplier or, as can often happen, with the purchasers themselves? Poor scheduling by the purchaser can allow insufficient time for either punctual delivery or proper quality inspections. Information concerning the receipt of wrong materials as well as items that have been damaged in transit, should also be relayed without delay to the production control and accounting departments.

Inventory Control

Businesses can only predict what customers will buy and when they will buy it. To overcome such uncertainty, stocks are kept to ensure that anticipated demand can be met. Stockholding can therefore be viewed as a buffer between supply and demand. For example, raw materials such as coal and fuel must be scheduled and stockpiled for the production of electricity, while banks have to maintain a certain level of cash inventory to meet customer needs. The main types of inventory are (i) raw materials (ii) work-in-progress (also called work-in-process or WIP) which represents partly finished products (iii) finished goods, i.e., completed products ready for shipment.

Controlling inventory is an important aspect of good management. In the past, inventories were often overstocked 'just in case' something went wrong, i.e., items were over-ordered to protect against supplier shortages or as a hedge against fluctuating price changes. However, excessive inventories tie up valuable capital as well as taking up expensive warehouse space. On the other hand, valuable sales may be lost if customer orders cannot be met because of insufficient stock. Likewise, production operations can be brought to a halt because an item is not available. Using computer models can help reduce inventory levels by providing more accurate forecasts on the quantity and timing of inventory transactions.

Common objectives of inventory control are (i) to ensure that there is a sufficient supply of finished goods to meet anticipated customer demand (ii) to ensure that there is a sufficient supply of materials to enable production operations to operate smoothly and (iii) to reduce inventory costs by taking advantage of quantity discounts or buying when prices are lower. Thus, inventory management strives to have exactly enough inventory on hand to satisfy all demands without having any excess.

There are two main classes of inventories, namely those with dependent-demand items and those with independent-demand items. Independent-demand items are those whose demands are unrelated to anything else which the company produces or sells. Independent-demand inventory usually consists of finished goods whose demand is based on uncertain environmental factors such as sales forecasts, consumer trends, etc. Independent demands are therefore full of uncertainties as to how much is needed and when it is required.

On the other hand, dependent-demand items are those that can be directly linked to a specific end-product such as the bicycle shown in Figure 1.5. In this situation, the product structure tree shows how many handlebars, spokes, tyres, etc., are required to make one bicycle. Here the demand for a bicycle automatically triggers demand for known quantities of parts and materials, i.e., there is no uncertainty associated with their demand. For example, if a customer orders six bicycles, then six handlebars, twelve tyres, 600 spokes, etc., must be in stock if the order is to be met.

Quality Control

In a manufacturing environment, the quality control (QC) function ensures that all products meet the standards specified by the engineering design department. The two main approaches to quality control are acceptance sampling and statistical process control. The term 'acceptance sampling' refers to statistical techniques that are used to accept or reject a batch of items on the basis of a sample test or inspection. This traditional approach to quality control involves randomly selecting a sample from a batch of items and applying various tests to each item in the sample to see if it works as intended. The QC manager then extends the sample's test results to the whole batch. For example, if 2% of a sample's items are found to be defective, the manager concludes that 2% of the whole batch are also faulty.

Acceptance sampling involves the risk of finding too many or too few defective items in a random sample. If the QC manager is unfortunate in picking out too many defectives, a wrong decision will be made when rejecting the whole batch unnecessarily. The same outcome applies to accepting a batch because a sample was lucky enough to include very few faulty items.

Recent developments in computer-based systems using mechanical, optical and electronic sensors can help in non-destructive quality control, i.e., in the measuring and testing of items. Technology in testing equipment has advanced to the point where many manufacturing companies can now check out all items, thus achieving 100% quality control. The same technology cannot of course be applied to destructive quality control whereby the testing of a product involves tearing it apart to see how well it is made, e.g., strength tests of materials. In this situation, acceptance sampling is used.

The well-known advocate of quality management, W. Edwards Deming, stated that management is responsible for 85% of quality problems in a factory environment with workers being responsible for only 15%. He pointed out that workers cannot extend quality beyond the limits of what any process is capable of producing. The quality-control function is now referred to as total quality management (TQM), emphasising the strategic importance of quality to the whole organisation – not just the factory floor. TQM involves an unending process of continuous improvement with the objective of achieving perfection. The fact that perfection is never reached is irrelevant – the setting and achieving of ever-higher goals is sufficient justification.

Statistical process control (SPC) is the application of statistical techniques to the control of processes. SPC is used to ensure that a process is meeting specified standards by measuring its performance. If the process is to produce quality products, its capabilities must be periodically measured to check that it is performing as planned. The quality of the process can be affected by natural variations that occur in almost every production process. As long as these variations remain within specified limits, the process is 'in control' and quality will not be affected. However, if the variations go outside the specified limits, the process is 'out of control' and the causes must be determined. Control charts are used to separate random causes of variation from non-random causes such as operator error, faulty setup, poor materials, and so forth.

Storage and Distribution (Logistics)

The logistics function is a key aspect of production operations. Logistics is concerned mainly with the handling, storage, and movement of products to markets and materials to manufacturing facilities. For example, the logistics of a retail company involves purchasing goods from suppliers, receiving and storing such goods, and then distributing them to customers. In a manufacturing company, the logistics function is more complex because raw materials and spare parts have to be purchased and stored before the production process can commence.

When finished goods start rolling off the production line, they also have to be warehoused and eventually distributed to customers. The storage term of 'storeskeeping' usually refers to the activities associated with the storing of materials and spare parts while 'warehousing' is used for the storage of finished goods. In managing logistics, several important issues arise.

- What should be the structure of the distribution system – centralised or decentralised?
- How can warehouse and storage layouts be optimised in order to maximise space while minimising material handling costs?
- Which geographic locations provide the best benefits to the organisation?
- How much inventory should be held at each location?
- Which modes of transportation should be used?

A strategic part of logistics planning is operations layout. A layout is the physical configuration of processes, equipment, and materials that facilitates the flow of materials and personnel within and between work areas. For example, it makes sense to group similar machines together so that jobs are routed to one particular work area rather than being scattered all over the place. Poor layouts cause bottleneck queues by interrupting the physical flow of materials, and consequently add extra costs to production activities. Layout decisions should therefore be made with efficiency of operations in mind. The various types of layout include process-orientated layout, product-orientated layout, warehouse layout, and office layout.

Project Management

Project management is an integral part of operations management. Projects may involve recurring activities, e.g., plant maintenance, or they may be large one-off projects such as the construction of a new manufacturing facility. Large-scale projects consist of numerous tasks that must be completed, some in parallel and others in sequence, by various individuals or groups. Because considerable expenditure is involved, projects must be managed carefully to ensure that the entire project is completed on time. Project management comprises the important activities of (i) planning (ii) scheduling and (iii) controlling project tasks. The initial phase of project planning involves setting objectives and performance criteria (usually measured in terms of costs and time), identifying resource requirements, and assigning areas of responsibility.

The practical phase of project control is basically a comparison between what has actually been completed against what was planned at the start. Project control uses *milestones* periodically to review a project's progress. Rather than allow a project to be completed without any control checks, management designates certain intermediate points, called milestones, at which progress will be evaluated. If a milestone check indicates that a project is running late, then corrective measures must be taken to bring the project back on course.

Project scheduling focuses on the activities that make up the project. A schedule shows when each task starts and ends and how long it will take to complete the task, i.e., the task's duration. Scheduling also shows how each task is related to others in the project. Because projects often have important deadlines to meet, scheduling is a critical aspect of project management. Where

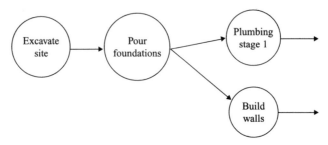

Figure 1.6   Partial network of nodes and arcs.

there is a large number of interrelated tasks, timing and co-ordination become very complex. Nowadays project managers use computer software to help them identify those tasks that must be finished on time in order to avoid delaying the entire project.

There are various mathematical techniques for scheduling projects. The two main approaches are the critical path method (CPM) and the project evaluation and review technique (PERT). These two techniques are very similar, the main difference being their assumptions concerning the accuracy of duration estimates for each task. PERT emphasises the uncertainty in estimating activity times while CPM assumes that task times can be accurately predicted. The type of questions that can be answered by using PERT/CPM are:

- When will the project finish?
- What are the critical activities, i.e., tasks which, if delayed, will delay the whole project?
- How is the overall project affected if a critical activity is delayed?
- What is the interrelationship between activities?

The CPM method is the scheduling approach used in virtually all project management software today, including Microsoft Project. All CPM and PERT models use a network to portray graphically the project's interrelationships. A network consists of nodes and arcs, also called arrows. Figure 1.6 shows the main features of a partial network. A node represents a project task (i.e., activity) and is depicted as a circle in the network. Arcs are shown as arrows and define the interrelationships between nodes, indicating what activity must end before another activity can start.

MANAGEMENT DECISION-MAKING

Management is responsible for setting an organisation's objectives. In order to achieve these objectives, management must make decisions. Decision-making is an integral part of management and occurs in every function and at different levels within the organisational structure. While the type of decisions that are made vary considerably, they can be linked to the following common managerial activities:

Planning involves (i) establishing organisational goals and objectives and (ii) developing policies and procedures for achieving those goals.

Organising is the process of (i) determining and co-ordinating activities and (ii) establishing organisational structures and procedures to ensure that the activities are carried out as planned.

Staffing entails the recruitment and training of personnel in order to achieve organisational goals and objectives.

Controlling involves (i) measuring performance against goals and objectives and (ii) developing procedures for adjusting goals or activities in order to bring them into line.

All of the above managerial functions need information to make decisions. Information provides vital input to the decision-making process by increasing knowledge and reducing uncertainty. While they are obviously interdependent, each managerial activity requires different information. For example, a planning decision utilises information concerning future events, e.g., sales forecasts, while control decisions need details of what is happening now or in the immediate past, e.g., information about machines that have suddenly broken down.

In the previous sections, the organisation was viewed from the functional perspective of marketing, production, finance/accounting, and human resources activities. Another popular way of looking at an organisation's structure is provided by the hierarchical framework of management. This hierarchical structure focuses on the decision-making process at three distinct levels namely top, middle, and lower management as shown in Figure 1.7 below. Because of the different types of decision taken at each level, top management is often referred to as strategic-level management. Similarly, middle and lower levels are also called tactical-level and operational-level management respectively.

Top Management

Top management includes the board of directors and the heads of the functional divisions of marketing, production, finance/accounting, and human resources activities. They exercise control over the long-term strategic direction of policies that determine the company's future direction. The information required for strategic decision-making is obtained largely from sources outside the company and includes such details as market trends, the competition, new product developments, etc. This external information contains a high level of uncertainty and in most cases is qualitative in nature. Information about the company's own operations is used primarily for forecasting.

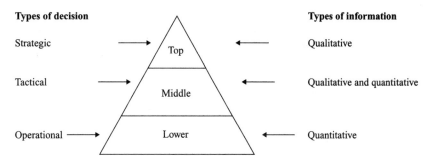

Figure 1.7 Hierarchical levels of management.

Table 1.1 Characteristics of decision-making information

| Characteristics | ← Management Decision Level → | | |
	Operational	Tactical	Strategic
Decision-makers	Supervisors, foremen	Departmental managers	Board of directors, divisional heads
Time horizon	Daily	Weekly/monthly	One year and beyond
Type of decision	Structured	Semi-structured	Unstructured
Decision level	Low	Moderate	Very high
Information source	Mainly internal	Internal/external	Mainly external
Information type	Quantitative	Quantitive and qualitative	Qualitative
Information complexity	Simple	Moderate	Complex
Breadth of control	Narrow	Intermediate	Broad

Top-level decisions depend to a large extent on the quality of managerial judgement based on past experience, intuition, and an element of luck. The term 'unstructured decision-making' is often used to describe strategic-level situations. Unstructured decisions involve complex processes for which no standard procedures exist to help the decision-maker, e.g., launching new products. Because strategic decisions occur infrequently, top management receives company information on an irregular basis, usually in the form of summary reports. The chief characteristics of decision-making information are shown in Table 1.1.

Middle Management

Middle or tactical management is responsible for implementing the decisions taken at the top level. It must ensure that organisational goals are achieved by obtaining and using resources in an efficient and effective way. Because middle management has the role of controlling and monitoring the organisation's various resources, it is sometimes referred to as 'management control'. Typical tactical-level decisions include planning working capital, scheduling production, formulating budgets, and making short-term forecasts. Middle management uses internal information to compare actual performance with planned goals. By analysing this information, managers are able to determine whether operations are proceeding as planned or if corrective action is needed.

Tactical-level decisions utilise both internal and external information. If a competitive advantage is to be gained, then middle management must obtain outside information on industry averages and other companies' productivity levels. By comparing these figures with their own internal productivity data, middle management is better placed to evaluate the organisation's position in the market-place. Because tactical-level decisions are based on a mixture of internal quantitative details and external qualitative information, they are sometimes called 'semi-structured'. A semi-structured problem is one where decision-makers have factual data to analyse but must also use their own judgement to arrive at a satisfactory solution.

Sensitivity or 'what if' analysis is a typical semi-structured approach in which the decision-maker asks a series of 'what if' questions in order to determine how key factors respond to assumed changes or conditions. The ability to experiment with quantitative data in order to gain greater insight into a semi-structured situation lets the decision-maker see the consequences of certain actions. For example, a manager may wish to see how an organisation might be affected if there was a 3% increase in labour costs. Some of the models in this book illustrate the benefits of using 'what if' analysis.

Operational Management

Operational-level decisions are 'structured', i.e., they are based on factual data. Structured problems are routine and repetitive, e.g., a payroll system. They utilise quantitative information which is regularly obtained from operational activities and their outcome is totally predictable. Although a structured decision may involve complex calculations, standard techniques already exist for finding a solution. Lower management therefore makes fairly straightforward decisions that follow specific rules and patterns requiring very little qualitative input. Activities at this level include the maintenance of inventory records, the preparation of sales invoices and shipping orders, and decisions on materials requirements.

Lower management measures the efficiency of factory-level operations and takes remedial action to improve their efficiency wherever possible. Like tactical management, lower-level management is also involved with control and is often referred to as 'operational control' management. An example of operational control is the cost control of an organisation's product. Cost accounting provides a standard (or expected) cost which may be obtained from the engineering design department or may be based on past records. Actual costs of manufacturing the product are produced at the end of the accounting period. By comparing expected costs with actual costs, lower management are able to calculate cost variances and hence determine if any corrective action is necessary.

In summary, much of an organisation's information is utilised by lower-level managers with only a small percentage being accessed by top management. Exception reports, i.e., reports that focus on out-of-control situations such as inventory shortages or machine breakdowns, are important information sources for lower and middle management. Top management may utilise *ad hoc* reports to deal with unexpected one-off situations that may arise. They also use organisational information, supplemented by external market research input, to assess sales forecasts.

ENTERPRISE RESOURCE PLANNING (ERP)

In today's competitive business environment, many organisations are turning to enterprise resource planning (ERP) systems to help them manage the increasingly complex processes created by the globalisation of markets. An ERP system extends the centralised database concept to include customers and suppliers as part of the business value chain. For example, a European manufacturer may use an ERP system to process an order from a Canadian customer requiring the purchase of extra components from its Chinese supplier. The ERP system will (i) handle all currency transactions (including exchange rate conversions), (ii) update inventory and MRP subsystems, (iii) provide distributors with the necessary supplier and customer details, and finally (iv) update all accounting processes.

The model of Figure 1.3 shows how information is shared among the various subsystems of a manufacturing business. In many cases, much of this organisational information is fragmented, with key departments having their own computer systems. These stand-alone systems can create inefficiencies in the management and control of information by encouraging data duplication and the proliferation of incompatible software applications. To overcome such a piecemeal approach, database systems have been developed whereby a company's information is integrated and stored in a single source, called the database (see Chapter 7). The database concept allows users to have immediate access to the entire business information resource.

The software company, SAP – an acronym for Systems, Applications, and Products – is a major supplier of ERP systems. Numerous large corporations including Coca-Cola, Microsoft, Kodak, IBM, Intel, and Exxon have implemented SAP's R/3 software package. The R/3 product includes a fully integrated suite of programs for finance and accounting, production and materials management, quality management and plant maintenance, sales and distribution, human resources management, and project management. It is also capable of handling different countries' languages and business regulations.

The successful implementation of an ERP system can be expensive, complex, and time-consuming. For example, an organisation that wants to implement the R/3 system must first produce a blueprint of its business, involving detailed models of how each process operates. While much of the R/3 system consists of standardised modules, it is sufficiently flexible to allow customisation to meet specific requirements.

REFERENCES AND FURTHER READING

Heizer, J. and Render, B. (2003) *Operations Management* (7th edn), Prentice Hall, New Jersey.
Lucey, T. (2005) *Management Information Systems* (9th edn), Thomson Learning, London.

2

Model-building tools

OVERVIEW

The success of an organisation depends to a large extent upon the quality of its managerial decision-making. Everyone makes a decision when choosing between two or more alternatives. An alternative is a course of action intended to solve a problem. Although few people analyse the decision-making process, all decisions follow a similar series of logical steps as shown in Figure 2.1. The decision-maker must first recognise that a problem exists. The next step is to establish the evaluation criteria, i.e., the necessary quantitative and qualitative information which will be used to analyse various courses of action. The third stage involves identifying various alternatives for consideration. Having assessed every situation, decision-makers then select the alternative that best satisfies their evaluation criteria. Finally, this optimal choice is implemented.

Business managers must choose the appropriate course of action which is most effective in attaining an organisation's goals. The types of decisions that have to be taken vary considerably and depend upon the complexity of the problem to be solved. Usually, the level of complexity increases proportionally with the level of qualitative information required to solve the problem. Even where a problem is based almost entirely on factual, quantitative information, decision-making can be difficult. For example, the construction of a large building contains so many interdependent activities that an overwhelming amount of time could be spent on gathering factual information about the situation. Luckily, computer models are now available to assist the managerial decision-making process!

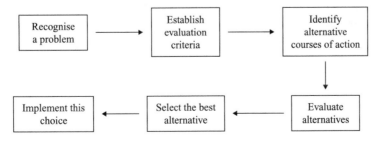

Figure 2.1   Stages in the decision-making process.

MODELLING CHARACTERISTICS

A model is a simplified representation of a real-world situation. It can be regarded as a substitute for the real system, stripping away a large amount of complexity to leave only essential, relevant details. A model is used to facilitate understanding of a real object or situation. A decision-maker is better able to evaluate the consequences of alternative actions by analysing the model's behaviour. For example, dummies which are used in car-crash simulations, allow engineers to test and analyse the safety of new features. The advantages of a model are (i) it is easy for the decision-maker to understand (ii) it can be modified quickly and cheaply, and (iii) there is less risk when experimenting with a model than with the real system.

Typical models showing the layout of a new housing or shopping complex can be found in architects' offices. Such models are referred to as 'physical' models because they are three-dimensional representations of real-world objects. They may be scaled-down versions of the real thing or, as in the case of the crash-testing dummy, they can be exact replicas. Types of models which are more suited to computers include (i) graphical models, which use lines, curves, and other symbols to produce flow charts, pie charts, bar charts, scatter diagrams, etc. and (ii) mathematical models which use formulae and algorithms to represent real-world situations. All of the models developed in this book are either graphical or mathematical.

Because a model is not an exact representation, it cannot contain all aspects of a problem. Models involve a large number of assumptions about the environment in which the system operates, about the operating characteristics of its functions, and the way people behave. These environmental assumptions are called uncontrollable variables because they are outside the decision-maker's control, e.g., interest rates, consumer trends, currency fluctuations, etc. On the other hand, controllable variables are those inputs that influence a model's outcome and are within the decision-maker's control. Examples of control variables are product price, the level of output, or acceptable profit levels.

Steps in Model-Building

The validity of a model's results will depend on how accurately the model represents the real situation. The ideal model is one which is neither too trivial in its representation of reality nor too complex to implement. There are three main steps in building a spreadsheet model as shown in Figure 2.2. The first step of problem formulation requires that the decision-maker adopt a systematic and rigorous approach to the selection of variables. One of the main sources of errors in model-building is the exclusion of important variables, due either to an oversight or a lack of understanding of the model's underlying logic. In either case, the results will be meaningless or at best, dubious.

The second step in model-building is the identification of the relationships among the variables. In many cases well-known formulae may already exist. For example, consider the amount due to an investor at the end of five years when £2000 is invested at a compound interest rate of 12% per annum. The general formula for basic compound interest states that if an amount P_0 is invested at a fixed rate of $r\%$, the principal P_n after n years is

$$P_n = P_0(1 + r/100)^n$$

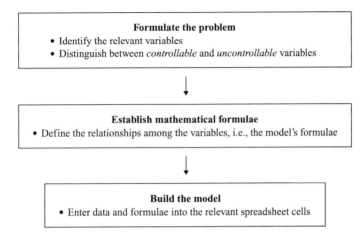

Figure 2.2 Steps in model-building.

The investor will thus get $2000(1.12)^5 = £3525$. In this case, the controllable variables are $P_0, r,$ and n. In situations where no known formula exists, the decision-maker must take great care in defining the relationships among the variables. A sensible precaution is to check out a newly-derived formula by using historical data and comparing the formula's result with an already-known answer.

The final step is to set up the model as a spreadsheet. The compound-interest example above is used as a demonstration model. A spreadsheet is usually depicted as a matrix or grid of cells, each uniquely numbered by reference to the column and row in which it is found. A cell can contain either a description, a fixed value, or a formula, e.g., cells A1, E3, and E7 in Figure 2.3 show each of these three features. The main source of errors in building a spreadsheet model is due to wrong cell cross-referencing, i.e., the user incorrectly identifies source cells when entering either input or formulae.

The advantage of the spreadsheet model is that the user can easily change any of the input data. Thus the compound interest for any values of $P_0, r,$ or n can be found by simply overwriting the current input values in cells E3, E4, and E5. The model also allows users to see instantly the

	A	B	C	D	E	F	G	H	I
1	Compound interest example								
2									
3	*Input data*		Initial principal, P_0		£2,00		Cell E7 contains the formula E3*(1 + E4) ^ E5 where the symbols *, ^ represent multiplication and ' to the power of'		
4			Interest rate, r		12%				
5			No. of years, n		5				
6									
7			Principal P_n after n years is		*£3,524.68*				
8									
9									

Figure 2.3 A spreadsheet model for compound interest.

Table 2.1   Characteristics of the decision-making environment.

| | ← The decision-making environment → | | |
Characteristics	Certainty	Risk	Uncertainty
Controllable variables	Known	Known	Known
Uncontrollable variables	Known	Probabilistic	Unknown
Type of model	Deterministic	Probabilistic	Nonprobabilistic
Type of decision	Best	Informed	Uncertain
Information type	Quantitative	Quantitative and qualitative	Qualitative
Mathematical tools	Linear programming	Statistical methods; Simulation	Decision analysis; Simulation

effects of their deliberations. By experimenting with various combinations of variables, the decision-maker can obtain a better understanding of the model's sensitivity.

RISK AND UNCERTAINTY IN DECISION-MAKING

In business decision-making, there are three classes of decision problems, namely

- decisions under conditions of certainty
- decisions under conditions of risk
- decisions under conditions of uncertainty.

There are various characteristics associated with each of these three classes of decision-making as shown in Table 2.1. If a decision-maker knows the exact values of all uncontrollable variables, then the model is said to be deterministic, i.e., the outcome is already determined because all variables – both controllable and uncontrollable – are known. The 'best decision' is thus made under conditions of certainty, i.e., there is no element of doubt associated with the outcome. A payroll system is a typical example of a deterministic application because all inputs are already quantified. Linear programming (LP) techniques, including integer and goal programming, are the most widely used tools for solving deterministic models.

Under conditions of certainty, the decision taken is always the best one. In many managerial decisions, however, there is an element of risk attached to future events because the uncontrollable variables are not known with certainty. Decision-makers should therefore be aware that in a risky environment where they do not have complete control over all inputs, bad outcomes will sometimes occur. To take an everyday example, there is a level of doubt associated with the outcome of most sporting events. Such 'decisions under risk' are made every week by racing punters who back horses to win races on the basis of recent performances. While the outcome is not known with certainty, the decision is an informed one, based on an analysis of previous events.

While 'decisions under risk' can have more than one outcome, it is assumed that decision-makers have some knowledge of how matters will turn out, i.e., they know the probability of events occurring. The decision-maker tries to make a good decision which will result in a good outcome by taking into account the probabilities associated with the uncontrollable inputs. In this situation, a model is said to be 'probabilistic' or 'stochastic'. The decision is an informed one because there is sufficient information available to allow probabilities to be assigned to the uncontrollable variables.

Statistical techniques, involving probabilities and probability distributions, are the main tools used in solving problems which have an element of risk attached to them. Simulation is another model-building tool which is used to analyse problems containing uncontrollable variables represented by probability distributions. A simulation model is designed to mimic the behaviour of a real-world situation. A major advantage of simulation models is that they can handle uncertainties by using random number generation. By running a model many times with different sequences of random numbers, a reasonable replication of what actually happens in the system is obtained. One common application of simulation is the behaviour patterns of supermarket queues.

The final class of decision problem – decisions under uncertainty – moves into the area of guesswork where very little, if any, information exists on which to base a decision. A typical example would be choosing numbers to win a national lottery. While probabilities can be assigned to uncontrollable variables in decisions under risk, the decision-maker is unable or lacks confidence to specify such probabilities in an environment of uncertainty. Even where all possible outcomes are known, probabilities still cannot be assigned to uncontrollable inputs because of the levels of uncertainty. For this reason, models which operate under conditions of uncertainty are called nonprobabilistic models.

Decision analysis – also called decision theory – is the chief model-building tool used in an environment of uncertainty. In decision analysis, uncontrollable variables are called 'events' or 'states of nature'. States of nature may result from economic, social, and political factors beyond the control of the decision-maker. There are three different criteria which can be applied to decisions under uncertainty, namely maximin, maximax, and minimax. All of these criteria can be used without specifying probabilities. They are usually associated with the 'theory of games' which, despite the name, has important applications, e.g., military strategies. Simulation techniques, which have been briefly discussed above, can also be used where conditions of uncertainty exist.

LINEAR PROGRAMMING (LP)

Managers often have to make decisions on how best to allocate scarce resources among competing activities. Limited resources such as machinery, time, materials, labour, and money are used to manufacture various products, or provide services such as investment plans and advertising strategies. Typically, there are many different ways to produce these products or services. Management's problem is to find the best way, given the limitations of the resources.

Linear programming (LP) is a widely used mathematical technique designed to help in the planning and allocation of key organisational resources. The word 'linear' refers to the fact that all equations and inequalities associated with an LP problem must have linear relationships. The 'programming' part refers to the iterative process that is used to derive an optimum solution.

All LP problems have two main aspects, namely

- to maximise or minimise some quantity such as profit or cost. Having decided upon the objective to be optimised, it is then necessary to define it mathematically, i.e., to formulate the 'objective function'. Typical objectives include:

  - how to find the optimal allocation of parts inventory to minimise production costs
  - how to create the most efficient personnel schedule to minimise costs while meeting business needs and individual scheduling requests
  - how to optimise allocation of funds in an investment portfolio to maximise profits.

- The use of scarce resources places restrictions on the alternative courses of action available to a manager. These resource limitations, called 'constraints', are described in terms of linear inequalities, expressed either as ≥ (greater-than-or-equal-to) or ≤ (less-than-or-equal-to). It is the presence of these resource inequalities that creates alternative solutions, with (usually) only one solution being optimal.

The best-known linear programming methods are the Simplex and graphical methods. Since the graphical method can be used only for problems with two or three variables, it is of limited use. The Simplex method, which was developed during the Second World War for use in military logistics, is capable of solving very large LP problems involving thousands of variables. It consists of a set of step-by-step rules, which are ideally suited for computerisation. Indeed, until the arrival of Karmarkar's Algorithm in 1984 (Winston, Chapter 10) most LP software packages were based on the Simplex method. However, Karmarkar's new algorithm takes significantly less computer time than the Simplex method to solve very large-scale problems, and a new generation of LP software, using Karmarkar's approach, has now been developed.

Applications of Linear Programming

Linear programming problems fall into two main categories: (i) blending or product-mix problems and (ii) transportation problems. Blending or product-mix problems focus on achieving an optimum combination of resources in order to maximise profits or minimise costs. A typical food-blending problem could involve a developing country wishing to produce a high-protein food mixture at the lowest possible cost. A popular business mix problem relates to portfolio management whereby a bank wants to allocate funds in order to achieve the highest possible return on its investment.

Transportation problems involve a number of supply sources (e.g., warehouses) and a number of destinations (e.g., retail shops). The objective is to minimise the transportation costs involved in moving wholesale products from warehouses to shops. Transportation problems are therefore concerned with selecting minimum-cost routes in a product-distribution network between sources and destinations. The special case of the transportation problem known as the 'assignment method', involves assigning employees or machines to different tasks on a one-to-one basis. In this situation, only one source item is assigned to each of the various destinations. Both transportation and assignment problems belong to the wider class of LP problems known as 'network flow problems'.

In many situations, solutions to LP problems make sense only if they have integer (whole number) values. Quantities such as $23^2/_3$ employees or $12^1/_2$ tables are unrealistic. Simply rounding off the LP solution to the nearest whole number may not produce a feasible solution. 'Integer programming' (IP) is the term used to describe an LP problem that requires the solution to have integer values. The LP model for the Acme Company developed below is an example of integer programming being applied to a product-mix situation.

One of the limitations of linear programming is that it allows only one objective function to be optimised. Thus, the decision-maker must focus on a single objective or goal at a time. However, managers frequently want to optimise several conflicting goals at the same time, e.g., how to maximise both production and profits or to maximise profits while minimising risk. 'Goal programming' (GP) is a variation of linear programming that provides for multiple objective optimisation. GP involves making trade-offs among several goals or objectives until a solution is found that satisfies the decision-maker. GP differs from LP in that it does not produce an optimum solution. Rather, it provides a method whereby the decision-maker can explore alternative solutions and then choose that solution which comes closest to meeting the goals under consideration.

While all LP problems contain only linear relationships, problems do exist in which equations and/or inequalities are nonlinear. Nonlinear programming (NLP) is a technique which can solve problems containing nonlinear relationships. A simple definition of a nonlinear relationship is any equation which does not conform to the straight-line relationship, $y = mx + c$. Formulating an NLP problem is exactly the same as formulating an LP problem, except that the objective and/or constraints may be nonlinear. Nonlinear programming is a collective term for many different categories, which include quadratic programming, geometric programming, convex programming, and calculus.

Most spreadsheet packages have built-in solvers. A solver is a powerful tool for analysing and solving various types of linear programming problems which contain many variables and constraints. Excel's solver – called simply 'Solver' – can analyse and solve three types of problems, namely linear programming (LP), integer programming (IP), and nonlinear programming (NLP). Because of its iterative nature, linear programming may not always converge to the best solution. It is worth remembering that there may be different optimal solutions to any LP problem and finding them will depend upon the values assigned to options such as the maximum time allowed, the maximum number of iterations allowed, the size of the residual error, etc.

Excel's Solver provides default settings for all options, which are appropriate for most problems. However, experimentation with the different Solver Option settings, which are shown in Figure 2.6 on page 26, may yield better results. Because of the complexity of nonlinear programming (NLP) problems, Solver's nonlinear option will not guarantee that the solution which it found is optimal. This is not a reflection on Solver's capabilities but rather on the fact that some NLP problems cannot be solved by any method.

EXAMPLE 2.1 *LP model for the Acme Company's problem*

The Acme Company manufactures two products – widgets and gadgets. The company earns a profit of £2 per box for widgets and £3 a box for gadgets. Each product is assembled and packaged. It takes 9 minutes to assemble a box of widgets and 15 minutes for a box of gadgets. The packaging department can package a box of widgets in 11 minutes, while a box of gadgets takes 5 minutes. Acme wants to find out what combination of boxes of widgets and gadgets will maximise total profit, given that there is a maximum of 1800 hours available in both the assembly and packaging departments. The company has decided to see if Excel's Solver can provide a satisfactory solution, so the first step is to formulate the problem as an LP exercise.

Let $x_1, x_2 =$ the optimum number of boxes of widgets, gadgets   (x_1, x_2 are positive *integers*)

Acme's objective is to maximise profit, i.e., maximise the objective function, Z (in £s), where

$$Z = 2x_1 + 3x_2$$

subject to the following four constraints:

- $9x_1 + 15x_2 \leq 108,000$ minutes   (Time constraint for assembly department)
- $11x_1 + 5x_2 \leq 108,000$ minutes   (Time constraint for packaging department)
- $x_1, x_2 \geq 0$ (x_1, x_2 must be positive values)
- $x_1, x_2 =$ int(eger)   (x_1, x_2 must be integer values)

Excel's Solver uses the same approach as outlined above except that it uses different terms.

Target cell In Solver, the target cell is a single cell containing the objective function which is to be either maximised or minimised.

Changing cells These cells contain the unknowns. In the Acme example, there are only two unknowns, x_1, x_2. Solver uses an iterative approach by changing the values in these cells in order to progress from one solution to a better solution. This process of changing x_1, x_2 values is repeated until an answer is eventually reached which cannot be improved upon, i.e., the optimum solution has been found. Note that the changing cells are usually left blank or are assigned zero values.

Constraints As described above, constraints are the limits which are imposed upon certain cells, and may include changing cells and/or the target cell.

Before using Solver, the first thing that must be done is to set up the spreadsheet model for the Acme Company problem, as shown in Figure 2.4. Note that the 'Solver Parameters' details and formulae given on lines 14 to 24 are not part of the model and are provided only for the user's benefit. For example, it should be clear that the model's changing cells are G5, G6 and the target cell is F11.

The model in Figure 2.4 shows the optimal solution calculated by Excel's Solver. The answer is 9000 boxes of widgets and 1800 boxes of gadgets, giving a maximum profit of £23,400. Note that the actual amount of time used in each department is 1800 hours, equalling the maximum time available. The answers are given in cells G5, G6, F11, C9 and D9 – though do not forget that these cells will initially display blanks or zeros when the model is first set up. Having entered the descriptive data and formatted the cells as shown in lines 1 to 11, complete the following tasks:

- Leave changing cells G5, G6 blank
- Enter formula C5*$G5 + C6*$G6 into cell C9

	A	B	C	D	E	F	G	H
1	**Example 2.1 - The Acme Company**							
2								
3			Assembly	Packaging				
4			Time (min)	Time (min)	Profit		*Solution*	
5		**WIDGETS**	9	11	£2		**9000**	$= x_1$
6		**GADGETS**	15	5	£3		**1800**	$= x_2$
7								
8		Time constraints	108,000	108,000	*User input cells are shaded*			
9		Actual values	108,000	108,000				
10								
11				*Objective: Maximize profits =*		*£23,400*		
12								
13								
14			*Solver Parameters*					
15			*Set Target Cell:*	F11				
16			*Equal to:*	Max				
17			*By Changing Cells:*	G5:G6				
18			*Subject to Constraints:*	C9 <= C8	= ASSEMBLY time constraint			
19				D9 <= D8	= PACKAGING time constraint			
20				G5:G6 >= 0	= Answers must be positive			
21				G5:G6 = int	= Answers must be integer			
22		*Cell*	*Formula*		*Copied to*			
23		C9	C5*$G5 + C6*$G6		D9			
24		F11	E5*G5 + E6*G6					
25								

Figure 2.4   LP model for the Acme Company.

- Copy the formula in cell C9 into D9
- Enter formula E5*G5 + E6*G6 into the target cell F11
- Enter the values shown in Figure 2.4 into shaded cells C5:E6 and C8:D8

The next step is to activate Solver. Select the Tools|Solver command to display the Solver_Parameters dialog box as shown in Figure 2.5. Next, enter the data as shown into the Solver_Parameters dialog box. The similarity between Figure 2.5 and lines 14–21 of Figure 2.4 should be noted! Click the 'Solve' button to start Solver and the results as displayed in Figure 2.4 will appear after a few seconds. Select the 'Keep Solver Solution' option on the 'Solver Results' dialog box in order to store the answer in the worksheet. For most problems, the default settings in the 'Solver Options' box (see Figure 2.6) are appropriate. However, remember that situations such as nonlinearity can arise which require some parameter settings to be altered in order to get an optimal result.

The Acme Company model is an example of a product-mix problem in which the company is trying to maximise profits, given the time constraints imposed by the assembly and

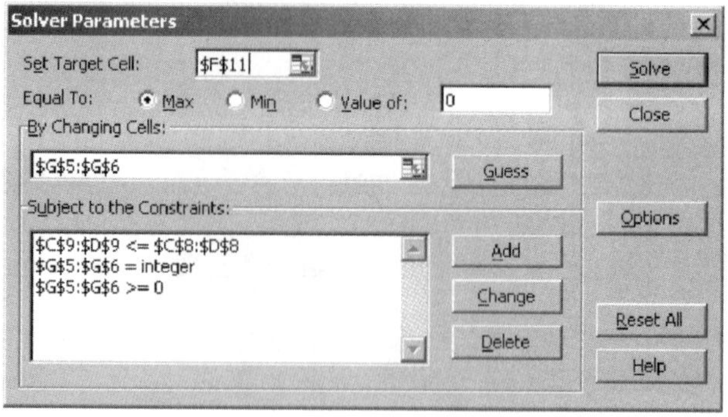

Figure 2.5

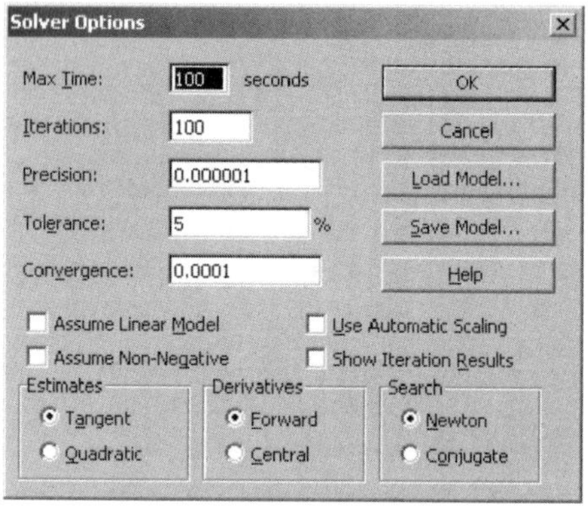

Figure 2.6

packaging departments. Since the answers relate to boxes of products, it is also an example of integer programming (IP). IP is a special form of LP in which the solution values are required to be integer. The alternative approach of accepting a 'rounded solution' whereby fractional answers such as 170.43 boxes are rounded down to 170 boxes, may not give the best answer.

USING EXCEL'S 'ANALYSIS TOOLPAK'

Excel provides some very powerful add-in tools such as Solver and the Analysis ToolPak, which contains a number of statistical and engineering functions. To activate the Analysis ToolPak, choose the Tools|Data Analysis command. If either Solver or Data Analysis do not appear on the Tools menu, then choose the Tools|Add-Ins command and click in the checkboxes next to the required add-ins. Depending upon the version of Excel being used, either a ✓ or ✗ symbol

Table 2.2   Analysis ToolPak: analysis tools.

Function	Function
ANOVA: Single factor	Correlation
ANOVA: Two-factor with replication	Covariance
ANOVA: Two-factor without replication statistics	Descriptive
F-Test Two-sample for variances smoothing	Exponential
Random number generation	Fourier analysis
Rank and percentile	Histogram
t-Test: paired two-sample for means	Moving average
t-Test: two-sample assuming equal variances	Regression
t-Test: two-sample assuming unequal variances	Sampling
z-test: two-sample for means	

will appear in the checkbox to indicate that the add-in is now ready to be installed. When finished, click the OK button to exit. The Analysis ToolPak provides the functions shown in Table 2.2.

STATISTICAL METHODS

The problem of information overload is a well-recognised symptom of the information era. Today's businesses create such large amounts of computer-generated information that management is often unable to make full use of all available data. The primary role of statistics is to provide managers with mathematical tools that will help them to organise and analyse data in an effective and meaningful way. By summarising the essential features and relationships of data, managers are better able to interpret details on product performance, patterns of consumer behaviour, sales forecasts, and other areas of interest. A brief summary of the main terms used in business statistics is now given.

A 'population' is a collection of all the items (data, facts or observations) of interest to the decision-maker. A 'sample' is a subset of a population. The set of measurements from the whole population is called a 'census'. Normally, taking a complete census is economically impossible. Even if a manager could take a census, there are obvious constraints, namely: (i) time constraints – it is quicker to ask a question of 100 people than 10,000; (ii) cost constraints – it is cheaper to ask 100 than 10,000 people!

Decision-making means choosing between two or more alternatives. Good decision-making is based on evaluating which alternative has the best chance of succeeding. When managers refer to the chance of something occurring, they are using probability in the decision-making process. Common methods associated with probability are permutations, combinations and various probability rules (including Bayes's Rule). Statistical sampling techniques include all those using random or probability sampling, whereby data items are selected by chance alone.

Statistics can be divided into three main areas, namely, (i) descriptive statistics, (ii) probability and (iii) inferential statistics.

Descriptive Statistics – Organising and Presenting Data

Descriptive statistics consist of techniques that help decision-makers to present data in a meaningful way. Frequency distribution tables, histograms, pie charts, scatter plots, and bar charts are some of the tools that allow data to be organised and presented in a manageable form (Groebner, Shannon et al., Chapters 1–3). The easiest method of organising data is to construct a frequency distribution table using classes. A class is simply a specified interval of interest, usually having an upper and lower limit. Presentation techniques such as frequency histograms can, however, be misleading when making comparisons between two different sets of data. For example, by varying the number and width of class intervals, histograms from two quite different sets of data may appear very similar!

   Other statistical techniques are needed to test for differences between data groups. The more common of these attempt to determine whether the two groups have the same distribution, i.e., have they the same central location and spread? The central location is simply the middle or centre of a set of data. Common measures of central location are the mode, median and arithmetic mean. Statistical measures of spread are also called measures of variation (or dispersion) because they focus on fluctuations that occur on either side of the central location. The more common measures of spread are the range, variance and standard deviation.

EXAMPLE 2.2   *Graphical presentation using Chart Wizard*

The Wheelie Company is about to introduce a new line of tyres for racing bicycles. The quality control manager has been asked to present the results of a recent test of tyres on a hundred bicycles competing in the Tour de France. The following is a list of how far the 100 bicycles got (to the nearest 100 km) before one of the tyres failed to meet minimum EC standards.

38	24	12	36	41	40	45	41	40	47
26	15	48	44	29	43	28	29	37	10
37	45	29	31	23	49	41	47	41	42
61	40	40	45	37	55	47	42	28	38
38	48	18	16	39	50	14	52	33	32
51	10	49	21	44	31	43	34	49	48
28	39	28	36	56	54	39	31	35	36
32	20	54	25	39	44	25	42	50	41
9	34	32	34	42	40	43	32	30	45
20	29	14	19	38	46	46	39	40	47

The quality control manager has decided to use a frequency histogram for his presentation. His first task is to convert the raw data into a number of groups or classes, and then count the number of values which fall into each class. The number of values in each class is called the 'class frequency'. The ideal number of classes N can be found by using the 'rule of thumb' inequality which states that 2^N must be greater than the number of observations, O. In this example, $O = 100$, and so $2^7 > 100$, i.e., $N = 7$.

$$\text{Class width} = \frac{\text{largest value} - \text{smallest value}}{\text{number of classes, } N} = \frac{61 - 9}{7} = 7.43$$

Rounding the class width of 7.43 down to 7 and then applying this value to the data range (9–16), the following frequency distribution table is obtained:

Range	9–16	17–24	25–32	33–40	41–48	49–56	57–64
Class frequency	8	7	19	26	28	11	1

The quality manager's next step is to enter this frequency table into a spreadsheet as shown in Figure 2.7. Excel's ChartWizard is used to obtain a histogram. The steps required to produce graphical output are given on lines 33–43.

Probability – Measuring Levels of Uncertainty

Probability is the chance that something will happen. Probabilities are expressed as fractions or decimals. If an event is assigned a probability of 0, this means that the event can never happen. If the event is given a probability of 1 then it will always happen. Classical probability defines the probability that an event will occur, given that each of the outcomes are equally likely, as

$$P \text{ (event)} = \frac{\text{number of ways that the event can occur}}{\text{total number of possible outcomes}}$$

For example, what is the probability of rolling a 4 on the first throw of a dice? Since the total number of possible outcomes is 6, and the number of ways that 4 can be achieved with one throw is 1, the answer is P (event) $= 1/6$.

A probability distribution is similar to a frequency distribution because each uses intervals to group data items into more meaningful form. Probability distributions can be either discrete or continuous. A discrete probability distribution describes instances where the variable of interest can take on only a limited number of values, e.g., the rolling of a dice is limited to one of six numbers. In a continuous probability distribution, the variable can take any value in a given range, e.g., measuring a child's growth over a specified time period. The mean of a discrete probability distribution is referred to as its 'expected value'.

There are many different probability distributions, both discrete and continuous. The four more commonly used are (i) the Binomial distribution, which is a discrete distribution used to describe many business activities, (ii) the Poisson distribution which is a discrete distribution often used to count the number of occurrences of some event in a given period of time, (iii) the exponential distribution which is a continuous distribution used to measure the length of time needed to perform some activity, and (iv) the important continuous distribution known as the normal distribution.

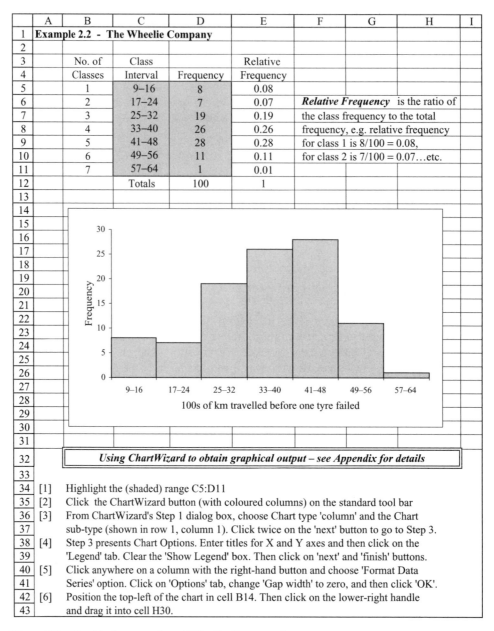

	A	B	C	D	E	F	G	H	I
1	**Example 2.2 - The Wheelie Company**								
2									
3		No. of	Class		Relative				
4		Classes	Interval	Frequency	Frequency				
5		1	9–16	8	0.08				
6		2	17–24	7	0.07	*Relative Frequency* is the ratio of			
7		3	25–32	19	0.19	the class frequency to the total			
8		4	33–40	26	0.26	frequency, e.g. relative frequency			
9		5	41–48	28	0.28	for class 1 is 8/100 = 0.08,			
10		6	49–56	11	0.11	for class 2 is 7/100 = 0.07…etc.			
11		7	57–64	1	0.01				
12			Totals	100	1				
13									
14									

Using ChartWizard to obtain graphical output – see Appendix for details

[1]   Highlight the (shaded) range C5:D11
[2]   Click the ChartWizard button (with coloured columns) on the standard tool bar
[3]   From ChartWizard's Step 1 dialog box, choose Chart type 'column' and the Chart
       sub-type (shown in row 1, column 1). Click twice on the 'next' button to go to Step 3.
[4]   Step 3 presents Chart Options. Enter titles for X and Y axes and then click on the
       'Legend' tab. Clear the 'Show Legend' box. Then click on 'next' and 'finish' buttons.
[5]   Click anywhere on a column with the right-hand button and choose 'Format Data
       Series' option. Click on 'Options' tab, change 'Gap width' to zero, and then click 'OK'.
[6]   Position the top-left of the chart in cell B14. Then click on the lower-right handle
       and drag it into cell H30.

Figure 2.7   Graphical presentation of Wheelie Company data.

	A	B	C	D	E	F	G	H	I
1	Example 2.3 - Using Excel's Binomial distribution function BINOMDIST								
2									
3			*BINOMDIST(number, size, probability, cumulative)*						
4			*where **number** is number of successful outcomes; **size** is the sample size;*						
5			**probability** *is the sample probability;* **cumulative** *is a logical value;*						
6			if **cumulative** is set to TRUE then the function returns the cumulative Binomial						
7			probability; if FALSE it returns the individual Binomial probability						
8									
9			In this example, **number** = no. of sales made per day, **size** = 20, **probability** = 0.1						
10								Answers	
11	(i)	Probability of no sales, P(0) =			BINOMDIST(0,20,0.1,FALSE) =			*0.1216*	
12	(ii)	Probability of four sales, P(4) =			BINOMDIST(4,20,0.1,FALSE) =			*0.0898*	
13	(iii)	Probability of more than 4 sales =		1 - BINOMDIST(4,20,0.1,TRUE) =				*0.0432*	
14	(iv)	Probability of 4 or more sales =		1 - BINOMDIST(3,20,0.1,TRUE) =				*0.1330*	
15									

Figure 2.8   Checking out sales data with the BINOMDIST function.

Probabilities can be either individual or cumulative as demonstrated by Excel's BINOMDIST function in Figure 2.8. The cumulative probability is the sum of all probabilities up to and including the particular probability. For example, consider the following probability distribution table which gives the individual probabilities of selling different numbers of items:

No. of items sold	20	18	15	10
Probability	0.1	0.2	0.3	0.4

The cumulative probability of selling 15 items or more, usually denoted as $P\ (\geq 15)$, is the sum of the probabilities of selling 15, 18 and 20, i.e., $P\ (\geq 15) = 0.3 + 0.2 + 0.1 = 0.6$. Similarly, the cumulative probability of selling 18 units or more, i.e., $P\ (\geq 18)$, is the sum of the probabilities of selling 18 and 20 $= 0.2 + 0.1 = 0.3$. Conversely, the probability of selling less than 18 items, $P\ (<18) = 1 - P\ (\geq 18) = 0.7$, which is the same as the sum of the probabilities of selling 10 and 15 items. Note that in any probability distribution table, the sum of all the probabilities is always unity, i.e., $0.1 + 0.2 + 0.3 + 0.4 = 1$.

EXAMPLE 2.3   *Using Excel's binomial distribution function BINOMDIST*

A salesperson makes twenty calls per day to randomly selected houses. If the probability of the salesperson making a sale is 0.1, use Excel's binomial distribution function BINOMDIST to find the probability of (i) no sales (ii) four sales (iii) more than four sales (iv) four or more sales. The spreadsheet of Figure 2.8 utilises both the individual and cumulative probability features of the distribution function BINOMDIST (click Excel's Function Wizard button f_x to activate BINOMDIST).

Inferential Statistics – Drawing Conclusions from Samples

Inferential statistics, usually abbreviated to inference, is a process by which conclusions are reached on the basis of examining only a part of the total data available. A typical example of inference is an opinion poll that is used to predict the voting pattern of a country's population during an election. Statistical inference can be divided into two main areas – estimation and hypothesis testing. Estimation is concerned with drawing conclusions from population samples. The objective of hypothesis testing is to use sample information to decide whether a manufacturer's claim about a product should be confirmed or refuted.

In operations management, quality-control testing relies heavily on statistical estimation to accept or reject production output. A quality-control manager will take a random sample of products and if it is found that the number of defective items is too high the batch will be rejected. Adjustments must then be made to the production process in order to eliminate, or at least reduce, the level of deficiency.

Most people at some time or other have purchased a box of matches with the label inscribed 'contents 100 approx'. If anyone bothered to count the number of matches in a random sample of six boxes, they would most likely find that the contents varied from, say 98 to 102. It would be most unusual, if not unique, if every one of the six boxes contained the same number of matches. Putting this observation into statistical terms, when the mean is calculated from a sample the value obtained, $\bar{X}$, depends on which sample (of the many possible samples that could be chosen) is observed.

The difference between the population mean, μ (pronounced mu), and the sample mean, $\bar{X}$, is called the sampling error. Two samples from the same population are likely to have different sample values and therefore possibly lead to different conclusions being drawn. Consequently, managers need to understand how sample means are distributed throughout the population, i.e., they need to understand the concepts of sampling distribution. Consider the following example.

EXAMPLE 2.4   *Sampling error model*

The investment manager of AstroReturns stockbrokers has been asked by a client to determine the average return on her portfolio investment of six stocks. The returns on each stock for last year are:

Stock	A	B	C	D	E	F
Return (%)	8	11	–3	18	3	5

The population mean μ for the six stocks is $(8 + 11 - 3 + 18 + 3 + 5)/6 = 7\%$.

In this example, in order to illustrate the concept of sampling error, the investment manager will base his report on a simple random sample of three stocks from the six available. Because the population is so small – consisting of only six stocks, the investment manager could easily have carried out a census (i.e., show that $\mu = 7$). In Table 2.3, the twenty possible combinations of samples, along with their sample means, $\bar{X}$, have been arranged in ascending order from 1.67 to 12.33.

When the sampling errors, $\mu - \bar{X}$, are calculated, they show a wide variation, ranging from $+5.33$ to -5.33. The client could therefore be seriously misled, depending upon which sample(s) the investment manager included in his report. Being aware that there will always be

Table 2.3

Stock sample	Average % return	Stock sample	Average % return	Stock sample	Average % return
CEF	1.67	CDE	6.00	DEF	8.67
ACE	2.67	BEF	6.33	ADE	9.67
ACF	3.33	CDF	6.67	ADF	10.33
BCE	3.67	ABE	7.33	BDE	10.67
BCF	4.33	ACD	7.67	BDF	11.33
ABC	5.33	ABF	8.00	ABD	12.33
AEF	5.33	BCD	8.67		

a sampling error, is only part of the problem. Since the investment manager cannot know in advance how large the sampling error will be, he must organise his $\bar{X}$ data in order to obtain a clearer picture of how the sample means are distributed.

The easiest way of presenting data is to construct a frequency distribution table. All of the sample means, $\bar{X}$, lie within the range 1–13. By taking six classes of interval size 2, ranging from 1–3 to 11–13, the graph of Figure 2.9 can be created to show the distribution of all possible $\bar{X}$ values, i.e., the sampling distribution of $\bar{X}$. It can be seen that the distribution follows a normal bell-shaped curve. This feature illustrates one of the characteristics of the important central limit theorem. Another aspect of the central limit theorem is that the 'mean of the means', i.e., the mean of the sampling distribution, is equal to the population mean, μ.

Using Excel's ChartWizard, follow the steps below to obtain the graph in Figure 2.9:

- Enter the data as shown on lines 1–11.

- Use Excel's SUM function for totals on line 12 (e.g., D12 contains the formula SUM (D6:D11)).

- Enter formula D6/D$12 in cell F6 and then copy into cells F7:F11.

- Cell H14 contains the 'mean of the means', i.e., the mean of the data, which has been grouped into a frequency distribution table. The formula for the mean of grouped data is

$$\text{mean (of grouped data)} = \left(\sum_{i=1}^{c} f_i M_i \right) / N$$

where: c = number of classes (= 6)
N = number of data points (= 20)
f_i = frequency in the ith class (cells D6:D11)
M_i = midpoint of the ith class (cells E6:E11)

- To draw the graph, firstly highlight the range C6:D11.

- Click the ChartWizard button (with coloured columns) on the standard toolbar.

- In ChartWizard's Step 1, click on the 'CustomTypes' tab and then select Chart type 'Smooth Lines'.

- Follow the instructions as requested by ChartWizard, positioning the chart's top-left corner in cell A16. Click on the lower-right handle and drag it into cell I32.

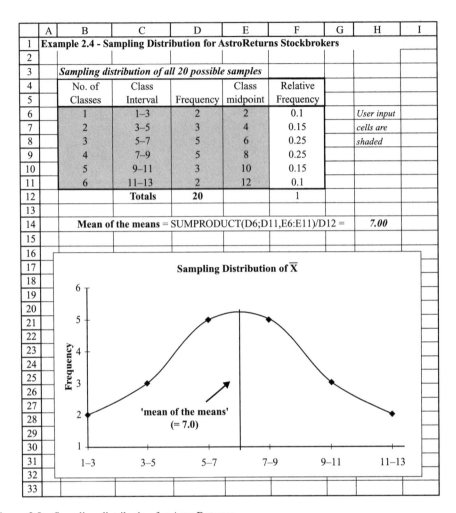

Figure 2.9   Sampling distribution for AstroReturns.

DECISION ANALYSIS

Decision analysis – also called decision theory – is one of the main tools used for decision-making in an uncertain environment (Groebner, Shannon et al., Chapters 19, 20). In making a decision, a manager must choose from a number of alternative courses of action that are intended to solve the problem. However, under conditions of uncertainty, the result of choosing any of the alternatives is unknown. Even where the possible outcomes are known, the manager may still be unable to make a prediction because there is insufficient information to allow probabilities to be assigned to the outcomes.

As an example, consider a supplier who has received a telephone order from customer A for 200 widgets. Shortly afterwards, another customer, B, arrives on the premises urgently requiring 200 widgets. Unfortunately, the supplier has none in stock except for the 200 items reserved for customer A. What should the supplier do? Should he sell the reserved items to customer B and hope that he can get a reorder in time to satisfy customer A? Should he refuse B and lose out on a definite sale? What if customer A decides to cancel the order? What if the reordered widgets are more expensive than current stock? All these questions contain such levels of uncertainty that the decision-maker can only answer them by drawing upon his or her own experience and judgement.

In order to build a model, a decision-maker must distinguish between controllable and uncontrollable variables (see Figure 2.2). In decision-analysis terminology, the uncontrollable variables are called 'events' or 'states of nature'. A future event is a possible outcome over which the decision-maker has no control. In an environment of uncertainty, identifying those future events that can occur is generally easier than identifying events that will occur. Having drawn up a list of possible events, the decision-maker usually constructs a payoff table (or matrix). A payoff table assigns some payoff (i.e., monetary value or weighting factor) to each event in order to quantify them more accurately. An example of a payoff table is given in Example 2.7.

The founder of modern decision analysis was an eighteenth-century amateur statistician called the Reverend Thomas Bayes whose best-known contribution is the Bayes rule (or theorem) for conditional probability. A more recent contribution to decision analysis is Von Neumann and Morgenstern's theory of games published in 1944. The game theory concept states that the 'right' decision in any situation depends upon the objectives of the decision-maker and the likely actions to be taken by the competitor(s), e.g., deciding which piece to move in a chess game. Game theory basically consists of three strategies called the maximax criterion, the maximin criterion, and the minimax regret.

Conditional Probability and the Bayes Rule

Before discussing conditional probability, it is helpful to restate some basic probability definitions. Two events are mutually exclusive if they cannot happen together, i.e., the probability of their occurring together is zero. For example, the probability that a tossed coin will show both a head and a tail simultaneously is zero. Two non-mutually exclusive events can happen together, e.g., the probability of two tossed coins showing a head and a tail is nonzero. Two events are independent if the outcome of one does not affect the outcome of the other, e.g., if a coin is tossed twice and a tail occurs the first time, then the probability of getting a tail on the second toss is still $1/2$. Two events are dependent if the outcome of one affects the outcome of the second, e.g., the probability of drawing a second consecutive spade from a deck of cards is affected if the first card is not returned to the pack. Two important rules of probability can be applied to independent events, namely the addition rule and the multiplication rule.

Addition Rule   The probability that one or other of two mutually exclusive events A and B occurring is the sum of their respective probabilities, i.e.,

$$P \text{ (A or B)} = P \text{ (A)} + P \text{ (B)}$$

For example, the probability of getting 2 or 5 when a dice is rolled is $P(2) + P(5) = 1/6 + 1/6 = 1/3$.

Multiplication Rule   The probability of two independent events A and B occurring together is the product of their respective probabilities, i.e.,

$$P \text{ (A and B)} = P \text{ (A)} . P \text{ (B)}$$

For example, if two coins are tossed, the probability of a head (H) on the first and a tail (T) on the second coin is $P \text{ (H and T)} = P \text{ (H)} . P \text{ (T)} = \frac{1}{2} \times \frac{1}{2} = \frac{1}{4}$. The probability of two or more events occurring simultaneously is usually called their joint probability.

Conditional probability   refers to two events A and B, where event A has already taken place. It is usually expressed in the form $P \text{ (B|A)}$. The conditional probability of event B, given that event A has occurred, is equal to the joint probability of A and B, divided by the probability of event A, i.e.,

$$P(B|A) = \frac{P(A \text{ and } B)}{P(A)} \quad \text{where } P(A) \neq 0$$

$$\text{i.e., } P \text{ (A and B)} = P \text{ (B|A)} . P \text{ (A)}$$

When the events are independent, then the conditional probability is the same as the remaining event. This is easily derived by substituting the RHS of the multiplication rule into the above equation, i.e.,

$$P \text{ (B|A)} = \frac{P(A \text{ and } B)}{P(A)} = \frac{P(A) . P(B)}{P(A)} = P(B)$$

A basic form of Bayes's rule can be obtained by interchanging the letters in the conditional probability equation to give

$$P(A|B) = \frac{P(B \text{ and } A)}{P(B)} \quad \text{where } P(B) \neq 0$$

Since $P \text{ (B and A)}$ is the same as $P \text{ (A and B)}$, the above equation can then be re-written as

$$P(A|B) = \frac{P(A \text{ and } B)}{P(B)} = \frac{P(B|A) . P(A)}{P(B)}$$

A more general form of Bayes's rule for two events, A and B, is given by the equation

$$P(A|B) = \frac{P(B|A) . P(A)}{P(B|A) . P(A) + P(B|\overline{A}) . P(\overline{A})}$$

where $\overline{A}$ is the converse, i.e., the opposite of A.

Decision-makers are better placed to make a decision if they are able to gather additional information about future events. Potential sources of more information include product sampling, materials testing, opinion polls, and updating event probabilities. In other words, as more knowledge about a situation becomes available, the more certain the decision becomes. Statistically, as an event's certainty increases, its probability moves closer to unity – and vice versa. If an event's probability can be revised to take account of new information, the revised probability will be greater than the previous value. Conditional probability and Bayes's rule are important processes in the updating of event probabilities. The following example shows how Bayes's rule can be used to derive a revised probability, based on an event that has already taken place.

EXAMPLE 2.5   *Using Bayes's rule*

A drilling company reckons that there is a 70% chance of finding a profitable reservoir of oil in a particular area. After drilling a first test bore-hole, the results are found to be favourable. From previous experience, the company estimates the bore-hole results to be 80% accurate. Use Bayes's rule to find a revised probability of finding oil in economic quantities. Here, the two events are A = oil and B = successful strike. The required conditional probability is given by $P(A|B)$. From the above data, $P(A) = P(\text{oil}) = 0.7$ and $P(\text{T}) = P(\text{no oil}) = 0.3$. $P(B|A) = P(\text{successful strike | oil}) = 0.8$ and $P(B|\text{T}) = P(\text{successful strike | no oil}) = 0.2$. Applying this data to Bayes's rule above,

$$P(A|B) = \frac{P(\text{successful strike|oil}).P(\text{oil})}{P(\text{successful strike|oil}).P(\text{oil}) + P(\text{successful strike|no oil}).P(\text{no oil})}$$

$$= \frac{0.8 \times 0.7}{0.8 \times 0.7 + 0.2 \times 0.3} = \frac{0.56}{0.62} = 0.9$$

(Note that the revised probability of 0.9 is greater than the original probability of 0.7.)

Expected Values and Decision Trees

Under conditions of uncertainty, a decision-maker often has to choose among a number of alternatives. Each alternative usually has some monetary value associated with it. A truer picture of the effects of choosing a particular alternative emerges when these monetary values are taken into account. The expected monetary value (EMV) of an event is simply its *weighted average*. The weighted average is obtained by multiplying each monetary value by its associated probability and then summing these products. For example, a company requires a new plant facility and must decide whether to choose between type A or type B on the basis of expected annual profits from each plant. The following probabilities and profits (in £000s) have been calculated and are shown in Table 2.4.

On the basis of each plant's EMV, plant type A would be favourite because of its higher profit returns. The EMV is a special monetary case of the more general expected value concept of a random variable. The expected value is the weighted average of the random variables, where the weights are the probabilities assigned to the values as shown in Table 2.5.

Table 2.4

	←Plant type A →		×	←Plant type B →		×
	Probability	Profit		Probability	Profit	
Optimistic	0.2	500	100	0.1	500	50
Most likely	0.5	250	125	0.6	300	180
Pessimistic	0.3	150	45	0.3	50	15
EMV (£000s)			270			245

Table 2.5

Random variable, x_i	0	1	2	3	4	Totals
Probability, p_i	0.1	0.3	0.2	0.3	0.1	1.0
Weighted value, $x_i p_i$	0.0	0.3	0.4	0.9	0.4	2.0
Expected value $= E(x) = \sum x_i p_i = 2.0$						

Table 2.6

		←Revenue (£m.) →	
Drilling options	**Probability of finding oil**	**Oil**	**Lease**
No further testing	50%	140	50
Further tests indicate oil	80%	120	70
Further tests indicate no oil	15%	−40	10

A decision tree is a graphical representation of the various alternative courses of action, along with the events and their probabilities which are associated with each alternative. In other words, a decision tree is basically a probability tree applied to the evaluation of expected values. Consider the following situation.

EXAMPLE 2.6   *Building a decision tree*

An oil company owns exploration rights to a particular field. Several well-bore tests have already been carried out in the area indicating that there is good potential. If further tests are conducted, the company reckons that there is a 70% chance of finding oil in economic quantities. The company has three options available to it: (i) perform further tests before drilling; (ii) start drilling without testing, or (iii) sell the exploration lease. The possible drilling options are listed in Table 2.6, along with their associated revenues (in £m.) from the sale of either oil or the lease.

The option of drilling without further testing will cost the company £32 million if no oil is found. Management has decided to use a decision tree to illustrate the above events and their associated EMVs. It will then evaluate the various options open to it and decide which option represents the best course of action.

The decision tree shown in Figure 2.10 uses standard symbols to represent the two types of nodes. Decision nodes are shown as squares while event nodes are shown as circles. Decision nodes are points where a choice has to be made between several alternatives, e.g., to drill, test, or sell. The event nodes are points from which various branches extend, each branch representing a possible outcome. Each outcome has a probability assigned to it as shown by the figures in parentheses in Figure 2.10. The EMVs associated with each final outcome are written alongside terminal nodes, represented by arrowheads. Instructions for drawing and

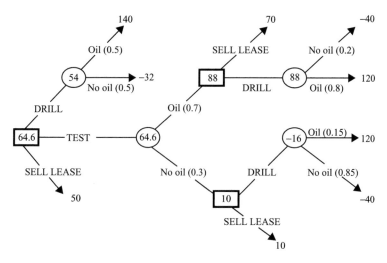

Figure 2.10   A decision tree for the oil company's options.

evaluating the decision tree are given below:

- First, draw the tree starting from left to right, showing the decision points and the various event nodes. This process is called a 'forward pass'. When the tree has been drawn and labelled with probability and monetary values, proceed to the next step.

- The general process for solving a decision tree problem is to work backwards through the tree, i.e., from right to left, calculating an EMV for each event and decision node. This solution procedure is known by different names – backward pass, rollback, or foldback.

- Initially, there will be no EMV values assigned to either decision or event nodes. Starting with the top right-hand *event node*, an EMV of £88m. is calculated by summing the expected profits from the two final outcomes as shown below:

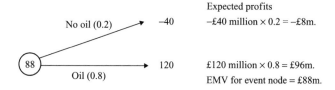

- The decision node at the top right-hand now has two EMV values to consider – either sell the rights for £70m. or drill to get an EMV of £88m. Always assign the largest EMV value to the decision node, i.e., £88m. in this case. Repeat this step for all event and decision nodes to obtain Figure 2.10.

The possible returns from the oil company's three options are 64.6, 54, and 50. From these figures, it can be seen that option (i) is the best, i.e., test before drilling. However, management may prefer the less risky option of selling the exploration rights for an immediate return of £50 million.

The Maximax, Maximin, and Minimax Decision Criteria

Several decisions fall into the nonprobabilistic category, i.e., the levels of uncertainty are such that probabilities cannot be assigned to any of the possible courses of action. While there may be insufficient quantitative information to establish probabilistic criteria, the decision-maker can still apply qualitative judgement and experience to the situation. It would be a very unusual problem indeed that would leave a decision-maker bereft of ideas! For cases where probabilities cannot be specified, the main decision criteria are maximin, maximax, and minimax. These decision rules characterise game theory which provides a framework for analysing conflict situations.

In order to gain competitive advantage, many business decisions involve a conflict between competing parties. In such cases, an organisation's actions can be influenced by choices made by its competitors whose objectives clash with the organisation's own goals. Business decisions, however, are also influenced by management's attitudes to risk. Some managers are very conservative and actively avoid risk taking. On the other hand, decision-makers such as speculators will take a high risk of losing a lot of money in order to make a substantial gain. Between these two extremes is the risk-neutral manager. A decision-maker who is concerned with achieving a balance between highest returns and lowest costs is considered to be risk-neutral. In decision analysis terminology, these risk-preference attitudes are referred to as 'risk-averse', 'risk-neutral', and 'risk-seeking'. Risk-preference attitudes can also be applied to the maximax, maximin, and minimax criteria (rules).

The maximax rule   A risk-seeking decision-maker will choose the adventurous maximax decision rule. The maximax criterion takes an optimistic view that 'everything will turn out right' regardless of what decision is taken. It looks only at the highest possible gain and ignores the opportunities that other alternatives might present. In monetary terms, a maximax decision looks for the 'best of the best' by evaluating the largest possible profit that each alternative can produce and then choosing the alternative with the highest profit. An organisation that adopts a maximax approach perceives a business opportunity and takes a gamble in trying to achieve its goal. It may become very profitable or it may go broke.

The maximin rule   A risk-averse decision-maker will use the conservative maximin criterion which often leads to a decision to do nothing. An organisation that adopts a 'maximin' attitude is non-competitive and will soon be overtaken by more innovative risk-taking competitors. The maximin criterion essentially takes a pessimistic view and considers the results of taking the 'wrong' alternative. It evaluates the worst outcome for each alternative and then chooses the alternative which leads to the best of these worst outcomes. In monetary terms, a maximin decision looks for the 'best of the worst' by choosing the alternative that yields the maximum profit from all minimum possible returns – hence the name maximin.

The minimax rule   The minimax criterion – also called minimax regret – can be considered as another conservative or pessimistic decision rule. It introduces the concept of regret or opportunity loss. To use the minimax rule, the payoff table must first be converted into a regret table. A payoff table is simply a matrix of values showing the profits or other benefits that would result from each possible combination of alternatives. A regret table summarises

Table 2.7 Payoff table for new Gizmo models.

Model Popularity	←**Expected profits (£000s)** →		
	G1	**G2**	**G3**
Excellent	120	100	60
Moderate	80	60	50
Poor	−30	−20	0

the regrets or lost opportunities that could result from choosing each alternative. In monetary terms, a minimax decision looks for the 'minimum of the maximums' by evaluating the largest possible opportunity loss that each alternative would produce and then choosing the alternative with the smallest loss. Thus, the minimax rule chooses the alternative with the smallest (or minimum) maximum regret – hence the name minimax.

EXAMPLE 2.7 *Using the maximax, maximin, and minimax rules*

The Gizmo Company is considering the introduction of three new models of its popular product, specified as prototypes G1, G2, and G3. However, the company has sufficient capacity to manufacture one model only. A payoff table has been prepared showing the estimated profits that can be expected on the basis of the prototypes' popularity (Table 2.7). Gizmo will use the table to find which is the most profitable model to make. It has decided to use all three decision rules.

Note that since the decision relates to the choice of best model, the decision alternatives are represented by the columns. The events or states of nature, i.e., product popularity, are represented by rows.

- The maximax rule chooses the 'best of the best', i.e., the value 120 is the best of the maximum values for G1 (120), G2 (100), and G3 (60) which all happen to be on row 1. The Gizmo Company should choose model G1 using the maximax criterion

- The maximin rule chooses the 'best of the worst', i.e., the value 0 is the best of the minimum values of G1 (–30), G2 (–20), and G3 (0). The Gizmo Company should choose model G3 using the maximin criterion

- The minimax rule requires that the payoff table be converted into a regret table of opportunity losses. A regret table is now developed using the following two steps.

  (i) Find the maximum value in each row, e.g., 120 is the maximum value in row 1.
  (ii) Calculate a new row by subtracting the current values from the maximum value found in (i), e.g., row 1 will now read 0 20 60.

The above two steps are applied to each row, giving the regret table shown in Table 2.8.

The minimax criterion chooses the 'minimum of the maximums' from the regret table, i.e., the value 20 is the minimum of the maximum values for G1 (30), G2 (20), and G3 (60). The Gizmo Company should choose model G2 using the minimax regret criterion.

Table 2.8   Regret table for new Gizmo models.

Model Popularity	←Expected profits (£000s) →		
	G1	**G2**	**G3**
Excellent	0	20	60
Moderate	0	20	30
Poor	30	20	0

It is interesting to note that the three decision rules each give a different answer, which does not appear to be very helpful to the Gizmo Company. The final decision may ultimately depend on the risk-preference attitudes of Gizmo's management.

SIMULATION

The final topic to be considered in this chapter is the versatile model-building tool of simulation. Many real-world situations contain so many unpredictable variables that it is impossible to solve them analytically. A typical example is the everyday queue problem that occurs in supermarkets, bus stations, and so on. In such cases, the best approach is to simulate or mimic the process by developing a model, and then use trial-and-error experiments in an attempt to understand the model's behaviour. Simulation is not an optimising technique but merely allows decision-makers to observe the results of their experimentation, similar to the 'what if?' approach of sensitivity analysis.

Simulation is very useful for analysing problems that contain elements of uncertainty, especially if some of the variables can be represented by probability distributions. Simulation modelling which uses probabilistic distributions and random number generation, is sometimes referred to as Monte Carlo simulation, after the casino in Monaco. Because simulation models are more representative of the real world, they are very popular among business managers. However, the simulation of many queuing or waiting-line systems is so complex that they require the use of special-purpose simulation software packages such as GPSS, SIMSCRIPT, or SIMFACTORY.

A simulation model uses random numbers to imitate uncertain events. The value of a random number or variable cannot be predicted with any certainty, e.g., the random numbers drawn in a national lottery. A simulation model will contain many input variables whose actual values are unknown. If the spreadsheet model is to be realistic, it must avoid bias in the selection of these variables by ensuring that they are truly random in their selection.

A random number generator (RNG) is used in simulation modelling to achieve unbiased selection. Excel has a mathematical function called RAND() which returns a uniformly distributed random number between 0.0 and 1.0. If the RAND() function is entered in any cell in a spreadsheet and the recalculation key F9 is then pressed repeatedly, a series of random numbers will appear in the cell. This repeated random selection of input variables and the recording of the resultant outputs is the basic philosophy underlying simulation. A decision-maker is thus able to gain a better understanding of the likely pattern of events. Consider the following staff allocation problem.

Table 2.9 Customer arrivals.

Number of customers	0	1	2	3	4	5	6
Number of intervals	5	6	8	10	12	9	4
Probability	0.09	0.11	0.15	0.19	0.22	0.17	0.07

Table 2.10 Purchases.

Value of purchases	zero	£10	£20	£30	£40	£50
Number of purchases	14	22	30	53	33	17
Probability	0.08	0.13	0.18	0.31	0.20	0.10

EXAMPLE 2.8 *Simulation model for the Bargain Store*

The Bargain Store is currently reviewing staffing levels in one of its departments. Because the volume of customer activity is unpredictable, management has problems in determining the correct number of sales staff to employ in order to provide an adequate service level. The store is open continuously from 9 a.m. to 6 p.m. Management have decided to collect customer information on a daily basis and have divided the 9-hour day into fifty-four 10-minute intervals. A record has been kept of the number of customers arriving during each 10-minute interval, as well as details on the amount purchased by each customer. Both sets of data are now converted into probability distributions.

The 'customer arrivals' table (Table 2.9) initially contains only data for the top two rows. However, the probabilities (or percentages) for each customer group can easily be calculated. Since the total number of intervals is 54, the probability for zero customers = 5/54 = 0.09, one customer = 6/54 = 0.11, two customers = 8/54 = 0.15, etc.

From the same customer records, information on the values of the 169 customers' purchases have been calculated and a 'purchases' table (Table 2.10) is also constructed. Customers are divided into groups, depending upon the value of their purchases, i.e., no purchase, ≤£10, ≤£20, etc. These purchase group values have been converted into probabilities using the same approach as in the 'customer arrivals' table, i.e., probability of £10 purchases = 22/169 = 0.13; £20 purchases = 30/169 = 0.18, etc.

Bargain Store would like to know how many sales staff should be assigned to the department in order to maximise profits. Management are concerned that customers may be leaving the store without purchasing anything because they cannot get served. They wonder if this situation is due to the fact that there are only two assistants in the department. When there are more than two customers in the department, staff can still only assist one person at a time. Sales may increase if more assistants were available. But how many? Since there is no pattern to customer arrivals or their purchasing habits, mathematical queuing models cannot be used. A simulation model using the Monte Carlo method is now developed.

The Monte Carlo method is a technique based on the selection of random numbers ranging from 00 to 99. The chance of selecting one of these 100 numbers is 1%. Series of the hundred numbers can be assigned to represent a probability. Consider the probability relating

Table 2.11

Number of customers	Probability P_i	Cumulative probability, CUM_i	Random number series
0	0.09	0.09	00–08
1	0.11	0.20	09–19
2	0.15	0.35	20–34
3	0.19	0.54	35–53
4	0.22	0.76	54–75
5	0.17	0.93	76–92
6	0.07	1.00	93–99

to customer arrivals. When the simulation model generates a random number using Excel's RAND function, the chance of a number being in the range 00–08 is 9%, corresponding to probability, $P_1 = 0.09$. Similarly, the chance of a number being in the range 09–19 is 11% corresponding to probability, $P_2 = 0.11$, etc.

Any random number generated must fall within one of the seven-number series shown in Table 2.11. The series in which the number falls determines the number of customers arriving during a 10-minute interval. For example, the RAND function may generate the random number 0.69 (RAND values are always between 0 and 1) for the first interval. This value is equivalent to 69 in the 'Random number series' column of Table 2.11. The number 69 falls within the 54–75 range, giving a value of four customer arrivals for the first 10-minute interval. The cumulative probability, CUM_i, is used to determine upper and lower limits for each of the seven-number series in the table. CUM_i is simply found by adding the current probability, P_i, to the previous cumulative probability CUM_{i-1}, e.g., $CUM_3 = CUM_2 + P_3 = 0.20 + 0.15 = 0.35$.

The same process is used to generate customer purchases. For each customer, a random number is generated and its location in the 'Purchases' table (see range H6:L12 in Figure 2.11) determines the amount of the purchase. For example, RAND numbers of 0.11 and 0.82 give customer purchases of £10 and £40 respectively. In the 'Random arrivals' table (cells B17:D34), the third column contains the number of customers arriving during each 10-minute interval. The 'Random purchases' table (cells F17:K34) consists of six columns, each column representing the number of assistants available to serve customers. The model calculates details of actual and lost sales for different numbers of sales staff.

To perform a cost-benefit analysis, assume that a sales assistant is paid £5 per hour. In the simulated three-hour period, the Bargain Store is currently losing £1000 in sales (see cell G40) by assigning only two departmental assistants who achieve sales of £1,060 (cell G39). An extra assistant, whose three hours would cost £15 in pay, could achieve sales of £1,540 (cell H39) – an increase of £480. Two extra assistants would bring in sales of £1,830 (cell I39) adding £770. Obviously, as sales figures increase the amount of lost sales decreases (cells G40:K40). As the model indicates, the amount of idle time, however, will increase as staff numbers increase. Idle time is defined as:

> Idle intervals = Cumulative no. of blank cells in each column of the 'Random purchases' table
>
> Idle time (hours) = (Number of idle 10-minute intervals × corresponding no. of assistants)/6

	A	B	C	D	E	F	G	H	I	J	K	L	M
1	Example 2.8 - A SIMULATION model for the Bargain Store												
2													
3		'Customer Arrivals' Table						'Purchases' Table					
4		<--Limits-->		Cust.				<--Limits-->		Purch.			
5		Lower	Upper	Nos.	Freq.	P_i		Lower	Upper	Value	Freq.	P_i	
6		0	0.09	0	5	0.09		0	0.08	£0	14	0.08	
7		0.09	0.20	1	6	0.11		0.08	0.21	£10	22	0.13	
8		0.20	0.35	2	8	0.15		0.21	0.39	£20	30	0.18	
9		0.35	0.54	3	10	0.19		0.39	0.70	£30	53	0.31	
10		0.54	0.76	4	12	0.22		0.70	0.90	£40	33	0.20	
11		0.76	0.93	5	9	0.17		0.90	1.00	£50	17	0.10	
12		0.93	1.00	6	4	0.07							
13				169	54			*User input cells are shaded*			169		
14													
15		**Random Arrivals**						**Random Purchases (£'s)**					
16		Interval	RAND	No.		*1*	*2*	*3*	*4*	*5*	*6*		
17		1	0.55	4		30	0	30	40				
18		2	0.34	2		50	10						
19		3	0.50	3		50	30	30					
20		4	0.66	4		20	40	30	30				
21		5	0.31	2		50	20						
22		6	0.47	3		10	30	30					
23		7	0.94	6		40	20	20	40	50	30		
24		8	0.52	3		0	40	30					
25		9	0.91	5		40	20	20	20	20			
26		10	0.81	5		50	30	40	30	40			
27		11	0.57	4		30	30	30	30				
28		12	0.74	4		10	30	20	20				
29		13	0.92	5		40	30	20	10	40			
30		14	0.88	5		30	40	40	10	0			
31		15	0.84	5		20	30	20	20	50			
32		16	0.45	3		10	40	40					
33		17	0.73	4		20	40	30	30				
34		18	0.63	4		30	50	50	10				
35				Purchase totals =		£530	£530	£480	£290	£200	£30		
36				Idle intervals =		0	0	2	8	20	37		
37													
38				Number of sales staff =			2	3	4	5	6		
39				Actual sales =			£1,060	£1,540	£1,830	£2,030	£2,060		
40				Lost sales =			£1,000	£520	£230	£30			
41				Idle Time (hours) =		0.00	0.00	1.00	5.33	16.67	37.00		
42													
43		*Note that the model contains data for only EIGHTEEN 10-minute intervals in lines 17--34.*											
44		*This small number of intervals has been chosen simply to illustrate the Monte Carlo method.*											
45		*In practice, a much larger number of intervals (54 intervals = 1 day) would be simulated.*											
46													

Figure 2.11   Simulation model for Bargain Store's staffing problem.

Table 2.12   Simulation model – worksheet formulae.

Cell	Formula	Copied to
C6	F6	
B7	C6	B8:B12
C7	C6 + F7	C8:C12
F6	E6/E$13	F7:F12
I6	L6	
H7	I6	H8:H11
I7	I6 + L7	I8:I11
L6	K6/K$12	L7:L11
D13	SUMPRODUCT(D6:D12,E6:E12)	
E13	SUM(E6:E12)	
K12	SUM(K6:K11)	
C17	RAND()	C18:C34
D17	VLOOKUP(C17,$B$6:$D$12,3)	D18:D34
F17	IF(F$16 > $D17,"",VLOOKUP(RAND(),$H$6:$J$11,3))	F17:K34
F35	SUM(F17:F34)	G35:K35
F36	COUNTBLANK($F17:F34)	G36:K36
G38	G16	H38:K38
G39	SUM($F35:G35)	H39:K39
G40	SUM(H35:$K35)	H40:J40
F41	G38*F36/6	G41:K41

The simulation model of Figure 2.11 is created from the formulae template shown in Table 2.12. Details of all Excel formulae used in the model are also given. The user should be aware of the RAND function's sensitivity. Any change to the original spreadsheet will cause new random values to be automatically generated, thus producing a different set of results.

EXCEL FUNCTIONS USED IN MODEL-BUILDING

The models developed in this chapter use eight Excel functions, each of which is explained below. The user should remember that a comprehensive on-line help facility is also provided by Excel.

1. BINOMDIST BINOMDIST (number, size, probability, cumulative)

returns the individual Binomial probability. Use BINOMDIST in problems with a fixed number of trials where the trial outcomes can only be either success or failure. For example, BINOMDIST can calculate the probability that a sample of twenty items will contain only two defectives.

number   = the number of successful outcomes.
size   = the number of trials.
probability = probability of success on each trial.
cumulative = a logical value which can be set equal to TRUE to give the cumulative
                  Binomial probability, or set to FALSE to give the individual Binomial
                  probability.

	A	B	C	D	E	F
1						
2		Product	No. in	Product	Product	
3		name	stock	price	code	
4		Gizmo	10	£10.00	G2	
5		Gadget	25	£12.50		
6		Widget	8	£20.00	W6	
7		Sprocket	40	£4.50		
8						
9				*Sample Figure*		

Figure 2.12　Sample figure.

Example: The probability of exactly 6 heads occurring when a coin is tossed 10 times is BINOMDIST(6, 10, 0.5, FALSE) = 0.2051 where probability of getting a head is 0.5.

2. COUNT: COUNT (ref1:ref2)

counts the number of cells containing numeric values in a range from ref1 to ref2. A blank cell is considered to be non-numeric.

Example: COUNT (D2:D7) in Figure 2.12 returns a value of 4 (i.e., cells D4, D5, D6, D7; note that cells D2 and D3 are ignored because they contain text).

3. COUNTBLANK: COUNTBLANK (ref1:ref2)

counts the number of blank cells in a range from ref1 to ref2. A blank cell is either an empty cell or a cell containing space characters or null text ("").

Example: COUNTBLANK (E2:E7) in Figure 2.12 returns a value of 2 (i.e., cells E5, E7).

4. IF: IF (Logical_test, TrueValue, FalseValue)

returns one of two values, depending upon the value of the initial logical argument.

Logical_test = A logical test between two variables, e.g., C2 < 45 or Exam = 'Fail'.
TrueValue　 = A statement which is returned if Logical_test is true. The statement can be a number, text, or another Excel function. Note that text is always enclosed in quote marks.
FalseValue　 = A statement, similar to TrueValue, which is returned if Logical_test is false.

Example 1: IF (A4<40, "Fail", "Pass") returns the word Fail if the value in cell A4 is less than 40, otherwise it returns the word Pass.

Example 2: IF (A4<40, "Fail", IF(A4<60, "Grade C", IF(A4<80, "Grade B", "Grade A"))) allocates grades A, B, C, and Fail depending upon the value of A4. This is an example of nested IF functions.

5. RAND: RAND()

   randomly generates numbers between (and including) 0 and 1, i.e., $0 \leq \text{RAND}() < 1$. To generate numbers between 0 and 100, simply multiply by 100, i.e., RAND() * 100. The RAND function, which uses a Uniform distribution, requires no input.

   Note that Excel's Analysis ToolPak also contains a 'Random Number Generation' (RNG) function which allows the user to choose from seven different distributions: Uniform, Normal, Bernoulli, Binomial, Poisson, Patterned, and Discrete. An important difference between the RAND function and the ToolPak RNG is that cells will contain functions when using RAND whereas cells contain only numbers when the ToolPak's RNG is used.

6. SUM: SUM (ref1:ref2)

   adds up all cell values in a range from ref1 to ref2.

   Example: SUM (C4:C7) in Figure 2.12 returns a value of 83 by adding 10, 25, 8, and 40.

7. SUMPRODUCT: SUMPRODUCT (ref1:ref2, ref3:ref4)

   returns the sum of the products of two corresponding cell ranges. Both ranges must contain the same number of cells. The first range is defined by ref3:ref2 and the second by ref3:ref4

   Example: SUMPRODUCT (C4:C7, D4:D7) in Figure 2.12 returns a value of £752.50 (i.e., 10*£10 + 25*£12.50 + 8*£20 + 40*£4.50)

8. VLOOKUP: VLOOKUP(Table_value, Lookup_table, Column_no, Nearest)

   searches the leftmost column of a range of cells (the Lookup_table) for a specific value (Table_value). It then returns a corresponding value from a different column in the table.

   Table_value   = The value being searched for in the first column of the Lookup_table. This value can be a constant, text, or another function as used in the simulation model example. Note that if an exact match is not found for Table_value, VLOOKUP then selects the largest value that is less than Table_value.
   Lookup_table = A rectangular range of cells.
   Column_no   = The column number that contains the required data (must be > 1).
   Nearest   = A logical value (i.e., TRUE or FALSE) that specifies whether the user wants to find an exact match (FALSE) or an approximate match (TRUE). If this argument is omitted, then the value TRUE is assumed. Note that for integer values 'Nearest' is always FALSE.

   Example: VLOOKUP("Widget",B4:D7,2) in Figure 2.12 returns a value of 8.
   Since 'Widget' is located in the third row of the lookup range, the corresponding value in the second column is 8. Note that the 'Nearest' argument has been omitted.

EXERCISES

2.1 Table 2.13 shows (i) the nutritional contents of five foods in grams per 100g (ii) their costs per 100g, and (iii) the minimum weekly requirements for an adult (in grams).

Table 2.13

	Protein	Fat	Carbohydrate	Cost (pence)
Wholemeal bread	8	1	56	8
Margarine	–	84	–	16
Cheese	25	35	–	38
Breakfast cereal	10	2	77	24
Diet snack bar	10	–	49	40
Weekly adult requirements (g)	500	600	2100	

Using Excel's Solver, find the cheapest combination of foods that will meet the weekly adult minimum requirements.

(Answer: 6250g of wholemeal bread and 640g of margarine, costing a total of £6.02.)

2.2 The Good-Nut Company sells dry-roasted nut mixes. Table 2.14 gives the price per bag and the ingredients in a 210g bag of its four best-selling nut mixes, along with current prices of a kilo of each nut type.

Table 2.14

Mixes	Cashews	Peanuts	Brazils	Walnuts	Almonds	Price
Cocktail Special	60	60	30	30	30	£2.20
Deluxe Mix	90			60	60	£2.50
Good-Nut Mix	90		60		60	£2.50
Party Special		120	90			£2.50
Price per kilo (£)	7.20	3.75	6.00	8.25	9.50	

The Good-Nut Company has the following stocks of bulk nuts (in kilos): 200 (cashews), 100 (brazils), 50 (walnuts), 150 (almonds) and an unlimited supply of peanuts. The Company cannot sell more than 800 bags of Cocktail Special in the current period. Recommend the best product mix to maximise profits. Solve this linear programming problem using Excel's Solver.

(Answer: maximum profit of £2,170 by selling 800 Cocktail Specials, 433 Deluxe Mix, 1255 Good-Nut and 7 Party Special bags.)

2.3 Mary Jones has been given the job of finding the best way to present the company's advertising expenses at a forthcoming meeting. She has obtained the data in Table 2.15.

Mary has access to a computer and Excel software. She has examined the various options offered by ChartWizard such as pie-charts, doughnuts, columns, and bar charts. Mary has decided on two options: (i) two three-dimensional pie charts, one for each year (ii) a line chart with the two sets of figures on the same chart. You are asked to help Mary create the charts and then choose between the two presentations, giving reasons for your choice.

Table 2.15

Advertising Medium	This year's expenses	Next year's expenses
Television	£60,000	£80,000
Newspapers	£35,000	£40,000
Trade Publications	£25,000	£20,000
Miscellaneous	£10,000	£10,000

2.4   A quality control manager estimates that a batch of items contains 15% defectives. A sample of eight items is taken at random from the batch. Using Excel's binomial distribution function BINOMDIST, find the probability that the sample contains (i) one defective (ii) two or more defectives.

(Answers: (i) probability of one defective is 0.3847 (ii) probability of two or more defectives is 0.3428.)

2.5   A manufacturing plant has two facilities, A and B which produce 30% and 70% of output respectively. On average, twelve out of every thousand components produced in facility A are defective while eight out of every thousand from facility B are defective. If a component is drawn at random from the plant's total output, use Bayes's rule to determine the probability that the component is from facility A.

(Hint: let the two events be A = from facility A and C = from total plant output, i.e., from either facility A or B. Find $P(A|C)$. Remember that $P(C|A)$ is the probability of C occurring, given the probability of A, hence $P(C|A) = 0.012$; also $P(T) = P(B) = 0.7$.)

(Answer: $P(A|C) = 9/23 = 0.3913$.)

2.6   If the Acme Company makes a profit in any given year, the probability that it will make a profit the following year is 0.9. On the other hand, if it makes a loss in any given year, the probability of a loss in the following year is 0.5. In year 1, the company made a profit. Use a decision tree diagram to illustrate Acme's profit and loss situations for the next three years, i.e., up to year 4. What is the probability that Acme made a loss in year 4? If it is known that Acme made a profit in year 2, what is the probability that it made a profit in year 4?

(Answers: (i) probability of a loss in year 4 is 0.156 (ii) probability of a profit in year 4 is 0.86.)

2.7   An hotel which caters for airline passengers has 40 rooms. Because of possible cancellations, the hotel takes up to 45 reservations on any given day. Analysis of past records indicate that the number of daily bookings varies from 36 to 45 with each value in this range having a probability of 0.1. The probability of cancellations is represented by the following distribution table.

Number of cancellations	0	1	2	3	4	5
Probability	0.1	0.2	0.2	0.3	0.1	0.1

Develop a model, utilising Excel's RAND() function, to simulate a fortnight's data and hence find (i) the average number of room bookings per night, and (ii) the percentage of nights when the hotel is overbooked.

(Because of the RAND() function's volatility, the answers may not correspond exactly (i) 40 (ii) 21.4%.)

REFERENCES AND FURTHER READING

Groebner, D., Shannon, P. *et al.* (2001) *Business Statistics: A Decision-Making Approach* (5th edn), Prentice Hall, New Jersey.

Urry, S. (1991) *Introduction to Operational Research*, Longman Scientific & Technical, Essex.

Winston, W. (2003) *Operations Research: Applications and Algorithms* (4th edn), Duxbury Press, California.

Part 1

Business models

3

Financial models

OVERVIEW

There are two main categories of accounting, namely financial accounting and management accounting. Financial accounting is concerned primarily with providing information for parties external to the business such as investors, banking institutions and government agencies. If a company wants to borrow money, it must provide the lending institutions with information to show that the company is a sound investment. Likewise, shareholders want to see financial statements indicating how well the company is doing and how much their investment is worth!

Company accounts consist essentially of two financial statements – the balance sheet and the profit and loss (P&L) statement, also called the income statement. The fact that there are only two main financial statements is often confused by the interchange of the equivalent terms – revenue account, P&L account, and income and expenditure account. Whereas the balance sheet reveals the financial position of the business at a certain date, the profit and loss statement summarises the transactions of the business over a fixed period (usually one year). Thus the balance statement represents a snapshot of the company's financial status at a particular moment in time whereas the income statement presents a fuller picture of the company's activities over a specified period.

All computerised accounting has three main ledgers

- The sales ledger records the sale of goods on credit and the cash received from customers.

- The purchases ledger records the purchase of goods on credit and cash paid to suppliers.

- The nominal ledger – also called the general ledger – records all accounts other than sales and purchases ledger accounts such as expenses, bank payments, and VAT paid and collected.

To add further confusion, the terms 'debtors' ledger' and 'accounts receivable' are sometimes used to refer to the sales ledger! Similarly, the purchases ledger is also known as the 'creditors' ledger' or 'accounts payable'.

The double-entry method of book-keeping recognises that every transaction has a dual effect on the business, i.e., every transaction will produce a debit entry and a credit entry which are equal. Thus all double-entry accounts contain two transaction columns. The left-hand column is called the debit and increases the account balance while the right-hand column is called the credit and reduces the account balance.

Computerised accounting does not need to use credits and debits as accuracy checks since the system automatically ensures that the double-entry rules are followed. This means that each time an alteration is made to an account, a compensating alteration will be made elsewhere to maintain the correct balance. For example, suppose a firm purchases goods from a supplier. This transaction will appear in two accounts – the purchases and nominal ledgers –as shown below:

- The total cost of the goods will be recorded on the debit side of a nominal ledger account called (say) 'goods' or 'stock', i.e., the goods are assets.

- The amount owed for the goods will be recorded on the credit side of the supplier's account within the purchases ledger, i.e., it will be recorded as a liability.

FINANCIAL STATEMENTS

Businesses need to measure and report income. The measurement of net income is an attempt to match the finances generated by a business (its revenue) over a specified period with the resources it consumes (its expenses) during the same period. A profit-and-loss account (i.e., income statement) summarises the transactions which a business has engaged in over a fixed period of time, and determines how much profit (or loss) has been made. Thus

$$\text{Profit (or loss)} = \text{Revenue} - \text{Expenses}$$

Revenue is defined as sales of goods or services to customers and also includes rent or investment revenue received. Expenses are the cost of wages, materials and overheads incurred over the specified period.

A balance sheet is required in order to calculate the projected profitability of a business. The word 'balance' in a balance sheet reflects the double-entry approach to book-keeping, i.e., assets must equal liabilities. The balance sheet is based on the formula

$$\text{Assets} = \text{Liabilities} + \text{Owner's equity}$$

There are two main types of assets, namely fixed and current assets. Fixed assets include land, buildings, plant and machinery, and motor vehicles. They are used by the company to generate profits and are not for resale. Current assets are assets acquired for conversion into cash in the ordinary course of business. They include stock, customers' debts, work-in-progress, and cash itself. Liabilities are obligations owed by the company and include creditors, bank overdrafts, and loans and mortgages. The difference between total assets (fixed + current) and total liabilities of a firm is its total net worth, also called owner's equity, shareholders' equity, or capital. Figure 3.1 shows typical layouts for the two financial statements.

RATIO ANALYSIS

The two main financial statements outlined provide considerable amounts of information in terms of their absolute amounts. However, accounting reports are more useful if they provide comparative figures. For example, accountants may want to compare a company's performance

	A	B	C	D	E	F	G	H	I	J
1	The ABC Company - FINANCIAL ACCOUNTS									
2										
3	➤ Profit and Loss Account									
4	For years ended				31 December 200X			31 December 200Y		
5					£'000	£'000		£'000	£'000	
6	Sales									
7	Cash				150			180		
8	Credit				330	480		420	600	
9	Less: Cost of goods sold									
10				opening inventory	200			195		
11				purchases	60			80		
12					260			275		
13				Less: closing inventory	30	230		10	265	
14										
15	Gross profit					250			335	
16	Less: Operating expenses									
17				administrative expenses	75			70		
18				financial expenses	18			20		
19				selling and distribution expenses	55	148		60	150	
20										
21	Net profit before tax					102			185	
22	Less: corporation tax					25			47	
23	Net profit after tax (earnings)					77			138	
24										
25										
26										
27	➤ Balance Sheet									
28	As at				31 December 200X			31 December 200Y		
29	Fixed assets				£'000	£'000		£'000	£'000	
30				buildings and land	60			90		
31				equipment	110	170		85	175	
32										
33	Current assets									
34				inventory	30			10		
35				debtors	50			90		
36				cash	150	230		100	200	
37	Total assets					400			375	
38										
39	Current liabilities & owner's equity									
40				creditors	80			55		
41				dividends	30			42		
42				overdraft	4	114		20	117	
43				owner's equity		286			258	
44	Total liabilities & owner's equity					400			375	
45										

Figure 3.1 Financial statements for the ABC Company.

with other firms, or perhaps with industry averages or predetermined standards. Such comparisons can provide important insights into a company's profitability and financial stability.

To help assess business performance, accountants use a technique called ratio analysis which examines the relationship between two sets of figures extracted from financial accounts. The two sets of figures may come from either one or both of the two main financial statements.

	A	B	C	D	E	F	G	H	I	J
47	*The ABC Company - FINANCIAL RATIOS*									
48										
49	*Ratio*				*31 December 200X*			*31 December 200Y*		
50	Business profitability		Formula							
51	Gross Profit Margin		F15/F8			52%			56%	
52	Net Profit Margin		F23/F8			16%			23%	
53	Return on Equity		F23/F43			27%			53%	
54										
55	Financial stability									
56	Current Ratio		F36/F42			2.0			1.7	
57	Debt/Equity Ratio		(F37 – F43)/F43			0.40			0.45	
58	Quick Ratio		(F36 – E34)/F42			1.8			1.6	
59										
60	Resource utilization									
61	Total Assets Turnover		F8/F37			1.2 times			1.6	
62	Inventory Turnover		F13/E34			7.7 times			26.5	
63	Debt Turnover		E8/E35			6.6 times			4.7	
64										

Figure 3.2   Financial ratios for the ABC Company.

The computation of financial ratios can reveal underlying relationships between items within the reports and trends in relationships at different points in time.

Ratios can be classified under the three headings of (i) business profitability which is usually the most important business objective (ii) financial stability, i.e., the ability to meet financial commitments in both the short and long term so that the business can continue to operate (iii) resource utilisation ratios which measure how efficient a company is in utilising its resources (assets).

Inventory turnover calculates the number of times during a year (or any other specified period) that a company replaces its inventories. A high turnover implies that goods are being sold quickly and that company assets are not being tied up in idle stock. Debt turnover measures the number of times per year that debts are collected. The debt turnover rate can be converted into a credit period, showing how long it takes customers to pay for goods. The credit control department can then use these credit periods to assess its own effectiveness. The cell formulae for the following ratio definitions are shown in Figure 3.2.

- Business profitability
    - Gross profit margin   = (Gross profit)/(Net sales)
    - Net profit margin   = (Net profit after tax)/(Net sales)
    - Return on equity   = (Net profit after tax)/(Owner's equity)
- Financial stability
    - Current ratio   = (Current assets)/(Current liabilities)
    - Debt/equity ratio   = (Total assets – Owner's equity)/(Owner's equity)
    - Quick (or acid test) ratio = (Current assets less inventory)/(Current liabilities)
- Resource utilisation
    - Total assets turnover   = (Net sales)/(Total assets)
    - Inventory turnover   = (Cost of goods sold)/(Inventory)
    - Debt turnover   = (Credit sales)/(Debtors)

NET PRESENT VALUE (NPV)

Compound interest measures the future value of invested money. However, it is also possible to look at money in the reverse direction, namely the present value of money to be received at some future point in time. The concept of time value of money recognises that cash today is more valuable than the same amount of cash available at a later date. The difference between present values and future sums is due to the accumulated interest that would have accrued if the money had been invested. The time value of money is summed up by the old Wall Street maxim 'a dollar today is worth more than a dollar tomorrow'.

Today's equivalent of a future payment is called its principal or present value P_0. Management often assesses a project's acceptability by converting future expenditure and income into their equivalent present values. This process of reducing principal amounts is known as discounted cash flow (DCF) and has the opposite effect of compound interest which increases the principal. All DCF methods use cash flows instead of accounting profits. A cash flow is simply the flow of cash into and out of a business. The interest rate used in DCF calculations is given the name 'discount rate' and is usually expressed as a decimal. The general formula for basic compound interest states that if an amount P_0 is invested at a fixed rate of $i\%$, expressed as a decimal, the principal P_n after n years is

$$P_n = P_0(1+i)^n$$

Rearranging this formula gives

$$P_0 = P_n/(1+i)^n$$

This important formula, which is often called the DCF formula, forms the basis of all discounted cash flow methods. The DCF equation finds the present value of money, P_0, that would yield amount P_n in n years time when invested at a compound interest rate of $i\%$. The expression $1/(1+i)^n$ is known as the present value factor. The DCF formula, as it currently appears, discounts only one amount P_n. However, there are many situations where a whole series of cash flows require to be discounted to a present value. In this case, the basic DCF formula can be extended to cover cash flows arising at the end of a number of years

$$P = \sum_{j=1}^{n} P_j/(1+i)^j$$

where P_j represents the cash flow occurring at the end of year j where $j = 1, 2, 3 \ldots n$. The net present value (NPV) method involves calculating the present values of expected cash inflows and outflows and establishing whether the total present value of cash inflows is greater than the total value of cash outflows. The word 'net' in NPV simply means the sum of the negative and positive present values.

Excel's financial PV function can be used to find the present value of an investment as demonstrated in the following examples. The input parameters for the PV function are fully explained at the end of the chapter. Use Excel's function wizard button f_x on the standard toolbar at the top of the screen to bring up the function categories. Then choose the 'financial' category and function name 'PV'. Always use the Help button if in any doubt!

EXAMPLE 3.1

Using Excel's financial function PV, find the present worth of £1331 received three years from now, if the sum is discounted at 10%. (Use the DCF formula above to check the answer).

$$\text{Answer: PV}(0.1,3,,1331) = -£1000$$

Note that the result is negative because it represents money that you would pay, i.e., a cash outflow. To achieve a positive answer, insert the principal into Excel's PV formula as a negative value, i.e., PV(0.1,3,,−1331) = £1000.

EXAMPLE 3.2

A motorist buys a new car for £12,000 and intends to keep it for six years. If the resale value at the end of that time is expected to be £4000, and the annual running costs (apart from depreciation) are £2000, what is the NPV of the car's costs over the six-year period? Take interest as 7%.

Answer:	PV of car		= £12,000 (outflow)
	PV of resale value	= PV(0.07, 6, 0, −4000)	= £2,665 (inflow)
	PV of running costs	= PV(0.07, 6, −2000, 0)	= £9,533 (outflow)
	NPV = PV of car − PV of resale value + PV of running costs		= £18,868

EXAMPLE 3.3

A company is considering an investment in a project for which the estimated cash flows (in £'000s) are as shown in the table below. Calculate the project's NPV, given that the discount rate is 10%. Is the project acceptable?

Project cash flows for year	0	1	2	3	4
(in £'000s)	−60	20	17	22	25

The answer can be derived using Excel's NPV function (details of how to use Excel functions are given at the end of the chapter). The NPV function assumes that all inflows occur at the end of each period. If a payment (i.e., cash outflow) occurs at the beginning of the first period – as is the case above – then the project's NPV is given by the formula

$$-60 + \text{NPV}(0.1, 20, 17, 22, 25) = 5.84(£'000s) = £5,840$$

The project would be considered acceptable because its NPV and all PV values are positive, i.e., each year yields an acceptable cash inflow (compared to negative and unacceptable cash outflows).

Internal Rate of Return

The internal rate of return (IRR) is one of the most common methods used for evaluating investment projects. It is also known as the discounted cash flow (DCF) yield. The IRR of an investment is defined as the discount rate that equates the present value of the expected cash outflows with the present value of the expected cash inflows. In other words, it is the interest rate i, such that

$$\sum_{j=0}^{n} P_j/(1+i)^j = 0$$

where P_j is the cash flow (in or out) for period j, $j = 0, 1, 2, 3 \dots n$. The internal rate of return can be calculated using Excel's IRR function, which will now be applied to Example 3.3 above.

EXAMPLE 3.3a

Calculate the internal rate of return (IRR) for the investment project for which the estimated cash flows (in £'000s) are as shown in the following table.

Project cash flows for year	0	1	2	3	4
(in £'000s)	−60	20	17	22	25

If the values −60, 20, 17, 22, 25 are entered into cells A1, B1, C1, D1, E1 of a spreadsheet, then Excel's IRR function calculates the internal rate of return as follows:

$$\text{IRR(A1:E1)} = 14.21\%$$

INVESTMENT APPRAISAL

Many firms make decisions on capital investments on an annual basis. Since capital is not free, companies require a return on any new proposed investments. The process of providing information which will assist decision-making in relation to the investment of capital funds is called capital budgeting. The capital expenditure budget is essentially a list of what management believes to be worthwhile projects for the acquisition of new facilities and equipment.

Proposals for capital investment may start at department level and pass through various stages of discussion and approval before finally being considered by top management. The board of directors usually have a number of such proposals to examine. To assist their decision-making, the firm needs to set a minimum required rate of return against which the profitability of the proposals can be measured.

Industry relies on borrowed capital to finance many of its projects, and the rate of interest on the loan is often referred to as the cost of capital. Investment appraisal (i.e., capital budgeting) involves management choosing among a number of alternative investments or projects in order to maximise the return, subject to constraints on the amount of capital available each year. The cash flows for each alternative are first converted into a net present value (NPV). The problem is then to find which options produce the largest NPV. Consider the following example.

EXAMPLE 3.4   *Evaluating proposals: an investment appraisal model*

Microtec is a small manufacturer of microcomputers. Its board of directors is faced with the problem of evaluating four proposals and deciding which, if any, of the alternatives are

Table 3.1   Annual cash flows.

Proposals	Year 1	Year 2	Year 3	Year 4
1	−60	0	40	70
2	−50	−30	50	100
3	−40	−80	100	90
4		−35	110	−50
Capital available for each year =	100	100	50	50

acceptable. Table 3.1 shows the expected annual cash flows and available capital (£'000s) over the next four years. Cash inflows are shown as positive values while outflows are negative. The cost of capital is taken to be 15% per annum.

Capital requirements appear as negative values in the above table while net receipts are positive. Management's objective is to maximise the rate of return, i.e., maximise the total NPV of the selected proposals. The solution to this problem is best obtained by using integer programming (IP) techniques. IP is a special case of linear programming (LP) with the added constraint that the solution contains only whole numbers, i.e., integers. Excel's Solver is an ideal tool for solving such LP problems. If NPV_1, NPV_2, NPV_3, NPV_4 are the net present values for each proposal, then Microtec's problem can be restated in LP terms as follows:

Let x_1, x_2, x_3, x_4 represent the logical integers associated with the four Microtec proposals where, $x_i = 1$ if proposal i is accepted and $x_i = 0$ if proposal i is not accepted.

The objective is to MAXIMISE investment returns, i.e., maximise Z, where

$$Z = x_1 NPV_1 + x_2 NPV_2 + x_3 NPV_3 + x_4 NPV_4$$

subject to constraints on the amount of capital available for each year, i.e.,

$$60x_1 + 50x_2 + 40x_3 \quad \leq 100 \quad \text{(Year 1 constraint)}$$

$$30x_2 + 80x_3 + 35x_4 \quad \leq 100 \quad \text{(Year 2 constraint)}$$

Since year 3 produces only inflows, there are no capital constraints

$$50x_4 \quad \leq 50 \quad \text{(Year 4 constraint)}$$

where: $x_i \leq 1, x_i \geq 0, x_i = \text{integer}$ for all $i = 1, 2, 3, 4$

The following steps illustrate how this LP logic is built into the spreadsheet model of Figure 3.3.

- Enter the cost of capital into cell F3 and copy the expected cash flows from Table 3.1 into the shaded cell range D7:G10.

- Enter the capital constraint values in cells D22:G22.

- Enter formulae into the relevant cells – see lines 37–42 of Figure 3.3. Excel's NPV function (as shown on line 37) is used to find the NPV value for each proposal. NPV values are initially calculated in cells C7:C10 and are then copied into C16:C19.

- Activate Excel's Solver by selecting the Tools|Solver command and then enter Solver parameter data as shown on lines 28–34.

	A	B	C	D	E	F	G	H	I
1		**Example 3.4 - An investment appraisal model for Microtec Computers**							
2									
3			*Cost of capital =*		*15%*			*User input cells*	
4								*are shaded*	
5					<------ Annual cash flows ------>				
6		Propasal	*NPV*	year 1	year 2	year 3	year 4		
7		1	*16.27*	−60	0	40	70		
8		2	*27.47*	−50	−30	50	100		
9		3	*25.23*	−40	−80	100	90		
10		4	*19.87*		−35	110	−50		
11		Capital required:		150	145	0	50		
12									
13								Select	
14				<--- Annual capital requirements --->				0=No	
15		Proposal	NPV	year 1	year 2	year 3	year 4	1=Yes	
16		1	16.27	60				*0*	
17		2	27.47	50	30			*1*	
18		3	25.23	40	80			*0*	
19		4	19.87		35		50	*1*	
20									
21		Capital required:		£50	£65	£0	£50		
22		Capital available:		£100	£100	£50	£50		
23									
24						*Objective: Maximise total NPV=*		47.34	
25									
26									
27		*Solver Parameters*							
28		*Set Target Cell:*	H24						
29		*Equal to:*	Max						
30		*By Changing Cells:*	H16:H19						
31		*Subject to Constraints:*	D21:G21<=D22:G22			= Capital available			
32			H16:H19<=1			= Answers must be <=1			
33			H16:H19>=0			= Answers must be positive			
34			H16:H19=int(eger)			= Answers must be integer			
35									
36		*Cell*	*Formula*				*Copied to*		
37		C7	NPV(F$3, E7:G7) + D7				C8:C10		
38		D11	ABS(SUMIF(D7:D10,"<0"))				E11:G11		
39		C16	C7				C17:C19		
40		D16	IF(D7<0,ABS(D7),"")				D16:G19		
41		D21	SUMPRODUCT(D16:D19,$H16:$H19)				E21:G21		
42		H24	SUMPRODUCT(C16:C19,H16:H19)						
43									

Figure 3.3 An investment appraisal model.

Note that the lower part of Figure 3.3 is provided only for the user's benefit and is not part of the model. If the user has any difficulty in following the Solver dialog boxes, the linear programming (LP) section of Chapter 2 should be revised. The proposals' NPV values (£'000s), i.e., $NPV_1 = 16.27$, $NPV_2 = 27.47$, $NPV_3 = 25.23$, and $NPV_4 = 19.87$ are derived in Figure 3.3. The solution achieves a maximum rate of return of £47,340 by choosing proposals 2 and 4, while rejecting projects 1 and 3.

PORTFOLIO MANAGEMENT

In the previous section, capital budgeting was assessed solely on the basis of the NPV method of investment appraisal. However, one very important factor was not considered, namely the element of risk attached to the success or failure of any proposal. Risk can be defined as the probability that a prediction will prove to be wrong, i.e., it is a measure of uncertainty attached to the outcome of future events.

Portfolio management deals with the selection of investments so as to satisfy two main criteria (i) minimise risk and (ii) maximise expected returns. The term 'portfolio' simply means a collection of investments. One of the key objectives in portfolio management is to balance the portfolio by choosing a combination of investments that cover the full spectrum of risk minimisation and returns maximisation. This policy of diversification means that a properly balanced portfolio should have a mixture of high-risk, medium-risk, and low-risk investments. The key question is, what is the ideal ratio of such investments?

This common financial management activity can be classified as a non-linear programming (NLP) problem that is best handled by using Excel's Solver. Linear programming (LP) assumes that all equations and inequalities (constraints) have linear relationships. However, there are many business problems where the variables have a nonlinear relationship, i.e., do not conform to the standard straight line equation of $y = mx + c$. In trying to distinguish between stocks that are stable (i.e., low-risk) and high-risk investments, investment managers often use nonlinear statistical methods to verify if stock variations are due either to seasonal trends or unknown circumstances.

EXAMPLE 3.5 *Portfolio management model*

Barney Briggs has recently inherited some money which he would like to invest in stock. Barney already holds stock in company A, and over the past ten years he has received an average annual return of 7.48% on his investment. He would like to improve on this figure and has informed his bank that an annual return of at least 12% is his desired objective. The bank's funds investment manager has forwarded details (Table 3.2) of two suitable companies B and C, whose stock performances meet Barney's requirements.

Table 3.2 Percentage annual return (over 10 years).

Company	1	2	3	4	5	6	7	8	9	10
A	8.5	15.3	11.5	−1.6	−3.6	8.4	6.8	11.9	6.1	11.5
B	6.7	9.2	11.3	17.7	7.4	13.0	19.5	15.1	19.4	15.2
C	15.1	27.8	38.6	−12.0	−5.9	12.7	−2.1	12.8	36.8	22.7

From the table, it is clear that there is a wide variation between the annual returns for each stock. On the basis of return fluctuations, stocks A, B, and C can be classified as medium, low, and high-risk, giving average annual returns of 7.48%, 13.45%, and 14.65% respectively. The investment manager's problem is to determine what is the best percentage of the total funds that should be invested in each stock. His main objective is to achieve an optimal balance between three criteria: (i) minimise risk; (ii) maximise returns; (iii) ensure that returns are not less than 12%.

The manager's first task is to determine how closely the three sets of stock data are related. To do this, he will use covariance analysis. Covariance analysis is a statistical technique for determining the relationship between two sets of data. It measures trend similarities between the data, showing how close the relationship is.

- A positive covariance means that the two data sets tend to move together in the same direction, i.e., as values increase/decrease in one set, the same pattern is repeated in the second set.

- A negative covariance means that the two data sets diverge, i.e., move in opposite directions. As values increase/decrease in one set, there is a corresponding decrease/increase in the second set.

- A covariance of zero or near-zero indicates that there is no relationship between the two sets of variables, i.e., they are totally independent of each other.

The investment manager's problem can now be viewed as a non-linear programming exercise in which he must minimise the variance between the different stocks in the portfolio (Diacogiannis, Chapter 8). He will use various statistical functions that are available in Excel. COVAR (abbreviation for covariance) establishes the strength of the relationship between two sets of data. While Excel's COVAR function determines variations between two sets of data, the variance function VAR determines variations within a single data set. Note that COVAR(A,A) is not the same as VAR(A).

The objective is to minimise the portfolio's risk by minimising the portfolio's total variance. For a portfolio consisting of n investments, the total variance is defined by the following equation:

$$\text{Total portfolio variance} = \sum_{i=1}^{n} \sigma_i^2 p_i^2 + 2 \sum_{i=1}^{n-1} \sum_{j=i+1}^{n} \sigma_{ij} p_i p_j$$

where: $p_i =$ the percentage of the portfolio invested in investment i
$\sigma_i^2 =$ the variance of investment i
$\sigma_{ij} = \sigma_{ji} =$ the covariance between investments i and j

By performing a variance analysis on A, B and C and a covariance analysis on all other combinations (AB, AC, and BC), a covariance matrix can be built up. Excel's matrix multiplication function MMULT has been used to simplify the computation of the model's rather complex objective function as defined by the portfolio-variance equation. The following steps are used

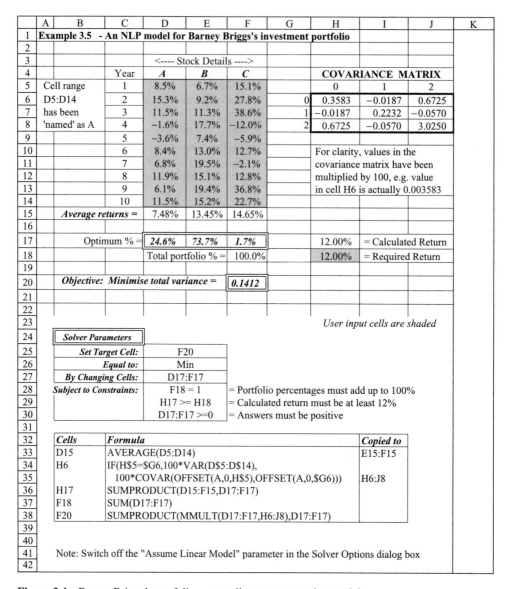

Figure 3.4   Barney Briggs's portfolio – a non-linear programming model.

to build the portfolio model of Figure 3.4:

- Enter the table of annual returns for the three stocks. Details for stock A are contained in cells D5:D14, stock B in E5:E14, and stock C in cells F5:F14.

- Find the average annual rate of return for each stock by averaging the return values over the ten years. The average returns, R_A, R_B, and R_C are contained in cells D15:F15.

- Set up the covariance matrix in cells H6:J8, using the formulae as shown below:

	A	B	C
A	VAR(A)	COVAR(A,B)	COVAR(A,C)
B	COVAR(B,A)	VAR(B)	COVAR(B,C)
C	COVAR(C,A)	COVAR(C,B)	VAR(C)

Note that COVAR(B,A) = COVAR(A,B), etc. Values in the covariance matrix have been multiplied by 100 for clearer presentation.

- The model is solved as an NLP problem using Excel's Solver. The objective is to find the best mixture of investments in stocks A,B, and C which will minimise risk. Note: when solving nonlinear problems, it is important that the 'Assume Linear Model' option is not selected!

- The optimum percentage amounts, p_A, p_B, and p_C are contained in the changing cells D17:F17.

- The objective function, as given by the equation for total portfolio variance, is contained in the target cell, F20. Note that Excel's matrix multiplication function MMULT has been used in cell F20. Details on how to use the various Excel functions are given at the end of the chapter.

- The NLP problem has three constraints:

  (a) Barney Briggs wants an annual return of at least 12%. Thus, the calculated return on the three stocks – as shown in cell H17 – must be at least 12%, i.e., $p_A R_A + p_B R_B + p_C R_C \geq 12\%$.

  (b) To ensure that all of Barney's money is invested, the total percentage amounts must add up to 100% (see cell F18), i.e., $p_A + p_B + p_C = 100\%$.

  (c) Since it is impossible to invest a negative amount, answers must be positive, i.e., p_A, p_B, and p_C must be greater than or equal to zero.

By varying the required annual return from 10% to 13% (cell H18), the results in Table 3.3 were obtained from the portfolio model of Figure 3.4.

These results are not surprising, given the average returns and the risk attached to each stock. Required returns of 10% and 11% give the same answer, both emphasising low-risk stock B with its average return of 13.45%, followed by medium-risk stock A, while ignoring high-risk stock C. As the required returns are increased to 12% and 13%, the emphasis focuses on those stocks with higher average returns, i.e., stocks B and C. The reluctance to give priority to high-risk stock C is obvious!

Table 3.3 Solver solutions.

Required return	Stock A	Stock B	Stock C
10%	39.1%	60.9%	0.0%
11%	39.1%	60.9%	0.0%
12%	24.6%	73.7%	1.7%
13%	8.9%	84.6%	6.5%

CAPITAL BUDGETING USING DECISION TREES

A decision tree is a graphical representation of the various possible courses of action available to the decision-maker. A decision tree is basically a probability tree whereby each possible outcome has a probability assigned to it. It provides a visual 'road map' of the decision problem. Consider the following situation.

EXAMPLE 3.6 *A decision tree for capital budgeting*

The KleenUp Company is currently evaluating an investment proposal. The project which will cost £100,000, has an expected duration of two years. A discount rate of 10% has been calculated for the project's duration. The project's estimated cash flows and associated probabilities are as follows. In year 1, the most likely estimate is a 50% probability of achieving a cash flow of £75,000. The optimistic view gives a 30% chance of generating £100,000, while the pessimistic outcome is a 20% probability of getting only £50,000.

Cash flows in year 2 are influenced by the financial outcome of year 1. If the pessimistic figure of £50,000 is realised, then there are three possible alternatives – £25,000, £35,000, or £50,000 with probabilities of 0.3, 0.3, and 0.4 respectively. If first-year profits of £75,000 are achieved, then it is possible to produce cash flows of £75,000, £100,000, or £125,000 with probabilities of 0.3, 0.5, and 0.2 respectively. Finally, if the optimistic target of £100,000 profits is reached, then second-year options can lead to cash flows of £75,000, £80,000, or £100,000 with associated probabilities of 0.2, 0.6, and 0.2.

This situation can be more easily interpreted when converted into a decision tree. Use the following basic steps and the formulae template of Table 3.4 to create Figure 3.5.

- Starting from left to right, draw the decision tree. Use Excel's Format|Cells|Border command to create the tree outline. Enter data for projected cash flows and associated probabilities.

- Calculate the present value (PV) for all combinations using Excel's PV function with a discount rate of 10%, e.g., (B11,D8), (B11,D10), (B11,D12), etc.

- Calculate the joint probability for each combination of net cash flows. The joint probability for a combination (of two possible outcomes) is the product of their probabilities.

Table 3.4 Decision tree – worksheet formulae.

Cell	Formula	Copied to
E8	PV(D$4, 1,, –B$11) + PV(D$4, 2,, –D8) – D$3	E10, E12
E14	PV(D$4, 1,, –B$17) + PV(D$4, 2,, –D14) – D$3	E16, E18
E20	PV(D$4, 1,, –B$23) + PV(D$4, 2,, –D20) – D$3	E22, E24
F8	B$10*C8	F10, F12
F14	B$16*C14	F16, F18
F20	B$22*C20	F22, F24
G8	E8*F8	G10:G24
G27	SUM(G8:G24)	
F29	SUM(F13:F24)	

	A	B	C	D	E	F	G	H
1	**Example 3.6 - Decision tree for KleenUp's investment proposal**							
2								
3		Initial investment =		£100,000		*User input cells are shaded*		
4		Fixed interest rate =		10%				
5						Joint	Weighted	
6		*Year 1*		*Year 2*	PV	Probab.	PV	
7								
8			0.3	£25,000	−£33,884	0.06	−£2,033	
9								
10		0.2	0.3	£35,000	−£25,620	0.06	−£1,537	
11		£50,000						
12		(pessimistic)	0.4	£50,000	−£13,223	0.08	−£1,058	
13								
14			0.3	£75,000	£30,165	0.15	£4,525	
15								
16		0.5	0.5	£100,000	£50,826	0.25	£12,707	
17		£75,000						
18		(most likely)	0.2	£125,000	£71,488	0.1	£7,149	
19								
20			0.2	£75,000	£52,893	0.06	£3,174	
21								
22		0.3	0.6	£80,000	£57,025	0.18	£10,264	
23		£100,000						
24		(optimistic)	0.2	£100,000	£73,554	0.06	£4,413	
25								
26								
27		Expected NPV (i.e., the sum of the weighted PVs) = £37,603						
28								
29		Probability of positive cash flows = 80%						
30								

Figure 3.5   A decision tree for capital budgeting.

The weighted PV values in column G of Figure 3.5 show a mixture of cash outflows (20%) for the pessimistic option and inflows (80%) for the other two options. These figures indicate that the project is not completely risk free. However, the 80% probability of positive cash inflows and the size of the project's returns (given by the NPV value) may convince management that the risk is worth taking.

CASH FLOW ANALYSIS

A business must have a steady flow of cash moving through the system in order to meet its regular commitments such as wages, raw materials, rates and rent, fuel and electricity, etc. If this cash flow slows down, e.g., due to bad debts, then a 'cash flow' problem occurs and the business may face serious difficulties. It therefore makes good business sense to carry out a regular cash flow analysis of the company's financial position. The terms 'cash flow forecasting' and 'cash budgeting' are synonymous with cash flow analysis.

A cash flow analysis is a financial statement of the cash expected to flow into and out of a business over a specified future period. When ascertaining a firm's economic health, cash flows are more objective than accounting profits. Profits are calculated on a periodic basis, usually quarterly or annually, whereas cash flows can be carried out at any time. Accounting procedures do not provide the ongoing view of a firm's activities which a cash flow analysis does. The term 'cash' usually refers to both cash in hand and cash in the bank. A typical cashflow forecast is short term, covering approximately six months to a year. The layout of a cash flow statement shows detailed cash inflows at the top with cash outflow details at the bottom.

CASE STUDY 3.1   *Cashflow model for Bill's Barbecues*

Bill Brown is the new owner of Bill's Barbecues, which manufactures barbecue units. He has capital of £7500 in his bank. Bill has just been informed that he has won £35,000 on the national lottery and, when he receives it in June, he intends to invest this money in his company. Bill plans to produce 60 units per month, but expects sales to start from 30 units in February, increasing in steps of 10 until May and then in steps of 20 in June and July when they will reach 100 per month. The barbecues will sell for £180 each but his customers' accounts will only be settled in the third month after the month of purchase.

Bill calculates that his overheads will be £1000 per month, to be paid one month in arrears. In April, he will spend £25,000 on equipment and machinery needed to run the business. His unit production costs, which are not anticipated to rise in the period under review, are: Materials, £50; Labour, £40; Variables, £30. He will buy materials as needed, paying for them two months later. Labour costs will have to be paid for in the month of production, as will his variable costs.

In order to satisfy his bank manager that his request for a £25,000 overdraft facility will be sufficient to meet the needs of his new enterprise, Bill Brown needs to draw up a cashflow analysis for the first six months of operations, i.e., from February to July. The bank's interest charges are 1.5% per month on the previous month's overdraft. Bill has asked you to help him. Having set up the cashflow model as shown in Figure 3.6, you now show Bill how to use the formulae template of Table 3.5 to build the model.

Further 'what-if' scenarios

By May, Bill Brown finds that the business is proceeding very much as he had anticipated. Advance orders suggest that sales are likely to be maintained at the July level during August and September, falling to 30 in October and 20 in November. This is extremely encouraging but leaves Bill with the problem of how he is going to be able to satisfy the demand. His production capacity of 60 barbecues per month has been sufficient in the start-up phase because he has built up enough stock to cope with the June/July demand. However, Bill anticipates that stocks will need to be increased if he is going to meet predicted sales for August and September.

Scenario 1
Having been impressed by your first cashflow forecast, Bill Brown has decided that he needs to extend the analysis until November. The current worksheet of Figure 3.6 must be modified in order to create this first scenario. To do this, extend the number of months in Figure 3.6

	A	B	C	D	E	F	G	H	I
1		Case Study 3.1 - Cashflow analysis model for Bill's Barbecues							
2									
3			**FEB**	**MAR**	**APR**	**MAY**	**JUN**	**JUL**	
4									
		Cash in Bank	£7,500	£3,300	−£1,900	−£35,129	−£38,455	−£5,032	
6									
7		*CASH INFLOW:*							
8		Sales Volume	30	40	50	60	80	100	
9									
10		Unit Price	£180	£180	£180	£180	£180	£180	
11		Sales Income				£5,400	£7,200	£9,000	
12		Lottery Winnings					£35,000		
13									
14		*Total Inflows*	£0	£0	£0	£5,400	£42,200	£9,000	
15									
16		*CASH OUTFLOW:*							
17		Production Volume	60	60	60	60	60	60	
18		Unit Costs							
19		materials	£50	£50	£50	£50	£50	£50	
20		labour	£40	£40	£40	£40	£40	£40	
21		variables	£30	£30	£30	£30	£30	£30	
22		Total Prod'n Costs	£4,200	£4,200	£7,200	£7,200	£7,200	£7,200	
23									
24		Fixed Overheads		£1,000	£1,000	£1,000	£1,000	£1,000	
25		New Machinery			£25,000				
26		Overdraft charges	£0	£0	£29	£527	£577	£75	
27									
28		*Total Outflows*	£4,200	£5,200	£33,229	£8,727	£8,777	£8,275	
29									
30		*C/F to Bank*	*£3,300*	*−£1,900*	*−£35,129*	*−£38,455*	*−£5,032*	*−£4,308*	
31									
30		*All user input cells are shaded*							

Figure 3.6   A cashflow model for Bill's Barbecues.

from July to November. Copy column H across into columns I to L. The extended spreadsheet should look similar to Figure 3.7 which has columns C to F hidden for clearer presentation. (Ignore the cell range in rows 19–23 which is part of the next scenario 2.)

Scenario 2

Overtime working, which will inevitably increase his labour costs, seems to be required and Bill starts to think about how this can be organised. Weekday and Saturday morning overtime will cost him time and a half; Saturday afternoon and Sunday morning, double time. With the employment situation as it is and summer holidays on the horizon, his workforce (currently working 5 eight-hour days) will be glad of the overtime but Bill's problem is how much, when, and how will it affect his overdraft? These questions are really examples of 'what-if' analysis. Bill has now asked you to carry out some further modifications to the original cashflow model.

Table 3.5   Cashflow analysis – worksheet formulae.

Cell	Formula	Copied to
D5	C30	E5:H5
D10	$C10	E10:H10
F11	C8*C10	G11:H11
C14	SUM(C11:C13)	D14:H14
D17	$C17	E17:H17
D19	$C19	D19:H21
C22	SUM(C20:C21)*C17	D22
E22	SUM(E19:E2l)*E17	F22:H22
E24	$D24	F24:H24
C26	IF(C5 < 0, ABS(0.015*C5), 0)	D26:H26
C28	SUM(C22:C27)	D28:H28
C30	C5 + C14 − C28	D30:H30

You may assume that only the labour cost will be affected by the overtime working, which will be limited to four-hour shifts during weekdays. You should remember that Bill cannot improve his cashflow by selling barbecues that he has not yet produced! Assume four working weeks per month, and do not forget to allow for summer holidays (1 week in July). In order that Bill Brown can better appreciate the logic behind your actions, keep a record of each alternative 'what-if' scenario that you have investigated, printing out hard copies with sub-headings. The following steps create scenario 2 of Figure 3.7.

- Insert six new rows after line 17 of Figure 3.6. First, place the cursor anywhere on line 18 and then use the Insert|Rows command repeatedly.

- Copy the text into cells B18:B23 as shown in Figure 3.7.

- Using the template of Table 3.6, enter formulae into the newly created rows and then format the new cells appropriately. Modify other rows as indicated.

To appreciate the logic behind scenario 2, the case study should be studied carefully and the following facts verified:

Table 3.6   Modified cashflow analysis – worksheet formulae.

Cell	Formula	Copied to
C20	IF(C19 > 36, 720 + (C19 − 36)*40, C19*20)	D20:L20
C21	C17 − C8 + C19	D21:L21
C22	C21	
D22	C22 + D21	E22:L22
C23	C36	D23:L23
G24	IF(H19 > 27, "Remember July holidays!", "")	
C28	SUM(C26:C27)*C17 + C20	D28
E28	SUM(E25:E27)*E17 + E20	F28:L28

	A	B	G	H	I	J	K	L	M
1		Case Study 3.1 - Further cashflow scenarios for Bill's Barbecues							
2									
3		Scenario 1	JUN	JUL	AUG	SEP	OCT	NOV	
4									
5		Cash in bank	−£38,455	−£5,032	−£4,308	−£1,772	£4,401	£14,201	
6									
7		*CASH INFLOW:*							
8		Sales Volume	80	100	100	100	30	20	
9									
10		Unit Price	£180	£180	£180	£180	£180	£180	
11		Sales Income	£7,200	£9,000	£10,800	£14,400	£18,000	£18,000	
12		Lottery Winnings	£35,000						
13									
14		*Total Inflows*	£42,200	£9,000	£10,800	£14,400	£18,000	£18,000	
15									
16		*CASH OUTFLOW:*							
17		Production Volume	60	60	60	60	60	60	
18		Scenario 2	*'What If' analysis: enter trial values in the 'Extra Production' row*						
19		Extra Production							
20		LABOUR Overtime (£)	£0	£0	£0	£0	£0	£0	
21		Surplus Units	−20	−40	−40	−40	30	40	
22		Cumulative Surplus	40	0	−40	−80	−50	−10	
23		*C/F to Bank*	*−£5,032*	*−£4,308*	*−£1,772*	*£4,401*	*£14,201*	*£24,001*	
24		Unit Costs							
25		materials	£50	£50	£50	£50	£50	£50	
26		labour	£40	£40	£40	£40	£40	£40	
27		variables	£30	£30	£30	£30	£30	£30	
28		Total Prod'n Costs	£7,200	£7,200	£7,200	£7,200	£7,200	£7,200	
29									
30		Fixed Overheads	£1,000	£1,000	£1,000	£1,000	£1,000	£1,000	
31		New Machinery							
32		Overdraft charges	£577	£75	£65	£27	£0	£0	
33									
34		*Total Outflows*	£8,777	£8,275	£8,265	£8,227	£8,200	£8,200	
35									
36		*C/F to Bank*	*−£5,032*	*−£4,308*	*−£1,772*	*£4,401*	*£14,201*	*£24,001*	
37									
38		Note that columns C to F have been hidden for clearer presentation							

Figure 3.7   Extended cashflow scenarios for Bill's Barbecues.

- Nine extra barbecues can be manufactured each week at an extra labour cost of £20 per unit. A further three barbecues can be produced weekly at an extra cost of £40 per unit. Since the workforce's month consists of four weeks, 36 extra barbecues can be produced each month at a total labour cost of £720, while a further 12 units will cost an extra £480.

- The normal monthly production of barbecues is 60, i.e., three units per day. The user should therefore calculate extra production in multiples of three units.

- Because of the July holidays, only three weeks' production can be achieved in July.

	FEB	MAR	APR	MAY	JUN	JUL	AUG	SEP	OCT	NOV
Scenario 2				*'What If' analysis: enter trial values in the 'Extra Production' row*						
Extra Production					*30*	*24*	*27*			
LABOUR Overtime (£)	£0	£0	£0	£0	£600	£480	£540	£0	£0	£0
Surplus Units	30	20	10	0	10	−16	−13	−40	30	40
Cumulative Surplus	30	50	60	60	70	54	41	1	31	71
C/F to Bank (£'000s)	*3.30*	*−1.90*	*−35.13*	*−38.46*	*−5.63*	*−5.40*	*−3.42*	*2.73*	*12.53*	*22.33*

	FEB	MAR	APR	MAY	JUN	JUL	AUG	SEP	OCT	NOV
Scenario 2 (cont.)				*'What If' analysis: enter trial values in the 'Extra Production' row*						
Extra Production				*27*	*18*	*18*	*18*			
LABOUR Overtime (£)	£0	£0	£0	£540	£360	£360	£360	£0	£0	£0
Surplus Units	30	20	10	27	−2	−22	−22	−40	30	40
Cumulative Surplus	30	50	60	87	85	63	41	1	31	71
C/F to Bank (£'000s)	*3.30*	*−1.90*	*−35.13*	*−39.00*	*−5.94*	*−5.59*	*−3.43*	*2.72*	*12.52*	*22.33*

Figure 3.8   Results of a 'what-if' analysis for Scenario 2.

- The circled information on line 22 of Figure 3.7 indicates a shortfall for the four months of August to November. This shortfall must be eliminated by extra production, subject to the following criteria:

  (a) the workers' appreciation of pre-holiday money during the months of June/July

  (b) the bank's lack of appreciation of an increasing overdraft during the June/August period!

The answers shown in Figure 3.8 were obtained by trial and error. The user enters various combinations into the 'Extra production' row (row 19 in Figure 3.7) over a number of months, ranging from April to September. Each 'what if' analysis will produce different results which are compared with previous answers. The user will then choose the combination that best meets Bob's objectives of satisfying both workers and the bank. Figure 3.8 shows that 27 extra units in May and further equal amounts of 18 in months June to August give an acceptable result.

INVESTMENT FINANCING: A SIMULATION MODEL

The MightyBig Corporation specialises in large construction projects. The company is planning to build a new production facility and must decide how it will finance the project. Construction costs are difficult to determine exactly because of potential delays and inflation. In recent years, variations in construction costs have shown a pattern similar to the probability table below. The company's financial division has decided on raising funds by (i) issuing bonds and (ii) borrowing from its bank. Bonds will yield 8.5% per annum for investors, while the bank's interest rate on a loan is 10% per annum. The bank has stipulated a lending condition that the bond flotation should not be more than $1^1/_2$ times the loan amount.

In the event of the MightyBig Corporation being unable to raise sufficient funds from these two options, it will borrow the remaining amount from an insurance company. Because insurance companies are relatively new to banking and are trying to increase their customer base, they offer competitive interest rates on loans. However, there is a wide variation in insurance interest rates, so the MightyBig Corporation has asked its financial division to draw up a table of probable rates. The company must now decide the cheapest way of financing the new production facility.

Probability table for construction costs

Construction cost (£ million)	10	15	20	25
Probability	0.2	0.4	0.3	0.1

Probability table for insurance company interest rates

Annual interest rate (%)	8	9	10	11	12
Probability	0.1	0.2	0.3	0.3	0.1

This simulation problem has the added complexity of linear programming (LP) constraints. The solution involves two steps, namely (i) building a simulation model using the probability tables shown above, and (ii) restating the problem as an LP exercise.

EXAMPLE 3.7   *Investment analysis for the MightyBig Corporation*

Step 1: Simulating the probability tables
The first step is to determine the most likely values for the random variables – construction cost C, and insurance company interest rate, i. These values are found by building a simulation model using the two probability tables shown above. The model of Figure 3.9 randomly generates values for the insurance rate and construction cost over a sample of 30 trials. In reality, a more precise estimate of the average values for construction cost C and interest rate i would be achieved by simulating several hundred trials.

Each time the recalculation key F9 is pressed, a new series of 30 random values will be generated for both interest rate i, and construction cost C. The average values of $i = 0.1$ and $C = 16.8$ are the most common figures appearing on line 31 of the model. These values will now be used as input to the next step. The formula template for the simulation model is shown in Table 3.7.

Step 2: Restating the problem as an LP exercise

Let $C =$ the uncertain construction cost of the new facility (£m.)
          (to be determined in step 1 by using simulation)
Let B, L_B, $L_I =$ the optimum amounts (in £m.) obtained from bonds (B), bank loan
          (L_B), and insurance loan (L_I)

The MightyBig Corporation's objective is to minimise total interest costs, i.e., minimise the objective function, Z (in £m.), where

$$Z = 0.085B + 0.1L_B + iL_I$$
and $i =$ the uncertain insurance interest rate
(to be determined in step 1 by using simulation)

	A	B	C	D	E	F	G	H	I	J	K
1	**Example 3.7 - A simulation model for investment financing - Step 1**										
2											
3		*Table 2:* Insurance interest rates					*Table 1:* Construction costs				
4		<-- Limits -->			Interest		<-- Limits -->			Cost	
5		Lower	Upper	Pi	rate, i		Lower	Upper	Pi	(£m)	
6		0	0.10	0.1	8.0%		0	0.20	0.2	10	
7		0.10	0.30	0.2	9.0%		0.20	0.60	0.4	15	
8		0.30	0.60	0.3	10.0%		0.60	0.90	0.3	20	
9		0.60	0.90	0.3	11.0%		0.90	1.00	0.1	25	
10		0.90	1.00	0.1	12.0%		*All user input cells are shaded*				
11											
12		*Insurance interest rate, i*					*Construction cost, C*				
13		Trial	Outcome	Trial	Outcome		Trial	Outcome	Trial	Outcome	
14		*1*	0.1	*16*	0.1		*1*	10	*16*	15	
15		*2*	0.11	*17*	0.09		*2*	25	*17*	15	
16		*3*	0.08	*18*	0.08		*3*	15	*18*	20	
17		*4*	0.09	*19*	0.11		*4*	10	*19*	20	
18		*5*	0.11	*20*	0.11		*5*	20	*20*	10	
19		*6*	0.09	*21*	0.08		*6*	15	*21*	25	
20		*7*	0.12	*22*	0.1		*7*	10	*22*	10	
21		*8*	0.08	*23*	0.12		*8*	20	*23*	15	
22		*9*	0.12	*24*	0.1		*9*	20	*24*	15	
23		*10*	0.11	*25*	0.1		*10*	15	*25*	25	
24		*11*	0.1	*26*	0.11		*11*	25	*26*	20	
25		*12*	0.1	*27*	0.11		*12*	15	*27*	20	
26		*13*	0.11	*28*	0.09		*13*	10	*28*	15	
27		*14*	0.1	*29*	0.1		*14*	15	*29*	15	
28		*15*	0.1	*30*	0.09		*15*	25	*30*	15	
29		***Totals:***	1.52		1.49		***Totals:***	250		255	
30											
31			Average interest, i =		**0.100**			Average construction, C =		**16.8**	
32											

Figure 3.9   A simulation model for investment financing (step 1).

subject to the following three constraints:

$$B \le 1.5L_B \quad \text{(Bank lending stipulation)}$$
$$B, L_I, L_B \ge 0 \quad \text{(All amounts must be positive)}$$
$$B + L_B + L_I \ge C \quad \text{(Loan must be as large as the total construction cost)}$$

The LP model of Figure 3.10 uses the simulated values found in step 1, i.e., an interest rate $i = 0.1$ (10%) and a construction cost $C = £16.8$m., as input parameters. The LP model has found a solution giving a minimum interest rate figure of £1.53m. This amount is achieved by the MightyBig Corporation borrowing £6.72m. from its bank and obtaining the rest by issuing £10.08m. worth of bonds.

Table 3.7 Simulation model – worksheet formulae

Cell	Formula	Copied to
C6	D6	
B7	C6	B8:B10
C7	B7 + D7	C8:C10
H6	I6	
G7	H6	G8:G9
H7	G7 + I7	H8:H9
C14	VLOOKUP(RAND(), $B$6:$E$10, 4)	C15:C28, E14:E28
H14	VLOOKUP(RAND(), $G$6:$J$9, 4)	H15:H28, J14:J28
C29	SUM(C24:C28)	E29, H29, J29
E31	(C29 + E29)/30	J31

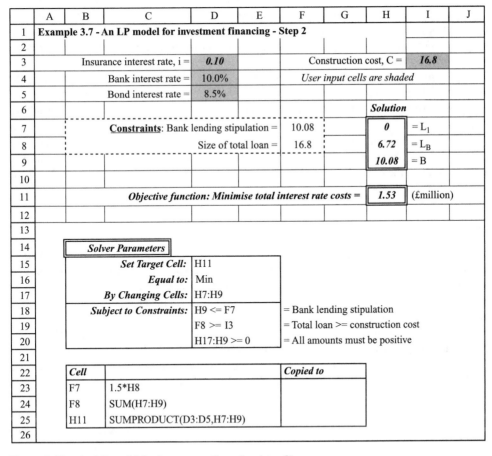

Figure 3.10 An LP model for investment financing (step 2).

FINANCIAL PLANNING

Financial planning and business forecasting are terms that are often used interchangeably. However, there is a clear distinction between planning – which is about formulating future activities over which the planner has control, and forecasting – which is about predicting events over which the planner has no control. For example, a family may plan a picnic outing on the basis of a weather forecast. How often are such plans spoilt because of poor forecasting? However, business forecasting which is based on the extrapolation of historical company data, is considered more reliable than weather forecasting! The main purpose of financial forecasting is to aid planning and decision-making. Business forecasting models are covered in Chapter 6.

Financial planning problems can be considered as semi-structured, i.e., they contain a set of assumptions, some of which are made with a high degree of confidence while others are little more than educated guesses. The purpose of creating a computer-based financial model is to allow the planner to 'play around with these educated guesses' by asking a number of 'what-if' questions until a clearer picture emerges. A model allows the planner to see immediately the results of his/her changes to variables which have a high degree of uncertainty. By developing a better understanding of how such variables can affect the result, their levels of uncertainty are accordingly reduced.

Sensitivity analysis involves a planner asking a series of 'what-if' questions in order to determine which variables have a major influence on the outcome, and which variables do not affect the result and can therefore be safely disregarded. For example, 'what-if' sensitivity analysis might uncover that the cost of a certain component used in product P is subject to quite large and unpredictable variations. However, the component's sensitivity to cost has very little affect on the pricing of product P because it represents such a small element of total cost. In this situation, the component can be disregarded. Consider the following case study which involves the development of a financial planning model.

CASE STUDY 3.2   *Financial planning model*

Kitchenware Products is a small manufacturer of stainless steel kitchen utensils. It is considering the production and marketing of a new type of carving knife. Initial estimates suggest that the company could sell 40,000 units the first year and expect to increase sales by as much as 10% per annum thereafter. The variable costs per unit are estimated as follows: raw materials, £3.00; packaging, £0.90; direct labour, £2.00; distribution, £1.00.

The inflation rates for the next three years are forecast to be 3%, 5% and 6%. Inflation will affect variable costs for the product but fixed costs are likely to remain at the same level of £10,000 over the next four years. In calculating profits over the next four years, the tax rate can be taken as 23%. Kitchenware Products intend to sell the carving knife at £8 for the first year with an annual increase of £0.30 thereafter.

Kitchenware Products have asked you to develop a financial planning model so that they can determine how net profits would be affected by changes in planned sales volume and product price over years 2 to 4. The given estimates represent the 'base case' for the four years. Because Kitchenware want to examine the model in terms of 'percentage changes' from this base case, there must be '% Change' factors for sales volume and product price built into the model (see double-surround cells in Figure 3.11). Column C contains the planning values (i.e., starting

	A	B	C	D	E	F	G	H	I
1		Case Study 3.2 - Financial planning model for Kitchenware Products							
2									
3			*Planning*	<------- Planning Horizon ------->					
4			*Values*	Year 1	Year 2	Year 3	Year 4	Totals	
5		*Sales*	40000						
6		Planned Growth	10%						
7	►	% Change Volume							
8		Planned Sales Vol		40,000	44,000	48,400	53,240	185,640	
9		Actual Sales Vol		40,000	44,000	48,400	53,240	185,640	
10									
11		*Product Price*	£8.00						
12		Price Increase	£0.30						
13	►	% Change Price							
14		Planned Price		£8.00	£8.30	£8.60	£8.90		
15		Actual Price		£8.00	£8.30	£8.60	£8.90		
16									
17		*Sales Revenue*		£320,000	£365,200	£416,240	£473,836	1,575,276	
18									
19	►	Inflation	0%	3%	5%	6%			
20									
21		*Variable Unit Costs*							
22		Raw Material	£3.00	£3.00	£3.09	£3.24	£3.44		
23		Labour Costs	£2.00	£2.00	£2.06	£2.16	£2.29		
24		Packaging	£0.90	£0.90	£0.93	£0.97	£1.03		
25		Distribution	£1.00	£1.00	£1.03	£1.08	£1.15		
26		*Total Unit Cost*		£6.90	£7.11	£7.46	£7.91		
27									
28		*Direct Costs*		£276,000	£312,708	£361,178	£421,133	£1,371,019	
29									
30		*Gross Profit*		£44,000	£52,492	£55,062	£52,703	£204,257	
31									
32		Fixed Costs	£10,000	£10,000	£10,000	£10,000	£10,000		
33									
34		Net profit before tax		£34,000	£42,492	£45,062	£42,703	£164,257	
35		Less: tax @	23%	£7,820	£9,773	£10,364	£9,822		
36									
37	►	*Net profit after tax*		£26,180	£32,719	£34,698	£32,881	£126,478	
38									
39		*Input data cells are shaded*							

Figure 3.11 Financial planning model for Kitchenware Products.

Table 3.8 Financial planning – worksheet formulae.

Cell	Formula	Copied to
D8	C5	
E8	D8*(1 + $C6)	F8:G8
H8	SUM(D8:G8)	H9
D9	D8*(1 + $C7)	E9:G9
D14	C11	
E14	D14 + $C12	F14:G14
D15	D 14*(1 + $C13)	E15:G15
D17	D15*D9	E17:G17
H17	SUM(D17:G17)	
D22	C22*(1 + C$19)	D22:G25
D26	SUM(D22:D25)	E26:G26
D28	D9*D26	E28:G28
H28	SUM(D28:G28)	H30
D30	D17 – D28	E30:G30
D32	$C32	E32:G32
D34	D30 – D32	E34:G34
H34	SUM(D34:G34)	H37
D35	$C35*D34	E35:G35
D37	D34 – D35	E37:G37

assumptions), column D represents year 1, columns E to G contain details for the three-year planning horizon, and column H contains the totals for all four years. Using the formulae template (Table 3.8), build the worksheet model of Figure 3.11.

Having built the financial planning model, Kitchenware Products now want to look at three 'what-if' scenarios.

- **Scenario 1**   Suppose inflation is predicted to be 6% during the second year and 8% thereafter. What would be the profitability of the new carving knife in these circumstances?

- **Scenario 2**   Suppose the company decides to sell 3% more units per year as well as increasing the current selling price by 10% per year. What would be the effect on 'net profit after tax' for each year?

- **Scenario 3**   Suppose that Kitchenware Products decides to vary the projected sales volume over a range from –5% to 10% of the initial assumption. The company wants to see how the 'Net profit after tax' would change as the projected sales volume changes.

The first task is to set up a 'results table' in rows 40–57 as shown in Figure 3.12. This results table will hold a permanent record of net profit after tax for each situation. Now copy the net-profit-after-tax figures from the worksheet (Row 37) into row 45 (copy by hand – do not use any Excel formulae!). Remember that all 'what-if' scenarios refer to the base case of Figure 3.11. It is important to check that all altered cells have been changed back to their original values, before proceeding to a new 'what-if' scenario.

Finally, in order to help Kitchenware Products visualise the table of figures in Scenario 3, draw a graph using Excel's Chart Wizard showing the 'comparison of profits' for the different

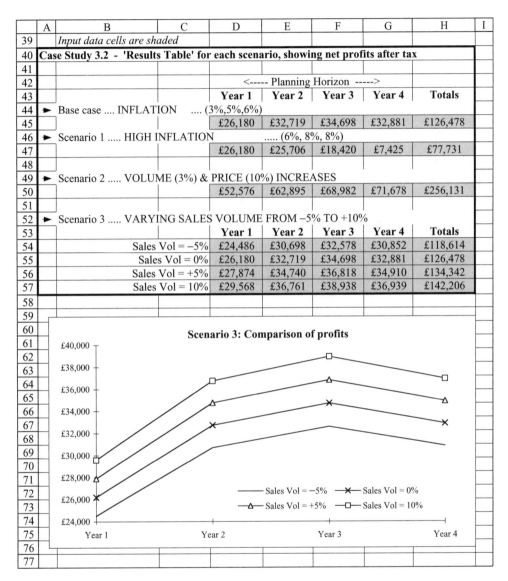

	A	B	C	D	E	F	G	H	I
39		*Input data cells are shaded*							
40	**Case Study 3.2 - 'Results Table' for each scenario, showing net profits after tax**								
41									
42				<----- Planning Horizon ----->					
43				**Year 1**	**Year 2**	**Year 3**	**Year 4**	**Totals**	
44	►	Base case .... INFLATION .... (3%,5%,6%)							
45				£26,180	£32,719	£34,698	£32,881	£126,478	
46	►	Scenario 1 ..... HIGH INFLATION		..... (6%, 8%, 8%)					
47				£26,180	£25,706	£18,420	£7,425	£77,731	
48									
49	►	Scenario 2 ..... VOLUME (3%) & PRICE (10%) INCREASES							
50				£52,576	£62,895	£68,982	£71,678	£256,131	
51									
52	►	Scenario 3 ..... VARYING SALES VOLUME FROM −5% TO +10%							
53				**Year 1**	**Year 2**	**Year 3**	**Year 4**	**Totals**	
54			Sales Vol = −5%	£24,486	£30,698	£32,578	£30,852	£118,614	
55			Sales Vol = 0%	£26,180	£32,719	£34,698	£32,881	£126,478	
56			Sales Vol = +5%	£27,874	£34,740	£36,818	£34,910	£134,342	
57			Sales Vol = 10%	£29,568	£36,761	£38,938	£36,939	£142,206	
58									

Figure 3.12   'Results table' for Kitchenware Products scenarios.

sales volumes (note that profits peak in year 3). In this case study, a summary report of each scenario's 'net profit after tax' is sufficient. However, if complete spreadsheet details are required for a scenario, then Excel's Scenario Manager can be used. When using the Scenario Manager, which is activated by the Tools|Scenarios command, the 'Base Case' scenario must also be included to ensure that original BASE CASE cell values are correctly restored.

COMMERCIAL ADD-IN PRODUCTS FOR EXCEL

An add-in, as the name implies, is not a standard part of Excel but is a separate component designed to seamlessly extend the capabilities of Excel. Excel comes with its own built-in library of add-ins including Solver, the Analysis ToolPak, and Internet Assistant. Add-in files, which always have an .XLA extension, can be installed or removed using the Tools|Add-Ins. . . command. The four major vendors of add-in software are Palisade (www.palisade-europe.com), Decisioneering (www.decisioneering.com), Frontline Systems (www.solver.com), and LINDO Systems (www.lindo.com). The first two companies offer risk and decision analysis tools while the latter two specialize in spreadsheet optimization.

The DecisionTools Suite of programs from Palisade contains seven products – @RISK, PrecisionTree, TopRank, RISKOptimizer, BestFit, RISKview, and @RISKAccelerator – that work together in an integrated environment to provide combined analyses and maximum functionality. The @RISK add-in for Excel provides risk analysis and Monte Carlo simulation, while PrecisionTree creates influence diagrams and decision trees in existing spreadsheets. Decisioneering's most popular product is Crystal Ball (CB) which performs risk analysis and Monte Carlo simulation. The software suite includes CB Predictor for analysing historical data to build models using time-series forecasting and multiple linear regression. The CB Tools feature is used to automate model building tasks, simulate variability, define correlations, and perform additional functions.

Frontline Systems claims to be a world leader in spreadsheet optimization, having developed the Solvers/Optimizers used in Excel, Lotus 1-2-3, and Quattro Pro. Its software products can handle the full range of optimization problems from linear, quadratic and mixed-integer programming to global, non-smooth, conic and convex optimization. LINDO systems offer three software products, namely LINDO API (optimization engine), LINGO (solver with its own modelling language) and What's *Best*! (spreadsheet solver).

EXCEL FUNCTIONS USED IN MODEL-BUILDING

The models developed in this chapter use the following ten Excel functions, each of which is explained below. The user should remember that a comprehensive on-line help facility is also provided by Excel.

1. ABS: ABS (Numb)

   returns absolute value of a real number Numb. The absolute value of a number is the number without its sign.

   Example: ABS(–3.6) returns the value 3.6.

2. AVERAGE: AVERAGE (array)

   returns the average (i.e., arithmetic mean) for cell range array.

   array = the range of cells for which the average is required. If the array contains text, logical values, or blanks, then all these cells will be ignored; however, cells with value zero are included

   Example: AVERAGE(C4:C7) in Figure 3.13 returns the value 20.75.

	A	B	C	D	E	F	G	H
1								
2		Product	No. in	Product		Year	Cash	
3		name	stock	price			flow	
4		Gizmo	10	£10.00		1	−300	
5		Gadget	25	£12.50		2	150	
6		Widget	8	£20.00		3	180	
7		Sprocket	40	£4.50		4	100	
8								
9				*Sample Figure*				

Figure 3.13   Sample figure.

3. COVAR: COVAR(ref1:ref2, ref3:ref4)

returns the covariance between two data sets, each set having the same number of data values. One set is contained in the cell range ref1:ref2 and the second set in the range ref3:ref4. Covariance measures the correlation, i.e., the strength of relationship, between two data sets. A positive covariance indicates that the two sets tend to go in the same direction. A negative covariance indicates that the two data sets diverge, i.e., tend to go in opposite directions. A covariance of zero indicates that there is no relationship between the two data sets.

Examples: COVAR($\{1, 2, 3, 4\}$, $\{13, 24, 51, 78\}$)   returns a value of 27.75
COVAR($\{1, 2, 3, 4\}$, $\{-99, 122, -1, -58\}$)   returns a value of 0
COVAR($\{13, 24, 51, 78\}$ $\{-99, 122, -1, -58\}$)   returns a value of −360

4. IRR: IRR(ref1:ref2)

returns the internal rate of return (IRR) – also called the yield – of a range of cell values ref1:ref2.

Example: IRR(G4:G7) in Figure 3.13 returns a value of 22%.

5. MMULT: MMULT(array1, array2)

returns the matrix product of two arrays. The result is a matrix (array) with the same number of rows as array1 and the same number of columns as array2. Note that the number of columns in array1 must be the same as the number of rows in array2. The MMULT function must be entered as an array formula. An array formula contains cell ranges, each range being treated as a single entity. This means that individual cells within the output matrix I3:K6 cannot be changed or deleted. A matrix is simply a cell range, with the notation x_{ij} representing the value of the matrix cell in row i, column j. Consider the two matrices in Figure 3.14.

The value in cell I3 = (row 1 of array 1) × (col. 1 of array 2)
$$= \{2, 3\} \times \{-2, 2\} = (2 \times -2) + (3 \times 2) = 2$$

The value in cell J3 = (row 1 of array 1) × (col. 2 of array 2)
$$= \{2, 3\} \times \{3, 1\} = (2 \times 3) + (3 \times 1) = 9, \text{ etc.}$$

	A	B	C	D	E	F	G	H	I	J	K	L
1												
2		*array1*				*array2*				*array1* × *array2*		
3		2	3			−2	3	−3		*2*	*9*	*9*	
4		−1	0			2	1	5		*2*	*−3*	*3*	
5		1	−3							*−8*	*0*	*−18*	
6		4	2							*−4*	*14*	*−12*	
7												
8		The result of multiplying array1 by array2 is a (4 row × 3 col.) matrix as shown										
9		by cell range I3:K6. Perform the following steps to obtain the required answer:-										
10												
11		[1] Highlight the cell range I3:K6.										
12		[2] Type =MMULT(B3:C6,E3:G4) into the formula bar at the top of the screen.										
13		[3] Press the three keys **Ctrl+Shift+Enter** at the same time. Curly brackets will										
14		automatically appear around the formulae in cells I3:K6, indicating that an **array**										
15		**formula** has been entered, i.e. each cell contains {=MMULT(B3:C6,E3:G4)}										

Figure 3.14   MMULT diagram.

6. NPV: NPV(discount, ref1:ref2)

returns the net present value (NPV) of an investment based on a series of periodic cash flows in the range ref1:ref2 and a discount rate of 'discount'. The NPV of an investment is today's value of a series of future payments (negative values) and income (positive values). All cash flows occur at the end of each period. If the first value in a series, e.g., B1:B6, occurs at the beginning of period 1, the NPV is given by B1+NPV (discount, B2:B6).

Example: NPV(12%,40,45,50) returns a value of £107.18, assuming all flows occur at the end of each period. If a payment (i.e., outflow) occurs at the beginning of the first period – as in Figure 3.13 – then the formula is G4 + NPV(10%, G5:G7) = £60.26.

7. PMT: PMT(rate, nper, pv, fv, type)

returns the periodic payment for an annuity based on fixed payments and a fixed interest rate. PMT is closely associated with the PV function below.

rate = The interest rate period.

nper = The total number of payments in the annuity.

pv = The present value, i.e., the total amount that a series of future payments is worth now.

fv = The future value that is required after the last payment is made. If *fv* is omitted, it is assumed to be 0, e.g. the *fv* of a loan is zero.

type = The number 0 or 1 and indicates when payments are due. If *type* = 0 or is omitted, payments are made at the end of the period. If *type* = 1 then payments are made at the beginning of the period.

Example: If a car loan of £3,000 is taken out for a period of two years at an annual interest rate of 7%, then the monthly payments are PMT(7%/12, 24, 3000), i.e., −£134.32. Note that units for 'nper' and 'rate' must be consistent, thus the monthly interest rate is 7%/12. The parameters 'fv' and 'type' have been omitted.

8. PV: PV(rate, nper, pmt, fv, type)

> returns the present value (PV) of an investment. The PV represents the time value of money, i.e., the total amount that a series of future payments is worth now.

rate	= The interest rate per period. For example, if payments are made monthly and the annual interest rate is 12%, then interest is entered as 12%/12, i.e., 1%.
nper	= The total number of payments in the annuity. For example, if monthly payments are made on a four-year car loan, then nper = 4*12 = 48.
pmt	= The fixed payment that is made each period.
fv	= The future value that is required after the last payment is made. If fv is omitted, it is assumed to be 0, e.g., the fv of a loan is zero.
type	= The number 0 or 1 and indicates when payments are due. If type = 0 or is omitted, payments are made at the end of the period. If type = 1 then payments are made at the beginning of the period.

Example: PV(10%, 3, 1000) returns a value of −£751.31, i.e., in order to receive £1000 in three years time, £751.31 must be paid out today, assuming an annual interest rate of 10%. Note that PV shows future cash received as positive while cash payouts are negative. The parameters 'pmt' and 'type' have been omitted.

9. SUMIF: SUMIF(range, criteria, sum_range)

> adds the cells specified by given criteria.

range	= Range of cells to be examined.
criteria	= Specified criteria in the form of a number, text, or an expression. For example, criteria can be specified in the form 32, "32", ">32", "apples".
sum_range	= Cell range being summed – only cells satisfying *criteria* are summed. If *sum_range* is omitted then *range* is examined.

Example: SUMIF(C4:C7, "<12") in Figure 3.13 returns 18, i.e., 10 + 8.
SUMIF(B4:B7, "=Gadget", C4:C7) in the Figure 3.13 returns 25, i.e., the sum of the values in column C which correspond to 'Gadget' in column B.

10. VAR: VAR(ref1, ref2)

> returns the variance between the values in a data set contained in the cell range ref1:ref2. Variance is a measure of dispersion, indicating the spread of individual data values. Note that the square root of the variance is the well-known *standard deviation*.

Example: Let C2:C6 contain the values 3, 3.1, 3.2, 3.3, 3.4 and D5:D9 contain the values –20, 0, 14, 45, 88. Then VAR(C2:C6) returns 0.025, a small number because the data is close together. VAR(D5:D9) returns 1784.8, a large number because the data is spread out.

EXERCISES

3.1 The net cash flows for a new project are estimated to be as follows:

Year	0	1	2	3	4
Net cash flow (£'000s)	–40	16	24	18	14

Use Excel's IRR function to calculate the yield on the investment. If the cost of capital is 14%, calculate the net present value of the investment using Excel's NPV function.
(Answers: 29%, £12,941.)

3.2 Fred Flint owns 1000 shares in the Bedrock Company. The shares are currently worth £2.80 each. Fred is considering whether to (i) hold the shares for one year and then sell, or (ii) sell the shares now and buy stock at £80 per stock in the MightyBig Corporation. He estimates that the price of the MightyBig stock in a year's time will be £87, £80, or £70 with probabilities of 0.5, 0.3, and 0.2 respectively. At the end of one year, Bedrock's share price and dividend depend upon Table 3.9.

Table 3.9

Share price	Probability	Share dividend
Up 20%	0.1	£0.5
Same	0.5	£0.2
Down 10%	0.4	None

Use Excel to draw a decision tree for Fred Flint's investment problem, and hence determine his best policy.

(Answer: best policy is to buy the MightyBig stock.)

3.3 Referring to Barney Briggs's investment portfolio of Example 3.5, show that you understand the concept of matrix multiplication by manually verifying the spreadsheet answer of Figure 3.4. Suggest another way in which the objective function might be calculated. (Note that details on Excel's MMULT function are given at the end of the chapter.)

3.4 Barney's cousin, Bette Briggs, has been impressed by his bank's portfolio management and has decided to avail herself of their expertise. Bette has informed the bank that she wants a return of 13% on her investment and she has been given details of three stocks X, Y and Z with average annual returns of 13.2%, 17.5%, and 9.7% respectively. Statistical information on these stocks is as follows: variances for X, Y, Z are 0.0012, 0.0023, and 0.00047, while covariances are $XY = -0.00019$, $XZ = 0.0009$, and $YZ = 0.000125$. Using the investment model for Barney Briggs's portfolio, find the percentage investments for X, Y and Z that will give Bette an overall return of 13%.

(Answer: 20% in X, 33.3% in Y, and 46.7% in Z with a portfolio variance of 0.000587.)

3.5 Willie Wong has recently purchased a microcomputer system and has decided to set up a cash flow spreadsheet which will allow him to analyse his personal finances over the next six months (January–June). His only source of income is his annual net salary of £18,000. After examining his bank statements for the past year, Willie has worked out average expenses. These include monthly payments for rent (£250), food (£150), car expenses (£90), and sundries (£100) as well as two-monthly bills for electricity (£100) and telephone calls (£70). Because of his recent microcomputer purchase, Willie has estimated that he will have a bank overdraft of £2000 on 1 January. Willie Wong intends to take a holiday in July and he would like to know how much money will be available. Set up a cash flow model showing net cash flows and balances at the end of each month. How much will Willie have for his holiday?

(Answer: Willie Wong will have £2,950 available for his July holiday.)

3.6 A company is considering the following five investment proposals for acceptance. The capital required for each project over the next five years is shown in Table 3.10, along with the amount of budgeted capital. Management wants to maximise the rate of return, i.e., maximise the total NPV of the selected proposals. Using Excel's linear programming tool – Solver – find the optimal set of investments and the resulting NPV of the investments.

Table 3.10

Proposals	Expected NPV (£'000s)	Capital (in £'000s) required in				
		Year 1	Year 2	Year 3	Year 4	Year 5
1	40	10	5	20	10	0
2	70	30	20	10	10	10
3	80	10	20	27	20	10
4	90	25	20	20	15	15
5	100	20	10	40	20	20
Capital available for each year =		50	45	70	40	30

(Answer: Accept proposals 1,2, and 3 which give a maximum NPV value of £190,000)

3.7 The Interstate Bank is planning its funds portfolio for next year. The bank has £20 million to invest and is considering five different funds as shown in Table 3.11. All of the funds are secured except the signature loans.

Table 3.11

Fund	Rate of return (%)
Signature loans	14
Vehicle instalment loans	13
Home improvement loans	13
Miscellaneous instalment loans	12.5
Government securities	12

Interstate wants to maximise the return on its investment portfolio while complying with the following banking regulations:

- Signature loans may not exceed 10% of total loans.
- Home improvement loans may not exceed 50% of total secured loans.
- Signature loans cannot exceed the investment in government securities.
- Government securities cannot exceed 40% of the total investment.

Solve the Interstate Bank's problem by linear programming methods using Excel's Solver.

(Answer: The maximum profit of £2.6m can be achieved in various ways, e.g., £2m in signature loans, £7m in vehicle instalments, £9m in home improvements, and £2m in government securities.)

3.8 Because of recent cash flow problems, Microtec Computers has decided to ask its bank for financial help over the next six months. However, Microtec must first estimate how large a loan is required. Past records of weekly receipts follow a pattern as shown in the probability table below. A similar table has been produced for cash outflows. Simulate Microtec Computers' cash flow situation for fifteen weeks and hence find the maximum loan required.

Cash Receipts (£'000s)	10	15	20	25	Cash Payments (£'000s)	8	12	15	20
Probability	0.3	0.4	0.2	0.1	Probability	0.1	0.3	0.4	0.2

(Answer: because of the volatility of the RAND function, answers will vary considerably.)

REFERENCES AND FURTHER READING

Carlberg, C. (2001) *Business Analysis with EXCEL* (2nd edn), Que Corporation, Indianapolis.

Diacogiannis, G. (1994) *Financial Management: A Modelling Approach Using Spreadsheets*, McGraw-Hill, UK.

Jackson, M. (1988) *Advanced Spreadsheet Modelling with Lotus 1-2-3*, John Wiley & Sons, Ltd, UK.

Ragsdale, C. (2004) *Spreadsheet Modeling and Decision Analysis* (4th edn), Thomson South-Western, USA.

4

Investment analysis models

OVERVIEW

The objective of financial management is twofold: (i) to ensure that there are sufficient funds available to meet the organisation's financial obligations and (ii) to maximise the returns on invested funds that are not needed to meet current commitments. In order to maximise profit, financial managers must decide whether the benefits accruing from any investment are sufficient to justify the original outlay. Investment situations include capital budgeting decisions relating to expansion plans or new product development, and long-term investments such as government bonds or shares in other companies.

Any business can be viewed as a collection (or portfolio) of assets which management tries to optimise through shrewd decision-making. Success depends upon the environmental conditions under which the investment decision is taken, i.e., certainty, risk, or uncertainty. A decision made under certainty is risk-free. The outcome depends solely on known quantitative information and is not affected by unpredictable events. For example, a company that has a fixed-term bank deposit or government bonds can forecast its exact return with certainty, i.e., the asset provides a riskless or risk-free rate of return.

Companies investing in assets such as shares are affected by the vagaries of the stock market, i.e., there is a lack of certainty attached to future events. Uncontrollable factors that contribute to business risk include general economic conditions, volatility of consumer demands, and personal attitudes to risk. Nevertheless, many investors are prepared to accept an increase in the level of risk if there is a strong probability of higher returns on their investment.

The final class of decision problem – decisions under uncertainty – moves into the area of guesswork where very little, if any, information exists on which to base a decision. A typical example would be a company considering an investment in a new product for which there is insufficient information on which to base probable future sales. In these situations, where the outcome is unpredictable and the probabilities unknown, qualitative as well as quantitative factors must be taken into account. While a mathematical model can provide valuable decision support for investment analysis, such decisions are heavily influenced by basic human traits that include irrationality, greed, and panic.

Basic Concepts in Financial Risk Management

Investors who trade in stocks and bonds are continuously looking for ways to increase their profits while minimising risk. Indeed, the main priority for many financial institutions is not to deal with cash and securities but to manage risk. The term 'security' is a generic name for any asset of monetary value such as stocks, shares, bonds, gold, property, etc. The activity of controlling or managing financial risk is often referred to as 'hedging'.

Recent developments in securities and trading strategies have allowed portfolio managers to be more efficient in hedging against uncertainty in the market place. The terms 'risk management' and 'financial engineering' are commonly used to describe these new strategies. The interrelated concepts of risk preference attitudes and utility theory are now examined.

RISK PREFERENCE ATTITUDES

Investment decisions are influenced by personal attitudes to risk. Investors who are very conservative and actively avoid risk-taking are said to have 'risk aversion'. On the other hand, some decision-makers such as speculators will take a high risk of losing a lot of money in order to make a substantial gain. Such aggressive investors are described as 'risk-seekers'. Most investors are assumed to be risk-averse. In order to avoid risk, an investor must be able to measure and assess investment performance. The quantitative measure of 'expected return' is used to find the rate of return expected from an investment.

Between these two extremes of risk-aversion and risk-seeking is the 'risk-neutral' person who makes decisions on the basis of an investment's expected return – not the risk involved. The risk-neutral person will choose the investment with the highest expected return because it represents the least risky alternative. For example, consider an investor who wants to purchase shares and would like to know which of three possible alternatives – A, B or C – gives the greatest expected return. The shares' returns for the next investment period are not known with certainty and can only be described by a probability distribution of possible outcomes, as shown in the top part of Figure 4.1.

The expected return, $E(R_i)$, which describes the most likely outcome from the probability distribution, is the weighted average of all possible returns, where the weights are the prob-

Share A		Share B		Share C	
Return (%) R_A	Probability p_j	Return (%) R_B	Probability p_j	Return (%) R_C	Probability p_j
9	0.2	8	0.5	11	0.4
12	0.4	11	0.3	12	0.4
17	0.4	13	0.2	13	0.2

Expected returns for shares A, B and C :-

$E(R_A)$ = $0.2 \times 0.09 + 0.4 \times 0.12 + 0.4 \times 0.17 = 0.134 = 13.4\%$
$E(R_B)$ = $0.5 \times 0.08 + 0.3 \times 0.11 + 0.2 \times 0.13 = 0.099 = 9.9\%$
$E(R_C)$ = $0.4 \times 0.11 + 0.4 \times 0.12 + 0.2 \times 0.13 = 0.118 = 11.8\%$

Figure 4.1   Calculating expected returns for shares A, B and C.

abilities assigned to the possible returns and n is the total number of outcomes, i.e., in this example $n = 3$. Thus,

$$E(R_{\mathrm{i}}) = \sum_{j=1}^{n} p_{\mathrm{j}} R_{ij}$$

where $R_{\mathrm{ij}} =$ possible return for share i for outcome j
$p_{\mathrm{j}} =$ probability associated with return R_{ij}

Applying the above formula for $E(R_{\mathrm{i}})$ to share details in Figure 4.1, share A gives the highest expected return of 13.4% while shares B and C give returns of 9.9% and 11.8%.

UTILITY THEORY

In the previous section, the investor's decision to choose share A was based on the maximisation of expected return. Decision-making, however, involves not only quantitative rules but also qualitative intangibles such as personal attitudes to risk. There are situations where numerical measures, such as an investment's return or expected monetary value, are not sufficient and could lead to the wrong course of action being taken.

Utility theory, as presented in Von Neumann and Morgenstern's theory of games, incorporates risk-preference attitudes into the decision-making process by introducing the concept of 'utility functions'. Every decision-maker is assumed to have a personal utility function which is used to convert quantitative values into non-monetary measures called utilities. A 'utility' expands the narrow monetary concept to include individual (or company) preferences to risk and return. The decision-maker then evaluates each alternative on the basis of its utility and identifies the best outcome by maximising expected utility rather than expected value. Because each decision-maker has a unique utility function, there can be a wide variation in the shape of utility curves.

Utility functions for the three most common risk-preference attitudes are shown in Figure 4.2. The risk-averse curve illustrates the concept of 'diminishing marginal utility' which states that the more a person has of a particular resource, the less satisfying becomes the next increment. For example, a salary increase of £1000 means less to a person earning £60,000 than to someone earning £15,000. The risk-averse graph shows that utility increases as monetary value increases. However, as monetary value continues to grow, the curve flattens out reflecting the decision-maker's desire to avoid the higher risks associated with larger monetary values.

The risk-seeking curve illustrates the characteristic of increasing marginal utility whereby utility increases faster than monetary value. This curve reflects the speculative nature of the risk-seeker who is prepared to let utility grow at a faster rate in order to gain some smaller monetary value. The risk-neutral function is a straight line with a constant marginal utility, indicating that the decision-maker is indifferent to risk. Because the risk-indifferent person is concerned with expected monetary value (EMV) rather than risk, utility and monetary values increase proportionately.

Some people can perceive the same situation differently. It is therefore possible to have all three risk-preference attitudes being applied to the same problem. Consider, for example, the reactions of individuals to the situation seen regularly on TV quiz shows. Each participant

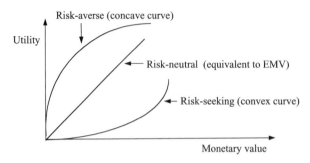

Figure 4.2   Utility functions for risk-preference attitudes.

has to choose between accepting some monetary value being offered by the quiz-master or opening a box which may contain either a star prize or a booby prize. Some contestants will gamble on winning the star prize regardless of the risk involved. On the other hand, if the quiz-master continues to increase the amount on offer, many participants will eventually change their mind and accept the money.

EXAMPLE 4.1   *Constructing a utility curve*

Joe Bloggs is a contestant on the 'Open the Box' quiz show. The star prize is a motor-car worth £16,000 while the booby prize is worth £5. The quiz-master has made an offer of £2000. Joe must now decide what to do. The first step in constructing a utility function is to determine two monetary values representing the worst and best outcomes to the problem. In Joe Bloggs's situation, the worst and best outcomes are described by the monetary values of £5 (booby prize) and £16,000 (car). A common practice is to assign utility values of 0 to represent the worst outcome and 1 to the best outcome. The associated utility U values are therefore given by the following two equations

$$U(5) = 0 \text{ and } U(16,000) = 1$$

Joe Bloggs has two alternatives, namely (i) accept the quiz-master's offer of £2000 with certainty, or (ii) gamble on winning the star prize, in which case he also has a 50% chance of receiving the booby prize. The expected utilities for each alternative are given by the following two equations:

First alternative, A_1 $U(A_1) = U(2,000)$

Second alternative, A_2 $U(A_2) = 0.5*U(5) + 0.5*U(16,000) = 0.5*0 + 0.5*1 = 0.5$

As matters stand, Joe prefers the second alternative which means that $U(A_1) < U(A_2)$, i.e., the utility of £2000 is less than 0.5. However, he waits to see if the quiz-master will increase the offer. When a new offer of £4000 is made, Joe immediately accepts. This decision implies that $U(4000) > U(A_2)$, i.e., the utility of £4000 is greater than 0.5. Because Joe has changed his mind, it can also be deduced that there is some value between £2000 and £4000, at which Joe is 'indifferent' to the two alternatives. Indifference implies that both alternatives are equally acceptable to Joe, i.e., each has a probability of 0.5. In this situation, Joe has adopted a risk-neutral attitude. If it is established that Joe's 'indifference value' is £3000, another utility value can be calculated as follows:

$$U(3000) = 0.5^*U(5) + 0.5^*U(16,000) = 0.5^*0 + 0.5^*1 = 0.5$$

Thus a new utility value, $U(3000)$, has been derived from the two known utility values, $U(5)$ and $U(16,000)$. A further point on the utility curve can be found by incorporating $U(3000)$ into a different monetary option. For example, if the booby prize is replaced by £3000 in cash, Joe Bloggs faces a new dilemma. In this situation, he prefers to gamble on winning the star prize unless the quiz-master increases the current offer of £4000. If Joe decides that his indifference value is now £7000, then:

$$U(7000) = 0.5^*U(3000) + 0.5^*U(16, 000) = 0.5^*0.5 + 0.5^*1 = 0.75$$

Other utility values may be found in a similar manner. The four points (5, 0), (3000, 0.5), (7000, 0.75) and (16000, 1) are used to construct Joe's utility curve as shown in Figure 4.3.

Joe Bloggs's indifference value(s) represents the minimum amount of money that he is prepared to accept for avoiding a risky alternative, i.e., opening the box. This minimum amount of money is called the 'certainty equivalent'. Because Joe is indifferent between opening or not opening the box, the certainty equivalent can also be interpreted as the maximum amount that a person is willing to forfeit in order to participate in a risky alternative. The term 'risk premium' is closely associated with the certainty equivalent. Risk premium is defined as the difference between the risky alternative's expected monetary value (EMV) and its certainty equivalent.

It should be noted that utility analysis is not easy to implement in practice because of its subjective nature. Finding the exact point of an individual's indifference can be a complex process. This problem is accentuated when trying to establish a company's utility function. Managers with different attitudes to risk usually find it very difficult to agree on a common utility function. Furthermore, a person's perspective can alter over time making any previous utility assessment obsolete.

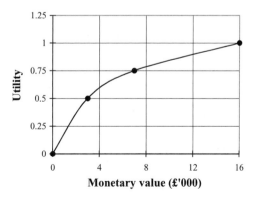

Figure 4.3 Utility curve

The Exponential Utility Function (EUF)

The concave curve of a risk-averse investor shown in Figure 4.2 can be approximated by an exponential utility function (EUF) as given by the equation

$$U(x) = 1 - e^{-x/R}$$

where   e = 2.71828 the base of natural logarithms
            R = the decision-maker's *risk tolerance* (R > 0)

The risk-tolerance parameter R controls the shape of the utility function. As R increases the curve flattens out, i.e., the decision-maker becomes less risk-averse. In order to use the exponential utility function, a suitable R-value must be found that best fits the decision-maker's risk tolerance. One approach is to find a value for X that will persuade the decision-maker to participate in the following gamble: toss a coin to win £X or lose £X/2. The value of X that convinces the decision-maker to accept this gamble can be taken as a reasonable estimate for R, e.g., a person who accepts a gamble to win £200 or lose £100, has an R-value of 200.

EXAMPLE 4.2   *Using the EUF to maximise expected utility*

AstroReturns stockbrokers has been asked by a long-standing client to invest £30,000. The company has provided details of three stocks X, Y and Z. Stock X is a government bond guaranteeing a fixed return of 8%. The returns from stocks Y and Z depend upon the prevailing market conditions. AstroReturns estimate the probability of a good, average, or poor market as 0.3, 0.6, and 0.1 respectively. The company has calculated relevant stock returns (%) for each market condition as shown in Table 4.1. Since the client wants all her money to be invested in the same stock, AstroReturns must now decide which of the three stocks will maximise her expected utility.

   Because the client is well known to AstroReturns, the company can use the exponential utility function. An R-value of 4000 has been assessed as the most reasonable figure for their client's risk tolerance. The expected utility model of Figure 4.4 has found that stock Z produces a maximum expected utility of 0.5 (see cell H27). If the client's R-value is reduced to 1500 (cell F11), i.e., she is now more risk-averse, stock X then has the largest utility.

PORTFOLIO THEORY: THE MARKOWITZ MODEL

Modern portfolio theory started in the early 1950s when Harry Markowitz published his mean-variance approach to portfolio management. Markowitz's model was the first to emphasise the

Table 4.1   Estimated stock returns (%).

Stock	← Market conditions →		
	Good	Average	Poor
Y	11	7.5	2
Z	16	9	-1

	A	B	C	D	E	F	G	H	I
1	Example 4.2 - **Maximising expected utility**								
2									
3			Stock	<--- Market conditions --->					
4				Good	Average	Poor			
5			X	8.0%	8.0%	8.0%		User input	
6			Y	11.0%	7.5%	2.0%		cells are	
7			Z	16.0%	9.0%	−1.0%		shaded	
8			Probability	0.3	0.6	0.1			
9									
10				Amount invested =		£30,000			
11			Client's risk-tolerance value, R =			4000			
12									
13									
14				**Payoff matrix of expected returns**					
15									
16				Good	Average	Poor		**EMV**	
17			X	£2,400	£2,400	£2,400		£2,400	
18			Y	£3,300	£2,250	£600		£2,400	
19			Z	£4,800	£2,700	−£300		£3,030	
20									
21			Convert the payoff matrix to an **'expected utility'**						
22			table using the exponential utility function						
23								**Expected**	
24				Good	Average	Poor		**utility**	
25			X	0.45	0.45	0.45		0.45	
26			Y	0.56	0.43	0.14		0.44	
27			Z	0.70	0.49	−0.08		0.50	
28									
29									
30		*Cell*	*Formula*					*Copied to*	
31		D17	$F$10*D5					D17:F19	
32		H17	SUMPRODUCT(D17:F17, D$8:F$8)					H18:H19	
33		D25	1 - EXP(-D17/$F$11)					D25:F27	
34		H25	SUMPRODUCT(D25:F25, D$8:F$8)					H26:H27	
35									

Figure 4.4   Maximising expected utility.

importance of diversification of securities within the portfolio. By combining a judicious mixture of securities that range from low-risk/low-return to high-risk/high-return investments, Markowitz showed how portfolio returns could be maximised while minimising risk at the same time. He described this trade-off between risk and return on stock portfolios as the 'efficient frontier' – a concept which is discussed below. The Markowitz model involves three phases:

- **Security analysis**   Quantifies the risk/return characteristics of an individual security by using statistical measures, i.e., mean, variance, and covariance (already discussed in Chapter 3). The variance is usually denoted by σ^2 or V, and its square root – called the standard deviation – by σ or SD. Both terms are often used interchangeably.

- **Portfolio analysis**   Utilises information from the first phase to identify the best portfolios, i.e., the optimal combination of securities that can be achieved through diversification. This second phase involves plotting a mean-variance graph which is then used to find the efficient frontier. Note that the terms 'mean/variance' and 'expected return/standard deviation' are synonymous.

- **Portfolio selection**   Examines the best portfolios identified in the second phase and selects the portfolio that maximises the investor's preferences, which may range from risk-averting (low-risk) to risk-seeking (high risk).

Security Analysis

A security's expected return, $E(R_i)$, is equivalent to the mean or average of a discrete probability distribution. For example, the expected return of 13.4% for share A in Figure 4.1 was found by using the weighted average formula. A security's risk is measured by its variance. The greater the variance of a security's expected return, the greater the security's risk. This observation is because a large variance means that the spread of values from the mean is large, i.e. the actual return moves further away from the expected return, $E(R_i)$. Conversely, the smaller the size of the variance, the closer the actual return is to $E(R_i)$, and so the smaller is the risk. The formula for the variance of the expected return of security i is

$$V_i = \sigma_i^2 \quad = \sum_{j=1}^{n} p_j \left(R_{ij} - E(R_i) \right)^2$$

where n = number of possible returns

The formula for the covariance, σ_{ij}, between the expected returns on two securities i and j is

$$COV_{ij} = \sigma_{ij} \quad = \sum_{k=1}^{n} p_k \left(R_{ik} - E(R_i) \right)^* \left(R_{jk} - E(R_j) \right)$$

where $i \neq j$

EXAMPLE 4.3   *A security analysis model*

A security analysis model is now developed, using the share details given in Figure 4.1 as input data. The spreadsheet in Figure 4.5 shows how a security analysis model can be constructed. The expected returns for the three shares are shown on line 5, while variances and covariances are calculated in column H. Because the standard deviation, σ, is generally expressed in the same units as the original data, σ-values are easier to interpret than variance values. The σ-values for shares A, B, and C are 3.14%, 2.02%, and 0.75% respectively. In terms of risk, share C is the least risky because it has the smallest σ-value of 0.75% while share A has the greatest risk with a σ-value of 3.14%. From the input data in cell range C8:C16, it can be seen that the return values cover a range of 8% for share A (9–17%), 5% for share B (8–13%), and only 2% for share C.

	A	B	C	D	E	F	G	H	I	J
1		Example 4.3 - Security analysis of three shares A, B, C								
2										
3						Expected Returns				
4		*User input cells are shaded*				E(R$_A$)	E(R$_B$)	E(R$_C$)		
5						**13.40%**	**9.90%**	**11.80%**		
6			Return	Probability			p$_i$ ×		Standard	
7			R$_i$	p$_i$	−1	R$_{ij}$ − E(R$_i$)	(R$_{ij}$ − E(R$_i$))	**Variance**	deviation	
8		*Share A*	9.0%	0.2	0	−0.0440	−0.0088	0.00098	3.14%	
9			12.0%	0.4	0	−0.0140	−0.0056			
10			17.0%	0.4	0	0.0360	0.0144			
11		*Share B*	8.0%	0.5	1	−0.0190	−0.0095	0.00041	2.02%	
12			11.0%	0.3	1	0.0110	0.0033			
13			13.0%	0.2	1	0.0310	0.0062			
14		*Share C*	11.0%	0.4	2	−0.0080	−0.0032	0.00006	0.75%	
15			12.0%	0.4	2	0.0020	0.0008			
16			13.0%	0.2	2	0.0120	0.0024			
17										
18								**Covariances**		
19		Cell ranges (F8:F10), (G11:G13),				Covariance COV$_{AABB}$ =		0.00060		
20		(F14:F16) have been named as				Covariance COV$_{AACC}$ =		0.00076		
21		AA, BB, CC				Covariance COV$_{BBCC}$ =		0.00016		
22										
23										
24		*Cell*	*Formula*					*Copied to*		
25		F5	SUMPRODUCT(C8:C10,D8:D10)							
26		G5	SUMPRODUCT(C11:C13,D11:D13)							
27		H5	SUMPRODUCT(C14:C16,D14:D16)							
28		F8	$C8 - OFFSET(F$5,0,$E8)					F9:F16		
29		G8	D8*F8					G9:G16		
30		H8	IF(E8=E7,"",SUMPRODUCT(F8:F10,G8:G10))					H9:H16		
31		I8	IF(H8="","",SQRT(H8))					I9:I16		
32		H19	SUMPRODUCT(AA,BB)							
33		H20	SUMPRODUCT(AA,CC)							
34		H21	SUMPRODUCT(BB,CC)							
35										

Figure 4.5 Security analysis of three shares.

PORTFOLIO ANALYSIS: THE EFFICIENT FRONTIER

In order to identify superior portfolios, formulae must first be derived for the (i) expected return and (ii) level of risk of a portfolio. The expected return of a three-asset portfolio, $E(R_p)$, is given by the following equation:

$$E(R_p) = w_1 E(R_1) + w_2 E(R_2) + w_3 E(R_3)$$

where w_1, w_2, and w_3 are the percentages of the portfolio invested in securities 1, 2 and 3 respectively. Assuming that all of the money is invested, then $w_1 + w_2 + w_3 = 100\% = 1$. The above equation can be extended to a portfolio consisting of n assets by simply adding extra terms to the right-hand side. As an example, consider a portfolio consisting of the three shares shown in Figure 4.5. Assume that the investment percentages (also called asset weights) are 45%, 20%, and 35% for shares A, B and C respectively. Then the expected return for this portfolio is

$$E(R_p) = 0.45^* E(R_A) + 0.2^* E(R_B) + 0.35^* E(R_C)$$

$$= 0.45^* 13.4\% + 0.2^* 9.9\% + 0.35^* 11.8\% = 12.14\%$$

An important objective in portfolio management is to balance the portfolio by choosing a combination of investments that cover the full spectrum of risk minimisation and return maximisation. This policy of diversification means that a well-balanced portfolio should contain a mixture of high-risk, medium-risk, and low-risk investments. A diversified portfolio reduces the risk of loss by ensuring that the investments do not have a very close correlation, i.e., they counterbalance each other. A portfolio's variance is used as a measure of risk. If a portfolio's variance is minimised then so also is its risk. For a portfolio consisting of n securities, total variance is defined by the equation

$$\text{portfolio variance} = \sigma_p^2 = \sum_{i=1}^{n} \sigma_i^2 w_i^2 + 2 \sum_{i=1}^{n-1} \sum_{j=i+1}^{n} \sigma_{ij} w_i w_j$$

where $\sigma_p^2 =$ the percentage of the portfolio invested in security i
    $\sigma_i^2 =$ the variance of security i
    $\sigma_{ij} = \sigma_{ji} =$ the covariance between securities i and j

Since most investors are considered to be risk-averse, they will choose a portfolio which minimises risk for a given level of expected return. Such a portfolio is called an efficient portfolio and is located on the 'efficient frontier'. The efficient frontier can be defined as the set of portfolios that minimises risk, σ_p, for a given level of expected return, $E(R_p)$.

EXAMPLE 4.4   *A model for the efficient frontier*

There are two steps involved in deriving the efficient frontier:

Step 1: Build a portfolio optimisation model
A non-linear programming (NLP) model is built in order to find the best mixture of investments that will minimise portfolio risk. The required spreadsheet is a simplified version of Barney Briggs's portfolio management model discussed in Chapter 3 (see Figure 3.4). Input data for this new model has already been derived in the security analysis model of Figure 4.5 (line 5 and column H). Details for each share, i.e., expected return $E(R_i)$, variance (V_{ii}), and covariance (V_{ij}), are copied into the appropriate (shaded) cells of Figure 4.6. The worksheet formulae and Solver parameters for the model are given in Table 4.2.

Step 2: Generate graphical data
The portfolio optimisation model is now run seven times. By varying the required rate of return (cell G11 in Figure 4.6) – from 10% to 13% in increments of 0.5% – a 'Results Table' (see

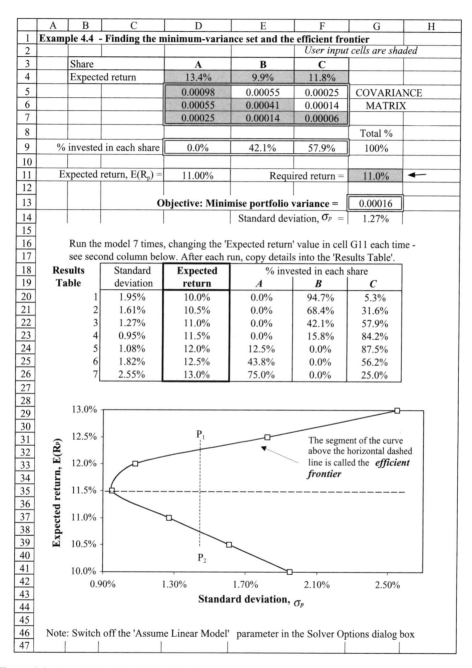

	A	B	C	D	E	F	G	H
1	**Example 4.4 - Finding the minimum-variance set and the efficient frontier**							
2							*User input cells are shaded*	
3		Share			**A**	**B**	**C**		
4		Expected return			13.4%	9.9%	11.8%		
5					0.00098	0.00055	0.00025	COVARIANCE	
6					0.00055	0.00041	0.00014	MATRIX	
7					0.00025	0.00014	0.00006		
8								Total %	
9		% invested in each share			0.0%	42.1%	57.9%	100%	
10									
11		Expected return, $E(R_p) =$			11.00%		Required return =	11.0%	←
12									
13				**Objective: Minimise portfolio variance =**				0.00016	
14						Standard deviation, σ_p =		1.27%	

Run the model 7 times, changing the 'Expected return' value in cell G11 each time - see second column below. After each run, copy details into the 'Results Table'.

Results		Standard		**Expected**		% invested in each share		
Table		deviation		**return**		*A*	*B*	*C*
	1	1.95%		10.0%		0.0%	94.7%	5.3%
	2	1.61%		10.5%		0.0%	68.4%	31.6%
	3	1.27%		11.0%		0.0%	42.1%	57.9%
	4	0.95%		11.5%		0.0%	15.8%	84.2%
	5	1.08%		12.0%		12.5%	0.0%	87.5%
	6	1.82%		12.5%		43.8%	0.0%	56.2%
	7	2.55%		13.0%		75.0%	0.0%	25.0%

The segment of the curve above the horizontal dashed line is called the *efficient frontier*

Note: Switch off the 'Assume Linear Model' parameter in the Solver Options dialog box

Figure 4.6   A model for the efficient frontier.

Table 4.2 Efficient frontier model – worksheet formulae and Solver parameters.

Cell	Formula	Copied to
E5	D6	(also set cells F5 = D7, F6 = E7)
G9	SUM(D9:F9)	
D11	SUMPRODUCT(D4:F4, D9:F9)	
G13	SUMPRODUCT(MMULT(D9:F9, D5:F7), D9:F9)	
G14	SQRT(G13)	

Solver parameters		
Set target cell:	G13	
Equal to:	Min	
By changing cells:	D9:F9	
Subject to constraints:	D11 = G11	= Expected and required returns must be equal
	G9 = 1	= Portfolio percentages must add up to 100%
	D9:F9 ≥ 0	= Answers must be positive

lines 18–26) is built up. Note that the expected return, $E(R_p)$, is set equal to the investor's required return. The trade-off between risk and expected return for a portfolio can be illustrated by plotting a $(\sigma_p, E(R_p))$ graph. Each Solver solution generates a $(\sigma_p, E(R_p))$ point that is used to plot the minimum-variance set.

Excel's ChartWizard (see Appendix) has produced the graph shown in Figure 4.6, using cell range B20:C26 as input. The vertical axis represents expected return values, $E(R_p)$, while corresponding σ_p-values are plotted along the horizontal axis. The resulting C-shaped curve is called the 'minimum-variance set' because it contains only portfolios with minimum risk. The positively-sloped segment (i.e., upper part) of this curve, which gives the greater expected return for a given level of risk, is called the 'efficient frontier'. It is also referred to as a trade-off curve.

Portfolio Selection

The last phase of the Markowitz model examines the portfolios lying on the minimum-variance set. Investors prefer efficient portfolios, i.e., portfolios that lie on the efficient frontier, because they give a higher expected return for a given level of risk. For example, portfolio P_1 in Figure 4.6 is preferred to portfolio P_2 because P_2 is not on the efficient frontier. However, the final preference of an efficient portfolio will be determined by the investor's attitude to risk.

A very risk-averse investor will choose a portfolio with minimum variance, i.e., minimum risk. The 'Results Table' in Figure 4.6 shows that a portfolio with an expected return of 11.5% produces the minimum standard deviation of 0.95% (line 23). On the other hand, a more adventurous risk-seeking investor will be prepared to accept a higher level of risk in order to get a higher expected return. Such an investor may well select a portfolio offering returns of 12.5% or 13% although corresponding standard-deviation (i.e., risk) values are high – see cells C25 and C26.

SINGLE INDEX MODEL (SIM)

The single index model (SIM), developed by William Sharpe, is a simplified version of the Markowitz model. The model's main benefit is that it greatly reduces the amount of computation. A SIM portfolio analysis of n securities requires only $(n + 1)$ calculations to build the variance-covariance matrix. On the other hand, the Markowitz model generates $n(n + 1)/2$ calculations to carry out a similar n-security analysis. For example, a portfolio containing 100 securities needs only 101 calculations using SIM but 5050 calculations for the Markowitz model.

The SIM model assumes that there is a linear relationship between the price movement of a security (or portfolio) and the price movement of the overall market. The market is represented by a market index such as the FTSE (UK), Dow Jones (USA), Nikkei (Japan), etc. The basic SIM straight-line equation is

$$R_i = \alpha_i + \beta_i R_m + \varepsilon_i$$

where $i = 1, 2, 3 \ldots n$

R_i = the rate of return for security i over a specified period

R_m = the rate of return of the market index over a specified period

α_i = the rate of return that is independent of the market movement

β_i = measures the expected change in R_i to a given change in R_m. β_i is usually called the *beta-coefficient* or simply 'beta'

ε_i = the residual (i.e., error) associated with R_i

This equation divides the return on a stock into two components. The first part ($\beta_i R_m$), which is due to market changes, is called the systematic or market risk. β_i measures how sensitive a stock's return is to the market return. A β_i of 3 means that a stock's return is predicted to increase (decrease) by 3% when the market increases (decreases) by 1%. The second part ($\alpha_i + \varepsilon_i$), which is independent of the market, is known as the unsystematic or diversifiable risk. This type of risk, which is specific to the individual stock, can be reduced or even eliminated by creating a well-balanced portfolio of diverse securities – hence the name diversifiable risk.

In co-ordinate geometry terms, β_i represents the slope of the line while α_i is the intercept value on the vertical y-axis. In the SIM model, the horizontal x-axis is represented by the market index returns, R_m, and the y-axis by the stock returns, R_i. The SIM model makes three important assumptions about the residuals, ε_i, which represent the difference between actual and predicted returns:

1. The mean of the residuals, ε_i is zero, i.e., $E(\varepsilon_i) = 0$.

2. Each residual is independent of the other, i.e., $E(\varepsilon_i \varepsilon_j) = 0$.

3. There is no correlation between the residuals, ε_i, and the market return, R_m, i.e., $\text{COVAR}(\varepsilon_i, R_m) = E(\varepsilon_i [R_m - E(R_m)]) = 0$.

EXAMPLE 4.5 *Determining beta and intercept values*

Bette Briggs invested in the XYZ Company some time ago and now wants to find out how her shares have been performing in relation to the overall market. Bette has collected monthly

Table 4.3

Month	1	2	3	4	5	6	7	8	9	10	11	12
R_i	9.33	6.72	−1.21	0.86	1.34	−4.73	7.56	5.39	2.4	−7.9	−1.7	6.58
R_m	7.98	4.55	1.04	4.42	5.76	−1.67	4.18	6.7	2.87	−3.89	−1.3	2.08

(percentage) returns over the past year on both shares (R_i) and the market index (R_m), as shown in Table 4.3.

In Figure 4.7, Bette uses (i) Excel's Chart Wizard to obtain a scattergraph of the tabulated data, and (ii) the 'Trendline' function to plot a regression line through the data using the least-squares method (see Case Study 6.1). The least-squares approach attempts to optimise the linear relationship between two variables by fitting a line through observed data so that it minimises $\sum \varepsilon_i^2$, i.e., the sum of the squares of the residuals. The regression line equation has been calculated as $y = 1.2351x - 0.0131$ which is equivalent to $R_i = \beta_i R_m + \alpha_i$. Thus, beta $= \beta = 1.2351$ and intercept $= \alpha = -0.0131$ (i.e., −1.31%). A security with a β value of 1.0 moves with the market, i.e., it follows the general trend of all security movements. While a β value of 1.235 implies that XYZ stock is more volatile than the overall market, it also means that XYZ should have relatively high returns. The speculative Bette Briggs is therefore pleased to see that her shares have been performing above the market index.

The coefficient of determination, R^2 (R-squared), measures the goodness of fit of the regression line. If the fit is good, R^2 will be close to 1; if the fit is poor then R^2 is close to 0. In this case, $R^2 = 0.7095$ which indicates a good line fit. R-squared is also a measure of systematic risk, i.e., 70.95% of the total variability in XYZ Company returns can be explained by the variability in the market index returns, R_m. The remaining percentage, i.e., $(1 - R^2) = 29.05\%$ is attributed to unsystematic risk.

Deriving the expected return, variance, and covariance for the SIM model

- Expected return (or mean) of a security i, $E(R_i)$

$$\begin{aligned} E(R_i) &= E(\alpha_i + \beta_i R_m + \varepsilon_i) && \text{by substitution} \\ &= \alpha_i + \beta_i E(R_m) + E(\varepsilon_i) && \text{since } \alpha_i \text{ and } \beta_i \text{ are constants} \\ &= \alpha_i + \beta_i E(R_m) && \text{since } E(\varepsilon_i) = 0 \text{ (assumption 1)} \end{aligned}$$

- Variance of a security's return, $\text{VAR}(R_i)$
  The variance of a random variable, X, can be defined as $\text{VAR}(X) = \sigma_x^2 = E[X - E(X)]^2$. The variances of the market index and residuals for security i are represented by σ_m^2 and $\sigma_{\varepsilon i}^2$ respectively. Thus,

$$\begin{aligned} \text{VAR}(R_i) = \sigma_i^2 &= E[R_i - E(R_i)]^2 \\ &= E[\{\alpha_i + \beta_i R_m + \varepsilon_i\} - \{\alpha_i + \beta_i E(R_m)\}]^2 \quad \text{by substitution} \\ &= E[\beta_i \{R_m - E(R_m)\} + \varepsilon_i]^2 \\ &= E[\beta_i^2 \{R_m - E(R_m)\}^2] + 2\beta_i E[\varepsilon_i \{R_m - E(R_m)\}] + E(\varepsilon_i)^2 \end{aligned}$$

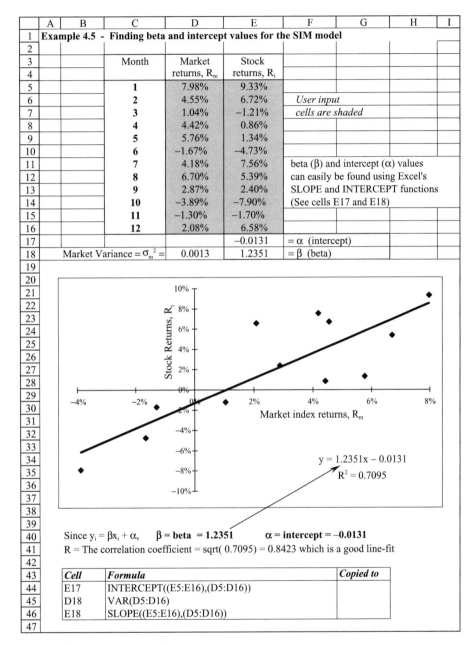

The spreadsheet shown in the figure contains the following:

	A	B	C	D	E	F	G	H	I
1	**Example 4.5 - Finding beta and intercept values for the SIM model**								
2									
3			Month	Market	Stock				
4				returns, R_m	returns, R_i				
5			1	7.98%	9.33%				
6			2	4.55%	6.72%	*User input*			
7			3	1.04%	−1.21%	*cells are shaded*			
8			4	4.42%	0.86%				
9			5	5.76%	1.34%				
10			6	−1.67%	−4.73%				
11			7	4.18%	7.56%	beta (β) and intercept (α) values			
12			8	6.70%	5.39%	can easily be found using Excel's			
13			9	2.87%	2.40%	SLOPE and INTERCEPT functions			
14			10	−3.89%	−7.90%	(See cells E17 and E18)			
15			11	−1.30%	−1.70%				
16			12	2.08%	6.58%				
17					−0.0131	= α (intercept)			
18	Market Variance = σ_m^2 =			0.0013	1.2351	= β (beta)			

Since $y_i = \beta x_i + \alpha$,   β = **beta = 1.2351**   α = **intercept = −0.0131**
R = The correlation coefficient = sqrt(0.7095) = 0.8423 which is a good line-fit

Cell	Formula		Copied to
E17	INTERCEPT((E5:E16),(D5:D16))		
D18	VAR(D5:D16)		
E18	SLOPE((E5:E16),(D5:D16))		

Figure 4.7   Determining beta and intercept values.

Using assumption 3 and the fact that $\sigma_{\varepsilon i}^2 = E(\varepsilon i)^2$, the above expression can be simplified to

$$= \beta_i^2 E[R_m - E(R_m)]^2 + E(\varepsilon_i)^2$$
$$= \beta_i^2 \sigma_m^2 + \sigma_{\varepsilon i}^2$$

- Covariance between the returns of securities i and j, COVAR(R_i, R_j)
  The covariance of two variables, X and Y, is COVAR(X,Y) $= E[\{X - E(X)\}\{Y - E(Y)\}]$.
  Thus, the SIM covariance between the returns of securities i and j is

$$\begin{aligned}
\text{COVAR}(R_i, R_j) = \sigma_{ij} &= E[\{R_i - E(R_i)\}\{R_j - E(R_j)\}] \\
&= E[\{\alpha_i + \beta_i R_m + \varepsilon_i\} - \{\alpha_i + \beta_i E(R_m)\}] \\
&\quad \times E[\{\alpha_j + \beta_j R_m + \varepsilon_j\} - \{\alpha_j + \beta_j E(R_m)\}] \\
&= \beta_i \beta_j E[R_m - E(R_m)]^2 + \beta_j E[\varepsilon_i\{R_m - E(R_m)\}] \\
&\quad + \beta_i E[\varepsilon_j\{R_m - E(R_m)\}] + E(\varepsilon_i \varepsilon_j) \\
&= \beta_i \beta_j \sigma_m^2 \qquad \text{using the SIM assumptions}
\end{aligned}$$

EXAMPLE 4.6   *Using SIM to find the covariance matrix*

Fred Flint has decided to invest his recent inheritance of £20,000 in three companies X, Y and Z. He has kept records of the movement of the companies' shares and the market index over the past twelve months as shown in the Table 4.4.

The matrices in Figure 4.8 require data for the securities' covariance, σ_{ij}, and variance, σ_i^2. The SIM formulae for σ_{ij} and σ_i^2 – derived in the previous section – require three inputs, namely (i) each security's β_i value (ii) the variance of the market index, σ_m^2, and (iii) the variance of the residuals, $\sigma_{\varepsilon i}^2$. Excel's SLOPE and VAR functions are used to find β_i and the market variance, σ_m^2. The variance of the residuals, $\sigma_{\varepsilon i}^2$, is easily derived by using Excel's STEYX function. STEYX returns the standard deviation of the residuals, $\sigma_{\varepsilon i}$ – also called the standard error (see cells E20:G20 in Figure 4.8).

A comparison has been made between the covariance matrix produced by the SIM model and the covariance matrix computed from share returns data. The difference between the two matrices is relatively small (see Table 4.5). To simplify input to the formulae used in each matrix, share and market returns have been 'named'. When a name is assigned to a range of cells, the cell range is treated as a single unit. For example, cell range D5:D16 containing the market returns data, has been named simply as 'M'. Similarly, share returns in ranges E5:E16, F5:F16, and G5:G16 have been named X, Y and Z. The covariance formula for shares X and Y is then simplified to COVAR(X, Y).

Table 4.4   Percentage annual returns for shares X, Y, Z and the market index.

Month	Share X	Share Y	Share Z	Market Index	Month	Share X	Share Y	Share Z	Market Index
1	5.92	13.07	2.98	7.17	7	9.59	27.04	−7.56	14.18
2	3.69	3.55	8.36	5.71	8	12.39	6.22	38.91	11.67
3	−2.64	−15.19	−10.25	−8.04	9	−6.46	−15.91	−11.50	−9.28
4	9.92	7.86	20.79	14.42	10	2.71	−1.85	−4.72	1.89
5	11.34	11.81	22.50	12.76	11	4.70	13.82	20.79	6.93
6	5.73	7.18	34.46	3.67	12	10.64	36.58	12.31	12.28

	A	B	C	D	E	F	G	H	I
1	Example 4.6 - Calculating the covariance matrix using the SIM model								
2									
3			Month	Market	Share **X**	Share **Y**	Share **Z**		
4				returns, R_m	returns, R_i	returns, R_i	returns, R_i		
5			1	7.17%	5.92%	13.07%	2.98%		
6	Market and		2	5.71%	3.69%	3.55%	8.36%	*User input*	
7	share return		3	−8.04%	−2.64%	−15.19%	−10.25%	*cells are*	
8	data have		4	14.42%	9.92%	7.86%	20.79%	*shaded*	
9	been 'named'		5	12.76%	11.34%	11.81%	22.50%		
10	as M, X, Y		6	3.67%	5.73%	7.18%	34.46%		
11	and Z (see		7	14.18%	9.59%	27.04%	−7.56%		
12	text)		8	11.67%	12.39%	6.22%	38.91%		
13			9	−9.28%	−6.46%	−15.91%	−11.50%		
14			10	1.89%	2.71%	−1.85%	−4.72%		
15			11	6.93%	4.70%	13.82%	20.79%		
16			12	12.28%	10.64%	36.58%	12.31%		
17	MarketVariance $= \sigma_m^{\,2} =$			0.00646	0.0141	−0.0159	0.03462	$= \alpha$ (intercept)	
18					0.6893	1.5431	1.1659	$= \beta$ (beta)	
19									
20	Standard deviation of residuals $= \sigma_{\varepsilon i} =$				0.01668	0.08901	0.15193		
21	Variance of residuals $= \sigma_{\varepsilon i}^{\,2} =$				0.00028	0.00792	0.02308		
22									
23					0	1	2		
24		**Covariance**		0	0.00335	0.00687	0.00519		
25		**Matrix**		1	0.00687	0.02330	0.01161		
26		(using SIM)		2	0.00519	0.01161	0.03186		
27									
28		**Covariance**			0.00332	0.00618	0.00599		
29		**Matrix**			0.00618	0.02258	0.00725		
30		(using share returns)			0.00599	0.00725	0.02976		
31									
32									
33		*Cell*	*Formula*					*Copied to*	
34		D17	VAR(M)						
35		E17	INTERCEPT((E5:E16),M)					F17:G17	
36		E18	SLOPE((E5:E16),M)					F18:G18	
37		E20	STEYX((E5:E16),M)					F20:G20	
38		E21	E20*E20					F21:G21	
39		E24	IF(E$23=$D24,E18^2*D$17 + E$21, $D$17*						
40			OFFSET($E$18,0,E$23)*OFFSET($E$18,0,$D24))					E24:G26	
41		E28	IF(E$23=$D24,VAR(E$5:E$16),COVAR(OFFSET(X,0,E$23),						
42			OFFSET(X,0,$D24)))					E28:G30	
43									

Figure 4.8   Calculating the covariance matrix using the SIM model.

Table 4.5   Difference between covariance matrices.

Share X	**Share Y**	**Share Z**
−0.00003	−0.00068	0.00080
−0.00068	−0.00072	−0.00436
0.00080	0.00436	−0.00210

THE CAPITAL ASSET PRICING MODEL (CAPM)

Investment analysis models so far have focused on individual investors and their preferences for maximising returns while minimising risk. Asset pricing models – also called equilibrium models – take a broader view of the market by examining the attitudes of investors as a whole. Asset pricing models assume that the capital market, i.e., the market for long-term securities, is perfect. A perfect market implies that the market is 'in equilibrium', i.e., demand equals supply and each asset has a single market-clearing price. If an asset's price is temporarily low/high, investors will buy/sell the asset until the forces of supply and demand restore equilibrium.

The best-known asset pricing model is William Sharpe's capital asset pricing model (CAPM) published in 1964. To simplify the complexity of capital markets, the CAPM assumes that everyone has equal access to the same information and can borrow or lend any amount of money at a risk-free interest rate. It is therefore concluded that all investors will make the same decisions and create identical portfolios using the Markowitz model. Today, such theoretical assumptions are regarded as being too restrictive and unrepresentative of real-world situations, and more realistic asset pricing models have subsequently been developed. The five assumptions are:

1. All assets are marketable. Marketable assets are much easier to quantify than non-marketable assets such as goodwill, patents, and copyrights.

2. The capital market is perfect, i.e., (i) there are no transaction or tax costs (ii) assets are infinitely divisible, i.e., there is no restriction on the size of the amount to be invested (iii) the same information is freely available to every investor (iv) no single investor can influence the market by buying or selling actions.

3. A risk-free interest rate exists; all investors can borrow or lend any amount at this fixed risk-free interest rate.

4. All investors are risk-averse and seek to maximise expected portfolio returns.

5. All investors have homogeneous expectations, i.e., they make identical portfolio decisions, using the Markowitz model over the same investment horizon.

The Capital Market Line (CML)

The models that were developed earlier in this chapter contained only risky securities. The third CAPM assumption adds a risk-free (riskless) asset to the portfolio. Investors can now choose a set of risky assets (e.g., stocks) as well as a risk-free asset (e.g., fixed-term bank deposit). Consider a portfolio P which consists of risky assets and one risk-free asset with an interest rate of R_f. The expected portfolio return $E(R_p)$ is then

$$E(R_p) = x E(R_y) + (1 - x)R_f$$

where: x = the percentage of the portfolio invested in risky assets
$(1 - x)$ = the percentage of the portfolio invested in the risk-free asset
$E(R_y)$ = the expected return of the risky-asset portfolio
R_f = the risk-free interest rate

Assumption 4 states that all investors are risk-averse and seek to maximise their expected portfolio returns, i.e., they prefer to invest in optimal portfolios lying on the efficient frontier. Because all investors make identical portfolio decisions (assumption 5), they will all derive the same efficient frontier of Markowitz. At this stage, all investors will hold their risky assets in the same proportions regardless of their risk preferences. These optimal proportions (or percentages) constitute the 'market portfolio', denoted by M in Figure 4.9. The market portfolio, M, is the optimal portfolio of risky assets. It should be noted that the derivation of suitable values for the expected return on the market portfolio, $E(R_M)$, and the risk-free interest rate, R_f , can be problematic.

Because the market is in equilibrium (assumption 2), the market portfolio must include all assets in the market. If an asset was not included in the market portfolio, i.e., implying that no one wanted to buy it, then total demand would not equal total supply. The proportion of each asset, w_i, in the market portfolio is given by

$$w_i = \frac{\text{market value of asset i}}{\text{total market value of all assets in the market}}$$

The capital market line (CML) is defined as the line that (i) has an intercept of R_f on the vertical axis and (ii) is tangential to the efficient frontier of Markowitz at point M (Diacogiannis, Chapter 9). All investors lie on the CML as shown in Figure 4.9. Whatever part of the line they occupy will depend upon investors' risk preference attitudes. They must decide how much to invest in (i) the risky-asset portfolio M and (ii) the risk-free asset, i.e., they must find a value for x as defined in the $E(R_p)$ equation above.

Very risk-averse investors will put most of their wealth into the risk-free asset while leaving a small percentage in the market portfolio, M. This means that they would choose a point on the line to the left of M such as C. On the other hand, less risk-averse investors will borrow in excess of their current wealth in order to increase their holdings in portfolio M. In this case, they would choose a point to the right of M, e.g., L. At point M, investors put all their wealth into the market portfolio and neither borrow nor lend at the risk-free interest rate.

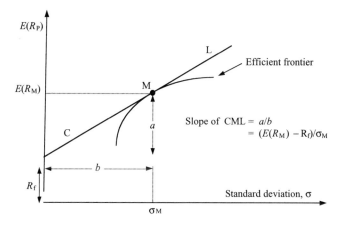

Figure 4.9 The capital market line and market portfolio.

EXAMPLE 4.7 *Using CAPM to calculate beta and expected return values*

Sharpe's original CAPM model is usually written as

$$E(R_i) = R_f + \beta_i[E(R_M) - R_f]$$

where: $E(R_i)$ = the expected return on asset i
R_f = the risk-free rate
$E(R_M)$ = the expected return on the market
β_i = beta coefficient (or beta) of asset i

The beta coefficient for asset i is defined as

$$\beta_i = \sigma_{iM}/\sigma_M{}^2$$

where: σ_{iM} = the covariance between asset and market returns R_i and R_M
$\sigma_M{}^2$ = the market variance, i.e., $VAR(R_M)$.

The riskless interest rate, R_f , and the 'market risk premium' defined as $[E(R_M) - R_f]$, are the same for all assets. However, β_i is different for each asset because of the unique covariance term σ_{iM}. It is therefore a measure of the systematic risk of asset i. Beta coefficient, β_i , is usually defined as 'a measure of the responsiveness of a security or portfolio to the market as a whole'. Assets with $\beta_i < 1$ are called defensive while those with $\beta_i > 1$ are aggressive assets. Where $\beta_i = 1$, the asset or security has the same risk as the market portfolio. Data for market and company share returns given in Table 4.4 are used as input to the CAPM model of Figure 4.10. The risk-free interest rate, R_f, is taken as 4% and the expected market return, $E(R_M)$, as 8%.

The security market line (SML)

The security market line (SML) shown in Figure 4.11 has been constructed using details from Example 4.7. The SML is derived by plotting expected return, $E(R_i)$, along the vertical axis and β_i values along the horizontal axis, i.e., replacing the σ-values of Figure 4.9 with β_i. Since the expected return of the market portfolio, $E(R_M)$, represents $\beta = 1$ and the vertical-axis intercept is the risk-free interest rate, R_f, drawing the SML is a straightforward exercise.

BOND VALUATION

Many organisations generate capital by issuing debt securities such as bonds, debentures, gilt-edged securities, US treasury bills, and so on. A bond is defined as a fixed-interest security, which may be issued by a government (a government bond) or a private company (a corporate bond or debenture). Corporate bonds generally offer a higher interest rate than government bonds, reflecting the reality that higher interest rates are associated with greater risks. In other words, a company is seen as more risky than a government. The life-time (or maturity) of a bond can vary from one to thirty years.

	A	B	C	D	E	F	G	H
1	**Example 4.7 - Calculating beta values and expected returns using CAPM**							
2								
3			Month	Market	Historical share returns, R_i			
4				returns, R_M	**A**	**B**	**C**	
5	*User input*		**1**	7.17%	5.92%	13.07%	2.98%	
6	*cells are*		**2**	5.71%	3.69%	3.55%	8.36%	
7	*shaded*		**3**	−8.04%	−2.64%	−15.19%	−10.25%	
8			**4**	14.42%	9.92%	7.86%	20.79%	
9			**5**	12.76%	11.34%	11.81%	22.50%	
10			**6**	3.67%	5.73%	7.18%	34.46%	
11			**7**	14.18%	9.59%	27.04%	−7.56%	
12			**8**	11.67%	12.39%	6.22%	38.91%	
13			**9**	−9.28%	−6.46%	−15.91%	−11.50%	
14			**10**	1.89%	2.71%	−1.85%	−4.72%	
15			**11**	6.93%	4.70%	13.82%	20.79%	
16			**12**	12.28%	10.64%	36.58%	12.31%	
17								
18			Market variance $= \sigma_M^2 =$		0.00646			
19			Covariance $(R_i, R_M) = \sigma_{iM} =$		0.00408	0.00913	0.00690	
20								
21			CAPM β_i values $= \sigma_{iM}/\sigma_M^2 =$		0.6319	1.4145	1.0687	
22								
23			Risk-free interest rate, $R_f =$		4.0%			
24			Expected market return, $E(R_M) =$		8.0%			
25								
26		Using the CAPM equation, $E(R_i) = R_f + \beta_i*[E(R_m) - R_f]$						
27			Share		**A**	**B**	**C**	
28			Expected return, $E(R_i)$		6.53%	9.66%	8.27%	
29								
30								
31		*Cell*	*Formula*				*Copied to*	
32		E18	VAR(D5:D16)					
33		E19	COVAR($D5:$D16,E5:E16)				F19:G19	
34		E21	E19/$E18				F21:G21	
35		E28	$F23 + E21*($F24 − $F23)				F28:G28	
36								

Figure 4.10   The capital asset pricing model (CAPM).

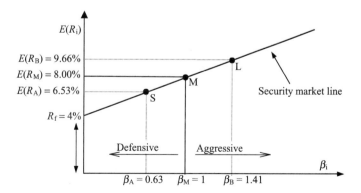

Figure 4.11   The security market line.

Each bondholder receives a printed certificate displaying the bond's face value (par value or maturity value). A bond certificate represents the issuer's promise to pay the holder fixed amounts periodically, e.g., half-yearly, and to repay the principal at maturity. In bond terminology, these regular interest payments are known as 'coupons' and the interest rate as coupon rate. The bond's maturity (or redemption) date is the date on which the last payment is made and the principal returned. A pure discount bond – also called a zero-coupon bond – makes a one-off payment on maturity, i.e., there are no interim coupon payments during the bond's life.

Bonds are not as risk-free as they might appear. There are two main sources of risk associated with bonds, namely (i) interest rate risk and (ii) default risk. Fluctuating interest rates directly affect a bond's value, with rising interest rates causing bond prices to fall (and vice versa). Default risk refers to the uncertainty about a bond issuer's ability to pay contracted amounts to certificate holders. The larger the uncertainty about default, the higher the interest offered by the issuer.

Bond valuation, which is the process of determining a bond's price, involves the two basic concepts of (i) time value of money (see 'Net Present Value' section, Chapter 3) and (ii) the risk-return trade-off represented by the efficient frontier. Bonds are priced according to the size and timing of the cash flows promised by the issuer and the interest rates available in the market.

Bond Prices and Yields

A bond's value or price is the present value of its future cash flows. These flows are discounted back to the present at a discount rate that reflects the bond's riskiness. The discount rate, r, is usually referred to as the 'yield' or 'required rate of return'. These future cash flows consist of (i) a series of periodic coupon payments made over the bond's life and (ii) a lump sum, i.e., the principal, which is paid at maturity. A bond's price is given by the following formula in which the first term represents the series of coupon payments and the second term the principal at maturity:

$$P = \sum_{t=1}^{n} \frac{C_t}{(1+r)^t} + \frac{M}{(1+r)^n}$$

where: P = price of bond
M = bond's face value (principal)
C_t = periodic coupon payment
r = required rate of return
n = total number of periods to maturity

The annual coupon (or interest) payment, C_a, on a bond is found by multiplying its face value by the coupon rate, i.e., $C_a = M \times r$. For bonds which make 'm' coupon payments per year, the size of each coupon payment is equal to C_a/m. The price of a zero-coupon bond is easily found because there are no interim coupon payments. The first term in the equation for a bond's price is now superfluous and the formula reduces to $P = M/(1 + r)^n$. For example, the price of a zero-coupon bond with a face value of £500, a coupon rate of 8%, and a maturity of 4 years is $500/(1.08)^4 = £367.51$. There are two main types of yields, namely (i) current yield and (ii) yield-to-maturity:

- **Current yield**   The current yield, y_c, is defined as the bond's annual coupon payment divided by its current price, i.e., $y_c = C_a/P$. Because the current yield ignores compound interest, it is usually regarded as a rough measure of return earned over the next year. The current yield is also called interest yield or running yield.

- **Yield-to-maturity**   The yield-to-maturity, r, is the rate of return that an investor will receive if the bond is held to maturity. The yield-to-maturity is also known as the redemption yield or simply 'yield'. Because this equation cannot be solved directly, an iterative process must be used to find a solution. Fortunately, Excel has a YIELD function which considerably simplifies the calculation of yield-to-maturity.

EXAMPLE 4.8   *Calculating a bond's price, yield, and duration*

A government bond has a maturity of four years, a coupon rate of 7.5%, and a face value of £1000. If interest is paid half-yearly, what is the value of this bond to an investor requiring a rate of return of 9%? In this case, $M = £1000$, $r = 9\%$, $n = 8$, $m = 2$, and coupon payment, $C_t = M \times r/m = £1000 \times 0.075/2 = £37.50$. In Figure 4.12, the first summation term in the equation for a bond's price is given in cell D24 and the second term in cell D25. The bond's price has been calculated as £950.53 (see cell D27). This answer is obtained more easily using Excel's PV or PRICE functions. A bond's duration, derived using Excel's DURATION function (cell F30), is discussed later.

It should be noted that PRICE gives the bond price per £100 face value. Since the face value of the bond is £1000, the answer in cell H27 must be multiplied by 10 (see the factor F7/F8 (=10) in front of the PRICE formula on line 42). The same factoring applies to the YIELD function, which expects the bond price to be given as 'per £100 face value'. Since the bond's face value in Figure 4.12 is £1000, the price parameter must be divided by 10 (see the factor F8/F7 (=1/10) in the YIELD formula on line 44). Both PRICE and YIELD functions require 'settlement' and 'maturity' dates instead of a specified number of years to maturity. The settlement date is the date on which a person purchases the bond while the maturity date is the date on which the bond expires.

EXAMPLE 4.9   *Calculating a bond's yield for unevenly spaced coupon periods*

All of the above calculations for bond prices have been made on the assumption that the settlement and issue dates are the same, i.e., a bond is purchased on the first day of its issue. In many cases, bonds are purchased months after the issue date. For example, suppose a 10-year bond is issued on 1st January 2005, and is purchased by a buyer six months later. The issue date would be 1st January 2005, the settlement (i.e., purchase) date would be 1st July 2005, and the maturity date would be 1st January 2015, which is 10 years after the issue date.

	A	B	C	D	E	F	G	H	I
1		Example 4.8 - Calculating a bond's price, yield-to-maturity and duration							
2									
3		**BOND PRICE**		Required rate of return, r =		9.0%		*User input*	
4				Coupon rate =		7.5%		*cells are*	
5				Maturity (years) =		4		*shaded*	
6			No. of coupon payments per year, m =			2			
7			Face value (principal), M =			£1,000			
8			Redemption per £100 of face value =			£100			
9			Periodic coupon payment, C =			£37.50			
10									
11									
12			**Using 'Bond Price' equation**				**Using Excel's PV and PRICE functions**		
13							The basic equation for a bond's price, P,		
14				Periodic coupon			is used to derive the bond's present		
15				payments, C_t, t = 1 to 8			value (see cells D15 to D26). The same		
16			No. of	1	£35.89		result can be obtained more easily by		
17			payments, t =	2	£34.34		using either of Excel's PV or PRICE		
18			(maturity x	3	£32.86		functions (see cells H23 and H26)		
19			frequency)	4	£31.45				
20			= 4 x 2	5	£30.09		Settlement Date =	25-Sep-04	
21				6	£28.80		Maturity Date =	25-Sep-08	
22				7	£27.56				
23				8	£26.37		Using PV function		
24			Total coupon payments =		£247.35		Bond price, P =	£950.53	
25			Principal at maturity =		£703.19				
26							Using PRICE function		
27			Bond price, P =		£950.53		Bond price, P =	£950.53	
28									
29		**YIELD &**							
30		**DURATION**		Duration, D =		3.51			
31				Yield-to-maturity, r =		9.00%	= Required rate of return,		
32							(as given in cell F3)		
33									
34		*Cell*		*Formula*				*Copied to*	
35		F9		F7*F4/F6					
36		D16		F$9/(1 + F$3/F$6)^C16				D17:D23	
37		D24		SUM(D16:D23)					
38		D25		F7/(1 + F3/F6)^(F5*F6)					
39		D27		D24 + D25					
40		H21		H20 + 365*F5 + F5/4					
41		H24		–PV(F3/F6, F5*F6, F9, F7, 0)					
42		H27		F7/F8*PRICE(H20, H21, F4, F3, F8, F6, 2)					
43		F30		DURATION(H20,H21,F4,F3,F6,2)					
44		F31		YIELD(H20, H21, F4, F8/F7*H27, F8, F6, 2)					
45									

Figure 4.12   Calculating a bond's price, yield-to-maturity and duration.

Figure 4.13 shows how the yield-to-maturity, r, can be calculated for uneven periods using Excel's XIRR function. XIRR returns the internal rate of return (yield) for a schedule of unevenly spaced coupon payments. In this case, the bond's current price is £1200, its face value is £1000, and the periodic coupon of £100 is paid on 1st January every year. Because the buyer has purchased the bond on 12th October 2004, there are only 81 days left until the next

	A	B	C	D	E	F	G	H	I
1	Example 4.9 - Calculating a bond's yield for uneven payment periods								
2									
3			Current bond price =		£1,200		*User input cells are shaded*		
4			Face value (principal), M =		£1,000				
5				Coupon =	£100		**Date**	**Payment**	
6			Current date (dd/mm/yy) =		12-Oct-04		12-Oct-04	–£1,200	
7			Next coupon date (dd/mm/yy) =		1-Jan-05		1-Jan-05	£100	
8							1-Jan-06	£100	
9							1-Jan-07	£100	
10							1-Jan-08	£100	
11			Time to first payment (days) =		81		1-Jan-09	£100	
12			Maturity date (dd/mm/yy) =		1-Jan-10		1-Jan-10	£1,100	
13									
14							Yield-to-maturity, r =	7.10%	
15									
16									
17		*Cell*	*Formula*	*Copied to*			*Cell*	*Formula*	*Copied to*
18		G6	E6				E11	E7 – E6	
19		H6	–E3				G11	G10 + 366	
20		G7	E7				G12	G11 + 365	
21		H7	E$5	H8:H11			H12	E4 + E5	
22		G8	G7 +365	G9:G10			H14	XIRR(H6:H12,G6:G12)	
23									

Figure 4.13   Calculating a bond's yield for uneven payment periods.

coupon payment on 1st January 2005. The bond's final payment includes the bond's principal as well as a coupon payment (£1000 + £100) and will be made on its maturity date, 1st January 2010. The model in Figure 4.13 has derived a yield-to-maturity value of 7.10% (see cell H14).

DURATION AND BOND VOLATILITY

Duration is a measure (in years) of a bond's price volatility with respect to changes in the bond's yield, r. Each year of duration represents the chance for a 1% gain or loss of principal for every 1% change in interest rates, i.e., it measures the interest rate risk of a bond. Duration assumes that the percentage change in bond price is proportional to the percentage change in one plus the interest rate. The formula for duration, D – as defined by F. Macaulay in 1938 – can be expressed as follows:

$$D = -\frac{\text{Percentage change in bond price}}{\text{Percentage change in } (1+r)} = -\frac{dP/P}{d(1+r)/(1+r)}$$

An expression for the derivative $dP/d(1+r)$ can be found by using the formula for bond price, P, given above. If it is assumed that the last coupon payment, C_n, also includes the principal on

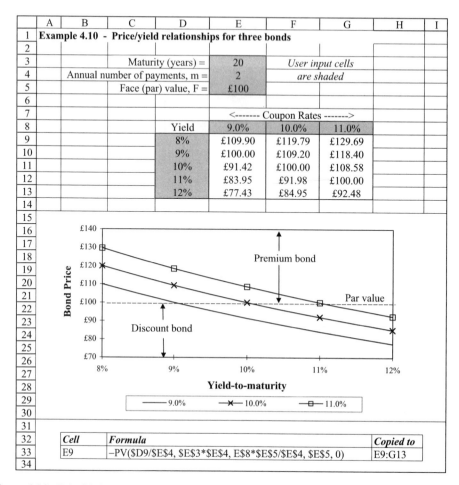

	A	B	C	D	E	F	G	H	I
1	**Example 4.10 - Price/yield relationships for three bonds**								
2									
3				Maturity (years) =	20	*User input cells*			
4			Annual number of payments, m =		2	*are shaded*			
5				Face (par) value, F =	£100				
6									
7					<------- Coupon Rates ------->				
8				Yield	9.0%	10.0%	11.0%		
9				8%	£109.90	£119.79	£129.69		
10				9%	£100.00	£109.20	£118.40		
11				10%	£91.42	£100.00	£108.58		
12				11%	£83.95	£91.98	£100.00		
13				12%	£77.43	£84.95	£92.48		
14									
15–31									
32	Cell	Formula						Copied to	
33	E9	–PV($D9/$E$4, $E$3*$E$4, E$8*$E$5/$E$4, $E$5, 0)						E9:G13	
34									

Figure 4.14   Price/yield relationships for three bonds.

maturity, then the second term in the expression for P can be included in the first term to give

$$P = \sum_{t=1}^{n} \frac{C_t}{(1+r)^t}$$

Differentiating,

$$\frac{dP}{d(1+r)} = -\sum_{t=1}^{n} \frac{tC_t}{(1+r)^{t+1}}$$

Substituting in the formula for duration,

$$D = -\frac{dP/P}{d(1+r)/(1+r)} = \left| \frac{dP}{d(1+r)} \cdot \frac{(1+r)}{P} \right| = \frac{1}{P} \sum_{t=1}^{n} \frac{tC_t}{(1+r)^t}$$

EXAMPLE 4.10 *Bond price behaviour: price and yield changes*

There is an inverse relationship between bond prices and yields, i.e., as a bond's yield increases, its price decreases, and vice versa. Yield changes are often expressed in terms of basis points. A 'basis point' is defined as one hundredth of a percent, e.g. a yield change from 10% to 10.5% is a change of 50 basis points. This price/yield relationship can be illustrated by considering three 20-year bonds offering coupon rates of 9%, 10%, and 11%.

The graph in Figure 4.14 shows how bond prices fall as the yield increases for each of the three bonds. When the yield, r, is greater (or less) than the coupon rate, the bond's value will be less (or greater) than its par or face value. When the coupon rate equals r, the bond is said to be 'selling at par'. The bond's par value of £100 – represented by the dashed line – cuts each curve at r-values of 9%, 10%, and 11% respectively. When a bond's price is above par (i.e., above the dashed line), it is called a premium bond, and when the price is below par, it is a discount bond.

EXAMPLE 4.11 *Bond price behaviour: duration and volatility*

An important relationship exists between a bond's duration and its price volatility. Bond volatility, V, can be defined as the absolute value of the percentage change in bond price associated with a specified change in the yield, r. This definition can be written as follows:

$$V = \left| \frac{dP/P}{dr} \right|$$

where $dP/P = \Delta P/P =$ percentage change in bond price, P, and $dr = \Delta r =$ the change in yield, r, where Δ means 'a change in'. The equation for a bond's duration, D, as derived above, can be rewritten as

$$\frac{dP}{P} = D \frac{d(1+r)}{1+r}$$

For small changes in yield, r, $\Delta(1+r)$ can be approximated by Δr, i.e., $d(1+r)$ can be replaced by dr in the above equation. The two equations for volatility and duration can now be combined to give

$$V \approx \frac{D}{1+r}$$

The above approximation for volatility, V, assumes that bonds make annual coupon payments, i.e., frequency $m = 1$. Where payments are semi-annual ($m = 2$) or quarterly ($m = 4$), then the yield, r, in the volatility formula should be divided by 'm'. The equation for V, which is often called the 'modified Macaulay duration', has been used to derive the Volatility Table shown in Figure 4.15 (lines 21 – 24). The same results could also have been obtained by using Excel's MDURATION function, as shown on lines 29–30. Figure 4.15 illustrates the following properties of duration:

- Duration, which is measured in years, can generally be equated to maturity, i.e.,, the longer the maturity (cells B11:B14), the greater the duration (e.g., cells D11:D14).

	A	B	C	D	E	F	G	H	I
1		**Example 4.11**	**- Bond duration and volatility**						
2									
3				Yield, r =	10.00%		*User input cells*		
4			No. of payments per year, *m* =		1		*are shaded*		
5									
6									
7			**DURATION TABLE (Years)**			Settlement date =	22/10/2004		
8									
9		Maturity	Maturity	<----------------------		Coupon Rates	---------------------->		
10		(Years)	Date	4.0%	6.0%	8.0%	10.0%	12.0%	
11		5	22/10/2009	4.57	4.41	4.28	4.17	4.07	
12		10	22/10/2014	7.95	7.42	7.04	6.76	6.54	
13		15	22/10/2019	10.12	9.28	8.74	8.37	8.09	
14		20	22/10/2024	11.30	10.32	9.75	9.36	9.09	
15									
16									
17			**VOLATILITY TABLE (% price change)**						
18									
19			Maturity	<----------------------		Coupon Rates	---------------------->		
20			(Years)	4.0%	6.0%	8.0%	10.0%	12.0%	
21			5	4.15	4.01	3.89	3.79	3.70	
22			10	7.22	6.75	6.40	6.14	5.94	
23			15	9.20	8.44	7.95	7.61	7.36	
24			20	10.28	9.39	8.86	8.51	8.27	
25									
26			The first two lines of the Volatility Table (lines 21-22) have been recalculated						
27			below using Excel's MDURATION function for the **modified Macaulay duration**						
28									
29				4.15	4.01	3.89	3.79	3.70	
30				7.22	6.75	6.40	6.14	5.94	
31									
32									
33		*Cell*	*Formula*					*Copied to*	
34		C11	G$7 + B11*365 + B11/4					C12:C14	
35		D11	DURATION($G$7, $C11, D$10, $E$3, $E$4, 4)					D11:H14	
36		D21	D11/(1 + $E$3/$E$4)					D21:H24	
37		D29	MDURATION($G$7, $C11, D$10, $E$3, $E$4, 4)					D29:H30	
38									

Figure 4.15   Bond duration and volatility.

- An increase in the coupon (interest) rate will reduce duration, i.e., the greater the interest rate, the larger will be the size of the coupon payments. By receiving larger initial cash flows, the time required to receive all payments is reduced, thereby lowering duration, e.g., cells D11:H11.

- Duration is proportional to bond volatility, i.e.,, duration (e.g., D11:D14) increases as volatility (D21:D24) increases. This property can be used to assess the sensitivity of a bond's price to yield changes and is therefore a useful tool for comparing bonds.

- The duration of a zero-coupon (pure discount) bond is equal to the bond's maturity (lifetime).

THE BLACK–SCHOLES OPTION PRICING MODEL

Derivative instruments are securities whose returns are derived – hence the name 'derivative' – from those of underlying securities. The primary aim of derivatives, which include options and futures, is to minimise financial risk while maximising expected return. An option on a security is a contractual agreement between two parties that gives one party the right (but not the obligation) to buy or sell an underlying asset from the other party at a price agreed at a future date or within a specified period of time. An option to buy is known as a 'call' while an option to sell an asset is called a 'put'.

The term 'to exercise' refers to the process by which an option is used to purchase (or sell) the underlying security. Whether or not a holder exercises an option depends on the price of the specified stock at the option's expiration. If the stock value is above the original agreed price, then the holder will exercise the call, otherwise the call will not be exercised. Because the right to exercise an option is contingent on how the underlying assets perform, options are often called contingent claims. Options are traded in organised markets similar to the stock market.

In 1973, Fischer Black and Myron Scholes published a paper, in which they presented a formula for the valuation of options. This formula – known as the Black–Scholes (B–S) option pricing model – had a major influence on modern finance and lead to the development of many other derivative instruments and hedging strategies. The basic premise of the B–S pricing model is that an option can be priced by forming a riskless portfolio consisting of shares and call options. The value of the call option is then equal to the expected value of the investments in the riskless portfolio minus the cost of this investment (Diacogiannis, Chapter 19).

The Black–Scholes pricing model requires five inputs as shown in Figure 4.16, namely the current stock price (S), the exercise price (E), the riskless (risk-free) interest rate (r), the time remaining before the option's expiration date (T), and the standard deviation (σ) of the underlying stock price, usually known as its volatility. The B–S option pricing model is based on the following five assumptions:

1. The capital market is perfect, i.e., (i) there are no transaction or tax costs (ii) assets are infinitely divisible, i.e., there is no restriction on the size of the amount to be invested (iii) the same information is freely available to every investor (iv) no single investor can influence the market by buying or selling actions.

2. A risk-free interest rate exists and is constant over the lifetime of the option; investors can borrow or lend any amount at this fixed risk-free interest rate.

3. The underlying security does not pay dividends.

4. The underlying security's rate of return follows a normal distribution, and it has a constant and known variance over the lifetime of the option.

5. The option is European. The difference between European and American options is that a European option can only be exercised at maturity, i.e., on the expiration date, whereas an American option can be exercised on any day during its life.

	A	B	C	D	E	F	G	H
1		**Example 4.12 - The Black-Scholes option pricing model**						
2								
3		Current stock price, S =		£40.00	*User input cells*			
4		Exercise price, E =		£40.00	*are shaded*			
5		Risk-free interest rate, r =		7.00%				
6		Time to expiration (in years), T =		0.40				
7		Stock volatility, σ =		30.0%				
8								
9		d_1 =	0.2424		d_2 =	0.0527		
10		$N(d_1)$ =	0.5958		$N(d_2)$ =	0.5210		
11		$N(-d_1)$ =	0.4042		$N(-d_2)$ =	0.4790		
12								
13		**Call price =**	£3.57		**Put price =**	£2.46		
14								
15								
16		*Cell*	*Formula*				*Copied to*	
17		C9	(LN(D3/D4) + (D5 + D7*D7/2)*D6)/(D7*SQRT(D6))					
18		D9	C9 – D7*SQRT(D6)					
19		C10	NORMSDIST(C9)				F10	
20		C11	NORMSDIST(–C9)				F11	
21		C13	D3*C10 – D4*EXP(–D5*D6)*F10					
22		F13	–D3*C11 + D4*EXP(–D5*D6)*F11					
23								

Figure 4.16   The Black–Scholes option pricing model.

EXAMPLE 4.12   *Using the Black–Scholes model for pricing options*

The Black–Scholes option pricing model for a call option is given by the following formula:

$$C = SN(d_1) - Ee^{-rT}N(d_2)$$

where

$$d_1 = \frac{\ln(S/E) + (r + \sigma^2/2)T}{\sigma\sqrt{T}}$$

$$d_2 = d_1 - \sigma\sqrt{T}$$

and C = the price of a call option
S = the current market price of the underlying stock
$N(d_i)$ = the value of the cumulative normal distribution evaluated at d_i ($i = 1,2$)
E = the exercise price of the option
e = the base value in natural logarithms, i.e., 2.7183
r = the risk-free interest rate
T = the time remaining before the expiry date expressed as a fraction of a year
$\ln$ = the natural logarithm operator (i.e., $\log_e$)
σ = the standard deviation of the continuously compounded annual rate of return, i.e., the stock's volatility

Table 4.6   Sensitivity analysis using the Black–Scholes model.

Stock volatility	Call price	Put price	Stock price	Call price	Put price
20%	2.59	1.49	£30	0.25	9.15
25%	3.08	1.97	£35	1.26	5.16
30%	3.57	2.46	£40	3.57	2.46
35%	4.06	2.95	£45	7.11	1.01
40%	4.55	3.44	£50	11.47	0.36

The B–S model can also be used to calculate the price of a put option. The formula for the value of a put option, P, is :

$$P = -SN(-d_1) + Xe^{-rT}N(-d_2)$$

The Black–Scholes model in Figure 4.16 can be used to carry out sensitivity analysis by varying each of the five inputs (see cells D3:D7). Table 4.6 contains option prices that were obtained by varying two of the inputs, namely stock volatility and price. It is clear that (i) as stock volatility increases, both call and put prices also increase, and (ii) as the stock price increases, the call price increases while the put price falls. The user should check what happens to option prices when the other three inputs are changed.

EXAMPLE 4.13   *Estimating the implied volatility of a stock*

Volatility is a key feature in options markets – the greater the volatility of the underlying stock, the greater the potential to increase profits. While volatility also implies that stock prices can fall as well as rise, any loss to the call-holder is restricted to the exercise price. In fact, the holder does not care how low the value of the stock falls below the exercise price. Because high stock volatility is more attractive to buyers, estimating a stock's volatility (i.e., its standard deviation, σ) is important.

There are two methods for estimating stock volatility: historical volatility and implied volatility. Historical volatility is defined as the standard deviation of a security that is obtained by estimation from historical data taken over a recent period of time. Implied volatility is found by calculating the standard deviation that – when used in the Black–Scholes model – makes the model's calculated price equal to today's actual price. Thus, the implied volatility is the volatility of the stock as implied by today's market price of the option.

In Figure 4.17, which is a modified version of the Black–Scholes model, Excel's Solver tool is used to find the implied volatility. Since there is no objective to either maximise or minimise, the volatility model does not have a target cell. For a call price of £3.08, volatility has been calculated correctly as 25.03% (cell D8) – see the Stock Volatility section in Table 4.6.

	A	B	C	D	E	F	G	H
1	**Example 4.13 - Estimating implied volatility using the Black-Scholes model**							
2								
3		Current stock price, S =		£40.00	*User input cells*			
4		Exercise price, X =		£40.00	*are shaded*			
5		Risk-free interest rate, r =		7.00%				
6	Time to expiration (in years), T =			0.40				
7								
8		Stock's implied volatility, σ =		25.03%	Enter any value into cell D8			
9								
10				Actual	Estimated			
11		Call option's price =		3.08	3.08			
12								
13		d_1 =	0.2560		d_2 =	0.0977		
14		$N(d_1)$ =	0.6010		$N(d_2)$ =	0.5389		
15								
16								
17		*Solver Parameters*						
18		*Set Target Cell:*	Leave Blank					
19		*Equal to:*	Value of					
20		*By Changing Cells:*	D8					
21		*Subject to Constraints:*	D11 = E11	= Actual call price = Estimated call price				
22			D8 >=0	= Answer must be positive				
23								
24		*Cell*	*Formula*				*Copied to*	
25		E11	D3*C14 – D4*EXP(–D6*D5)*F14					
26		C13	(LN(D3/D4) + (D5 + D8*D8/2)*D6)/(D8*SQRT(D6))					
27		F13	C13 – D8*SQRT(D6)					
28		C14	NORMSDIST(C13)				F14	
29								

Figure 4.17   Estimating implied volatility.

EXCEL FUNCTIONS USED IN MODEL-BUILDING

The models developed in this chapter introduce ten Excel functions for the first time, each of which is explained below. If any of the functions is not available, and returns the #NAME? error, then install and load the Analysis ToolPak add-in.

1. DURATION: DURATION (settlement, maturity, coupon, yield, frequency, basis)

returns a security's annual duration. Duration is defined as the time-weighted average of the present value of the cash flows. Duration is used as a measure of the sensitivity of a security's price to changes in the yield to maturity.

settlement = the security's date of purchase, expressed as a serial date number.
maturity   = the security's date of maturity, expressed as a serial date number.
coupon   = the security's annual coupon rate.
yield   = the security's annual yield to maturity.
frequency = the number of coupon payments per year, i.e., for annual payments, frequency = 1; for semi-annual payments, frequency = 2; and for quarterly payments, frequency = 4.

basis = the type of day count basis to use. If basis = 0 or omitted, US (NASD) 30/360; basis = 1, Actual/actual; basis = 2, Actual/360; basis = 3, Actual/365; basis = 4, European/360.

Example: A five-year bond, which was purchased today, has a coupon rate of 8% and a yield of 9%. Find the bond's duration, given that payments are semi-annual. If cells B3 and B4 contain the settlement and maturity dates, then the answer is DURATION(B3, B4, 8%, 9%, 2, 4) = 4.198878 where cells B3, B4 contain the formulae TODAY() and B3 + 365*5 + 5/4 respectively.

2. INTERCEPT: INTERCEPT (y-values, x-values)

calculates the point at which a line will intersect the y-axis by using known x-values and y-values. The intercept point is based on a best-fit regression line plotted through the known x-values and y-values.

y-values = an array of known y-values.
x-values = an array of known x-values.

Example: Cell ranges (X1:X5) contain (5, 8, 10, 4, 2) and (Y1:Y5) contains (9, 3, 7, 6, 4). The formula INTERCEPT(Y1:Y5, X1:X5) returns an intercept value of 5.401961.

3. MDURATION: MDURATION (settlement, maturity, coupon, yield, frequency, basis)

returns the modified Macaulay duration of a security. The modified Macaulay duration is defined as

$$\text{MDuration} = \frac{\text{Duration}}{1 + (\text{yield/frequency})}$$

settlement = the security's date of purchase, expressed as a serial date number.
maturity = the security's date of maturity, expressed as a serial date number.
coupon = the security's annual coupon rate.
yield = the security's annual yield to maturity.
frequency = the number of coupon payments per year, i.e., for annual payments, frequency = 1; for semi-annual payments, frequency = 2; and for quarterly payments, frequency = 4.
basis = the type of day count basis to use. If basis = 0 or omitted, US (NASD) 30/360; basis = 1, Actual/actual; basis = 2, Actual/360; basis = 3, Actual/365; basis = 4, European/360.

Example: An eight-year bond has a coupon rate of 8% and a yield of 9%. Find the bond's modified Macaulay duration, given that payments are semi-annual. If cells B3 and B4 contain the settlement and maturity dates, then the answer is MDURATION(B3, B4, 8%, 9%, 2, 4) = 5.73567 where cells B3, B4 contain the formulae TODAY() and B3 + 365*8 + 8/4 respectively.

4. NORMSDIST: NORMSDIST(Z)

returns the standard normal cumulative distribution function. The function computes the area or probability less than a given Z value and is used in place of a table of areas under the standard normal curve

Z = the value for which the distribution is required

Example: Sales of an item are known to be normally distributed with a mean of 12 and a standard deviation of 5. What is the probability of selling 14 or more items? $P(X \geq 14)$ = 1 − NORMSDIST([14 - 12]/5) = 1 − 0.6554 = 0.3446 = 34.46%.

5. PRICE: PRICE (settlement, maturity, coupon, yield, redemption, frequency, basis)

returns the price per £100 face value of a security that pays periodic interest.

settlement = the security's date of purchase, expressed as a serial date number.
maturity   = the security's date of maturity, expressed as a serial date number.
coupon   = the security's annual coupon rate.
yield   = the security's annual yield to maturity.
redemption = the security's redemption value per £100 face value.
frequency = the number of coupon payments per year, i.e., for annual payments, frequency = 1; for semi-annual payments, frequency = 2; and for quarterly payments, frequency = 4.
basis   = the type of day count basis to use. If basis = 0 or omitted, US (NASD) 30/360; basis = 1, Actual/actual; basis = 2, Actual/360; basis = 3, Actual/365; basis = 4, European/360.

Example: A bond, which has a face value of £100, has eight years remaining to maturity. The annual coupon rate is 8% and the investor's annual required rate of return on the bond is 10%. Assuming that interest is paid at the end of each year, what is the bond's present value? If cells B3 and B4 contain the settlement and maturity dates, then the answer is PRICE(B3, B4, 8%, 10%, 100, 1, 4) = 89.33015 = £89.33 where cells B3, B4 contain the formulae TODAY() and B3 + 365*8 + 8/4 respectively.

6. SLOPE: SLOPE (y-values, x-values)

returns the slope of the linear regression line through data points in known y-values and x-values. The slope is the vertical distance divided by the horizontal distance between any two points on the line, which is the rate of change along the regression line.

y-values = an array of known y-values.
x-values = an array of known x-values.

Example: Cell ranges (X1:X5) contain (5,8,10,4,2) and (Y1:Y5) contains (9,3,7,6,4). The formula SLOPE(Y1:Y5, X1:X5) returns the slope of the regression line as 0.068627.

7. STDEV: STDEV (array)

estimates the standard deviation based on a sample.

array = cell range containing the sample values

Example: STDEV(C4:C7) returns the value 14.91 where cells C4, C5, C6, and C7 contain the values 10, 25, 8, and 40 respectively.

8. STEYX: STEYX (*y*-values, *x*-values)

returns the standard error of the predicted *y*-value for each *x* in the regression. The standard error is also known as the standard deviation of the estimation errors (i.e., residuals) in linear regression analysis.

y-values = an array of known *y*-values.
x-values = an array of known *x*-values.

Example: Cell ranges (X1:X5) contain (5, 8, 10, 4, 2) and (Y1:Y5) contains (9, 3, 7, 6, 4). The formula STEYX(Y1:Y5, X1:X5) returns a standard error of 2.745168.

9. YIELD: YIELD (settlement, maturity, coupon, price, redemption, frequency, basis)

returns the price per £100 face value of a security that pays periodic interest.

settlement = the security's date of purchase, expressed as a serial date number.
maturity = the security's date of maturity, expressed as a serial date number.
coupon = the security's annual coupon rate.
price = the security's price per £100 face value.
redemption = the security's redemption value per £100 face value.
frequency = the number of coupon payments per year, i.e., for annual payments, frequency = 1; for semi-annual payments, frequency = 2; and for quarterly payments, frequency = 4.
basis = the type of day count basis to use. If basis = 0 or omitted, US (NASD) 30/360; basis = 1, Actual/actual; basis = 2, Actual/360; basis = 3, Actual/365; basis = 4, European/360.

Example: A six-year bond has a coupon rate of 7% and a redemption value of £100. If the bond's price is £95.30 and coupon payments are semi-annual, what is the bond's yield to maturity? The answer is YIELD(B3, B4, 7%, 95.30, 100, 2, 4) = 0.080016 = 8% where cells B3, B4 contain the settlement and redemption dates, given by the formulae TODAY() and B3 + 365*6 + 6/4 respectively.

10. XIRR: XIRR (values, dates, guess)

returns the internal rate of return (yield-to-maturity) for a schedule of cash flows that is not necessarily periodic.

values = a series of cash flows that correspond to a schedule of payment dates. The first payment is optional. It corresponds to a cost or payment that occurs at the beginning of the investment and must be entered as a negative value. All succeeding payments are discounted and based on a 365-day year. The series of values must contain at least one positive and one negative value.

dates = a series of payment dates that corresponds to cash flow payments. All
dates should be entered into cells which are formatted as dates.

guess = a number that you guess is close to the result of XIRR. If omitted, guess
is assumed to be 0.1 (10 percent).

Example: Cell range (A1:A5) contains values (−500, 100, 120, 200, 200) and cells
(B1:B5) contain dates (1-Jan-06, 1-Mar-06, 15-Feb-07, 30-Oct-07, 1-Jan-08). XIRR(A1:A5,
B1:B5) returns a internal rate of return (yield) of 16.05%. Note that 'guess' has been omitted.

EXERCISES

4.1   Joe Bloggs, who is risk-averse, is a contestant on the 'Open the Box' quiz show. The worst
and best outcomes on the show are £1,000 and £9,000. What is the lower bound for Joe's utility U
value of £4000? It is known that Joe is indifferent between an offer of £4000 from the quiz-master
and the show offering probabilities of 0.3 and 0.7 for the worst and best outcomes respectively.
What is the lower bound of Joe's utility value for an offer of £5000 from the quiz-master?
(Hint: utility U values for risk-averse are greater than those for risk-indifferent)

(Answer: $U(4000) \geq 0.375$; $U(5000) \geq 0.76$)

4.2   Fred Flint recently inherited £20,000 from a wealthy relative. His stockbroker has advised
him to invest in three particular stocks. Because of the volatility of the market, Fred requests the
stockbroker to provide him with historical data for these stocks over the past four years, as shown
in Table 4.7.

Table 4.7

Year	Stock A	Stock B	Stock C
1	20.2%	10.9%	15.3%
2	2.4%	18.7%	6.8%
3	15.9%	9.8%	18.5%
4	4.6%	12.1%	5.7%

Fred decides to build a simple security analysis model using three of Excel's functions – SUMPROD-
UCT, AVERAGE, and STDEV. He wants to perform 'what-if' analysis to see what happens when
different amounts are invested in each stock. Being risk-averse, Fred knows that a lower standard
deviation (σ-value), means a less risky stock. He thus wants the highest expected return that can
be achieved without increasing the portfolio's riskiness. Set up Fred's 'what-if' model and then use
it to find an acceptable solution.

(Answer: Investing 10%, 70% and 20% in stocks A, B, and C respectively gives Fred an expected
return of 12.41% with a σ-value of 1.9%. Other combinations may give higher returns but also higher
σ-values)

4.3   Fred Flint has been talking to his neighbour Barney Briggs about investment options. Barney
explains that he has several investment analysis models, which Fred is welcome to borrow. Fred
decides to install Barney's portfolio analysis model (see Example 3.5) and use his own historical data
given in Table 4.7. He wants to find out if Barney's model produces an answer close to the solution

derived by his simple 'what-if' model. Use the model of Exercise 3.5 to verify (or otherwise) that the answer to Exercise 4.2 is acceptable.

(Answer: Barney's model confirms that Fred's 'what-if' model has found an optimal solution.)

4.4 Having successfully implemented Barney Briggs's portfolio analysis model, Fred Flint is now feeling more adventurous. He asks Barney if it is possible to find a range of portfolios based on the two objectives of (i) maximising expected returns and (ii) minimising risk. Barney tells Fred that his 'efficient frontier' model will provide the required information. Modify the SIM model of Figure 4.8 in order to utilise Fred's stock returns (see Table 4.7) as input. Next, use the results derived from this Markowitz model as input data to Figure 4.6. Since Fred would like a return of around 12% on his investment, run the model seven times in order to create the graph of the efficient frontier.

(Answer: Expected returns of 12.1%, 12.3% and 12.5% produce σ-values of 2.22, 2.24 and 2.44 respectively.)

4.5 Merlene Olonga, who is studying financial modelling, has been given an assignment by her tutor. She is required to calculate the covariance matrix using the single index model (SIM) and then check the accuracy of the SIM covariance matrix against the Markowitz matrix. Merlene's input (see Table 4.8) contains returns for four companies over the past eight years, as well as the market returns for the same period.

Table 4.8

Year	Company 1	Company 2	Company 3	Company 4	Market
1	7.6%	14.4%	20.3%	19.7%	17.2%
2	−3.4%	8.7%	33.6%	8.8%	9.1%
3	23.7%	28.1%	5.9%	−3.1%	10.8%
4	11.3%	15.7%	4.6%	16.2%	9.5%
5	−7.8%	8.5%	9.4%	21.5%	8.9%
6	10.5%	1.7%	−3.2%	29.7%	5.7%
7	25.9%	13.8%	28.5%	−4.3%	13.3%
8	20.1%	9.2%	15.9%	12.6%	11.8%

(Answer:

Covariance matrix (using SIM)

0.01710	0.00116	0.00232	−0.00149
0.00116	0.00678	0.00206	−0.00132
0.00232	0.00206	0.01778	−0.00264
−0.00149	−0.00132	−0.00264	0.01607

Covariance matrix (using Markowitz)

0.01484	0.00397	−0.00101	−0.00744
0.00397	0.00596	−0.00003	−0.00560
−0.00101	−0.00003	0.01582	−0.00646
−0.00744	−0.00560	−0.00646	0.01402

4.6 Merlene Olonga's next assignment requires her to modify the capital asset pricing model (CAPM) in order to find beta and expected return values for each of the four companies, using the data in Table 4.8 as input. The risk-free rate, R_f, is to be taken as 3.3% and the market risk premium, $(E(R_M) - R_f)$, as 6.3%.

(Answer: CAPM beta values and expected returns for companies 1–4 are (i) 0.9232, 0.8185, 1.6337, −1.0527 (ii) 9.12%, 8.46%, 13.59%, −3.33%.)

4.7 Bert Namagong has decided to invest £5,000 in some bonds, each having a face value of £1000. Since he would like a required return of 10%, Bert wants to find what is the maximum amount that he should pay for each of the four bonds shown in Table 4.9. He will use Excel's function, PRICE, and the simple formula for the price of a zero-coupon bond, to help in his bond valuation.

Table 4.9

Bond	Maturity	Coupon rate	Interest payments
A	2 years	8.2%	Semi-annual
B	5 years	8.5%	Semi-annual
C	10 years	9.2%	Annual
D	5 years	10.2%	Zero coupon

(Answer: The prices of the bonds A, B, C, and D are £968.09, £942.09, £950.84, and £615.31 respectively.)

4.8   Using the formulae for bond duration and the price of a zero-coupon bond, B_z, show that the duration of bond, B_z, is equal to its maturity.

4.9   Bert Namagong has been told recently that a bond's duration can be used as a measure of its volatility to changes in yield. The larger its duration, the more volatile is the bond. Bert would like to find the most volatile bond in Table 4.9. He will first use Excel's DURATION function and the information given in Exercise 4.8 to find each bond's duration. He will then use the volatility-duration equation, $V = D/(1 + r)$, to find bond volatility.

(Answer: The durations of bonds A, B, C, and D are 1.88, 4.15, 6.86, and 5.0 respectively – showing that bond C is the most volatile. The bonds' volatilities (1.71, 3.77, 6.24, and 4.55) confirm this fact.)

4.10   Fiona Brown, who regularly invests in the options market, knows that a higher stock price usually leads to a higher call price and a lower put price. She would like to see how an increase in the exercise price, E, of a stock will effect call and put options. Fiona has already built a worksheet of the Black–Scholes option pricing model (see Figure 4.16) containing data of her favourite stock. She will use this model to perform some sensitivity analysis, varying the current exercise price of £40 from £30 to £50. Next day, Fiona sees that the option's call price has risen from its original value of £3.57 to £3.88. She now wishes to find the stock's implied volatility.

(Answer: For exercise prices of (30, 35, 40, 45, 50) call prices are (10.96, 6.73, 3.57, 1.63, 0.66) and put prices are (0.13, 0.77, 2.46, 5.39, 9.28). Fiona is pleased to see that the stock's implied volatility has risen from 30% to 33.2% as greater volatility means a greater potential to increase profits.)

REFERENCES AND FURTHER READING

Benninga, S. (2000) *Financial Modeling* (2nd edn), The MIT Press, Massachusetts.

Diacogiannis, G. (1994) *Financial Management: A Modelling Approach Using Spreadsheets*, McGraw-Hill, UK.

Elton, E., Gruber, M., *et al.* (2002) *Modern Portfolio Theory and Investment Analysis* (6th edn), John Wiley & Sons Inc., New York.

Jackson, M., and Staunton, M. (2001) *Advanced Modelling in Finance using Excel and VBA*, John Wiley & Sons, Ltd, UK.

5

Worksheet applications in cost accounting

OVERVIEW

Cost accounting is defined as 'that part of management accounting which establishes budgets and standard costs and actual costs of operations, processes, departments or products and the analysis of variances, profitability or social use of funds'. The primary purpose of cost accounting is to provide information that managers can use to plan and control manufacturing operations, make decisions, and evaluate performance. In a cost accounting system, the cost of each product is accumulated as it flows through the production process, and is referred to as 'product costing'. Product costs consist of three basic elements, (i) raw materials costs (ii) labour costs, and (iii) manufacturing overhead costs such as equipment depreciation, heating, light, power, etc. The first two cost types are usually referred to as direct costs while manufacturing overheads are called indirect costs.

A typical costing system starts with the recording of product costs (i.e., materials acquisition, labour and overheads). It moves to the next stage of costing the resources that are used in the production process, as well as the work-in-progress (also called work-in-process) inventory. Work-in-progress inventory are goods that are in the intermediate stages of production. The third stage assigns a value to the finished goods inventory and finally, the income from product sales is recorded.

One important control function of cost accounting is budgeting. Budgeting is the practical outcome of business planning and is used to ensure that expenditure does not exceed income. While the budget provides projected data, the cost accounting system produces actual data. A key aspect of budgetary control is variance analysis. Variances from set targets are found by comparing actual costs with budgeted or standard costs. For example, a negative or unfavourable variance occurs if actual production uses materials that are more costly than planned. On the other hand, if actual labour hours used in the manufacture of a product are less than budgeted figures, then a positive or favourable variance results.

COST-VOLUME-PROFIT ANALYSIS

Cost-volume-profit (CVP) analysis – also called break-even analysis – is a method of examining the relationships between revenue and costs based on the equation

$$\text{profit} = \text{sales} - \text{variable costs} - \text{fixed costs}$$

Volume is usually measured by either the number of units sold (unit sales) or the amount of revenue generated by sales (sales value). As volume increases so also do costs and revenues. Costs can be divided into two categories; fixed and variable. Fixed costs remain constant regardless of the size of sales volume – they include heating, lighting, salaries, depreciation, building insurance, and interest on loans. Variable costs are those that vary directly and proportionately with volume – typical variable costs are direct labour and raw materials.

CVP analysis is closely associated with 'contribution analysis' which emphasises the distinction between variable and fixed costs. The contribution margin is defined as the sales revenue less the variable costs, while unit contribution is the margin contributed by each unit sold. Both CVP and contribution analyses are decision-making techniques which provide management with valuable information on how costs can be reduced and profits increased. For example, companies often manufacture several products, and an analysis of each product's contribution to total sales or profits would be beneficial. A sales mix analysis is simply the ratio of each product's contribution to total company sales revenue. Consider the following example.

EXAMPLE 5.1   *Cost-volume-profit model*

The Gizmo Company produces three versions of its popular product – large, medium, and small. Total fixed costs for the coming year are budgeted at £50,000. Table 5.1 contains details of sales estimates and variable costs involved in the manufacture of the three products. Gizmo would like to perform an analysis on each product's contribution to overall company sales in order to determine which products should be marketed more actively.

Finding the Break-Even Points

The Gizmo Company would also like to perform some break-even analysis. The break-even point is defined as the output level where total costs are exactly equal to total revenues received, i.e., there is neither a profit nor a loss. Break-even analysis identifies the level of sales that are required to cover total costs. It also shows the level of sales needed to reach a desired level of profitability.

Table 5.1

| Model version | Estimated sales | Unit price | ←Variable costs per unit → | |
			Parts/materials	Labour
Large	5,000	£27.50	£12	£8
Medium	6,000	£22.00	£8	£7
Small	10,000	£15.50	£5	£5

There are two main formulae that are used to calculate the break-even point in terms of the number of units sold (BEP_u) and in terms of sales revenue ($BEP_£$).

$$BEP_u = \text{Total fixed costs}/(p - v) \qquad \text{where } p = \text{unit selling price},$$
$$BEP_£ = \text{Total fixed costs}/(1 - v/p) \qquad v = \text{unit variable costs}$$

The formulae required to build the CVP model for the Gizmo Company are given at the bottom of Figure 5.1.

	A	B	C	D	E	F	G	H
1		**Example 5.1 - A cost-volume-profit model for the Gizmo Company**						
2								
3		*Model version*		Large	Medium	Small		
4		Sales		5,000	6,000	10,000	*User input cells*	
5		Unit price		£27.50	£22.00	£15.50	*are shaded*	
6		Parts/Materials		£12.00	£8.00	£5.00		
7		Labour		£8.00	£7.00	£5.00		
8		Unit variable cost =		£20.00	£15.00	£10.00		
9							*Totals*	
10		Sales (£s)		£137,500	£132,000	£155,000	£424,500	
11		Contribution margin		£37,500	£42,000	£55,000	£134,500	
12		As % of sales		27%	32%	35%		
13						*Less Fixed Costs =*	£50,000	
14						*Profit =*	*£84,500*	
15								
16		*Sales mix =*		32.4%	31.1%	36.5%		
17								
18		*Calculating the breakeven points*						
19			*$BEP_u =$*	6667	7143	9091		
20			*$BEP_£ =$*	£183,333	£157,143	£140,909		
21								
22								
23		*Cell*	*Formula*			*Copied to*		
24		D8	D6 + D7			E8:F8		
25		D10	D4*D5			E10:F10		
26		G10	SUM(D10:F10)			G11		
27		D11	D4*(D5 – D6 – D7)			E11:F11		
28		D12	D11/D10			E12:F12		
29		G14	G11 – G13					
30		D16	D10/$G10			E16:F16		
31		D19	$G13/(D5 – D8)			E19:F19		
32		D20	$G13/(1 – D8/D5)			E20:F20		
33								

Figure 5.1 Cost-volume-profit (CVP) model for the Gizmo Company.

DEPRECIATION

Fixed assets such as vehicles or computers usually last for a number of years before they are replaced. It would therefore be unfair to charge their whole acquisition cost in any one month or year. This problem is overcome by charging a proportion of the cost, called depreciation, in the profit-and-loss account of each year of the asset's expected life. Depreciation can be defined as an accounting procedure for reducing the book value of an asset by charging it off as an expense over time. Depreciation is a reduction in the value of a fixed asset due to its use. This may be caused by wear and tear as in the case of a vehicle or it may be due to obsolescence as in the case of computers.

In order to determine the amount of depreciation for an accounting period, four items of information must be available for each depreciable asset.

1. The asset's useful (or expected) life, i.e., over how many accounting periods will the asset be useful to the business?

2. The asset's original cost, i.e., how much did the business initially pay to acquire the asset?

3. The asset's residual (scrap or salvage) value, i.e., how much will the asset be worth at the end of its useful life?

4. The depreciation method used to calculate an asset's depreciation over its useful life.

Excel provides five functions for calculating depreciation on equipment. All are time-based, and in order to use the functions correctly, values must be available for the equipment's initial cost, useful life, and scrap value.

1. *The straight-line method using Excel's SLN function.* This method is based on the (rather unrealistic) assumption that the reduction in value is the same for each year. For example, suppose a van is bought for £20,000 with an estimated life of eight years and a residual value of £4000. The function SLN(20000,4000,8) returns a constant depreciation amount of £2000 for each year.

2. *The declining (reducing) balance method using the DB function.* This method adopts a more practical approach by ensuring that each year's depreciation value is less than the previous year's figure. The assumption is that equipment operates more efficiently when it is new. It therefore follows that the equipment's contribution to the creation of revenue will decline as it gets older and less useful. Using the above example, depreciation in year 1 is DB(20000,4000,8,1) = £3640; depreciation in year 2 = DB(20000,4000,8,2) = £2978; year 3 = £2436, etc.

3. *The sum-of-the-years' digits method (SYD).* This method produces a depreciation pattern that is very similar to the declining-balance (DB) method. Thus, depreciation in year 1 is SYD(20000,4000,8,1) = £3556; year 2 = £3111; year 3 = £2813.

4. *The double-declining balance method using the DDB function.* The DDB approach gives an even faster depreciation in the first few years of the life of the equipment than either of the previous two methods. It doubles the rate that equipment would depreciate under the straight-line method. Depreciation in year 1 is DDB(20000,4000,8,1) = £5000; year 2 = £3750; year 3 = £2813.

5. *The variable-declining balance (VDB) method* is the most flexible (and the most complex) of Excel's depreciation functions. VDB returns the depreciation on equipment for any specified period, including partial periods, using the double-declining method or some other method specified by the user. The VDB function includes a logical switch, which if set to FALSE, causes VDB to use straight-line depreciation when straight-line depreciation is greater than the declining balance value. For example, VDB(20000, 4000, 8, 0, 3, 2, TRUE) returns £11,563, which is the accumulated depreciation figure for years 1 to 3 using the DDB method.

Some firms use one type of depreciation for financial reporting (e.g., straight-line) and another such as declining balance (DB) for tax purposes. The choice of which depreciation approach to use depends upon the tax laws, which allow different methods to be applied to different types of asset. A comparison between Excel's different depreciation methods is shown in Figure 5.2.

	A	B	C	D	E	F	G	H
1		**Comparing Excel's depreciation functions**						
2								
3			Purchase price of van =	£20,000		SLN = straight-line method		
4			Salvage value =	£4,000		DB = declining balance method		
5			Estimated life (years) =	8		SYD = sum-of-the years' digits		
6						DDB = double-declining balance		
7		*User input cells are shaded*				VDB = variable-declining balance		
8								
9		*YEAR*	<-------------- *Depreciation Methods* -------------->					
10		0	*SLN*	*DB*	*SYD*	*DDB*	*VDB*	
11		1	£2,000	£3,640	£3,556	£5,000	£2,500	
12		2	£2,000	£2,978	£3,111	£3,750	£2,188	
13		3	£2,000	£2,436	£2,667	£2,813	£1,914	
14		4	£2,000	£1,992	£2,222	£2,109	£1,675	
15		5	£2,000	£1,630	£1,778	£1,582	£1,465	
16		6	£2,000	£1,333	£1,333	£746	£1,282	
17		7	£2,000	£1,090	£889	£0	£1,122	
18		8	£2,000	£892	£444	£0	£982	
19								
20								
21								
22		*Cell*	*Formula*				*Copied to*	
23		C11	SLN(D$3,D$4,D$5)				C12:C18	
24		D11	DB(D$3,D$4,D$5,B11)				D12:D18	
25		E11	SYD(D$3,D$4,D$5,B11)				E12:E18	
26		F11	DDB(D$3,D$4,D$5,B11)				F12:F18	
27		G11	VDB(D$3,D$4,D$5,B10,B11,1,TRUE)				G12:G18	
28								
29								

Figure 5.2 Comparison of different depreciation methods.

EQUIPMENT REPLACEMENT

The topic of equipment replacement is a very common business problem that can be placed into several categories. In operations management, it is associated with maintenance and product reliability involving quality control and statistical probability distributions. In a business environment, replacement analysis is usually seen as a fixed asset problem involving depreciation and the time value of money. When complex leasing arrangements are introduced, linear programming techniques are the best option for finding an optimal solution to equipment replacement. In this situation, replacement becomes a shortest route problem with the objective being to find the least-cost path through a network of cost nodes.

In many situations such as a hospital or factory, it makes sense to replace equipment and machines on a regular basis before they become unreliable and breakdowns occur. Just when to replace items is an exercise in cost-effectiveness. Some equipment may be technologically obsolete but still functioning effectively. However, effectiveness has to be weighed up against the machine's efficiency, which will not be as good as a new machine. The main purpose of replacement analysis is to determine the optimal time-interval at which equipment should be replaced in order to minimise costs. There are two main approaches to replacement analysis.

- *Deteriorating items.* Many businesses utilise items of equipment, e.g., components, vehicles, or machine tools that wear out over a period of several years. Such items are usually expensive but can be kept functioning with increasing amounts of maintenance. In the first year or two, depreciation of a 'deteriorating item' is usually high while maintenance costs are low. Towards the end of its useful life, the situation changes around, with the item's depreciation rate being low while repair bills start rising! Here, an accounting approach to replacement analysis involving depreciation is more appropriate.

- *Sudden failure items.* In this situation, components which have been functioning correctly, suddenly fail, e.g., light bulbs or fan belts. Such items are usually inexpensive but the consequences of their failure can be considerable. Decisions in these circumstances will depend upon considerations of probability, and statistical replacement methods are then used.

EXAMPLE 5.2   *Replacement analysis model using depreciation*

MeadowSweet Creameries have recently acquired a new van at a cost of £25,000. The dealer has provided Table 5.2 showing estimated annual maintenance costs and resale value of the van over the next eight years. Taking the cost of capital as 9%, find the best time at which MeadowSweet should replace the van.

The 'replacement analysis' model of Figure 5.3 has found that the minimum annual cost of £6,850 occurs in the fifth year and so Meadowsweet should replace their van every five

Table 5.2

Year	1	2	3	4	5	6	7	8
Maintenance (£)	800	1000	1200	2000	3500	4500	6500	8000
Resale value (£)	20,000	15,000	12,000	9000	7000	5000	4000	3000

	A	B	C	D	E	F	G	H	I	J
1		**Example 5.2 - Replacement analysis model using depreciation**								
2										
3			Capital cost of equipment, CC =			£25,000	MC = Maintenance cost			
4			Annual interest rate, IR =			9%	RV = Resale value			
5							PV = Excel's *present value* function			
6			*User input cells are shaded*				PMT = Excel's *periodic payment* function			
7										
8				*Resale*						
9		*Year*	*MC*	*Value*	*PV$_{MC}$*	*CUM*	*PV$_{RV}$*	*NPV*	*PMT*	
10		0				£25,000				
11		1	£800	£20,000	£734	£25,734	£18,349	£7,385	£8,050	
12		2	£1,000	£15,000	£842	£26,576	£12,625	£13,950	£7,930	
13		3	£1,200	£12,000	£927	£27,502	£9,266	£18,236	£7,204	
14		4	£2,000	£9,000	£1,417	£28,919	£6,376	£22,543	£6,958	
15		5	£3,500	£7,000	£2,275	£31,194	£4,550	£26,644	£6,850	
16		6	£4,500	£5,000	£2,683	£33,877	£2,981	£30,896	£6,887	
17		7	£6,500	£4,000	£3,556	£37,433	£2,188	£35,245	£7,003	
18		8	£8,000	£3,000	£4,015	£41,448	£1,506	£39,942	£7,217	
19										
20		*Replace item in year =*			5		*Minimum annual cost =*		*£6,850*	
21										
22										
23			*Cell*	*Formula*					*Copied to*	
24			E11	PV(F$4,B11,, −C11)					E12:E18	
25			F10	F3						
26			F11	F10 + E11					F12:F18	
27			G11	PV(F$4,B11,,−D11)					G12:G18	
28			H11	F11−G11					H12:H18	
29			I11	PMT(F$4,B11, −H11)					I12:I18	
30			E20	MATCH(I20,I11:I18,0)						
31			I20	MIN(I11:I18)						
32										

Figure 5.3   Replacement analysis model using depreciation.

years. Column E and F relate to maintenance costs with cells E10:E18 containing the present values of maintenance costs (PV$_{MC}$) over the eight-year period. Column F cumulates outgoings (CUM) for both van purchase price (£25,000) and the annual maintenance costs of column E. The present values of the van's resale figures (PV$_{RV}$) are stored in cell range G10:G18 while column H gives the net present value (NPV), i.e., PV outflows (CUM) minus PV inflows (PV$_{RV}$).

EXAMPLE 5.3   *A leasing approach to equipment replacement*

The shortest route (or least-cost) approach to equipment replacement is usually associated with leasing costs. The decision-maker must choose between leasing (i) newer equipment at higher rental cost but lower maintenance costs, or (ii) more used equipment with lower rental costs but higher maintenance costs. The main objective of the shortest-route method is to determine

Table 5.3

Year	$j = 2$	$j = 3$	$j = 4$	$j = 5$
$i = 1$	£9,000	£15,000	£20,000	£24,000
$i = 2$		£9,500	£16,500	£21,500
$i = 3$			£10,000	£16,000
$i = 4$				£11,000

the least-cost path through a network of costs, i.e., which of the various leasing policies is the least costly.

A network consists of points (called nodes) and lines (called arcs) which join up pairs of nodes. A typical everyday example of a network is a road map in which the roads represent the arcs and the towns are the nodes. When distances are replaced by costs, then the problem of finding the least-cost path is the same as finding the shortest route between two towns. For more details on the shortest-route method, see the section 'Other network flow applications' in Chapter 10.

Merlene Olonga has been given the job of updating her company's microcomputer system. She has a four-year time horizon to consider. She will trade in her company's current system at the start of year one, and then lease the latest technology from the suppliers Microtec. Since computer technology can quickly become obsolescent, Merlene would like to know what policy to choose in order to keep her company's system up-to-date, while minimising total costs. Total costs include both leasing and maintenance costs. For new equipment, maintenance is free for the first year, £2000 per year for the next two years, and £4000 per year thereafter.

The first step is to define C_{ij} as the cost of leasing new equipment in year i ($i = 1, 2, 3, 4$) and keeping it to the beginning of year j ($j = i + 1, \ldots 5$). Thus C_{12} and C_{15} represent leasing costs for one and four years respectively. Microtec have provided Merlene with the table of leasing costs shown in Table 5.3.

Merlene Olonga has several options open to her.

- Lease equipment in year 1 and keep it for the four years, i.e., the only leasing cost, C_{15}, incurred is the initial outlay of £24,000. Maintenance costs for the four years are £0, £2000, £2000, £4000, giving a total cost of £32,000. This is a policy of low leasing costs and high maintenance costs.

- Lease new micros at the beginning of each year. This is a policy of high leasing costs and low maintenance costs. The total leasing cost of this policy would be $C_{12} + C_{23} + C_{34} + C_{45}$, i.e., £39,500. Since maintenance costs are zero, the total cost is still £39,500.

- Adopt an intermediate policy. For example, lease new equipment at the beginning of years 1 and 3, i.e., total leasing cost is $C_{13} + C_{35} = £15,000 + £16,000 = £31,000$. When the maintenance costs of £4000 are added, the total policy cost is then £35,000.

The ten C_{ij} options available to Merlene are shown in Table 5.4 with their values given in £'000s.

The equipment-leasing model of Figure 5.4 shows that Merlene Olonga's problem is really a linear programming exercise with the objective of minimising costs. The answer is given by the non-zero values in cells L5:L14, i.e., arc$_4$. The model has found that option C_{15}, i.e., low leasing/high maintenance, is the cheapest policy – even though maintenance costs of £8000

Table 5.4

	C_{12}	C_{13}	C_{14}	C_{15}	C_{23}	C_{24}	C_{25}	C_{34}	C_{35}	C_{45}
Leasing costs	9.0	15.0	20.0	24.0	9.5	16.5	21.5	10.0	16.0	11.0
Maintenance costs	–	2.0	4.0	8.0	–	2.0	4.0	–	2.0	–
Total costs	9.0	17.0	24.0	32.0	9.5	18.5	25.5	10.0	18.0	11.0

	A	B	C	D	E	F	G	H	I	J	K	L	M	N
1		**Example 5.3 - An equipment-leasing model**												
2														
3		*<- Nodes ->*		*Cost*		*<--------------- Nodes ----------------->*								
4		From	To	*arcs*		*1*	*2*	*3*	*4*	*5*				
5		1	2	£9,000		−1	1	0	0	0		**0**	$=arc_1$	
6		1	3	£17,000		−1	0	1	0	0		**0**	$=arc_2$	
7		1	4	£24,000		−1	0	0	1	0		**0**	$=arc_3$	
8		1	5	£32,000		−1	0	0	0	1		**1**	$=arc_4$	
9		2	3	£9,500		0	−1	1	0	0		**0**	$=arc_5$	
10		2	4	£18,500		0	−1	0	1	0		**0**	$=arc_6$	
11		2	5	£25,500		0	−1	0	0	1		**0**	$=arc_7$	
12		3	4	£10,000		0	0	−1	1	0		**0**	$=arc_8$	
13		3	5	£18,000		0	0	−1	0	1		**0**	$=arc_9$	
14		4	5	£11,000		0	0	0	−1	1		**0**	$=arc_{10}$	
15														
16				**£32,000**		= *Objective: Minimise total costs*								
17												Start node = −1		
18		*User input cells*				−1	0	0	0	1		End node = 1		
19		*are shaded*				−1	0	0	0	1		All other nodes = 0		
20														
21														
22			*Solver Parameters*											
23			*Set Target Cell:*	D16										
24			*Equal to:*	Min										
25			*By Changing Cells:*	L5:L14										
26			*Subject to Constraints*	F18:J18 = F19:J19			= Define Start, End & other nodes							
27				L5:L14 >= 0			= Answers must be positive							
28														
29		*Cell*		*Formula*								*Copied to*		
30		F5		IF($B5=F$4,−1,IF($C5=F$4,1,0))								F5:J14		
31		D16		SUMPRODUCT(D5:D14,$L$5:$L$14)										
32		F18		SUMPRODUCT(F5:F14,$L$5:$L$14)								G18:J18		
33														
34		**Note:** Switch on the 'Assume Linear Model' parameter in the Solver Options dialog box												

Figure 5.4 Equipment-leasing model.

represent 25% of the total cost. The same equipment is retained for the four-year time horizon, and this may not be acceptable to Merlene who wants to keep her company's system up-to-date. For example, the intermediate policy of changing equipment after two years, i.e., $C_{13} + C_{35}$, gives a total cost of £35,000 which is only slightly dearer than the C_{15} cost of £32,000. Note that Figure 5.4 contains all the necessary formulae, including Excel's Solver parameters, required to build the model.

STATISTICAL REPLACEMENT ANALYSIS

In the accounting/leasing approaches to equipment replacement, the decline in a machine's performance is gradual and there is usually a predictable pattern of deterioration. On the other hand, in statistical replacement analysis, the equipment's deterioration is rapid and unexpected, and in many cases, may cause serious problems. For example, the sudden failure of an electronic component in an airline, could have catastrophic results. For this reason, companies often perform preventative (preventive) maintenance, i.e., routine inspections are carried out and items are replaced before they fail. This is in contrast to breakdown maintenance which occurs when equipment fails, and only then do repairs/replacement of failed components become a priority.

The success of any product depends to a large degree on its reliability and the manufacturer's warranty, guaranteeing the product's capabilities. It is therefore important to model the product's lifetime behaviour in order to find out when it is mostly likely to fail. Statistical information on a product's life history is usually collected during pre-release tests and a chart of lifetime failure rates is then produced.

The next step is to select a least-cost replacement policy based on the 'mean time between failure' probability distribution. This is usually based on the consequences of a breakdown. The failure of a few light bulbs is neither expensive nor critical, and it may be more economical to carry out preventative maintenance and replace all the light bulbs at once. On the other hand, the breakdown of a vital piece of equipment such as a bank's mainframe computer requires immediate attention. To help minimise downtime, history-profile records showing the cost, type and timing of the computer's maintenance requirements, should be available.

EXAMPLE 5.4   *Statistical approach to equipment replacement*

The Gizmo Company operates fifty machines which incorporate a special component that is liable to sudden failure. Records of 200 components have been kept, showing how long they were operating before failure:

Length of life (months)	1	2	3	4
No. of components	30	50	60	60
Probability of failure, P_t	0.15	0.25	0.3	0.3

It is assumed that component lives are an exact number of months, i.e., they fail at the end of each month. It costs Gizmo £20 to replace an individual component or £200 to replace all the components at the same time. Gizmo would like to find a replacement policy that will guarantee a near 100% operation of their machines at minimum cost.

Let $L =$ the maximum length of life of a component (i.e., $L = 4$ months in Gizmo's case)
$n =$ the total number of components under consideration, i.e., the no. of machines ($n = 50$)
$P_t =$ the probability of failure at the end of the time-period, i.e., month

The number of failures, F_m in any month m is then given by the following two equations (Wilkes, Chapter 8):

$$\text{for } m \leq L, \; F_m = nP_m + \sum_{t=1}^{m-1} P_t F_{m-t} \quad \text{for } m > L, \; F_m = \sum_{t=1}^{L} P_t F_{m-t}$$

Note that a component failure is the same as a component replacement and that the maximum number of component failures equals the number of available machines. From the model shown in Figure 5.5 it can be seen that the expected number of failures over the 15-month period (cells I15:I29) converges towards the average number of failures, F_{av}, where

$$F_{av} = n/\sum_{t=1}^{L} tP_t = 50/(1^*0.15 + 2^*0.25 + 3^*0.3 + 4^*0.3) = 18.18$$

In some situations, the convergence pattern may take longer to become apparent because of its oscillatory nature. The formulae required to build the 'expected failures' model are given at the bottom of Figure 5.5.

Cost Replacement Table: Extending the 'Expected Failures' Model

The two main replacement policies available to the Gizmo Company are:

- Replace components only when they fail. The cost of this option is $F_{av} \times$ (component cost), where F_{av} is the average monthly failure rate. From Figure 5.5, it can be seen that $F_{av} = 18.18$, so the total monthly cost is $18.18 \times £20 = £363.60$.

- Replace components when they fail but also replace all components at fixed periods whether they have failed or not. This second option involves finding the optimal time interval (i.e., the number of months) which will minimise costs.

The Gizmo Company can now use the data contained in the 'expected failures' model to build a table of equipment replacement costs (see Figure 5.6) for different months using the extended template given at the bottom of the diagram. Since it is impossible to replace a fraction of a component, values such as 7.5 or 13.63 are meaningless and must be rounded up to the nearest integer (see cells D44:D49).

The cost replacement table of Figure 5.6 shows that the optimal replacement interval is two months with an average monthly cost of £320. It is uneconomical to replace all components in month 1 because the number of failures is small compared to an average of around 18 failures. Eight components need replacing in the first month at a total cost of £160. The probability failure distribution (see cells G7:J7) confirms this answer by indicating a first-month failure probability of 0.15 which is low compared with the other months.

Generally, the failure distribution can be used to give an accurate indication of the optimal replacement interval. For example, consider a component which has a life of six periods and a

	A	B	C	D	E	F	G	H	I	J	K	L	M
1	**Example 5.4 - An 'expected failures' model for the Gizmo Company**												
2													
3				Number of machines, n =			50		*User input cells are shaded*				
4													
5				Length of life (months) =			1	2	3	4	Total		
6				No. of components =			30	50	60	60	200		
7				Probability of failure =			0.15	0.25	0.3	0.3			
8													
9				Average life of a component (months) =					2.75				
10				Average no. of failures per month, F_{av} =					18.18				
11													
12			**Probability matrix, P_t**						**Failure matrix, F_m**				
13			1	2	3	4			1	2	3	4	
14		1	0.15						50.00				
15		2	0.15	0.25				F_1 =	7.50	50.00			
16		3	0.15	0.25	0.30			F_2 =	13.63	7.50	50.00		
17		4	0.15	0.25	0.30	0.30		F_3 =	18.92	13.63	7.50	50.00	
18		5	0.15	0.25	0.30	0.30		F_4 =	23.49	18.92	13.63	7.50	
19		6	0.15	0.25	0.30	0.30		F_5 =	14.59	23.49	18.92	13.63	
20		7	0.15	0.25	0.30	0.30		F_6 =	17.83	14.59	23.49	18.92	
21		8	0.15	0.25	0.30	0.30		F_7 =	19.05	17.83	14.59	23.49	
22		9	0.15	0.25	0.30	0.30		F_8 =	18.74	19.05	17.83	14.59	
23		10	0.15	0.25	0.30	0.30		F_9 =	17.30	18.74	19.05	17.83	
24		11	0.15	0.25	0.30	0.30		F_{10} =	18.34	17.30	18.74	19.05	
25		12	0.15	0.25	0.30	0.30		F_{11} =	18.41	18.34	17.30	18.74	
26		13	0.15	0.25	0.30	0.30		F_{12} =	18.16	18.41	18.34	17.30	
27		14	0.15	0.25	0.30	0.30		F_{13} =	18.02	18.16	18.41	18.34	
28		15	0.15	0.25	0.30	0.30		F_{14} =	18.27	18.02	18.16	18.41	
29		16	0.15	0.25	0.30	0.30		F_{15} =	18.21	18.27	18.02	18.16	
30									F_m has converged to the average F_{av}				
31													
32		F_m is the expected no. of failures (i.e. replacements) in month 'm'											
33													

Cell	Formula	Copied to
K6	SUM(G6:J6)	
G7	G6/$K6	H7:J7
I9	SUMPRODUCT(G5:J5,G7:J7)	
I10	G3/I9	
C14	IF($B14<C$13,"",G$7)	C14:F29
I14	G3	
I15	SUMPRODUCT(C14:F14,I14:L14)	I16:I29
J14	IF(J$13>$B14,"",OFFSET(J14,-1,-1))	J14:L29

Figure 5.5 Statistical 'components failure' model.

	A	B	C	D	E	F	G	H	I	J	K	L	M
34	**Cost Replacement table for the Gizmo Company**												
35													
36			Cost of replacing one component, C_i =					£20		*User input cells*			
37			Group replacement costs, C_g =					£200		*are shaded*			
38													
39			Cheapest monthly average =					£320					
40			Best policy is to replace every					2	months				
41													
42				Integer	Cost		<- Individual and group costs for each month ->						
43			Month	F_i	of F_i		1	2	3	4	5	6	
44			1	*8*	£160		160	160	160	160	160	160	
45			2	*14*	£280			280	280	280	280	280	
46			3	*19*	£380				380	380	380	380	
47			4	*24*	£480					480	480	480	
48			5	*15*	£300						300	300	
49			6	*18*	£360							360	
50				Group cost			200	200	200	200	200	200	
51				Total cost			£360	£640	£1,020	£1,500	£1,800	£2,160	
52				Average monthly cost			£360	£320	£340	£375	£360	£360	
53													
65													
66			Template for Cost Replacement Table										
67			*Cell*	*Formula*						*Copied to*			
68			H39	MIN(G52:L52)									
69			H40	MATCH(H39,G52:L52,0)									
70			D44	ROUNDUP(I15,0)						D45:D49			
71			E44	H$36*D44						E45:E49			
72			G44	IF($C44>G$43,"",$E44)						G44:L49			
73			G50	$H37						H50:L50			
74			G51	SUM(G44:G50)						H51:L51			
75			G52	G51/G43						H52:L52			
76													

Figure 5.6 Cost replacement table for the Gizmo Company.

probability failure distribution of 0.05, 0.05, 0.1, 0.2, 0.3, and 0.3 over the six periods. Because the probability of failure in the first three periods is low compared with the remaining three periods, a reasonable assumption is that all components should be replaced every three periods. This assumption should of course be confirmed by creating a new 'expected failures' model.

The optimal replacement policy also depends on costs remaining constant which is not normally the case. The final 'what if' analysis table (Table 5.5) in this section shows how monthly cost-replacement figures alter as the cost of group replacement is increased from £200 to £400. When group cost rises to £300, the cheapest cost is £370 which is now greater than an individual replacement policy cost of £363.60. When group cost becomes £400, the

Table 5.5   'What-if' analysis: increasing group replacement costs from £200 to £400.

Costs	←Cost variations over 6-month period→					
	1	2	3	4	5	6
£200	360	320	340	375	360	360
£300	460	370	373	400	380	377
£400	560	420	407	425	400	393

optimal policy is to replace every six months at an average cost of £393. The figures in this 'what if' table are found simply by changing the value in cell H37. Further sensitivity analysis can be performed on the component's cost by changing cell H36. Other considerations, such as the disruption to operations caused by group replacement, must also be taken into account when arriving at an optimal policy.

SIMULATION MODEL FOR REPLACEMENT/REPAIRS

In the Gizmo Company problem above, it was assumed that the lives of components followed a discrete probability distribution. Discrete distributions assume that the variable (machine life) falls into specific categories, e.g., a machine can fail in one, two, or three months but cannot fail in 0.3, 1.2, or 2.7 months! Clearly, this is not the case. Machine life is measured by time which is a continuous variable and can take on any value within a specified range. A more appropriate way of achieving a continuous probability distribution is to use simulation over a large number of time intervals.

EXAMPLE 5.5   *Simulation approach to equipment replacement/repairs*

The management of Figtree Shopping Centre have collected data on the breakdown of the ten escalators in their busy shopping mall. The probability failure rates in the table relate to 10-week intervals where intervals 1 to 5 represent weeks 1–10, 11–20, 21–30, 31–40, 41–50.

Interval (10-weeks)	1	2	3	4	5
Probability	0.05	0.10	0.20	0.30	0.35

If all escalators are overhauled and repaired at the weekend, the cost is £200 for each escalator. If they fail during the week, the repair cost is £1000 for each escalator. Management would like to know what is the most economical policy to adopt. Should preventative maintenance be carried out, i.e., overhaul all escalators before they break down, and if so, when?

In order to achieve a continuous probability distribution, a mathematical equation must be found that best fits the given escalator data. A cumulative probability is added to the above table and a graph is plotted with the interval values along the x-axis and cumulative probability values along the y-axis.

Interval (10-weeks)	1	2	3	4	5
Cumulative Probability	0.05	0.15	0.35	0.65	1.00
Probability	0.05	0.10	0.20	0.30	0.35

Step 1
The solution to Figtree's escalator problem involves four steps. The first step requires the user to set up the graphical part of the model as shown in Figure 5.7; this initial phase (lines 1–33) does not involve any formulae. Use Excel's Chart Wizard to create the cumulative probability curve, depicted as a solid line. Follow the instructions given in the spreadsheet.

Step 2
Excel's Trendline function is next used to fit a 'power' curve to the data. The Trendline function provides six different trend types namely: linear, logarithmic, polynomial, power, exponential, or moving average. The mathematical equation, $y = 0.0462x^{1.88}$ is found. Since the y-value is the known value and the x-value the unknown, the equation must be rearranged as shown

$$x = (y/0.0462)^{0.532}$$

To obtain a power expression of the form $y = ax^b$, use Excel's regression analysis facility by performing the following steps. Note that all clicks are with the mouse's left-hand button unless otherwise stated.

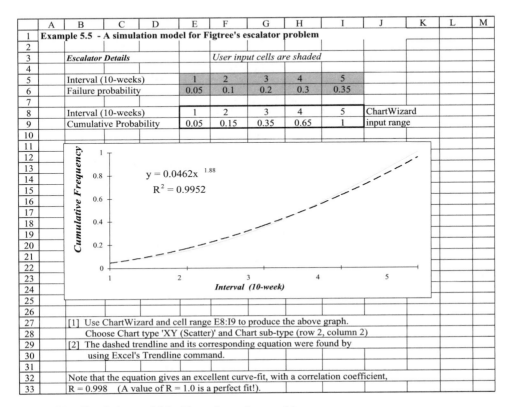

	A	B	C	D	E	F	G	H	I	J	K	L	M
1	Example 5.5 - A simulation model for Figtree's escalator problem												
2													
3		*Escalator Details*				*User input cells are shaded*							
4													
5		Interval (10-weeks)			1	2	3	4	5				
6		Failure probability			0.05	0.1	0.2	0.3	0.35				
7													
8		Interval (10-weeks)			1	2	3	4	5	ChartWizard			
9		Cumulative Probability			0.05	0.15	0.35	0.65	1	input range			
10													
11													
12													
13					$y = 0.0462x^{1.88}$								
14													
15					$R^2 = 0.9952$								
16													
17													
18													
19													
20													
21													
22													
23													
24													
25													
26													
27		[1] Use ChartWizard and cell range E8:I9 to produce the above graph.											
28		Choose Chart type 'XY (Scatter)' and Chart sub-type (row 2, column 2)											
29		[2] The dashed trendline and its corresponding equation were found by											
30		using Excel's Trendline command.											
31													
32		Note that the equation gives an excellent curve-fit, with a correlation coefficient,											
33		R = 0.998 (A value of R = 1.0 is a perfect fit!).											

Figure 5.7 Simulation model for Figtree's escalator problem.

	A	B	C	D	E	F	G	H	I	J	K	L	M
34													
35		Escal.	Rand.	Failure		*Failures Table*		for five 10-week periods					
36		No.	No.	period		1	2	3	4	5			
37		1	0.61	3.9		0	0	0	1	0			
38		2	0.10	1.5		0	1	0	0	0			
39		3	0.22	2.3		0	0	1	0	0			
40		4	0.80	4.6		0	0	0	0	1			
41		5	0.27	2.6		0	0	1	0	0			
42		6	0.91	4.9		0	0	0	0	1			
43		7	0.74	4.4		0	0	0	0	1			
44		8	0.77	4.5		0	0	0	0	1			
45		9	0.57	3.8		0	0	0	1	0			
46		10	0.72	4.3		0	0	0	0	1			
47				Failure Totals =		*0*	*1*	*2*	*2*	*5*			
48													
49		Copy cells (F47:J47) into the simulation blocks below - 10 times											
50													
51	Trial		Results of 10 simulations:-				Trial						
52	1	0	0	5	2	3	6	0	4	0	4	2	
53	2	1	0	2	1	6	7	0	0	1	4	5	
54	3	0	0	5	2	3	8	1	1	1	6	1	
55	4	0	0	3	3	4	9	0	2	2	2	4	
56	5	1	1	1	3	4	10	1	2	3	2	2	
57				Totals for 10 simulations =				4	10	23	29	34	
58				Average period values =				0.4	1	2.3	2.9	3.4	
59				Integer F$_i$ values =				*1*	*1*	*3*	*3*	*4*	
60													
61		►	**Cost replacement table**										
62			Cost of overhauling one escalator, C $_i$ =			£1,000							
63			Group maintenance cost, C $_g$ =			£2,000		*User input cells are shaded*					
64			Cheapest 10-week average =			£2,000							
65			Best policy is to group overhaul every			2		periods, i.e. after 20 weeks					
66													
67			Integer	Cost		Individual & group costs for each 10-week period							
68		Period	F$_i$	of F$_i$		1	2	3	4	5			
69		1	*1*	£1,000		1000	1000	1000	1000	1000			
70		2	*1*	£1,000			1000	1000	1000	1000			
71		3	*3*	£3,000				3000	3000	3000			
72		4	*3*	£3,000					3000	3000			
73		5	*4*	£4,000						4000			
74				Group cost		2,000	2,000	2,000	2,000	2,000			
75				Total cost		£3,000	£4,000	£7,000	£10,000	£14,000			
76			Average 10-week cost			£3,000	£2,000	£2,333	£2,500	£2,800			
77													

Figure 5.7   (cont.)

- Place the mouse-pointer anywhere on the curve and then click the mouse's right-hand button to activate the shortcut menu.
- Choose the 'Add Trendline ...' option from the menu.
- Click the 'Type' tab and then click on the 'Power' option.
- Click the 'Options' tab and select (i) Display equation on chart (ii) Display $\underline{R}$-squared value.
- Finally, click the OK button to return to the scattergraph.

The trendline equation represents a continuous cumulative probability graph which allows for escalator breakdowns at any point in time. Excel's RAND() function generates random numbers in the range 0.0–0.99 which are used to represent the relative frequency range. Random numbers correspond to randomly chosen breakdown points. For example, the first escalator may be assigned the random number 0.58, which is the y value in the equation $x = (y/0.0462)^{0.532}$. The corresponding x value – the escalator's life or breakdown point – is calculated as 3.8, i.e., the escalator fails in 3.8×10 weeks = the 38th week.

Step 3
The next step is to set up the simulation section of the model as shown in lines 34 to 58 of Figure 5.7, using the formula template of Table 5.6. Excel's RAND function (in C37:C46) assigns a random number to each of the ten escalators from which its breakdown point is calculated (see cells D37:D46). Each breakdown point is automatically copied into its appropriate period in the 'failures table' (F37:J46). The first simulation distributes the ten escalator breakdowns over the five periods giving totals of 0, 0, 5, 2, 3. These five values must be copied by the user into an appropriate position in the simulation cell block (B52:L56), and the whole process is repeated 10 times; in practice, many more times would be required! The average for each set

Table 5.6   Escalator simulation – worksheet formulae.

Cell	Formula	Copied to
E8	E5	F8:I8
E9	E6	
F9	E9 + F6	G9:I9
C37	RAND()	C38:C46
D37	(C37/0.0462)^ 0.532	D38:D46
F37	IF(ROUNDUP($D37, 0) = F$36, 1, 0)	F37:J46
F47	COUNTIF(F37:46, "> 0")	G47:J47
H57	SUM(B52:B56) + SUM(H52:H56)	I57:L57
H58	H57/10	I58:L58
H59	ROUNDUP(H58, 0)	I59:L59
G64	MIN(F76:J76)	
G65	MATCH(G64, F76:J76, 0)	
C69	H59 (C70 = I59, C71 = J59, C72 = K59, C73 = L59)	
D69	C69*G$62	D70:D73
F69	IF($B69 > F$68, "" , $D69)	F69:J73
F74	$G63	G74:J74
F75	SUM(F69:F74)	G75:J75
F76	F75/F68	G76:J76

of ten simulated failures, F_i is then calculated, giving values of 0.4, 1, 2.3, 2.9, 3.4 (see cells H58:L58) over the five periods. Since fractional breakdowns are meaningless, the averages are rounded up.

Step 4

The logic behind Figtree's cost replacement table (lines 61–76) is similar to the Gizmo Company's table (see Figure 5.6). The individual cost of repairing one escalator is £1000 while the group cost for all escalators is $10 \times £200 = £2000$. The expected number of failures, F_i for each time period i ($i = 1$, 5), are rounded up to the nearest integer to give, $F_1 = 1$, $F_2 = 1$, $F_3 = 3$, $F_4 = 3$, $F_5 = 4$. These F_i values are automatically copied into cells C69:C73 to give the optimal answer:

Group overhaul all escalators after 20 weeks (two 10-week periods) at a total cost of £2000.

COMPARISON BETWEEN SIMULATION AND STATISTICAL RESULTS

A worthwhile exercise is to perform a comparison between results obtained by (i) simulation as above, and (ii) the use of mathematical formulae as in the previous Gizmo example. A modified version of the Gizmo model has been created for Figtree's escalator problem. The simulation F_i values shown in Table 5.7 were obtained from Figure 5.7 (see cells H59:L59), while the statistical results are found in Figure 5.8 (cells D43:D48).

Optimal Maintenance Policy

Simulation: overhaul all escalators after 20 weeks at an average cost of £2000 per period.

Statistical: overhaul all escalators after 20 weeks at an average cost of £2500 per period.

BUDGETING

Budgeting is the practical outcome of business planning. A detailed financial plan which contains quantitative information can be described as a budget. Through planning, budgets are prepared and targets are set that enable the business to work towards its stated goal. Management usually prepares a variety of budgets, each with a differing time span. Sales budgets, production budgets, and cash budgets are short term, covering a period from one month to a year. Other budgets, such as capital investment in plant and equipment are long term covering periods up to ten years or more.

Budgets are one of the traditional controls of business, being used to ensure that expenditure does not exceed income on an ongoing basis. Budgetary control is exercised through reports. These control reports are based on a comparison between actual results and planned

Table 5.7

	F_1	F_2	F_3	F_4	F_5	F_6	Average
F_i values – simulation	1	1	3	3	4	–	2.4
statistical	1	2	3	4	5	2	2.83

Example 5.5 - An 'expected failures' model for the Figtree escalator problem

Number of escalators, n=	10		User input cells are shaded			

Breakdown (10-week) period =	1	2	3	4	5	Total
Probability of failure =	0.05	0.1	0.2	0.3	0.35	1.0

Average length of breakdown =	3.8	periods
Average no. of breakdowns per period, F_{av} =	2.63	

Probability matrix, P_t · **Failures/breakdowns matrix, F_m**

	1	2	3	4	5			1	2	3	4	5
1	0.05							10.00				
2	0.05	0.10					F_1 =	*0.50*	10.00			
3	0.05	0.10	0.20				F_2 =	*1.03*	0.50	10.00		
4	0.05	0.10	0.20	0.30			F_3 =	*2.10*	1.03	0.50	10.00	
5	0.05	0.10	0.20	0.30	0.35		F_4 =	*3.31*	2.10	1.03	0.50	10.00
6	0.05	0.10	0.20	0.30	0.35		F_5 =	*4.23*	3.31	2.10	1.03	0.50
7	0.05	0.10	0.20	0.30	0.35		F_6 =	*1.45*	4.23	3.31	2.10	1.03
8	0.05	0.10	0.20	0.30	0.35		F_7 =	*2.15*	1.45	4.23	3.31	2.10
9	0.05	0.10	0.20	0.30	0.35		F_8 =	*2.83*	2.15	1.45	4.23	3.31
10	0.05	0.10	0.20	0.30	0.35		F_9 =	*3.07*	2.83	2.15	1.45	4.23
11	0.05	0.10	0.20	0.30	0.35		F_{10} =	*2.78*	3.07	2.83	2.15	1.45
12	0.05	0.10	0.20	0.30	0.35		F_{11} =	*2.16*	2.78	3.07	2.83	2.15
13	0.05	0.10	0.20	0.30	0.35		F_{12} =	*2.60*	2.16	2.78	3.07	2.83
14	0.05	0.10	0.20	0.30	0.35		F_{13} =	*2.81*	2.60	2.16	2.78	3.07
15	0.05	0.10	0.20	0.30	0.35		F_{14} =	*2.74*	2.81	2.60	2.16	2.78

➤ **Cost replacement table for the Figtree Shopping Centre's escalators**

Cost of overhauling one escalator, C_i =	£1,000	User input cells
Group overhaul costs, C_g =	£2,000	are shaded

Lowest cost =	£2,500	
Best policy is to group-overhaul every	2	periods, i.e. after 20 weeks

Month	Integer F_i	Cost of B_i	< Individual & group costs for each 10-week period >					
			1	2	3	4	5	6
1	*1*	£1,000	1000	1000	1000	1000	1000	1000
2	*2*	£2,000		2000	2000	2000	2000	2000
3	*3*	£3,000			3000	3000	3000	3000
4	*4*	£4,000				4000	4000	4000
5	*5*	£5,000					5000	5000
6	*2*	£2,000						2000
		Group cost	2,000	2,000	2,000	2,000	2,000	2,000
		Total cost	£3,000	£5,000	£8,000	£12,000	£17,000	£19,000
	Average 10-week cost		£3,000	£2,500	£2,667	£3,000	£3,400	£3,167

Figure 5.8 Statistical model for the Figtree escalator model.

performance. The reports analyse the differences that occur, usually called variances, giving reasons for such deviations from the plan. Where there are significant and unfavourable variances, the control reports will also give details of the corrective action that is necessary to eliminate (or at least reduce) the variances.

The preparation of budgets involves the creation of pro forma financial statements, i.e., financial statements prepared for future periods on the basis of assumptions contained in budgets. To give a true picture of the company's financial health, budgets should also include the main financial statements, i.e., the profit and loss (P & L) account and balance sheet as well as a cash flow analysis. The following case study shows the benefits of combining the two main financial statements into a single spreadsheet.

CASE STUDY 5.1 *Budgeting model*

Fine Furniture is a small family business involved in the manufacture of pine furniture. Its balance sheet at the end of 31st December can be summarised as follows:

Balance Sheet

As at		31 December 200X
Fixed assets		£25,000
Current assets		
stock		£4,300
debtors		£6,300
cash		£2,000
Total assets		£37,600
Current liabilities and equity		
creditors	£5,800	
overdraft	£1,000	
equity	£30,800	
Total liabilities and equity		£37,600

Fine Furniture want to work out their budgets for the next four months to see what levels of overdraft are required at the bank. Sales in November and December were £3,800 and £4,200 respectively. They have estimated sales for the next six months, i.e., January to June, as follows: £4,500, £5,000, £5,500, £5,000, £6,000, and £6,500. Fine Furniture would like to know how sensitive profits are to changes in these estimates.

Cost of materials is normally taken to be 25% of this month's sales, while purchases refer to next month's materials costs. Variable expenses are calculated as 6% of this month's sales, while fixed expenses for each month amount to £2,000. All Fine Furniture's sales are for credit. Debtors take on average about 60 days (two months) to pay whereas Fine Furniture has to pay its creditors within 30 days (one month). Depreciation works out at 0.5% per month of fixed assets and the interest rate on any overdraft is fixed at 0.8% per month.

Step 1: Set up the budget model for the month of January

The Fine Furniture Company wants to develop a budget worksheet so that it can explore the effect on profits when changes are made to the estimated sales figures. The budget worksheet is to consist of a combined profit-and-loss account and balance sheet. The first task is to set up the integrated worksheet as shown in Figure 5.9, using the formulae template of Table 5.8. Note that the arrow in cell D6 indicates the current month, in this case January.

	A	B	C	D	E	F	G	H	I	J	K
1	Case Study 5.1 - Budget model for Fine Furniture–January										
2											
3		*Estimated Sales*				*Current month*		*PLANNING VALUES*			
4		November	£3,800		November	£3,800		Cost of materials			25%
5		December	£4,200		December	£4,200		Variable expenses			6%
6		January	£4,500		January	£4,500		Fixed expenses			£2,000
7		February	£5,000		February	£5,000		Interest rate/month			0.80%
8		March	£5,500		March	£5,500		Depreciation/month			0.50%
9		April	£5,000		April	£5,000		Cash calculations			£2,472
10		May	£6,000		May	£6,000		Overdraft required?			No
11		June	£6,500		June	£6,500		*Debtor period = 2 months (i.e. 60 days)*			
12								*Creditor period = 1 month (i.e. 30 days)*			
13		*User input cells are shaded*									
14											
15		*January*		<------ ASSETS ------>				<------ LIABILITIES ------>			
16				*Fixed Assets*	*Stock*	*Debtors*	*Cash*	*Overdraft*	*Creditors*	*Equity*	*P&L*
17		*Opening Balance*		**£25,000**	**£4,300**	**£6,300**	**£2,000**	**£1,000**	**£5,800**	**£30,800**	**£0**
18		Sales				£4,500					£4,500
19		Cost of materials			-£1,125						-£1,125
20		Purchases			£1,250				£1,250		£0
21		Creditors					-£1,050		-£1,050		£0
22		Debtors				-£3,800	£3,800				£0
23		Variable expenses					-£270				-£270
24		Fixed expenses					-£2,000				-£2,000
25		Depreciation		-£125							-£125
26		Interest					-£8				-£8
27		Overdraft					£0	£0			£0
28		Profit & Loss								£972	-£972
29		*Closing Balance*		**£24,875**	**£4,425**	**£7,000**	**£2,472**	**£1,000**	**£6,000**	**£31,772**	**£0**
30		Totals		£38,772				£38,772			
31											

Figure 5.9 Budget model for Fine Furniture.

Table 5.8   Budgeting – worksheet formulae.

Cell	Formula	Copied to
G1	E6	
E4	B4	E5:E11
F4	C4	F5:F11
J9	SUM(G17:G26)	
J10	IF(J9 < 0, "Yes", "No")	
B15	E6	
K17	SUM(D17:G17) – SUM(H17:J17)	K18:K28
F18	F6	
E19	– J4*F6	
E20	J4*F7	
I20	E20	
G21	–F5*J4	
I21	G21	
F22	–F4	
G22	–F22	
G23	–J5*F6	
G24	–J6	
D25	–J8*D17	
G26	–H17*J7	
G27	IF($J10 = "No", 0, ABS($J9))	H27
J28	SUM(K17:K27)	
D29	SUM(D17:D28)	E29:K29
D30	SUM(D29:G29)	H30

Table 5.9   Budgeting – extended worksheet formulae.

Cell	Formula	Copied to
E36	B37	E37:E42
F36	C37	F37:F42
E43	Delete contents of this cell	
F43	Delete contents of this cell	
D49	D29	E49:J49

Step 2: Extend the model for the months of February, March and April

To extend the model for months February to April is relatively straightforward. Firstly, copy the budget model (range A1:K30) down into cell range A33:K62. Then use the simple template of Table 5.9 to perform the following two tasks:

- Update the copied 'Current month' table (cells E36:F43) by moving all table values upwards.
- Set February's opening balance equal to January's closing balance.

The worksheet should now look like Figure 5.10. Note that the current month has been automatically updated to February. To obtain results for the next two months of March and April,

	A	B	C	D	E	F	G	H
33	Case Study 5.1 - Budget model for Fine Furniture - February							
34								
35		*Estimated Sales*			*Current month*			*PLAN*
36		November	£3,800		December	£4,200		Cost of mate
37		December	£4,200		January	£4,500		Variable exp
38		January	£4,500	→	February	£5,000		Fixed expen
39		February	£5,000		March	£5,500		Interest rate
40		March	£5,500		April	£5,000		Depreciation
41		April	£5,000		May	£6,000		Cash calcula
42		May	£6,000		June	£6,500		Overdraft re
43		June	£6,500					*Debtor peric*
44								*Creditor per*
45								
46								
47		**February**		<----------- *ASSETS* ----------->				<-----------
48				Fixed Assets	Stock	Debtors	Cash	Overdraft
49		*Opening Balance*		*£24,875*	*£4,425*	*£7,000*	*£2,472*	*£1,000*
50		Sales				£5,000		
51		Cost of materials			–£1,250			
52		Purchases			£1,375			
63		Creditors					–£1,125	
54		Debtors				–£4,200	£4,200	
55		Variable expenses					–£300	
56		Fixed expenses					–£2,000	
57		Depreciation		–£124				
58		Interest					–£8	
59		Overdraft					£0	£0
60		Profit & Loss						
61		*Closing Balance*		*£24,751*	*£4,550*	*£7,800*	*£3,239*	*£1,000*
62		**Totals**		£40,340				£40,340
63								

Figure 5.10   Extended budget model for February.

copy February's closing balance figures longhand (i.e., don't use the Excel's 'Copy' command) into January's opening balance, i.e., cells D17:J17. Next repeat step 2, i.e., update the 'Current month' tables by removing the months of December (for March results) and January (for April results).

The complete summary of Fine Furniture's budget model for the four months (January to April) is shown in Figure 5.11. The standard accounting format has been used for clarity. It should be noted that the profit and loss figures are simply copied from column K, i.e., cell ranges K18:K28 and K50:K60 while the balance sheet details are the same as the closing balance figures contained in cells D29:J29 and D61:J61. Finally, cashflow accounting can be easily performed by calculating the difference between the opening and closing cash values for each month, i.e., January net cashflow (ncf) = cell G17 – cell G29 = £2000 – £2472 (£472); February ncf = £2472 – £3239 = (£767), etc.

	A	B	C	D	E	F	G	H
1		Case Study 5.1 - Summary of budget details for Fine Furniture						
2								
3		**Profit and Loss Account**						
4		For month ended		*January*	*February*	*March*	*April*	
5								
6		*Sales*		£4,500	£5,000	£5,500	£5,000	
7		*Less: Cost of Materials*		£1,125	£1,250	£1,375	£1,250	
8								
9		*Gross Margin*		£3,375	£3,750	£4,125	£3,750	
10		*Less: Operating Expenses*						
11		Variable expenses		£270	£300	£330	£300	
12		Fixed expenses		£2,000	£2,000	£2,000	£2,000	
13		Depreciation		£125	£124	£124	£123	
14		Interest		£8	£8	£8	£8	
15				£2,403	£2,432	£2,462	£2,431	
16		*Gross profit*		£972	£1,318	£1,663	£1,319	
17								
18		**Balance Sheet**						
19		As at end of		*January*	*February*	*March*	*April*	
20		*Fixed assets*		£24,875	£24,751	£24,627	£24,504	
21		*Current assets*						
22		stock		£4,425	£4,550	£4,425	£4,675	
23		debtors		£7,000	£7,800	£8,800	£8,800	
24		cash		£2,472	£3,239	£4,151	£5,468	
25								
26		*Total assets*		£38,772	£40,340	£42,003	£43,447	
27								
28		*Current liabilities & equity*						
29		overdraft		£1,000	£1,000	£1,000	£1,000	
30		creditors		£6,000	£6,250	£6,250	£6,375	
31		equity		£31,772	£33,090	£34,753	£36,072	
32								
33		*Total liabilities & equity*		£38,772	£40,340	£42,003	£43,447	
34								

Figure 5.11   Summary of Fine Furniture's budget model.

JOB COSTING

Job costing is an essential aspect of cost accounting. Job costing is used where goods or services are provided on a one-off basis as opposed to being mass produced. In order to determine whether a particular job will make a profit or loss, a business manager must be able to make reasonably accurate estimates of the costs involved in performing the job. The materials used in the job, the labour requirements, as well as overheads such as heating, electricity, fuel, etc., must all be costed. The manager determines the unit cost for each input and then estimates how many units of each input are required to carry out the job. By adding profit margins, the company can arrive at an acceptable cost estimate for any job. Consider the following case study which involves the creation of a spreadsheet for job estimating and costing.

	A	B	C	D	E	F	G	H
1		Case Study 5.2 - Job quotation model for Murphy Builders						
2								
3		**Details of Job:**			**Quotation:**			*No. 0001*
4		Fittings/Furnishings	£3,000		Client No:			999
5		Job duration (days)	3		Date:			25-Mar-0X
6		Workers required (daily)	3					
7		Distance to job (miles)	20		Price:			5723.51
8		Labour (hours)	60		+ VAT			1201.94
9					Total Price:			**£6,925**
10								
11		**Fixed Costs:**			**Cost Estimate:**			
12		Labour rate:			Total Labour Cost			378.00
13		- Paid/hour	£4.50		Fittings/Furnishings			3000.00
14		- Labour factor	140%		Materials Cost			283.50
15		Materials:			Travel Costs			
16		- Materials factor	75%				vehicle	102.00
17		Transport:					travel time	90.72
18		- Rate/mile	£0.85					
19		- Hours/mile	0.04		Total Direct Cost:			**£3,854**
20								
21		**Profit Margins:**						
22		Labour	25%		Profit on Labour			94.50
23		Fittings/Furnishings	25%		Profit on Fittings/Furnish			750.00
24		Materials	25%		Profit on Materials			70.88
25		Overall job	20%		Total Profit			915.38
26								
27		VAT rate	21%		Full Cost			4769.60
28					Overall Job Profit			953.92
29					VAT			1201.94
30					**Job Price**			**£6,925**
31								
32		Note: Totals are rounded to the nearest pound						

Figure 5.12   Job quotation model for Murphy Builders.

CASE STUDY 5.2   *Job quotation model for Murphy Builders*

Joe Murphy owns a small firm that specialises in the renovation of houses. While Murphy Builders (MB) gets many requests to provide free job estimates, many of the quotations do not convert into actual orders. MB has therefore decided to ask your help in developing a spreadsheet job quotation model using a recently purchased copy of Excel. Joe hopes that the program will improve the quality of his company's estimating procedures by producing quotations quickly and accurately.

The job pricing for a house depends on making practical estimates of the various costs involved; the cost of furnishings and other building materials used, labour costs, and travelling expenses associated with the job. In particular, the time required for plastering, carpentry, and plumbing work as well as redecoration costs must be estimated.

Joe Murphy is pleased with the estimation model as shown in Figure 5.12, which was built using the formula template of Table 5.10. The worksheet has been divided into two parts – input and output – separated by column D. Columns B and C form the input part of the model

Table 5.10   Job quotation model – worksheet formulae.

Cell	Formula	Copied to
H7	H27 + H28	
H8	H29	
H9	H7 + H8	
H12	C$8*C13*C14	
H13	C$4	
H14	H12*C16	
H16	2*C$7*C$5*C18	
H17	2*C$7*C$5*C$6*C19*C14*C13	
H19	SUM(H12:H17)	
H22	H12*C22	H23:H24
H25	SUM(H22:H24)	
H27	H19 + H25	
H28	H27*C25	
H29	(H27 + H28)*C27	
H30	SUM(H27:H29)	

containing 'Details of Job' which can only be filled after Joe or one of his colleagues has visited the customer and calculated job requirements. There are four main cost elements, namely, costs of fittings and furnishings, cost of building materials, labour costs, and travel costs. The 'Fixed Costs' section contains permanent data about labour rates, materials and travelling costs as well as acceptable profit margins.

Labour costs are factored by 140% to cover employee insurance, holiday pay and other employment costs. The 'Materials factor' is associated with building materials that are used on the job, e.g., timber, plaster, etc. From Joe's experience, he has found that such sundry materials usually amount to about 75% of labour costs. Travelling costs involve two elements (i) the cost of running the Murphy van and (ii) the cost associated with the time spent travelling to and from the job. This latter cost must be paid for at the going labour rate for each travelling worker. There are two journeys each day.

Columns E to H represent the output part of the model. All output values are derived from formulae using the model's input section. The final 'Job Price' (see line 30, Figure 5.12) is the Full Cost together with the overall job profit and VAT. Note that the costs associated with travel time are calculated by multiplying (total distance travelled by all workers for job duration) by (hours/mile) by (average labour rate).

Improving the Model's Flexibility

The current model uses a standard labour rate of £8.00 per hour. However, tradesmen normally have differing rates, e.g., a plasterer may command a rate of £9.50 while a labourer may only get £5.20 per hour. To make job estimation more accurate, Joe Murphy wants to introduce a range of pay rates covering the different labour grades.

Over the years, Joe has noticed that the age of the house to be renovated has a direct bearing on the estimated hours put in by plasterers, carpenters, and plumbers. For example, a 150-year-old house usually has very thick stone walls which increases the workload considerably. On the other hand, modern houses have cavity-block walls which are much easier to alter or remove. Joe has therefore decided to categorise properties according to their age, reflecting more accurately the degree of difficulty that each type of house presents. Houses are divided into four age categories: (0–25), (26–50), (51–100), over 100 years old.

When visiting a property, Joe records details not only of the house's age but also of its decorative condition, which will directly affect the estimated hours for painters only. A decorative scale of 1 (poor condition) to 4 (good) will give a more accurate estimation of the amount of labour required for painting and decorating.

Carry out the following three steps to improve the model's capabilities.

- Create a copy of the existing job quotation model (Figure 5.12) and use the Insert/Row command to insert eleven new lines after line 10. Firstly, place the cursor anywhere on line 11.

- Now insert the new data blocks surrounded with heavy borders as shown in Figure 5.13. Only cell block G19:H35 requires new formulae as given in the template of Table 5.11.

- Finally, add the three LOOKUP tables (cell range B44:G55) to handle the additional information for (i) different labour pay-rates (ii) age of property, and (iii) decorative condition. (Use Excel's HLOOKUP function to access table information. HLOOKUP is identical to VLOOKUP, except that it searches a row for a given value, whereas VLOOKUP searches a column.) The new improved model should look like Figure 5.13.

Because Joe is using confidential data in his model, he would like to 'hide' the model's logic from clients. His first objective is to provide protection against the user inadvertently overwriting the model's logic. The second objective is to show only the job quotation details to the customer, not sensitive data such as profit margins and estimates! To hide the relevant information, select rows 17–55 and then use the Format|Row|Hide command. To unhide these hidden rows, select rows 16–56 (only rows 16 and 56 will be visible) and choose the Format|Row|Unhide command.

Table 5.11 Modified quotation model – worksheet formulae.

Cell	Formula	Copied to
G19	HLOOKUP(C$8,C$50:F$51, 2)*C11	G20:G22
G23	HLOOKUP(C$8,C$54:F$55, 2)*C15	
G24	SUM(G19:G23)	
H19	C$25*HLOOKUP(C19, C$45:G$46, 2)*G19	H20:H23
H24	SUM(H19:H23)	
H25	H24/G24	
H26	C$4	
H27	H24*C27	
H29	2*C$7*C$5*C29	
H30	H24*(2*C$7*C$5*C$6*C30*C25)	
H31	H24 + SUM(H26:H30)	
H33	H24*C33	
H34	H26*C34	H35

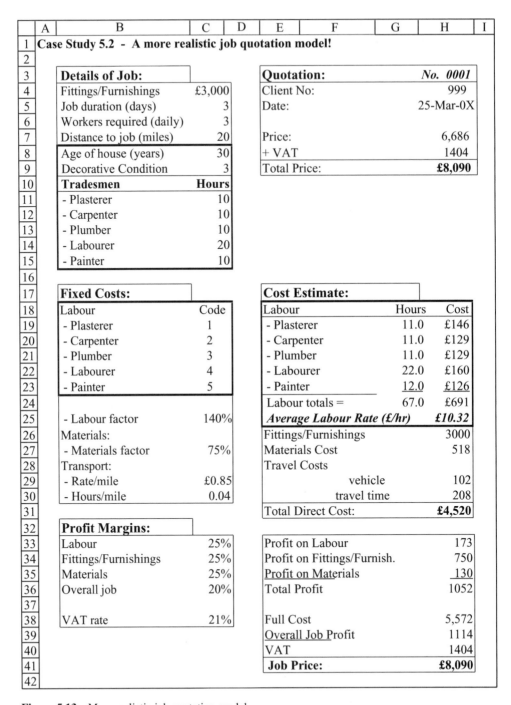

	A	B	C	D	E	F	G	H	I
1	Case Study 5.2 - A more realistic job quotation model!								
2									
3	**Details of Job:**				**Quotation:**			*No. 0001*	
4	Fittings/Furnishings		£3,000		Client No:			999	
5	Job duration (days)		3		Date:			25-Mar-0X	
6	Workers required (daily)		3						
7	Distance to job (miles)		20		Price:			6,686	
8	Age of house (years)		30		+ VAT			1404	
9	Decorative Condition		3		Total Price:			**£8,090**	
10	**Tradesmen**		**Hours**						
11	- Plasterer		10						
12	- Carpenter		10						
13	- Plumber		10						
14	- Labourer		20						
15	- Painter		10						
16									
17	**Fixed Costs:**				**Cost Estimate:**				
18	Labour		Code		Labour		Hours	Cost	
19	- Plasterer		1		- Plasterer		11.0	£146	
20	- Carpenter		2		- Carpenter		11.0	£129	
21	- Plumber		3		- Plumber		11.0	£129	
22	- Labourer		4		- Labourer		22.0	£160	
23	- Painter		5		- Painter		12.0	£126	
24					Labour totals =		67.0	£691	
25	- Labour factor		140%		*Average Labour Rate (£/hr)*			*£10.32*	
26	Materials:				Fittings/Furnishings			3000	
27	- Materials factor		75%		Materials Cost			518	
28	Transport:				Travel Costs				
29	- Rate/mile		£0.85			vehicle		102	
30	- Hours/mile		0.04			travel time		208	
31					Total Direct Cost:			**£4,520**	
32	**Profit Margins:**								
33	Labour		25%		Profit on Labour			173	
34	Fittings/Furnishings		25%		Profit on Fittings/Furnish.			750	
35	Materials		25%		Profit on Materials			130	
36	Overall job		20%		Total Profit			1052	
37									
38	VAT rate		21%		Full Cost			5,572	
39					Overall Job Profit			1114	
40					VAT			1404	
41					**Job Price:**			**£8,090**	
42									

Figure 5.13 More realistic job quotation model.

	A	B	C	D	E	F	G	H	I
43									
44		**Table 1**: Tradesmens' rate of pay					(C45:G46)		
45		Tradesman code	1	2	3	4	5		
46		Hourly rate of pay	£9.50	£8.40	£8.40	£5.20	£7.50		
47									
48		**Table 2**: Age of house				(C50:F51)			
49		Age Range (years)	0-25	26-50	51-100	over 100			
50		Lower Limit	02	65	1	101			
51		Labour Factor	1.0	1.1	1.2	1.3			
52									
53		**Table 3**: Decorative condition				(C54:F55)			
54		Condition Scale	1	2	3	4			
55		Labour (Painters) Factor	1.6	1.4	1.2	1.0			
56									

Figure 5.13   (cont.)

THE LEARNING CURVE

Everyone learns from experience. The first time that a complicated job is undertaken, mistakes will be made and progress will be slow. The next time the same job is carried out, work should proceed at a faster pace. By the time the job has been repeated, say 20 times, job time will have reduced considerably! However, the 'law of diminishing returns' has to be applied, and eventually no further reductions will be possible. Learning curves, or experience curves as they are sometimes called, are based on the principle that people and businesses become more efficient at performing tasks as the tasks are repeated. The learning curve states that 'as an organisation gains experience in manufacturing a product, the resource inputs required to produce each additional unit diminish over the life of the product'. This effect can be shown graphically (Figure 5.14).

The learning curve can provide valuable insights into company and employee performance as well as helping to determine pricing strategies of future products. If a company is planning to introduce a new model of an existing product, then the learning curve, i.e., the experience gained in the manufacture of the original version, can help reduce production costs of the new model. The concept of the learning curve originated in the aircraft manufacturing industry when

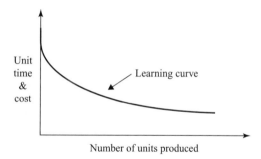

Figure 5.14

it was observed that the costs of assembling an aircraft decreased in a steady and predictable manner (Heizer and Render, Chapter 12).

The learning curve calculates production time only. However, in any task, time is a measure of labour-hours and can be easily converted into a resource cost. The terms, time, labour-hours, and manufacturing costs, are often used interchangeably. The reduction in the average time taken to produce subsequent items is referred to as a 'learning rate'. The learning rate, which is not the same in all manufacturing applications, is usually specified in percentage terms and is based on a doubling of the cumulative volume of the product. It should be noted that a lower learning rate means more efficient performance levels because production times have decreased.

The arithmetic approach to learning curves is the simplest and uses the fact that each time production doubles, the labour requirements per unit decrease by the learning-rate percentage. For example, if the 10th widget takes 100 hours to manufacture, under a learning rate of 80%, the time required to produce the 20th widget would be 80% of the 10th widget, i.e., 80 hours. Similarly the time for the 40th widget is 80% of the 20th widget (64 hours), and so on. The drawback with the arithmetic method is that production times can only be calculated for multiples of units, e.g., 1, 2, 4, 8, 16, ... etc. A more acceptable technique is the logarithmic approach which allows the production time for any unit to be calculated. The logarithmic formula, which uses natural logs, is

$$T_n = T_1 n^b$$

where: T_n is the production time for the n th unit and T_1 is the production time for the first unit.

b is the slope of the learning curve and is defined as $b = \log$ (learning rate)/log2.

L_r, the learning rate, is expressed as a decimal, e.g., $L_r = 80\% = 0.8$.

This formula can be used to calculate the production time for any unit, T_n. For example, suppose the learning rate of a particular process is 80% and the first unit of production takes 50 hours, then the number of hours required to produce the fifth unit, T_5, is given by the formula

$$T_5 = T_1 n^b = 50(5)^b \qquad \text{where } b = \log(0.8)/\log(2) = -0.322$$
$$= 50(5)^{-0.322}$$
$$= 29.78 \text{ hours}$$

If the learning rate is unknown, a second option exists for finding the learning curve equation. If the production times, T_1 and T_j, for the first unit and any other unit j are known, then the three values T_1, T_j and j can be used to derive a learning curve by replacing the formula for b with the new formula

$$b = -\log(T_1/T_j)/\log(j)$$

The learning rate L_r, is found from the equation, $L_r = 2^b$. The learning curve model of Figure 5.15 contains both options for finding (i) unit production time (ii) total time (iii) total average time for any number of units. The total cumulative time, CUM_t, is simply the sum of the unit production times, i.e., $\sum T_i$, while the average cumulative time, CUM_{av}, for the n th unit equals CUM_t/n.

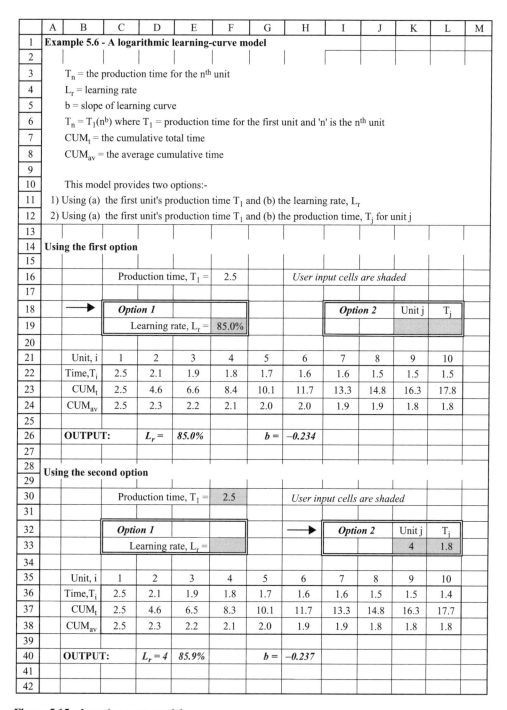

	A	B	C	D	E	F	G	H	I	J	K	L	M
1	**Example 5.6 - A logarithmic learning-curve model**												
2													
3		T_n = the production time for the nth unit											
4		L_r = learning rate											
5		b = slope of learning curve											
6		$T_n = T_1(n^b)$ where T_1 = production time for the first unit and 'n' is the nth unit											
7		CUM_t = the cumulative total time											
8		CUM_{av} = the average cumulative time											
9													
10		This model provides two options:-											
11		1) Using (a) the first unit's production time T_1 and (b) the learning rate, L_r											
12		2) Using (a) the first unit's production time T_1 and (b) the production time, T_j for unit j											
13													
14	**Using the first option**												
15													
16			Production time, T_1 =		2.5			*User input cells are shaded*					
17													
18		→	*Option 1*						*Option 2*	Unit j	T_j		
19			Learning rate, L_r =		85.0%								
20													
21		Unit, i	1	2	3	4	5	6	7	8	9	10	
22		Time,T_i	2.5	2.1	1.9	1.8	1.7	1.6	1.6	1.5	1.5	1.5	
23		CUM_t	2.5	4.6	6.6	8.4	10.1	11.7	13.3	14.8	16.3	17.8	
24		CUM_{av}	2.5	2.3	2.2	2.1	2.0	2.0	1.9	1.9	1.8	1.8	
25													
26		**OUTPUT:**		L_r =	85.0%			b =	-0.234				
27													
28	**Using the second option**												
29													
30			Production time, T_1 =		2.5			*User input cells are shaded*					
31													
32			*Option 1*				→		*Option 2*	Unit j	T_j		
33			Learning rate, L_r =							4	1.8		
34													
35		Unit, i	1	2	3	4	5	6	7	8	9	10	
36		Time,T_i	2.5	2.1	1.9	1.8	1.7	1.6	1.6	1.5	1.5	1.4	
37		CUM_t	2.5	4.6	6.5	8.3	10.1	11.7	13.3	14.8	16.3	17.7	
38		CUM_{av}	2.5	2.3	2.2	2.1	2.0	1.9	1.9	1.8	1.8	1.8	
39													
40		**OUTPUT:**		$L_r = 4$	85.9%			b =	-0.237				
41													
42													

Figure 5.15   Learning curve model.

Table 5.12   Learning curve model – worksheet formulae.

Cell	Formula	Copied to
C22	$F16*C21^$H26	D22:L22
C23	C22	
D23	C23 + D22	E23:L23
C24	C23/C21	D24:L24
E26	IF(F19 = "", 2^H26, F19)	
H26	IF(F19 = "", –LN(F16/L19)/LN(K19), LN(F19)/LN(2))	

EXAMPLE 5.6   *Learning curve model*

The Acme Company is producing a new model of its popular gadget. The learning rate is 85%. Given that it took 2.5 hours to make the first gadget, how long will it take the Acme Company to make (i) the 10th gadget (ii) the first 10 gadgets? The answers are contained in Figure 5.15, i.e., the 10th gadget takes 1.5 hours (cell L22) while the first ten gadgets take a total of 17.8 hours (cell L23).

How would the above answers differ if the Acme Company had no learning curve details other than observed data, indicating that it took 2.5 hours to make the first gadget and 1.8 hours to make the fourth gadget? Using $T_1 = 2.5$ and $T_4 = 1.8$ produces a learning rate of 84.9% (cell E40) with the 10th gadget taking 1.4 hours and the first 10 gadgets taking a total time of 17.7 hours. The formula template of Table 5.12 creates the learning curve model of Figure 5.15. The second option section in cells A28:N40 is obtained by copying cell range A14:N26. The model is currently limited to 10 production units but this number can be extended indefinitely by copying the relevant formulae into other cells.

CHECKING THE ACCURACY OF LEARNING CURVES

In the learning-curve model above, it is assumed that the learning rate is a uniquely defined value that can be safely used to derive production times. It is also assumed that unit production times have been achieved under identical conditions, i.e., the same machinery, personnel, production process, and materials are always used in the manufacture of every unit. Clearly, this is not the case. There are many factors which influence the learning curve and all of these factors are subject to modification. For example, a new model may incorporate more up-to-date design techniques that significantly reduce production time. The learning rate will alter accordingly.

One of the first problems in analysing data is to determine whether a learning curve actually exists. The use of scatter diagrams can help to give a visual picture of the collected data. Once a trend has been established, the next step is to derive a logarithmic expression that best fits the observed data. Regression analysis is an ideal tool for this activity. Consider the following example.

EXAMPLE 5.7 *Getting the true picture!*

The production manager of ABC Manufacturing has observed that workers become more efficient as they produce more units of item X, but he is unsure just how much more efficient they have become. He has collected the following data and would like to know how much the workers have improved so that he can use this information in planning future production runs.

Unit Number	3	6	8	9	12	13	14	15	17	20
Time (minutes)	7.0	6.5	5.2	5.0	4.5	4.4	4.3	4.2	4.0	3.8

The first task is to use Excel's Chart Wizard to produce a scattergraph showing how the above data is actually distributed (see Case Study 5.1). When the data is entered into the model of Figure 5.16 the distribution of points does appear to follow a pattern – with the exception of

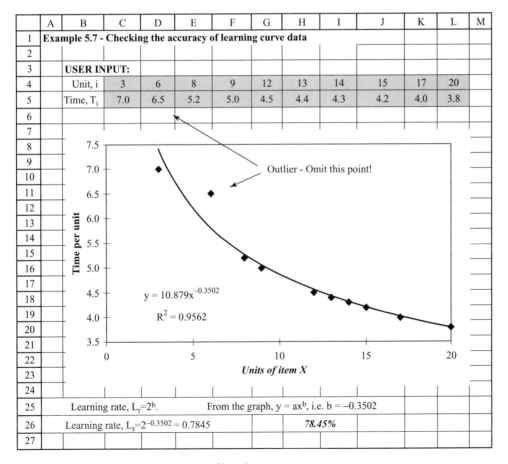

Figure 5.16 Checking out the accuracy of learning curves.

the second data point, i.e., unit 6 and its production time of 6.5 minutes. There could be any number of reasons why this unit number is out of step with the other data – the production time may have been wrongly recorded, an inexperienced employee may have produced the unit, equipment may have temporarily broken down, etc. This 'outlier' – as it is normally called – will be deleted from the data. By carrying out the steps below, a 'power' trendline is produced and the following expression obtained:

$$y = 10.879x^{-0.3502}$$

The production time, T_1, for the first unit is obtained by setting $x = 1$ in the above equation, i.e., $T_1 = 10.88$ and the learning rate, $L_r = 2^b$ where $b = -0.3502$, i.e., $L_r = 78.45\%$.

To obtain a logarithmic expression of the form $y = ax^b$, use Excel's regression analysis facility by performing the following steps:

- Place the cursor on one of the points in the scattergraph and click the right-hand button to activate the shortcut menu.
- Click the 'Add_Trendline...'option to display the Add_Trendline dialog box.
- Click on the 'Type' tab and select the 'Power' option.
- Click on the 'Options' tab and select (i) Display equation on chart (ii) Display R-squared value on chart.
- Finally, click the OK button to return to the scattergraph.

The importance of having a visual representation of observed data points can now be illustrated. Suppose that the production manager of ABC Manufacturing has only a few recorded observations from which to derive a learning rate, L_r, namely production times $T_1 (= 10.9)$, T_3, T_6, T_8, T_9, and T_{12}. He has decided to use the second option provided in the learning curve model of Figure 5.15, and obtains the following results:

Unit pairs (T_i, T_j)	(T_1, T_3)	(T_1, T_6)	(T_1, T_8)	(T_1, T_9)	(T_1, T_{12})
Learning rate, L_r	75.6%	81.9%	78.1%	78.2%	78.1%

From these calculations, it is clear that the production times for units 3 and 6 are unreliable, giving learning rates that vary by -2.85% and $+3.45\%$ from the trendline value of 78.45%. This same conclusion can also be reached by simply observing the 'closeness of fit' of units 3 and 6 in the scattergraph of Figure 5.16. These two points are furthermost from the trendline.

EXCEL FUNCTIONS USED IN MODEL-BUILDING

The models developed in this chapter use Excel's five depreciation functions – SLN, DB, SYD, DDB and VDB – which have been fully discussed in the section on 'Depreciation'. The following eight Excel functions are used for the first time and are explained below. The user should remember that a comprehensive on-line help facility is also provided by Excel.

	A	B	C	D	E	F	G	H
1								
2		Product	No. in	Product		Year	Cash	
3		name	stock	price			flow	
4		Gizmo	10	£10.00		1	−10	
5		Gadget	25	£12.50		2	4	
6		Widget	8	£20.00		3	3	
7		Sprocket	40	£4.50		4	6	
8								
9				*Sample Figure*				

Figure 5.17 Sample figure.

1. COUNTIF: COUNTIF(range, criteria)

> searches a cell range and counts cells specified by given criteria

range   = the range of cells to be examined
criteria = the specified criteria in the form of a number, text, or an expression. For
            example criteria can be specified in the form 32, "32", ">32", "apples".

Examples: COUNTIF(C4:C7, ">20") in Figure 5.17 returns 2, i.e., the number of cells greater than 20.

COUNTIF(B4:B7, "=Gadget") in Figure 5.17 returns 1, i.e., the number of cells containing the word 'Gadget'.

2. EXP: EXP(number)

> returns *e* raised to the power of *number* where *e* is the base of the natural logarithm.

Examples: EXP(1) = 2.7183 (the approximate value of *e*); EXP(2) = 7.3891; EXP(LN(3)) = 3

3. HLOOKUP: HLOOKUP((Table_value, Lookup_table, Column_no, Nearest)

> searches the top row of a range of cells (the Lookup_table) for a specific value (Table_value). It then returns a corresponding value from a different row in the table.

Note: HLOOKUP is very similar to the VLOOKUP function, which has been fully documented in Chapter 2.

Example: HLOOKUP("Gizmo", B4:D7, 4) in Figure 5.17 returns *Sprocket*. Since 'Gizmo' is located in the first column of the lookup range, the corresponding value in the fourth row is *Sprocket*.

4. LN: LN(number)

returns the natural logarithm of *number*.

Examples: LN(2.7183) = 1.   LN(86) = 4.454347.   LN(EXP(4)) = 4

5. MATCH: MATCH(value, array, type)

returns the position of *value* in the one-dimensional cell range *array*. Use MATCH instead of one of the LOOKUP functions when the position of a matched item is required instead of the item itself.

value = the value to be matched. 'value' can be a number, text, or logical value.
array = the specified one-dimensional cell range.
type = 0 in which case, search for an exact match.
     = 1 in which case, search for the largest value that is less than or equal to *value*.
     = −1 in which case, search for the smallest value that is greater than or equal to *value*. If *type* is omitted, it is assumed to be 1.

Example: MATCH("Widget", B4:B7) in Figure 5.17 returns 3 because 'Widget' is in the third position of the cell range B4:B7.

6. MIN: MIN(array)

returns the smallest number in an array.

Example: MIN(D4:D7) in Figure 5.17 returns the value £4.50.

7. OFFSET: OFFSET(cellRef, rowOffset, colOffset, height, width)

examines a cell range and returns a cell value which is offset from a given starting point by a specified number of rows and columns.

cellRef   = the starting position in a cell range from which the offset is required.
rowOffset   = the vertical offset. A positive number moves down; a negative number moves up; zero performs no movement.
colOffset   = the horizontal offset. A positive number moves right; a negative number moves left; zero performs no movement.
height,width = the number of rows, columns in the offset range. If these values are omitted, the offset range is assumed to be the same size as the *cellRef* range.

Examples: OFFSET(B7, −2, 2) in Figure 5.17 returns £12.50 which is the value in cell D5. OFFSET(D4, 0, −2) returns 'Gizmo' which is the contents of cell B4.

8. ROUNDUP: ROUNDUP(number, digits)

rounds a number up, away from zero.

number = the real number which is to be rounded up.

digits = the number of digits to which the number is to be rounded. If $digits > 0$, the number is rounded up to the specified number of decimal places. If $digits = 0$, then the number is rounded up to the nearest integer. If $digits < 0$, the number is rounded up to the left of the decimal point.

Examples: ROUNDUP(27.2, 0) = 28; ROUNDUP(3.142, 2) = 3.15; ROUNDUP (465.83, −1) = 470.

EXERCISES

5.1 The MightyBig Company is considering three sites for the location of its new manufacturing plant. Annual estimated revenue along with fixed and variable costs for each site are shown in Table 5.13. Sales volume is expected to be 30,000 units per year. Set up a cost-volume-profit model and hence find the best location using break-even analysis.

Table 5.13

Site location	Revenue per unit	Fixed costs (£'000s)	Variable costs per unit
A	£70	300	£65
B	£70	500	£45
C	£68	700	£30

(Answer: For locations A,B,C the break-even points are: BEP_u = 60,000, 20,000, 18,421 and $BEP_£$ = £4,200,000, £840,000, £536,842. Corresponding profit (loss) figures are −£150,000, £250,000, £440,000. The best site is C even though annual fixed costs are much higher than for the other two sites.)

5.2 A bakery is considering the purchase of a new delivery van costing £20,000. The estimated running costs of the van are £3000 in the first year, rising annually by 15% thereafter. If the van's depreciation is 20% per annum and the cost of capital is 9%, how often should the van be replaced? How would your answer be affected if (i) the rate of depreciation decreased/increased (ii) the cost of capital altered? (Vary depreciation from 15% to 25% and capital cost from 6% to 12%).

(Answer: Modify the equipment-depreciation model of Figure 5.3 by introducing a 'rate of depreciation' factor, DR. Cells C11:D18 will now contain appropriate formulae.)

Rate of depreciation	15%	20%	25%	Capital cost	6%	9%	12%
Minimum annual cost (£s)	7580	7988	8205		7566	7988	8399
Replace item in year	4	6	7		5	6	6

5.3 A hospital has a permanent need for a piece of theatre equipment costing £48,000. The fixed annual running cost is £2000 and maintenance charges are estimated at £3000 in the first year, rising annually at a rate of 15% thereafter. The equipment's useful life is eight years and equipment cost is written off on a straight-line depreciation basis. If the cost of capital is calculated to be 10%, when is the best time to replace the equipment, and what is the annual equivalent cost? Would the answer change if the equipment's life was extended to 12 years, given that depreciation is zero over this extended period?

(Answer: Modify the equipment-depreciation model of Figure 5.3 by introducing a 'fixed running cost', FC. Cells C11:D18 will now contain appropriate formulae. When an eight-year period is considered, the equipment should be replaced after five years with a corresponding equivalent cost of £15,653. When a twelve-year period is considered, the optimum replacement period now becomes eleven years with a corresponding cost of £15,216.)

5.4   Bloggs Engineering has recently carried out a detailed cost analysis of its machinery. Having studied past records of the maintenance costs and depreciation of its machines, the company has found that for a machine with a capital cost C, the maintenance cost and resale value at the end of year 'n' of its life can be expressed by the following formulae:

$$\text{Maintenance cost} = 0.08C(1.2^n + 2) \quad \text{Resale value} = C/\log_e(1.5n + 2)$$

Bloggs Engineering wants to find the optimum replacement time for the machines over a period of eight years, given that the annual cost of capital is 10%.

(Answer: Take a copy of Figure 5.3 and use the template of Table 5.14 to make the necessary modifications. Note that any value can be assigned to capital cost C, e.g., £10,000. Equipment should be replaced every six years, with the minimum cost being £4,867.)

Table 5.14   Replacement analysis – Bloggs Engineering.

Cell	Formula	Copied to
C11	0.08*F$3*(1.2^B11 + 2)	C12:C18
D11	F$3/LN(1.5*B11 + 2)	D12:D18

5.5   Consider Merlene Olonga's equipment-leasing problem discussed earlier in the chapter. She is not satisfied with the answer obtained by the model of Figure 5.4, which found that a four-year leasing policy was the most economical solution. Merlene knows that her company's microcomputer system must be kept up to date and has decided that any equipment can be retained only for a maximum period of three years. By modifying the C_{ij} cost options to reflect Merlene's new request, re-run the model and find Merlene's best option under these new conditions.

(Answer: Set the current option of C_{15} equal to a very large cost, say £99,999, and re-run the model. The new policy is $C_{12} + C_{25}$, giving a total cost of £34,500.)

5.6   The GreenFingers Garden Centre hires out lawnmowers over a period of five months. Because of maintenance, many of the lawnmowers are out of service for varying lengths of time and are therefore losing money. GreenFingers' table of hire rates, shown in Table 5.15, reflect these hidden expenses. The table also takes supply and demand into account, with hire rates being reduced towards the end of the summer. Unfortunately, the complexity of GreenFingers' costs table presents a problem for Fred Flint. He would like to know the cheapest way of hiring out a lawnmower for a period of five months. Use the equipment leasing model of Figure 5.4 to help solve Fred's problem.

(Answer: The cheapest option for Fred Flint is to hire out a lawnmower three times – at the beginning of months 1, 2, and 4 giving a total cost of £145, i.e., $C_{12} + C_{24} + C_{46}$.)

Table 5.15 Hire rates – GreenFingers Garden Centre.

Month	$j = 2$	$j = 3$	$j = 4$	$j = 5$	$j = 6$
$i = 1$	£30	£65	£95	–	£155
$i = 2$		£40	£60	£95	£120
$i = 3$			£45	–	£100
$i = 4$				–	£55
$i = 5$					£22

5.7 The Bedrock Company's headquarters contains 1000 electric light bulbs. When any bulb fails, it is immediately replaced. From past records of 500 bulbs, the following failures table has been obtained:

Age at failure (months)	2	3	4	5
No. of failed bulbs	100	200	150	50

(i) Calculate the expected number of bulbs to be replaced in each of the first seven months. What rate of failure can be expected in the long run?

(ii) Replacement of individual bulbs costs £0.50 each. What is the average monthly replacement cost? An alternative policy is to replace all the bulbs after a fixed number of months at a cost of £200, as well as replacing any units that fail at the individual price of £0.50 each. Is this preventative maintenance policy justified, and if so, in what month should it come into operation?

(Answer: In order to be consistent, the failures table above must also include month 1 with zero failures. Failures in the first 7 months are 0, 200, 400, 340, 260, 288, and 328. In the long run, the average number of failures per month is 303. The average monthly individual replacement cost is therefore £151.50. The cheapest replacement policy is group replacement every two months at an average monthly cost of £150.)

5.8 Barry Lime is marketing manager of SuperMicros, which has recently begun to lease micro-computers. The company has set aside a total of 200 micros for this purpose. Barry has obtained recent market research data, showing the distribution of 100 similar micro leasing policies:

Length of lease (years)	1	2	3	4
No. of policies	20	40	30	10

Barry would like to find (i) the number of new leasing policies required each year for the next four years in order to maintain SuperMicros' rentals at 200 (ii) the average length of the leasing period (iii) the average number of new leasing policies required each year.

(Answer: This exercise is equivalent to a statistical equipment replacement problem and is solved using the model of Figure 5.5. (i) 40, 88, 94, 86 (ii) 2.3 years (iii) 87.)

5.9 The Things A'Plenty Company has recently received several orders for its new solar-assisted car. The number of customer orders for the next five months are 2, 6, 10, 10, and 15 respectively. The first three cars have already been manufactured and their production times have been found to be 500, 400, and 350 hours respectively. Having studied these times, the Company's engineers estimate that an 80% improvement in production time can be achieved. Things A'Plenty would like to know how much labour is required to meet its commitments to customers. The company has asked its engineers to draw up a table of monthly labour requirements. Company data shows that an employee works twenty 8-hour days each month, i.e., 160 labour-hours per month. If production-time data for the next three units is found to be 320, 298, and 280 respectively, use the model of Figure 5.16 to check out the accuracy of the Company's assumption of an 80% learning curve.

(Answer: Extend the model in Figure 5.15 to include details for 45 units.)

Month	1	2	3	4	5
No. of cars required	2	6	10	10	15
Actual unit nos.	1–2	3–8	9–18	19–28	29–43
Production hours	900.0	1773.0	2185.1	1815.5	2373.5
No. of employees	5.6	11.1	13.7	11.3	14.8

When the first six production times (500, 400, 350, 320, 298, 280) are entered into the model of Figure 5.16, a learning curve value of 79.96% is obtained, confirming the engineers' estimation of 80%. The curve fit is almost perfect with a correlation coefficient of $R = 0.9999$. The equation is $y = 500x^{-0.3227}$.

5.10   Sharon Smith is sales manager of the KleenUp Company. Sharon intends to launch a monthly sales campaign during the coming year. She is currently preparing a budget for the labour costs required to handle the sales campaigns and has estimated that the first one will require 100 hours at a cost of £15 per hour. From previous experience, Sharon knows that the salesforce's learning experience follows a 78% learning curve. The KleenUp Company would like to know what the first four campaigns will cost.

(Answer: Using the learning curve model of Figure 5.15, the total time required for the first four campaigns, $\text{CUM}_4 = 306.3$. Total costs $= 306.3 \times £15 = £4594.50$.)

REFERENCES AND FURTHER READING

Heizer, J. and Render, B. (2003) *Production & Operations Management* (7th edn), Prentice Hall, New Jersey.

Jackson, M. (1988) *Advanced Spreadsheet Modelling with Lotus 1-2-3*, John Wiley & Sons, Ltd, UK.

Ragsdale, C. (2004) *Spreadsheet Modeling and Decision Analysis* (4th edn), Thomson South-Western, USA.

Urry, S. (1991) *Introduction to Operational Research*, Longman Scientific & Technical, Essex.

Wilkes, F. (1980) *Elements of Operational Research*, McGraw-Hill, UK.

Winston, W. (2003) *Operations Research: Applications and Algorithms* (4th edn), Duxbury Press, California.

6

Marketing models

OVERVIEW

Marketing is one of the most complex areas of business decision-making. Many input variables are qualitative in nature and cannot be accurately measured, e.g., changing consumer patterns, increasing competition, and sales forecasting in an uncertain economic environment. Some managers view marketing as an art form, with the qualities of experience and good judgement being considered more important than analytical model-building. However, spreadsheet modelling is an ideal tool for combining managerial knowledge with uncertain marketing information. Because many marketing decisions are based on a mixture of both quantitative details (e.g., past sales data) and qualitative predictions of a volatile market-place, they are called semi-structured. A semi-structured problem is one where the decision-maker has factual data to analyse but must use his or her own judgement to arrive at a satisfactory solution.

Sensitivity or 'what-if' analysis is a typical semi-structured approach in which the decision-maker asks a series of 'what-if' questions in order to determine how key factors respond to assumed changes in conditions. The ability to experiment with quantitative data in order to gain greater insight into a semi-structured situation lets the decision-maker see the consequences of certain actions. For example, how would a 5% increase in production costs affect product pricing?

Many companies have multiple and often contradictory goals. For example, they may seek to maximise sales at minimum cost or, perhaps to maximise profits while minimising risk. Goal programming (GP) which is a variation of linear programming, allows the decision-maker to specify multiple objectives which can then be placed in whatever order the decision-maker wishes. Although GP answers are non-optimal, they come as close as possible to meeting goals in the order specified by the decision-maker.

ORGANISING AND PRESENTING DATA

Statistics play an important part in marketing decisions. Descriptive statistics consists of techniques and measures that help decision-makers describe data. Unfortunately too much data can confuse rather than clarify, i.e., the decision-maker can't see the information for the data! Frequency distributions, histograms, pie charts, scatter plots, tables and bar charts are some of the tools that decision-makers use to help convert data into meaningful information. The easiest method of organising data is to construct a frequency distribution, using classes. A class is simply a specified interval of interest, usually having an upper and lower limit.

EXAMPLE 6.1   *Interpreting sales data*

Fred Doherty has been asked by his boss to make a presentation at next week's end-of-year meeting of the Little Manufacturing Company. The presentation concerns the company's sales figures for this year, and how they compare with last year's sales. As sales manager, Fred must be in a position to answer any questions that may arise during the meeting. Fred has decided to use a standard line chart presentation containing both sets of sales figures for easier interpretation and analysis (see Figure 6.1). During the end-of-year meeting, Fred is asked to explain (i) the reason for the sudden fall-off in last year's May sales, and (ii) why have sales improved so much in the latter part of this year?

Fred reminds the first questioner of the flood damage that was done to the company's warehouse during last year's storms. With so much stock damaged, sales for May were seriously affected. However, the sales force made considerable efforts during July and August to recoup lost sales. This year's improved sales from September onwards are due to the introduction of a new sales strategy in mid-August. To date, the new dynamic sales approach is producing very satisfactory results.

Measures of Location and Spread

Presentation techniques such as frequency histograms can be misleading when making comparisons between two different sets of data. For example, by varying the number and width of class intervals, histograms from two quite different sets of data may appear very similar. Other statistical techniques are needed to test for differences between data groups. The most common of these attempt to determine whether the two groups have the same distribution, i.e., have they the same central location and spread? The central location is simply the middle or centre of a set of data.

Common measures of central location are the mode, median and mean. The mean is often referred to as the arithmetic average. Statistical measures of spread are also called measures of variation (or dispersion) because they focus on fluctuations that occur on either side of the central location. The best known measures of spread are the range, variance and standard deviation, which is the square root of the variance.

EXAMPLE 6.2   *Calculating the mean, variance, and standard deviation*

A sales manager has examined past records for product X, and has calculated that sales (in '000s) for the new version of product X will follow the pattern as shown in the probability table below:

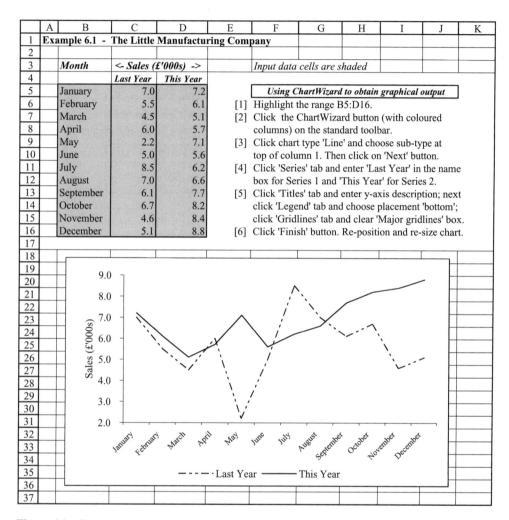

Figure 6.1 Graphical presentation of sales data.

Sales, S_i	5	10	15	20	25	30
Probability, P_i	0.1	0.3	0.3	0.15	0.1	0.05

The sales manager is interested in the spread of data, i.e., how tightly packed or scattered is the data around the mean? She has decided to set up a simple spreadsheet as shown in Figure 6.2 to find the expected value (or mean), variance, and standard deviation of a probability distribution. The table's sales data, S_i, and probabilities, P_i, are used to define the standard formulae as follows:

	A	B	C	D	E	F	G	H	I	J	K
1		**Example 6.2 - Finding the mean, variance, and standard deviation of sales data**									
2											
3		Sales ('000s), S$_i$		5	10	15	20	25	30	*User input cells*	
4		Probability, P$_i$		0.1	0.3	0.3	0.15	0.1	0.05	*are shaded*	
5											
6			Expected value, E, or Mean =			*15*					
7											
8			(S$_i$ – E)^2 =	100	25	0	25	100	225		
9											
10				Variance =		*42.5*					
11				Standard deviation =		*6.52*					
12											
13											
14		*Cell*	*Formula*				*Copied to*				
15		F6	SUMPRODUCT(D3:I3, D4:I4)								
16		D8	(D3 –$F6)^2				E8:I8				
17		F10	SUMPRODUCT(D4:I4, D8:I8)								
18		F11	SQRT(F10)								
19											

Figure 6.2   Mean, variance, and standard deviation of a probability distribution.

$$\text{Mean or expected value, } E = \sum_{i=1}^{n} P_i S_i \quad n = 6 \text{ (number of values in sales distribution table)}$$

$$\text{Variance, } \sigma^2 = \sum_{i=1}^{n} P_i (S_i - E)^2$$

$$\text{Standard deviation, } \sigma = \text{square root of the variance}$$

CORRELATION ANALYSIS AND LINEAR REGRESSION

Correlation analysis and linear regression are two of the most widely used statistical tools for determining the linear relationship between two or more variables. When there are only two variables involved, the technique for prediction is called simple regression analysis. The quantitative measure of strength in a linear relationship between two variables is called the correlation coefficient. The closer the correlation coefficient is to $+1.0$ or -1.0, the stronger the linear relationship. If two variables have no linear relationship, the correlation between them is zero.

As an example, consider the sales manager of a manufacturing company who notices that there is a wide variation in monthly sales figures. He (or she) also notices that the company's advertising expenditures change each month. The sales manager is interested in determining if a relationship exists between sales and advertising. If he could successfully define the relationship, he might be able to use this information to improve predictions of monthly sales and, therefore, do a better job of planning.

A popular method for selecting the best regression line for a sample of data is the 'least squares' approach. It is a line-fitting technique that attempts to optimise the linear relationship between two variables. The 'least squares' method states that the best regression line is the one that minimises the sum of the squared distances between the observed (x, y) points and the regression line. Consider the following case study.

CASE STUDY 6.1   *Predicting sales with Excel's CORREL and TRENDLINE functions*

Sharon Smith has just taken over from Harry Locke as sales manager of the KleenUp Company which manufactures household detergents and sells them directly to retail stores via a large force of salespeople. The owners have been concerned for some time about the company's varying quarterly sales figures and have asked Sharon to look into the situation. To help clarify her ideas, Sharon has tabulated sales data for ten randomly selected sales areas as shown in Table 6.1.

The tabulated sales data is rather uninspiring, and Sharon has decided to plot the data to get a clearer picture. While looking through Harry Locke's notes on previous sales data, Sharon notices that he was convinced that there could well be a direct link between sales figures and the number of stores visited by the company's sales force. Unfortunately, he had no way of proving if such a connection did in fact exist, and as Harry was close to retirement age, his enthusiasm was not what it used to be!

Being new to the job, Sharon wants to impress the owners with her initiative. She has decided to find out if there is indeed a close relation between area sales and the number of retail outlets visited by the salespeople. If true, then Sharon could improve sales revenue by making sure that her sales force visit more stores in future. Not only would she be helping the owners but also her own reputation.

Sharon recently attended a business computing course and knows that statistical software can help her make some sense of the data which she has collected. For example, she would like

Table 6.1

Sales area	No. of retail stores visited	Last quarter's sales (£'000s)	Population of sales area ('000s)
1	39	15	110
2	44	9	65
3	50	10	90
4	64	12	100
5	65	3	160
6	55	13	130
7	66	15	105
8	12	2	20
9	92	20	240
10	81	17	95

a way of measuring how close a relationship there is between the two variables, i.e., she needs to find if there is a strong correlation. Sharon starts checking through her course handouts and discovers that Excel's statistical function CORREL gives her what she wants. Firstly, she enters her data table into a worksheet (see Figure 6.3). Then Sharon uses the following steps to create a scattergraph in order to see what the data looks like:

- Select cell range D6:E15 in Figure 6.3 and then click the Chart Wizard button (with coloured columns) on the standard toolbar.

- In Chart Wizard's Step 1, select chart-type XY (Scatter) and chart sub-type in (row 1, column 1). Click the 'Next' button twice to proceed to Step 3.

- In Chart Wizard's Step 3, click on the following tabs: (i) 'Titles' tab and enter titles for Chart, X-axis, and Y-axis as shown in Figure 6.3; (ii) 'Legend' tab and clear the 'Show Legend' box; (iii) 'Gridlines' tab and clear the Y-axis (Major gridlines) box.

- Click the 'Finish' button to exit from Chart Wizard. (For further information on formatting charts with Chart Wizard, see Appendix).

When the function CORREL is applied to the relevant data, Sharon views the initial correlation coefficient of 0.68 as encouraging but not as high as she would have liked. On closer examination of the scattergraph, Sharon identifies two 'rogue' sales areas (1 and 5) – usually referred to as 'outliers' – that do not conform to the general pattern. At a later stage, Sharon will try to establish why these areas are 'out of step' with the rest of the data. Meanwhile, having deleted the data for these two areas from the table, Sharon finds an almost perfect correlation of 0.99; so old Harry Locke was right after all!

The scattergraph of Figure 6.3 indicates a linear trend. Sharon Smith would now like to go one step further and find the linear regression equation, She has decided to use Excel's 'trendline' feature to help her find this equation. A trendline smoothes out fluctuations in a set of data and allows the user to see performance trends more clearly. Once an equation has been found, Sharon can extrapolate data backwards or forwards. She will then be able to predict, with at least some degree of accuracy, what value of sales will be generated by, for example, a sales force visiting 80 retail outlets regularly.

This knowledge will also help her to identify a sales area that seems to be 'the exception to the rule'. Where, for instance, the appropriate sales volume is not being generated considering the number of outlets that are claimed to be visited. On the other hand, where sales are higher than expected, Sharon might identify the existence of a more subtle sales strategy. For example, the exceptional sales in area 1 could be due to sophisticated marketing techniques being used by individual salespeople; techniques about which the company's own marketing division may know very little.

Excel's TRENDLINE function is not restricted to lines, and also allows various curves to be fitted to observed data. Excel provides six options, namely linear, logarithmic, polynomial, power, exponential, and moving average. Since the scattergraph of Figure 6.3 indicates a linear trend, Sharon will select the trendline's linear option. The trendline function not only displays the regression equation but also the value of R^2 where R is the correlation coefficient. R^2 (R-squared) is called the coefficient of determination. The various steps for adding a trendline to a data series are given at the bottom of Figure 6.4, which is a copy of Figure 6.3. Note that all mouse clicks are with the left-hand button unless otherwise stated.

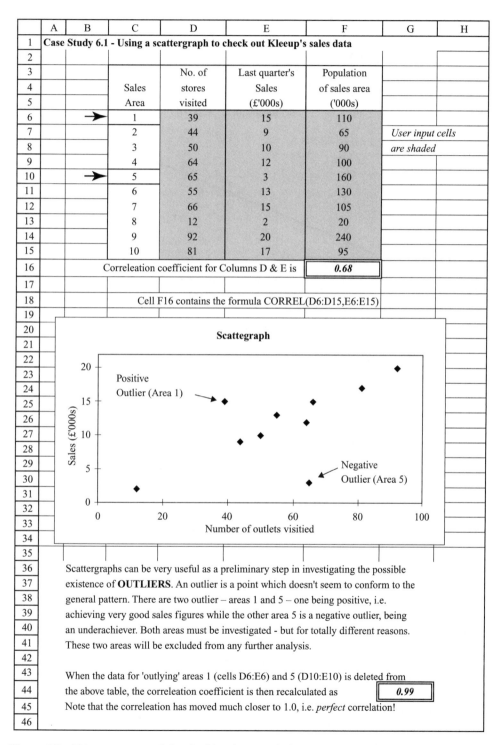

	A	B	C	D	E	F	G	H
1	Case Study 6.1 - Using a scattergraph to check out Kleeup's sales data							
2								
3				No. of	Last quarter's	Population		
4			Sales	stores	Sales	of sales area		
5			Area	visited	(£'000s)	('000s)		
6		➡	1	39	15	110		
7			2	44	9	65	*User input cells*	
8			3	50	10	90	*are shaded*	
9			4	64	12	100		
10		➡	5	65	3	160		
11			6	55	13	130		
12			7	66	15	105		
13			8	12	2	20		
14			9	92	20	240		
15			10	81	17	95		
16		Correleation coefficient for Columns D & E is				**0.68**		
17								
18			Cell F16 contains the formula CORREL(D6:D15,E6:E15)					
19								
20								
21								
22								
23								
24								
25								
26								
27								
28								
29								
30								
31								
32								
33								
34								
35								
36		Scattergraphs can be very useful as a preliminary step in investigating the possible						
37		existence of **OUTLIERS**. An outlier is a point which doesn't seem to conform to the						
38		general pattern. There are two outlier – areas 1 and 5 – one being positive, i.e.						
39		achieving very good sales figures while the other area 5 is a negative outlier, being						
40		an underachiever. Both areas must be investigated - but for totally different reasons.						
41		These two areas will be excluded from any further analysis.						
42								
43		When the data for 'outlying' areas 1 (cells D6:E6) and 5 (D10:E10) is deleted from						
44		the above table, the correleation coefficient is then recalculated as			**0.99**		
45		Note that the correleation has moved much closer to 1.0, i.e. *perfect* correlation!						
46								

Figure 6.3   Using a scattergraph for checking data correlation.

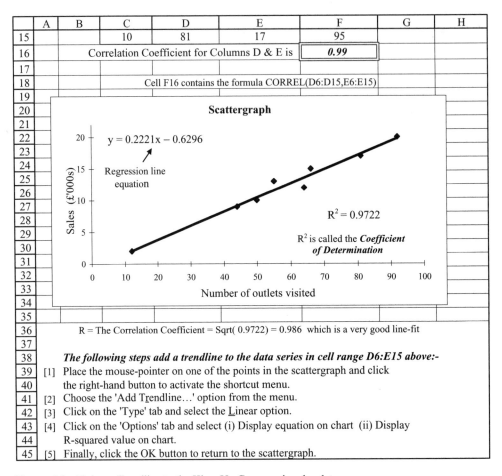

	A	B	C	D	E	F	G	H
15			10	81	17	95		
16		Correlation Coefficient for Columns D & E is				*0.99*		
17								
18			Cell F16 contains the formula CORREL(D6:D15,E6:E15)					

Scattergraph

$y = 0.2221x - 0.6296$

Regression line equation

$R^2 = 0.9722$

R^2 is called the *Coefficient of Determination*

Sales (£'000s)

Number of outlets visited

R = The Correlation Coefficient = Sqrt(0.9722) = 0.986 which is a very good line-fit

The following steps add a trendline to the data series in cell range D6:E15 above:-

[1] Place the mouse-pointer on one of the points in the scattergraph and click the right-hand button to activate the shortcut menu.

[2] Choose the 'Add Trendline...' option from the menu.

[3] Click on the 'Type' tab and select the Linear option.

[4] Click on the 'Options' tab and select (i) Display equation on chart (ii) Display R-squared value on chart.

[5] Finally, click the OK button to return to the scattergraph.

Figure 6.4   Fitting a Trendline to the KleenUp Company's sales data.

FORECASTING – TIME SERIES AND EXPONENTIAL SMOOTHING

No company can function effectively without a forecast for its goods or services. Forecasting is the process of predicting the future. On the other hand, planning is the process of deciding in advance what is to be done and how it is to be done. Forecasts provide valuable input into the planning process. Practically all management decisions depend on forecasts, either quantitative or qualitative.

Forecasts can be either short range, i.e., with a forecast horizon of up to one year, or long range extending over several years. Statistical quantitative techniques, e.g., moving average, trend extrapolation, and exponential smoothing, are best suited to short-term forecasting. Qualitative or judgemental forecasts depend almost exclusively on human judgement, intuition, and experience. These qualities are better suited to long-range forecasting where trends and seasonal cycles become blurred and ill defined, making mathematical models unreliable.

In the previous study of the KleenUp Company, Sharon Smith was able to make predictions on the basis of linear regression, i.e., fitting a straight line through her data. However, not all data follows a straight-line pattern, e.g., some data may exhibit a pattern which is best described as a curved or exponential trend. To make predictions on the basis of a straight-line fit to such data could well produce disastrous results! To overcome these non-linear situations, two well-known forecasting techniques are examined in the next two sections, namely time series and exponential smoothing.

A time-series is defined as a set of observations that have been collected at regular intervals such as every week, month, or quarter. Statistical forecasting models assume that the time series follows a stable pattern, such as a trend or seasonal cycle, that can be extrapolated into the future. In analysing a time-series, two major components must be identified, namely, the trend and the seasonal variation. The trend reflects the general overall movement of the data (i.e., in an upwards or downwards direction) while the seasonal variation is a cyclical subset (of the observed data) repeating itself in a regular way over the observed period of time. Seasonal variations often occur at definite intervals, e.g., toy sales are higher at Xmas while ice-cream sales usually peak during the summer.

One popular way of calculating the trend is the moving-average technique, which smoothes out fluctuations in the data to reveal whatever trend there may be. Using the moving-average approach, the forecast at any period is simply the average of previous observations in the time series. For example, if a three-month moving average is chosen, then the forecast for April is the average for the months of January, February and March. The terms 'time-series techniques' and 'extrapolation models' are synonymous and are often used interchangeably. The moving average and exponential smoothing functions are contained in Excel's Analysis ToolPak (see Chapter 2 for ToolPak details).

CASE STUDY 6.2 *Using Excel's ToolPak moving-average function*

Fred Flint is in charge of inventory at the Bedrock Company. As part of his job, he must obtain demand forecasts for the products stocked in inventory. Fred has decided to use a three-month moving average to help him find a feasible sales forecast for product P over the next two months, i.e., November and December. Fred has heard that forecasting techniques can be unreliable. He has therefore decided to compute the moving average for the previous 10 months sales data and then see how accurate the moving-average method was in predicting sales during that period.

Having studied the output in Figure 6.5, Fred is not very impressed with the moving-average method as a way of forecasting future sales. It appears only to be effective for planning one month (or period) ahead. While he can see the benefits of having a long-term trend, his impression is that the moving-average method generally tends to underestimate sales on a month-by-month basis. Fred has decided to use a larger moving average of nine months to see if there is any change to the trend. A nine-month moving average produced values of 482, 524, and 576 for October, November, and December, reinforcing Fred's view that the moving-average approach is too simplistic to provide a worthwhile forecast. These values are easily found by using Excel's AVERAGE function, e.g., referring to cell values in Fig. 6.5, AVERAGE(C4:C12) = 482, AVERAGE(C5:C13) = 524, etc.

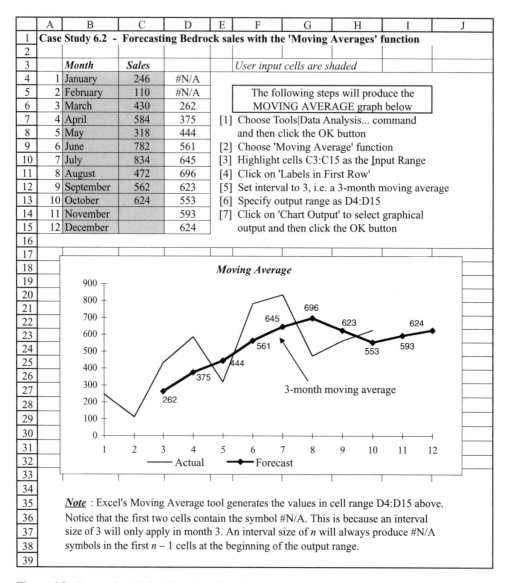

Figure 6.5   Forecasting Bedrock's sales with a 3-month moving average.

Fitting a Trendline to Bedrock's Sales Data

Fred Flint has decided to see if there is a long-term trend to sales of product P. His first task is to collect all the available sales data relating to product P, which comes to almost four years in total. To simplify his model, Fred has grouped the monthly data into fifteen quarterly figures. Having entered his data into the spreadsheet of Figure 6.6 (see range D4:E18), he then uses Chart Wizard to produce the graph as shown.

	A	B	C	D	E	F	G	H
1	**Case Study 6.2 - Fitting a trendline through Bedrock's seasonal variations**							
2								
3			*Quarterly periods*		*Sales*			
4			200W - Q1	1	490			
5			Q2	2	370			
6			Q3	3	330			
7			Q4	4	610	*User input cells*		
8			200X - Q1	5	571	*are shaded*		
9			Q2	6	482			
10			Q3	7	557			
11			Q4	8	861			
12			200Y - Q1	9	895			
13			Q2	10	753			
14			Q3	11	1190			
15			Q4	12	1255			
16			200Z - Q1	13	786			
17			Q2	14	1684			
18			Q3	15	1868			
19								
20								

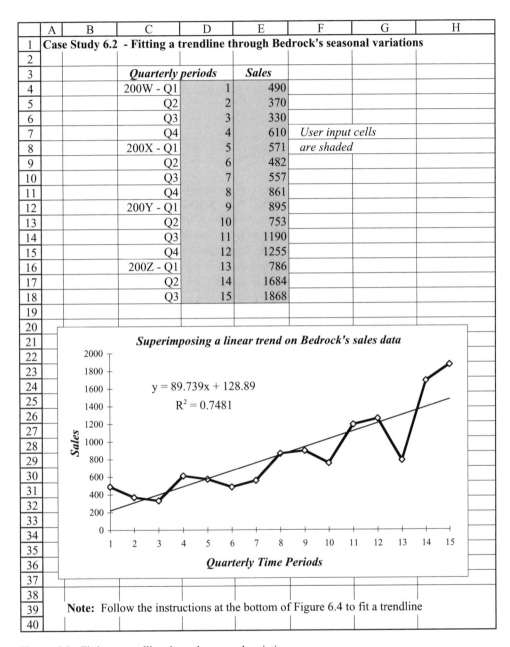

Superimposing a linear trend on Bedrock's sales data

$y = 89.739x + 128.89$

$R^2 = 0.7481$

Sales

Quarterly Time Periods

Note: Follow the instructions at the bottom of Figure 6.4 to fit a trendline

Figure 6.6   Fitting a trendline through seasonal variations.

To draw a trendline through the graph, Fred uses the same procedure as Sharon Smith – see Figure 6.4. Note that all mouse clicks are with the left-hand button unless otherwise stated. When the linear graph has been superimposed on product P's actual sales data, Fred Flint can see that the Bedrock Company can be optimistic about future sales. The trend line is in an upwards direction, indicating that sales, although 'up and down' in the short term, have been steadily increasing over the past four years.

FORECASTING – EXPONENTIAL SMOOTHING

Fred Flint has also discovered the importance of 'weighting data'. He has been told by marketing colleagues that old data is considered to be less important than recent data. In his moving-average model, Fred used unweighted data and he now knows that a more accurate forecast might have been obtained if he had assigned weighting factors to reflect the age of the data. While a weighted moving average does indeed provide more flexibility, it also complicates matters. For example, how does Fred decide what is a good weight for a particular item of data? This problem will be examined later.

There are limitations in using the moving-average approach for forecasting, as Fred Flint has discovered. The need to experiment both with the number of months (periods) and also with weighting factors, creates serious problems. Exponential smoothing is a short-term forecasting method that overcomes these difficulties by automatically weighting data, with recent data being weighted more heavily than old data. It is an adaptive approach in which the forecast for a given period is adjusted to take account of the error made in the preceding period. This process of adjustment is repeated until the errors are minimised. The general rule for exponential smoothing is

$$\text{new forecast} = \text{old forecast} + \alpha \ (\text{latest observation} - \text{old forecast})$$

where α (alpha) is the smoothing constant. This equation is written mathematically as

$$y_{t+1} = y_t + \alpha(y_o - y_t)$$

where y_t = old forecast; y_o = latest observation, i.e., actual value for time period t.

The value of α can lie between 0 and 1. The closer α is to 1, the more responsive the forecast is to recent observations. On the other hand, if α is close to 0, the forecast becomes more insensitive and will not reflect recent data. Fred has used the last 18 months of product P's data to examine these two extreme situations. Figure 6.7 shows how Excel's exponential smoothing function performs at the extremities when using α values of 0.1 and 0.9. Note that instead of the smoothing constant α, Excel's function uses a damping factor which is equal to $1 - \alpha$. Reasonable values for α are considered to be between 0.2 and 0.3.

Follow the instructions below to create the exponential smoothing model of Figure 6.7.

- Activate Excel's 'Analysis ToolPak' by choosing the Tools|Data Analysis command.

- Click on the 'Exponential Smoothing' option and then click the OK button. A table will appear on the screen. Fill in the following data, leaving other options blank. When all data has been entered, click the OK button to exit.

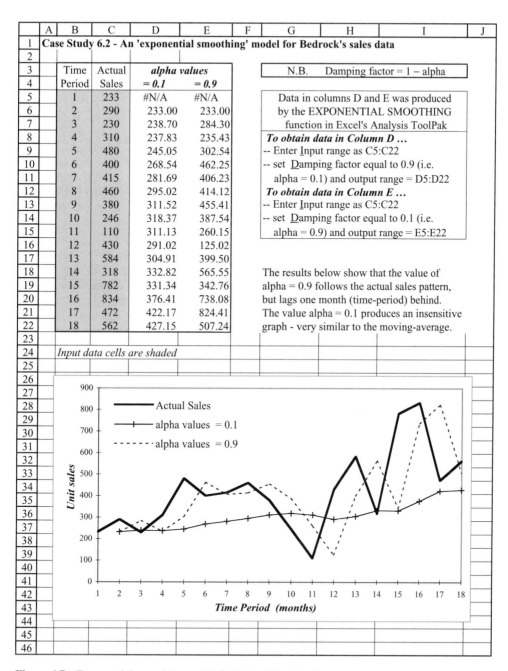

	A	B	C	D	E	F	G	H	I	J
1		Case Study 6.2 - An 'exponential smoothing' model for Bedrock's sales data								
2										
3		Time	Actual	*alpha values*			N.B.	Damping factor = 1 – alpha		
4		Period	Sales	*= 0.1*	*= 0.9*					
5		1	233	#N/A	#N/A		Data in columns D and E was produced			
6		2	290	233.00	233.00		by the EXPONENTIAL SMOOTHING			
7		3	230	238.70	284.30		function in Excel's Analysis ToolPak			
8		4	310	237.83	235.43		***To obtain data in Column D …***			
9		5	480	245.05	302.54		-- Enter Input range as C5:C22			
10		6	400	268.54	462.25		-- set Damping factor equal to 0.9 (i.e.			
11		7	415	281.69	406.23		alpha = 0.1) and output range = D5:D22			
12		8	460	295.02	414.12		***To obtain data in Column E …***			
13		9	380	311.52	455.41		-- Enter Input range as C5:C22			
14		10	246	318.37	387.54		-- set Damping factor equal to 0.1 (i.e.			
15		11	110	311.13	260.15		alpha = 0.9) and output range = E5:E22			
16		12	430	291.02	125.02					
17		13	584	304.91	399.50					
18		14	318	332.82	565.55		The results below show that the value of			
19		15	782	331.34	342.76		alpha = 0.9 follows the actual sales pattern,			
20		16	834	376.41	738.08		but lags one month (time-period) behind.			
21		17	472	422.17	824.41		The value alpha = 0.1 produces an insensitive			
22		18	562	427.15	507.24		graph - very similar to the moving-average.			
23										
24		*Input data cells are shaded*								

Figure 6.7 Exponential smoothing model for Bedrock's sales data.

Input   Input range: C5:C22
              Damping factor: 0.9   (A damping factor of 0.9 is the same as $\alpha = 0.1$)

Output   Output range: D5:D22

- Repeat the above step with the following input:

Input   Input range: C5:C22
              Damping factor: 0.1   (A damping factor of 0.1 is the same as $\alpha = 0.9$)

Output   Output range: E5:E22

- Select cell range C3:E22 and use it as input to Chart Wizard to produce the graph as shown.

Evaluating a Forecast's Accuracy Using MAD and MSE

The question of which forecasting technique will best fit Fred's data is really a matter of evaluating each forecast's accuracy. There are many methods available for modelling time-series data. The best approach to time-series analysis is therefore to try out several methods on past data and then compare the different results to see how accurate they were in predicting already-known answers. Two popular techniques for measuring forecast accuracy are the mean absolute deviation (MAD) which gives equal weight to each error, and the mean squared error (MSE) – as its name suggests – which squares the errors. The MSE approach is more practical than MAD because it puts more emphasis on large errors. To illustrate how MAD and MSE are obtained, consider Table 6.2 which uses a two-month moving average forecast.

Fred's colleagues in Bedrock's information systems department have told him that Excel's Solver can help him to find optimal weighting factors by minimising either the MAD or MSE values. In the moving-average technique, the number of weights depends upon the number of time intervals being used, e.g., a 3-month moving average requires 3 weighting factors.

Table 6.2

Period	Data X_i	Forecast F_i	Error, $E_i = X_i - F_i$	Absolute error $|E_i|$	Squared error E^2_i
June	17	#N/A			
July	16	#N/A			
August	22	16.5	5.5	5.5	30.3
September	14	19.0	−5.0	5.0	25.0
October	23	18.0	5.0	5.0	25.0
November	22	18.5	3.5	3.5	12.3
December	24	22.5	1.5	1.5	2.3

$\text{MAD} = \sum |E_i|/N = 20.5/5 = 4.1 \text{ for } i = 3, 7$ $\sum 20.5$ $\sum 94.9$

$\text{MSE} = \sum E^2_i/N = 94.9/5 = 19.0$

Because the exponential-smoothing method has only one weighting factor – the smoothing constant α (alpha) – Fred has decided to find an optimal value for α. Having familiarised himself with Excel's Solver, Fred has set up the Solver model of Figure 6.8. He is now able to find the value of α that minimises the mean squared error (MSE).

The non-linear programming (NLP) model is first solved to find the optimal α value of 0.422 (damping-factor = 0.578). The standard formula for exponential smoothing, i.e., $y_{t+1} = y_t + \alpha(y_o - y_t)$, is used to obtain the values in cells D5:D22 of Figure 6.8. For comparison purposes, the model also shows graphs for (i) actual sales and (ii) results using an α value of 0.9 (see cells E5:E22). As usual, the graph was produced using Chart Wizard with the cell range C3:E22 being used as input.

Excel's GROWTH Function

Exponential smoothing should be used in situations where there is no obvious trend. If the data shows a dramatic upward (or downward) trend, then the relationship is probably exponential, in which case Excel's GROWTH function can be used. An example of the GROWTH function is now given.

EXAMPLE 6.3 *Using Excel's GROWTH function*

The huge popularity of the new version of the Gizmo Company's main product has caused serious production problems. Since its launch six months ago, monthly sales figures (in '000s) are 200, 360, 558, 925, 1430, and 2100. The company wants to plan production runs in order to meet future demand and has decided to use Excel's GROWTH function to help find sales forecasts for the next three months. The company will verify these results by first plotting a scattergraph and then fitting an exponential trendline through the points. The resulting exponential equation will be used to obtain a second set of forecast figures.

Figure 6.9 shows that the GROWTH function found sales forecasts (in '000s) of 3577, 5715, and 9131 for the next three months (see cells C10:C12). The exponential equation gives almost identical forecasts of 3578, 5716, and 9133 which is hardly surprising since GROWTH also fits an exponential curve to user data. The exponential equation was obtained as follows (all mouse clicks are with the left-hand button unless otherwise stated).

- Place the mouse-pointer on one of the points in the scattergraph and then click the mouse's right-hand button to activate the shortcut menu.
- Choose the 'Add Trendline . . . ' option from the menu.
- Click the 'Type' tab and then click on the 'Exponential' option.
- Click the 'Options' tab and select (i) Display equation on Chart (ii) Display R-squared value on chart.
- Finally, click the OK button to return to the scattergraph.

	A	B	C	D	E	F	G	H	I	J	K
1	Case Study 6.2 - Fred Flint finds the optimal value for *alpha* (α)!										
2											
3		Time	Actual	*alpha values*			This is a nonlinear (NLP) problem because				
4		Period	Sales	*0.422*	*0.9*		MSE represents a nonlinear objective function				
5		1	233	#N/A	#N/A						
6		2	290	233.00	233.00						
7		3	230	257.06	284.30		Solver parameters				
8		4	310	245.64	235.43		Set Target Cell:	D25			
9		5	480	272.80	302.54		Equal to:	Min			
10		6	400	360.25	462.25		By Changing Cells:	J23			
11		7	415	377.02	406.23		Subject to Constraints:	J23 <= 1			
12		8	460	393.05	414.12			J23 >= 0			
13		9	380	421.31	455.41						
14		10	246	403.87	387.54		Cell	Formula		Copied to	
15		11	110	337.24	260.15		D6	$C5		E6	
16		12	430	241.34	125.02		D7	J$23*C6 + (1− J$23)*D6		D8:D22	
17		13	584	320.96	399.50		E7	E$4*E6 + (1 − E$4)*E6		E8:E22	
18		14	318	431.97	565.55		D23	SUMXMY2(C6:C22,D6:D22)			
19		15	782	383.87	342.76		D25	D23/COUNT(D6:D22)			
20		16	834	551.90	738.08		J24	1 − J23			
21		17	472	670.96	824.41						
22		18	562	586.99	507.24						
23		$(C_i − D_i)^2 =$		532898					*alpha =* α =	*0.422*	
24									Damping factor =	0.578	
25				31346.9	= Objective: Minimise MSE values						

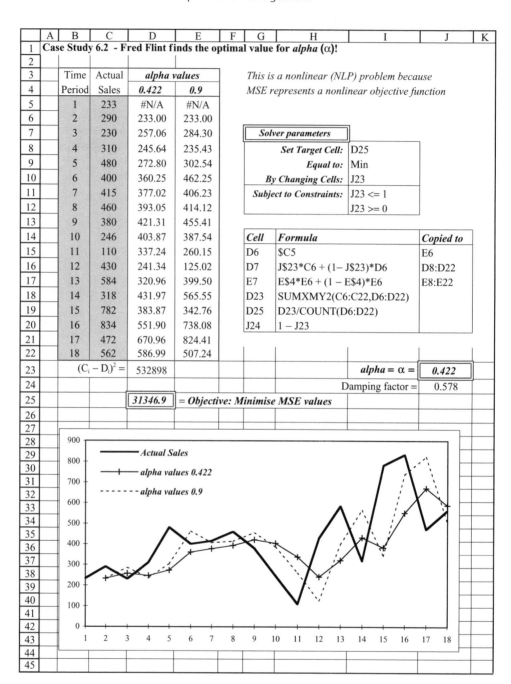

Figure 6.8   Using Solver to find an optimal α value for exponential smoothing.

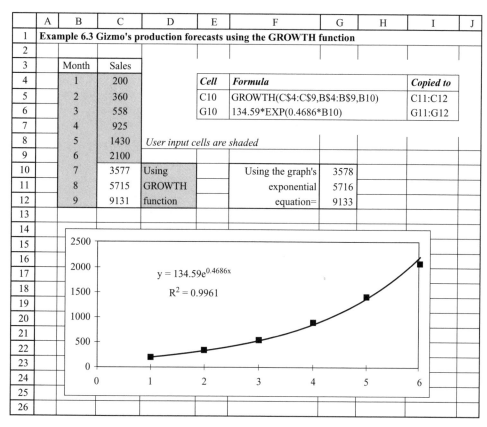

	A	B	C	D	E	F	G	H	I	J
1	**Example 6.3 Gizmo's production forecasts using the GROWTH function**									
2										
3		Month	Sales							
4		1	200		*Cell*	*Formula*			*Copied to*	
5		2	360		C10	GROWTH(C$4:C$9,B$4:B$9,B10)			C11:C12	
6		3	558		G10	134.59*EXP(0.4686*B10)			G11:G12	
7		4	925							
8		5	1430		*User input cells are shaded*					
9		6	2100							
10		7	3577	Using		Using the graph's	3578			
11		8	5715	GROWTH		exponential	5716			
12		9	9131	function		equation=	9133			
13										

Figure 6.9   Sales forecasting with Excel's GROWTH function.

EXAMPLE 6.4   *A model for the Holt-Winters' exponential smoothing method*

Fred Flint has recently come across a forecasting technique known as the Holt-Winters' exponential smoothing method. Being in charge of inventory at the Bedrock Company, Fred is very interested in this method as it is often used to forecast a company's inventory. In order to work properly, the Holt-Winters' model requires a minimum of three years data that must be either monthly or quarterly. The model also utilises three smoothing constants, α (alpha), β (beta) and γ (gamma) which can all vary between 0 and 1.

The Holt-Winters' method is based on four equations that compute, for time period t, (i) the expected level of the time series, L_t, (ii) a trend factor, T_t, (iii) a seasonality component, S_t, and (iv) the forecasting function, F_t. The four equations are:

$$L_t = \alpha(Y_t/S_{t-p}) + (1 - \alpha)(L_{t-1} + T_{t-1})$$
$$T_t = \beta(L_t - L_{t-1}) + (1 - \beta)T_{t-1}$$

$$S_t = \gamma(Y_t/L_t) + (1 - \gamma)S_{t-p}$$

$$F_{t+n} = (L_t + nT_t)S_{t+n-p}$$

where: $F_{t+n} =$ forecast for time period $(t + n)$
$Y_t =$ observation (sales data) for time period t
$p = 4$ or 12 (for quarterly or monthly data)
$n = 1, 2, 3, \ldots, p$

Fred Flint has decided to use the quarterly data of Figure 6.6 as input to the Holt-Winters' model, i.e., $p = 4$. Due to the time lag in the expected level (L_t) and seasonality (S_t) equations above, initial estimates for S_{t-p} will be required, i.e., either four or twelve S_t values depending on whether data is quarterly or monthly. Since the model of Figure 6.10 uses quarterly data, the first S_t equation will start in time period 5, i.e., $S_5 = \gamma(Y_5/L_5) + (1 - \gamma)S_1$.

Initial estimates for the smoothing constants are taken as $\alpha = 0.3$, $\beta = 0.4$, and $\gamma = 0.5$. However, Excel's Solver will be used later to find more feasible α, β, and γ values. Fred now has to compute initial seasonality S_t values as well as trend and level estimates T_0 and L_0 (see dashed rectangle in Figure 6.10). The following formulae are used to find Fred's estimates:

$$S_t = Y_{Wt}/\text{Average(200W sales)}$$

$$T_0 = (\text{Average (200X sales)} - \text{Average(200W sales)})/p$$

$$L_0 = Y_{Wt}/S_t$$

where: $Y_{Wt} =$ sales data for year 200W, in time period $t(t = 1, 2, 3, \ldots p)$

Table 6.3   Holt-Winters' model – worksheet formulae and Solver parameters.

Cell	Formula	Copied to
E11	D11/AVERAGE(D$11:D$14)	E12:E14
F14	(AVERAGE(D15:D18) – AVERAGE(D11:D14))/4	
G14	D14/E14	
G15	D$5*D15/E11 + (1−D$5)*(G14 + F14)	G16:G26
E15	D$7*D15/G15 + (1−D$7)*E11	E16:E26
F15	D$6*(G15-G14) + (1−D$6)*F14	F16:F26
H15	(G14 + F14)*E11	H16:H26
H28	SUMXMY2(D15:D26,H15:H26)/COUNT(H15:H26)	

Solver parameters		
Set target cell:	H28	
Equal to:	Min	
By changing cells:	D5:D7	
Subject to constraints:	D5:D7 $\geq$ 0	= smoothing constants must be ≥ 0
	D5:D7 $\leq$ 1	= smoothing constants must be ≤ 1

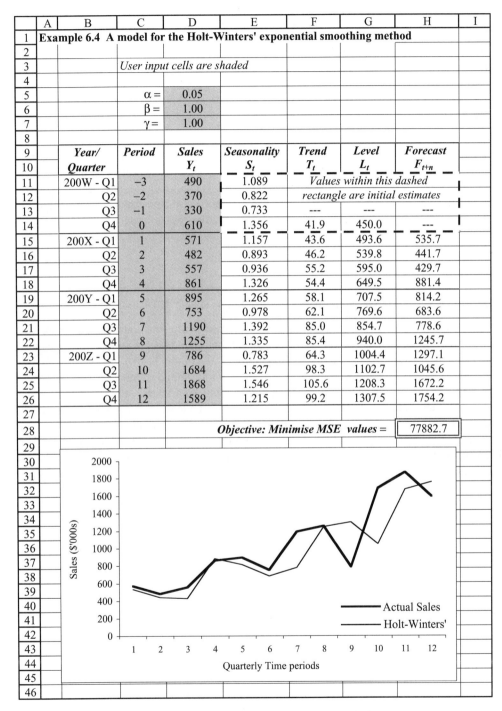

	A	B	C	D	E	F	G	H	I
1		**Example 6.4 A model for the Holt-Winters' exponential smoothing method**							
2									
3			*User input cells are shaded*						
4									
5			α =	0.05					
6			β =	1.00					
7			γ =	1.00					
8									
9		*Year/*	*Period*	*Sales*	*Seasonality*	*Trend*	*Level*	*Forecast*	
10		*Quarter*		Y_t	S_t	T_t	L_t	F_{t+n}	
11		200W - Q1	−3	490	1.089	*Values within this dashed*			
12		Q2	−2	370	0.822	*rectangle are initial estimates*			
13		Q3	−1	330	0.733	---	---	---	
14		Q4	0	610	1.356	41.9	450.0	---	
15		200X - Q1	1	571	1.157	43.6	493.6	535.7	
16		Q2	2	482	0.893	46.2	539.8	441.7	
17		Q3	3	557	0.936	55.2	595.0	429.7	
18		Q4	4	861	1.326	54.4	649.5	881.4	
19		200Y - Q1	5	895	1.265	58.1	707.5	814.2	
20		Q2	6	753	0.978	62.1	769.6	683.6	
21		Q3	7	1190	1.392	85.0	854.7	778.6	
22		Q4	8	1255	1.335	85.4	940.0	1245.7	
23		200Z - Q1	9	786	0.783	64.3	1004.4	1297.1	
24		Q2	10	1684	1.527	98.3	1102.7	1045.6	
25		Q3	11	1868	1.546	105.6	1208.3	1672.2	
26		Q4	12	1589	1.215	99.2	1307.5	1754.2	
27									
28					*Objective: Minimise MSE values =*			77882.7	

Figure 6.10   A model for the Holt-Winters' exponential smoothing method.

Excel's Solver is used to minimise the mean squared error (MSE) – similar to the model of Figure 6.8. Solver has found smoothing constant values of $\alpha = 0.05$, $\beta = 1.0$, and $\gamma = 1.0$. The worksheet formulae and Solver parameters for the Holt-Winters' model of Figure 6.10 are given in Table 6.3.

SALESFORCE MODELS

The salesforce represents a large investment for most companies, especially in the manufacturing industry. In many instances, salesforce expenditure is the highest of all the marketing functions. The size of a salesforce is a major contributing factor to this large expenditure. Many companies face problems in deciding how many temporary staff to employ when promoting new products, or trying to meet seasonal sales increases. The following salesforce sizing model focuses on the importance of integer programming when the model's variables happen to be people.

EXAMPLE 6.5 *Salesforce sizing – a non-linear programming (NLP) model*

Bob's Builders Providers requires trained sales staff to market its construction equipment. Sales tend to be seasonal. Bob estimates that the minimum numbers of salespeople, as shown in Table 6.4, are required for the first eight months of the coming year.

After hiring salespeople, Bob first sends them on a four-month training course. Following training, the salespeople begin active selling. Each month, some sales staff (10% approx.) find the job too demanding and quit. Bob wants to determine the least number of new trainees that have to be hired over the next four months, while still maintaining the minimum salesforce requirements as indicated in Table 6.4. At the beginning of January, the salesforce consists of 50 sales staff and 90 trainees (30 trainees will begin active selling on 1st March and the rest will start on 1st April). Build an integer programming model and then use Excel's Solver to solve Bob's problem.

Table 6.4

Month	Minimum no. of salespeople required
Jan	30
Feb	20
Mar	40
Apr	90
May	110
Jun	120
Jul	120
Aug	100

Step 1: Derive mathematical expressions for each month

Redefine the problem, remembering that there cannot be any fractions of people, i.e., only whole numbers are acceptable! Since Excel's integer function INT always rounds down, the mathematical function ROUNDUP will be used instead. Determine the number of staff available for each month as follows:

January	= 50 salespeople		
February	= 90% of (January total) salespeople		
March	= 90% of (February total)	+ 30 finished trainees	
April	= 90% of (March total)	+ 60 finished trainees	
May	= 90% of (April total)	+ x_1	
June	= 90% of (May total)	+ x_2	where x_1, x_2, x_3, x_4 are the
July	= 90% of (June total)	+ x_3	number of new trainees hired
August	= 90% of (July total)	+ x_4	for May, June, July and August

The above calculations are contained in cells D6:D12 of Figure 6.11. The model has found that 31 new trainees are required to meet minimum staff requirements. To allow for the four-month training course, 20 new trainees should be hired to start training on 1st February so they will be available as active sales staff in June. Similarly, 11 new trainees should be hired to start training on 1st March to eliminate the July deficit.

EXAMPLE 6.6 *Salesforce allocation model*

The KleenUp Company has divided the Upper State region into three sales areas, namely A, B and C. Sharon Smith, who is sales manager for the region, has observed that area sales depend upon the amount of time spent by salespeople in each area. She has determined that area sales figures (in £'000s) can be estimated from the following three equations:

$$\text{Area A} \quad S_A = 2 \log_e(T_A + 1)$$

$$\text{Area B} \quad S_B = 3 \log_e(T_B + 2)$$

$$\text{Area C} \quad S_C = 4 \log_e(T_C + 2)$$

where S_A, S_B, and S_C are the monthly sales (£'000s) achieved in each area and T_A, T_B, and T_C are the times spent by sales personnel in each area, expressed in days.

   The salesforce in Upper State consists of seven people who normally spend up to four days each week visiting customers. The salesforce consists of two grade G1 employees with annual salaries of £24,000, three grade G2 with a salary of £21,000, and two grade G3 at £18,000. Areas B and C always have a grade G1 and a grade G2 staff member assigned to them while area A always has a grade G2. Sharon Smith is under pressure to reduce her sales budget by 10%, while maintaining sales as near to current levels as possible. She has decided to reduce the amount of time spent by the salesforce in each area while minimising the level of disruption to their work schedule.

	A	B	C	D	E	F	G	H
1		Example 6.5 - A salesforce sizing model for Bob's Builders Providers						
2								
3		*Month*	*Mininum*	*Actual*			*User input cells*	
4			*staff*	*staff*		*Trainees*	*are shaded*	
5		January	30	50		*available*		
6		February	20	45		0		
7		March	40	71		30		
8		April	90	124		60		
9		May	110	112		**0**	$=x_1$	
10		June	120	121		**20**	$=x_2$	
11		July	120	120		**11**	$=x_3$	
12		August	100	108		**0**	$=x_4$	
13								
14		*Objective: Minimise no. of new trainees =*				31		
15								
16								
17		*Solver parameters*						
18		*Set Target Cell:*	F14					
19		*Equal to:*	Min					
20		*By Changing Cells:*	F9:F12					
21		*Subject to Constraints:*	D5:D12 >= C5:C12		= Minimum staff requirements			
22			F9:F12 = int(eger)		= Answers must be integer			
23			F9:F12 >=0		= Answers must be positive			
24								
25		Cell	Formula		Copied to			
26		D6	ROUNDUP(0.9*D5,0) + F6		D7:D12			
27		F14	SUM(F9:F12)					
28								
29		This is an NLP model so switch off the 'Assume Linear Model' in the Options box						

Figure 6.11   Salesforce sizing model.

This problem involves both (i) non-linear programming (NLP) constraints as represented by the logarithmic equations for sales, and (ii) integer programming (IP) constraints as represented by the number of whole days spent in each area, i.e., T_A, T_B, and T_C.

Step 1: Find the current level of monthly sales
Current sales (£'000s) are found by restating the problem as a NLP exercise.

Let T_A, T_B, T_C = optimum no. of days spent by the salesforce in each area

Sharon Smith's objective is to maximise Z where $Z = S_A + S_B + S_C$ subject to the following three constraints:

$$T_A + T_B + T_C \leq 112 \qquad \text{(112 days per month = 7 people} \times \text{4 days} \times \text{4 weeks)}$$
$$T_A, T_B, T_C = \text{int(eger)} \qquad \text{(no. of days must be integer, i.e., a whole number)}$$
$$T_A, T_B, T_C \geq 0 \qquad \text{(no. of days must be positive)}$$

	A	B	C	D	E	F	G	H	I
1	**Example 6.6 - A salesforce allocation model with NLP constraints - Step 1**								
2									
3			*Area*	*Area sales*		Optimum			
4				*(£'000s)*		no. of days			
5			A	6.52		**25**	$=T_A$		
6			B	10.99		**37**	$=T_B$		
7			C	15.80		**50**	$=T_C$		
8						112			
9									
10		*Objective: Maximise regional sales (£'000s) =*				*33.31*			
11									
12									
13		**Solver parameters**							
14			*Set Target Cell:*	F10					
15			*Equal to:*	Max					
16			*By Changing Cells:*	F5:F7					
17			*Subject to Constraints:*	F5:F7 = int(eger)		= Answers must be integer			
18				F5:F7 >= 0		= Answers must be positive			
19				F8 <= 112		= Total no. of workforce days <= 112			
20									
21		*Cell*	*Formula*		*Copied to*				
22		D5	2*LN(F5 + 1)						
23		D6	3*LN(F6 + 2)						
24		D7	4*LN(F7 + 2)						
25		F8	SUM(F5:F7)						
26		F10	SUM(D5:D7)						
27									
28	Note: This is a non-linear (NLP) model so switch off the 'Assume Linear Model' parameter								

Figure 6.12   Salesforce allocation model – Step 1.

Using Excel's Solver, the non-linear programming (NLP) model of Figure 6.11 finds an optimum sales figure of £33,310 for the Upper State region with the salesforce spending 25, 37 and 50 days in areas A, B and C respectively.

Step 2: Introduce staff costing constraints for each area
The Upper State sales budget is tied up totally in salesforce salaries. The monthly salary bill can be expressed in £s per month as follows:

$$2 \text{ grade G1 staff} = 2 \times £24,000 = £48,000 \text{ pa}$$
$$3 \text{ grade G2 staff} = 3 \times £21,000 = £63,000 \text{ pa}$$
$$2 \text{ grade G3 staff} = 2 \times £18,000 = £36,000 \text{ pa}$$

$$\text{Total salary costs} = £147,700$$
$$= £12,250 \text{ per month}$$

Sharon Smith must therefore achieve savings of 10% of £12,250, i.e., she must reduce the total monthly salary figure to £11,025. Given that sales staff work a 48-week year, the daily rate for each grade is

$$\text{Grade G1} = £24,000/(48 \times 4) = £125.00 \text{ per day}$$
$$\text{Grade G2} = £21,000/(48 \times 4) = £109.38 \text{ per day}$$
$$\text{Grade G3} = £18,000/(48 \times 4) = £93.75 \text{ per day}$$

The allocation of salesforce personnel is shown in the following table:

Area	← Staff grade →		
	G1	G2	G3
A	–	1	(?)
B	1	1	(?)
C	1	1	(?)

The allocation of the two grade G3 employees depends on where they are most needed.

The number of days spent by staff in each area, i.e., T_A, T_B, T_C, must now be expressed in financial terms. If the current values of T_A, T_B, T_C are taken as an example, then area costs are calculated as follows:

Area	T_i		G1		G2		G3		Total
A	25	=			16		9		
					£1750	+	£843.75	=	£2593.75
B	37	=	16		16		5		
			£2000	+	£1750	+	£468.75	=	£4218.75
C	50	=	16		16		18		
			£2000	+	£1750	+	£1687.50	=	£5437.50

The 'area cost' formulae of Step 2 are contained in cells G5:G7 of the modified salesforce model (Figure 6.13). The revised answer shown in this new salesforce model indicates that monthly sales of £32,230 can be achieved using only 99 workforce days, compared to the original figures of £33,310 requiring 112 days. The monthly salary costs have been reduced from £12,250 to £10,984 – a saving of £1,266 per month. The lost sales revenue of £1,080 per month is compensated by this salary reduction. However, the major benefit is the availability of 13 free days that will allow sales personnel to be allocated to other areas, with the potential of achieving higher sales figures.

GOAL PROGRAMMING

Linear programming (LP) can handle only one objective or goal, as defined by the objective function Z. However, many business problems involve several goals which usually conflict with each other, e.g., maximise profits while minimising costs. This limitation is overcome by using goal programming (GP) – sometimes referred to as multiple objective linear programming (MOLP) – which can solve multiple-goal problems. Goal programming requires that goals are

	A	B	C	D	E	F	G	H	I	J	K
1	Example 6.6 - A salesforce model with cost constrains - Step 2										
2											
3		*Staff*	*Pay rate*		*Area*	*Area sales*	*Area*			Optimum	
4		*grade*	*per day*			*(£'000s)*	*Costs*			no. of days	
5		G1	£125.00		A	6.36	£2,406.25		$T_A =$	23	
6		G2	£109.38		B	10.30	£3,421.88		$T_B =$	29	
7		G3	£93.75		C	15.57	£5,156.25		$T_C =$	47	
8						Totals =	£10,984			99	
9		Budgetary constraints (i.e., new salary costs) =					£11,025				
10											
11											
12				*Objective: Maximise regional sales (£'000s) =*				32.23			
13											

	Solver parameters	
Set Target Cell:	H12	
Equal to:	Max	
By Changing Cells:	J5:J7	
Subject to Constraints:	J5:J7 = int(eger)	= Answers must be integer
	J5:J7 >= 0	= Answers must be positive
	J8 <= 112	= Total no. of workforce days <= 112
	G8 <= G9	= New salary costs <= £11,025

Cell	Formula	Copied to
F5	2*LN(J5 + 1)	
F6	3*LN(J6 + 2)	
F7	4*LN(J7 + 2)	
G5	IF(J5<=16, J5*C6, 16*C6 + (J5–16)*C7)	
G6	IF(J6<=16, J6*C$5,IF(J6<=32, 16*C$5 = *(formula continued on next line)*	
	(J6–16)*C$6, 16*(C$5+C$6) + (J6–32)*C$7))	G7
G8	SUM(G5:G7)	
H12	SUM(F5:F7)	

Figure 6.13 Allocating staff costs in the salesforce model – Step 2.

ranked in order of priority. GP constraints are very similar to LP constraints with one major exception – GP goal constraints are flexible, whereas LP resource constraints are fixed. Goal constraint targets have to be flexible because they are competing against each other, with the most important goal being achieved at the expense of less important goals.

Target values, t_i, representing the right-hand side of goal constraint equations, are estimated or expected targets set by the decision-maker. Goal constraints must exist for every goal in a GP problem. Likewise, if the problem contains any LP resource constraints, then there must also be corresponding resource equations. A goal constraint allows a decision-maker to determine how close a given solution comes to achieving that goal. GP introduces the concept of deviations, d_i, from the required targets t_i.

Deviations can be positive, d_{+i}, (i.e., the goal is overachieved) or negative d_{-i}, (the goal is underachieved). Goal programming then tries to minimise the deviations from the targets. Since target deviations usually measure totally different things (e.g., a profit target of £10,000 is disproportionate to a product target of 50 units), a modification must be made. A proportional deviation, d_i/t_i, is introduced whereby deviations are divided by their target values, t_i, ($t_i > 0$). The proportional deviation thus establishes the correct proportionality for each deviation value. Consider the following example.

EXAMPLE 6.7   *Advertising – a media selection model using goal programming*

The Gizmo Company is introducing a new product and plans to mount an advertising campaign both on television and in magazines. However, the two media are not equally effective in reaching potential (high-income) buyers. The company plans to spend a maximum of £200,000 on promoting the new product. Table 6.5 gives the advertising costs and potential audiences (in thousands) for every £1000 spent in each advertising medium.

The Gizmo Company has prioritised its three goals as follows:

1. Reach an audience of at least 3 million.

2. Spend around 40% of the advertising budget on magazines.

3. Reach a high-income audience of approximately 500,000.

Step 1: Check if all of the goals can be met simultaneously
Step 1 is achieved by restating the problem as a linear programming (LP) exercise.

Let x_1, x_2 = the total amounts spent (in £'000s) on TV, magazines respectively

Because the Gizmo Company wants to achieve three goals or objectives, its situation differs from the normal LP problem which has only one objective to meet. However, it is reasonable to focus on the highest-priority goal and try to meet it first. The objective then is to maximise total audience, i.e., to maximise the objective function, Z, where $Z = 20x_1 + 7x_2$ subject to the following three constraints:

$$x_2 \geq 0.4^*200 \quad \text{(Goal 2: magazine expenditure constraint)}$$
$$2x_1 + 3x_2 \geq 500,000 \quad \text{(Goal 3: high-income audience constraint)}$$
$$x_1 + x_2 \leq 200 \quad \text{(Total advertising budget constraint)}$$

Apply Excel's Solver to the model of Figure 6.14, switching on the 'Assume Linear Model' parameter in the Solver Options dialog box. A message will then be displayed on the screen

Table 6.5   Potential audience ('000s) per £1000 expenditure.

	TV	Magazines
Total audience	20	7
High-income audience	2	3

	A	B	C	D	E	F	G	H
1	**Example 6.7 - A media selection model - with GP constraints - Step 1**							
2								
3			Advertising budget (£'000s) =		£200		*All user input cells*	
4							*are shaded*	
5				*Television*	*Magazines*			
6				(audience in '000s)				
7			Total audience	20	7			
8			High-income audience	2	3			
9						Total amount		
10			Amounts spent, x_1, x_2 =	**£120**	**£80**	£200		
11								
12			*Objective: Maximise total audience (in '000s) =*			**2960**		
13								
14		**Goal achievements**		**Target**	**Actual**			
15		[1]	Total audience	3000	2960	Goal not achieved		
16		[2]	Magazine budget	£80	£80	OK		
17		[3]	High-income audience	500	480	Goal not achieved		
18								
19								
20			**Solver Parameters**					
21			**Set Target Cell:**	F12				
22			**Equal to:**	Max				
23			**By Changing Cells:**	D10:E10				
24			**Subject to Constraints:**	F10 = E3		= Advertising budget constraint		
25				E16 >= D16		= Magazine expenditure constraint		
26				E17 >= D17		= High-income audience constraint		
27				D10:E10 >= 0		= Answers must be positive		
28								
29		**Cell**	**Formula**				**Copied to**	
30		F10	SUM(D10:E10)					
31		F12	SUMPRODUCT(D7:E7,D10:E10)					
32		E15	F12					
33		E16	E10					
34		D16	0.4*E3					
35		F15	IF(D15<=E15,"OK","Goal not achieved")				F16:F17	
36		E17	SUMPRODUCT(D8:E8,D10:E10)					
37								

Figure 6.14 Media selection model – Step 1.

stating that 'Solver could not find a feasible solution'. This message appears because only the second goal has in fact been met. When the 'goal achievement' results are examined in the model (cells D15:E17), it can be seen that goals 1 and 3 have not been achieved. If the constraints could be ignored then it should be obvious that (i) investing all advertising funds in TV would produce a total audience of 4 million, while (ii) a total investment in magazines would give a high-income audience figure of 600,000.

Step 2: Introduce goal programming (GP) with prioritised goals

Returning to the Gizmo Company's priorities, deviations are now assigned as shown below:

1. Reach an audience of at least 3 million   (with deviations $= d_{-1}, d_{+1}$)

2. Spend around 40% of the advertising budget on magazines   (with deviations $= d_{-2}, d_{+2}$)

3. Reach a high-income audience of 500,000 approximately   (with deviations $= d_{-3}, d_{+3}$)

Formulate the problem as a GP problem as follows:

Let $x_1, x_2, =$ the optimum amounts (£'000s) spent on TV and magazines respectively.

The GP objective is to minimise the sum of the proportional deviations, i.e., minimise the objective function, Z, where

$$Z = \sum_{i=1}^{3} (d_{-i} + d_{+i})/t_i$$

subject to the following six constraints:

1. $20x_1 + 7x_2 + d_{-1} - d_{+1} \geq 3000$ (Goal 1 constraint with $t_1 = 3000$)

2. $x_2 + d_{-2} - d_{+2} \geq 0.4{*}200$ (Goal 2 constraint with $t_2 = 0.4{*}200 = 80$)

3. $2x_1 + 3x_2 + d_{-3} - d_{+3} \geq 500$ (Goal 3 constraint with $t_3 = 500$)

4. $x_1 + x_2 = 200$ (Advertising budget (LP resource) constraint)

5. All variables ≥ 0 (i.e., all x_i, d_i must be positive)

6. $d_{-1} = 0.0$ (Ensure that goal 1 is not underachieved.)

The above GP problem has been converted into the spreadsheet model of Figure 6.15. While the first ten lines of the GP model are the same as in Figure 6.14, the following additions are necessary to create Figure 6.15.

- A new block representing the (d_{-i}, d_{+i}) goal deviations is added, showing the amount by which each goal is underachieved (cells D15:D17) or overachieved (cells E15:E17). These cells are designated as extra changing cells whose values will be calculated by Excel's Solver. They are added to the initial changing cells D10:E10, which will contain optimal values for x_1 and x_2.

- The '(d_{-i}, d_{+i}) deviations' block is used to obtain proportional deviations, by dividing each set of (d_{-i}, d_{+i}) goal deviations by their corresponding target value, t_i. For example, Goal 1 (total audience) deviations in cells D15 and E15 are divided by the goal's target value of 3000 which is contained in cell G15. The same procedure applies to the other two goals. This new 'proportional deviations' block is shown as percentages in cells B20:E23.

- To ensure that the highest-priority goal (i.e., reach an audience of at least 3 million) is achieved, an extra constraint is added. This extra constraint sets the underachieving deviation, d_{-1}, to zero, i.e., the calculated target value cannot be less than 3 million.

- The GP model's objective is to minimise the sum of the proportional deviations, i.e., to minimise the sum of all values in cells D21:E23.

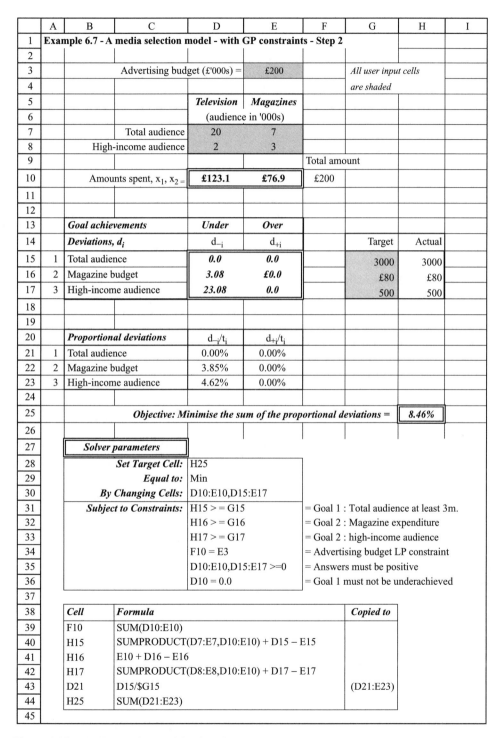

	A	B	C	D	E	F	G	H	I
1	**Example 6.7 - A media selection model - with GP constraints - Step 2**								
2									
3			Advertising budget (£'000s) =		£200		*All user input cells*		
4							*are shaded*		
5				*Television*	*Magazines*				
6				(audience in '000s)					
7			Total audience	20	7				
8			High-income audience	2	3				
9						Total amount			
10			Amounts spent, x_1, x_2 =	**£123.1**	**£76.9**	£200			
11									
12									
13		*Goal achievements*		*Under*	*Over*				
14		*Deviations, d_i*		d_{-i}	d_{+i}		Target	Actual	
15	1	Total audience		*0.0*	*0.0*		3000	3000	
16	2	Magazine budget		*3.08*	*£0.0*		£80	£80	
17	3	High-income audience		*23.08*	*0.0*		500	500	
18									
19									
20		*Proportional deviations*		d_{-i}/t_i	d_{+i}/t_i				
21	1	Total audience		0.00%	0.00%				
22	2	Magazine budget		3.85%	0.00%				
23	3	High-income audience		4.62%	0.00%				
24									
25			*Objective: Minimise the sum of the proportional deviations* =					8.46%	
26									
27		Solver parameters							
28			*Set Target Cell:*	H25					
29			*Equal to:*	Min					
30			*By Changing Cells:*	D10:E10,D15:E17					
31			*Subject to Constraints:*	H15 > = G15		= Goal 1 : Total audience at least 3m.			
32				H16 > = G16		= Goal 2 : Magazine expenditure			
33				H17 > = G17		= Goal 2 : high-income audience			
34				F10 = E3		= Advertising budget LP constraint			
35				D10:E10,D15:E17 >=0		= Answers must be positive			
36				D10 = 0.0		= Goal 1 must not be underachieved			
37									
38		*Cell*	*Formula*				*Copied to*		
39		F10	SUM(D10:E10)						
40		H15	SUMPRODUCT(D7:E7,D10:E10) + D15 – E15						
41		H16	E10 + D16 – E16						
42		H17	SUMPRODUCT(D8:E8,D10:E10) + D17 – E17						
43		D21	D15/$G15				(D21:E23)		
44		H25	SUM(D21:E23)						
45									

Figure 6.15   Media selection model – Step 2.

Since the GP model of Figure 6.15 is linear, the user should switch on the 'Assume Linear Model' parameter in the Solver Options dialog box. The answers show that £123,100 must be spent on television and £76,900 on magazines in order to meet goal 1. The Gizmo Company's second and third goals are underachieved by 3.85% (cell D22) and 4.62% (cell D23) respectively. The actual amounts are shown in cells D16 and D17, i.e., £3,080 and 23,080. Both these shortfalls are relatively small and should be accepted by the company. However, the Company may choose to add another constraint – as in the sixth constraint above – to see if another goal can be achieved.

EXAMPLE 6.8 *Product pricing model*

Few marketing decisions have more critical consequences than those associated with product pricing. Setting and adapting prices in a competitive market-place is a classical semi-structured situation involving both quantitative modelling and intuitive skills. Consider the following example.

Bill Brown is the owner of Bill's Barbecues, which manufactures barbecues. Bill has recently introduced a new barbecue model – marketed as Hotplate – to complement his popular BBQ model. Unit production costs are as shown in Table 6.6.

Bill initially employed a firm of marketing research consultants to test the strength of consumer demand for his new product. Having examined Bill's past sales records and manufacturing costs, the consultants have recommended maximum unit prices of £180 and £220 for the BBQ and HotPlate models respectively . They have also provided Bill with the following two price-demand equations:

BBQ model $\text{Demand}_{BBQ} = 325 - 1.45P_1$ where P_1 = price of BBQ model
Hotplate model $\text{Demand}_{HP} = 290 - 1.15P_2$ P_2 = price of Hotplate model

Bill's staff are paid at a rate of £5 per hour and he has a total of 850 labour hours available. His limited storage space restricts him to a maximum of 130 barbecue units at any time. Bill wants to know how many of each type he should manufacture every month and what price he should charge for each product in order to maximise his profits.

First of all, restate the problem as a nonlinear programming (NLP) exercise.

Let x_1, x_2 = optimum demands for BBQ, HotPlate barbecues respectively

Bill Brown's objective is to maximise profits Z where unit profits are found by subtracting unit production costs of £110 (for BBQ) and £140 (for HotPlate) from unit prices P_1 and P_2, i.e.,

$$\text{Maximise } Z = (P_1 - 110)x_1 + (P_2 - 140)x_2$$

Table 6.6 Unit production costs.

	Materials	Labour	Overheads
BBQ model	£60	£30	£20
HotPlate model	£75	£40	£25

	A	B	C	D	E	F	G	H	I	J
1	Example 6.8 - A product pricing model for Bill's Barbecues									
2										
3					*BBQ*	*Hotplate*				
4					*model*	*model*		*Input data cells*		
5			Maximum unit price =		£180	£220		*are shaded*		
6			Unit production costs =		£110.00	£140.00				
7			Unit profit =		£67.91	£65.22		*Constraints*		
8			Unit prices P_1, P_2 =		*£177.91*	*£205.22*		Used	Available	
9								121	130	
10			Demands x_1, x_2 =		67	54		834	850	
11										
12			*Objective: Maximise profits =*			*£8,072*				
13										
14										
15			*Solver parameters*							
16			*Set Target Cell:*		F12					
17			*Equal to:*		Max					
18			*By Changing Cells:*		E8:F8					
19			*Subject to Constraints:*		E7:F7 >= 0		= Profits must be positive			
20					E8:F8 <= E5:F5		= Maximum unit prices			
21					H9:H10 <= I9:I10		= Storage/Labour constraints			
22										
23		Cell	Formula				Copied to			
24		E7	E8 – E6				F7			
25		E10	INT(325 – 1.45*E8)							
26		F10	INT(290 – 1.15*F8)							
27		H9	E10 + F10							
28		H10	6*E10 + 8*F10							
29		F12	E7*E10 + F7*F10							
30										
31	Remember to switch off the 'Assume Linear Model' parameter in the Solver dialog box									

Figure 6.16 Product pricing model with NLP variables.

subject to the following five constraints:

1. $6x_1 + 8x_2 \leq 850$ (Labour resource constraint)

2. $x_1 + x_2 \leq 130$ (Storage space constraint)

3. $P_1, P_2 \leq 180, 220$ (Maximum unit prices)

4. $P_1 - 110 \geq 0$ (Profit on BBQ model must be positive)

5. $P_2 - 140 \geq 0$ (Profit on HotPlate model must be positive)

The pricing model of Figure 6.16 has found that Bill should sell 67 BBQ units at £177.91 each and 54 HotPlate units at £205.22 each to make a maximum monthly profit of £8,072.

Table 6.7

Selling price	Probability	Variable cost	Probability	Sales	Probability
£22	0.3	£18	0.4	40,000	0.25
£24	0.4	£20	0.4	45,000	0.50
£27	0.3	£22	0.2	50,000	0.25

EXAMPLE 6.9 *Simulating marketing conditions for a new product*

The MightyBig Corporation has decided to make a major capital investment in the introduction of a new product, ProtoC. There is usually a large amount of uncertainty associated with the development and marketing of any new product, e.g., the size of potential sales, the ideal selling price of the product, and the manufacturing costs. These uncertain factors are best represented by appropriate probability distributions, and the project's profitability can then be investigated using simulation. Such an approach is generally referred to as 'risk analysis'.

Maria Lopez has been asked by her company to perform a risk analysis on the marketing of the new product ProtoC. The capital investment required to market the product is £120,000. There are three main risk-analysis factors associated with the new product, namely selling price, variable cost, and annual sales volume. The probabilities for each factor are given in Table 6.7.

Maria has decided to simulate the marketing conditions using the Monte Carlo method. For demonstration purposes, the model of Figure 6.17 contains only 20 trial simulations. In reality, many hundreds of trials would be performed – press the recalculation F9 key to generate new trial values. Profits for product ProtoC are found from the equation

$$\text{Profit} = (\text{Price} - \text{Cost}) \times \text{Volume} - \text{Capital investment}$$

Table 6.8   Simulating a new product – worksheet formulae.

Cell	Formula	Copied to
C6	E6	
B7	C6	B8
C7	C6 + E7	C8
H6	J6	
G7	H6	G8
H7	H6 + J7	H8
C13	E13	
B14	C13	B15
C14	C13 + E14	C15
D19	VLOOKUP(RAND(),B$6:D$8, 3)	D20:D38
E19	VLOOKUP(RAND(),G$6:I$8, 3)	E20:E38
F19	VLOOKUP(RAND(),B$13:D$16, 3)	D20:D38
H19	0.001*((D19 − E19)*F19 − I$14)	H20:H38
H39	SUM(H19:H38)/COUNT(H19:H38)	

	A	B	C	D	E	F	G	H	I	J	K
1	**Example 6.9 - Simulating marketing conditions for a new product**										
2											
3		*Table 1: Product selling price*					*Table 2: Variable costs*				
4		<-- Limits -->					<-- Limits -->				
5		Lower	Upper	Price	P_i		Lower	Upper	Costs	P_i	
6		0	0.30	£22.00	0.30		0	0.40	£18.00	0.40	
7		0.30	0.70	£24.00	0.40		0.40	0.80	£20.00	0.40	
8		0.70	1.00	£27.00	0.30		0.80	1.00	£22.00	0.20	
9					1.00					1.00	
10											
11		*Table 3: Product sales*					*User input cells are shaded*				
12		Lower	Upper	Sales	P_i						
13		0	0.25	40,000	0.25		Capital				
14		0.25	0.75	45,000	0.50		Investment =		£120,000		
15		0.75	1.00	50,000	0.25						
16					1.00						
17											
18			Trial	Price	Cost	Volume	Profit (£'000s)				
19			1	£27	£20	40,000	£160				
20			2	£27	£18	45,000	£285				
21			3	£22	£18	50,000	£80				
22			4	£24	£22	45,000	−£30				
23			5	£22	£20	45,000	−£30				
24			6	£22	£20	50,000	−£20				
25			7	£24	£22	45,000	−£30				
26			8	£22	£20	45,000	−£30				
27			9	£24	£18	50,000	£180				
28			10	£22	£18	45,000	£60				
29			11	£27	£22	40,000	£80				
30			12	£27	£18	40,000	£240				
31			13	£22	£22	40,000	−£120				
32			14	£27	£18	45,000	£285				
33			15	£24	£22	45,000	−£30				
34			16	£27	£22	40,000	£80				
35			17	£22	£22	45,000	−£120				
36			18	£24	£18	50,000	£180				
37			19	£27	£18	50,000	£330				
38			20	£22	£18	45,000	£60				
39				*Average profit (£'000s) =*			£80.5				
40											

Figure 6.17   Simulating market conditions for a new product.

	A	B	C	D	E	F	G	H
1								
2		Product	No. in	Product		Year	Cash	
3		name	stock	price			flow	
4		Gizmo	10	£10.00		1	1	
5		Gadget	25	£12.50		2	4	
6		Widget	8	£20.00		3	4	
7		Sprocket	40	£4.50		4	16	
8						5		
9				*Sample Figure*				

Figure 6.18   Sample figure.

EXCEL FUNCTIONS USED IN MODEL-BUILDING

The following six Excel functions appear for the first time in this chapter and are explained below. The user should remember that a comprehensive on-line help facility is also provided by Excel.

1. CORREL: CORREL(array1, array2)

   returns the correlation coefficient between two sets of data array1 and array2.

   array1 = a cell range to be compared with a second cell range array2.

   Example: CORREL(F4:F7, G4:G7) in Figure 6.18 returns 0.973. Note that the closer the correlation coefficient is to -1 or $+1$ the stronger is the linear relationship. If there is no linear relationship, then the correlation coefficient is near to zero.

2. FORECAST: FORECAST(x-point, y-values, x-values)

   returns a predicted value for x-point, based on a linear regression of known (x, y) data stored in arrays or cell ranges.

   x-point   = the x-value point for which the predicted value is required.
   y-values = an array or range of known y-values used to derive the linear regression
                    equation.
   x-values = an array or range of known x-values used to derive the linear regression
                    equation.

   Example: FORECAST(F8, G4:G7, F4:F7) in Figure 6.18 returns 19.5 for the value in cell F8, i.e., year 5. The y-values are the cash flows and the x-values are the years.

3. GROWTH: GROWTH(y-values, x-values, new-x's, const)

fits an exponential curve to known (x, y) data and returns corresponding y-values along the curve for a new set of x-values specified by the user. Note that the function returns an error value if any of the y-values are zero or negative.

y-values	= an array of known y-values in the relationship $y = bm^x$.
x-values	= an array of known x-values in the relationship $y = bm^x$.
new-x's	= the new x-values – entered either as a single value or as an array for which GROWTH will return corresponding y-values.
const	= a logical value specifying whether to force the constant b in the equation $y = bm^x$ equal to 1. If const = TRUE or omitted, b is calculated normally. If const = FALSE, b is set equal to 1 and the m-values are adjusted so that $y = m^x$.

Example: GROWTH(G4:G7, F4:F7, F8) in Figure 6.18 returns 45.3 for the value in cell F8, i.e., year 5. The y-values are the cash flows and the x-values are the years.

4. INT: INT(number)

rounds *number* down to the nearest integer, i.e., whole number.

Examples: INT(17.8) = 17; INT(–8.9) = –9.

5. SQRT: SQRT(number)

returns the square root of a positive number.

number = the number for which the square root is required.

Examples: SQRT(C4) in Figure 6.18 returns 3.1623. Also, SQRT(87.45) = 9.3515.

6. SUMXMY2: SUMXMY2(array1, array2)

returns the sum of the squares of the differences between two sets of data.

array1	= the first array or range of values.
array2	= the second array or range of values.

Examples: SUMXMY2(F4:F7, G4:G7) in Figure 6.18 returns 173. This value is found by adding $(1 - 1)^2 + (2 - 4)^2 + (3 - 8)^2 + (4 - 16)^2 = 0 + 4 + 25 + 144 = 173$.

EXERCISES

6.1 Sharon Smith from the KleenUp Company has collected sales data for area 9 over the past seven quarters. The sales figures are 11, 14, 12, 20, 15, 19, 24. She would like to know what the sales forecast will be in quarter 8 and has decided to use Chart Wizard to obtain a scattergraph. She will then fit a linear regression line, get the regression line equation, check its 'goodness of fit', and then find the sales forecast for quarter 8.

(Answer: $y = 1.8571x + 9$; 'goodness of fit' = $R = 0.85$; when $x = 8$, $y = $ forecast = 23.86.)

6.2   The Acme Company has collected monthly sales data for widgets over the past nine months. The sales figures (in '000s) are 14, 11, 23, 39, 33, 40, 61, 48, and 66. The company would like to find a sales forecast for the next three months but is unsure which forecasting technique to use, i.e., either linear regression or an exponential trend. The Acme Company has decided to produce a scattergraph of its data and then fit both a linear regression line and an exponential curve through the data. Which method gives the more accurate forecasts, and why?

(Answer: Using linear regression, $R^2 = 0.8807$ and $y = 6.6x + 4.222$. Thus when $x = 10, 11, 12$ then $y = 70.22, 76.82$, and 83.422. Using an exponential curve, $R^2 = 0.8459$ and $y = 11.201e^{0.21x}$. Thus when $x = 10, 11, 12$ then $y = 91.47, 112.84, 139.21$. These exponential y-values are much greater than current widget sales and are therefore suspect. The line equation is more accurate because its R^2 value is closer to 1.0.)

6.3   Barry Lime is marketing manager of SuperMicros, manufacturers of the popular ZXZ micro. Barry has tabulated some sales and advertising figures for the ZXZ micro as shown in Table 6.9. Barry Lime has been told that he has £1750 to spend next month (i.e., month 6) on advertising, and he would like to get a feasible forecast for next month's ZXZ sales. He would also like to find out if the amounts spent on advertising are justified. Having previously used Excel's FORECAST and CORREL functions, Barry doesn't anticipate any problems.

Table 6.9

Month	Sales ('000s)	Advertising (£'000s)
1	251	2.4
2	139	1.4
3	171	1.5
4	119	1.0
5	206	2.1

(Answer: Forecast = 184; Correlation = 0.98.)

6.4   Fred Flint has now decided that he should know how to calculate the MAD and MSE values of a time series using Excel. He has chosen the 9 time periods 2 to 10 from the Bedrock data for product P in Figure 6.8 as his sample. His data table includes only actual sales and exponential smoothing figures with $\alpha = 0.1$ (i.e., cell range C6:D14). Which of the two methods, in Fred's view, is better and why?

(Answer: MAD = 104.82; MSE = 15103.7; MAD gives equal weight to each error, while MSE gives more weight to errors by squaring them. If large forecast errors remain undetected, serious problems can arise, so Fred chooses MSE.)

6.5   The Holt-Winters' exponential smoothing method is a popular forecasting technique that is often used for forecasting a company's inventory. Being in charge of inventory at the Bedrock Company, Fred Flint wants to find out how accurate this method really is. He has collected monthly data covering a period of three years as shown in Table 6.10. Fred will assign initial values of $\alpha = 0.3$, $\beta = 0.4$, and $\gamma = 0.5$ for the three smoothing constants. However, he will eventually use

Excel's Solver to find more feasible values for α, β, and γ that minimise the mean squared error (MSE).

Table 6.10 ←—————— Monthly data (£'000s) —————→

Year	1	2	3	4	5	6	7	8	9	10	11	12
200A	12	5	11	20	19	32	29	37	29	22	20	8
200B	11	14	19	22	36	34	47	30	33	35	30	33
200C	20	12	31	40	61	85	91	98	78	62	43	37

(Answer: MSE = 115.4 with smoothing constants $\alpha = 0.02$, $\beta = 1.0$, and $\gamma = 0.15$. The Holt-Winters method gives a good fit for Fred's historical data.)

6.6 Sharon Smith would like to be sure that the forecast that she obtained in Example 6.1 above is accurate. She has chosen to get another forecast for quarter 8 using Excel's EXPONENTIAL SMOOTHING function. Taking Sharon's sales data from Example 6.1 and an alpha value of 0.4 (i.e., damping factor = 0.6), help Sharon find this new forecast. Plot the graphs of both the actual sales and the exponential smoothing forecast.

(Answer: Sales forecast for quarter 8 is 19.62.)

6.7 A grocery store operates seven days a week. A minimum number of employees is required each day, depending upon the day of the week (Table 6.11). The store requires staff to work five consecutive days, followed by two days off, e.g., an employee working Monday through Friday gets Saturday and Sunday off. Using Solver, formulate and solve so as to minimise the number of employees needed, while meeting the minimum staff requirements (remember that employee numbers must be integers).

Table 6.11

Day	Minimum no. of staff required
Monday	15
Tuesday	13
Wednesday	13
Thursday	15
Friday	19
Saturday	14
Sunday	9

(Answer: Minimum of 21 employees; there are several arrangements which fulfil all constraints. For example, Mon, Tues, Wed, . . . Sun: 7,4,1,7,0,2,0; 7,5,1,2,6,0,0; 6,1,5,3,4,1,1, etc.)

6.8 The Acme Company manufactures two products, widgets and gadgets. The company earns a profit of £2 per box for widgets and £3 a box for gadgets. Each product is assembled and packaged. It takes 9 minutes to assemble a box of widgets and 15 minutes for a box of gadgets.

The packaging department can package a box of widgets in 11 minutes, while a box of gadgets takes 5 minutes. The Acme Company has prioritised its two main goals as follows: (i) achieve a profit of around £23,000 (ii) ensure that the number of boxes of gadgets and widgets produced are equal. The company has a maximum of 1800 hours available in both the assembly and packaging departments. Acme has decided to see if Excel's Solver can provide a satisfactory solution to this goal programming (GP) exercise.

   (Hint: First of all, re-read examples 2.1 and 6.7 and then formulate the problem as a GP exercise.)

   (Answer: The first goal is underachieved by 2.17%, i.e., a profit of £22,500 results, while the second goal is fully realised with an answer of 4,500 boxes for both widgets and gadgets.)

6.9   MeadowSweet Creameries manufactures yogurt at its two plants located at Riversdale and Greenhills. Riversdale has a maximum weekly output of 2000 cartons while Greenhills can produce up to 3000 cartons per week. Weekly production costs at each plant are given by the following equations:

   Greenhills: Production costs $= 2.7q_1 + 4q_1^{1/2} + 400$
   Riversdale: Production costs $= 3.2q_2 + 1.5q_2^{1/2} + 250$

where q_1, $q_2 =$ number of cartons produced each week at Greenhills and Riversdale respectively. MeadowSweet Creameries has a weekly demand of 4000 cartons. The company would like to know how much to produce at each plant in order to minimise production costs. Set up this nonlinear programming (NLP) problem and find the answer to MeadowSweet's problem using Excel's Solver.

   (Answer: Minimum production costs of £12,217 are achieved by producing 3000 cartons at Greenhills and the remaining 1000 cartons at Riversdale.)

6.10   The KleenUp Company has divided Upper State into three main sales areas, namely A, B, and C. The company has determined that sales of its product depend upon the amount spent on advertising in each area, and can be defined as follows:

   Sales ('000s) in area A $= 2.0a^{1/2} + 30$
   Sales ('000s) in area B $= 1.75b^{1/2} + 40$
   Sales ('000s) in area C $= 1.6c^{1/2} + 15$

where a, b, c represent the amounts (in £'000s) spent on advertising in areas A, B, and C.
   The product sells for £2.50, £3.10, and £2.95 in areas A, B, and C respectively. The KleenUp Company, which spends £100,000 on advertising in Upper State, would like to maximise its income. It has decided to find a solution by modelling the situation as a nonlinear programming (NLP) problem. Formulate the problem and solve using Solver. Is it worthwhile for the KleenUp Company to increase its advertising expenditure in Upper State by 10%?

   (Answer: The maximum income is £331 thousand and the advertising budget (£'000s) is 33 (area A), 38 (area B), 29 (area C) with sales ('000s) of 41 (area A), 51 (area B), and 24 (area C). When the budget is increased by 10%, income increases to £335 thousand with advertising expenditures of 36 (A), 42 (B), and 32 (C). Thus the advertising budget goes up by £10,000, but total income increases by only £4,000. Therefore it is not worth while increasing the advertising budget.)

REFERENCES AND FURTHER READING

Groebner, D., Shannon, P. *et al.* (2001) *Business Statistics: A Decision-Making Approach* (5th edn), Prentice Hall, New Jersey.

Levine, D., Stephan, D. *et al.* (2002) *Statistics for Managers Using Microsoft Excel*, (3rd edn), Prentice-Hall, New Jersey.

Ragsdale, C. (2004) *Spreadsheet Modeling and Decision Analysis* (4th edn), Thomson South-Western, USA.

7

Purchase order processing: a database application

OVERVIEW

Most users view Excel as a tool for spreadsheet modelling without being aware of the package's database capabilities. Excel is a powerful development tool that can be used to create practical business information systems. When combined with Microsoft's programming language – Visual Basic for Applications (VBA) – developers are able to make full use of Excel's library of inbuilt objects to design flexible information systems involving complex data analysis. Although there is a limitation on the number of records that an Excel database can contain (under twenty thousand), an Excel application can still be used as a user-friendly interface to larger specialised databases without the need for any further modification.

A database is simply a base for data, i.e., it stores business data in an integrated and organised way so that data can be easily accessed by all users. The purpose of this chapter is to introduce the reader to Excel's internal database capabilities and the benefits of using macros. Excel distinguishes between two types of databases, namely (i) internal databases that are stored in worksheets – usually called lists in Excel terminology, and (ii) external databases such as dBASE, FoxPro, or Access. Excel communicates with external databases through the Microsoft Query program which uses a technology called Open Database Connectivity (ODBC).

The tabular structure of a worksheet is ideally suited to the development of a relational table-based application. The first step in creating a list or database is to analyse the information which will form the database. Can this information be written down in lists, tables or on index cards? A database approach to file design is similar to a card index system, with each card holding, say, supplier details such as name, address, discount levels, etc. The products sold by each supplier are NOT included in the supplier index system. The reason for having a separate products list is that several suppliers will sell the same product – but perhaps at different prices. If a product list is included as part of the supplier table, then duplication of data occurs! One of the key objectives of database technology is to reduce data duplication (also called data redundancy) by including each piece of data only once in the database.

The main consideration when planning a database is to remove repeating data items. When two tables are created, one each for supplier and product details, then wasted disk space is eliminated. The technique of separating repetitive data items into their own tables is called 'data normalisation'. Data normalisation is the key to good relational database design. Too often, users do not give sufficient thought to this fundamental process which not only saves on disk space but also on processing time. Any good textbook on information technology will show how the process of normalisation can be applied to raw data. The purchase order processing (POP) application developed in this chapter makes use of macros which are now discussed.

CREATING A SIMPLE MACRO

A macro can be defined as a set of instructions to perform some operation, e.g., hand calculators contain macros to perform mathematical functions such as sin, cos, tan, log, e^x, etc. The objective of a macro is to automate routine tasks so that the user does not have to enter the same commands over and over again. Macros, which are really mini-programs written in the Visual Basic programming language, are sometimes called procedures or subroutines.

Microsoft Excel provides a built-in macro recorder which can be used by everyday users, who have no programming experience, to automate simple tasks. When macros are generated by Excel, a new worksheet called a 'module' is created in the active workbook. This new module does not appear with the other sheets in the workbook and must be accessed through the VBA Editor, normally called the Visual Basic Editor. The following steps show how a simple macro can be created.

1. Open a new worksheet and select cell Al.
2. Choose the Tools|Record Macro|Record_New_Macro command. A dialog box appears displaying the default macro name and a macro description.
3. Enter the title *Colour_Cells* in the Macro Name box. Note that the name of the macro cannot contain spaces, so use the underscore character as shown.
4. Leave the next line as currently shown. The 'Short key:' box should be empty and the 'Store macro in:' box should contain the words 'This Workbook'.
5. The Description box already displays the user's name and current date. Add the following comment to explain the purpose of the macro: ***This macro colours user-defined cells BLUE.*
6. Click OK. The 'Stop Recording' toolbar appears on the screen and the word 'Recording' appears on the status bar at the bottom of the screen, indicating that any action that the user performs from now on will be recorded.

   - Click the *Format* tab on the menu bar at the top of the screen.
   - Click the *Cells . . .* tab and then the Patterns tab in the *Format* Cells dialog box.
   - Click the BLUE colour displayed on the second line of the colour palette.
   - Click OK.
   - Click the small blue button on the left of the 'Stop Recording' toolbar.

The macro is complete and the cell A1 should now be coloured blue. It is very important that the user remembers to stop recording. If the user forgets this last command, a huge macro will continue to be created, taking up valuable storage space and may eventually interfere with the running of the computer. The user has two ways to stop recording, either (i) click the square blue button on the 'Stop Recording' toolbar, or (ii) choose the Tools|Macro|Stop_Recording command.

Running the Macro

The following steps show how to use the macro Colour_Cells.

- Select the range D4:F6.
- Choose the Tools|Macro|Macros . . . command. A Macro dialog box will appear, displaying the name *Colour_Cells*, which is the only macro in the current worksheet.
- Click on the *Colour_Cells* macro and then click the *Run* button.
- The selected cell range D4:F6 should now be coloured blue.

The Macro Listing

To see the macro listing choose the Tools|Macro|Macros . . . command, select the Colour_Cells macro and then click on the Edit button. The macro listing as shown below appears in the right-hand window. To return to the worksheet, choose the command File|Close_and_Return_ to_Microsoft Excel.

```
Sub Colour_Cells ()
'
'Colour_Cells Macro
'Macro recorded 28-10-200X by Joe Soap
'***This macro colours user-defined cells BLUE
'
'
    With Selection.Interior
      .ColorIndex = 5
      .Pattern = x1Solid
      .PatternColorIndex = x1Automatic
    End With
End Sub
```

The six lines that start with apostrophes at the beginning of the macro are comments. Comments are ignored by Visual Basic and are there to indicate when and by whom the macro was written, and what the macro actually does. The user's name and current date will replace those of Joe Soap and the displayed date. On the VDU screen, comments are displayed in green, while Visual Basic statements like *End Sub* are in blue.

A macro always begins with word *Sub* (short for subroutine) and ends with the words *End Sub*. Note that the 'xl' in x1Solid are the letters 'x' as in xmas and 'l' as in learn. While the Colour_Cells macro was generated by clicks (keystrokes), an experienced programmer would have achieved the same result by typing the Visual Basic instructions directly into a macro worksheet. Having introduced the concept of macros, a practical application will now be developed.

PURCHASE ORDER PROCESSING

The purchase order processing (POP) database application consists of a workbook, named 'Purchase', containing four macro worksheets and the following seven worksheets.

1. Worksheet 'Title'   – displays the title screen and option buttons
2. Worksheet 'Suppliers'   – contains *supplier* details
3. Worksheet 'Products'   – contains *product* details
4. Worksheet 'OrderEntry'   – displays a blank purchase order form
5. Worksheet 'Database'   – allows already-entered orders to be amended
6. Worksheet 'AmendOrder'   – contains details of all purchase orders
7. Worksheet 'PrintOrder'   – prints out one or more orders as requested

Both Excel and Visual Basic will be used to create the POP system. For readers who are unfamiliar with Visual Basic, there are now many good textbooks available (see Walkenbach), which provide a quick and easy introduction to Visual Basic for Applications (VBA). While some programming experience would be a help, it is not a necessary prerequisite as many of the macros will be automatically generated using keystrokes. Where the user has to enter programming code, it is a simple matter of copying the Visual Basic instructions that are provided into a macro spreadsheet.

Figure 7.1 shows the typical data flows in a purchase order processing (POP) system.

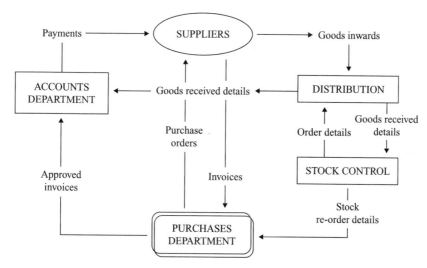

Figure 7.1   A simple purchase order processing system.

CREATING THE TITLE SCREEN

Step 1: Creating a title
Note: all clicks are with the mouse's left button unless otherwise stated.

- Open a new workbook and rename the first sheet as 'Title'. Check that all cells have a standard column width of 8.5 and row height of 12.75.

- Choose the View|Toolbars command and click on the Drawing toolbar.

- Click the 'Shadow Style' symbol on the toolbar (second last), choose 'shadow style 6', position the cursor in cell B5 and then drag it to cell J7. A rectangular box should now appear on the screen. Enter the title PURCHASE ORDER PROCESSING in the box.

- Click on the edge of the rectangle with the mouse's right-hand button to activate the shortcut menu. From the menu list, choose 'Format Text Box . . . ' and perform the following:

  - Click on the 'Font' tab, and choose *Font:* Times New Roman, *Style:* Bold Italic, *Size:* 20.

  - Click on the 'Alignment' tab, and in the Text Alignment section, click *Center* on both the Horizontal and Vertical boxes.

  - Click on the 'Colors and Lines' tab, and in the Color section, choose a light-red (coral) colour (or any other colour that you like). Finally click the 'OK' button.

Step 2: Adding a clipart image
To brighten up the POP presentation, add a piece of clipart.

- Select the Insert|Picture|Clipart . . . command to bring up the 'Clip Art' dialog box. Type the word 'Business' into the 'Search for:' edit box and click the 'Go' button.

- Choose a suitable picture and then click on it. The image will now be placed on the worksheet.

- Click on the top button (Insert Clip) and the clipart image is now embedded on the screen.

- To reduce the object's size, click anywhere on the clipart to activate its frame, and then use the frame's diagonal arrow to reduce the image's size.

- Position the clipart in the range B12:F22.

Step 3: Colouring the screen background

- Highlight the range A1:M33.

- Choose the Format|Cells|Pattern command and colour the range light yellow.

- Save the workbook, giving it the name 'Purchase'. At this stage, the title should look similar to Figure 7.2.

Step 4: Adding buttons
The next step is to add the five buttons which will be used to run the macros for performing the various activities as shown in Figure 7.2. Buttons perform the same function as a menu.

- Open the workbook 'Purchase', choose the View|Toolbars command and click on the Forms toolbar.

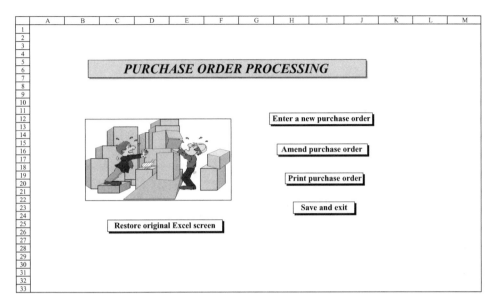

Figure 7.2   Title screen for the POP system.

- Click the 'Create Button' symbol on the Forms toolbar (second row, right) and then position the mouse on the Title screen to the right of the clipart (use Figure 7.2 as a guideline).

- Drag the cursor so as to create a reasonable-sized button. At this stage, it is better to make the button too large rather than too small – it will be modified in any case!

- An 'Assign Macro' screen will now appear. Since no macros have yet been created, click the Cancel button.

- Click inside the button and overwrite the default name *Button_1* with a new title: *Enter a new purchase order*.

- Enlarge the button if necessary by clicking anywhere on the button and then using the frame's handles (for more information on objects, see Appendix – 'Object Linking and Embedding').

- Convert the current format to Bold/Times New Roman. The first button should now look like the one in Figure 7.2.

- Repeat the above steps for the other four buttons.

Step 5: Creating a macro
The MACRO RECORDER will now be used to automatically generate a Visual Basic macro, based on the user's keystroke actions. The screen as it appears is cluttered up with toolbars, status bars, worksheet tabs, etc. To create a macro that will maximise the screen display area, perform the following tasks:

- Choose the Tools|Macro|Record_New_Macro command. A dialog box appears showing the default macro name.

- Enter the title *Maximise_Screen*. Note that the name of the macro cannot contain spaces, so use the underscore character as shown.

- Leave the next line as currently shown, i.e., the *Short key:* box should be empty and the words 'This Workbook' should appear in the *Store_macro_in:* box.

- The Macro_description box already contains the user's name and current date. Add the following comment: ****Maximises screen area and then displays the title screen.*

- Click OK. The word 'Recording' appears on the status bar at the bottom of the screen, indicating that any action that the user performs from now on will be recorded.

- Click the worksheet 'Title' tab at the bottom of the screen.   (Action recorded!)
- Click the *View* tab and then click the *Full Screen tab*.   (Action recorded!)
- Click the *Tools* tab, *Options* tab, and then the *View* tab.   (Action recorded!)
- Now click each of the following four boxes to turn them off:
  Row and Column Headers; Horizontal Scroll Bar; Vertical Scroll
  Bar; Sheet Tabs.   (Action recorded!)
- Click OK.   (Action recorded!)
- Click in cell A1 to position the screen correctly.   (Action recorded!)
- Click the *Tools* tab, then the *Macro* tab and finally the
  Stop_Recording tab.

                                                                    (Action recorded!)

The first macro is complete. The screen is almost totally clear with the exception of the menu bar at the top. At this stage, it is important that the user knows how to stop recording otherwise a huge macro will be created. *It is very easy to forget to stop recording!* The listing of the macro Maximise_Screen that has just been created can be viewed by choosing the Tools|Macro|Macros ... command and then clicking on the Edit button. To return to the worksheet, choose the command File|Close_and_ Return_to _ Microsoft Excel. Another macro will now be created to undo the actions of the first macro. In other words, the screen will be returned to its original appearance by reversing the above actions.

Step 6: Restoring the original screen
Repeat the initial steps for creating a macro as shown in Step 5 above. Enter a macro name Restore_Screen_Defaults and a macro description ****Restores the normal screen display.* Click OK to start recording.

- Click the *View* tab and then click the *Full Screen* tab to turn it off.

- Click the *Tools*, *Options* and *View* tabs.

- Activate the following four options by clicking in the relevant boxes: Row and Column Headers; Horizontal Scroll Bar; Vertical Scroll Bar; Sheet Tabs.

- Click OK.

- Click the left-hand button on the 'Stop Recording' toolbar to stop recording.

The screen should now be restored to its original appearance. A second macro, called 'Restore_Screen_Defaults' is created, similar to the first macro, by simply reversing the logical True/False statements. Most of the Visual Basic statements should be self-evident. For example, in the Maximise_Screen macro the statement '*DisplayVerticalScrollBar = False*' means that the vertical scroll bar has been turned off. In the second macro the word *False* has been replaced by *True*, i.e., turn this option back on again. The six lines at the top of each macro, starting with apostrophes, are *comments*. For clearer presentation, the POP application starts every user-inserted comment with three asterisks.

Look at the macro listings using the commands shown above. The VBA Editor refers to the two newly created macros as *Module1* and *Module2*. These titles appear in the upper left-hand window of the screen. Double-click on either title to see the relevant macro code. Print out the VBA Basic listings for both modules and check that they are the same as the macros printed below. There may be slight variations, depending upon the order in which the keys were pressed. Finally, and most importantly, save the workbook 'Purchase'.

Macro Listings for (i) Screen Maximisation and (ii) Screen Restoration

Sub Maximise_Screen()
```
'
' Maximise_Screen Macro
' Macro recorded 22-11-200X by Joe Soap
'
'***Maximises screen area and then displays the title screen
'
    Sheets("Title").Select
    Application.DisplayFullScreen = True
    With ActiveWindow
        .DisplayHeadings = False
        .DisplayHorizontalScrollBar = False
        .DisplayVerticalScrollBar = False
        .DisplayWorkbookTabs = False
    End With
    Range("A1").Select
End Sub
```

Sub Restore_Screen_Defaults()
```
'
' Restore_Screen_Defaults Macro
' Macro recorded 22-11-200X by Joe Soap
'
'***Restores the normal screen display
'
    Application.DisplayFullScreen = False
    With ActiveWindow
        .DisplayHeadings = True
        .DisplayHorizontalScrollBar = True
```

```
        .DisplayVerticalScrollBar = True
        .DisplayWorkbookTabs = True
      End With
    End Sub
```

PRODUCTS AND SUPPLIERS WORKSHEETS

The Products and Suppliers worksheets are created by renaming *Sheet2* as Products and *Sheet3* as Suppliers. Both worksheets are simple tables, consisting of one record per row. The Products sheet contains details of up to twenty products – in this case personal computing supplies – including product code, description, price, VAT rate, percentage discount (if applicable), type, and some inventory information. The sheet layout, including column widths, for the Products table is shown in Figure 7.3 while similar details for the Suppliers worksheet are given in Figure 7.4.

The data in these two worksheets will be accessed by other worksheets as the database is developed. Because it is easier to refer to a table by a single name rather than as a range of cells, the data tables will be assigned names as follows:

- Go to the 'Products' worksheet, and choose the *Insert|Name|Define* command to activate the *Define Name* dialog box.

- Enter the name 'Prodata' in the 'Names in Workbook:' box. Next, clear out the contents of the 'Refers to:' box and enter the formula = ***Products!$B$3:$H$22***.

- Finally, click the OK button.

	A	B	C	D	E	F	G	H	I
1		**Product**	**Price**	**VAT**	**Discount**	**Type**	**On**	**On**	
2	Code	**Description**		**%**	**%**		**Hand**	**Order**	
3	S512	MS Windows XP	£125.00	23.0	5	Software	35	40	
4	S173	Lotus SmartSuite	£290.00	23.0		Software	90		
5	B38	Using MS Excel	£30.55	0.0	10	Book	42	25	
6	H65	Epson Stylus Colour	£155.00	23.0		Hardware	10	10	
7	S238	MS Works Suite	£95.00	23.0		Software	79	20	
8	B12	Using Word for Windows	£25.95	0.0	10	Book	15	20	
9	S21	Borland Delphi Personal	£90.00	23.0		Software	55		
10	S191	Sage Instant Accounts	£130.00	23.0		Software	46	25	
11	S217	Norton Internet Security	£55.00	23.0		Software	92	20	
12	CD21	MS Encarta Encyclopedia	£25.00	23.0	5	CD-ROM	129		
13	S72	MS Office Pro	£390.00	23.0		Software	25		
14	B51	Users Guide to the Internet	£22.45	0.0	5	Book	45		
15	A33	Ink Cart -HP DeskJet (black)	£24.00	23.0	10	Accessory	120		
16	A33a	Ink Cart -HP DeskJet (color)	£29.00	23.0	10	Accessory	165		
17									
18									
19									
20									
21									
22									
23									
24	-- The **PRODUCTS table**, as currently set up, can accept details of up to 20 products - stored in cell range A3:H22								
25	-- For clearer presentation, the cell range B3:H22 has been named **'Prodata'**								
26	-- Column widths are currently set as A (7), B(31), C(10), D(7.5), E(8), F(12), G(7), H(7)								
27	-- The above parameters can be adjusted as required.								
28									

Figure 7.3 The Products worksheet.

	A	B	C	D	E	F
1	Code	Suppliers Name	Address1	Address2	Address3	Telephone
2	SN2	Things A'Plenty Company	Unit 61, Eastwood Estate	North Uplands	North Island	0123-9876
3	SN3	The MightyBig Corporation	Blackwater	Atlantic Drive	North Island	0123-8585
4	SP1	The Bedrock Company	Ancient Boulevard	Craggy Creek	North Ridge	0987-6542
5	SP3	The KleenUp Company	Whitewater	Riverside	Newgate	0345-6677
6	SS2	Supplies Unlimited	Unit 55 - Industrial Estate	Sunset City		0678-1252
7						
8						
9						
10						
11						
12						
13						
14						
15						
16						
17						
18						
19						
20						
21						
22						
23	-- The **SUPPLIER table**, as currently set up, can accept details of up to 20 suppliers - stored in cell range A2:F21					
24	-- For clearer presentation, the cell range B2:F21 has been named '**Suppdata**'					
25	-- Column widths are currently set as A(6), B(26), C(23), D(18), E(18), and F(10).					
26	-- The above parameters can be adjusted as required.					
27						

Figure 7.4   The Suppliers worksheet.

Repeat the above steps for the 'Suppliers' worksheet, giving the name 'Suppdata' to the cell range Suppliers!$B$2:$F$21. The data in the two worksheets can now be accessed by simply using the names Prodata and Suppdata.

CREATING THE PURCHASE ORDER FORM

A new Excel workbook contains only three worksheets. Since the POP application will eventually contain seven worksheets, four new sheets (Sheet4 to Sheet7) must be added to the 'Purchase' workbook. Use the Insert|Worksheet command to add these new worksheets. The purchase order form, as shown in Figure 7.5, is the most important worksheet in the POP application. It will be used to create both the AmendOrder and PrintOrder worksheets.

Step 1: Creating the order form
Using Figure 7.5 as a template, create the basic layout contained in cell range A8:J42. The column widths are A(8), B(7.5), C(7), D(9), E(5.5), F(8), G(8), H(9), I(11), J(5), K(5). Enter only the company name, address and telephone, box titles and column headings. Most of the data inside the various boxes and columns, will be generated automatically by the POP system, using the Supplier and Product worksheets that were created in the previous section.

Step 2: Adding list boxes
List boxes appear at the top of Figure 7.5. There are two list boxes, one for Supplier details and one for Product details. List boxes are important Excel control objects that allow the user to (i) select an item from a list, and then (ii) specify a linked cell which will contain the item's position in the list. In the Gizmo Company example, the linked cell, D2, shows that the Bedrock Company is the third record in the Suppliers table of Figure 7.4. Similarly, linked cell, H2, shows that

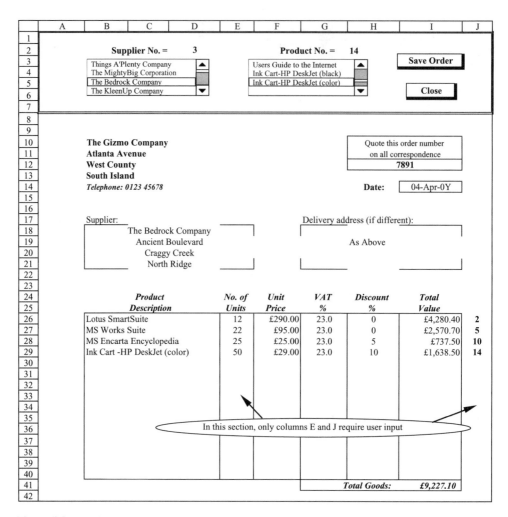

Figure 7.5 Purchase order form.

the product 'Ink Cart – HP DeskJet (color)' is record 14 in the Products table (Figure 7.3). Check that these linked values are correct – be careful not to confuse record numbers with row numbers.

- Choose the View|Toolbars command, and then click on the Forms toolbar.
- Click the 'List Box' symbol on the Forms toolbar (fourth row, left) and then position the mouse in cell B3 and drag the cursor over to cell D6. A list box should now appear.
- Click the mouse's right-hand button to activate the shortcut menu, choose the 'Format Control' option, and then click on the 'Control' tab. The Format Control dialog box will now appear requesting input for (i) **_Input range_**. Since the supplier names are stored in the

Suppliers table called 'Suppdata', enter Suppdata as the input range (ii) *Cell link*. As stated above, the cell link is D2, so enter D2 in this box. (iii) *Selection type*. The default value of <u>S</u>ingle is acceptable, so no action is required. (iv) *<u>3</u>D shading*. To activate three-dimensional shading around the list box, click on this option. Finally, click the OK button.

- Repeat the above step for the Products list box, entering (i) Prodata (the named Products table) into the *<u>I</u>nput range* box and (ii) H2 for the *<u>C</u>ell link*. The relevant information, which can be scrolled in either direction, should now be displayed in the list boxes.

Step 3: Adding a scroll bar facility

Currently, only part of the purchase order can be seen on the screen. To facilitate the viewing of the whole purchase order, a scroll bar is now created at row 8. Position the cursor in cell A8, and choose the command <u>W</u>indows|<u>S</u>plit. A broad scroll-line will appear at the top of row 8. Next choose the command <u>W</u>indows|<u>F</u>reeze Panes to lock cell range A1:J7. Only the lower part of the screen can now scroll up or down.

Step 4: Entering cell formulae

Supplier and product information can now be automatically generated from the Supplier and Product tables. The record numbers for the supplier and each product – stored in cells D2 and H2 – are the key indexes which are used to locate other relevant details such as supplier address, product price, etc. Table 7.1 should be used to complete the purchase order form. In this model, an order is restricted to eight items, i.e., only eight lines (lines 26 to 33 in Figure 7.5) are used for product details. If desired, the number of items can be extended to 15 by copying the appropriate formulae down into cells B34:I40.

Step 5: Adding buttons

As with the Title worksheet, two buttons must be added at the top-right of Figure 7.5 to allow the user to (i) generate multiple purchase orders using the Save Order button (ii) exit from the worksheet and return to the main menu using the Close button. Note that input data for the current order will be cleared from the screen when the Save Order button is clicked. To add the two buttons, follow the same instructions of Step 4 in the section 'Creating the Title Screen' on page 210. Again, macros will be added at a later stage to the buttons.

Table 7.1 Purchase order processing – worksheet formulae.

Cell	Formula	Copied to
B18	IF(D$2 = "", "", INDEX(Suppdata, D$2, 1))	
B19	IF(D$2 = "", "", INDEX(Suppdata, D$2, 2))	
B20	IF(D$2 = "", "", INDEX(Suppdata, D$2, 3))	
B21	IF(D$2 = "", "", INDEX(Suppdata, D$2, 4))	
B26	IF(J26 = "", "", INDEX(Prodata, J26, 1))	B27:B33
F26	IF(J26 = "", "", INDEX(Prodata, J26, 2))	F27:F33
G26	IF(J26 = "", "", INDEX(Prodata, J26, 3))	G27:G33
H26	IF(J26 = "", "", INDEX(Prodata, J26, 4))	H27:H33
I26	IF(J26 = "", "", E26*(1 + G26/100 – H26/100)*F26)	I27:I33
I41	SUM(I26:I33)	

Step 6: Protecting the OrderEntry worksheet

It is all too easy for users to forget that certain cells contain formulae and then overwrite them by mistake. To prevent such errors happening, the worksheet will be protected, allowing users to enter data only into those cells that require user input. Such user-input cells, usually called unlocked cells, are: D2 (the Supplier Number), H2 (the Product Number), H12 (the Order Number), I14 (Date of order), J26:J33 (the eight user product numbers) and E26:E33 (the number of units ordered for each product). Finally, the cell range (B8:T8) on line 8 must be unlocked (unprotected). Line 8 has been arbitrarily chosen as a temporary transfer area for data being copied from the purchase order worksheet into the Database worksheet.

- To unlock or unprotect a cell or cells, firstly highlight the relevant cell(s), choose the Format|Cells|Protection command, and turn off the Locked option (cells are locked by default).

- When all the relevant cells have been unlocked, choose the Tools|Protection|Protect_Sheet command and click OK. An optional Password is best ignored. This command protects the whole worksheet with the exception of the unlocked cells specified above.

Step 7: Saving the Purchase Order worksheet

Clear up the screen by using the Tools|Options|View command to switch off the options for gridlines and row/column headings; then choose the command View|Full_Screen. Finally, save the Purchase Order form of Figure 7.5, giving it the name OrderEntry. Until a macro is created that will transfer data from the OrderEntry screen to the Database worksheet, no database records will be generated. Users can therefore familiarise themselves with the purchase order worksheet by creating as many sample purchase orders as they wish. The next step shows how to produce a purchase order.

Step 8: Using the OrderEntry worksheet

The final step is to use the purchase order form of Figure 7.5. The following steps explain how a purchase order is created.

- Scroll through the Supplier's list box (located at the top of the screen in cells B3:D6) and click on a suppliers name, e.g., the Bedrock Company. Details of the supplier's address will automatically appear in the supplier window (cells B18:E21).

- Enter an order number and order date in cells H12 and I14.

- Scroll through the Products list box (located in cells F3:H6) and click on any product, e.g., Lotus SmartSuite. The product number for Lotus SmartSuite is 2 and will be displayed in cell H2. When (product number) 2 is entered in cell J26, product details are filled in automatically on line 26, with the exception of the 'No. of units' in column E. This value must be entered by the user. In this case, 12 units of Lotus SmartSuite are required, so the value 12 is entered in cell E26.

- Repeat the above step for the rest of the purchase order, choosing 'MS Works Suite (Product No. 5) ordering 22 items, 'MS Encarta Encyclopedia' (Product No. 10) ordering 25 items, etc. Currently, cell H2 contains the value 14, i.e., the product number for accessory 'Ink Cart – HP DeskJet (color)'. This is the last product that has been entered in the purchase order.

	A	B	C	D	E	F	G	H	I	J	K	L	M	N	O	P	Q	R	S
1	Order	Order	Supp.	<------- Product code numbers for 8 products ------->								< Number of units ordered for each product ->							
2	No.	Date	Code	1	2	3	4	5	6	7	8	1	2	3	4	5	6	7	8
3																			
4	7891	04-Apr-0Y	3	2	5	10	14					12	22	25	50				
5	7566	22-Mar-0Y	1	11	2	5	9					25	10	15	30				
6	7120	03-Feb-0Y	4	3	7	5	9	10	12			25	10	15	35	22	17		
7	6891	21-Jan-0Y	4	11	1	6	9	4				16	21	5	20	10			
8	6541	19-Dec-0X	5	1	4							35	10						
9	3265	12-Nov-0X	2	4	5	3						20	10	5					
10																			
11																			
12																			
13																			
14																			
15																			
16																			
17																			
18																			
19																			

20 -- The **DATABASE** can accept up to 50 records - stored in cell range A4:S53 - and up to 8 product lines per order.
21 -- For clearer presentation, the cell range A4:S53 has been named **Basedata'**
22 -- Column widths are currently set as A(8), B(9.5), C(5.5), columns D to S(4.5).
23 -- The aboveparameters can be adjusted as required.
24
25 Supplier and Product code numbers represent the positions of the records in each list table.
26 *To understand the database setup, consider the record details entered in line 8.*
27 Order No. 6541, created on 19th December 200X, deals with products ordered from supplier code 5, i.e. Supplies Unlimited.
28 Order details are:-   35 units of product code number 1 (i.e. MS windows XP)
29   10 units of product code number 4 (i.e. Epson Stylus Colour)
30

Figure 7.6   Database worksheet containing six purchase orders.

- A product can be removed from the purchase order by simply deleting the contents of the relevant cells in columns E and J. For example, if the 'MS Encarta' item is not required, then clear the contents of cells E28 and J28 and line 28 will become blank.

- All calculations, including the total value of the purchase order, are performed automatically.

CREATING THE DATABASE AND ITS ASSOCIATED MACROS

Open a new worksheet and name it *Database*. Like the Suppliers and Products worksheets, the Database worksheet consists of a simple table with each row holding purchase order details, most of which are code numbers. Figure 7.6 contains formatting instructions for the data table. Column widths and headings are given at the bottom of the spreadsheet, along with an explanation of how each record is stored in the database. Using Figure 7.6 as a template, copy across the information as shown, ignoring formats such as underlining, shading, etc., (data is centred in each cell).

All database information is generated automatically by the POP system. The six orders, already in the database, have been included solely for demonstration purposes. The top two lines in the worksheet explain the purpose of each column. Line 3 is used as a temporary storage area for transfer of data from the purchase order (i.e., OrderEntry) worksheet. Note that the Database worksheet allows details of only eight products. As explained above, this number can be increased (up to 15 product items) if so desired.

To simplify data access within the Database worksheet, the cell range will be assigned a name, similar to the Suppliers (*Suppdata*) and Products (*Prodata*) tables. There is, however, one major difference between the contents of the database and the two previous worksheets. The Supplier and Product tables contain relatively static data with additions and modifications to existing records being infrequent. On the other hand, the data in the *Database* worksheet is dynamic with purchase orders being continually added, updated, and eventually deleted.

Because the number of *Database* records is variable, a formula must be created to dynamically change the list of purchase orders appearing in any subsequent list boxes. This formula, named *Basedata*, can be defined in the same way as the Suppdata and Prodata tables. Each time the Database worksheet is accessed via the formula *Basedata*, the current number of records will be calculated by the COUNTA function. Note that the values 50 and 19 appearing in the formula below represent the maximum number of rows (records) and columns (fields) in the Database table.

- Go to the 'Database' worksheet, and choose the *Insert|Name|Define* command to activate the *Define Name* dialog box.

- Enter the name 'Basedata' in the 'Names in Workbook:' box. Next, clear out the contents of the 'Refers to:' box and then enter the following formula:

  =OFFSET(Database!$A$1,3,0,COUNTA(OFFSET(Database!$A$1,3,0,50,1)),19)

- Finally, click the OK button.

The COUNTA function is identical to the COUNT function except that it counts the number of non-blank cells, i.e., cells which contain text, numbers, or error values. It is now time to generate a few more macros. The following three macros will be created by entering VBA instructions directly into a macro module. Commands for entering macro code are (i) Tools|Macro|Visual_Basic_Editor and (ii) Insert|Module. Type the Display_OrderEntry code as shown below into the blank window to the right of the VBA screen. When finished, choose the following command (iii) File|Close_and_Return_to_Microsoft_Excel.

1. Display_OrderEntry	(displays worksheet OrderEntry, i.e., enter a new purchase order).
2. CopyData	(copies *and* transposes cell range X1:X2 into range Y1:Y2; then clears out the contents of cell range X1:X2).
3. Copy_OrderEntry	(copies *and* transposes of cell X1:X2 the contents of worksheet OrderEntry into the Database worksheet).

The user should be aware that a macro does not require its own module, i.e. several macros can share the same module. When one macro has been entered, simply insert a blank line after its *End Sub* statement and continue typing in VBA code for another macro. A line will automatically appear to distinguish between each macro listing. The names of macros sharing one module will still appear in the Macro list box.

Macro Listing for Display_OrderEntry

This simple macro (i) opens the worksheet OrderEntry and (ii) activates the vertical scroll bar.

```
Sub Display_OrderEntry()
'
' Display_OrderEntry Macro
' Macro recorded 26/11/200X by Joe Soap
'
' ***Displays the purchase order worksheet "OrderEntry"
'
    Sheets("OrderEntry").Select
    With ActiveWindow
    .DisplayVerticalScrollBar = True
    End With
End Sub
```

MACROS FOR TRANSFERRING DATA INTO THE DATABASE

The two macros – CopyData and Copy_OrderEntry – transfer data from the order form (OrderEntry) to the database (Database). Because it is easier to transfer data from one worksheet to another as a single row, line 8 in the OrderEntry worksheet is used as a temporary storage area. The macro CopyData performs two main functions: (i) copies and transposes a range of vertical cells, e.g. J26:J33, into a horizontal range, say E8:L8, and (ii) clears out current input data from the OrderEntry worksheet, enabling the user to create further new orders. This flexibility is achieved by adding ARGUMENTS (parameters) to the macro. Arguments are associated with flexibility, allowing a macro to be used in many different ways. It is worth noting that macros which contain arguments cannot appear in the Assign Macro list box (used to assign macros to buttons).

When creating the first two macros, Maximise_Screen and Restore_Screen_Defaults, the user may have observed that there was a considerable amount of screen activity as the macro commands were being executed. While a macro is running, such *screen updating* can be hidden from the user's view by using the VBA command, Application.ScreenUpdating = False. When the screen display is suppressed, the macro runs faster and the user is unaware of macro activity. This feature has been incorporated into the Restore_Screen_Defaults macro (see end-of-chapter macro listing) and is now used in the CopyData macro below.

Macro Listing for CopyData

In this macro, three features need clarification.

1. In the term 'x1All' (see sixth last line of macro), the letters are x = xmas, 1 = last, All = Allow.

2. The same line, i.e., 'Selection.PasteSpecial . . . . . . ∇_' ends with a space (the symbol for a space is ∇) followed by an underscore symbol (_). These two characters (∇_) must be used when a long statement is split over two (or more) lines.

3. A cell range that has the same values, e.g., B8:B8, represents a single cell. For example, the following CopyData command copies cell H12 into cell B8:

$$\text{Copy Data } X1 := \text{``H12'', } X2 := \text{``H12'', } Y1 := \text{``B8'', } Y2 := \text{``B8''}$$

```
Sub CopyData(X1, X2, Y1, Y2)
'
' Macro recorded 02-12-200X by Joe Soap
'***Copies and transposes cell range (X1:X2) into range (Y1:Y2) and then
'***clears out the contents of cell range (X1:X2)
'***The "Screen Updating" feature hides macro actions from the user
'
    Application.ScreenUpdating = False
    Range(X1, X2).Select
    Selection.Copy
    Range(Y1, Y2).Select
    Selection.PasteSpecial Paste:=xlAll, Operation:=xlNone, _
        SkipBlanks:=False, Transpose:=True
    Application.CutCopyMode = False
'***Clear the contents of cell range (X1:X2)
    Range(X1,X2).ClearContents
End Sub
```

Part of the CopyData macro can be generated automatically by using keystrokes.

- Open the Purchases workbook and choose a new worksheet. Enter the letters A,B,C,D into cells A1:A4.

- Start recording the macro by choosing the Tools|Macro|Record_New_Macro command. Enter the macro name CopyData and the description (as shown in the macro listing above) into the macro_dialog box.

- Highlight the cell range A1:A4 and click on the Edit tab. Then click on the Copy option.

- Next, click in cell C5.

- Click the Edit tab again, and click on the Paste Special option.

- The Paste_Special dialog box now appears with the default All button already activated. Click the Transpose box at the bottom of the dialog screen and then click OK. The letters A,B,C,D should now be copied across into cells C5:F5.

- Stop recording by clicking on the blue square on the left of the 'Stop recording' toolbar.

To print out a copy of the macro, choose the Tools|Macro|Macros . . . command, then select the CopyData macro and click on the Edit button. The printout should contain code similar to the CopyData listing above. Modify the automatically generated macro CopyData so that it is exactly the same as the listing. The name of any macro that contains arguments, such as the modified version of CopyData, will not appear in either the (i) Macro dialog box or (ii) Assign Macro list box (used to assign macros to buttons). It is therefore practical to store an 'argumented' macro in the same module as other procedures that utilise it.

Macro Listing for Copy_OrderEntry

The last macro in this session, *Copy_OrderEntry*, transposes and transfers data from various cells in the OrderEntry worksheet and places them in the unused row 8, i.e., in cell range B8:T8. Line 8 is used as a temporary storage area because it is easier to move data from one worksheet to another as a contiguous row. The macro then transfers (cuts) this cell range over into the Database worksheet where it inserts a blank row to prevent overwriting of the order details. Having created an order, the user has the option of exiting without saving the order by using the Close button. At this stage, it is simpler to enter VBA instructions by hand into a macro module rather than use the macro recorder. Again, the logic of the VBA instructions should be obvious. Comments have been inserted as guidelines.

```
Sub Copy_OrderEntry()
'
' Copy_OrderEntry Macro
' Macro recorded 02-12-200X by Joe Soap
'
'***Transfers user-input from the OrderEntry sheet into the Database sheet.
'***Line 8 in the OrderEntry worksheet is arbitrarily chosen as a temporary
'***transfer line (it is easier to move data as a single contiguous row)
'
'***Transfer the Order number (cell H12), the Order date (cell I14), and the
'***Supplier code number (cell D2) into cells B8,C8,D8
'
    CopyData X1:="H12", X2:="H12", Y1:="B8", Y2:="B8"
    CopyData X1:="I14", X2:="I14", Y1:="C8", Y2:="C8"
    CopyData X1:="D2", X2:="D2", Y1:="D8", Y2:="D8"
'
'***Transpose and transfer the 8 product numbers (J26:J33) into cells (E8:L8)
'***The number of product lines can be increased to 15 if so desired
    CopyData X1:="J26", X2:="J33", Y1:="E8", Y2:="L8"
'
'***Transpose and transfer the 8 "No. of Units Ordered" (E26:E33) into cells (M8:T8)
'***If the number of product lines is altered, also modify the two CopyData lines
    CopyData X1:="E26", X2:="E33", Y1:="M8", Y2:="T8"
'
'***Transfer row 8 ("OrderEntry" sheet) to row 3 ("Database" worksheet)
    Range("B8:T8").Cut Sheets("Database").Range("A3")
'
'***Insert a blank row in the database – to prevent overwriting the current order
    Sheets.("Database").Range("A3").EntireRow.Insert
End Sub
```

Save the Purchase workbook. The above macros – along with previously created procedures – give a total of five macros. The macro modules do not appear in the Purchase workbook but are accessed through the VBA Editor.

ADDING MACROS TO BUTTONS

Excel has two specially reserved macros – Auto_Open and Auto_Close. If there is a macro named Auto_Open in a workbook, it runs automatically when the workbook is opened. Similarly, if the workbook contains a macro named Auto_Close, it runs automatically before the workbook is closed. The POP system will use only the Auto_Open macro to open the title screen and hide screen activity from the user. The following two simple macros are entered manually into the macro worksheet.

Macro Listing for Auto_Open

```
Sub Auto_Open()
'
'Auto_Open Macro
'***Automatically displays the Title screen when the Purchases workbook is opened.
'***The "Screen Updating" command hides macro actions from the user
    Application.ScreenUpdating=False
    Maximize_Screen
End Sub
```

Macro Listing for Save_Quit

```
Sub Save_Quit()
'
'Save_Quit Macro
'***Macro recorded 04/12/200X by Joe Soap
'
    Restore_Screen_Defaults
'***The following two lines SAVE and CLOSE the workbook (to exit completely
'***from EXCEL, use Application.Quit instead of ActiveWorkbook.Close)
    ActiveWorkbook.Save
    ActiveWorkbook.Close
End Sub
```

Seven macros have so far been created in the POP system. They can now be assigned to buttons in both the Title and OrderEntry worksheets by following the instructions below.

- Activate the Title worksheet by clicking on its tab.

- Place the cursor on the 'Enter a new purchase order' button and click the right-hand button. The button's shortcut menu will now appear.

- Click on the Assign Macro ... option to bring up the Assign_Macro ... dialog box. The list should contain six macros (the missing macro is CopyData which contains arguments and is therefore omitted from the list).

- Click on the Display_OrderEntry macro to assign it to the 'Enter a new purchase order' button, and then click OK.

- Click somewhere outside the button to deactivate the button's shortcut menu.

- Click the 'Enter a new purchase order' button again and the OrderEntry screen will appear.

- Repeat the above steps to assign (i) the Copy_OrderEntry macro to the 'Save order' button (ii) the Maximise_Screen macro to the 'Close' button – both buttons being in the OrderEntry sheet.

- When the relevant macros have been assigned to these two buttons, click on the 'Close' button to return to the Title screen.

- The Title screen now occupies almost all of the screen. To return to the original screen format assign the macro 'Restore_Screen_Defaults' to the 'Restore original Excel screen' button.

- Finally, assign the macro 'Save_Quit' to the 'Save and exit' button, and when this task has been completed, click the 'Save and exit' button to end the current session.

AMENDING PURCHASE ORDERS

Occasionally, purchase orders have to be amended. A sudden and unexpected increase in sales may have a knock-on effect, causing readjustments in purchase order details. Government changes in VAT levels can necessitate alterations to the VAT data stored in the POP system, as can product discounts which are an everyday occurrence in today's business world. Amendments include changing, deleting, or adding items to the purchase order.

The final two POP functions to be developed are the Amend and Print options. The Amend option is a modification of the OrderEntry worksheet, so the first task is to create a copy of the OrderEntry worksheet in Sheet6 and rename the sheet AmendOrder. Before any changes can be made to AmendOrder, it must be unprotected by using the command Tools|Protection|Unprotect_Sheet. Column widths in the AmendOrder worksheet are the same as those in the OrderEntry worksheet.

Step 1: Modifying the Suppliers list box
Since details of all orders to be amended are already stored in the database, this step involves modifying the List Boxes section in cells A1:J7 (see Object Linking and Embedding (OLE) in Appendix). Start by changing the contents of the Suppliers list box into an Orders list box to display order numbers, as shown in Figure 7.7.

- Place the cursor in the Suppliers list box. Click the mouse's right-hand button to activate the shortcut menu and choose the Format Control . . . option.

- The Format Control. . . dialog box now appears displaying: (i) *Input Range*: Suppdata (ii) *Cell Link*: D2. Change this data to read (i) *Input Range*: Basedata (ii) *Cell Link*: D2 and then click OK.

- A list of purchase order numbers should now have replaced suppliers' names in the list box. Reduce the size of the Orders list box using one of its *handles* (small black squares located

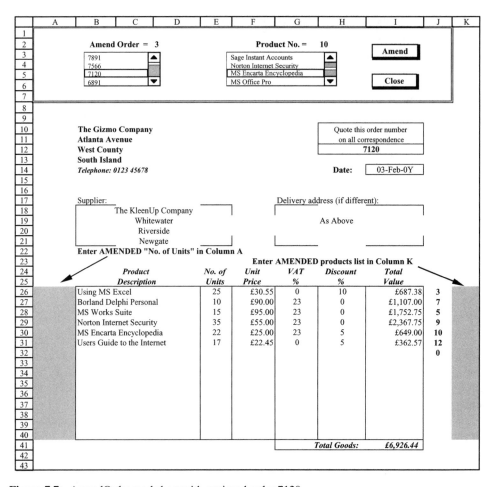

Figure 7.7   AmendOrder worksheet with retrieved order 7120.

around the object's perimeter) and then click anywhere outside the list box to deactivate its shortcut menu.

- Change the contents of cell C2 from 'Supplier No. =' to 'Amend Order ='.

Step 2: Renaming the 'Save Order' button
The next step is to rename the 'Save Order' object (i.e., button) as an 'Amend' button, as shown in the AmendOrder worksheet of Figure 7.7.

- Place the cursor in the 'Save Order' object and click the mouse's right-hand button to activate the shortcut menu.

- Choose the Format Control . . . option and when the dialog box appears, click the OK button. The button's perimeter should now be highlighted, indicating that it is in edit mode.

- Place the cursor inside the button and change the description 'Save Order' to 'Amend'.

- Reduce the size of the button by activating the button's frame and then using the object handles.
- De-activate the shortcut menu by clicking anywhere outside the object.

Step 3: Retrieving data from the worksheets

Cell formulae must be altered in Figure 7.7 in order to retrieve stored data from the Database and Products worksheets, as shown in Table 7.2. The key index, showing the record's location in the Database worksheet, is contained in cell D2 of the AmendOrder sheet.

Step 4: Protecting the AmendOrder worksheet

The AmendOrder worksheet must now be protected. Previous unlocked user-input cells E26:E33 and J26:J33 will first be locked since they contain data already stored in the

Table 7.2   Amend purchase orders – worksheet formulae.

Cell	Formula	Copied to
H12	INDEX(Basedata, D2, 1)	
I14	INDEX(Basedata, D2, 2)	
B18	INDEX(Suppdata, INDEX(Basedata, D2, 3), 1)	
B19	INDEX(Suppdata, INDEX(Basedata, D2, 3), 2)	
B20	INDEX(Suppdata, INDEX(Basedata, D2, 3), 3)	
B21	INDEX(Suppdata, INDEX(Basedata, D2, 3), 4)	
B26	IF(J26 = 0, IF(K26 = 0, "", INDEX(Prodata, K26, 1)), INDEX(Prodata, J26, 1))	B27:B33
F26	IF(J26 = 0, IF(K26 = 0, "", INDEX(Prodata, K26, 2)), INDEX(Prodata, J26, 2))	F27:F33
G26	IF(J26 = 0, IF(K26 = 0, "", INDEX(Prodata, K26, 3)), INDEX(Prodata, J26, 3))	G27:G33
H26	IF(J26 = 0, IF(K26 = 0, "", INDEX(Prodata, K26, 4)), INDEX(Prodata, J26, 4))	H27:H33
I26	IF(E26 = "", "", E26*F26*(1 + (G26 − H26)/100))	I27:I33
I41	SUM(I26:I33)	
*E26	IF(J26 = 0, "", INDEX(Basedata, D$2, 12))	E27:E33
*J26	INDEX(Basedata, D$2, 4)	J27:J33
E26	IF(J26 =0, "", INDEX(Basedata, D$2, 12))	
E27	IF(J27 = 0, "", INDEX(Basedata, D$2, 13))	
E28	IF(J28 = 0, "", INDEX(Basedata, D$2, 14))	
. . . . etc. down to cell E33		
E33	IF(J33 = 0, "", INDEX(Basedata, D$2, 19))	
J26	INDEX(Basedata, D$2, 4)	
J27	INDEX(Basedata, D$2, 5)	
J28	INDEX(Basedata, D$2, 6)	
. . . . etc. down to cell J33		
J33	INDEX(Basedata, D$2, 11)	

* These two lines need further clarification. The extended template shows the pattern of formulae changes in cells E27:E33 and J27:J33. The only characters to change in each formula are: (i) Cell E26 – the number 26 in J26 and the number 12 in the INDEX formula (ii) Cell J26 – the number 4 in the INDEX formula.

Database. Highlight each cell range, and using the F<u>o</u>rmat|C<u>e</u>lls|Protection command, turn on the <u>L</u>ocked option. The new USER INPUT cells are A26:A33 and K26:K33. Unlock these cells by using the above commands but turning off the <u>L</u>ocked option. Finally, choose the <u>T</u>ools|Protection|Protect_Sheet command to protect the AmendOrder worksheet and click OK. Again, the optional password is best ignored.

Step 5: Creating two new macros
Another two macros are created to complete the AmendOrder facility. Like the AmendOrder worksheet itself, they are modifications of objects that already exist, namely the Display_ OrderEntry and Copy_OrderEntry macros. In this situation, the modifications to the macros are straightforward. The new macros are called Display_AmendOrder and Copy_ AmendOrder.

Macro Listing for Display_AmendOrder

```
Sub Display_AmendOrder()
'
'Display_AmendOrder Macro
'Macro recorded 04-12-200X by Joe Soap
'
'***Displays the amend order worksheet "AmendOrder"
'
    Sheets("AmendOrder").Select
    With ActiveWindow
    .DisplayVerticalScrollBar = True
    End With
End Sub
```

Macro Listing for Copy_AmendOrder

```
Sub Copy_AmendOrder()
'
' Copy_AmendOrder Macro
' Macro recorded 04-12-200X by Joe Soap
'
'***Copies user-input from the AmendOrder sheet into the Database sheet.
'***Line 8 in the AmendOrder worksheet is arbitrarily chosen as a temporary
'***transfer line (it is easier to transfer a single line over to another sheet)
'
'***Transpose and transfer product numbers (K26:K33) into cells (E8:L8)
'***Note that the no. of product lines can be increased to 15 if so desired
        CopyData X1:="K26", X2:="K33", Y1:="E8", Y2:="L8"
'
'***Transpose and transfer the AMENDED "No. of Units Ordered" (A26:A33)
```

'*** into cells (M8:T8)
      CopyData X1:="A26", X2:="A33", Y1:="M8", Y2:="T8"
'

'***Transfer row 8 ("AmendOrder" sheet) into the "Database" sheet. To find the
'***correct row to alter in the "Database" sheet, use the amended order's index
'***number (in cell D2 of "AmendOrder" sheet) . . . (correct column is 4, i.e., D)
'

    Range("E8:T8").Select
    Selection.Cut
    CorrectRow = Range("D2").Value + 3
    Sheets("Database").Select
    Cells(CorrectRow,4).Select
    ActiveSheet.Paste
'

'***Return to the "AmendOrder" worksheet
    Display_AmendOrder
End Sub

Step 6: Assigning buttons

Both these macros will now be assigned to buttons. The Copy_AmendOrder macro is assigned to the *Amend* button in the AmendOrder worksheet, and the Display_AmendOrder macro is assigned to the 'Amend purchase order' button in the Title worksheet. Note that the Close button in the AmendOrder worksheet does not need modification as the previously assigned Maximise_Screen macro is OK. If help is required, go back to the previous section, entitled 'Adding macros to buttons'.

Step 7: Using the AmendOrder worksheet

Finally, to demonstrate how the AmendOrder worksheet operates, examine the details of Purchase Order number 7120 shown in Figure 7.7. Suppose the order needs to be modified as follows:

Using MS Excel	– number of units to be increased from 25 to 30
Borland Delphi Personal	– OK
MS Works Suite	– number of units to be increased from 15 to 25
Norton Internet Security	– number of units to be increased from 35 to 40
MS Encarta Encyclopedia	– Delete this unwanted item!
Users Guide to the Internet	– OK

All relevant values are entered in columns A and K:

- Item OK: If the item details are OK, simply enter the same values in columns A and K.

- Modifying an item: If the item is to be modified, enter the amended details.

- Deleting an item: If the item is to be deleted either (i) overwrite the corresponding cells in columns A and K with details of another item (see unwanted item 'MS Encarta Encyclopedia' in Figure 7.8), or (ii) leave the A,K cells blank. Items that have their A,K cells blank are deleted.

BEFORE *clicking the Amend button*

Enter AMENDED 'No. of Units' in Column A

Enter AMENDED products list in Column K

	Product Description	No. of Units	Unit Price	VAT %	Discount %	Total Value		
30	Using MS Excel	16	£30.55	0	10	£439.92	3	3
10	Borland Delphi Personal	10	£90.00	23	0	£1,107.00	7	7
25	MS Works Suite	15	£95.00	23	0	£1,752.75	5	5
40	Norton Internet Security	35	£55.00	23	0	£2,367.75	9	9
17	MS Encarta Encyclopedia	22	£25.00	23	5	£649.00	10	12
	Users Guide to the Internet	17	£22.45	0	5	£362.57	12	
							0	
	The item 'MS Encarta Encyclopedia' is no longer required. Its details in columns A and K have been overwritten with the details for the item below, i.e. 'Users Guide to the Internet'						0	

AFTER *clicking the Amend button*

Enter AMENDED 'No. of Units' in Column A

Enter AMENDED products list in Column K

Product Description	No. of Units	Unit Price	VAT %	Discount %	Total Value	
Using MS Excel	30	£30.55	0	10	£824.85	3
Borland Delphi Personal	10	£90.00	23	0	£1,107.00	7
MS Works Suite	25	£95.00	23	0	£2,921.25	5
Norton Internet Security	40	£55.00	23	0	£2,706.00	9
Users Guide to the Internet	17	£22.45	0	5	£362.57	12
						0
						0
				Total Goods:	£7,921.67	0

Figure 7.8   Amending order no. 7120: BEFORE & AFTER.

- Adding an item: If an item is to be added, either (i) enter the details of the new item in columns A and K at the end of the current list or (ii) overwrite the cells of an unwanted item with the new item's details.

The two diagrams in Figure 7.8 show sections of purchase order number 7120 (i) with the amended values entered in columns A and K BEFORE the *Amend* button is clicked (ii) AFTER the *Amend* button has been clicked. It is usually easier to experiment with an application to see how it works, rather than read explanatory notes!

PRINTING PURCHASE ORDERS

The PrintOrder worksheet is a modified version of the AmendOrder worksheet. Therefore, the first task to do is to copy the AmendOrder sheet (Figure 7.7) into Sheet7 and rename this new worksheet PrintOrder.

Step 1: Modifying list boxes
As with the AmendOrder in the previous section, the next step is to modify the objects at the top of the worksheet.

- Delete the Products list box as follows. Place the cursor in the list box and click the mouse's right-hand button to activate the shortcut menu. Click the *Clear* command.

- Move the Amend Order list box to the centre and enter the description '*Print Order =*' in cell E2.

- Place the cursor in the newly-created Print Order list box and activate its shortcut menu. Choose the *Format Control . . .* option.

- The Format_Control dialog box now displays: (i) *Input Range*: Basedata (ii) *Cell Link*: D2. Change the contents of the *Cell Link* from D2 to F2 and then click OK.

- Delete the contents of cells C2 and D2, i.e., Amend Order = 3.

- Rearrange the buttons as shown in Figure 7.9, renaming the *Amend* button as the *Print* button.

- Finally, clear AmendOrder details out of cell ranges B22:I23, A26:A33, K26:K33, using the Edit|Clear|All command. The PrintOrder worksheet should now look like Figure 7.9.

Step 2: Creating two new macros

To complete the POP system, two simple macros are now created to (i) display the PrintOrder screen and (ii) to print out the purchase order. The Print_PurchaseOrder macro is then assigned

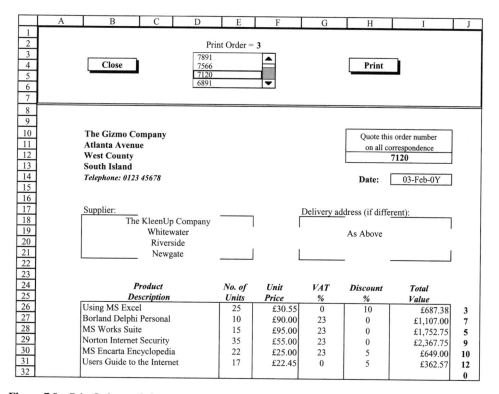

Figure 7.9 PrintOrder worksheet.

to the *Print* button in the PrintOrder worksheet while the Display_PrintOrder macro is assigned to the 'Print purchase order' button in the Title worksheet.

Macro Listing for Display_PrintOrder

```
Sub Display_PrintOrder()
'
'Display_PrintOrder
'Macro recorded 04-12-200X by Joe Soap
'
'***Displays the 'PrintOrder' worksheet
'
    Sheets("PrintOrder").Select
    With ActiveWindow
    .DisplayVerticalScrollBar = True
    End With
End Sub
```

Macro Listing for Print_PurchaseOrder

```
Sub Print_PurchaseOrder()
'
'Print_PurchaseOrder
'Macro recorded 04-12-200X by Joe Soap
'
'***Prints out the purchase order displayed in the "PrintOrder" worksheet
'
    Sheets("PrintOrder").Select
    Range("A8:I42").Select
    Selection.PrintOut Copies:=1
End Sub
```

PROTECTING THE POP DATABASE APPLICATION

To prevent the POP system being overwritten by mistake, protect each worksheet – with the important exception of the Database worksheet – ensuring that all user-input cells are first unlocked! Remember that protected cells cannot be altered. Since the Database worksheet is changed every time a new order is created or an existing order is amended, the Database must remain unprotected. If required, the Database worksheet can be hidden from the user's view by using the Format|Sheet|Hide command.

A complete listing of the eleven macros used in the Purchase Order Processing system now follows.

Sub Maximise_Screen()

```
'

'Maximise_Screen Macro
'Macro recorded 22-11-200X by Joe Soap
'

'***Maximises screen area and then displays the title screen
'

    Sheets("Title").Select
    Application.DisplayFullScreen = True
    With ActiveWindow
       .DisplayHeadings = False
       .DisplayHorizontalScrollBar = False
       .DisplayVerticalScrollBar = False
       .DisplayWorkbookTabs = False
    End With
    Range("A1").Select
End Sub
'
```

Sub Restore_Screen_Defaults()

```
'Restore_screen_Defaults Macro
'Macro recorded 22-11-20X by Joe Soap
'

'***Restores the normal screen display
'***The "Screen Updating" command hides macro activity from the user
    Application.ScreenUpdating = False
    Application.DisplayFullScreen = False
    With ActiveWindow
       .DisplayHeadings = True
       .DisplayHorizontalScrollBar = True
       .DisplayVerticalScrollBar = True
       .DisplayWorkbookTabs = True
    End With
End Sub
'
```

Sub Display_OrderEntry()

```
'Display_OrderEntry Macro
'Macro recorded 26-11-200X by Joe Soap
'

'***Displays the purchase order worksheet "OrderEntry"
'

    Sheets("OrderEntry").Select
    With ActiveWindow
    .DisplayVerticalScrollBar = True
    End With
End Sub
```

'

Sub CopyData(X1, X2, Y1, Y2)
'CopyData Macro(X1, X2, Y1, Y2)
'Macro recorded 02-12-200X by Joe Soap
'

'Copies and transposes cell range (X1:X2) into range (Y1:Y2)
'

'***The "Screen Updating" feature hides macro actions from the user
    Application.ScreenUpdating = False
    Range(X1, X2).Select
    Selection.Copy
    Range (Y1, Y2).Select
    Selection.PasteSpecial Paste = x1All, Operation: = xlNone, _
        SkipBlanks: = False, Transpose: = True
    Application.CutCopyMode = False
'***Clear contents of cell range (X1:X2)
    Range(X1, X2).ClearContents
End Sub
'

Sub Copy_OrderEntry()
'Copy_OrderEntry Macro
'Macro recorded 02-12-200X by Joe Soap
'

'Transfers user input from the OrderEntry sheet into the Database sheet.
'Line 8 in the OrderEntry worksheet is arbitrarily chosen as a temporary
'transfer line (it is easier to move data as a single contiguous row)
'

'***copy the Order number(cell H12), the Order date (cell I14), and
'***the Supplier code number (cell D2) into cells B8,C8,D8
        CopyData X1: = "H12", X2:="H12", Y1:="B8", Y2:="B8"
        CopyData X1: = "I14", X2:="I14", Y1:="C8", Y2:="C8"
        CopyData X1: = "D2", X2:="D2", Y1:="D8", Y2:="D8"
'***Copy and transpose the first 8 product numbers (J26:J33) into cells (E8:L8)
'***The number of Product lines can be increased to 15 if so desired
        CopyData X1: = "J26", X2: = "J33", Y1: = "E8", Y2: = "L8"
'***Copy and transpose the 8 "No. of Units Ordered" (E26:E33) into cells (M8:T8)
'***If the number of product lines is altered, also modify the two CopyData lines
        CopyData X1: = "E26", X2: = "E33", Y1: = "M8", Y2: = "T8"
'***Transfer row 8 ("OrderEntry" sheet) to row 3 ("Database" worksheet)
        Range("B8:T8").CutSheets("Database").Range("A3")
'***Insert a blank row in the database – to prevent overwriting the current order
        Sheets("Database").Range("A3").EntireRow.Insert
End Sub
'

```
Sub Auto_Open()
'Auto_Open Macro
'***Automatically displays the Title screen when the PURCHASE workbook is opened
'***The "Screen Updating" feature hides macro actions from the user
'
    Application.ScreenUpdating = False
    Maximise_Screen
End Sub
'

Sub Save_Quit()
'Save_Quit Macro
'Macro recorded 04-12-200X by Joe Soap
'
'***Before leaving the POP system, restore Excel's screen to its original format
    Restore_Screen_Defaults
'***The following two lines SAVE and CLOSE the workbook (to exit completely
'***from EXCEL, use Application.Quit instead of ActiveWorkbook.Close)
    ActiveWorkbook.Save
    ActiveWorkbook.Close
End Sub
'

Sub Display_AmendOrder()
'Display_AmendOrder Macro
'Macro recorded 04-12-200X by Joe Soap
'
'Displays the AMEND order worksheet "AmendOrder"
'
    Sheets("AmendOrder").Select
    With ActiveWindow
    .DisplayVerticalScrollBar = True
    End With
End Sub
'

Sub Display_PrintOrder()
'Display_PrintOrder Macro
'Macro recorded 04-12-200X by Joe Soap
'
'Displays the "PrintOrder" worksheet
'
    Sheets("PrintOrder").Select
    With ActiveWindow
    .DisplayVerticalScrollBar = True
    End With
End Sub
'
```

Sub Copy_AmendOrder()
'Copy_AmendOrder Macro
'Macro recorded 04-12-200X by Joe Soap
'
'Copies user input from the AmendOrder sheet into the Database sheet.
'Line 8 in the AmendOrder worksheet is arbitrarily chosen as a temporary
'transfer line (it is easier to transfer a single line over to another sheet)
'
'***Transpose and transfer product numbers (cells K26:K33) into cells E8:L8
     CopyData X1: = "K26", X2: = "K33", Y1: = "E8", Y2: = "L8"
'***Transpose and transfer the AMENDED "no. of units ordered" (cells A26:A33)
'***into cells M8:T8
     CopyData X1: = "A26", X2: = "A33", Y1: = "M8", Y2: = "T8"
'
'***Transfer row 8 ("AmendOrder" sheet) into the "Database" worksheet. To find
'***correct row to alter in the "Database" sheet, use the amended order's index
'***number (in cell D2 of "AmendOrder" sheet) . . . (correct column is 4, i.e., D)
'
   Range("E8:T8").Select
   Selection.Cut
   CorrectRow = Range("D2").Value + 3
   Sheets("Database").Select
   Cells(CorrectRow, 4).Select
   ActiveSheet.Paste
'
'***Return to the 'AmendOrder' worksheet
   Display_AmendOrder
End Sub
'
Sub Print_PurchaseOrder()
'Print_PurchaseOrder Macro
'Macro recorded 04-12-200X by Joe Soap
'***Prints out the purchase order displayed in the "PrintOrder" worksheet
'
   Sheets("PrintOrder").Select
   Range("A8:I42").Select
   Selection.PrintOut Copies: = 1
End Sub

EXCEL FUNCTIONS USED IN MODEL-BUILDING

The Excel function TRANSPOSE appears for the first time in this chapter. It is found in the macro CopyData and was activated by using the Transpose: = True command. However, the TRANSPOSE function is not restricted to macros and can also be usefully applied to any spreadsheet as explained below. The TRANSPOSE function is found under the function category of 'Lookup & Reference'.

1. TRANSPOSE: TRANSPOSE(array)

> returns the transpose of an array, i.e., it converts a column array into a row array and vice versa. The TRANSPOSE function must be entered as an array formula. An array formula is used to manipulate a range of cells, which is treated as a single entity. This means that individual cells within the output array (e.g., F3:H3) cannot be changed or deleted.

array   = the cell range to be transposed

Example 1: Step 1: Select the horizontal output range F3:H3 by highlighting it.
Step 2: Type the following formula into the formula bar at the top of the screen, =TRANSPOSE(B4:B6). Note that the two arrays must be the same size – in this example, each array consists of three cells.
Step 3: Enter the formula into the first cell of the selected range (cell F3) by pressing the three keys Ctrl+Shift+Enter all at once. The curly brackets will then appear automatically to indicate that an array formula has been entered into cell F3.

Example 2: Transpose the column array C2:C4 into the row array F6:H6 as shown in Figure 7.10.

Example 3: To delete an array formula, select the entire array, and then use the delete key. Try deleting the array formula in cells F3:H3.

EXERCISES

7.1 The current POP system assumes that *all* suppliers sell *all* products. This is not normally the case. Some suppliers may be chosen on the basis of their after-sales support services for particular products, combined perhaps with a particularly attractive discount price range. Consider how the current Supplier table and POP system might be modified to cater for suppliers selling

	A	B	C	D	E	F	G	H	I
1									
2		Product	No. in	Product					
3		name	stock	price		Gizmo	Gadget	Widget	
4		Gizmo	10	£10.00					
5		Gadget	25	£12.50					
6		Widget	8	£20.00		No. in stock		10	
7		Sprocket	40	£4.50					
8									
9		Cells F3:H3 contain the array formula {=TRANSPOSE(B4:B6)}							
10		Cells F6:H6 contain the array formula {=TRANSPOSE(C2:C4)}							
11									
12		*Sample Figure*							

Figure 7.10   Sample figure.

specific products. For example, when Supplier X is chosen from the Suppliers list in the OrderEntry worksheet, only products which supplier X sells should appear in the Products list box.

7.2   The Products table contains some inventory information such as the number of items on hand and items on order. How might the current purchase order information that is stored in the Database worksheet be utilised so as to update such inventory details in the Products worksheet?

7.3   The purchase order contains an address area for the '*Delivery address (if different)*'. At present, the only information that appears here is the phrase 'As Above'. Show how the Database worksheet could accommodate details for Delivery Addresses (such as warehouses) that are different from the Gizmo Company's headquarters address at Atlanta Avenue, West County, South Island.

7.4   Supplier, product, and database tables contain information that has been stored in no particular order. Discuss how Excel's database functions (see Data̲Sort . . . Filter . . . Con̲solidate . . . etc.) could be used to sort data into some meaningful order, using, for example, code numbers. Is there any benefit to sorting data by more than one key (index)?

7.5   How might the POP system be modified so that purchase order transactions that have been fully completed, i.e., all goods received and paid for, can be deleted from the Database worksheet?

7.6   Mary Jones is the owner of a small electrical business. She has recently been awarded a contract and wants to know what parts she has in stock and their prices. She has asked you to design a simple stock retrieval system that will allow her to keep track of her inventory. The final system should look similar to Figure 7.11.

	A	B	C	D	E	F	G	H	I	J
1	*Exercise 7.6 - A simple stock retrieval system*						**STOCK DATABASE**			
2										
3	*Order No:* EL6125						**Part No.**	**Units**	**Cost/Unit**	
4		**Part No.**	**Units**	**Cost/Unit**	**Value**		3216	45	£12.50	
5		3218	10	£6.75	£67.50		3218	34	£6.75	
6		3223	12	£21.00	£252.00		3220	22	£25.00	
7		3226	22	£9.50	£209.00		3221	29	£30.20	
8		3230	12	£17.35	£208.20		3223	81	£21.00	
9							3225	75	£32.25	
10							3226	37	£9.50	
11				*Total Order Value =*	£736.70		3227	19	£40.80	
12							3229	22	£50.00	
13	The Excel functions required for the model are:-						3230	9	£17.35	
14	(a) IF (b) VLOOKUP (c) SUMPRODUCT						**Total stock value =**		**£8,720.40**	
15	(d) SUM									
16										

Figure 7.11

7.7   The stock retrieval system in Exercise 7.6 does not take stockouts into account. Modify Mary Jones's model to include

- an option to update the stock database to reflect current inventory levels
- reorder levels for each part in the stock database (add column J say, to the stock database)

- a message 'Reorder now!' to be printed out whenever a 'no. of units' value in cells H5:H13 falls below its corresponding reorder value in cell range J5:J13.

7.8 Data consolidation is used to summarise data from several sources. Consolidating information from multiple sources is a task that Excel can handle quite easily using its Data|Consolidate command. Consider how the POP system might use data consolidation as a means of interfacing with other workbooks containing information from associated areas such as accounting, sales, and inventory control.

REFERENCES AND FURTHER READING

Walkenbach, J. (2004) *Excel 2003 Power Programming with VBA*, John Wiley & Sons, Inc., New Jersey.

Part 2

Models for operations management

8

Statistical applications in quality control

OVERVIEW

In today's competitive market-place, quality of goods and services is a critical success factor. In a manufacturing environment, the quality control (QC) function ensures that all products meet the standards specified by the engineering design department. The quality of products at various stages of production are, however, subject to a certain amount of variability. No two items will be identical in every respect even though they conform to their specifications. Traditionally, quality control involved carrying out inspections to ensure that products met minimum quality requirements. This approach had the disadvantage of determining product quality only when the manufacturing process was completed. Today, quality control involves continuous inspection, i.e., monitoring the product's progress at regular stages throughout its manufacturing life cycle, and taking corrective action where necessary.

The well-known advocate of quality management, W. Edwards Deming, stated that management is responsible for 85% of quality problems in a factory environment with workers being responsible for only 15%. He pointed out that workers cannot extend quality beyond the limits of what any process is capable of producing. The quality control function is now referred to as total quality management (TQM), emphasising the strategic importance of quality to the whole organisation, not just the factory floor. TQM involves an unending process of continuous improvement with the objective of achieving perfection. The fact that perfection is never reached is irrelevant, the setting and achieving of ever-higher goals is sufficient justification.

The two main approaches to quality control are (i) acceptance sampling and (ii) statistical process control. The term 'acceptance sampling' refers to statistical techniques that are used to accept or reject a batch of items on the basis of a sample test or inspection. This traditional approach to quality control involves randomly selecting a sample from a batch of items and applying various tests to each item in the sample to see if it works as intended. The QC manager then extends the sample's test results to the whole batch. For example, if 2% of a sample's items are found to be defective, the manager concludes that 2% of the whole batch are also faulty.

Statistical process control (SPC) is the application of statistical techniques to the control of processes. SPC is used to ensure that a process is meeting specified standards by measuring its performance. If the process is to produce quality products, its capabilities must be periodically measured to check that it is performing as planned. The quality of the process can be affected by natural variations that occur in almost every production process. As long as these variations remain within specified limits, the process is 'in control' and quality will not be affected. However, if the variations go outside the specified limits, the process is 'out of control' and the causes must be determined. Control charts are used to separate random causes of variation from non-random causes such as operator error, faulty setup, poor materials, and so forth.

PROBABILITY DISTRIBUTIONS

Probability is the chance that something will happen. Probabilities are expressed as fractions or decimals. If an event is assigned a probability of 0, this means that the event can never happen. If the event is given a probability of 1 then it will always happen. Classical probability defines the probability that an event will occur, given that each of the outcomes are equally likely, as

$$P(\text{event}) = \frac{\text{number of ways that the event can occur}}{\text{total number of possible outcomes}}$$

For example, what is the probability of rolling a 4 on the first throw of a dice? Since the total number of possible outcomes is 6, and the number of ways that 4 can be achieved with one throw is 1, the answer is P (event) $= 1/6$. A probability distribution extends the concepts of frequency distributions into an uncertain environment where events can have several possible outcomes. Probability distributions can be either discrete or continuous. A discrete probability distribution describes instances where the variable of interest can take on only a limited number of values, e.g., the rolling of a dice is limited to one of six numbers. In a continuous probability distribution, the variable can take any value in a given range, e.g., measuring growth over a specified time period. There are many different probability distributions, both discrete and continuous. The four most commonly used distributions are:

1. The Binomial distribution is a discrete distribution which is used to describe many applications including games of chance, product quality control, and finance.

2. The Poisson distribution is a discrete distribution which is often used to count the number of occurrences of some event in a given period of time, e.g., predicting the number of arrivals at a service facility such as a filling-station.

3. The Exponential distribution is a continuous distribution used to measure the length of time needed to perform some activity. It is widely used in queuing (waiting-line) models.

4. The Normal distribution is a continuous distribution providing the basis for many important statistical decisions, e.g., the central limit theorem. It is bell-shaped and symmetrical in appearance.

Probabilities can be either individual or cumulative. The cumulative probability is the sum of all the individual probabilities up to and including the particular probability. Consider the following situation: the probabilities of selling 20, 18, 15 and 10 items have been estimated as 0.1, 0.2, 0.3 and 0.4. The cumulative probability of selling 15 items or more is then determined to be 0.6, i.e., the sum of the probabilities of selling 15, 18 and 20 items. Expressed mathematically, the probability of selling 18 items or more, i.e., $P(\geq 18)$ equals $P(18) + P(20) = 0.2 +$

$0.1 = 0.3$. Conversely, the probability of selling less than 18 items, $P(<18)$ is $1 - P(\geq 18) = 1 - 0.3 = 0.7$, i.e., $P(10) + P(15)$.

EXAMPLE 8.1   *Using Excel's HISTOGRAM function to obtain a frequency distribution*

The Wheelie Company is about to introduce a new line of tyres for racing bicycles. The Company's quality control manager has been asked to present the results of a recent test of tyres on a hundred bicycles competing in the Tour de France. In order to save time and effort, he has decided to use Excel's Histogram option. The Histogram converts raw data into a number of groups or classes, and then counts the number of values which fall into each class. These class values are called the class frequencies. The QC manager has decided to use a standard group width and limit of 5, i.e., for any data point x_i, $5 < x_i \leq 10$, $10 < x_i \leq 15$, $15 < x_i \leq 20$, etc. The following table contains a list of how far the 100 bicycles got (to the nearest 100 km) before one of the tyres failed to meet minimum EC standards.

38	24	12	36	41	40	45	41	40	47
26	15	48	44	29	43	28	29	37	11
37	45	29	31	23	49	41	47	41	42
59	40	40	45	37	55	47	42	28	38
38	48	18	16	39	50	14	52	33	32
51	13	49	21	44	31	43	34	49	48
28	39	28	36	56	54	39	31	35	36
32	20	54	25	39	44	25	42	50	41
11	34	32	34	42	40	43	32	30	45
20	29	14	19	38	46	46	39	40	47

Although the number of classes is an optional parameter when using Excel's Histogram function, it is better to define a suitable set of classes, called 'bins' in Histogram terminology. Bin ranges should be in ascending order. Excel counts the number of data points between the current bin number, B_i, and the adjoining higher bin, B_{i+1}. A number N is counted in bin B_{i+1} if it lies in the range $B_i < N \leq B_{i+1}$. The Histogram function is found in Excel's Analysis ToolPak which is activated by clicking on the Tools menu in the spreadsheet and then clicking Data Analysis in the options list. Inputs to Figure 8.1 include formula template Table 8.1 and Histogram details as given below.

Excel's Histogram input

INPUT	Input range:	Select (or enter) cell range C3:L12
	Bin range:	D16:N16
	Labels:	Click OK with mouse
OUTPUT	Output range:	A18
	New worksheet ply:	
	New workbook:	
	Pareto (sorted histogram):	
	Cumulative percentage:	Click OK with mouse
	Chart output:	Click OK with mouse

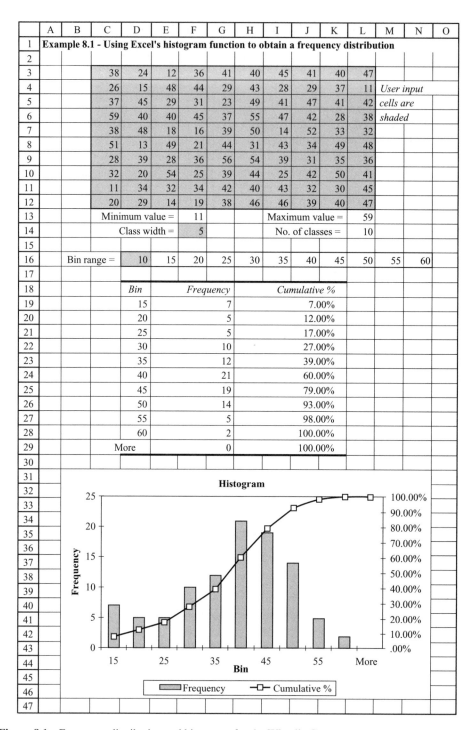

	A	B	C	D	E	F	G	H	I	J	K	L	M	N	O
1	Example 8.1 - Using Excel's histogram function to obtain a frequency distribution														
2															
3			38	24	12	36	41	40	45	41	40	47			
4			26	15	48	44	29	43	28	29	37	11	*User input*		
5			37	45	29	31	23	49	41	47	41	42	*cells are*		
6			59	40	40	45	37	55	47	42	28	38	*shaded*		
7			38	48	18	16	39	50	14	52	33	32			
8			51	13	49	21	44	31	43	34	49	48			
9			28	39	28	36	56	54	39	31	35	36			
10			32	20	54	25	39	44	25	42	50	41			
11			11	34	32	34	42	40	43	32	30	45			
12			20	29	14	19	38	46	46	39	40	47			
13			Minimum value =			11			Maximum value =			59			
14			Class width =			5			No. of classes =			10			
15															
16		Bin range =		10	15	20	25	30	35	40	45	50	55	60	
17															
18				*Bin*		*Frequency*			*Cumulative %*						
19				15		7			7.00%						
20				20		5			12.00%						
21				25		5			17.00%						
22				30		10			27.00%						
23				35		12			39.00%						
24				40		21			60.00%						
25				45		19			79.00%						
26				50		14			93.00%						
27				55		5			98.00%						
28				60		2			100.00%						
29				More		0			100.00%						

Figure 8.1   Frequency distribution and histogram for the Wheelie Company.

Table 8.1 Frequency distribution – worksheet formulae.

Cell	Formula	Copied to
F13	MIN(C3:L12)	
L13	MAX(C3:L12)	
F14	ROUNDUP((L13–F13)/F14, 0)	
E16	D16 + $F14	F16:N16

The Histogram's output in Figure 8.1 has been rearranged to make it more presentable. The Frequency column (cells G19:G29) contains the number of observations that fall into each class or bin as defined in column D. For example, cells G19, G20, G21 show that 7, 5, 5 observations lie in bins 11–15, 16–20, 21–25 respectively. The Cumulative % column shows the percentage of observations that are less than or equal to the values listed in column D. For example, cell J21 contains the value 17% which is the percentage of observations that are less than or equal to 25 (cell D21). These cumulative values, shown as white squares, have also been plotted on the histogram using the graph's right-hand scale.

EXAMPLE 8.2 *Checking out defective inventory items*

Barbara Blair is the quality control manager for the Gizmo Company. One of her jobs is to check out inventory for defective items. If she thinks that more than 2% of items in a batch of 1000 gizmos are defective, then she rejects the batch. She usually takes a random sample of 50 items to check out the whole batch. Barbara has decided to use Excel's Binomial distribution function BINOMDIST to obtain answers (see double-border cells in Figure 8.2) to the following:

- the probability of finding (i) one defective item (ii) more than one defective item (iii) from 1 to 3 defective items
- the expected number of defectives in a sample of 50, given that 2% of all batch items are defective. (Note: the term 'expected value' is the same as the sample mean.)

Barbara would now like to determine a standard value, N, which she can use as a reference for batch rejection. If N or more defectives are found in any sample of 50 items, then the batch can be rejected with at least 90% confidence that it is truly defective. Barbara has decided that Excel's Poisson function is more appropriate than BINOMDIST for finding an acceptable value for N. If Barbara is to be at least 90% confident that the consignment is truly defective, then there must be less than a 10% chance of finding N or more defectives in the batch. The answer is $N = 3$, as shown in Figure 8.3.

The Poisson distribution can be applied to situations where the number of successful outcomes is known but not the number of failures, or vice versa. The converse applies in Barbara's case because she is interested in unsuccessful outcomes, i.e. defective items. The Poisson function can be used to solve this part of the problem since it requires that only the average number (i.e., mean) of defectives be known. Barbara's sample mean, which is defined as (sample size) × (probability), has already been calculated (=1) in the first part of the exercise (see cell G24 in Figure 8.2).

	A	B	C	D	E	F	G	H
1						**Example 8.2 - Using Excel's binomial distribution function to check out defective items**		
2								
3		BINOMDIST(number, size, probability, cumulative) where						
4		**number** = the number of defectives **size** = the sample size						
5		**probability** = the sample probability **cumulative** is a logical value						
6		If **cumulative** = TRUE, the function returns the cumulative Binomial probability						
7		If **cumulative** = FALSE, it returns the individual Binomial probability						
8								
9		*Sample size* =	50	*Probability* =	2%	*Cumulative* =	FALSE	
10								
11		Probability of	0	defectives, P(0) = BINOMDIST(0,50,0.02,FALSE) =			0.3642	
12		Probability of	1	defectives, P(1) = BINOMDIST(1,50,0.02,FALSE) =			0.3716	
13		Probability of	2	defectives, P(2) = BINOMDIST(2,50,0.02,FALSE) =			0.1858	
14		Probability of	3	defectives, P(3) = BINOMDIST(3,50,0.02,FALSE) =			0.0607	
15		Probability of more than one defective item = 1 – [P(0) + P(1)] =					0.2642	
16								
17						*Cumulative* =	TRUE	
18		Prob. of up to	3	defectives, CUM_3 = BINOMDIST(3,50,0.02,TRUE) =			0.9822	
19		Prob. of up to	0	defectives, CUM_0 = BINOMDIST(0,50,0.02,TRUE) =			0.3642	
20		Probability of between 1 to 3 defective items = $CUM_3 - CUM_0$ =					0.6181	
21		The above answer is the same as summing the individual probabilities, i.e.						
22		Probability of between 1 to 3 defective items = P(1) + P(2) + P(3) =					0.6181	
23								
24				Sample mean = (sample size)*(probability) = 50(0.02) =			1	
25								
26			*Cell*	*Formula*			*Copied to*	
27			G11	BINOMDIST(C11,C$9,E$9,G$9)			G12:G14	
28			G16	1 – G11 – G12				
29			G18	BINOMDIST(C18,C$9,E$9,G$17)			G19	
30			G20	G18 – G19				
31			G22	G12 + G13 + G14				
32			G24	C9*E9				
33								

Figure 8.2   Checking out defective inventory items using BINOMDIST.

EXAMPLE 8.3   *Calculating probabilities with Excel's NORMDIST function*

The life of an electronic component used in product X was found to be normally distributed with a mean of 4,500 hours and a standard deviation of 1000 hours. Calculate the probability that the component will last for between 5,000 and 6,000 hours. If average annual usage of product X is 1500 hours, what is the probability that the component will last for five years?

Customers can purchase a five-year guarantee for product X for an additional charge of £40. The guarantee provides free component replacement if failure occurs during the first three years, but there will be an extra charge of £45 to the customer if the component has to be replaced in either the fourth or fifth year. How much will this offer cost the company, given that a component costs £80, and assuming that the average usage of product X is 1500 hours per year?

	A	B	C	D	E	F	G	H
1	**Example 8.2 - Using Excel's Poisson distribution to find a standard value**							
2								
3		POISSON(**x, mean, cumulative**) where						
4		**x** = the number of defectives, **mean** = the sample mean						
5		**cumulative** is a logical value						
6		If **cumulative** = TRUE, the function returns the cumulative Poisson probability						
7		If **cumulative** = FALSE, it returns the individual Poisson probability						
8								
9		**Sample mean =**	1				%	
10		Probability of	0	or more defectives = certainty =		1,0000	100.00%	
11		Probability of	1	or more defectives = 1 – POISSON(0,1,TRUE) =		0.6321	63.21%	
12		Probability of	2	or more defectives = 1 – POISSON(1,1,TRUE) =		0.2642	26.42%	
13		Probability of	3	or more defectives = 1 – POISSON(2,1,TRUE) =		0.0803	*8.03%*	
14		Probability of	4	or more defectives = 1 – POISSON(3,1,TRUE) =		0.0190	1.90%	
15								
16								
17		The Poisson probabilities in column G indicate, for example in cell G12, that there is a 26.42%						
18		chance that two or more defectives will occur in a random sample of 50 with a 2% defect rate. Thus,						
19		if sample contain two or more defectives, then the whole batch can be rejected with a 73.58%						
20		confidence level. Since Barbara wants to be at least 90% confident, **the standard should be**						
21		**set at three defectives per sample.** This level can only occur randomly in 8.03% of occasions						
22		(see cell G13), i.e. Barbara can be 91.97% confident that the whole batch is truly defective.						
23								
24		*Cell*		*Formula*		*Copied to*		
25		F11		1 – POISSON(C10, C$9,TRUE)		F12:F14		
26		G10		F10		G11:G14		
27								

Figure 8.3   Finding a standard value using the Poisson function.

The answers, as calculated in Figure 8.4, are (i) 24.2% chance that the component will last between 5000 and 6000 hours (ii) 99.87% probability of component lasting for five years (iii) the company will make a loss of £17.45 on each guarantee offer.

ACCEPTANCE SAMPLING

Acceptance sampling is normally used to monitor the quality of incoming materials or products. A random sample is selected from a shipment of items. The sample items are then inspected and tested to see if they conform to predetermined standards. The quality of the sample is used to determine whether the entire shipment should be accepted or rejected. Since acceptance sampling can also be used in the final inspection of outgoing finished goods, it applies to the input/output stages of the manufacturing cycle. Statistical process control completes the cycle by monitoring the middle stage of the 'input-process-output' system.

A sampling plan is simply a decision rule which specifies (i) the size of the random sample n, and (ii) an acceptable number of defectives in the sample, usually called the 'acceptance

	A	B	C	D	E	F	G	H
1		**Example 8.3 - Using the normal distribution NORMDIST to solve for Product X**						
2								
3		NORMDIST(*x, mean, standard_dev, cumulative*) where						
4		*x* = the value for which the normal distribution is required						
5		*mean* = the distribution mean, *standard_dev* = the standard deviation						
6		If *cumulative* = TRUE, the function returns the cumulative Normal probability						
7		If *cumulative* = FALSE, it return the individual Normal probability						
8								
9		*mean* =	4500	*standard deviation* =	1000	*cumulative* =	TRUE	
10								
11			Probability of component lasting up to	6000	hours = P(6000) =	0.9332		
12			Probability of component lasting up to	6000	hours = P(5000) =	0.6915		
13			Prob. of lasting between 5000 and 6000 hours = P(6000) − P(5000) =			0.2417		
14								
15			Probability of component lasting 5 years is	7500	hours = P(7500) =	0.9987		
16			i.e. there is a 99.87% probability that the component will last up to 5 years					
17								
18		The probability of the component *failing in 3 years* is the same the						
19			probability of the component lasting up to	4500	hours =P(4500) =	0.5000		
20								
21			Probability of *failing in years 4 and 5* = P(7500) − P(4500) =			0.4987		
22								
23		Using the values in cells G19 and G21, the expected payout by the company for the						
24		5-years gurantee can be calculated as follows: (£80 × 0.5) + (£35 × 0.4987) = *£57.45*						
25		Since the charge for the guarantee is only £40, the company can *expect to make*						
26		*a loss of (£57.45 – £40), i.e. £17.45 on each guarantee*						
27								
28		*Cell*	*Formula*			*Copied to*		
29		G11	NORMDIST(E11,C$9,E$9,G$9)			G12, G15, G19		
30		G13	G11– G12					
31		G21	G15 – G19					
32								

Figure 8.4   Using Excel's normal distribution function NORMDIST.

number' c. If the sample contains c or fewer defectives, then the whole batch is accepted. Conversely, if the sample contains more than c defectives then the batch is rejected. A typical sampling plan could be stated as 'select a random sample of 50 items and count the number of defectives, c, in the sample. If $c \leq 3$, accept the shipment, otherwise reject it'. The objective of any sampling plan is to help the customer or consumer in deciding whether a batch is good or bad.

Sampling plans involve a degree of uncertainty, i.e., there is a risk of finding too many or too few defective items in the random sample. A customer may accept a shipment because a sample was lucky enough to include very few faulty items. In such situations, the customer's decision to accept a bad batch is called the 'consumer's risk' (or, in statistical terms, a type II error – see later section 'Hypothesis testing – checking out a claim!'). On the other hand, if the customer's sample is unfortunate enough to contain too many defectives, a wrong decision will be made when rejecting a good batch unnecessarily. The producer of the product will then have to replace the rejected shipment even though it meets specified standards. For obvious reasons, the customer's decision to reject a good batch is called the 'producer's risk' (or, in statistical terms, a type I error).

Operating Characteristic (OC) Curves

An operating characteristic (OC) curve is a graph showing the features of a specific sampling plan and its associated risks. Every sampling plan has its own OC curve. The shape of an OC curve depends primarily upon the values given to n and c by the sampling plan. Assigning numerical values to n and c is not an easy task and depends to a large extent on managerial judgement and experience. Increasing the sample size, n, will lower the consumer's risk but increase the producer's risk. Decreasing n has the opposite effect, i.e., a small sample size favours the producer. Generally, as n increases and c decreases, the curve will be lowered (see Figure 8.5). Lowering the curve means that the probability of acceptance will also be reduced, i.e., the quality requirements become more stringent.

In order to interpret the results of an OC curve, it is necessary to specify performance requirements as defined by the following four parameters:

1. *Acceptable quality level* (AQL) – defines 'good quality' and batch acceptance, e.g., if AQL = 3%, then a good-quality batch of 500 items must contain 15 defective items or less ($0.03 \times 500 = 15$).

2. *Lot tolerance percent defective* (LTPD) – defines 'bad quality' and batch rejection, e.g., if LTPD = 5%, then a bad-quality batch of 500 items must contain 25 defectives or more ($0.05 \times 500 = 25$).

3. *Producer's risk* – the probability of rejecting a good batch as described above. Producer's risk is usually designated by α (alpha) with a typical upper limit for α being 5%, i.e., $\alpha = 0.05$.

4. *Consumer's risk* – the probability of accepting a bad batch as described above. Consumer's risk is usually designated by β (beta) with a typical upper limit for β being 10%, i.e., $\beta = 0.1$.

An OC curve can be plotted using either the Binomial or Poisson distribution. The Poisson distribution is more suitable for solving problems in which the sample size, n, is large (>20) and the probability, p (of randomly selecting a defective) is small. The probability, p, has the same meaning as percent defective. Note that the Poisson mean is defined as (sample size) $\times$ (probability) $= np$. The OC curve plots the 'percent defective' values along the x-axis and the 'probability of accepting the shipment' along the y-axis.

EXAMPLE 8.4   *OC curve model for the Gizmo Company's sampling plans*

The Gizmo Company has recently received a batch of 5000 components which are used in the manufacture of its product. Management have specified percent defective limits of 2% and 6% for batch acceptance and rejection respectively. This means that the sample must contain 2% or less defectives for the whole consignment to be accepted, i.e., AQL = 2%. On the other hand, if the sample contains 6% or more defectives, then the consignment will be rejected, i.e., LTPD = 6%.

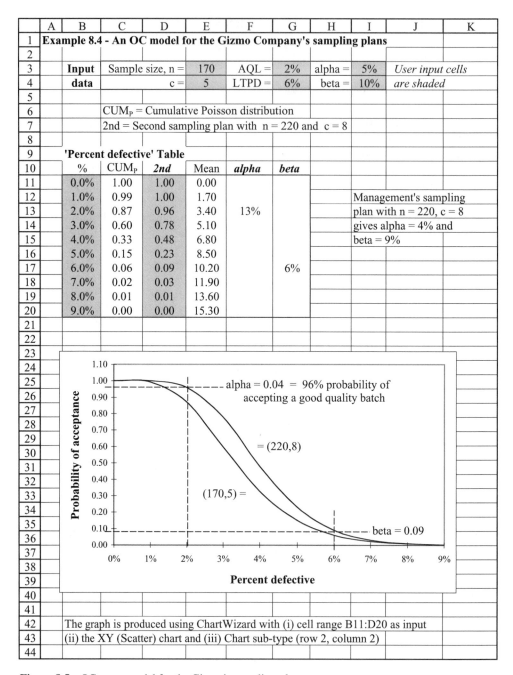

	A	B	C	D	E	F	G	H	I	J	K
1		**Example 8.4 - An OC model for the Gizmo Company's sampling plans**									
2											
3		**Input**	Sample size, n =		170	AQL =	2%	alpha =	5%	*User input cells*	
4		**data**		c =	5	LTPD =	6%	beta =	10%	*are shaded*	
5											
6			CUM_P = Cumulative Poisson distribution								
7			2nd = Second sampling plan with n = 220 and c = 8								
8											
9		**'Percent defective' Table**									
10		%	CUM_P	*2nd*	Mean	*alpha*	*beta*				
11		0.0%	1.00	1.00	0.00						
12		1.0%	0.99	1.00	1.70				Management's sampling		
13		2.0%	0.87	0.96	3.40	13%			plan with n = 220, c = 8		
14		3.0%	0.60	0.78	5.10				gives alpha = 4% and		
15		4.0%	0.33	0.48	6.80				beta = 9%		
16		5.0%	0.15	0.23	8.50						
17		6.0%	0.06	0.09	10.20		6%				
18		7.0%	0.02	0.03	11.90						
19		8.0%	0.01	0.01	13.60						
20		9.0%	0.00	0.00	15.30						
21											
22											
23											
...											
42		The graph is produced using ChartWizard with (i) cell range B11:D20 as input									
43		(ii) the XY (Scatter) chart and (iii) Chart sub-type (row 2, column 2)									
44											

Chart labels: alpha = 0.04 = 96% probability of accepting a good quality batch; = (220,8); (170,5) =; beta = 0.09. Y-axis: Probability of acceptance (0.00 to 1.10). X-axis: Percent defective (0% to 9%).

Figure 8.5   OC curve model for the Gizmo's sampling plans.

Table 8.2 OC curve model – worksheet formulae.

Cell	Formula	Copied to
C11	POISSON(E$4, F11, TRUE)	C12:C20
E11	E$3*B11	E12:E20
F11	IF(B11 = G$3, 1–C11, "")	F12:F20
G11	IF(B11 = G$4, C11, "")	G12:G20

The company wants to find a sampling plan that gives at least a 95% probability of accepting good shipments but only a 10% probability of accepting bad goods, i.e., $\alpha = 5\%$ and $\beta = 10\%$. The quality control manager has suggested a sampling plan specifying a sample size of $n = 170$ with an acceptance number, $c \leq 5$. However, management are not convinced that this plan will meet both specifications for good ($\alpha \leq 5\%$) and bad ($\beta \leq 10\%$) quality acceptance, and have suggested another plan with $n = 220$ and $c \leq 8$.

All OC curves are created from a 'percent defective' table. The model of Figure 8.5, which is built using the formulae template of Table 8.2, contains a '% defective' table (cells B11:B20) with values ranging from 0%–9%. Because the proposed sample sizes are large (>20) and the percent-defective is small (2%), the Poisson distribution is used to plot the OC curve. The model has found that the quality control manager's plan with $n = 170$, $c = 5$ yields values of $\alpha = 13\%$ and $\beta = 6\%$. While β is within the limit of 10%, α is well outside the 5% limit. However, management's sampling (220,8) plan is within both acceptance probabilities for good ($\alpha = 4\%$) and bad ($\beta = 9\%$) quality shipments. The graph for management's plan was obtained by entering the appropriate (n, c) values into cells E3:E4 and then copying cell range C11:C20 into D11:D20 by hand.

EXAMPLE 8.5 *Using an OC curve to find acceptable AQL and LTPD values*

Fred Flint has recorded details of defective items in recent batches of product P. He always takes a sample size of 200 items and rejects the lot if more than 5 defectives are found. Having set both consumer's and producer's risk at 10%, he has decided to plot an operating characteristic (OC) curve using the following 'Percent Defective' table:

Average no. of defectives	1	2	4	6	10	18
% defective	0.5	1	2	3	5	9

Fred wants to use his curve to find acceptable values for measuring good (AQL) and bad (LTPD) quality. A 10% producer's risk is equivalent to a 90% probability of accepting only good-quality items. A 10% consumer's risk is the same as a 10% probability of accepting bad-quality items. Using the OC curve of Figure 8.6 to read 'percent defective' values gives AQL = 1.5% and LTPD = 4.8%.

ESTIMATION – DRAWING CONCLUSIONS FROM SAMPLES

Statistical inference, usually abbreviated to inference, is a process by which conclusions are reached on the basis of examining only a part of the total data available. A typical example of

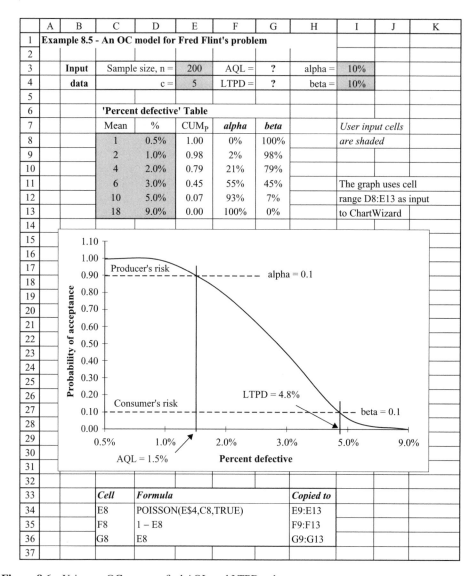

	A	B	C	D	E	F	G	H	I	J	K
1	**Example 8.5 - An OC model for Fred Flint's problem**										
2											
3		**Input**	Sample size, n =		200	AQL =	?	alpha =	10%		
4		**data**	c =		5	LTPD =	?	beta =	10%		
5											
6			**'Percent defective' Table**								
7			Mean	%	CUM$_P$	*alpha*	*beta*		*User input cells*		
8			1	0.5%	1.00	0%	100%		*are shaded*		
9			2	1.0%	0.98	2%	98%				
10			4	2.0%	0.79	21%	79%				
11			6	3.0%	0.45	55%	45%		The graph uses cell		
12			10	5.0%	0.07	93%	7%		range D8:E13 as input		
13			18	9.0%	0.00	100%	0%		to ChartWizard		
14											
33			**Cell**	**Formula**				**Copied to**			
34			E8	POISSON(E$4,C8,TRUE)				E9:E13			
35			F8	1 − E8				F9:F13			
36			G8	E8				G9:G13			

Figure 8.6 Using on OC curve to find AQL and LTPD values.

inference is an opinion poll that is used to predict the voting pattern of a country's population during an election. Statistical inference can be divided into two main areas, statistical estimation and hypothesis testing. This section examines estimation, i.e., drawing conclusions from population samples.

Most people at some time or other have purchased a box of matches containing the label inscription 'contents 100 approx'. If anyone bothered to count the number of matches in a random sample of six boxes, they would most likely find that the contents varied from, say 98 to 102. It would be most unusual, if not unique, if every box contained the same number of matches. Putting this observation into statistical terms: when the mean is calculated from a sample, the value that results, $\overline{X}$, depends on which sample (of the many possible samples that could be chosen) is observed.

The difference between the population mean, μ, and the sample mean, $\overline{X}$, is called the sampling error. Two samples from the same population are likely to have different sample values and could therefore lead to different conclusions being drawn. Because random samples are selected by chance alone, there is a level of uncertainty attached to sampling errors. The concept of 'confidence limits' is introduced to reflect this uncertainty.

Confidence limits define an interval within which managers can be confident that that any conclusions drawn from sampling data will be right for $x\%$ of the time. The most common values given to x are 95% and 99%. It should be noted that the terms 'confidence limits' and 'significance levels' are complementary, one being the reciprocal of the other. Thus, the phrase 'there is a 95% confidence that the sampling error is not due to chance' can be restated as 'the sampling error is significant at the 5% level'. Similarly, a 99% confidence limit has the same meaning as a significance level of 1%. Generally, confidence limits are used when discussing statistical estimation while significance levels are associated with hypothesis testing.

In operations management, quality control testing relies heavily on statistical estimation to accept or reject production output. A quality control manager will take a random sample of products and if he finds that the number of defective items is too high, the batch will be rejected. His job is then to make adjustments to the production process in order to eliminate (or at least reduce) the level of deficiency. The only practical way of reducing the size of a sampling error without decreasing the level of confidence is to increase the size of the sample.

EXAMPLE 8.6 *Determining confidence limits with Excel's CONFIDENCE function*

The expected life of a component was tested using a sample of 100 units. The following results were obtained:

Component life (hours)	< 85	< 90	< 95	< 100	< 105	< 110	≥ 110
No. of components	3	10	17	39	18	9	4

On the basis of this sample, the ABC Company would like to determine 95% confidence limits for the mean life of the component. If the component's life is normally distributed, should the company accept a large order from a regular customer who requires that all components last for at least 90 hours?

Since the component data is grouped into classes, the usual Excel formulae do not apply. The model of Figure 8.7 uses the standard formulae for the mean and standard deviation of a grouped frequency table.

$$\text{Grouped data:} \quad \text{Mean, } \overline{X} = \left(\sum_{i=1}^{c} F_i M_i \right) / N$$

$$\text{and Variance, } \sigma^2 = \left\{ \sum_{i=1}^{c} F_i (M_i - \overline{X})^2 \right\} / N$$

	A	B	C	D	E	F	G	H	I	J	K	L
1		**Example 8.6 - Determining confidence limits using the CONFIDENCE function**										
2											Totals	
3		Component life (hours)		< 85	< 90	< 95	< 100	< 105	< 110	>= 110		
4		No. of Components, F		3	10	17	39	18	9	4	100	
5												
6		Mid-point of interval, M =		82	87	92	97	102	107	112		
7			F*M =	246	870	1564	3783	1836	963	448	9710	
8			F*(M–m$_s$)² =	684	1020	442.2	0.39	432.2	882.1	888	4349	
9												
10						sample mean, m$_s$ =	97.1		User input cells			
11					standard deviation of sample =		6.59		are shaded			
12												
13		CONFIDENCE(**alpha, standard_dev, size**) where										
14		**alpha** = significance level (which is the complement of *confidence limits*)										
15		= 0.05 = 5% significance level = 95% *confidence limits*										
16		**standard_dev** = standard deviation of the sample						**size** = sample size				
17												
18			CONFIDENCE(0.05, G11, K4) =				1.29					
19												
20		CONFIDENCE returns the confidence interval which is a range on either side of the										
21		sample mean of 97.1. Thus the ABC Company can be 95% confident that the population										
22		mean lies in the range (97.1 – 1.29) to (97.1 + 1.29), i.e. between 95.81 and 98.39 hours.										
23												
24		Assuming that the component's life is normally distributed, then the probability of a										
25		component lasting up to 90 hours (i.e. failing within 90 hours) is										
26		NORMDIST(90, G10, G11, TRUE) =					0.14	= 14%				
27												
28		The failure rate of 14% (see cell G26) seems rather high and so the ABC Company										
29		should not accept the customer's order.										
30												

Figure 8.7 Using Excel's CONFIDENCE function to determine confidence limits.

where: $\overline{X}$ = sample mean
C = number of classes
N = sample size
M_i = midpoint of the ith class
F_i = frequency of the ith class
$\sum$ = 'the sum of'
σ = standard deviation, i.e., the square root of the variance

The model of Figure 8.7 has found (i) sample mean = 97.1, standard deviation = 6.59 (ii) 95% confidence limits are (95.81, 98.39) (iii) because component failure rate is high (14%, see cell H26), the customer order should not he accepted. The template of Table 8.3 is used to build the model of Figure 8.7.

Table 8.3 Confidence limits – worksheet formulae.

Cell	Formula	Copied to
K4	SUM(D4:J4)	
E6	D6 + 5	F6:J6
D7	D4*D6	E7:J7
K7	SUM(D7:J7)	K8
D8	D4*(D6–$G10)^2	E8:J8
G10	K7/K4	
G11	SQRT(K8/K4)	
G18	CONFIDENCE(0.05, G11, K4)	
G26	NORMDIST(90, G10, G1, TRUE)	

HYPOTHESIS TESTING – CHECKING OUT A CLAIM!

It is common for businesses to make claims about their products. For example, a manufacturer of widgets may claim that only 2% of his products are defective. When such a claim, or hypothesis, is made managers must be able to substantiate their claim. To check out the manufacturer's assertion, it is not feasible to test every widget and so a random sample is normally selected. The objective of a hypothesis test is to use sample information to decide whether the claim should be confirmed or refuted. But the key question in hypothesis testing is, how do decision-makers decide whether the sample information itself is reliable? As was seen in the previous section, different conclusions can be drawn from different samples.

When checking out a claim, there can only be four outcomes:

- Accept a TRUE hypothesis   – a CORRECT decision
- Do NOT accept a FALSE hypothesis – a CORRECT decision
- Do NOT accept a TRUE hypothesis – an INCORRECT decision, called a TYPE I error
- Accept a FALSE hypothesis   – an INCORRECT decision, called a TYPE II error

An error can only be either Type I or Type II – not both. The errors are divided into two types because there are situations where, if a mistake has to be made, it is much better that one type of error is made rather than the other. For example, the consequences of a Type I error for the claim that 'the house is on fire!' could be disastrous, which is not the case if a Type II error was made.

When a sample is taken to check out a claim, it is possible that the sample mean, $\overline{X}$, does not support the claim. For example, a random sample of widgets might show a defective level of 4%, which is at odds with the manufacturer's claim of 2%. The difference could be due to either (i) the manufacturer's claim being wrong or (ii) the sample is a 'rogue' sample and does not represent the true situation. It is important to be able to check out which of these two possibilities is the most likely. Hypothesis testing will show whether the sample is indeed a 'rogue' sample or whether it is truly representative, in which case the difference is said to be statistically significant.

Hypothesis tests are of two types, one-tailed and two-tailed. A one-tailed test is interested in only one direction, either the lower or upper limit of a confidence interval. A typical one-tailed test checks if a claim conforms to a minimum or maximum standard, i.e., the rejection zone occurs in only one tail of the sampling distribution, see the MeadowSweet Creameries example below. On the other hand, a two-tailed test uses both upper and lower interval limits, i.e., a check is carried out in both directions to ensure that the claim lies within the confidence interval. In this case, the rejection zone occurs in both tails of the sampling distribution. For example, a production manager would use a two-tailed test to check out the accuracy of tooling equipment. In order to pass quality control specifications, tooled items must lie within the upper and lower limits specified by the equipment's tolerances.

CASE STUDY 8.1   *Using hypothesis-testing to check out a claim*

MeadowSweet Creameries use a machine to fill their one-litre cartons of milk. Some customers have complained that their cartons do not contain a full litre. MeadowSweet are concerned that their filling machine may not be functioning correctly and so have taken a random sample of 200 cartons. The mean volume of the 200 cartons was found to be 1.05 litres with a standard deviation of 0.15 litres. MeadowSweet would like to claim that all their cartons contain at least one litre of milk. Because the company is only interested in establishing a minimum standard, the hypothesis test will be one-tailed with a rejection zone in the left-hand tail. They have decided to perform a significance test at the 5% level. The first step is to restate MeadowSweet Creameries problem as two hypotheses:

1. The cartons on average are filled with one litre or more (the machine is operating correctly).

2. The cartons on average are filled with less than one litre (the machine is faulty).

The first hypothesis is called the 'null hypothesis', written as H_0, and simply confirms MeadowSweet Creameries' claim. The second hypothesis is known as the 'alternative hypothesis' and is written as H_1. These two hypotheses are commonly shown as

$$\text{Null hypothesis, } H_0: \quad \mu \geq 1 \text{ litre} \quad \text{where } \mu = \text{the population mean}$$
$$\text{Alternative hypothesis, } H_1: \quad \mu < 1 \text{ litre}$$

The null hypothesis will be tested and if it is found to be true, H_1 is rejected. Otherwise, if H_0 is found to be false, then H_1 is accepted and MeadowSweet's claim is rejected. The solution in Figure 8.8 shows that the confidence limits are (0.979, 1.021). Since the sample mean of 1.05 litres is well above the lower limit of 0.979 litres, MeadowSweet's claim is therefore accepted.

ANALYSIS OF VARIANCE (ANOVA)

Managers are often faced with the problem of comparing data collected from three or more populations. For example, consider a production manager who must make a purchasing decision among three machines. He may want to ascertain whether there are any significant differences among the equipment, even though the suppliers all make identical claims for their particular

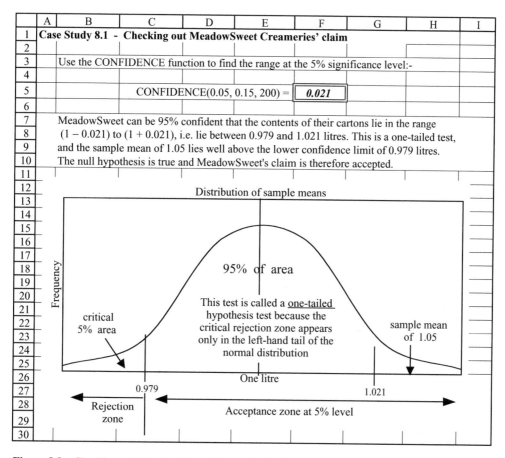

	A	B	C	D	E	F	G	H	I
1	**Case Study 8.1 - Checking out MeadowSweet Creameries' claim**								
2									
3	Use the CONFIDENCE function to find the range at the 5% significance level:-								
4									
5			CONFIDENCE(0.05, 0.15, 200) =			**0.021**			
6									
7	MeadowSweet can be 95% confident that the contents of their cartons lie in the range								
8	(1 – 0.021) to (1 + 0.021), i.e. lie between 0.979 and 1.021 litres. This is a one-tailed test,								
9	and the sample mean of 1.05 lies well above the lower confidence limit of 0.979 litres.								
10	The null hypothesis is true and MeadowSweet's claim is therefore accepted.								

Distribution of sample means

Frequency

95% of area

This test is called a one-tailed hypothesis test because the critical rejection zone appears only in the left-hand tail of the normal distribution

critical 5% area

sample mean of 1.05

One litre

0.979   1.021

Rejection zone

Acceptance zone at 5% level

Figure 8.8   Checking out MeadowSweet Creameries' claim (continued).

product. Because hypothesis testing is such a useful statistical technique, managers need to be able to extend the hypothesis-testing procedure to more than two populations. Analysis of variance (ANOVA) allows this extension.

By using ANOVA, managers are able to determine whether the sample data came from the same population or different populations. ANOVA allows managers to separate data into categories and see whether this separation explains some of the variation in the sample data. The ability to test for significant relationships between sample data falling into different categories makes ANOVA a powerful decision-making tool. In order to use ANOVA, three conditions must be satisfied:

1. The samples must be independent random samples.

2. The samples must be selected from populations with normal distributions.

3. The populations must have equal variances (i.e., $\sigma^2_1 = \sigma^2_2 = \sigma^2_3 \ldots = \sigma^2$ where $\sigma^2 = $ variance).

Table 8.4 Sample time readings

Sample	Machine 1	Machine 2	Machine 3
1	14.8	17.1	15.1
2	17.2	15.8	15.7
3	14.9	18.1	14.5
4	16.1	15.7	15.2
5	15.6	16.9	14.9
6	16.3	16.4	14.4
Totals	94.9	100.0	89.8
Mean	$\mu_1 = 15.82$	$\mu_2 = 16.67$	$\mu_3 = 14.97$

μ_T = total (sample) mean = $284.7/18 = 15.82$
N = sample size (= 6)
K = number of groups (i.e., no. of machines = 3)

Note: Variance, which can be calculated using Excel's VAR function, is a measure of data dispersion and is defined as the average of the squared differences between the N individual measurements, X_i, and the mean μ, i.e., variance $\sigma^2 = \left\{ \sum (X_i - \mu)^2 \right\} / N$.

CASE STUDY 8.2   *Using ANOVA to check out the carton-filling process*

MeadowSweet Creameries have studied the results of the recent hypothesis test regarding the amount of milk contained in their one-litre cartons. While they are justifiably pleased that their claim has been accepted, the test results have raised another problem. Management is now concerned that the cartons contain too much rather than too little milk! The 200-carton sample has shown that on average, a carton contains 1.05 litres which is well above the confidence-interval's upper limit of 1.021 as indicated in Figure 8.8. Perhaps the carton-filling machine is faulty and needs to be replaced.

MeadowSweet's production manager, Willie Wong, has contacted three equipment suppliers to obtain information on their carton-filling machines. The suppliers are willing to provide their equipment on a trial basis so that MeadowSweet can better evaluate their products. Having installed the three machines, Willie has found that their capabilities are almost identical except for one important detail – the filling process – which varies considerably. He has recorded six sample readings of the times (in seconds) taken by each machine to fill a batch of ten cartons, as shown in Table 8.4.

The table's eighteen sample times show three main sources of variation:

1. All recorded times in the table are not the same. Thus variation exists in all eighteen sample values. This variation is called total variation.

2. For each machine, the six recorded times are not the same. Thus there is variation within each machine's sample data. This variation is called within-group variation (or within-sample variation).

3. The means for the three machines are not all equal, so there is variation between the machines. This variation is called between-group variation (or between-sample variation).

These three sources of variation can be combined into one equation, which defines the basic principle of one-way ANOVA:

$$\text{total variation} = \text{within-group variation} + \text{between-group variation}$$

i.e., $\quad TV = WGV + BGV$

Modifying and applying the variance (σ^2) formula to Willie Wong's two-dimensional sample table above, the total variation (TV) is given by the equation:

$$TV = \sum_{i=1}^{K}\sum_{j=1}^{N}(X_{ij} - \mu_T)^2$$

Likewise, two further equations can be derived for the within-group variation (WGV) and between-group variation (BGV) as shown below:

$$WGV = \sum_{i=1}^{K}\sum_{j=1}^{N}(X_{ij} - \mu_i)^2 \qquad BGV = N\sum_{i=1}^{K}(\mu_i - \mu_T)^2$$

Entering the MeadowSweet Creameries' data into these equations produces the results as shown below. These values have also been computed by the ANOVA analysis model of Figure 8.9 (see cells C35:C38).

$$TV = (14.8 - 15.82)^2 + (17.2 - 15.82)^2 + (14.9 - 15.82)^2 + \ldots(14.4 - 15.82)^2$$

$$= 18.025$$

$$BGV = 6[(\mu_1 - 15.82)^2 + (\mu_2 - 15.82)^2 + (\mu_3 - 15.82)^2]$$

$$= 8.67$$

$$WGV = TV - BGV = 18.025 - 8.67 = 9.355$$

Willie Wong wants to find out whether there is any difference among the machines' average filling times. He has only the sample data recorded in his table on which to base the decision. He will propose a null hypothesis H_0, stating that the average filling times for the three machines are equal. This null hypothesis H_0 will be tested using Excel's ANOVA function. If it is found to be true, then the alternative hypothesis H_1, i.e., that the average filling times are not equal, will be rejected. Set up the null hypothesis H_0 to be tested, i.e., all of the means are the same.

$$H_0 : \mu_1 = \mu_2 = \mu_3$$

$$H_1 : \text{Not all of the means are equal}$$

Two important parameters are calculated by ANOVA – the calculated F value (called simply 'F') and the critical F value (abbreviated to 'F crit'). If the calculated F value is greater than the critical F value, then the null hypothesis H_0 is rejected, otherwise it is accepted. The decision rule is

$$\text{If } F > F_{\text{crit}} \text{ reject} H_0 - \text{otherwise, accept } H_0$$

	A	B	C	D	E	F	G	H	I
1		**Case Study 8.2 - Using ANOVA to check out the carton-filling process**							
2									
3		Sample	Machine 1	Machine 2	Machine 3				
4		1	14.8	17.1	15.1		*User input cells*		
5		2	17.2	15.8	15.7		*are shaded*		
6		3	14.9	18.1	14.5				
7		4	16.1	15.7	15.2				
8		5	15.6	16.9	14.9				
9		6	16.3	16.4	14.4				
10		Mean =	15.82	16.67	14.97				
11		Total sample mean =	15.82						
12									
13	[1]	Click the Tools menu and then Data_Analysis to activate the Analysis ToolPak							
14	[2]	Choose the 'Anova: Single Factor' option and fill in the dialog box as follows:-							
15									
16		*INPUT*	*Input Range:*	Highlight (or enter) the range C3:E9					
17			*Grouped by:*	Columns					
18			*Labels in First Row:*	Click OK with mouse					
19			*Alpha:*	Enter the required significance level (leave at 5%)					
20									
21		*OUTPUT*	*Output Range:*	Click OK with mouse					
22				Enter a suitable output cell, e.g. B24					
23									
24		Anova: Single Factor							
25									
26		SUMMARY							
27		*Groups*	*Count*	*Sum*	*Average*	*Variance*			
28		Column 1	6	94.9	15.8167	0.8297			
29		Column 2	6	100.0	16.6667	0.8107			
30		Column 3	6	89.8	14.9667	0.2307			
31									
32									
33		ANOVA							
34		*Source of Variation*	*SS*	*df*	*MS*	*F*	*P-value*	*F crit*	
35		Between Groups	8.67	2	4.335	**6.9508**	0.0073	**3.6823**	
36		Within Groups	9.355	15	0.62367				
37									
38		Total	18.025	17					
39									
40		Using the decision rule: Reject the null hypothesis H_0 if $F > F_{crit}$							
41									
42		F (= 6.95) $> F_{crit}$ (= 3.682), therefore H_0 is rejected, i.e. there is a significant							
43		difference among the three machines' filling times.							
44									

Figure 8.9   Using ANOVA to check out the carton-filling process.

Firstly, enter Willie Wong's table into the spreadsheet as shown in Figure 8.9. Next, activate Excel's Analysis ToolPak by using the Tools|Data Analysis command, and choose 'Anova: Single Factor' from the list of options. Fill in the ANOVA dialog box as given in Figure 8.9 to obtain the answers for 'F' (cell F35) and 'F crit' (cell H35). On the basis of the calculated values, $F(= 6.95)$ is seen to be greater than $F_{crit}(= 3.68)$ and so the null hypothesis is rejected. Willie Wong may therefore conclude that there is indeed a significant difference in the average times taken by each machine to fill ten cartons. (Note: the real benefits of ANOVA are seen when sample sizes are much larger than those used in the MeadowSweet Creameries situation.)

STATISTICAL PROCESS CONTROL

In the previous sections, acceptance sampling focused on the acceptability of inputs (e.g., raw materials) and outputs, i.e., finished goods. Statistical process control (SPC), however, is applied to a process during the manufacturing operation, i.e., the important middle stage of the 'input-process-output' life cycle. A process is a sequence of steps that describe an activity from beginning to completion. SPC uses statistical techniques to measure a process's performance and thereby ensure that the process is meeting specified standards. The two people associated most closely with quality control are Walter Shewhart and Edwards Demming.

Shewhart pioneered the early use of statistical control methods in the 1920s and is honoured by having control charts named after him. He was the first person to distinguish between natural (or random) and assignable (or non-random) causes of variation. Natural variations occur randomly within almost every manufacturing process and are accepted as part of the system's normal behaviour. These variations are due to changes in the production environment such as temperature and humidity, floor vibration, lubricants, etc. As long as the random variations remain within specified limits, the process is 'in control' and quality will not be affected. However, if the variations go outside the specified limits, the process is 'out of control' and the reasons for the fluctuations must be determined.

Assignable variations are not inherent to the process and can be traced to specific causes – hence the name 'assignable'. These non-random variations are due to identifiable factors such as machine wear, process misalignment, poor operator skills, improper materials, etc. The main purpose of SPC is to ensure that the process is 'operating in statistical control', i.e., the only source of process variation is due to natural causes. Corrective action should only be applied to genuine non-random causes. To mistakenly interpret a naturally occurring variation as an assignable cause, can lead to over-correction of the process and to even greater variation. Control (or Shewhart) charts help management to monitor a process, and thereby determine the difference between natural and assignable variation.

Control Charts

Control charts, which are the primary means of process control, ensure that process patterns are correctly interpreted. By monitoring the behaviour of the process over a period of time, any deviation from predetermined limits – usually referred to as upper and lower control limits – may indicate that the process is drifting out of control. In order to specify such control limits, management must have a reasonable understanding of how the process actually works. In many situations, a company may not know what the process is capable of doing. It must therefore carry out a 'capability study' to determine tolerance limits, which represent the process's natural variations.

The first step in a capability study is to take sample data, i.e., selecting and measuring representative units of output. Sample units are measured according to some important product characteristic, e.g., diameter, pressure, strength, weight, etc. Because of natural and assignable variations, it may not be possible to detect shifts or trends using individual data points. Sample data therefore uses averages of mini-samples, containing perhaps five or six data points. The well-known statistical measures of central location (mean or average) and spread (standard deviation) are then used to record the characteristic's movement or shift over the time interval.

Control charts can be divided into two main categories, namely (i) variable and (ii) attribute control charts. A variable control chart plots the specific characteristic (pressure, strength, weight) along the Y-axis and the various sample numbers along the X-axis. The most common variable charts are the $\overline{X}$ and R charts.

An attribute control chart depends upon an item being classified as being either defective or non-defective. An attribute control chart involves counting the number of defectives that occur in say, a particular batch, rather than measuring some product characteristic as in variable charts. The two main types of attribute chart are the p-chart, which calculates the percent defective in the samples taken, and the c-chart which counts the number of defectives in the samples. The samples for attribute control charts are usually greater than those for variable charts by at least a factor of 10, e.g., 50 to 100 or more units.

Variable Control Charts: the $\overline{X}$-chart and R-chart

The $\overline{X}$-chart plots the average of each sample showing variation among samples while the R-chart shows variation within samples. In an R-chart, the letter 'R' stands for the statistical term, *range*, which is the simplest measure of spread in a set of data. The range is the difference between the largest and smallest values in a sample. Both charts are often used together to provide a clearer view of a process's behaviour patterns.

The theoretical basis for both $\overline{X}$ and R charts is the well-known 'central limit theorem', which can be stated in general terms as: If random samples of size n are taken from any population with mean μ and standard deviation σ, then the sampling distribution will closely follow a normal curve with a mean of μ and a standard deviation of $\sigma/\sqrt{n}$. While a common value for n is 30, many quality control procedures use much smaller sample sizes of $n = 4$ or 5. In simpler terms, a typical control chart sets control limits that are within 3 standard deviations of the average of the sample means, i.e.,

$$\text{Upper control limit (UCL)} = \overline{\overline{x}} + 3\sigma$$

$$\text{Lower control limit (LCL)} = \overline{\overline{x}} - 3\sigma$$

where $\overline{\overline{x}}$ = average of the sample means. The choice of ± 3 standard deviations relates to confidence limits discussed earlier in the chapter. If the process has only random variations, then a manager can be 99% confident that sample averages will fall within $\pm 3\sigma$ (3-sigma).

Similarly, for a manager to be 95% confident requires the sample averages to fall within $\pm 2\sigma$ of the mean of the sample means. Consider the MeadowSweet case study.

EXAMPLE 8.7   *Using $\overline{X}$- and R-charts to check out the carton-filling process*

The production manager, Willie Wong, has decided to use control charts to check MeadowSweet Creameries' own carton-filling machine in order to be certain that it is faulty and should be replaced. He would like to be 99% certain that the machine is not 'out of control'. Having collected twenty samples of size $n = 10$, Willie has then calculated the average time (in seconds) taken by the machine to fill each batch of ten cartons. The following table contains average (mean) times for the 20 samples

Samples	1	2	3	4	5	6	7	8	9	10
1 to 10	1.72	1.58	1.62	1.83	1.91	1.65	1.77	1.57	1.85	1.64
11 to 20	1.92	1.71	1.57	1.69	1.59	1.85	1.90	1.63	1.75	1.74

From the table, the average of the twenty means, $\overline{\overline{X}}$ is $(1.72 + 1.58 + 1.62 + \ldots 1.75 + 1.74)/20 = 1.725$ and the standard deviation for the twenty values, σ, is 0.119. The upper and lower control limits for the $\overline{X}$-chart are therefore

$$\text{Upper control limit (UCL)} = 1.725 + 3 * 0.119 = 2.082$$

$$\text{Lower control limit (LCL)} = 1.725 + 3 * 0.119 = 1.368$$

The $\overline{X}$-chart produced in Figure 8.10 shows that there is considerable variation both above and below the mean of the means value of 1.725. However, all variations are well within the lower and upper control limits of (1.367, 2.082). On the basis of the $\overline{X}$ plot, Willie Wong can conclude with 99% certainty that there is no shift – gradual or sudden – in the carton-filling process. Even with a reduced certainty of 95% (i.e., number of standard deviations $= 2$), there are no data points outside the control limits. Willie Wong is aware that the $\overline{X}$-chart shows only that the process is continuing to produce average output. It does not indicate whether there is any change in individual output from 'normal' levels.

Willie has decided to use the R-chart to detect individual changes in data. He will then be able to evaluate within-sample variation, i.e., to see how each sample's range varies. The sample range is simply the difference between the largest and smallest values in the sample. In order to calculate a sample range, the individual measurements for every carton in the sample must be examined. Willie Wong's table above, which contains 10-carton sample averages, must be expanded to show data for individual items. The table below shows the original values for every carton in the first two samples. This information is used to illustrate how sample ranges, R, are derived.

Sample	1	2	3	4	5	6	7	8	9	10	Average
1	1.69	1.68	1.75	1.79	1.68	1.72	1.81	1.61	1.79	1.68	1.72
2	1.61	1.55	1.59	1.59	1.52	1.60	1.54	1.60	1.57	1.63	1.58

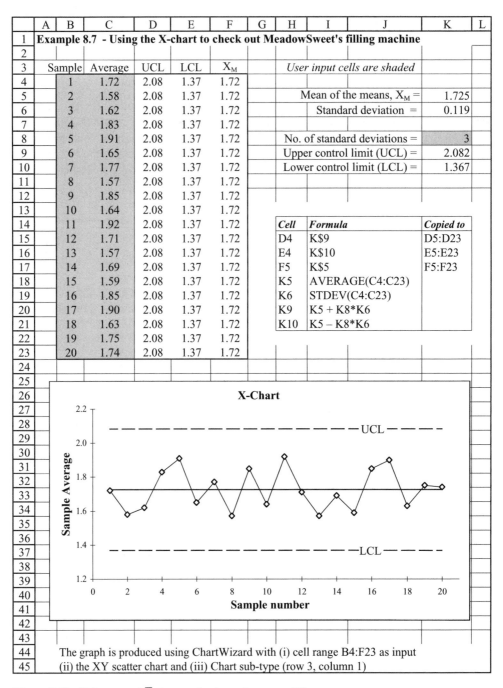

	A	B	C	D	E	F	G	H	I	J	K	L
1			Example 8.7 - Using the X-chart to check out MeadowSweet's filling machine									
2												
3		Sample	Average	UCL	LCL	X_M			User input cells are shaded			
4		1	1.72	2.08	1.37	1.72						
5		2	1.58	2.08	1.37	1.72			Mean of the means, X_M =		1.725	
6		3	1.62	2.08	1.37	1.72			Standard deviation =		0.119	
7		4	1.83	2.08	1.37	1.72						
8		5	1.91	2.08	1.37	1.72			No. of standard deviations =		3	
9		6	1.65	2.08	1.37	1.72			Upper control limit (UCL) =		2.082	
10		7	1.77	2.08	1.37	1.72			Lower control limit (LCL) =		1.367	
11		8	1.57	2.08	1.37	1.72						
12		9	1.85	2.08	1.37	1.72						
13		10	1.64	2.08	1.37	1.72						
14		11	1.92	2.08	1.37	1.72		Cell	Formula		Copied to	
15		12	1.71	2.08	1.37	1.72		D4	K$9		D5:D23	
16		13	1.57	2.08	1.37	1.72		E4	K$10		E5:E23	
17		14	1.69	2.08	1.37	1.72		F5	K$5		F5:F23	
18		15	1.59	2.08	1.37	1.72		K5	AVERAGE(C4:C23)			
19		16	1.85	2.08	1.37	1.72		K6	STDEV(C4:C23)			
20		17	1.90	2.08	1.37	1.72		K9	K5 + K8*K6			
21		18	1.63	2.08	1.37	1.72		K10	K5 – K8*K6			
22		19	1.75	2.08	1.37	1.72						
23		20	1.74	2.08	1.37	1.72						

X-Chart

The graph is produced using ChartWizard with (i) cell range B4:F23 as input (ii) the XY scatter chart and (iii) Chart sub-type (row 3, column 1)

Figure 8.10 Using control $\overline{X}$-chart to check out the carton-filling process.

Table 8.5   Factors for computing control chart limits (Copyright ASTM. Reprinted with permission)

Sample size n	$\overline{X}$-chart factor A_2	Factors of R-chart	
		Lower limit D_3	Upper limit D_4
2	1.880	0	3.267
3	1.023	0	2.575
4	0.729	0	2.282
5	0.577	0	2.114
6	0.483	0	2.004
7	0.419	0.076	1.924
8	0.373	0.136	1.864
9	0.337	0.184	1.816
10	0.308	0.223	1.777
15	0.223	0.348	1.652
20	0.180	0.414	1.586
25	0.153	0.459	1.541

The largest and smallest values in each 10-carton sample are underlined. Thus the range for the first sample, $R_1 = 1.81 - 1.61 = 0.20$, and similarly $R_2 = 1.63 - 1.52 = 0.11$. The full set of ranges R_i for the 20 samples have been calculated in the same way to give the following range table.

Samples	R_1	R_2	R_3	R_4	R_5	R_6	R_7	R_8	R_9	R_{10}
1 to 10	0.20	0.11	0.15	0.21	0.23	0.09	0.17	0.19	0.12	0.33
11 to 20	0.12	0.22	0.17	0.29	0.19	0.15	0.09	0.13	0.30	0.14

R-charts require two factors that can be found from a table of predetermined control chart values as shown by Table 8.5. The two factors – called D_3 and D_4 – are required to find control limits for an R-chart and vary, depending upon the size of the sample. The values contained in Table 8.5 are derived for 99% confidence limits, i.e., ± 3 standard deviations. The upper and lower control limits for R-charts can be calculated from the following two equations:

$$\text{Upper control limit (UCL)} = D_4\overline{R} \qquad \text{Lower control limit (LCL)} = D_3\overline{R}$$

where $\overline{R}$ = average of the sample ranges. For Willie Wong's situation, $\overline{R}$ is found from the range table, i.e., $\overline{R} = (0.2 + 0.11 + 0.15 + 0.21 + \ldots + 0.30 + 0.14)/20 = 0.18$. Since each sample consists of 10 cartons, the D_3, D_4 values in Table 8.5, appropriate for a sample size of 10, are $D_3 = 0.223$ and $D_4 = 1.777$. Control limits for the R-chart are UCL $= 1.777*0.18 = 0.32$ and LCL $= 0.223*0.18 = 0.04$.

The R-chart model of Figure 8.11 shows a data point beyond the upper limit and an increasing oscillatory pattern, indicating that the process is starting to drift out of control. The cause for this variation should be determined and, if possible, corrected. Willie Wong may yet have to buy a new filling machine!

	A	B	C	D	E	F	G	H	I	J	K	L
1		**Example 8.7 - An R-chart model for MeadowSweet's filling machine**										
2												
3		Sample	Range,R_i	UCL	LCL	X_M						
4		1	0.20	0.32	0.04	0.18			*User input cells are shaded*			
5		2	0.11	0.32	0.04	0.18						
6		3	0.15	0.32	0.04	0.18			Mean of the ranges, R_M =		0.180	
7		4	0.21	0.32	0.04	0.18			For a sample size of 10,			
8		5	0.23	0.32	0.04	0.18			Table value, D_3 =		0.223	
9		6	0.09	0.32	0.04	0.18			Table value, D_4 =		1.777	
10		7	0.17	0.32	0.04	0.18						
11		8	0.19	0.32	0.04	0.18			Upper control limit (UCL) =		0.320	
12		9	0.12	0.32	0.04	0.18			Lower control limit (LCL) =		0.040	
13		10	0.33	0.32	0.04	0.18						
14		11	0.12	0.32	0.04	0.18						
15		12	0.22	0.32	0.04	0.18						
16		13	0.17	0.32	0.04	0.18			*Cell*	*Formula*	*Copied to*	
17		14	0.29	0.32	0.04	0.18			D4	K$11	D5:D23	
18		15	0.19	0.32	0.04	0.18			E4	K$12	E5:E23	
19		16	0.15	0.32	0.04	0.18			F4	K$6	F5:F23	
20		17	0.09	0.32	0.04	0.18			K6	AVERAGE(C4:C23)		
21		18	0.13	0.32	0.04	0.18			K11	K6*K9		
22		19	0.30	0.32	0.04	0.18			K12	K6*K8		
23		20	0.14	0.32	0.04	0.18						
24												
25												

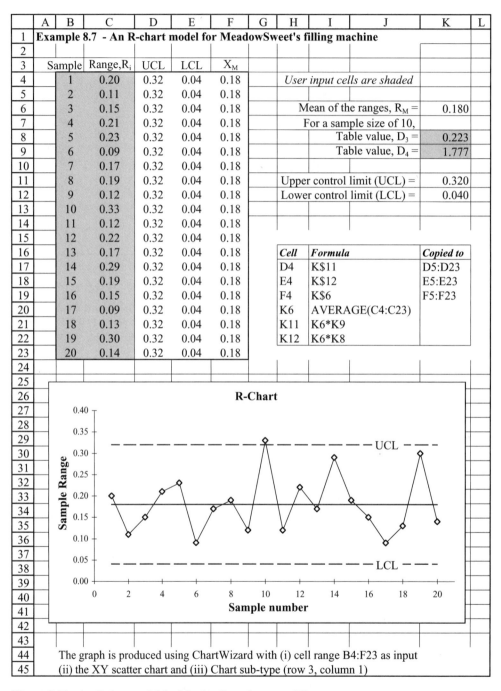

The graph is produced using ChartWizard with (i) cell range B4:F23 as input
(ii) the XY scatter chart and (iii) Chart sub-type (row 3, column 1)

Figure 8.11   An *R*-chart model for MeadowSweet's carton-filling process.

Constructing and Interpreting Variable Control Charts

The following steps show how to construct and interpret $\overline{X}$ and R control charts:

1. Collect a number (20 to 30) of samples of size $n = 4$ or 5 taken at regular time intervals.
2. Compute the mean, $\overline{X}$ and the range, R for each of these small samples.
3. Compute the overall mean, $\overline{\overline{X}}$, i.e., the mean of the means and overall range, $\overline{R}$, i.e., the mean of the sample ranges.
4. Choose confidence limits, usually 99%, and calculate upper and lower control limits.
5. Plot the $\overline{X}$ and R control charts and determine if any data points fall outside the control limits. Investigate the reason why any point is outside the control limits.
6. Check if data points exhibit any pattern – either as an increasing, decreasing, or oscillatory trend – that might indicate that the process is drifting out of control.
7. Collect further samples and, if necessary, repeat the above steps.

Attribute Control Charts: the *p*-chart and *c*-chart

Attribute control charts are normally used when there is no obvious characteristic to measure. In this situation, the attribute characteristic is defined in terms of whether the product is defective or not. The measure then becomes a simple task of counting how many defective items occur in a particular sample. The two main types of attribute control charts are the *p*-chart which measures the percent defective in a sample and the *c*-chart which counts the number of defective items in a sample.

Attribute charts assume that a product can only have one of two states – either good or bad, success or failure, acceptance or rejection. Any process that can have only two possible outcomes is called a Bernoulli process. The two probability distributions that are used to model a Bernoulli process are the Poisson and Binomial distributions. The Binomial distribution is generally associated with a Bernoulli process. Under certain conditions, however, the Poisson distribution is more appropriate. Where the size of the sample is large or unknown, and the probability of finding a defective item is very small, then the Poisson distribution should be used instead of the Binomial distribution. The Binomial distribution is more suitable for *p*-chart situations while the Poisson distribution is used for *c*-charts.

The procedure for calculating the control limits for the *p*-chart is similar to that of $\overline{X}$-charts. To set control limits that are within ± 3 standard deviations of the average of the sample means, the same equation is again applied, i.e.,

$$\text{Upper control limit (UCL)} = \overline{p} + 3\sigma$$

$$\text{Lower control limit (LCL)} = \overline{p} - 3\sigma$$

where: $\overline{p} =$ mean proportion of defectives
$\sigma = \sqrt{\overline{p}(1 - \overline{p})/n}$ ($n =$ sample size)

Table 8.6   Sprocket production details

Day	Production	Defectives
1	1020	39
2	1076	33
3	988	45
4	1205	39
5	1092	36
6	1145	41
7	1086	50
8	1220	38
9	1176	43
10	1112	35
11	1105	42
12	1007	38
13	1201	36
14	1075	42
15	1121	40
16	1185	50
17	1130	39
18	1083	45
19	1112	41
20	1214	46

The equation for σ is the standard deviation of the Binomial distribution. The choice of ± 3 standard deviations (called 3-sigma) is used when a manager wants to be 99% confident that sample averages are within the control limits. Similarly, for a manager to be 95% confident requires that the sample averages fall within $\pm 2\sigma$ of the mean of the sample means.

EXAMPLE 8.8   *Using a p-chart to monitor defective levels*

The Acme Company has recently carried out an inspection of its production process for sprockets. Over the past month, a daily check was kept on the number of sprockets produced as well as the number of defective items. The results are shown in Table 8.6.

The Acme Company has decided to produce a p-chart of the above data in order to determine if defective levels are at an acceptable level. A p-chart is appropriate for this particular situation because both production and defective levels are known for each sample. The sample sizes for this situation are all different, being equal to the daily number of sprockets produced. An average sample size is found by adding up all daily production values and dividing by the total number of days, i.e., $n = 22, 353/20 = 1117.65$.

The p-chart of Figure 8.12 does not indicate anything unusual. All data points are well within the control limits and are evenly distributed around the percent-defective average of 3.66%. Since there is no discernible pattern, the Acme Company can conclude that the production process is 'operating in statistical control'. It is worth noting that the sample sizes for attribute control charts are much greater than those for variable charts – in this example by a factor of 100.

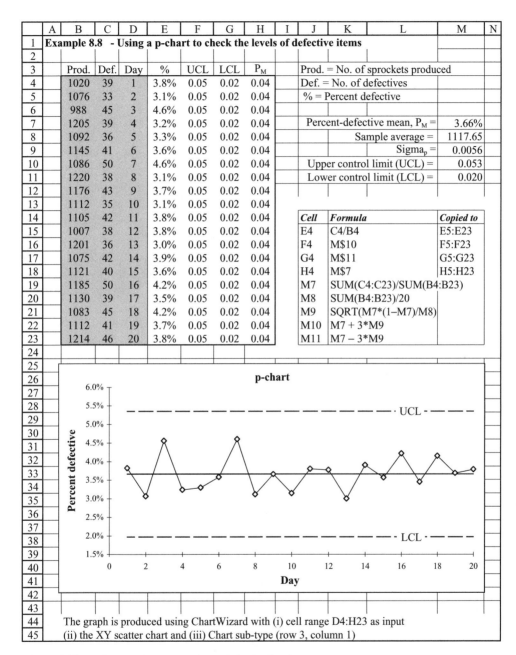

The graph is produced using ChartWizard with (i) cell range D4:H23 as input
(ii) the XY scatter chart and (iii) Chart sub-type (row 3, column 1)

Figure 8.12   Using a *p*-chart to check out defective levels.

Table 8.7   Equipment breakdown details

Week	Breakdowns
1	3
2	1
3	2
4	2
5	7
6	1
7	9
8	5
9	4
10	10

EXAMPLE 8.9   *Using a c-chart to monitor equipment breakdown levels*

Bloggs Engineering is concerned at the number of equipment breakdowns that have occurred in its production division over recent months. Management have decided that they want to be 95% certain that breakdowns are not getting unacceptably high. The company has recorded equipment breakdown details for the past ten weeks as shown in Table 8.7.

Because of the limited amount of information, the Poisson distribution is appropriate in this situation. For the Poisson distribution, the standard deviation, σ, is equal to the square root of the mean. The procedure for calculating the control limits for the c-chart is similar to p-charts. Because Bloggs Engineering want to be only 95% certain that the situation is getting out of control, the c-chart control limits are set at $\pm 2\sigma$ instead of the normal 99% certainty values of ± 3 standard deviations. The usual equation is modified as shown:

$$\text{Upper control limit (UCL)} = \bar{c} + 2\sigma$$

$$\text{Lower control limit (LCL)} = \bar{c} - 2\sigma$$

where : $\bar{c} =$ mean of the breakdowns
     and $\sigma = \sqrt{\bar{c}}$

The mean of the breakdowns, $\bar{c} = (3 + 1 + 2 + 2 \ldots 5 + 4 + 10)/10 = 4.4$ and the standard deviation $\sigma = \sqrt{4.4} = 2.10$. The control limits are therefore UCL $= 4.4 + 2*2.1 = 8.6$ and LCL $= 4.4 - 2*2.1 = 0.2$. In the event of a model having a negative value for the lower control limit, the LCL is set to zero because it is impossible to have a negative number of breakdowns. The c-chart in Figure 8.13 shows that two points are outside the upper control limit, confirming the company's fears that equipment breakdowns are becoming too frequent. Would the situation alter, if Bloggs Engineering wanted to be 99% certain that the process was in control? Run the c-chart model with ± 3 standard deviations instead of the 2-sigma values.

EXCEL FUNCTIONS USED IN MODEL-BUILDING

The models developed in this chapter introduce four Excel functions for the first time, each of which is explained below. The user should remember that a comprehensive on-line help facility is also provided by Excel.

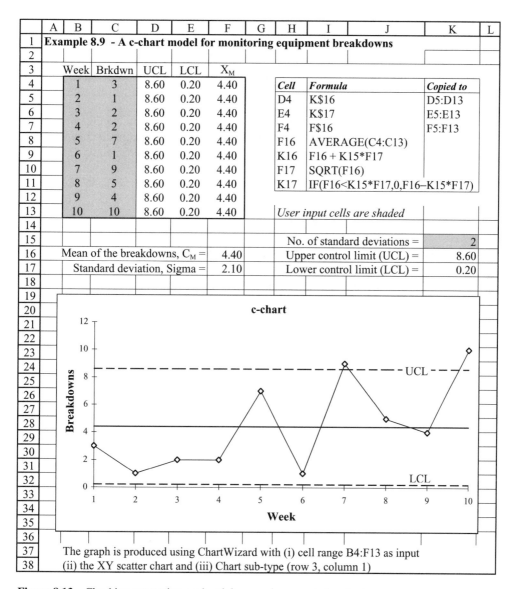

	A	B	C	D	E	F	G	H	I	J	K	L
1		Example 8.9 - A c-chart model for monitoring equipment breakdowns										
2												
3		Week	Brkdwn	UCL	LCL	X_M						
4		1	3	8.60	0.20	4.40		Cell	Formula		Copied to	
5		2	1	8.60	0.20	4.40		D4	K$16		D5:D13	
6		3	2	8.60	0.20	4.40		E4	K$17		E5:E13	
7		4	2	8.60	0.20	4.40		F4	F$16		F5:F13	
8		5	7	8.60	0.20	4.40		F16	AVERAGE(C4:C13)			
9		6	1	8.60	0.20	4.40		K16	F16 + K15*F17			
10		7	9	8.60	0.20	4.40		F17	SQRT(F16)			
11		8	5	8.60	0.20	4.40		K17	IF(F16<K15*F17,0,F16−K15*F17)			
12		9	4	8.60	0.20	4.40						
13		10	10	8.60	0.20	4.40		User input cells are shaded				
14												
15								No. of standard deviations =			2	
16		Mean of the breakdowns, C_M =				4.40		Upper control limit (UCL) =			8.60	
17		Standard deviation, Sigma =				2.10		Lower control limit (LCL) =			0.20	

The graph is produced using ChartWizard with (i) cell range B4:F13 as input
(ii) the XY scatter chart and (iii) Chart sub-type (row 3, column 1)

Figure 8.13   Checking out equipment breakdowns using a control c-chart.

1. CONFIDENCE CONFIDENCE (alpha, standard_dev, size)

returns the confidence interval for a population mean. The confidence interval is a range
on either side of a sample mean. For example, if a commuter takes a bus to work each
day, then he or she can predict, with a particular level of confidence, the earliest and latest
times when the bus will arrive.

alpha   = the significance level used to compute the confidence level. A
                 significance level is the complement of a confidence level. For example,
                 an alpha value of 0.05 indicates a confidence level of 95%.
standard_dev = the standard deviation of the population, which is assumed to be known.
size   = the sample size.

Example: A commuter has observed over the last 50 journeys that the average time taken
to travel to work is 30 minutes with a standard deviation of 2.5. The commuter can be 95%
confident that the average time lies in the interval 30 ± CONFIDENCE (0.05, 2.5, 50) =
30 ± 0.693, i.e., between 29.3 and 30.7 minutes.

2. MAX MAX (array)

   returns the largest number in an array.

   Example: MAX(D4:D7) in Figure 8.14 returns the value 20.00.

3. NORMDIST NORMDIST (x, mean, standard_dev, cumulative)

   returns the normal cumulative distribution for a given mean and standard deviation. This
   bell-shaped, symmetrical distribution is widely used in statistical applications.

   x   = the value for which the distribution is required.
   mean   = the arithmetic mean of the distribution.
   standard_dev = the standard deviation of the distribution.
   cumulative   = a logical value which can be set equal to TRUE to give the cumulative
                    exponential probability, or set to FALSE to give the individual
                    exponential probability.

   Example: The life of a component follows a normal distribution with a mean of 800 hours
   and standard deviation of 70 hours. The proportion of components that will fail before 900
   hours is NORMDIST (900, 800, 70, TRUE) = 0.9234 = 92.34%.

	A	B	C	D	E	F	G	H
1								
2		Product	No. in	Product		Year	Cash	
3		name	stock	price			flow	
4		Gizmo	10	£10.00		1	1	
5		Gadget	25	£12.50		2	4	
6		Widget	8	£20.00		3	8	
7		Sprocket	40	£4.50		4	16	
8						5		
9				*Sample Figure*				

Figure 8.14   Sample figure.

4. NORMINV NORMINV (probability, mean, standard_dev)

> returns the inverse of the normal cumulative distribution for a given mean and standard deviation.

probability   = the probability for which the normal distribution is required.
mean   = the arithmetic mean of the distribution.
standard_dev = the standard deviation of the distribution.

Example: The life of a component is normally distributed with a mean of 800 hours and a standard deviation of 70 hours. Find the average life that will ensure that no more than 10% of components fail before 800 hours. Answer = NORMINV (0.9, 800, 70) = 889.7 hours.

EXERCISES ▬▬▬▬▬▬▬▬▬▬▬▬▬▬▬▬▬▬▬▬▬▬▬▬

8.1 Fred Flint has agreed a sampling plan with the producer of component X. The sampling plan specifies α, β values of 5% and 10% respectively and (n, c) values of (100, 2). Fred would now like to determine values for measuring good and bad quality. He has decided to plot an operating characteristic (OC) curve, from which he can calculate acceptable values for AQL (good quality) and LTPD (bad quality).

(Answer: AQL = 0.8% and LTPD = 5.3%.)

8.2 A sampling plan for batch production states: 'select a random sample of 30 items and count the number of defectives, c, in the sample. If $c \leq 2$, accept the batch, otherwise reject it'. Plot the operating characteristic (OC) curve for this plan. What is the consumer's risk of accepting a batch containing 15% defectives?

(Answer: Consumer's risk = 17.5%)

8.3 The EverLite Company manufactures electric light bulbs. A batch of 2000 bulbs was found to have a mean life of 1000 hours and a standard deviation of 75 hours. Using Excel's normal distribution function NORMDIST, calculate how many bulbs will fail (i) before 900 hours (ii) between 950 and 1000 hours (iii) given the same mean life, what would the standard deviation have to be to ensure that not more than 20% of bulbs fail before 915 hours?

(Answer: (i) 182 (ii) 495 (iii) standard deviation = 101.)

8.4 Fiona estimates that, on average, she can serve five customers per hour in her FineFood restaurant. Using Excel's Poisson distribution function, find the probability that, in any one hour, Fiona will serve (i) more than 8 customers (ii) between 3 and 6 customers (iii) less than 3 customers in half an hour.

(Answer: (i) 0.0681 (ii) 0.6375 (iii) 0.5438.)

8.5 The GreenFingers Garden Centre has ordered 50kg bags of lawn fertiliser. A random sample of eight bags was taken and it was found that the sample mean was 49.1kg with a standard deviation of 1.6kg. GreenFingers would like to test whether the average weight of the bags is significantly less than the specified weight of 50kg. Use Excel's Confidence function to check out the situation, taking a 5% level of significance. If the sample size was doubled, would the situation be different?

(Answer: Bags are acceptable; if sample $= 16$, then bags are NOT acceptable!)

8.6 The KleenUp Company has decided to carry out an analysis on the operating costs of its fleet of cars. It has taken a random sample of 12 cars which can be divided into three types. The operating costs for the twelve cars in pence per mile are shown in Table 8.8.

Table 8.8

Type 1	Type 2	Type 3
13.3	12.4	13.9
14.3	13.4	15.5
13.6	13.1	14.7
12.8		14.5
14.0		

Perform an analysis of variance on the above data using Excel's Anova function – take a significance level of 1%. Does the table's data provide any evidence that the operating costs per mile for the three types of cars are different?

(Answer: Let $H_0 =$ 'operating costs per mile for 3 types of car are equal'; since $F(7.236) < F_{crit}(8.0215)$, H_0 is accepted.)

8.7 MeadowSweet Creameries sells 10-litre catering containers of milk for £4 each. Because of the recent problems with the filling machine, the amount of milk in each container varies from the 10-litre mean. The volumes are normally distributed with a standard deviation of 0.2 litres. Having reassured customers that only one in every hundred containers will contain less than 10 litres, MeadowSweet must now find the average container volume that will satisfy this guarantee. Furthermore, the company has an option of purchasing a new part for the filling machine that would reduce the standard deviation to 0.15 litres. MeadowSweet is undecided whether this new component, costing £5000, is worthwhile since it lasts for only 100,000 container fillings. The company has asked its production manager Willie Wong for advice on both problems.
    (Hint: use the NORMINV function – see end-of-chapter functions for NORMINV details.)

(Answer: (i) 10.465 litres (ii) Total savings = £4,653. Since the part costs £5000, it is not worthwhile.)

8.8 Barbara Blair, who is the quality control manager for the Gizmo Company, uses a sample size of twenty items when checking out production batches of an electronic component. Over recent months, a total of 20 defectives has been found in two hundred random samples. Barbara wants to be 95% confident that the process is operating under normal conditions. She has therefore constructed a p-chart using this sample data and the standard formula where $\sigma = \sqrt{\bar{p}(1 - \bar{p})/n}$ and $\bar{p} =$ average number of defectives. After plotting details of the five latest samples containing

3, 5, 2, 0, and 6 defectives on her *p*-chart, what conclusion should Barbara draw about the production process?

(Answer: Since two of the sample averages are outside the upper control limit, Barbara can conclude that the process is out of control. The oscillatory trend also confirms this view.)

8.9   MeadowSweet Creameries are aware of the problems with their filling machine. The company has been keeping records of one-litre milk cartons that have been rejected because of low-volume content. Table 8.9 contains daily records for the past month, showing (i) the total number of cartons filled, and (ii) the number of rejected cartons.

Table 8.9

Day	Total	Rejects
1	8042	349
2	7944	297
3	7848	277
4	8101	360
5	7932	451
6	7545	364
7	8290	482
8	7887	289
9	8003	363
10	7798	475
11	8135	358
12	7937	481
13	7712	476
14	8075	362
15	7191	360
16	8189	417
17	7633	397
18	8108	421
19	7762	455
20	7941	387

MeadowSweet has decided to set up a *p*-chart to check if the level of rejected cartons has reached unacceptable levels. The company wants to be 99% sure that the filling process is not out of control.

(Answer: The system is clearly out of control. The oscillatory pattern shows numerous values above and below the control limits. On the basis of this *p*-chart, MeadowSweet urgently needs a new filling machine!)

8.10   The EverLite Company has collected information on the mean life (in hours) of their electric light bulbs. Table 8.10 shows details for mini-samples of five light bulbs, including the average life and range for each mini-sample. The company wants to see how their manufacturing process is performing and has asked you to plot control charts for both the average $(\overline{X})$ and range (R). Having examined the output, what advice can you give to the EverLite Company?

Table 8.10

Sample	Mean ($\bar{X}$)	Range (R)
1	1232	59
2	1178	61
3	1096	84
4	1211	97
5	1050	73
6	1244	64
7	1190	40
8	1078	58
9	1101	77
10	1079	51
11	1095	58
12	1137	81
13	1221	76
14	1201	62
15	1191	60
16	1189	57
17	1236	49
18	1098	55
19	1262	71
20	1115	69

(Answer: The system is operating well inside the control limits for both X- and R-charts. Each data set is clustered around its respective mean, indicating that the EverLite Company has no cause for concern with its manufacturing process.)

REFERENCES AND FURTHER READING

Groebner, D., and Shannon, P. *et al.* (2001) *Business Statistics: A Decision-Making Approach* (5th edn), Prentice Hall, New Jersey.

Heizer, J. and Render, B. (2003) *Production & Operations Management* (7th edn), Prentice Hall, New Jersey.

Levine, D., Stephen, D. *et al.* (2002) *Statistics for Managers Using Microsoft Excel* (3rd edn), Prentice-Hall, New Jersey.

9

Inventory control models

OVERVIEW

Businesses can only predict what customers will buy and when they will buy it. To overcome such uncertainty, stocks are kept to ensure that anticipated demand can be met. Stockholding can therefore be viewed as a buffer between supply and demand. For example, raw materials such as coal and fuel must be scheduled and stockpiled for the production of electricity, while banks have to maintain a certain level of cash inventory to meet customer needs. The main types of inventory are (i) raw materials (ii) work-in-progress (also called work-in-process or WIP) which represents partly finished products (iii) finished goods, i.e., completed products ready for shipment.

Most companies appreciate that capital can be wastefully tied up in inventories which sit around gathering dust. For example, it is uneconomical to stock an item when the cost of keeping it in stock is greater than the profit made from selling it. In such situations, a company may adopt a back-order policy allowing planned shortages to occur, with customer demand being met after an order has been placed. A back-order policy assumes that customers are willing to wait for delivery, i.e., it is a strategy for negative inventory. Computer models are now being used to reduce inventory levels by providing more accurate forecasts on the quantity and timing of inventory transactions.

In the past, inventories were often overstocked 'just in case' something went wrong, i.e., items were over-ordered to protect against poor production performance resulting from un-reliable quality. Some industries now consider inventory to be an expensive luxury, and have asked their suppliers to deliver components only when they are needed. This 'just-in-time' (JIT) approach is seen as a way to eliminate waste, synchronise manufacturing processes, and reduce inventory holding costs. JIT has been adopted by car manufacturers, but it means that any interruption in the supply of a single component can bring a production line to a halt. The reliability of suppliers is therefore a key factor in JIT systems.

The primary purpose of inventory control is to ensure that the right amount of the right item is ordered at the right time. But what constitutes the right items, the right time, and the right amount? The basic questions that have to be asked are

- What items should be ordered?
- When should an order be placed?
- How much should be ordered?

The first question focuses on the importance of ensuring that only relevant items are ordered. Reasons for holding stock items are (i) to enable production processes to operate smoothly and efficiently (ii) to take advantage of quantity discounts (iii) to protect against possible shortages in the future (iv) to absorb seasonal fluctuations in demand and supply (v) to protect against inflation and price changes. Since holding stock is expensive, procedures such as cost-benefit analysis, should be carried out to ensure that inventories can be economically justified. For example, to stock components for a microcomputer which has become obsolescent is impractical.

The two most common approaches to the second question regarding the timing of orders are (i) the fixed-quantity system, and (ii) the fixed-period or periodic review system. In the fixed-quantity system, the same constant amount is ordered every time. Any variation in demand is overcome by changing the time between orders. In the periodic review system, orders are placed at fixed intervals regardless of stock size. Any variation in demand is overcome by changing the size of the order. The periodic review system is sometimes called the periodic order quantity (POQ) system.

The third question focuses on the order quantity, i.e., how much should be ordered? The best-known mathematical model for determining an optimal order size by minimising costs is the 'economic order quantity' (EOQ) method. Note that the terms 'order quantity', 'lot size', and 'batch size' are synonymous and are used interchangeably. The basis underlying all inventory control models is summarised by the last two questions above, i.e., how much and when?

GLOSSARY OF INVENTORY TERMS

There are many terms used in inventory control which, if not properly defined, can cause confusion. For example the terms 'stock control' and 'inventory control' are often used to mean the same thing. Strictly speaking, stock consists of the physical goods and materials held for future use by an organisation, while inventory is a list of all the items held in stock. To remove any ambiguity, a glossary of basic terms used in inventory control is now given. The first five terms below define the various costs involved in the holding of stock.

Unit cost   is the price charged by suppliers for one unit of the item.

Ordering (or setup) cost   ordering cost includes costs arising from the preparation and despatch of the order, checking of the goods on delivery, and other clerical support activities. Setup cost refers to the cost of preparing a machine or process for manufacturing an order.

Holding (or carrying) cost   the cost of holding one unit of an item in stock for one period of time. A typical holding cost would be expressed as, say, £20 a unit per year. A holding cost may also be expressed as a percentage of the unit cost of the item. Holding costs include interest on the capital tied up in stock, insurance, storage charges (rent, lighting, heating, refrigeration, etc.), deterioration and obsolescence of stock.

Shortage (or stockout) cost   running out of stock can prove costly. Factory production can be halted by a shortage of a single component or the lack of spare parts for broken machine tools. Shops may lose business if they are unable to supply goods when required, i.e., the customer may not wait for out-of-stock items which are met by placing a back-order.

Discounts   some suppliers offer discounts when items are purchased in large batches. Buying in bulk will lead to higher storage costs but the increase may be outweighed by the savings on the purchase price.

Other basic terms used in inventory control are

Lead time   represents the time between placing an order and getting the item in stock ready for use. Lead times are normally taken as constant values, e.g., two weeks. However, it should be remembered that lead times involve many activities which can give rise to uncertainty such as order preparation, item production, packaging, transportation, checking on arrival, etc. In practice, uncertainty exists in almost all inventory systems.

Demand   is the number of units to be supplied from stock in a given time period, e.g., ten units per week. Estimates of the rate of demand during the lead time are critical factors in inventory control systems.

Allocated stock   represents stock which has been set aside to satisfy an order until such time as the stock can be despatched. Although allocated stock may be physically present in the stockroom, it should not be included as 'in stock' (i.e., on hand) since it has already been earmarked!

Order (or reorder) quantity   i.e., 'How much should be ordered so as to minimise total costs?' When an order is placed and stock is replenished, the quantity to be ordered can be calculated using the classic economic order quantity (EOQ) equation. The EOQ is the best-known of several techniques aimed at deriving an optimal order quantity.

Re-order level (or order point)   i.e., 'When should orders be placed?' An item's lead time will affect the timing of an order's placement. The reorder level is the minimum level that stocks on hand are allowed to reach before a new order is placed. When an order is placed, the stock on hand must just cover demand until the order arrives.

Cycle time   the time taken between two consecutive orders. A cycle time, T_a, can be found for the year by dividing the order quantity Q by the annual demand D, i.e., T_a (in weeks) = $52^*Q/D$.

Safety (minimum or buffer) stock   a backup supply of items which are held for use in an emergency, i.e., to protect against uncertainties.

Maximum stock   a stock level selected as the maximum desirable amount, which is then used as an indicator to show when stocks have risen too high.

CHARACTERISTICS OF INVENTORY MODELS

Inventory models have two main characteristics, both associated with product demand. As shown in Figure 9.1, demand can be (i) independent or dependent (ii) deterministic or probabilistic.

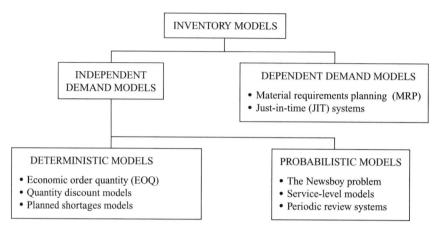

Figure 9.1   Types of inventory models.

- An independent demand model assumes that demand for an item is independent of the demand for other items. Independent demand inventory usually consists of finished goods, whose demand is based on uncertain environmental factors such as sales forecasts, consumer trends, etc. Such models use mathematical techniques to relate forecast demand, order size and costs.

- A dependent demand model assumes that demand for an item is dependent on existing production plans or operating schedules. For example, the demand for wheels in a car assembly plant is directly related to the number of cars being produced. Raw materials, components, and subassemblies that are used in the production of finished goods have a dependent demand.

- A deterministic model is one in which the demand for an item is assumed to be constant and uniform, i.e., the values of variables are known exactly.

- A probabilistic model is one in which the demand for an item varies, i.e., there is a degree of uncertainty attached to demand variables. The product (item) demand is then specified by a probability distribution.

DETERMINISTIC MODELS

Economic Order Quantity (EOQ) Model

The economic order quantity (EOQ) model is the oldest and best-known model for finding an optimal order size that minimises costs. The two basic costs involved in the management of inventory are (i) the ordering cost, and (ii) the holding cost. Unfortunately, both these costs operate to the disadvantage of each other, i.e., there is a conflict of interests! The ordering cost does not vary with the size of the order. Thus in any year, as the order quantity increases, fewer orders need to be placed and the ordering cost accordingly decreases. On the other hand, as the

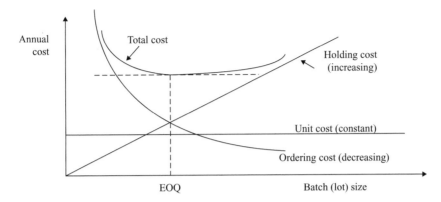

Figure 9.2

order quantity increases, the amount of stock being held also increases which in turn causes an increase in the carrying cost. The unit cost remains constant regardless of batch size and is therefore a fixed cost. This situation is shown in Figure 9.2.

The objective of most inventory models is to minimise total cost. In the EOQ model, the optimal order size represents the minimum point on the total cost (TC) curve where total cost is given by the equation

$$\text{total-cost} = \text{ordering-cost} + \text{holding-cost} + \text{purchase-cost}$$

In the total-cost equation above, purchase-cost is fixed while ordering-cost and holding-cost are variable. The EOQ model assumes that the following conditions are met:

- Annual demand is known and occurs at a constant rate.
- A single item is considered.
- All costs are known exactly and do not vary.
- There is no delay in receiving and using an order, i.e., replenishment is instantaneous.
- No shortages (stockouts) are allowed.

EXAMPLE 9.1

Each order placed throughout the year will be always be for a fixed quantity Q. Because the EOQ model does not allow any shortages, the quantity Q is assumed to arrive whenever the quantity on hand reaches zero. Since demand rate is taken to be constant, the on-hand inventory will follow a sawtooth pattern as shown in Figure 9.3. Note that the average inventory level is $Q/2$.

The basic EOQ equation, which is found by using calculus, is

$$Q_0 = \sqrt{2DS/H}$$

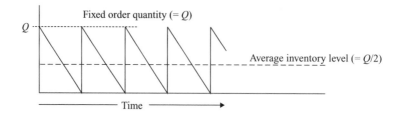

Figure 9.3

where: Q_0 = the optimal order quantity
S = ordering cost for each order
D = annual demand for the item
H = holding cost per unit per year

Using the above definitions, annual ordering cost = DS/Q_0, annual holding cost = $HQ_0/2$ and annual purchase cost = DC where C = unit cost. The total annual cost TC to purchase and stock an item can now be written mathematically as

$$TC = DS/Q_0 + HQ_0/2 + DC$$

The formula template of Table 9.1 is used to build the EOQ model shown in Figure 9.4. Because the annual purchase cost is usually much larger than the other two costs, it is omitted when plotting the EOQ graph. The annual cost (representing the y-axis in Figure 9.4) includes only the first two terms of the above equation, i.e., ordering and holding costs.

PRODUCTION ORDER QUANTITY MODEL

In the EOQ model described above, the whole inventory order was placed at one time, instantaneously raising the stock levels. This situation is typical of wholesalers who operate with large inventories, large quantities, and large turnovers. However in a manufacturing environment,

Table 9.1   Economic order quantity (EOQ) – worksheet formulae.

Cell	Formula	Copied to
F3	INT(D13/4)	
F7	F3	
F8	F7 + F$3	F9:F14
G7	0.5*F7*D$10	G8:G14
H7	D$4*D$5/F7	H8:H14
I7	G7 + H7	I8:I14
D10	IF(D9 = "",D8, D6*D9)	
C11	IF(D10 = 0,"Holding cost cannot be zero!", "")	
D13	SQRT(2*D4*D5/D10)	
D14	D4/D13	
D15	D4*D5/D13 + 0.5*D10*D13 + D4*D6	

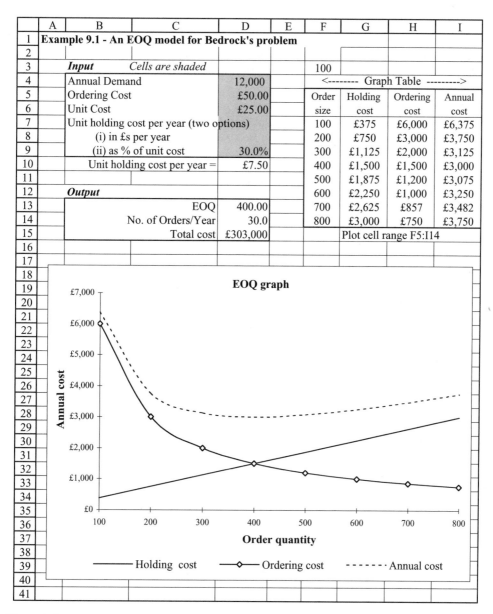

The table and graph contents:

	A	B	C	D	E	F	G	H	I
1	Example 9.1 - An EOQ model for Bedrock's problem								
2									
3		*Input*	*Cells are shaded*			100			
4		Annual Demand		12,000		<-------- Graph Table -------->			
5		Ordering Cost		£50.00		Order	Holding	Ordering	Annual
6		Unit Cost		£25.00		size	cost	cost	cost
7		Unit holding cost per year (two options)				100	£375	£6,000	£6,375
8		(i) in £s per year				200	£750	£3,000	£3,750
9		(ii) as % of unit cost		30.0%		300	£1,125	£2,000	£3,125
10		Unit holding cost per year =		£7.50		400	£1,500	£1,500	£3,000
11						500	£1,875	£1,200	£3,075
12		*Output*				600	£2,250	£1,000	£3,250
13			EOQ	400.00		700	£2,625	£857	£3,482
14			No. of Orders/Year	30.0		800	£3,000	£750	£3,750
15			Total cost	£303,000			Plot cell range F5:I14		

EOQ graph

Holding cost — Ordering cost — - - - - - Annual cost

Figure 9.4 Economic order quantity (EOQ) model.

the situation is somewhat different. If a firm's rate of production is greater than its customer demand, the firm can meet its customers' inventory requirements on an ongoing basis, while also building up an inventory from surplus stock. When this surplus inventory becomes large enough to meet customer demands for a reasonable period of time, production of the item can stop until all excess stock has been used up. On the other hand, if the production rate falls below customer demand, there will be no surplus goods, and some customer orders may not be fully met.

The production order quantity (PROQ) model differs only from the EOQ model in that replenishment is not instantaneous, otherwise the same conditions hold, i.e.,

- A single item is considered.
- All costs are known exactly and do not vary.
- No shortages (stockouts) are allowed.

The basic PROQ equation, which is found by equating the setup (ordering) cost to the holding cost and solving for Q_0, is

$$Q_0 = \sqrt{2DS/H} * \sqrt{P/(P - D)}$$

where: Q_0 = the optimal order quantity
S = setup (ordering) cost
P = annual production rate
D = annual demand for the item
H = holding cost per unit per year

The PROQ equation is very similar to the EOQ, the only difference being the factor $\sqrt{P/(P - D)}$.

Since $Q = PR$ where R is the production run time, then the optimal production run time, $R_0 = Q_0/P$. Using the cycle time definition, $T = Q/D$, an optimal cycle time, T_0, can also be found, i.e., $T_0 = Q_0/D$. There is only one production setup cost. Deriving the holding cost element of the total cost formula is complicated by the fact that the maximum stock level is never reached because units are continuously being removed to meet demand (see Waters, Chapter 4). In the PROQ model, the maximum stock level equals $Q_0^*(P - D)/P$. If C = unit cost, then the PROQ total cost equation can be written as

$$TC = DS/Q_0 + HQ_0^*(P - D)/2P + DC$$

which is very similar to the total cost equation for the EOQ model. The only difference is the extra term $(P - D)/P$ in the holding cost element, caused by Q_0 being replaced by $Q_0^*(P - D)/P$.

EXAMPLE 9.2

The Gizmo Company manufactures gizmos with an annual demand of 2100 units. The gizmo is manufactured at a rate of 2500 units per year. Unit cost for a gizmo is £30, setup cost is £450, and the annual holding cost is 20% of its value. Using the formula template provided at the bottom of Figure 9.5, create the PROQ model, and hence find the optimal batch size, cycle time, and total cost for a gizmo (see cells E12:E18).

	A	B	C	D	E	F	G
1			**Example 9.2 - The PROQ model and solution to Gizmo's problem.**				
2							
3		*Input*	Annual Demand		2,100		
4			Setup Cost		£450.00		
5			Unit Cost		£30.00	*User input*	
6			Annual production rate		2,500	*cells are*	
7			Unit holding cost per year (two options)			*shaded*	
8			(i) in £s per year				
9			(ii) as % of unit cost		20.0%		
10			Annual unit holding cost =		£6.00		
11							
12		*Output*	PROQ		1403.12		
13			Production run time, R_o (in weeks)		29.18		
14			Optimal cycle time, T_o (in weeks)		34.74		
15			Maximum inventory level		224.5		
16			Annual holding cost		£673		
17			Annual setup cost		£673		
18			Total cost		£64,347		
19							
20							
21		*Cell*	*Formula*			*Copied to*	
22		E10	IF (E9="",E8,E5*E9)				
23		E11	IF(E10=0,"Holding cost cannot be zero!","")				
24		E12	SQRT(2*E3*E4/E10)*SQRT(E6/(E6 – E3))				
25		E13	52*E12/E6				
26		E14	52*E12/E3				
27		E15	E12*(E6 – E3)/E6				
28		E16	0.5*E10*E15				
29		E17	E3*E4/E12				
30		E18	E16 + E17 + E3*E5				
31							

Figure 9.5   Production order quantity (PROQ) model.

Quantity Discount Models

Many suppliers offer discounts for large orders and these should be taken into account when calculating the economic order quantity. If the batch size is increased by the minimum amount necessary to qualify for a discount, the saving so achieved may cancel out the increases in both holding and ordering costs.

The EOQ model assumes that all costs are fixed whereas quantity discount models allow costs to vary. The most common cost-variation model considers discounted unit costs, i.e., order costs can vary with the size of the order quantity. However, order costs can also vary because of extra delivery charges being incurred due to the order's size, i.e., large orders may require two deliveries instead of one! In other situations, the benefits of quantity discounts

Table 9.2

Order	Quantity	Discount	Unit cost
1	0–999	0%	£10
2	1000–1999	20%	£8
3	2000 and over	40%	£6

may be cancelled out due to inadequate storage space. The effects of quantity discounts in unit costs are now considered.

EXAMPLE 9.3   *Deterministic model for quantity discounts*

The Wheelie Company has an annual demand for 1500 tyres for racing bicycles. The cost of placing an order is £80 and annual holding cost is 30% of unit cost. Unit costs will vary, depending upon the size of the order, as shown in Table 9.2. Find the optimal order quantity that will minimise total cost.

Taking advantage of the largest discount does not necessarily give the lowest cost. This is due to the fact that the holding cost and purchase cost conflict with each other. When an order size is increased to take advantage of discounts, the order's purchase cost will go down but its holding cost will go up. Consider the basic EOQ equation

$$\overline{Q} = \sqrt{2DS/H}$$

where: $\overline{Q}$ = the optimal order quantity
S = ordering cost for each order
D = annual demand for the item
H = holding cost, expressed as a % of unit cost, C

The holding cost, H, for any item is based on its unit cost, which varies in a quantity discount model. The holding cost therefore cannot be expressed as a fixed value, as is often the case. Instead, it must be expressed as a percentage of unit cost, as given in this example.

Use the formula template given at the bottom of Figure 9.6 to set up the inventory model for quantity discounts as shown and hence solve the Wheelie Company's problem. The model of Figure 9.6 uses the following four steps to find the optimal order size, cycle time, and minimum total cost.

1. From the Discount Table of Figure 9.6 (lines 9–11), calculate I_i for each discount unit cost, $i = 1, 3$ (see cells F13:H13).

2. If $\overline{Q}_i > Min_i$ then enter $\overline{Q}_i$ otherwise enter Min_i where Min_i is the minimum value to qualify for a discount, e.g., $Min_2 = 1000$. These values represent the adjusted order quantities and are stored in cell range F14:H14.

3. Use the total cost equation, $TC = DS/\overline{Q} + \overline{Q}H/2 + DC$ to calculate the total cost, T_i for each adjusted order quantity (see cells F15:H15).

4. Choose the minimum total cost, T_3, i.e., cell H15. The corresponding adjusted order quantity of 2000 (cell H14) is the optimal order size.

	A	B	C	D	E	F	G	H	I
1	Example 9.3 - A quantity discount model for the Wheelie Company								
2									
3		*Input*	Annual Demand				1,500	*User input cells*	
4			Ordering Cost				£80.00	*are shaded*	
5			Unit holding cost per year (two options)						
6			(i) in £s per year						
7			(ii) as % of unit cost				30.0%		
8									
9		*DISCOUNT TABLE*			Unit Cost =	*£10.00*	*£8.00*	*£6.00*	
10			Minimum discount quantity, Min$_i$ =			*0*	*1000*	*2000*	
11			Annual unit holding cost =			£3.00	£2.40	£1.80	
12									
13		*Output*			$\overline{Q}_i$=	282.8	316.2	365.1	
14			Adjusted order quantities =			282.8	1000.0	2000.0	
15			Total costs =			£15,849	£13,320	£10,860	
16									
17					Minimum total cost is	*£10,860*		2	
18					Optimal order quantity is	*2000.0*			
19					Cycle time is	*69.3*	weeks		
20									
21									
22		*Cell*	*Formula*					*Copied to*	
23		F11	IF ($G6="",$G7*F9,$G6)					G11:H11	
24		F12	IF(F11=0,"Holding cost cannot be zero!","")						
25		F13	SQRT(2*$G3*$G4/F11)					G13:H13	
26		F14	IF(F13>F10,F13,F10)					G14:H14	
27		F15	$G3*$G4/F14 + 0.5*F14*F11 + $G3*F9					G15:H15	
28		F16	MIN(F15:H15)						
29		H17	MATCH(F17,F15:H15,0) − 1						
30		F18	OFFSET(F18,−4,H17)						
31		F19	52*F18/G3						
32									

Figure 9.6   Quantity discount model for the Wheelie Company.

EXAMPLE 9.4   *Increasing delivery costs – a variation of the discount model*

A producer of limestone for agricultural use, supplies a farmers' co-operative with 3 tonnes of lime per day. Each lorry can deliver up to 10 tonnes of lime. For any delivery, the charge is £80 for the first lorry-load and £50 for subsequent lorry-loads. A tonne of lime costs £100 with a holding cost of £1.50 per day. What is the cheapest way of meeting the co-operative's daily demand?

Costs usually increase as the size of a delivery order increases. For example, the delivery of 30 tonnes of lime requiring several lorry-loads will be more costly than a single delivery of

	A	B	C	D	E	F	G	H	I
1		\multicolumn{8}{l}{**Example 9.4 - A delivery charge model for the farmer's co-operative**}	
2									
3		*Input*	Daily Demand (in tonnes)				3.0	*User input cells*	
4			Unit Cost				£100.00	*are shaded*	
5			Unit holding cost per day (two options)						
6			(i) in £s per day				£1.50		
7			(ii) as % of unit cost						
8									
9		*DELIVERY TABLE*			Reorder Cost =	*£80.00*	*£130.00*	*£180.00*	
10			Maximum delivery quantity, Max$_i$ =			*10*	*20*	*30*	
11			Daily unit holding cost =			£1.50	£1.50	£1.50	
12									
13		*Output*			$\overline{Q}_i$ =	17.9	22.8	26.8	
14			Adjusted order quantities =			10.0	20.0	26.8	
15			Total costs =			£332	£335	£340	
16									
17			Minimum total cost is			*£332*		0	
18			Optimal order quantity is			*10.0*			
19			Cycle time is			*3.3*	days		
20									
21			*Cell*	*Formula*				*Copied to*	
22			F13	SQRT(2*$G3*$F9/F11)				G13:H13	
23			F14	IF(F13<F10,F13,F10)				G14:H14	
24			F15	$G3*F9/F14 + 0.5*F14*F11 + $G3*$G4				G15:H15	
25			F19	F18/G3					
26									

Figure 9.7 Delivery charge model for the farmers' co-operative.

10 tonnes. In this situation, the unit cost is fixed but the reorder cost varies, depending upon the number of deliveries required. Example 9.4 can be considered as a discount application 'in reverse'. The previous 'unit cost' discount table in Figure 9.6 is now replaced by an increasing 'delivery cost' table. Note that the inequality in step 2 above is reversed, i.e., to find the adjusted order quantities, the inequality is now $\overline{Q}_i < Max_i$. When this inequality is satisfied, i.e., $\overline{Q}_3 < Max_3$, the Delivery Table of Figure 9.7 is complete.

Inventory Model with Planned Shortages

The basic EOQ model does not allow any deliberate shortages. Many shortages or stockouts can be handled by back-ordering, i.e., meeting outstanding orders by shipping a (late) order after a customer has placed the order. Such an approach makes sense where items are expensive and/or bulky, e.g., cars. The size of the back-order depends largely on the ratio between holding cost, H, and shortage cost, B. If H is equal to B, then the back-order size equals the maximum stock level, M. If H is larger (or smaller) than B, then the size of the back-order also becomes proportionally larger (or smaller). If back-orders do not incur too high a penalty, it is worthwhile modifying the EOQ model by adding a back-order factor to the total variable cost as shown in the equation below:

$$Q_0 = \sqrt{2DS/H} * \sqrt{(B+H)/B}$$

where: Q_0 = the optimal order quantity
      S = ordering cost for each order
      B = shortage cost per unit per year
      D = annual demand for the item
      H = holding cost per unit per year
      C = Unit cost

The maximum stock level, M, is calculated from the formula $M = BQ_0/(B+H)$ and the back-order size is then $Q_0 - M$ (see Waters, Chapter 4). The total cost is found from the equation:

Total cost = Ordering cost + Holding cost +   Shortage cost   + Purchase cost
i.e., TC = DS/Q_0 + $HM^2/2Q_0$ + $B(Q_0 - M)^2/2Q_0 + DC$

EXAMPLE 9.5 *Inventory model with planned shortages*

The Bedrock Company has an annual demand of 12,000 units for product X which costs £25. The ordering cost is £50 and the annual holding cost for one item is 30% of the product's purchase price. Bedrock would like to reduce its inventory costs by adopting a back-order policy which allows shortages to occur. The annual shortage cost per unit is £4. Build a model to find an optimal order size, the optimal back-order size, the cycle time, and total cost. Use the formula template provided in Figure 9.8 to create the EOQ model with planned shortages.

INVENTORY MODELS WITH CONSTRAINTS

All the models that have been developed so far apply to a single product. In practice, the assumption that a production facility will sit idle between manufacturing one batch of a single product and the next, is unrealistic. In a typical manufacturing environment, several products will usually be made in batches on the same production line, i.e., multiple items will compete for the same scarce resources. Because of resource limitations, these multiple-item problems involve constraints on storage space, investment in stock, machine availability, delivery capacity and frequency, etc. The following model demonstrates how complex inventory applications can be solved using linear and non-linear programming techniques. Inventory problems which involve constraints are best solved using Excel's Solver program.

	A	B	C	D	E	F	G	H
1		**Example 9.5 - An inventory model with shortages allowed**						
2								
3		*Input*	Annual Demand		12,000			
4			Setup/Ordering Cost		£50.00	*User input cells*		
5			Unit Cost		£25.00	*are shaded*		
6			Holding cost (two options)		2,500			
7			(i) in £s per year					
8			(ii) as % of unit cost		30.0%			
9			Shortage cost per unit per year		£4.00			
10			Unit holding cost per year =		£7.50			
11								
12								
13		*Output*	Optimal order size, Q_o		678.2			
14			Maximum stock level		235.9			
15			Back-order size		442.3			
16			No. of orders/year		17.7			
17			Cycle time		2.9	weeks		
18			Annual cost................					
19			Setup/ordering cost		£884.65			
20			Holding cost		£307.70			
21			Shortage cost		£576.95			
22			Purchase cost		£300,000			
23			Total cost		£301,769			
24								
25								
26		*Cell*	*Formula*				*Copied to*	
27		E10	IF (E8="",E7,E8*E5)					
28		E11	IF(E10=0,"Enter a value in either cell E7 or E8!","")					
29		E13	SQRT(2*E3*E4*(E9 + E10)/(E9*E10))					
30		E14	E9*E13/(E9 + E10)					
31		E15	E13 − E14					
32		E16	E3/E13					
33		E17	52/E16					
34		E19	E3*E4/E13					
35		E20	0.5*E10*E14*E14/E13					
36		E21	E9*(E13 − E14)^2/(2*E13)					
37		E22	E3*E5					
38		E23	SUM(E19:E22)					
39								

Figure 9.8   Deterministic model with planned shortages.

Table 9.3

Item	Annual demand	Unit cost	Space per unit (cubic metres)
Widget	10,000	£18	0.3
Gadget	8,000	£15	0.2
P	3,000	£10	0.15

EXAMPLE 9.6 *Multiple-product model with storage space constraint*

The Acme Company has recently added a new product P to its stock of widgets and gadgets. Expected annual demand for each item is given in Table 9.3. Because there is limited warehouse capacity of 600 cubic metres, Acme must reduce its current inventory levels of widgets and gadgets in order to accommodate product P. The company would like to know by what factor demand must be reduced if the demand ratio between the three products is to be maintained. It would also like to know how variable costs will be affected by these changes to inventory levels. The setup and annual holding costs, which are the same for all three items, are £1500 and 30% of unit cost respectively. Product details, including the storage space required for each item, are given in Table 9.3. The following steps are used to create the multiple-product model of Figure 9.9.

- Calculate the average space requirements for current demand. Since the average inventory level is $Q_0/2$, the average space is given by $S^*Q_0/2$ where Q_0 is the basic EOQ equation and S is the space required for one item (see cells H8:H10).

- Enter the formulae as given in the template of Figure 9.9 – copy the cell range B6:I11 down into B13:I18 and modify cell ranges C15:C17 and I15:I17 as shown.

- Create a scaling factor and initially set it equal to 1.0 (see cell E23).

- Finally, activate Excel's Solver, enter the Solver parameters as shown in Figure 9.9 and solve.

The model has found that an optimal scaling factor of 0.705 (70.5%) fully utilises the available warehouse space of 600 cubic metres (see cell H18). The levels of inventory have been reduced to 7054 widgets, 5643 gadgets, and 2116 units of product P (cells C15:C17). Variable costs increase by 1.53% (see cell I20).

PROBABILISTIC MODELS

In business decision-making, there are three classes of decision problems, namely (i) decisions under certainty (ii) decisions under risk, and (iii) decisions under uncertainty. In the inventory applications considered so far, it was assumed that future demand was constant and uniform, i.e., demand was known with certainty. All deterministic models such as the EOQ and PROQ models involve 'decisions under certainty'. The third class of decision problem – decisions

	A	B	C	D	E	F	G	H	I	J
1		**Example 9.6 - An inventory model with storage space constraints**								
2										
3			Setup cost				£1,500.0	*User input cells*		
4			Holding cost (as % of unit cost)				30.0%	*are shaded*		
5										
6		Product	Demand	Unit	Space		EOQ	Average	Variable	
7				cost	(per unit)		(Q_o)	space	costs	
8		Widget	10,000	£18.00	0.3		2357.0	353.6	£12,728	
9		Gadget	8,000	£15.00	0.2		2309.4	230.9	£10,392	
10		P	3,000	£10.00	0.15		1732.1	129.9	£5,196	
11							Totals =	714.4	£28,316	
12										
13		Product	Demand	Unit	Space		EOQ	Average	Variable	
14				cost	(per unit)		(Q_o)	space	costs	
15		Widget	7054	£18.00	0.3		1979.6	296.9	£12,922	
16		Gadget	5643	£15.00	0.2		1939.6	194.0	£10,551	
17		P	2116	£10.00	0.15		1454.7	109.1	£5,275	
18							Totals =	*600.0*	£28,749	
19										
20					Percentage increase in variable costs =				*1.53%*	
21										
22										
23			*Scaling Factor =*		**0.705**		(Initially, set Scaling Factor = 1)			
24										
25										
26		**Solver Parameters**								
27			*Set Target Cell:*		E23					
28			*Equal to:*		Max					
29			*By Changing cells:*		E23					
30			*Subject to Constraints:*		H18 <= 600		= Storage space constraint			
31					E23 >= 0		= Answer must be positive			
32										
33		*Cell*	*Formula*						*Copied to*	
34		G8	SQRT(2*C8*G$3/(G$4*D8)						G9:G10	
35		H8	0.5*E8*G8						H9:H10	
36		I8	C8*G$3/G8 + 0.5*G8*D8*G$4						I9:I10	
37		H11	SUM(H8:H10)						I11	
38		Copy range B6:I11 into B13:I18								
39		C15	C8*E$23						C16:C17	
40		I15	C8*G$3/G15 + 0.5*G15*D15*G$4						I16:I17	
41		I20	(I18 − I11)/I11							
42										
43										

Figure 9.9 Multiple-product model with storage space constraint.

under uncertainty – moves into the area of guesswork where very little, if any, information exists on which to base a decision. A typical example would be choosing numbers to win a national lottery.

In some situations, however, there is a lack of certainty (i.e., risk) attached to future events. For example, a level of doubt is associated with the outcome of many sporting events. Such 'decisions under risk' are made every week by racing punters who back horses to win races on the basis of recent performances. While the outcome is not known with certainty, the decision is an informed one, based on an analysis of previous events.

While 'decisions under risk' can have more than one outcome, it is assumed that the decision-maker has some knowledge of how matters will turn out, i.e., he or she knows the probability of events occurring. Because there is often an element of uncertainty associated with customer demand, order deliveries, inventory costs, etc., probabilistic – also called stochastic – models are used to solve inventory decisions involving risk. A classic example of a risk analysis model is the 'Newsboy problem' which is now examined.

The Newsboy Problem – A Probabilistic Model with Discrete Demand

The newsboy problem involves a newsboy selling papers on a street corner. The newsboy has to find the right amount of newspapers to buy from his supplier in order to maximise profits. If he buys too many, the newsboy is left with worthless inventory at the end of the day. If he orders too few, then he will run out of papers and lose money because he has missed opportunities to sell more newspapers. The newsboy's problem can be solved using probability (i.e., risk) analysis.

Discrete probability distributions describe situations where the variable of interest – newspapers in the newsboy problem – can only be chosen from a list of specified values. On the other hand, the variable of interest in a continuous probability distribution can take any value, e.g., the variable, time, in a forecasting model. The newsboy problem is typical of many seasonal situations where any products that are not sold over a short period will quickly lose their value, e.g., Easter eggs, calendars or perishable foods.

EXAMPLE 9.7

Bill's Bookshop is about to place an order for next year's diaries. Each diary costs the bookshop £3 and is sold for £5. At the end of January, Bill can return any unsold diaries to the printers and claim a refund of £0.75 per diary. In previous years, the demand for diaries has shown the following probability pattern:

No. of diaries sold	10	20	30	40	50	60	70	80
Probability	0.05	0.1	0.15	0.2	0.2	0.15	0.1	0.05

Bill would like to know how many diaries he should buy in order to maximise his profit.

Let   optimal quantity $= Q_0$ unit selling price $= S$ unit cost $= C$
          product demand $= D$ scrap value $= V$

P_i is the probability associated with demand D_i, e.g., $P_3 = 0.15$, $P_7 = 0.1$, etc. and CUM_i is the cumulative probability for demand D_i. The cumulative probability of selling, say 60 diaries or more, is the sum of all probabilities of selling 60, 70 and 80 diaries, i.e.

$$CUM_6 = P(\geq 60) = P_6 + P_7 + P_8 = 0.15 + 0.1 + 0.05 = 0.3$$

The expected profit for demand D_i is defined as EP_i and is given by the following equation:

$$\text{Expected profit} = \text{Selling price}^* \{\text{Expected sales}\} - \text{Expected cost} + \text{Expected scrap value}$$

$$\text{i.e., } EP_i = S^* \left\{ \sum_{j=1}^{i} D_j^* P_j + D_i^* CUM_{i+1} \right\} - C^* D_i + V^* (D_i - \text{Expected sales})$$

Since the optimal order quantity Q_0 will maximise expected profit EP (see Waters, Chapter 5), EP_i is calculated for each demand D_i.

Bill has decided to set up a model for the newsboy problem using the formula template provided in Figure 9.10. To simplify the equation for the expected profit, EP_i, the formula has been split into two parts. The expected sales, which is the part inside the curly brackets, is contained in cells F11:F18, while the rest of the expected profit formula is in cells G11:G18. The model has found that the maximum profit of £59 is obtained when demand for diaries is 40, i.e., $Q_0 = 40$.

Probabilistic Model with Shortages

This problem can be solved using a modified version of the newsboy problem (see Waters, Chapter 5). The sum of the probabilities, SUM_i, in this model is defined as

$$SUM_i = P_1 + P_2 + P_3 + \ldots + P_i \text{ where } P_i \text{ is the probability associated with demand } D_i$$

The optimal value, D_i, is now found when the following inequality is satisfied:

$$SUM_{i-1} \leq (\text{shortage cost})/(\text{shortage cost} + \text{holding cost}) \leq SUM_i$$

EXAMPLE 9.8

The KleenUp Company is reviewing its policy on cars used by its salesforce. The company regularly supplements its own car fleet by hiring extra vehicles from a local leasing company at a cost of £40 per car per day. The cost to the company of hiring out too few cars is £500 per car per day – the average income lost when a salesperson is unable to visit customers. If too many cars are hired then the KleenUp Company has still to pay the leasing company for the unused cars.

	A	B	C	D	E	F	G	H	I	J
1		Example 9.7 - The newsboy problem: a probabilistic model with discrete demand								
2										
3		*Input*	Unit cost, C =		£3.00					
4			Selling price, S =		£5.00	User input cells are shaded				
5			Scrap value, V =		£0.75					
6										
7										
8		*Output*			<- Probabilities ->		<-- Expected -->			
9				Indiv.	Cumul.	profit, EP_i				
10			Demand, D_i	P_i	CUM_i	Sales	Profit			
11		1	10	0.05	1	10	£20			
12		2	20	0.1	0.95	19.5	£38			
13		3	30	0.15	0.85	28	£52			
14		4	40	0.2	0.7	35	£59			
15		5	50	0.2	0.5	40	£58			
16		6	60	0.15	0.3	43	£48			
17		7	70	0.1	0.15	44.5	£32			
18		8	80	0.05	0.05	45	£11		4	
19										
20		*Optimal demand, Q_o =*	40			*Maximum profit =*		£59		
21										
22										
23		*Cell*	*Formula*						*Copied to*	
24		E11	SUM(D11:D$18)						E12:E18	
25		F11	SUMPRODUCT(C$11:C11,D$11:D11) + C11*E12						F12:F17	
26		F18	SUMPRODUCT(C$11:C18,D$11:D18)							
27		G11	E$4*F11 − E$3*C11 + E$5*(C11 − F11)						G12:G18	
28		I18	MATCH(H20,G11:G18,0)							
29		D20	OFFSET(C10,I18,0)							
30		H20	MAX(G11:G18)							
31										

Figure 9.10   The newsboy problem – a probabilistic model with discrete demand.

Past records have been examined and the following table of car-usage data produced.

No. of cars hired	3	4	5	6	7	8	9	10
Usage probability	0.40	0.25	0.13	0.11	0.05	0.04	0.01	0.01

KleenUp would like to find the optimal number of cars to hire that will balance the costs of oversupply and shortages. Copy the newsboy model of Figure 9.10 and modify it using the formula template provided at the bottom of Figure 9.11. The model has found an optimum answer of seven cars.

	A	B	C	D	E	F	G	H	I
1		**Example 9.8 - A probabilistic model with shortages**							
2									
3		*Input*	Holding cost, H =		£40.00	*All users input cells*			
4			Shortage cost, B =		£500.00	*are shaded*			
5			B/(B + H) =		0.93				
6									
7									
8		*Output*		<- Probabilities ->					
9				Indiv.	Sum				
10			Demand, D_i	P_i	SUM_i				
11		1	3	0.4	0.4				
12		2	4	0.25	0.65				
13		3	5	0.13	0.78				
14		4	6	0.11	0.89				
15		5	7	0.05	0.94	= Optimal amount			
16		6	8	0.04	0.98				
17		7	9	0.01	0.99				
18		8	10	0.01	1				
19									
20									
21		*Cell*	*Formula*					*Copied to*	
22		E5	E4/(E4 + E3)						
23		E11	SUM(D$11:D11)					E12:E18	
24		F11	IF(E11>=H$5)," = Optimal amount","")						
25		F12	IF(AND(E11<H$5,E12>=H$5)," = Optimal amount","")					F13:F18	
26									

Figure 9.11 Probabilistic model with shortages.

Service-Level Models

The probabilistic models considered in the above sections have (i) discrete demands, i.e., demand was chosen from a table of specified values, and (ii) zero lead times, i.e., the time taken between ordering and receiving goods was assumed to be instantaneous. Service-level models assume that (i) demand is variable and can be specified by a probability distribution, and (ii) lead times are non-zero, i.e., replenishment is not instantaneous and can be fixed or variable.

Since demand in a service-level model is probabilistic and uncertain, the possibility of stockouts or shortages will increase. A 'service level' is simply a probability estimate for stockouts that management is willing to tolerate. For example, if management requests a 95% service level, this means that they are willing to accept only a 5% probability of being out of stock. Service level can therefore be considered as the complement of the probability of a stockout.

Reorder Levels and Safety Stock

Service-level systems maintain a current record of the inventory level of each item on an ongoing basis. When the amount on hand drops below a predetermined level – called the reorder level or order point – a fixed quantity, e.g., an EOQ amount, is ordered. A reorder level is defined as the stock level at which a replenishment order should be placed. When a reorder is made, there must be sufficient stock on hand to cover demand until the order arrives. There must also be a certain amount of surplus stock – called safety stock – to protect against shortages caused by unexpectedly high demand or late deliveries.

A reorder level, R_L, can be found by multiplying the average demand, D_A, by the lead time, L_t, and then adding safety stock, S_s, where both D_A and L_t are expressed in the same time-units, i.e.,

$$\text{Reorder level} = (\text{average demand}) \times (\text{lead time}) + \text{safety stock}$$

i.e., $\quad R_L = D_A{}^*L_t + S_s \quad (D_A, L_t \text{ are expressed in the same time-units})$

For example, if the annual demand for an item is 5200, its lead time is two weeks, and safety stock is 15, then the reorder level is given by $(5200/52) \times 2 + 15 = 215$ units. As soon as the item's stock level declines to 215 units, an (EOQ) order should then be placed.

Normally Distributed Demand

If the demand during lead time, L_t, is assumed to be continuous and normally distributed, then Excel's statistical function NORMSINV can be used. NORMSINV(slpercent) calculates the inverse of the standard cumulative normal distribution at a service-level percentage of 'slpercent'. Recalling that 'sigma' or σ is the standard deviation of the normally distributed demand, then the formula for safety stock is given by

$$S_s = \text{NORMSINV(slpercent)}{}^*\sigma{}^*\sqrt{L_t}$$

EXAMPLE 9.9   *Service-level model with variable demand/fixed lead-time*

The Wheelie Company has a normally distributed demand for tyres with a mean of 500 units per week and standard deviation of 60 units per week. Lead time is constant at five weeks. A tyre costs £10 with an annual holding cost of 30% of unit cost. Reorder cost is £100 for each order. Calculate an ordering policy that will give the Wheelie Company a service level of 95%.

In the service-level model, safety stock must be held because demand is uncertain, i.e., it is represented by a statistical probability function. It is important that all input data is given in consistent time units, e.g., month, week, day, etc. Using the formula template given in Figure 9.12, set up the model and hence show that Wheelie's ideal order policy is to order 1317 tyres whenever stock levels drop to 2721 units (see cells D13, D14).

	A	B	C	D	E	F	G	H	I	J	K
1			**Example 9.9 - A service-level model with variable demand/fixed lead-time**								
2											
3			*Input - must be in consistent time units*								
4			Time (day, week, month, year)		week		*Demand is normally-distributed*				
5			Ordering/Setup Cost		£100.00		Mean =			500	
6			Unit Cost		£10.00		Standard deviation =			60	
7			Holding cost (two options)				Service Level %, S_L =			95%	
8			(i) in £s per year				Lead Time, L_t =			5	week
9			(ii) as % of unit cost		30.0%						
10			Unit holding cost per	week	£0.058		52				
11											
12			*Output*								
13			Reorder level/point, R	2721.0			Holding cost of saftey stock			£13	
14			Order quantity, Q	1316.6			Holding cost of normal stock			£38	
15			Safety stock	221.0			Ordering/setup costs			£38	
16							**Total costs per week**			£89	
17											
18											
19		*Cell*	*Formula*					*Copied to*			
20		D8	E4					D10, K8, H16			
21		E10	IF(E9="",E8/G10,E9*E6/G10)								
22		G10	IF(E4="day",365,IF(E4="week",52,IF(E4="month",12,1)))								
23		E11	IF(E10=0,"Enter a value in either cell E8 or E9!","")								
24		D13	J5*J8 + D15								
25		D14	SQRT(2*J5*E5/E10)								
26		D15	ROUNDUP(NORMSINV(J7)*J6*SQRT(J8),0)								
27		J13	D15*E10								
28		J14	D14*E10/2								
29		J15	IF(D14=0,"",E5*J5/D14)								
30		J16	SUM(J13:J15)								
31											

Figure 9.12   Service-level model with variable demand/fixed lead-time.

EXAMPLE 9.10   *Service-level model with fixed demand/variable lead-time*

In many situations, a supplier cannot guarantee that an order will always be met exactly on time, i.e., the lead time is uncertain. Delivery of an order can be delayed by common occurrences such as vehicle breakdowns, heavy traffic, shortage of raw materials, etc. In this service-level model, the objective is to ensure that no shortages occur. This goal can be achieved by ensuring that the reorder point (or level) is greater than the lead-time demand. The lead-time demand is found by simply multiplying the lead-time by the expected demand. In the previous Wheelie Company model, the lead-time was five weeks and the expected weekly demand was 500 units. Lead-time demand is therefore calculated as $5 \times 500 = 2500$ items (note that both values must be in the same time-units – in this case, weeks).

This example uses the same basic input as the previous model of Figure 9.12. The main difference between the two models is that the lead-time – and not demand – is now variable.

	A	B	C	D	E	F	G	H	I	J	K
1			Example 9.10 - A service-level model with fixed demand/variable lead-time								
2											
3			*Input - must be in consistent time units*								
4			Time (day, week, month, year)		week		*Lead-time normally-distributed*				
5			Demand		500			Mean =		5	
6			Ordering/Setup Cost		£100.00		Standard deviation =			1	
7			Unit Cost		£10.00		Service Level %, S_L =			95%	
8			Holding cost (two options)								
9			(i) in £s per year				*User input cells are shaded*				
10			(ii) as % of unit cost		30.0%						
11			Unit holding cost per	week	£0.058		52				
12											
13		*Output*									
14		Lead time		6.6	week		Holding cost of normal stock			£38	
15		Reorder level/point, R		3322.4			Ordering/setup costs			£38	
16		Order quantity, Q		1316.6			**Total costs per week**			£76	
17											
18											
19		*Cell*	*Formula*						*Copied to*		
20		D14	J5 + NORMSINV(J7)*J6								
21		E14	E4								
22		D15	E5*D14								
23		D16	SQRT(2*E5*E6/E11)								
24		J14	D16*E11/2								
25		J15	E6*E5/D16								
26		J16	SUM(J14:J15)								
27											

Figure 9.13   Service-level model with fixed demand/variable lead-time.

The demand is fixed at 500 units per week, while lead time is normally distributed with a mean of five weeks and a standard deviation of one week. To build the model of Figure 9.13, first make a copy of the previous service-level model (Figure 9.12). The next step is to modify the spreadsheet, using the supplied formula template shown in Figure 9.13. The answers produced by this new model show a lead-time of 6.6 weeks and a reorder level of 3322 units. Both these values have increased when compared with the previous model's figures of five weeks and 2721 respectively.

Periodic Review Models

All of the inventory models developed so far can be classified as fixed-order quantity systems, i.e., an order of fixed size is placed whenever stocks decline to a particular level. Any variation in demand is met by changing the order cycle, i.e., the time between orders. In many real-world situations, a fixed-period approach – usually referred to as a periodic review system – is used whereby orders are placed at regular intervals, e.g., every month. The amount of stock ordered will vary for each order and will depend upon the amount of stock on-hand. This fixed-period approach is often used in supermarkets, where stock is reviewed periodically, e.g., at the end of each week, and goods are then ordered to replace the sold items.

The advantage of a periodic review system is that a physical count of on-hand stock is carried out only once – at the end of a given period just before the next order is placed. This means that there is no need for a continual adjustment of inventory levels after each item is sold. However, because no account of item levels is kept during the time between orders, there is a possibility of stock shortages. Thus, the fixed-period system has the disadvantage of having to maintain a higher level of safety stock than the fixed-order approach.

EXAMPLE 9.11 *Periodic review model*

An electronic component has a normally distributed demand that averages 40 units per day with a standard deviation of 15 units per day. The component costs £10 and its annual holding cost is estimated at £20. Setup costs are £50 per order. Stock is checked every 16 days and lead time is constant at 8 days. Describe an ordering policy that gives a 95% service level, given that there are 60 units on hand at the time of reorder. How would this ordering policy be affected if the service level is increased to 99%?

To create the periodic-review model, first make a copy of Figure 9.12 and then modify the input section as shown in Figure 9.14. Use the spreadsheet's template to enter the correct

	A	B	C	D	E	F	G	H	I	J	K
1			Example 9.11 - A periodic review (i.e. fixed-period) model								
2											
3			*Input - must be in consistent time units*				*Demand is normally-distributed*				
4			Time (day, week, month, year)		day			Mean =		40	
5			Ordering/Setup Cost		£50.00		Standard deviation =			15	
6			Unit Cost		£10.00		Service Level %, S_L =			95%	
7			Holding cost (two options)				Lead Time, L_t =			8	day
8			(i) in £s per year		£20.00		Review Period =			16	day
9			(ii) as % of unit cost				Stock On-hand =			60	
10			Unit holding cost per	day	£0.055		365				
11											
12		*Output*									
13		Reorder level/point, R		1081.0			Holding cost of safety stock			£6.63	
14		Order quantity, Q		1021.0			Holding cost of normal stock			£27.97	
15		Safety stock		121.0			Ordering/setup costs			£1.96	
16							Total costs per day			£36.56	
17											
18											
19		Cell	Formula					Copied to			
20		D13	J4*(J7 + J8) + D15								
21		D14	D13 – J9								
22		D15	ROUNDUP(NORMSINV(J6)*J5*SQRT(J7+J8),0)								
23											

Figure 9.14   Periodic review (fixed-period) model.

formulae. Note that the annual holding cost of £20 has been automatically converted to £0.055 per day to maintain consistency in input units (i.e., days). The model has found the following answers: (i) for a 95% service level, an order for 1021 items should be placed when stock levels drop to 1081. A surplus quantity of 121 should be maintained as safety stock at a daily holding cost of £6.63. (ii) for a 99% service level, an order for 1071 items should be placed when stock levels drop to 1131. Safety stock of 171 should be maintained at a daily holding cost of £9.37.

EXAMPLE 9.12 *Multi-period model with several constraints*

The ABC Company has an annual demand of 3600 units for a product with an ordering cost of £5. The product's holding cost is 20% of unit cost. The company operates a periodic review policy with orders being placed at the end of each month. Quantity discounts are available on orders of 270 items or more, at a unit cost of £2. The ABC Company has sufficient storage space for a maximum of 360 items. It has two priorities, namely (i) shortages are not allowed, and (ii) surplus stock must be kept to a minimum. The company has decided to set up a linear programming model to solve its problem.

The model of Figure 9.15 has found an answer giving an annual surplus of 420 items (see cell F27) at a total cost of £7274. It is interesting to compare this total cost with the EOQ value of £7320 (cell I9). Both values are almost the same, showing that there is very little difference between the fixed-quantity and fixed-period methods in this case. The formula template and Solver parameters for the model are given in Table 9.4.

Table 9.4 Multi-period model with constraints – worksheet formulae and Solver parameters.

Cell	Formula	Copied to
I6	SQRT(2*F4*F5/F10)	
I8	12*I6/F4	
I9	F4*F5/I6 + 0.5*F10*I6 + F4*F6	
F10	IF(F9 = "", F8, F6*F9)	
F11	IF(F10 = 0,"Enter a value in either cell F8 or F9!"," ")	
F14	SUM(E$14:E14 – SUM(D$14:D14)	F15:F25
G14	F$5 F14*F$10/12 E14*F$6	G15:G25
D26	SUM(D14:D25)	G26
F27	SUM(F14:F25)	

Solver parameters		
Set target cell:	F27	
Equal to:	Min	
By changing cells:	E14:E25	
Subject to constraints:	E14:E25 ≥ 270	= Quantity discount constraint
	E14:E25 ≤ 360	= Storage space constraint
	E14:E25 = int(eger)	= Answers must be integer
	F14:F25 ≥ 0	= No stockouts are allowed

	A	B	C	D	E	F	G	H	I	J
1	Example 9.12 - A multi-period model with several constraints									
2										
3		*Input*		*User input cells are shaded*						
4		Annual demand				3,600				
5		Ordering cost				£5.00		*Output*		
6		Unit cost				£2.00		EOQ	300.00	
7		Unit holding cost per year (two options)						Cycle time		
8		(i) in £s per year						(in months)	1.0	
9		(ii) as % of unit cost				20.0%		Total cost	£7,320	
10				Unit holding cost per year		£0.40				
11										
12				Monthly	Order	Ending	Cost per			
13			Month	Demand	Quantity	Inventory	Period			
14			1	240	*270*	30	£546			
15			2	270	*330*	90	£668			
16			3	450	*360*	0	£725			
17			4	210	*270*	60	£547			
18			5	240	*270*	90	£548			
19			6	300	*270*	60	£547			
20			7	330	*330*	60	£667			
21			8	420	*360*	0	£725			
22			9	240	*270*	30	£546			
23			10	330	*300*	0	£605			
24			11	300	*300*	0	£605			
25			12	270	*270*	0	£545			
26		Annual demand =		3,600			£7,274	= Annual cost		
27		*Objective: Minimise surplus stock =*				420				
28										
29	Note: Switch on the 'Assume Linear Model' parameter in the Solver Option dialog box									

Figure 9.15 Multi-period model with several constraints.

INVENTORY CONTROL: A SIMULATION APPROACH

Simulation models do not find optimal solutions as in linear programming but mimic the behaviour of real-world situations. A simulation model's output is studied over a number of time periods and a decision is made, based on the plausibility of the results. Many inventory control models cannot be accurately represented by mathematical equations. In practice, both product demand and reorder lead times are often so unpredictable that simulation is the only solution.

EXAMPLE 9.13 *Simulation model for inventory control*

Fred is in charge of inventory at the Bedrock Company. He would like to be able to guarantee a high service level, say at least 98%, for product P. This means that Fred must find a policy which will ensure that there is always sufficient stock on hand to meet a variable demand pattern, as well as the uncertainty associated with delivery times.

Fred's current policy is to place an order for 30 units of product P whenever on-hand inventory falls to the reorder level of 15 units or less. Having studied sales records for product P over the past six months, Fred has now produced the following data tables for (i) demand, and (ii) lead times:

Demand for product P	0	1	2	3	4	5	6
Probability	0.03	0.05	0.13	0.25	0.22	0.20	0.12
Lead time (days)	1	2	3				
Probability	0.20	0.50	0.30				

For the sake of clarity, the inventory model of Figure 9.16 contains simulation data for only fourteen days. This value can be extended indefinitely by copying the formulae in row 31 down the worksheet. In the simulation model, random numbers are used to generate (i) product demand (see column E in the Output Table), and (ii) lead-times (column K). Note that the formulae in column K simultaneously generate both random numbers and the corresponding lead-times.

Lost sales occur when there is insufficient stock on hand to meet demand. Service level, expressed as a percentage, is defined as

$$\text{Service-level} = 1 - (\text{lost sales})/(\text{total demand})$$

For example, if total demand is 60 and lost sales are 2, then service level $= 1 - 2/60 = 96.7\%$. Table 9.5 is used to create the simulation model of Figure 9.16.

The following eight steps show how the simulation model works:

1. A beginning inventory of 30 (= order quantity) for day 1 is automatically entered in cell D18.

2. Calculate the ending inventory for each day. Ending-inventory is simply the beginning-inventory minus demand, i.e., in the output table of Figure 9.16, column G = column D – column F.

3. Whenever the ending-inventory is equal to or less than Fred Flint's reorder point of 15, a new order for 30 items is placed. All orders are recorded in column J in the Output table.

4. To prevent the generation of surplus orders, it is important to keep track of both on-hand inventory and scheduled receipts. The 'new-level' column H prevents surplus-order generation

	A	B	C	D	E	F	G	H	I	J	K	L
1		Example 9.13 - A simulation model for inventory control										
2												
3		Demand table					Lead-time table					
4		<-- Limits -->		Dem-			<-- Limits -->		No. of			
5		Lower	Upper	and	P$_i$		Lower	Upper	days	P$_i$		
6		0	0.03	0	0.03		0	0.20	1	0.20	*User input*	
7		0.03	0.08	1	0.05		0.20	0.70	2	0.50	*cells are*	
8		0.08	0.21	2	0.13		0.70	1.00	3	0.30	*shaded*	
9		0.21	0.46	3	0.25					1.00		
10		0.46	0.68	4	0.22							
11		0.68	0.88	5	0.20			Reorder level =		15		
12		0.88	1.00	6	0.12			Order quantity =		30		
13					1.00							
14												
15		Output table										
16			Units	Begin.	RAND	Dem-	Ending	New	Lost		Lead	Recpt.
17		Day	Recvd.	Invntry.	No.	and	Invntry.	Level	sales	Order?	time	Day
18		1		30	0.25	3	27	27	0	No		
19		2	0	27	0.85	5	22	22	0	No		
20		3	0	22	0.75	5	17	17	0	No		
21		4	0	17	0.31	3	14	14	0	Yes	3	8
22		5	0	14	0.03	1	13	43	0	No		
23		6	0	13	0.46	4	9	39	0	No		
24		7	0	9	0.91	6	3	33	0	No		
25		8	30	33	0.82	5	28	28	0	No		
26		9	0	28	0.55	4	24	24	0	No		
27		10	0	24	0.84	5	19	19	0	No		
28		11	0	19	0.74	5	14	14	0	Yes	2	14
29		12	0	14	0.12	2	12	42	0	No		
30		13	0	12	0.02	0	12	42	0	No		
31		14	30	42	0.43	3	39	39	0	No		
32						51			0			
33												
34					*Service Level =*		100.0%					
35												

Figure 9.16   Simulation model for inventory control.

by adding any scheduled receipt to the ending-inventory. For example, the new-level entry of day 5 (cell H22) is 43, i.e., ending-inventory (13) plus scheduled receipt (30).

5. Simulate the lead-time for the new order (see column K). For example, the inventory model of Figure 9.16 shows that an order is placed on day 4 with a lead-time of 3 days.

6. Receipt days (see column L) take lead-times into account. Column L shows when goods are actually received. Although a new order has been placed on day 4, it has a lead-time of three days and will not arrive until receipt-day 8 (see cell L21). Such a 'delayed' order is called a scheduled receipt because, although it is already on order, it has not yet been received.

Table 9.5   Inventory simulation model – worksheet formulae.

Cell	Formula	Copied to
C6	E6	
B7	C6	B8:B12
C7	C6 + E7	C8:C12
H6	J6	
G7	H6	G8
H7	H6 + J7	H8
J9	SUM(J6:J8)	
E13	SUM(E6:E12)	
C19	COUNTIF($L$18:L18, B19)*$J$12	C20:C31
D18	J12	
D19	D18 + C19 – F18	D20:D31
E18	RAND()	E19:E31
F18	VLOOKUP(E18, B$6:D$12, 3)	F19:F31
G18	IF(D18 – F18) > 0, D18 – F18, 0)	G19:G31
H18	G18	
H19	H18 – F19 + IF(J18 = "Yes", J$12, 0)	H20:H31
I18	IF(D18 – F18) < 0, F18 – D18, 0)	I19:I31
J18	IF(H18 > $J$11,"No","Yes")	J19:J31
K18	IF(J18 ="No", "",VLOOKUP(RAND(),G$6:J$8, 3))	K19:K31
L18	IF(K18 ="", "",K18 + B18 + 1)	L19:L31
F32	SUM(F18:F31)	I32
G34	1 – I32/F32	

7. Column I contains any lost sales. Lost sales occur when there is insufficient on-hand inventory to meet demand, i.e., (beginning-inventory – demand) is negative.

8. Finally, the service-level percentage is calculated by totalling both demand (column F) and lost sales (column I) and then using the service-level equation defined above.

Fred Flint can examine the sensitivity of the model's service level by repeatedly changing the reorder point and order quantity (cells J11, J12). These cells have been initially set to Fred's current policy levels of 15 and 30 respectively. As it turns out, Fred has chosen wisely and the current service level is 100% – even with several sets of newly generated random numbers. To generate new random numbers, simply press the recalculation F9 key repeatedly.

MATERIAL REQUIREMENTS PLANNING

In manufacturing situations, there is usually an inventory of parts (or raw materials) which are used solely in the production of finished products, i.e., end-items. Since there is no outside demand for this inventory, there is no sense in stocking it until it is needed for production. The problem of scheduling the arrival of such inventory to meet production deadlines is known as material requirements planning (MRP).

MRP is an important tool because of the complexity of product assemblies that consist of many sub-assemblies, components, and sub-components. MRP is classified as a dependent

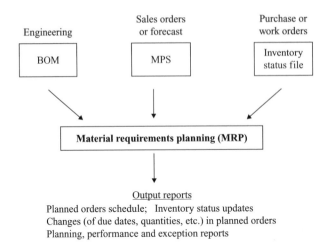

Figure 9.17 Basic structure of an MRP system.

demand model because the relationship between the sub-components, sub-assemblies, etc., is fixed and the schedule of the finished product is also known. Therefore, once management can make a forecast of the demand for the end-product, the required quantities of components can be calculated due to the interdependence of all items. For example, if the ABC Car Company manufactures two cars per week, then the operations manager knows all the requirements – down to the last rivet!

An MRP system has three major inputs – the master production schedule (MPS), the bill of materials (BOM) and the inventory status file – as shown in Figure 9.17. The MPS dictates gross requirements for end-items to the MRP system. Gross requirements do not take account of any inventory on hand or on order. The MRP spreadsheet uses the BOM to 'explode' the end-item demands into requirements for parts and materials by processing all relevant BOM details on a level-by-level basis. Net requirements are then calculated by adjusting for 'on hand' inventory and scheduled receipts as indicated in the inventory status file. The basic equation for net requirements is

$$\text{Net requirements} = \text{gross requirements} - \text{on-hand} - \text{scheduled receipts}$$

For example, consider car engines. Net requirements equals the total number required for final car assembly less those in inventory and those on order from subcontractors.

Glossary of MRP Terms

Master production schedule (MPS)   i.e., what is to be made and when. The MPS for-malises the production plan and translates it into specific end-item requirements over a short-to-intermediate planning horizon, e.g., an 8-week period. It lists the number of end-items that must be ready for delivery by specific dates, usually the end of a particular week.

Bill of materials (BOM)   i.e., how to make the product. A BOM is a listing of all the materials, components (parts) and subassemblies that are needed to make one product (i.e., end-item). A BOM provides the product structure tree (PST). This structure tree shows how the various parts, sub-components, etc., fit together to make up the end-product.

Inventory status file (ISF)   i.e., what is in stock. The ISF provides up-to-date information on every item. It contains such details as identification number, quantity on hand, safety stock level, quantity allocated, lead time.

Lead time   i.e., how long it takes to get an item. Each product assembly, sub-assembly, component, etc., has its own lead time, which is the time required to purchase, produce, or assemble an item.

On-hand/available   refers to the quantity of an item expected to be available at the end of a given period. If the item is a finished good, receipts from planned production are excluded.

Gross requirements   is the total number of materials, components, subassemblies or finished goods required by the end of a given period. Gross requirements come from the master production schedule (for end-items) or from the combined needs of other items.

Scheduled receipts (or open orders)   refers to parts/materials already on order from suppliers and due for delivery in a given period.

Planned order receipts   refers to parts/materials that will be ordered from suppliers during a given period.

Planned order releases   refers to the plan (i.e., the quantity and timing) initiating the purchase of parts/materials. The timing of the plan is adjusted to take care of lead-times to ensure that items will be received on schedule.

CASE STUDY 9.1 *Material requirements planning (MRP) model*

Fine Furniture manufactures kitchen furniture. One of its products is a pine table as shown in Figure 9.18 below. The production manager wants to develop an MRP plan to meet the following customer order schedule.

End of week	3	4	5
No. of tables required	180	180	100

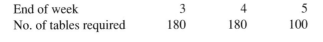

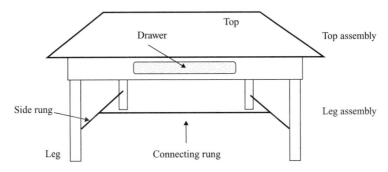

Figure 9.18 Kitchen table assembly.

At present, there are fifty tables on hand, as well as 50 top assemblies, 180 table tops, 200 drawers, 100 leg assemblies, 250 legs, 50 side rungs, and 110 connecting rungs. A scheduled receipt of 100 top assemblies and 100 legs is due in week 2. The manager wants the inventory to be zero at the end of week 5. Lot sizes are determined by using the traditional lot-for-lot (LFL) approach of ordering exactly what is required in every period, i.e., an item's lot size is the same as its net requirements (see 'lot-sizing methods' section).

Bill of Materials (BOM)

Two common methods of describing a BOM are a product structure tree (PST), and a BOM table. Both depict the parent–component relationships on a hierarchical basis, showing what components are needed for each higher-level parent assembly. The product structure tree for the kitchen table is shown in Figure 9.19. Level 0 is the highest level, containing the end-product, while level 2 is the lowest level for this example (obviously there could be many lower levels, depending upon the complexity of the product's structure). The numbers in brackets below indicate how many units of that particular component are needed to make the item immediately above it. For example, one top assembly and one leg assembly are needed to make one table.

When assigning codes to components, a widely accepted practice is to assign values 1–999 for level-0 end-items, values 1000–1999 for level-1 components, values 2000–2999 for level-2 components, 3000–3999 for level-3 parts, etc. In the product structure tree, the end-item (kitchen table) has an Id Code of 1 while the level-2 item (drawer) has an Id Code of 2002. When the same component appears in two or more products, then it is coded at the lowest level at which it is used (for details on low-level coding, see Heizer and Render, Chapter 14).

To simplify data entry into a spreadsheet model, a BOM table is normally used. The BOM table for the kitchen example is shown in Table 9.6. The positioning of the items in the BOM table is very important. Items are always placed directly underneath their parent, e.g., two level-2 items have 'Top Assembly' as their parent and thus come immediately below 'Top Assembly' in the table. The BOM table also contains details of each part's lead time (in weeks), how many units are required, and how many of each part are in stock.

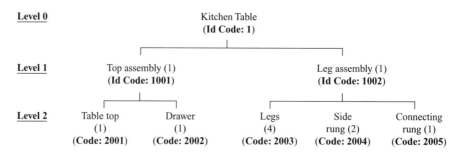

Figure 9.19   Product structure tree (PST) for the kitchen table.

Table 9.6 Bill of materials (BOM) for the kitchen table.

Part description	BOM level	Id. code	No. of units	Lead time	On hand
Table	0	1	1	1	50
Top assembly	1	1001	1	2	50
Table top	2	2001	1	1	180
Drawer	2	2002	1	1	200
Leg assembly	1	1002	1	1	100
Legs	2	2003	4	1	250
Side rung	2	2004	2	1	50
Connecting rung	2	2005	1	1	110

The MRP spreadsheet in Figure 9.20 contains one named cell range B6:H13 called BOM. This named area contains all the details of Table 9.6 with one addition, column H, which contains the row numbers of planned order releases (PORs) for the relevant parents. The following points explain the logic behind this last column's presence.

- The lot-for-lot (LFL) rule for ordering is used in the kitchen table problem.
- The gross requirements for the end-item (kitchen table) are obtained from the Master Production Schedule (see row 20 in Figure 9.20).
- The gross requirements for other lower-level items are found by multiplying the number of units required (as listed in BOM table) by the PORs of the item's parent. A link must therefore exist between every component and its parent. For example, level-1 items will have the PORs of the level-0 end-item (kitchen table) as their gross requirements. Similarly, all level-2 items will have the PORs of their level-1 parent as their gross requirements. Note that values in column H (cells H7:H13) are the last to be entered by the user! Default values of 25 are initially entered in the column for each item.

Step 1: Building the MRP model

At a glance, the MRP spreadsheet may appear rather complicated. In fact, most of the worksheet is achieved by copying individual cells and cell ranges. The MRP spreadsheet's key area is the cell range B17:K25 which is now examined in more detail.

User input   (i) BOM table details in rows 6–13, (ii) the master production schedule (MPS) in row 20, and (iii) any scheduled receipts of items in row 21 (as well as rows 31, 41, 51, etc.).

On-hand inventory   Cell D22 contains the initial on-hand (i.e., available) inventory as shown in column G of the BOM table. The following formula is used to calculate the on-hand inventory for week n. It is initially entered in cell E22 and then copied across into cells F22:K22 as shown in the formula template of Table 9.7

$$\text{on-hand}_n = \text{on-hand}_{n-1} + \text{receipts}_{n-1} - \text{gross requirements}_{n-1}$$

where receipts includes both scheduled and planned receipts.

	A	B	C	D	E	F	G	H	I	J	K	L
1		Case Study 9.1 - A material requirements planning (MRP) model										
2												
3	►	*The BOM Table*										
4		*Part Number: Description*	*BOM*	*Id.*	*No. of*	*Lead*	*On*	*Planned*				
5			*Level*	*Code*	*Units*	*Time*	*Hand*	*Order*		*User input*		
6		Table	0	1	1	1	50	*Rel. Row*		*cells are*		
7		Top Assembly	1	1001	1	2	50	25		*shaded*		
8		Table Top	2	2001	1	1	180	35				
9		Drawer	2	2002	1	1	200	35				
10		Leg Assembly	1	1002	1	1	100	25				
11		Legs	2	2003	4	1	250	65				
12		Side Rung	2	2004	2	1	50	65				
13		Connecting Rung	2	2005	1	1	110	65				
14												
15												
16	►	*The MRP Output Table*										
17		1										
18		*Table*				*Lead Time =*			*1*			
19		Week Number	Overdue	1	2	3	4	5	6	7	8	
20		**Master Production Schedule**		**0**	**0**	**180**	**180**	**100**	**0**	**0**	**0**	
21		Scheduled Receipts		0	0	0	0	0	0	0	0	
22		On Hand		50	50	50	0	0	0	0	0	
23		Net Requirements		0	0	130	180	100	0	0	0	
24		Planned Order Receipts		0	0	130	180	100	0	0	0	
25		Planned Order Releases	0	0	130	180	100	0	0	0	0	
26												
27		2										
28		*Top Assembly*				*Lead Time =*			*2*			
29		Week Number	Overdue	1	2	3	4	5	6	7	8	
30		Gross Requirements		0	130	180	100	0	0	0	0	
31		Scheduled Receipts		0	**100**	0	0	0	0	0	0	
32		On Hand		50	50	20	0	0	0	0	0	
33		Net Requirements		0	0	160	100	0	0	0	0	
34		Planned Order Receipts		0	0	160	100	0	0	0	0	
35		Planned Order Releases	0	160	100	0	0	0	0	0	0	
36												
37		3										
38		*Table Top*				*Lead Time =*			*1*			
39		Week Number	Overdue	1	2	3	4	5	6	7	8	
40		Gross Requirements		160	100	0	0	0	0	0	0	
41		Scheduled Receipts		0	0	0	0	0	0	0	0	
42		On Hand		180	20	0	0	0	0	0	0	
43		Net Requirements		0	80	0	0	0	0	0	0	
44		Planned Order Receipts		0	80	0	0	0	0	0	0	
45		Planned Order Releases	0	80	0	0	0	0	0	0	0	
46												

Figure 9.20 MRP model for the kitchen table example.

	A	B	C	D	E	F	G	H	I	J	K	L
47		4										
48		*Drawer*				*Lead Time =*		*1*				
49		Week Number	Overdue	1	2	3	4	5	6	7	8	
50		Gross Requirements		160	100	0	0	0	0	0	0	
51		Scheduled Receipts		0	0	0	0	0	0	0	0	
52		On Hand		200	40	0	0	0	0	0	0	
53		Net Requirements		0	60	0	0	0	0	0	0	
54		Planned Order Receipts		0	60	0	0	0	0	0	0	
55		Planned Order Releases	0	60	0	0	0	0	0	0	0	
56												
57		5										
58		*Leg Assembly*				*Lead Time =*		*1*				
59		Week Number	Overdue	1	2	3	4	5	6	7	8	
60		Gross Requirements		0	130	180	180	0	0	0	0	
61		Scheduled Receipts		0	0	0	0	0	0	0	0	
62		On Hand		100	100	0	0	0	0	0	0	
63		Net Requirements		0	30	180	100	0	0	0	0	
64		Planned Order Receipts		0	30	180	100	0	0	0	0	
65		Planned Order Releases	0	30	180	100	0	0	0	0	0	
66												
67		6										
68		*Legs*				*Lead Time =*		*1*				
69		Week Number	Overdue	1	2	3	4	5	6	7	8	
70		Gross Requirements		120	720	400	0	0	0	0	0	
71		Scheduled Receipts		0	100	0	0	0	0	0	0	
72		On Hand		250	130	0	0	0	0	0	0	
73		Net Requirements		0	490	400	0	0	0	0	0	
74		Planned Order Receipts		0	490	400	0	0	0	0	0	
75		Planned Order Releases	0	490	400	0	0	0	0	0	0	
76												
77		7										
78		*Side Rung*				*Lead Time =*		*1*				
79		Week Number	Overdue	1	2	3	4	5	6	7	8	
80		Gross Requirements		60	360	200	0	0	0	0	0	
81		Scheduled Receipts	10	0	0	0	0	0	0	0	0	
82		On Hand		50	0	0	0	0	0	0	0	
83		Net Requirements		10	360	200	0	0	0	0	0	
84		Planned Order Receipts		10	360	200	0	0	0	0	0	
85		Planned Order Releases	10	360	200	0	0	0	0	0	0	
86												
87		8										
88		*Connecting Rung*				*Lead Time =*		*1*				
89		Week Number	Overdue	1	2	3	4	5	6	7	8	
90		Gross Requirements		30	180	100	0	0	0	0	0	
91		Scheduled Receipts		0	0	0	0	0	0	0	0	
92		On Hand		110	80	0	0	0	0	0	0	
93		Net Requirements		0	100	100	0	0	0	0	0	
94		Planned Order Receipts		0	100	100	0	0	0	0	0	
95		Planned Order Releases	0	100	100	0	0	0	0	0	0	
96												

Figure 9.20   (*Cont.*)

Table 9.7   Material requirements planning – worksheet formulae.

Cell	Formula	Copied to
B17	INT(ROW(B17)/10)	
B18	INDEX(BOM, B17, 1)	
H18	INDEX(BOM, B17, 5)	
C21	IF(AND(COLUMN(D23) – 4 < H18, D23 <> 0), D23,'''')	
C22	IF(AND(COLUMN(E23) – 4 < H18, E23 <> 0), E23,'''')	
C23	IF(AND(COLUMN(F23) – 4 < H18, F23 <> 0), F23,'''')	
C24	IF(AND(COLUMN(G23) – 4 < H18, G23 <> 0), G23,'''')	
C25	SUM(C21:C24)	
D22	INDEX(BOM, $B17, 6)	
E22	IF(D21 + D22 + D24 – D20 < 0, 0, D21 + D22 + D24 – D20)	F22:K22
D23	IF(D22 + D21 > D20,0, D20 – D21 – D22)	E23:K23
D24	D23	E24:K24
D25	OFFSET(D25, –1, $H18)	E25:K25

Net requirements   Cell D23 contains the following conditional statement for calculating an item's net requirements.

$$\text{IF (net requirements)} > 0 \text{ THEN (net requirements) OTHERWISE } 0$$

where (net requirements) = (gross requirements) – (on-hand) – (scheduled receipts). If there is sufficient stock available (either as on-hand or scheduled receipt items) to meet the gross requirements, then obviously the net requirements are zero.

Planned order releases (PORs)   PORs must be adjusted to take care of lead-time offsets so that items will be received on schedule, i.e., they must coincide with the planned order receipts. Excel's OFFSET function is ideally suited to this situation.

Overdue items   The 'overdue' column at the beginning of the current planning horizon is used to highlight shortages caused by lead-times projecting backwards into the previous planning horizon, i.e., weeks 0, –1, –2, etc. The model can handle lead-times of up to four weeks/periods. The spreadsheet checks each of the first four columns (D to G) of the net requirements row (rows 23, 33, 43 . . .) for two criteria (i) does the column come within the item's lead-time offset? (ii) are there any net requirements for this week? Only if both criteria are satisfied will a value appear in the 'overdue column', otherwise it is left blank.

The overdue column is simply used to highlight shortages which might otherwise be overlooked at the beginning of the current planning horizon. Such outstanding requirements can usually be found by comparing the 'planned order receipts' with the 'planned order releases'. This situation is best illustrated by looking at the kitchen table example.

Overdue items occur at the 'side-rung' level, which has a lead time of one week. There are only 50 side-rungs on hand (cell D82) to meet a gross requirement of 60 (cell D80). Thus, there is a net requirement of 10 items in the first week of the current planning horizon. This shortfall will have to be met from the previous planning horizon, i.e., week 0! This amount appears twice in the overdue column C, in cell C81 and again in the 'overdue totals' cell C85. In this

Table 9.8 Materials requirements planning – worksheet formulae (cont.)

Cell	Formula	Copied to
B30	"Gross requirements"	
D30	INDEX(BOM, $B27, 4)*OFFSET(D30, INDEX(BOM, $B27, 7)–ROW(D30), 0)	E30:K30

case there is one overdue amount because the item's lead time is only one week. However, if lead times are longer, say 3 or 4 weeks, PORs may extend over several weeks of the previous planning horizon.

Use the formula template of Table 9.7 to create the initial part of the MRP model of Figure 9.20 (down to line 26). Remember to name the cell range B6:H13 as BOM. Then follow the instructions in Step 2 to complete the model.

Step 2: Modifying and copying cell ranges

Having completed step one above (i) copy the cell range B17:K26 into cell range B27:K36, and then (ii) modify line 30 as shown in Table 9.8.

Finally, all that now remains to be done is to copy the modified cell range B27:K36 down the worksheet for each remaining part, i.e., six times for the kitchen table example. When this final step has been completed, don't forget to fill in the correct POR values in cells H7:H13 of the BOM table. The POR values are found by studying the product structure tree to determine the correct parent–component relationship. The MRP spreadsheet is now complete and can be used again for other problems by entering new details in the following cells:

- BOM table details (cells B6:G13)
- master production schedule (cells D20:K20)
- POR row values from the product structure tree (cells H7:H13)
- scheduled receipts (if any) (rows 31, 41, 51, etc.).

LOT-SIZING METHODS

Lot-sizing is the term used in material requirements planning to define economic order quantities or batch sizes. The five most commonly used methods are:

1. Economic order quantity – the oldest and best-known method
2. Fixed order quantity – in the fixed order quantity (FOQ) approach, an order of fixed size is placed whenever stock falls to a certain level. The lot size may be influenced by economic reasons, e.g., an FOQ of 500 might be chosen because the quantity-discount level is 500 units.
3. Period order quantity – the period order quantity (POQ) method produces a different order quantity for each order issued. For example, consider the following net requirements for twelve months: 15, 26, 0, 12, 0, 23, 8, 15, 35, 0, 0, and 32. A three-month POQ simply sums

up the net (non-zero) requirements for months 1, 2, 4 ($= 53$), months 6, 7, 8 ($= 46$), and months 9, 12 ($= 67$). Orders for amounts of 53, 46, and 67 are then placed in months 1, 6, and 9 respectively. Since some months have no requirements, periods will not necessarily have the same duration. The POQ method should not be confused with the fixed-interval periodic review system discussed earlier.

4. Lot-for-lot – the lot-for-lot (LFL) policy represents the traditional MRP way of ordering exactly what is needed in every period, i.e., lot sizes are the same as the net requirements.

5. Part period balancing – the part-period balancing (PPB) method uses the ratio of ordering cost to holding cost to derive a part-period number which is then used as a basis for cumulating requirements. A model is now developed for the PPB algorithm.

EXAMPLE 9.14 *A model for the part-period balancing (PPB) method*

The part-period balancing method (PPB) is a lot-sizing policy in which order quantity varies according to a comparison between holding costs and ordering costs. The PPB method uses the ratio between ordering (or setup) cost to holding cost to derive an economic part period (EPP), i.e.,

$$EPP = \text{(ordering or setup cost)/(holding cost)}$$

The PPB uses the EPP ratio to achieve a balance between setup and holding costs. Product requirements are accumulated over a number of periods until the accumulated value is as close to the EPP value as possible. The PPB model of Figure 9.21 is developed using the following five steps.

1. For each period P, weight its net requirement, REQ_P, by $(P - 1)$. For example in Figure 9.21, the weighted requirement for period 2, $WREQ_2 = (2 - 1) \times REQ_2 = 1 \times 100 = 100$ (see cell E11). Similarly, $WREQ_3 = (3 - 1) \times REQ_3 = 2 \times 150 = 300$ (cell F11), etc.

2. Cumulate the weighted requirements $WREQ_i$ i.e., $CUM_i = \sum WREQ_i$ for $i = 1, 2, 3 \ldots$

Table 9.9 Part period balancing (PPB) – worksheet formulae.

Cell	Formula	Copied to
H5	INT(H3/H4)	
D11	IF(AND(D$8 = 0, D9 = 0), −1, D$8*(D9 − 1))	E11:L11
D12	IF(D11<0, 0, D11)	
E12	IF(E11<0, 0, E11 + D12)	F12:L12
D13	(D12 − $H$5)/$H$5	E13:L13
B14	MIN(D14:L14)	
D14	ABS(D13)	E14:L14
D15	IF(AND(D17 = 0, D11>= 0), D$8,"")	E15:L15
B16	COUNTIF(D11:L11, "<0")	
H16	SUM(D15:L15)	
K16	B16 + 1	
D17	IF(D13 > $B14, C17 + 1, 0)	E17:L17

	A	B	C	D	E	F	G	H	I	J	K	L
1	Example 9.14 - A model for the part period balancing (PPB) method											
2												
3		Input			Ordering (or setup) cost =			£200		User input cells		
4					Unit holding cost =			£1.00		are shaded		
5					Economic part period (EPP) =			200				
6												
7				<---------- Net requirements, REQ_P for each period P -------------->								
8		REQ_P		150	100	150	0	50	75	100	25	20
9		Period, P		1	2	3	4	5	6	7	8	9
10												
11		Weighted REQ_i		0	100	300	0	200	375	600	175	160
12		CUM_i		0	100	400	400	600	975	1575	1750	1910
13		$(CUM_i - EPP)/EPP$		-1.0	-0.5	1.0	1.0	2.0	3.9	6.9	7.8	8.6
14		0.5		1.0	0.5	1.0	1.0	2.0	3.9	6.9	7.8	8.6
15		Order Data =		150	100							
16	0			Answer: Place an order for				250	units in period		1	
17		New Factor, NF_i		0	0	1	2	3	4	5	6	7
18												
19		Weighted REQ_i		-150	-100	0	0	100	225	400	125	120
20		CUM_i		0	0	0	0	100	325	725	850	970
21		$(CUM_i - EPP)/EPP$		-1.0	-1.0	-1.0	-1.0	-0.5	0.6	2.6	3.3	3.9
22		0.5		1.0	1.0	1.0	1.0	0.5	0.6	2.6	3.3	3.9
23		Order Data =				150	0	50				
24	2			Answer: Place an order for				200	units in period		3	
25		New Factor, NF_i		0	0	0	0	0	1	2	3	4
26												
27		Weighted REQ_i		-150	-100	-150	-1	-50	0	100	50	60
28		CUM_i		0	0	0	0	0	0	100	150	210
29		$(CUM_i - EPP)/EPP$		-1.0	-1.0	-1.0	-1.0	-1.0	-1.0	-0.5	-0.3	0.1
30		0.1		1.0	1.0	1.0	1.0	1.0	1.0	0.5	0.3	0.1
31		Order Data =							75	100	25	20
32	5			Answer: Place an order for				220	units in period		6	
33		New Factor, NF_i		0	0	0	0	0	0	0	0	0
34												
35												
36		Copy cell range B11:L17 repeatedly down the spreadsheet, placing the cursor in cells B19,										
37		B27.... until the 'New Factor, NF_i' row contains nothing but zeros (e.g. see row 33 above).										
38												

Figure 9.21 Model for the part-period balancing (PPB) method.

3. Calculate a proportional ratio defined as $(CUM_i - EPP)/EPP$ for each $i = 1, 2, 3 \ldots$

4. Cumulate the requirements REQ_i until the smallest value of $ABS(CUM_i - EPP)/EPP$ is reached. The first part-period order has now been found (see line 16 of the spreadsheet model). The smallest value of $ABS(CUM_i - EPP)/EPP$ is 0.5 (see cell E14), and the cumulated amount is $REQ_1 + REQ_2 = 150 + 100 = 250$.

5. Repeat the above four steps until all periods have been assigned a part-period order.

JUST-IN-TIME (JIT) APPROACH TO INVENTORY MANAGEMENT

Just-in-time (JIT) systems are similar to material requirements planning in that they can only operate in a 'dependent demand' situation. The main objective of just-in-time systems is to minimise wastage. Inventory carrying costs can be greatly reduced by ensuring that raw materials and components which are used in the manufacture of the end-product arrive just at the time they are needed.

The implementation of a JIT system is complex and wide-ranging, being seen not only as a set of manufacturing rules but also as a philosophy requiring organisational commitment and discipline. While computers can make significant contributions to JIT manufacturing, the successful implementation of a JIT system goes far beyond the mechanisation of routine operations. In order to function properly, the following activities must also be carried out.

- Identify customer needs in terms of quality, quantity, and timing, i.e., what, how much, and when?

- Obtain the exact amount of material needed to meet today's production requirements, i.e., all lead times are zero!

- Perform work measurement and time studies to synchronise work flow, i.e., reduce time-wasting and motion-wasting as much as possible.

- Ensure that everything that is made is needed by the customer, i.e., there is no finished goods inventory.

- Ensure that there is total quality control, i.e., no defective materials/components are accepted and no defective end-products are manufactured.

EXCEL FUNCTIONS USED IN MODEL-BUILDING

The models developed in this chapter introduce four Excel functions for the first time, each of which is explained below. The user should remember that a comprehensive on-line help facility is also provided by Excel.

1. COLUMN COLUMN (reference)

> returns the column number of the given reference. Where the reference is a range of cells, COLUMN returns the starting column number of the named range.

reference = the cell or range of cells for which the column number is required.
Example: COLUMN(B3) returns the value 2; COLUMN(D5:F9) returns the value 4.

2. INDEX INDEX (LookupRange, rowNo, colNo)

> returns the contents of the cell given by (rowNo, colNo) in the range of cells.

LookupRange = the range of cells defining the lookup table
rowNo   = the row number within the LookupRange
colNo   = the column number within the LookupRange

Example: INDEX(B4:D7, 2, 3) in Figure 9.22 returns a value of £12.50 (i.e., the contents of cell D5 in the lookup cell range B4:D7).

	A	B	C	D	E	F	G	H
1								
2		Product	No. in	Product		Year	Cash	
3		name	stock	price			flow	
4		Gizmo	10	£10.00		1	1	
5		Gadget	25	£12.50		2	4	
6		Widget	9	£20.00		3	8	
7		Sprocket	40	£4.50		4	16	
8						5		
9				*Sample Figure*				

Figure 9.22 Sample figure.

3. NORMSINV NORMSINV (probability)

 returns the inverse of the normal cumulative distribution for a specified probability. The distribution has a mean of zero and a standard deviation of one.

 probability = the probability for which the inverse of the normal cumulative distribution is required.

 Example: NORMSINV(0.95) returns the value 1.6449.

4. ROW ROW (reference)

 returns the row number of a given reference. Where the reference is a range of cells, ROW returns the starting row number of the named range.

 reference = the cell or range of cells for which the row number is required.
 Example: ROW(B3) returns the value 3; ROW(D5:F9) returns the value 5.

EXERCISES

9.1 The ABC Company has an annual demand of 1200 units for a product with average order cost of £9 per order and a carrying cost of £0.10 per unit per year. Help ABC to find the economic order quantity (EOQ) for the product. What would be the EOQ if a supplier offers the following pricing schedule: £0.50 unit cost for orders under 500; £0.45 unit cost for orders of 500 and over?

 (Answers: (i) EOQ = 465 with total cost of £646.48 (ii) EOQ = 500 with total cost of £586.60.)

9.2 The Acme Company finds that it can produce widgets costing £5.50 each at the rate of 60 units per day. The annual demand is 6500, i.e., about 25 units per day. Acme's setup cost for widget production is £180 per run, and its annual carrying cost is 18% of unit cost. Use the PROQ model to find (i) the production lot size (ii) the maximum inventory level, and (iii) the length of each production run.

 (Answers: (i) 2013 (ii) 1174.2 (iii) 6.71 weeks.)

9.3 Production costs for the monthly magazine *Gardening Today* are £0.90 per unit with a selling price of £1.20. Monthly demand for the magazine has been calculated as follows:

No. of magazines sold	500	600	700	800	900	1000
Probability	0.1	0.15	0.2	0.25	0.2	0.1

If unsold copies have a scrap value of £0.50, how many copies of *Gardening Today* should be produced every month in order to maximise profits?

(Answer: 700 copies – giving a maximum profit of £186.)

9.4 The New Products Company has an annual demand for a product of 4000 with setup costs of £500 and carrying costs of 10% of unit cost. The cost of the product is £10 but the company offers discounts of 3% and 7% on unit cost for orders of 1000 and over, and 2500 and over respectively. Find the optimal size that will minimise total cost.

(Answer: 2500 giving a minimum cost of £39,163.)

9.5 Bloggs Engineering manufactures a product with a unit cost of £30. Demand averages 280 units per week. Lead time is two weeks and demand during the lead time is normally distributed with a standard deviation of 60 units. Bloggs Engineering estimates its ordering cost at £8 per order, carrying cost at £1 per unit per week, and stockout cost at £2.00 per unit. Find (i) the optimal order quantity and back-order size when planned shortages are allowed (disregard lead-time details) (ii) the order quantity, Q, and reorder level, R, when a continuous lead time is included with a service-level requirement of 95%.

(Answer: (i) Optimal order quantity $= 82$ with back-order size $= 27.3$ (i.e., 28) (ii) Optimal order quantity, $Q = 67$ and reorder level, $R = 700$.)

9.6 The Ajax Company sells two products, widgets and gadgets. The company stores the items in a warehouse with a capacity of 350 cubic metres (m^3). What would be the best ordering policy for the Ajax Company, given that a widget contributes £25 and a gadget £20 to the company's profits? In order fully to meet demand, by how much would storage space need to be increased, and what would be the corresponding increase in profits? Inventory details are given in the table below.

	Annual demand	Holding cost	Ordering cost	Storage requirements
Widget	5000	£10	£120	1.5 m^3
Gadget	4000	£15	£200	1.0 m^3

(Hint: this is an inventory problem with constraints. Solve using SOLVER.)

(Answer: (i) Each order consists of 240 widgets and 340 gadgets giving a total profit of £12,799 (ii) In order fully to meet demand, the Ajax Company requires total storage space of 412 m^3 increasing profits by £2272.)

9.7 The weekly demand for a product is normally distributed with a mean of 200 and a standard deviation of 30. The product's lead time is one week and orders can be produced at little or no additional cost. The product costs £300 and its carrying charge per unit per month is £8. Using a fixed-period model, calculate (i) the order quantity for a required service level of 98%. How would this answer be affected if (ii) the cost of placing an order is £100 (iii) the lead time is increased to two weeks?

(Note: review period and stock on-hand are zero.)

(Answer: (i) Order quantity is 262 at a weekly cost of £386 (ii) Weekly cost increases to £462.34 (iii) Order quantity = 488.)

9.8 MeadowSweet Creameries have recently experienced problems with overstocking resulting in product spoilage. They have collected historical data in order to determine the ideal amount that should be produced. Overstocking costs the company £2 per box through carrying costs and spoilage. On the other hand, understocking results in lost profits amounting to £2.40 per box.

Weekly demand	500	600	700	800	900	1000
Probability	0.1	0.2	0.3	0.3	0.05	0.05

(Answer: 700 boxes.)

9.9 The Bedrock Company has an annual demand of 7,500 units for its product P which costs £20. Bedrock estimates its ordering cost at £50 per order, holding cost at £10 per unit per year, and stockout cost at £15 for each lost sale. Fred Flint would like to find an optimal order policy which includes (i) the order size (ii) the cycle time (iii) the maximum inventory level.

(Answer: (i) 354 (ii) 2.5 weeks (iii) 212.)

9.10 Joe Bloggs is the owner of Micros Unlimited, which uses various components to make its main product, a microcomputer. The micro's main parts are a colour monitor, a CPU, and a keyboard. The CPU assembly includes a motherboard, a disk drive and a CD-ROM drive. Details of Micros Unlimited current inventory and component lead times (LT) are: 60 micros (LT = 1), 100 keyboards (LT = 1), 60 CPU Assembly (LT = 2), 50 monitors (LT = 2), 100 motherboards(LT = 1), and 90 of each type of drive (LT = l). Joe has to meet the order schedule as shown.

Week	1	2	3	4	5	6
Micro		40	80	90	80	

(i) Construct a product structure tree for Joe's micro (ii) set up the BOM table, and (iii) use the MRP model (with a lot-for-lot sizing method) to identify Joe's requirements.

(Answer: BOM table is Table 9.10.)

Table 9.10

Part description	BOM level	Id. code	No. of units	Lead time	On-hand	POR row
Microprocessor	0	1	1	1	60	
Monitor	1	1001	1	2	50	25
Keyboard	1	1002	1	1	100	25
CPU Assembly	1	1003	1	2	60	25
Motherboard	2	2001	1	1	100	55
Disk drive	2	2002	1	1	90	55
CD-ROM drive	2	2003	1	1	90	55

9.11 The Gizmo Company has to meet the following requirements schedule for its product. Ordering cost is £50 per order and holding cost is £0.70 per unit per week. Use the part period balancing (PPB) model to find an acceptable planned order schedule.

Week	1	2	3	4	5	6	7	8
No. of units	40	30	20	30	25	30	20	25

(Answer: 90 units in week 1; 85 units in week 4; 45 units in week 7.)

9.12 The GreenFingers Garden Centre sells lawn mowers. Since demand for lawn mowers is seasonal, the Garden Centre has decided to check sales data over the past fifteen months in order to get a better picture of the demand pattern. It has found that weekly demand varies according to the following probability table.

Demand	0	1	2	3	4	5
Frequency (weeks)	12	9	9	15	12	3
Probability	0.2	0.15	0.15	0.25	0.2	0.05

The current inventory policy is to order ten lawn mowers whenever on-hand inventory falls to the reorder level of five or less. When placing an order, there can be a delay of 1–3 weeks. Having examined delivery dates for the past 30 orders, the Centre has produced the following lead-time table.

Lead time (weeks)	1	2	3
Frequency	6	18	6
Probability	0.2	0.6	0.2

Using the inventory simulation model, simulate GreenFingers' sales for a 20-week period, and hence find (i) the average ending inventory per week (ii) lost sales for the 20-week period, and (iii) the number of orders placed during the 20-week period (iv) the service level.

(Answer: Due to the volatile nature of Excel's RAND function, answers may not be the same as those now given (i) 4.5 units/week (ii) 6 units (iii) 5 orders (iv) 87.0%.)

REFERENCES AND FURTHER READING

Heizer, J. and Render, B. (2003) *Production & Operations Management* (7th edn), Prentice Hall, New Jersey.

Waters, C.D. (2003) *Inventory Control and Management* (2nd edn), John Wiley & Sons, Ltd, UK.

10

Models for production operations

OVERVIEW

Managers often have to make decisions on how best to allocate scarce resources among competing activities. Limited resources such as machinery, time, materials, labour, and money are used to manufacture various products, or provide services such as investment plans and advertising strategies. Typically, there are many different ways to produce these products or services. Management's problem is to find the best way, given the limitations of the resources. Production operations are the processes by which inputs are converted into outputs as shown in Figure 10.1.

Production operations involve a wide spectrum of activities, ranging from the initial decision of where best to build the company (i.e., facility location planning) to the final stages of distribution when finished goods are shipped to the customer. Between these outer limits, other important activities occur:

- logistics planning and queuing systems

- production planning and scheduling

- materials purchasing and inventory control

- quality assurance and control

- project management.

Operational control decisions ensure that specific tasks are performed effectively and efficiently. Efficiency means that input resources are used in such a way as to produce the optimum (i.e., maximum) output. Put simply, efficiency is 'doing the thing right'. Effectiveness is a measure of how well a production system performs its functions. Being effective implies that management is 'doing the right thing'.

Figure 10.1

LOGISTICS MODELS

A key aspect of production operations is the logistics function which provides an integrated view of materials supply and product distribution. Logistics is concerned mainly with the handling, storage, and movement of materials to manufacturing facilities and products to markets. In managing logistics, several important issues arise.

- What should be the structure of the distribution system – centralised or decentralised?
- How can warehouse and storage layouts be optimised in order to maximise space while minimising material handling costs?
- Which geographic locations provide the best benefits to the organisation?
- How much inventory should be held at each location?
- Which modes of transportation should be used?

A key aspect of logistics planning involves the two critical areas of facility location planning and operations layout. The objective of 'facility location planning' is to find that site which will be most beneficial to the company. Locational analysis includes careful evaluation of market factors such as labour availability, proximity to raw materials and customers, government incentives, high-grade access routes, environmental regulations, etc. Since the costs of many input resources are determined by an organisation's location, the efficiency and effectiveness of production operations depend heavily upon the choice of location.

Operations layout is the physical configuration of processes, equipment, and materials that facilitates the flow of materials and personnel within and between work areas. For example, it makes sense to group similar machines together so that jobs are routed to one particular work area rather than being scattered all over the place. Poor layouts cause bottleneck queues by interrupting the physical flow of materials, and consequently add extra costs to production activities. Layout decisions involve the analysis of queues in terms of queue length, average waiting time, and queuing costs.

EXAMPLE 10.1   *Facility location model*

There are many factors, both qualitative and quantitative, to be considered when choosing a location, e.g., distribution costs, resource availability, distance from ports, etc. The weighted-distance (WD) method is a mathematical technique for finding the optimal location (X_0, Y_0) that will minimise distribution costs. It uses the standard co-ordinate geometry equation for the distance, d, between two points (x_1, y_1) and (x_2, y_2), i.e.,

$$\text{distance}, d = \sqrt{(x_2 - x_1)^2 + (y_2 - y_1)^2}$$

The weighted-distance method incorporates a weighting factor into the above equation. A standard map is converted into an (x, y) graph by placing a grid over the area under consideration. It then calculates the weighted distance, wd_i, of each location i, from the optimal location (X_0, Y_0), using the following weighted straight-line equation

$$\text{weighted distance}, wd_i = w_i\sqrt{(X_0 - x_i)^2 + (Y_0 - y_i)^2}$$

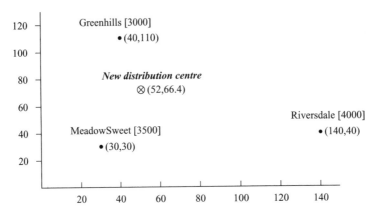

Figure 10.2   An (x, y) graph showing the best location for the new centre.

where w_i is the weighting factor, based on the volume of goods moved to/from location i, and (x_i, y_i) are the co-ordinates of location i.

Meadowsweet Creameries are currently planning a new distribution centre for their dairy products. They already have two production plants located at Greenhills and Riversdale and want to find the best location for the new warehouse facility. The (x, y) diagram of Figure 10.2 shows the location of Meadowsweet and its two subsidiaries, with goods-supplied data shown in square brackets. Because the wd_i formula is nonlinear, the facility location model is a nonlinear programming (NLP) exercise. Excel's Solver can be used to find the optimal values X_0, Y_0 that will minimise the total distance $\sum wd_i$. The facility location model of Figure 10.3 has found an optimal location of (52, 66.4) which has then been placed on the (x, y) diagram for clarification purposes.

The weighting factor, w_i, should be varied in order to see how sensitive the optimal location is to changes in the volume of goods. It is also advisable to find the best location when distance is the only consideration, by omitting the weighting factor, w_i. In this situation, Objective 2 in Figure 10.3 has found that the best location is (56.2, 58.6) which is close to the previous answer of (52, 66.4).

Transportation and Assignment Models

A method that is particularly useful in facility location planning is the transportation (or distribution) method of linear programming. The transportation problem involves a number of supply sources (e.g., warehouses) and a number of destinations (e.g., retail shops). The objective is to minimise the transportation costs involved in moving materials or products from warehouses to factories or shops. The transportation problem is therefore concerned with selecting minimum-cost routes in a product-distribution network between sources and destinations. Sources can be factories, warehouses, airports, or any other points from which goods can be shipped. Destinations are the points which receive the goods. The title 'transportation'

	A	B	C	D	E	F	G	H	I
1	Example 10.1 - A facility location model for MeadowSweet's new distribution centre								
2									
3		Creameries	Volume	Co-ordinates				Weighted	
4			of goods	X	Y		Distance	Distance	
5		MeadowSweet	3500	30	30		42.53	148840	
6		Greenhills	4000	40	110		45.24	180949	
7		Riversdale	3000	140	40		91.86	275581	
8									
9			Changing cells =	52.0	66.4		*User input cells are shaded*		
10									
11		*Objective 1: Minimise the weighted distances =*					605371		
12									
13		*Objective 2: Minimise distances only =*					179.62		
14									
15									
16		*Solver Parameters*							
17		*Set Target Cell:* G11				Change to G13 for objective 2			
18		*Equal to:* Min							
19		*By Changing Cells:* D9:E9							
20		*Subject to Constraints:*				There are no constraints			
21									
22		*Cells*	*Formula*				*Copied to*		
23		G5	SQRT((D$9–D5)^2 + (E$9–E5)^2)				G6:G7		
24		H5	G5*C5				H6:H7		
25		G11	SUM(H5:H7)						
26		G13	SUM(G5:G7)						
27									
28	Remember to switch off the 'Assume Linear Model' parameter in the Solver dialog box								

Figure 10.3 Facility location model for MeadowSweet Creameries.

is rather misleading in that the transportation technique can be applied to other areas such as inventory control, cash flow analysis, and production scheduling problems.

The special case of the transportation problem, known as the 'assignment method', involves assigning people or machines to different tasks on a one-to-one basis. In this situation, only one source item is assigned to each of the various destinations. Both transportation and assignment problems belong to the wider class of linear programming (LP) problems known as *network flow problems*. A typical transportation problem is now considered.

EXAMPLE 10.2 *Transportation model*

A producer of limestone for agricultural use has three lime quarries which supply five warehouses. Weekly production capacity (in tonnes) and transportation costs per tonne from each quarry to each warehouse are given in Table 10.1. The warehouses (1 to 5) need lime on a

Table 10.1

Quarry	Production capacity	Cost per tonne to warehouses (£s)				
		1	2	3	4	5
1	200	5	1	6	3	1
2	100	2	3	4	5	4
3	150	4	2	3	2	3

weekly basis in the following quantities: 80, 90, 100, 70, 60 tonnes respectively. Set up the exercise as an LP model and then use Excel's Solver to find the minimum total transportation costs that satisfy each warehouse's requirements.

The answer in Figure 10.4 shows that a minimum transportation cost of £770 (see cell I23) is obtained when quarry 1 ships 90, 20, and 60 tonnes to warehouses 2, 4, and 5 respectively; quarry 2 ships 80 tonnes to warehouse 1; and quarry 3 ships 100, 50 to warehouses 3 and 4. Most transportation situations, including assignment problems, involve the setting up and multiplication of two matrices. A matrix is simply a cell range, with the notation x_{ij} representing the value of the matrix element in row i, column j. Since Excel's SUMPRODUCT function is normally used in transportation and assignment problems, it is good practice to name matrices. (Note: To name matrices, first select the required cell range, and then use the Insert|Name|Define commands.)

Let the (3 × 5) matrix, named 'cost_matrix', represent the table of transportation costs as defined in cells C6:G8 of Figure 10.4, and let the (3 × 5) matrix named 'solution_matrix' (cells C14:G16) contain the required answers x_{ij} ($i = 1$ to 3; $j = 1, 5$). The objective is then to minimise transportation costs, i.e., minimise the objective function, Z (in £s) where

$$Z_{ij} = (\text{cost\_matrix})_{ij} \times (\text{solution\_matrix})_{ij} \quad \text{for all } i = 1, 3; j = 1, 5$$

$$= \text{SUMPRODUCT}(\text{cost\_matrix}, \text{solution\_matrix})$$

EXAMPLE 10.3 *Unbalanced transportation model*

In the previous limestone producer's transportation problem, demand was less than supply. The warehouses' weekly requirement was for 400 tonnes of limestone whereas the quarries could supply 450 tonnes between them. Excel's Solver can solve transportation applications in which demand is less than or equal to supply. But what happens when total demand exceeds total supply? The model of Figure 10.4 will not find a feasible solution because it is impossible to satisfy demand when the supply is insufficient.

The key to solving an unbalanced transportation model in which demand exceeds supply is to create a fictitious or dummy supply source whose capacity will be exactly equal to the deficient amount. Consider the following example.

ABC Transportation operates a containerisation service between seven depots. At the end of most weekends, their 24 wagons are located as follows:

Depot	D1	D2	D3
Number of wagons at depot	4	12	8

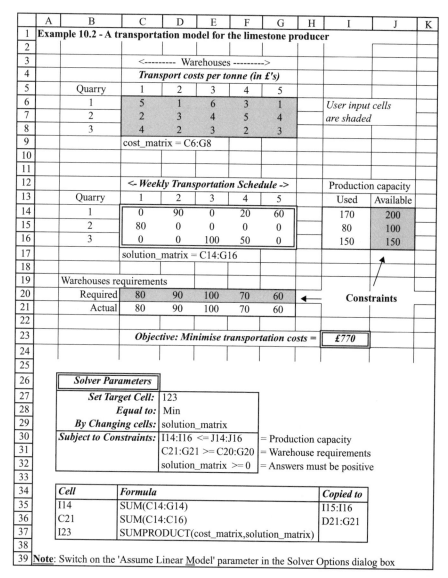

	A	B	C	D	E	F	G	H	I	J	K
1	Example 10.2 - A transportation model for the limestone producer										
2											
3			<-------- Warehouses -------->								
4			*Transport costs per tonne (in £'s)*								
5		Quarry	1	2	3	4	5				
6		1	5	1	6	3	1		User input cells		
7		2	2	3	4	5	4		are shaded		
8		3	4	2	3	2	3				
9			cost_matrix = C6:G8								
10											
11											
12			*<- Weekly Transportation Schedule ->*						Production capacity		
13		Quarry	1	2	3	4	5		Used	Available	
14		1	0	90	0	20	60		170	200	
15		2	80	0	0	0	0		80	100	
16		3	0	0	100	50	0		150	150	
17			solution_matrix = C14:G16								
18											
19		Warehouses requirements									
20		Required	80	90	100	70	60	←	Constraints		
21		Actual	80	90	100	70	60				
22											
23			*Objective: Minimise transportation costs =*						£770		
24											
25											
26		*Solver Parameters*									
27		*Set Target Cell:*	I23								
28		*Equal to:*	Min								
29		*By Changing cells:*	solution_matrix								
30		*Subject to Constraints:*	I14:I16 <= J14:J16			= Production capacity					
31			C21:G21 >= C20:G20			= Warehouse requirements					
32			solution_matrix >= 0			= Answers must be positive					
33											
34		*Cell*	*Formula*					*Copied to*			
35		I14	SUM(C14:G14)					I15:I16			
36		C21	SUM(C14:C16)					D21:G21			
37		I23	SUMPRODUCT(cost_matrix,solution_matrix)								
38											
39	Note: Switch on the 'Assume Linear Model' parameter in the Solver Options dialog box										

Figure 10.4 Transportation model for the limestone producer.

For the next stage of their operations, ABC would like to have five wagons at depot D4, six at depot D5, and eight wagons in both depots D6 and D7 but unfortunately they do not have 27 wagons! The distance (in kilometres) between the various depots is given in Table 10.2.

The company's main priority is to minimise the total costs involved in transferring the wagons from their current locations to the required destinations. Since costs can be equated with distance, the problem can be formulated as a transportation problem as shown in Figure 10.5.

Table 10.2

Depots	D4	D5	D6	D7
D1	190	95	30	80
D2	250	170	80	95
D3	340	290	210	190

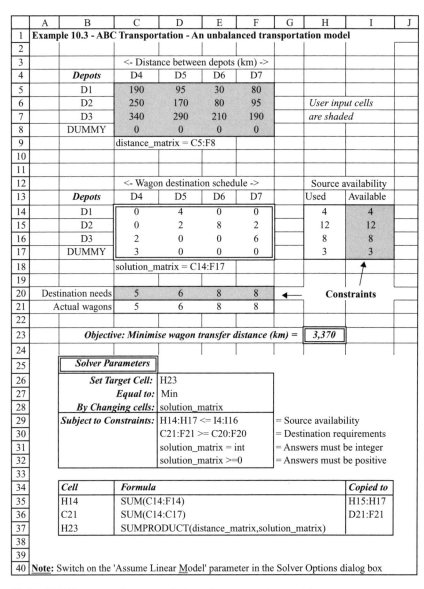

Figure 10.5   ABC Transportation – an unbalanced transportation model.

A dummy source is introduced to make up for the shortfall of 3 wagons, with zero distances being assigned between the dummy source and all other destinations. The answer shows that the non-existent dummy wagons are all sent to depot D4 (see cell C17). If ABC Transportation requires that there must be a minimum number of wagons at each destination, then extra constraints can be added to satisfy such a request.

EXAMPLE 10.4 *Assignment model*

Assignment problems are special cases of the transportation problem discussed above. The assignment problem involves assigning products to machines, salespeople to areas, vehicles to routes, etc. The main criterion is that the assignment process must operate on a one-to-one basis, i.e., each machine or person must be assigned exclusively to one and only one task. The objective is to allocate, say, jobs to machines so as to minimise the total time (or cost) taken for the jobs. An important aspect of any assignment problem is that the number of rows and columns must always be the same. This restriction does not apply to transportation situations. Another important point worth noting is that any assignment solution contains only the integer 1 in a row or column, with all other values being zero. Consider the following example.

The New Products Company has received an order for the manufacture of six products. The company has six assembly machines each operating at different levels of speed. Table 10.3 gives the time it would take (in hours) to manufacture any of the six products on any of the six machines.

Table 10.3

Product	Machines					
	1	2	3	4	5	6
1	7	6	2	8	5	5
2	6	8	4	5	4	6
3	9	9	8	12	10	6
4	1	3	1	2	1	1
5	16	18	10	14	19	12
6	12	14	12	18	20	24

The company wants to determine the assignment – one product to a machine – which will minimise total manufacturing time. The answer in Figure 10.6 shows that a minimum manufacturing time of 40 hours is achieved by assigning products P1, P2, P3, P4, P5, and P6 to machines M2, M4, M6, M5, M3, and M1 respectively. (Note: since only one product can be assigned to any one machine, product allocation for each product is 1, and the machine capacity for each machine is also 1.)

OTHER NETWORK FLOW APPLICATIONS

Transportation and assignment problems are a part of a larger class of special linear programming (LP) applications called network flow problems. Included in this category are transhipment problems, travelling salesman applications, minimal spanning trees, maximal

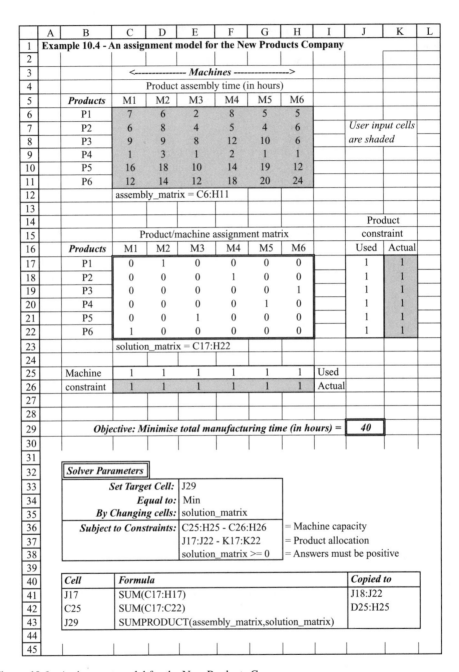

	A	B	C	D	E	F	G	H	I	J	K	L
1		**Example 10.4 - An assignment model for the New Products Company**										
2												
3					<--------------- *Machines* ----------------->							
4					Product assembly time (in hours)							
5		*Products*	M1	M2	M3	M4	M5	M6				
6		P1	7	6	2	8	5	5				
7		P2	6	8	4	5	4	6		*User input cells*		
8		P3	9	9	8	12	10	6		*are shaded*		
9		P4	1	3	1	2	1	1				
10		P5	16	18	10	14	19	12				
11		P6	12	14	12	18	20	24				
12			assembly_matrix = C6:H11									
13												
14										Product		
15					Product/machine assignment matrix					constraint		
16		*Products*	M1	M2	M3	M4	M5	M6		Used	Actual	
17		P1	0	1	0	0	0	0		1	1	
18		P2	0	0	0	1	0	0		1	1	
19		P3	0	0	0	0	0	1		1	1	
20		P4	0	0	0	0	1	0		1	1	
21		P5	0	0	1	0	0	0		1	1	
22		P6	1	0	0	0	0	0		1	1	
23			solution_matrix = C17:H22									
24												
25		Machine	1	1	1	1	1	1	Used			
26		constraint	1	1	1	1	1	1	Actual			
27												
28												
29			*Objective: Minimise total manufacturing time (in hours) =*							40		
30												
31												
32		**Solver Parameters**										
33		*Set Target Cell:*	J29									
34		*Equal to:*	Min									
35		*By Changing cells:*	solution_matrix									
36		*Subject to Constraints:*	C25:H25 - C26:H26			= Machine capacity						
37			J17:J22 - K17:K22			= Product allocation						
38			solution_matrix >= 0			= Answers must be positive						
39												
40		*Cell*	*Formula*							*Copied to*		
41		J17	SUM(C17:H17)							J18:J22		
42		C25	SUM(C17:C22)							D25:H25		
43		J29	SUMPRODUCT(assembly_matrix,solution_matrix)									
44												
45												

Figure 10.6   Assignment model for the New Products Company.

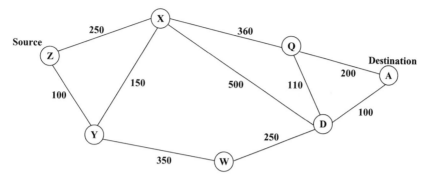

Figure 10.7   Finding the shortest route from depot Z to depot A.

flow, and shortest route situations. In many cases, there are geographical junction points such as warehouses, plants, pumping stations, etc., that can be connected in a number of different ways. The decision-maker wants to find the most economical way of linking up the different junction points, usually referred to as nodes, i.e., a network analysis has to be performed.

Networks consist of points (nodes) and lines (called *arcs*) which join up pairs of nodes. A typical everyday example of a network is a road map in which the roads represent the arcs and the towns are the nodes. In Figure 10.7, nodes are shown as letters, and the distances (not to scale) between nodes are written along each arc, e.g., distance ZX is 250 km. Other network examples include water distribution pipes connected to pumping stations, telecommunications and the Internet. A *route*, or path, between two nodes is any sequence of arcs connecting the two nodes.

In network flow applications, there is one variable, x_{ij}, associated with each (i, j) arc in the network. This x_{ij} variable represents the flow from node i to node j. The basic balance-of-flow rule applies to every node in the network, i.e., inflow − outflow = supply or demand. For example, in a town's water distribution system, the reservoir is a supply node whereas each household represents a demand node. When the node is neither a supply point nor a demand point (i.e., supply = demand = 0), then the balance-of-flow equation simplifies to inflow = outflow. This constraint states that whatever flows into a node must also flow out of the same node. Nodes that are neither demand nor supply nodes are often called 'transhipment' nodes.

Each unit that flows from node i to j in a network incurs a cost, c_{ij}, representing either transportation costs, distance, capacity, etc. The objective is then to find the lowest total cost, distance, capacity, etc. A network flow application can be restated as an LP exercise as follows. For every (i, j) arc in a network consisting of n nodes and m arcs, let c_{ij} be the associated cost and x_{ij} $(i \neq j)$ be the flow variable. The LP objective is to minimise total cost, C_t, i.e.,

$$\text{Minimise } C_t = \sum_i \sum_{j \neq i} c_{ij} x_{ij} \quad \text{for all } x_{ij} \geq 0$$

$$\text{subject to the constraint } \sum_j x_{ij} - \sum_k x_{ki} = R_i$$

for each node i in the network. R_i represents the inflow/outflow to/from node i. If $R_i > 0$, then node i is called a demand, destination, or end node; if $R_i < 0$, then node i is a supply, source, or start node; and if $R_i = 0$, then node i is a transhipment node. Since total demand must equal total supply, it also follows that

$$\sum_{i=1}^{n} R_i = 0$$

EXAMPLE 10.5 *Shortest-route model*

Harry van Heineken is managing director of ABC Transportation which operates a containerisation service between seven depots. At the end of a hard week, Harry finds himself in depot Z,
many kilometres from his company headquarters in location A. He can travel back via various
routes as shown in Figure 10.7. As it is the beginning of a bank-holiday weekend, he would
like to return home as quickly as possible, i.e., he wants to find the shortest route. In any
shortest-route problem, the decision-maker is trying to find the shortest path from source to
destination through a connecting network, e.g., air travel or courier delivery services. Shortest route applications can also be applied to cost minimisation problems such as equipment
replacement analysis.

Let the $(m \times n)$ matrix represent all arcs in the network, where m is the number of arcs and
n is the number of nodes. In the 'shortest-route' model of Figure 10.8, the network is described
by the (10×7) matrix shown in cell range F6:L15. Each node in the matrix can take any one of
three values, (i) a start node has the value -1, (ii) an end node is assigned the value 1, and (iii)
all other nodes are zero. Each row of the matrix defines an arc, e.g., the arc ZX is represented
by the row F6:L6, in which start-node Z is -1 (cell F6), end-node X is 1 (cell H6), and all other
nodes are 0.

The positioning of the nodes in the node list (cells B6:C15) is important. The user should
start at the source node – node Z in this example – and work systematically towards the
destination node A. In Figure 10.8, the distances in cells D6:D15 represent the arc costs c_{ij}
while the shortest-route arcs x_{ij} are assigned the value 1 in cells N6:N15. The model has found
that route Z–Y–W–D–A is the shortest distance between locations Z and A with a minimum
value of 800 km.

The above shortest-route problem is not the famous travelling salesman's problem which
involves the salesman visiting every city on his itinerary. The travelling salesman problem is
a shortest tour (loop) – not a shortest-route – problem. It should be treated as an assignment
problem in which each town to be visited represents both a source and a destination, i.e., the
towns appear along the horizontal as well as the vertical edges of the assignment matrix. Since
visiting the same town twice is not allowed, diagonal cells are assigned very large values to
make them unattractive alternatives for the travelling salesman. It then becomes a branch-
and-bound (B & B) problem involving iteration, in which modified assignment problems are
successively solved and their solutions analysed until an optimal tour, i.e., loop, is found. (For
an example, see Exercise 10.6 at the end of the chapter.)

Maximal-Flow Problem

The shortest-route algorithm found the shortest route from a start node to a destination node in
the network. The maximal-flow method finds the maximum flow from one supply (source) node
to one demand (sink) node. Typical examples of this application include traffic flow situations,

	A	B	C	D	E	F	G	H	I	J	K	L	M	N	O	P
1	Example 10.5 - A shortest-route model for Harry van Heineken's situation															
2																
3		*User input cells are shaded*														
4		*<-Nodes->*				*<------------- Nodes ------------->*										
5		*From*	*To*	*Distance*		*Z*	*Y*	*X*	*W*	*Q*	*D*	*A*				
6		Z	X	250		−1	0	1	0	0	0	0		**0**	=arc$_1$	
7		Z	Y	100		−1	1	0	0	0	0	0		**1**	=arc$_2$	
8		Y	X	150		0	−1	1	0	0	0	0		**0**	=arc$_3$	
9		Y	W	350		0	−1	0	1	0	0	0		**1**	=arc$_4$	
10		X	Q	360		0	0	−1	0	1	0	0		**0**	=arc$_5$	
11		X	D	500		0	0	−1	0	0	1	0		**0**	=arc$_6$	
12		W	D	250		0	0	0	−1	0	1	0		**1**	=arc$_7$	
13		Q	A	200		0	0	0	0	−1	0	1		**0**	=arc$_8$	
14		Q	D	110		0	0	0	0	−1	1	0		**0**	=arc$_9$	
15		D	A	100		0	0	0	0	0	−1	1		**1**	=arc$_{10}$	
16																
17				**800**		= Objective: Minimise total distance										
18																
19						−1	0	0	0	0	0	1				
20				Start Node Z = −1		−1	0	0	0	0	0	1		End Node A = 1		
21														All other nodes = 0		
22																
23																
24			*Solver Parameters*													
25			*Set Target Cell:*	D17												
26			*Equal to:*	Min												
27			*By Changing Cells:*	N6:N15												
28			*Subject to Constraints:*	F19:L19 = F20:L20			= Define Start, End & other nodes									
29				N6:N15 >= 0			= Answers must be positive									
30																
31			*Cells*	*Formula*								*Copied to*				
32			F6	IF($B6=F$5,−1,IF($C6=F$5,1,0))								F6;L15				
33			D17	SUMPRODUCT(D6:D15,N6:N15)												
34			F19	SUMPRODUCT(F6:F15,$N6:$N15)								G19:L19				
35																
36			The answer is determined by those arcs which have the value '1' assigned													
37			to them in cells N6:N15. Thus the four arcs - arc$_2$, arc$_4$, arc$_7$, arc$_{10}$ - give a													
38			shortest route (Z - Y - W - D - A) with a minimum distance of 800 kilometres													
39																
40		**Note:** Switch on the 'Assume Linear Model' parameter in the SOLVER Options dialog box														

Figure 10.8   Shortest-route model.

and any fluid flow involving oil, water, gas, etc. Note that both these network algorithms must have only one supply (start) node and one demand (destination) node.

EXAMPLE 10.6

The State Gas Company owns a pipe network that is used to pump natural gas from its main exploration site (located at source 1) to several storage facilities, as shown in Figure 10.9. The amount of gas flowing along the pipes is dictated by the diameters of the pipes which differ

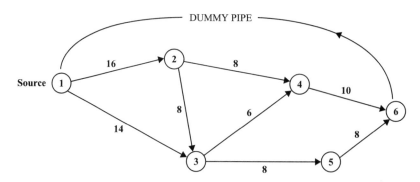

Figure 10.9   State Gas Company's pipe network.

from location to location. The company would like to know the maximum amount of gas that can be pumped to the storage facility located at node 6, given the maximum capacity (in 1000 cubic metres/hour) of each pipe. What is the maximum flow to facility 6 if pipe 2–4 has to be temporarily shut down for repairs?

The trick to solving this problem is to introduce a dummy pipe connecting nodes 1 and 6, and then assign a very large capacity to it. By maximising the flow in the dummy pipe, the flow through the network is also maximised! This is based on the principle that what flows into any node must also flow out of the same node.

The answer in Figure 10.10 is dictated by the capacity of the pipes bringing gas into storage facility 6, i.e., pipes 4–6 and 5–6 which have a combined capacity of 18 thousand cubic metres/hour (tcm/hr). When pipe 2–4 is closed for repairs, the maximum flow is dictated by the capacity of the remaining inflow pipes 3–4 and 3–5, i.e., 14 tcm/hour. Note that pipe flow patterns are not unique.

Transhipment Model

In the shortest-route and maximal-flow algorithms, each node can be (i) a supply node (ii) a demand node or (iii) neither. In the transhipment model, a new node is introduced, called a transhipment node, which can both receive from and send to other nodes in the network. A transhipment node can have either a supply or a demand, but not both. The word 'tranship' means to transfer from one location to another, i.e., to deliver goods in transit. For example, if goods are being shipped from location A to D, then it makes sense to deliver goods to B and C if they happen to be en route to destination D.

Goods at any node are represented by positive or negative numbers, depending upon whether it is a demand node (positive) or a supply node (negative). Supply must always equal or exceed demand. The transhipment model – often called the network model – is a generalised version of several of the previous models, namely the transportation model, the assignment model, and the shortest-route problem. The maximal-flow problem is also closely related.

EXAMPLE 10.7   *Transhipment model*

Ruth Radetsky is the distribution manager for SuperSteel Distributors. Her job is to ensure that steel beams are distributed as cheaply as possible to the four construction sites T, S, Y,

	A	B	C	D	E	F	G	H	I	J	K	L	M	N	O
1	Example 10.6 - A maximal-flow model for the State Gas Company														
2															
3		<-Nodes->		Pipe		<-----------Nodes----------->									
4		From	To	Capacity		1	2	3	4	5	6				
5		1	2	16.0		−1	1	0	0	0	0		4.0	=arc$_1$	
6		1	3	14.0		−1	0	1	0	0	0		14.0	=arc$_2$	
7		2	4	8.0		0	−1	0	1	0	0		4.0	=arc$_3$	
8		2	3	8.0		0	−1	1	0	0	0		0.0	=arc$_4$	
9		3	4	6.0		0	0	−1	1	0	0		6.0	=arc$_5$	
10		3	5	8.0		0	0	−1	0	1	0		8.0	=arc$_6$	
11		4	6	10.0		0	0	0	−1	0	1		10.0	=arc$_7$	
12		5	6	8.0		0	0	0	0	−1	1		8.0	=arc$_8$	
13		6	1	999.0		1	0	0	0	0	−1		18.0	=dummy pipe	
14															
15						0	0	0	0	0	0				
16															
17				18.0		= Objective: Maximise flow									

Solver Parameters

Set Target Cell:	D17
Equal to:	Max
By Changing Cells:	M5:M13
Subject to Constraints:	F15:K15 = 0 — = Balancing inflows and outflows
	M5:M13 <= D5:D13 — = Pipe capacity constraints
	M5:M13 >= 0 — = Answers must be positive

Cells	Formula	Copied to
F5	IF($B5=F$4,−1,IF($C5=F$4,1,0)	F5:K13
F15	SUMPRODUCT(F5:F13,$M5:$M13)	G15:K15
D17	M13	

Note: Switch on the 'Assume Linear Model' parameter in the Solver Options dialog box

Figure 10.10 Maximal-flow model for the State Gas Company.

and Z as shown in Figure 10.11. SuperSteel have two warehouses, with the main warehouse W_1 supplying the smaller warehouse W_2. The supply and demand values are written alongside each node. Shipping costs vary over each route, with the cost of shipping one beam between locations (nodes) as shown in Table 10.4. Warehouse W_2 is a transhipment node since it receives its supply of beams from W_1 and then distributes them to other sites. Similarly, sites T, Y and Z are also transhipment nodes.

The answer to the transhipment model is shown in Figure 10.12. The cheapest way to ship the steel beams is contained in cells M5:M14 where arc$_1$ = W_1 to W_2, arc$_2$ = W_1 to Z, arc$_3$ = W_1 to Y, etc. For clarification purposes, these values may be superimposed on the network diagram of Figure 10.11.

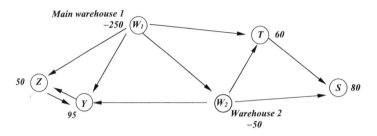

Figure 10.11 Details of SuperSteel's distribution network.

	A	B	C	D	E	F	G	H	I	J	K	L	M	N	O
1		Example 10.7 - A transhipment model for SuperSteel distributors													
2															
3		<-Nodes->		Unit		<-------------- Nodes ------------>							*Ship*		
4		From	To	Cost		W_1	W_2	Y	Z	S	T		*Goods*		
5		W_1	W_2	£50		−1	1	0	0	0	0		**0**	=arc$_1$	
6		W_1	Z	£35		−1	0	0	1	0	0		**145**	=arc$_2$	
7		W_1	Y	£60		−1	0	1	0	0	0		**0**	=arc$_3$	
8		W_1	T	£45		−1	0	0	0	0	1		**90**	=arc$_4$	
9		W_2	Y	£45		0	−1	1	0	0	0		**0**	=arc$_5$	
10		W_2	S	£60		0	−1	0	0	1	0		**50**	=arc$_6$	
11		W_2	T	£40		0	−1	0	0	0	1		**0**	=arc$_7$	
12		T	S	£40		0	0	0	0	1	−1		**30**	=arc$_8$	
13		Y	Z	£35		0	0	−1	1	0	0		**0**	=arc$_9$	
14		Z	Y	£20		0	0	1	−1	0	0		**95**	=arc$_{10}$	
15															
16		Supply/Demand Quantities				−235	−50	95	50	80	60	Used			
17						−250	−50	95	50	80	60	Available			
18															
19				£15,225		= Objective: Minimise costs									
20													*User input cells*		
21													*are shaded*		
22			*Solver Parameters*												
23			*Set Target Cell:*	D19											
24			*Equal to:*	Min											
25			*By Changing Cells:*	M5:M14											
26			*Subject to Constraints:*	F16:K16 >= F17:K17			= Assign supply & demand quantities								
27				M5:M14 >= 0			= Answers must be positive								
28															
29		*Cell*		*Formula*								*Copied to*			
30		F5		IF($B5=F$4,−1,IF($C5=F$4,1,0))								F5:K14			
31		F16		SUMPRODUCT(F5:F14,$M5:$M14)								G16:K16			
32		D19		SUMPRODUCT(D5:D14,M5:M14)											
33															
34		Note: Switch on the 'Assume Linear Model' parameter in the Solver Options dialog box													

Figure 10.12 Transhipment model for the SuperSteel distributors.

Table 10.4   Shipping costs for SuperSteel's network.

From:	To:	T	S	Y	Z	W₂
Warehouse W_1		£45		£60	£35	£50
Warehouse W_2		£40	£60	£45		
Site T			£40			
Site Y					£35	
Site Z			£20			

PRODUCTION PLANNING AND SCHEDULING

The goals of production planning can be stated simply as: determining which products to produce, when to produce them, and how much of each to produce. However, the task of achieving these goals is not so simple. The volume and timing of product output must fit in with the resource constraints of labour and materials availability, machine capacity and cost competitiveness. For a production plan to be effective, it must meet its demand obligations on time and at low cost. While production planning is concerned with determining output levels, capacity planning establishes whether there are sufficient resources to meet the planned output. If production capacity is less than output requirements, then the production plan is not feasible.

Very few organisations produce a single product at a fixed demand rate. The term 'aggregate capacity planning' is used when management has to decide how best to allocate resources in order to meet variable demand forecasts. The situation is further complicated if the company manufactures several products, all of which are competing for the same scarce resources. An *aggregate plan* combines the appropriate resources into general, or overall, terms. It translates an output plan into resource requirements, giving a general indication of how much resource capacity will be needed to meet each order. If the company does not have the overall capacity to meet its customer demand, it can overcome this situation in several ways. Extra part-time staff can be hired, overtime or extra shifts can be scheduled, or the company can subcontract with other organisations to fill the shortfall.

While output plans specify what products are needed, these general specifications must be converted into practical operations that can be implemented on the shop floor. Customer orders are initially aggregated to establish whether there are sufficient resources available. Detailed scheduling, usually referred to as master production scheduling (MPS), then refines the overall terms of aggregate planning into specific order details about capacities, demand, and materials availability. Start and finish dates for each customer order are determined. The order's progress is then tracked through the various manufacturing processes to ensure that it is completed on time.

EXAMPLE 10.8 *Production scheduling model*

Projected sales ('000s) for the Gizmo Company's main product over the next four months are shown in the table below.

Month	1	2	3	4
Demand ('000s)	5	6	9	5

Gizmo has a production capacity of 4,000 items per month which can be extended to 7,000 per month by utilising overtime. However, overtime adds £80 to the normal cost of producing 1000 items. Inventory of the finished goods can be stored indefinitely but incurs monthly

	A	B	C	D	E	F	G	H	I	J
1		**Example 10.8 - A production scheduling model for the Gizmo Company**								
2										
3		**Input**	On-hand stock			5				
4		(per 1000	Normal labour costs			£300		*User input cells*		
5		items)	Overtime labour costs			£380		*are shaded*		
6			Holding costs per month			£20				
7										
8			NT_1 = Normal shift in month 1, etc							
9			OT_2 = Overtime shift in month 2, etc							
10										
11			<------- *Monthly production costs* ------->							
12		**Shifts**	Month 1	Month 2	Month 3	Month 4				
13		On-hand stock		£20	£40	£60				
14		NT_1	£300	£320	£340	£360				
15		OT_1	£380	£400	£420	£440				
16		NT_2	£9,999	£300	£320	£340				
17		OT_2	£9,999	£380	£400	£420				
18		NT_3	£9,999	£9,999	£300	£320				
19		OT_3	£9,999	£9,999	£380	£400				
20		NT_4	£9,999	£9,999	£9,999	£300				
21		OT_4	£9,999	£9,999	£9,999	£380				
22			cost_matrix = C13:F21							
23										
24								Production capacity		
25		**Shifts**	Month 1	Month 2	Month 3	Month 4		Used	Available	
26		On-hand stock	5	0	0	0		5	5	
27		NT_1	0	2	2	0		4	4	
28		OT_1	0	0	0	0		0	3	
29		NT_2	0	4	0	0		4	4	
30		OT_2	0	0	0	0		0	3	
31		NT_3	0	0	4	0		4	4	
32		OT_3	0	0	3	0		3	3	
33		NT_4	0	0	0	4		4	4	
34		OT_4	0	0	0	1		1	3	
35			solution_matrix = C26:F34					↑		
36										
37		Product demand ('000s)								
38		Demand	5	6	9	5	←	**Constraints**		
39		Actual	5	6	9	5				
40										
41			*Objective: Minimise holding costs =*			**£6,440**				
42										
43		**Note:** Switch on the 'Assume Linear Model' parameter in the SOLVER Options dialog box								

Figure 10.13   Production scheduling model for the Gizmo Company.

Solver Parameters		
Set Target Cell:	F41	
Equal to:	Min	
By Changing Cells:	solution_matrix	
Subject to Constraints:	H26:H34 <= I26:I34	= Production capacity
	C39:F39 = C38:F38	= Monthly product demand
	solution_matrix >= 0	= Answers must be positive

Cell	Formula	Copied to
H26	SUM(C26:F26)	H27:H34
C39	SUM(C26:C34)	D39:F39
F41	SUMPRODUCT(cost_matrix,solution_matrix)	

Figure 10.14   Solver parameters and formulae for production scheduling model.

holding costs of £20 per 1000 units. Normal labour costs are £300 per 1000 items. The Gizmo Company currently has 5000 items in stock. The company would like to find a production schedule that will minimise the total overtime production and inventory storage costs over the next four months.

The transportation method of linear programming can be used in aggregate planning and production scheduling to allocate resources to meet sales forecasts. The Gizmo Company has therefore decided to set up the problem as a transportation model and solve it using Excel's Solver. The supply sources are now the monthly on-hand stock and the labour shifts, both regular and overtime. The destinations are the monthly sales forecasts.

The supply constraints are 5000 (current inventory), 4000 (regular shift), and 3000 (overtime shift). The overtime requirements for each month, which the user enters into cell range C13:F21 in Figure 10.13, are calculated from the following equation,

$$\text{Overtime} = \text{Demand} - \text{On-hand inventory} - \text{Regular production capacity}$$

To ensure that production follows a logical monthly pattern, enter very large values (e.g., 9999) wherever appropriate. For example, month 1 can only utilise items produced in the first month while month 2 can only utilise items produced in the first two months, etc. Note that the holding costs for month 1 are zero and then increase by £20 for each subsequent month.

The production scheduling model of Figure 10.13 obtained a minimum cost of £6440. All regular shifts are fully utilised. Note that the first month's unused production run of 4000 has been carried over into the second and third months (see cells D27 and E27). To meet monthly demand, overtime was required in months 3 and 4, in which 3000 and 1000 extra items were produced respectively. The model's formulae and Solver parameters are given in Figure 10.14.

EXAMPLE 10.9   *Aggregate planning model*

The sales department of Bloggs Engineering has estimated that demand (in hundreds) for its sprockets over the next four months is 5, 9, 10, and 7. Because sprocket sales are subject to demand fluctuations, the company has difficulty in meeting customer orders during peak periods. In an effort to overcome labour shortages, Bloggs Engineering employs temporary workers on a monthly basis at a cost of £770 per person. There are four working weeks in every month. The company's four full-time employees work a 35-hour week at a pay rate of £7 per hour. Every full-time employee has the option of working up to five hours overtime each week at a rate of £12 per hour.

Bloggs Engineering currently has 300 sprockets in stock which incur holding costs of £15 per month for every hundred sprockets. To make one sprocket requires one hour of labour and £1.50 of raw materials. The company is faced with the problems of (i) estimating the number of temporary workers to employ and (ii) keeping production costs to a minimum. Bloggs Engineering has decided to develop an aggregate planning model in order to find a feasible production schedule that can help reduce labour shortages and production costs. It will then use Excel's Solver to find an answer to this linear programming (LP) problem.

The first step is to divide the model into three distinct areas, giving monthly details for (i) labour resource requirements (ii) the production schedule and (iii) production costs.

1. Labour resource details (in hours)

   Total full-time hours   = (No. of full-time employees) × (weekly hours) × (no. of weeks per month)

   = $4 \times 35 \times 4 = 560$ hours

   Maximum overtime   = (No. of full-time employees) × (overtime hours) × (no. of weeks per month)

   = $4 \times 5 \times 4 = 80$ hours

   If t_i = the number of temporary workers hired for month i, then

   Total temporary hours   = (No. of temporary workers) × (weekly hours) × (no. of weeks per month)

   = $t_i \times 35 \times 4 = 140t_i$ hours

   Total labour hours   = $560 + 140t_i + h_i$ where h_i = total overtime hours worked in month i

2. Production schedule details (per 100 units)

   Production capacity   = (Total labour hours)/(No. of hours required to make 100 sprockets)

   = $(560 + 140t_i + h_i)/100$

   Monthly demand   = 5, 9, 10, and 7 as provided by the sales department

   On-hand stock   = Current stock + current production − current demand

   (Note: a necessary constraint is that on-hand stock cannot be negative)

3. Production costs (per 100 units)

   Full-time: regular shift   = £7 × 560 hours = £3920

   Full-time: overtime shift   = £12 × h_i hours where h_i=overtime hours worked in month i

   Temporary workers   = £770 × t_i where t_i = no. of workers hired for month i

Table 10.5 Aggregate planning – worksheet formulae.

Cell	Formula	Copied to
D16	4*35*$F3	E16:G16
D18	4*$F3*$F6	E18:G18
D21	4*35*D20	E21:G21
D22	D16 + D17 + D21	E22:G22
D26	D22/$F8	E26:G26
D28	F10 + D25 – D27	
E28	D28 + E25 – E27	F28:G28
D31	$F4*D16	F31:G31
D32	$F5*D17	F32:G32
D33	$F7*D20	F33:G33
D34	$F9*D25	F34:G34
D35	$F11*D28	E35:G35
D36	SUM(D31:D35)	E36:G36
F38	SUM(D36:G36)	

Raw materials costs   = £150 × current sprocket production
Holding costs   = £15 × on-hand stock (initially on-hand stock = 3)
The formulae template for the aggregate model is given in Table 10.5.

The aggregate model of Figure 10.16 shows that Bloggs Engineering must employ three temporary workers in the third month and one temporary worker in month 4 (see line 20) if customer orders are to be met. No full-time employees have been offered overtime. This is not surprising since the company must pay £12 per hour for overtime compared to a temporary worker's rate of £5.50 per hour (£770/{4 × 35}). The minimum total production costs are £23,017. The user should perform some 'what if' analysis on the model to ascertain under what circumstances overtime might be a feasible option. The Solver parameters for the aggregate planning model are given in Figure 10.15.

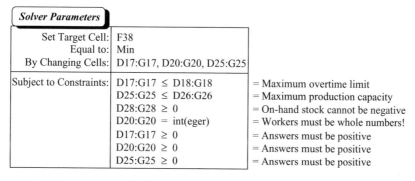

Figure 10.15 Solver parameters for the aggregate planning model.

	A	B	C	D	E	F	G	H
1			**Example 10.9 - An aggregate planning model for Bloggs Engineering**					
2								
3		**Input**	No. of full-time employees			4		
4		**details**	Full-time employee: hourly payrate			£7		
5			Full-time employee: overtime payrate			£12		
6			Maximum overtime hours per week			5	*User input cells*	
7			Monthly pay for temporary worker			£770	*are shaded*	
8			Production hours for 100 sprockets			100		
9			Raw material costs for 100 sprockets			£150		
10			Current stock ('00s)			3		
11			Holding costs per month (per 100)			£15		
12								
13				Month 1	Month 2	Month 3	Month 4	
14		► **Labour resource details (in hours)**						
15				<--------- *Full-time employee details* -------->				
16		Total monthly hours		560	560	560	560	
17		Overtime hours		*0*	*0*	*0*	*0*	
18		Maximum overtime hours		80	80	80	80	
19				<--------- *Temporary worker details* --------->				
20		Number available		*0*	*0*	*3*	*1*	
21		Total monthly hours		0	0	420	140	
22		Total labour hours		560	560	980	700	
23								
24		► **Production schedule (in '00s)**						
25		Sprocket production		*5.6*	*5.6*	*9.8*	*7.0*	
26		Production capacity		5.6	5.6	9.8	7.0	
27		Sprocket demand		*5.0*	*9.0*	*10.0*	*7.0*	
28		On-hand stock		3.6	0.2	0.0	0.0	
29								
30		► **Production costs (per 100)**						
31		Full-time: regular shift		£3,920	£3,920	£3,920	£3,920	
32		Full-time: overtime shift		£0	£0	£0	£0	
33		Temporary worker costs		£0	£0	£2,310	£770	
34		Raw materials costs		£840	£840	£1,470	£1,050	
35		Holding costs		£54	£3	£0	£0	
36		*Totals*		*£4,814*	*£4,763*	*£7,700*	*£5,740*	
37								
38				*Objective: Minimise total costs =*		*£23,017*		
39								
40								
41		**Note:** Switch on the 'Assume Linear Model' parameter in the SOLVER Options dialog box						
42								

Figure 10.16 Aggregate planning model for Bloggs Engineering.

EXAMPLE 10.10 *Capacity planning model*

The Acme Company manufactures two products – widgets and gadgets – which utilise seven electronic components in their construction. However, the company does not have sufficient production capacity or technical expertise to manufacture all components in its own factory. It must therefore purchase the shortfall from outside suppliers. The company is restricted to

Table 10.6 Capacity planning details.

Component no.	C1	C2	C3	C4	C5	C6	C7
Resource requirements (hours)							
Machining	4	2	1	3	1	0	2
Assembly	1	1	3	0	4	2	1
Testing	0	0	2	3	2	2	1
Technical supervision	1	1	3	2	2	3	1
Variable costs, V_i	25	25	50	25	50	45	20
Purchase price, P_i	55	70	85	50	120	95	50
No. of units required	30	15	50	25	20	15	20

a maximum number of hours of 210, 210, 120, and 180 for machining, assembly, testing, and technical supervision respectively. Table 10.6 below gives details of each of the seven components, including their resource requirements, number of units required, variable costs and purchase costs to be paid to the outside suppliers.

The problem facing the Acme Company is how many, if any, of these components should be purchased from outside suppliers? The company has decided to set up a linear programming model and then use Solver to find a feasible solution. Note that company savings for each component manufactured in-house is found from the equation: Unit savings = Purchase price − Variable costs. The capacity model of Figure 10.17 has found that the Acme Company must buy in 3, 39, and 25 units of components C1, C3 and C4 respectively at a total cost (less variable costs) of £2,080 (see cell D16).

EXAMPLE 10.11   *Production planning model with back-orders*

Fred Flint has used his forecasting model to determine sales of product P over the next six months. The model has produced the following figures: 6000, 4000, 5500, 5200, 4000, and 3500. Fred currently has 400 items in stock. Product P involves (i) high holding costs and (ii) variable production costs. The monthly holding cost of one item is 15% of the monthly unit production costs. Because of these factors, the Bedrock Company operates a back-order policy for product P. A back-order policy allows planned shortages to occur with customer demand being met later than requested. A back-order policy assumes that customers are prepared to wait for delivery without cancelling the order. The company imposes a shortage cost of £4.50 for each negative inventory item. This shortage cost covers extra administration, loss of goodwill, some loss of future orders, etc.

The Bedrock Company has estimated that unit production costs over the next six months will be £5, £5.25, £5.50, £5.75, £5.65, and £5.60 respectively. The company can manufacture up to 5000 units of product P each month. Because back-orders are acceptable, on-hand stock is allowed to be negative during the first five months. However, to ensure that all demand is met over the six-month planning horizon, on-hand stock at the end of the sixth month must be either zero or positive (i.e., cell H20 $\geq$ 0 in Figure 10.18). Bedrock wants to determine a production schedule that will minimise total production costs, holding costs, and shortage costs over the next six months.

	A	B	C	D	E	F	G	H	I	J	K	L	M	N
1		Example 10.10 - A capacity planning model for the Acme Company												
2														
3		Components no.		C1	C2	C3	C4	C5	C6	C7		Used	Available	
4		- matching		4	2	1	3	1	0	2		209	210	
5		- assembly		1	1	3	0	4	2	1		205	210	
6		- testing		0	0	2	3	2	2	1		112	120	
7		- technical supervision		1	1	3	2	2	3	1		180	180	
8		Variable costs, V_i		£25	£25	£50	£25	£50	£45	£20				
9		Purchase price, P_i		£55	£70	£85	£50	£120	£95	£50				
10		Units required		30	15	50	25	20	15	20		*Resource*		
11				*User input cells are shaded*								*constraints*		
12														
13		Units savings ($p_i - V_i$) =		£30	£45	£35	£25	£70	£50	£30				
14		In-house production =		27	15	11	0	20	15	20				
15		Outside purchases =		3	0	39	25	0	0	0				
16		Total costs ($P_i - V_i$) =		£2,080										
17														
18		Objective: maximise in-house production =						£4,620						

Solver Parameters

Set Target Cell: H18	
Equal to: Max	
By Changing Cells: D14:J14	
Subject to Constraints: L4:L7 <= M4:M7	= Resource limits
D14:J14 <= D10:J10	= Maximum units required
D14:J14 = int(eger)	= Answers must be integers
D14:J14 >= 0	= Answers must be positive

Cell	Formula	Copied to
L4	SUMPRODUCT(D4:J4,D$14:J$14)	L5:L7
D13	D9 - D8	E13:J13
D15	D10 - D14	E15:J15
D16	SUMPRODUCT(D13:J13,D15:J15)	
H18	SUMPRODUCT(D13:J13,D14:J14)	

Figure 10.17 Capacity planning model for the Acme Company.

In this back-order model, Solver uses two sets of changing cells to find (i) the optimal production schedule (cells C14:H14), and (ii) the optimal balance between overstocking and understocking (cells C17:H18). Remaining stock (row 19) is defined as on-hand stock (row 17) minus shortages (row 18). This remaining stock must equal the ending inventory (row 20) which is found by adding the amount produced (row 14) to current stock (cell G3) minus sales forecasts (row 10). The model has found a minimum total cost of £155,955 with stock shortages occurring in months 1, 3, and 4. Solver parameters are contained in the model of Figure 10.18, while the formulae template is given in Table 10.7.

	A	B	C	D	E	F	G	H	I
1		Example 10.11 - A production planning model with back-orders							
2									
3		*User input cells*	Current on-hand stock				400		
4		*are shaded*	Holding cost (% of production costs)				15%		
5			Shortage cost per month (per item)				£4.50		
6			Production capacity (per month)				5,000		
7									
8					<-------------- Six-month planning horizon -------------->				
9			1	2	3	4	5	6	
10		Sales forecasts	6000	4000	5500	5200	4000	3500	
11		Unit production cost	£5.00	£5.25	£5.50	£5.75	£5.65	£5.60	
12		Unit holding cost	£0.75	£0.79	£0.83	£0.86	£0.85	£0.84	
13									
14		Unit produced	*5000*	*5000*	*5000*	*5000*	*4300*	*3500*	
15		Production capacity	5,000	5,000	5,000	5,000	5,000	5,000	
16									
17		On-hand stock	*0*	*400*	*0*	*0*	*0*	*0*	
18		Shortages	*600*	*0*	*100*	*300*	*0*	*0*	
19		Remaining stock	−600	400	−100	−300	0	0	
20		Ending inventory	−600	400	−100	−300	0	0	
21									
22		Holding costs	£0	£60	£0	£0	£0	£0	
23		Shortage costs	£2,700	£0	£450	£1,350	£0	£0	
24									
25		Total production costs =	£151,395						
26		Total holding costs =	£60						
27		Total shortage costs =	£4,500						
28		*Objective: Minimise total costs =*	£155,955						
29									
30									
31		*Solver Parameters*							
32		*Set Target Cell:* E28							
33		*Equal to:* Min							
34		*By Changing Cells:* C14:H14, C17:H18							
35		*Subject to Constraints:* C14:H14 <= C15:H15			= Production capacity				
36		H20 >= 0			= Ending inventory >= 0				
37		C19:H19 = C20:H20			= Inventories must be equal				
38		C14:H14, C17:H18 = int(eger)			= Answers must integer				
39		C14:H14, C17:H18 >= 0			= Answers must be positive				
40									
41		**Note:** Switch off the 'Assume Linear <u>M</u>odel' parameter in the Solver Options dialog box							

Figure 10.18   Production planning model with back-orders.

Job Sequencing

An important aspect of production scheduling is job sequencing. While scheduling allocates jobs to relevant work centres, job sequencing specifies the order in which jobs are to be carried out. The simplest sequencing problem involves deciding in what order jobs are to be processed

Table 10.7   Production model with back-orders – worksheet formulae.

Cell	Formula	Copied to
C12	$G4*C11	D12:H12
C15	$G6	D15:H15
C19	C17 − C18	D19:H19
C20	G3 + C14 − C10	
D20	C20 + D14 − D10	E20:H20
C22	$G4*C17	D22:H22
C23	$G5*C18	D23:H23
E25	SUMPRODUCT(C11:H11, C14:H14)	
E26	SUM(C22:H22)	E27
E28	SUM(E25:E27)	

on a single facility. Should jobs be assigned on a first-come, first-served basis, or perhaps on a priority basis with the most urgent jobs being given preference? The total time for processing all jobs will not change regardless of their place in the queue. However, different job sequencing can affect delivery speed and reliability as well as customer satisfaction.

A job's completion (or flow) time is the time it takes for the job to flow through the system; processing time or 'duration' is the length of time it takes to process a job. The job's 'due date' is the required date of delivery to the customer, while 'lateness' is defined as the job's actual completion date minus its due date. Since lateness cannot be negative, jobs that finish ahead of schedule are assigned a lateness value of zero. 'Utilisation' is the ratio of (total job processing time) to (total flow time). The 'average number of jobs in the system' is the reciprocal of utilisation. The process of prioritising jobs is usually made on the basis of a set of 'priority rules'. The most common priority rules (given below) require only details of a job's duration and due date:

- **FIFO: First-in, First-out.** The first job to arrive at the work area is the first job to be processed.

- **SPT: Shortest processing time**. The shortest jobs are completed first with the longest jobs being placed last in the queue.

- **EDD: Earliest due date**. The job with the earliest due date is processed first. This rule usually improves delivery reliability but some jobs may have to wait a long time.

- **LPT: Longest processing time**. The longer jobs are often bigger and more important and should therefore be completed first.

- **CR: Critical ratio**. Jobs with the smallest critical ratio are completed first. The critical ratio is (time remaining until a job is needed) divided by (time required to complete the job), i.e.

$$CR = \frac{\text{time remaining}}{\text{work remaining}} = \frac{\text{due date} - \text{today's date}}{\text{remaining processing time}}$$

If CR > 1.0, the job is ahead of schedule; if CR < 1.0, then the job is behind schedule; if CR = 1.0, the job is on schedule.

Table 10.8   Job sequencing through one facility.

Job	A	B	C	D	E
Processing Time (days)	8	4	11	6	12
Due Date (days)	10	7	16	14	20

EXAMPLE 10.12   *Job sequencing through one facility*

Bloggs Engineering wants to determine a processing sequence for five jobs – A, B, C, D, and E – using the above five priority rules. Today is day 5 of the current month's production schedule. Standard processing time and due date for each job are given in Table 10.8. Solutions for all five priority rules are easily found by using Excel's SORT facility as explained in Figure 10.19 (lines 16–27). The best solution was achieved by the SPT priority rule (see the summary table on lines 29–37).

EXAMPLE 10.13   *Johnson's rule for job sequencing on two facilities*

The previous example sequenced jobs through a single facility such as a machine or work centre. Johnson's rule, developed by S. M. Johnson in 1954, extends the sequencing problem to cover a two-facility situation. The jobs must pass through each facility in the same order. The rule finds the correct job sequencing that will minimise the total processing time for all jobs. Johnson's rule involves the following four steps:

1. List the time required to process each job on each facility.

2. Select the job, J_s, with the shortest time for either facility. If J_s occurs on the first facility, J_s is placed first in the queue. If J_s occurs on the second facility, J_s is placed last in the queue. If two jobs have the same shortest time, then an arbitrary choice is made.

3. Remove job J_s from the list.

4. Repeat steps 1–3 until all jobs have been sequenced.

The New Products Company has five urgent jobs – A, B, C, D, and E – that require the use of two different machines. The times for processing each job on each machine are given in Table 10.9. The Company wants to find the quickest way of processing the jobs. A Visual Basic program has been written to simulate Johnson's four rules. The answers (see Figure 10.20) include the correct job sequencing (cells C15:C21), total sequencing time (cell G25), and total idle time (cell G24) where total idle time is defined as the amount of time that both facilities remain unused. The model can handle up to seven jobs but this number can be easily extended if so desired. A listing of the VBA program for Johnson's rule is given below.

Table 10.9   Johnson's rule.

Job	A	B	C	D	E
Machine 1 (hours)	6	4	12	6	10
Machine 2 (hours)	3	8	5	11	6

	A	B	C	D	E	F	G	H	I
1		**Example 10.12 Job sequencing through one facility**							
2									
3			Today's date =	5		*User input cells are shaded*			
4									
5			*(Job duration)*			*Completion*	*Job*	*Time*	
6		*Job*	*Processing Time*	*Due Date*	*CR*	*Time*	*Lateness*	*Remaining*	
7		A	8	10	0.63	8	0	5	
8		B	4	7	0.50	12	5	2	
9		C	11	16	1.00	23	7	11	
10		D	6	14	1.50	29	15	9	
11		E	12	20	1.25	41	21	15	
12					Averages:	22.6	9.6		
13					Utilisation =	36.3%	4	= No. of late jobs	
14			Average number of jobs in system =			2.76			
15									
16		The following steps are used to find the correct job sequencing:							
17		[1]	Highlight the cell range B7:E11 (contained inside the double-line border)						
18		[2]	Activate Excel's Sort facility by clicking on the Data\Sort tabs						
19		[3]	Click the arrow on the 'Sort By' box and, from the drop-down list select the						
20			relevant heading for the required rule. Ensure that the default option, i.e.						
21			"Ascending", is switched on for the first four rules. Finally, click "OK".						
22									
23		[4] *	**FIFO Rule** - Click 'Job'.						
24		*	**SPT Rule** - Click 'Processing Time'.						
25		*	**EDD Rule** - Click 'Due Date'.						
26		*	**CR Rule** - Click 'CR'.						
27		*	**LPT Rule** - Click 'Processing Time' & 'Descending' option.						
28									
29		**SUMMARY**		Average	Average	Average			
30				Completion	Job	No. of Jobs	No. of	Utilisation	
31		Rule	Job Sequence	Time	Lateness	in System	late jobs	(%)	
32		FIFO	A, B, C, D, E	22.6	9.6	2.76	4	36.3	
33	▶	SPT	B, D, A, C, E	20.4	8.4	2.49	3	40.2	
35		EDD	B, A, D, C, E	20.8	8.0	2.54	4	39.4	
36		CR	B, A, C, E, D	23.0	10.2	2.80	4	35.7	
37		LPT	E, C, A, D, B	28.8	17.0	3.51	4	28.5	
38									
39			*Cell*	*Formula*			*Copied to*		
40			E7	H7/C7			E8:E11		
41			F7	C7					
42			F8	F7 + C8			F9:F11		
43			G7	IF(F7 – D7 < 0, 0, F7 – D7)			G8:G11		
44			H7	D7 – D$3			H8:H11		
45			F12	AVERAGE(F7:F11)			G12		
46			F13	SUM(C7:C11)/SUM(F7:F11)					
47			G13	COUNTIF(G7:G11, ">0")					
48			F14	1/F13					
49									

Figure 10.19 Job sequencing through one facility.

Macro Listing for Johnson's Rule

```
Sub Johnson()
'
'*** Input details for facilities 1 & 2 are copied into temporary "named" arrays
'*** "Fac1" & "Fac2". The correct job sequence is stored in range "List", i.e.
'***cells B15:B21. The current program can handle up to 7 jobs, i.e. Njobs = 7.
'
    Dim COUNT1 As Integer, COUNT2 As Integer, POSI As Integer
    Sheets("Fig. 10.20").Select
    Names.Add "Fac1", "=H4:H10"
    Names.Add "Fac2", "=I4:I10"
    Names.Add "List", "=B15:B21"
    Range("E4:E10").Copy Range("Fac1")
    Range("F4:F10").Copy Range("Fac2")
    Range("List").ClearContents
    COUNT2 = Application.Count(Range("Fac1"))
    Max1 = Application.Max(Range("Fac1"))
    Max2 = Application.Max(Range("Fac2"))
    Maxx = Application.Max(Max1, Max2) + 10
    COUNT1 = 1
    Njobs = COUNT2
For K = 1 To Njobs
    Min1 = Application.Min(Range("Fac1"))
    Min2 = Application.Min(Range("Fac2"))
    If Min1 < Min2 Then
        POSI = Application.Match(Min1, Range("Fac1"), 0)
        Range("List").Item(COUNT1) = POSI
        Range("Fac2").Item(POSI) = Maxx
        Range("Fac1").Item(POSI) = Maxx
        COUNT1 = COUNT1 + 1
Else
        POSI = Application.Match(Min2, Range("Fac2"), 0)
        Range("List").Item(COUNT2) = POSI
        Range("Fac2").Item(POSI) = Maxx
        Range("Fac1").Item(POSI) = Maxx
        COUNT2 = COUNT2 − 1
End If
Next K
    Range("Fac1").Clear
    Range("Fac2").Clear
End Sub
```

	A	B	C	D	E	F	G	H	I	J
1	**Example 10.13 - Johnson's Rule for sequencing N Jobs on 2 facilities**									
2										
3				Job	Facility 1	Facility 2				
4			1	A	6	3				
5			2	B	4	8	*User input cells*			
6			3	C	12	5	*are shaded*			
7			4	D	6	11				
8			5	E	10	6				
9			6							
10			7							
11										
12										
13		Correct Job								
14		Sequence			Sequencing Times		Idle Time			
15		2	**B**		4			4		
16		4	**D**		6	8	−2			
17		5	**E**		10	11	−1			
18		3	**C**		12	6	6			
19		1	**A**		6	5	1			
20						3		3		
21										
22										
23							4	= Intermediate Idle Time		
24							11	= Total Idle Time		
25					**Total sequencing time =**		**41**			
26										
27										
28										

	Cell	*Formula*	*Copied to*
29			
30	C15	IF(B15="","", OFFSET(D$3,B15,0))	C16:C21
31	E15	IF(C15="","",VLOOKUP(C15,D$4:F$10,2))	E16:E21
32	H15	E15	
33	F16	IF(C15="","",VLOOKUP(C15,D$4:F$10,3))	F17:F22
34	G16	IF(E16="","",E16 – F16)	G17:G22
35	H16	IF(E16="",F16,"")	H17:H22
36	G23	SUM(G16:G22)	
37	G24	G23 + SUM(H15:H22)	
38	G25	IF(E15="","",E15 + SUM(F16:F22) + IF(G23>0,G23,0))	

39

40 Note: This spreadsheet utilises a VBA program called 'Johnson'.

41 [1] To run the model, click the Tools|Macro|Macros... to bring up the Macro list box.

42 [2] Next, click on the 'Johnson' macro and finally click the 'Run' button.

43

Figure 10.20 Johnson's Rule for sequencing N jobs on two facilities.

QUEUING MODELS

Queues or waiting lines are a common feature in everyday life. Queues occur because a facility that is required is unavailable to provide the service, e.g., a machine has broken down or a supermarket checkout is already busy. Many queuing situations can be simulated using mathematical models which are then used to predict actual behaviour patterns. The main objective in a queuing model is to balance the costs of providing a service against the costs associated with waiting for the service. For example, should a store employ an extra checkout clerk to reduce waiting lines? If the queue gets too long, customers may leave without buying anything because the quality of service is poor.

Queues are caused by delays which in turn can cause lost revenue. While queues could in practice be eliminated, there must be a cost-benefit trade-off between the cost of providing extra facilities and the benefits – both qualitative and quantitative – that would ensue. Queues consist of discrete (or distinct) items such as people, cars or components. Queuing theory is concerned with the mathematical analysis of queuing or waiting-line systems. The objective of such analysis is to find out important characteristics of the queue such as the number of items in the queue, the average waiting time, and the percentage of time that the service facility is busy. The characteristics of a simple queue are shown in Table 10.10.

The three main components of a queuing system are population, queue, and service facility. The population is the input source, e.g., customers, telephone calls, airline traffic, etc. A finite population is one in which the number of potential customers is limited, e.g., the number of people who own a Rolls-Royce car. On the other hand, the amount of traffic arriving at a busy roundabout can be considered as unlimited, i.e., there is an infinite population.

The length of a queue depends not only on the arrival pattern but also on physical constraints such as storage space or room for waiting customers. If a queue has reached its capacity limit then arrivals cannot enter the system, e.g., a full up waiting room in a doctor's surgery. The third component, i.e., the service facility, is typical of any shopping situation. For example, a small grocer's shop, which has only one serving counter, will operate a first-come, first-served (FIFO) facility at a constant speed. On the other hand, a large supermarket usually provides a multi-server checkout facility whereby several customers can be served at the same time.

Any queuing system requires a certain amount of time to build up to a normal level of operation, rather like a car accelerating to its cruising speed. Because a queue's behaviour

Table 10.10

Component	Characteristics	Details
• Population	Arrival pattern	Scheduled or random
	System capacity	Finite or infinite
	Queue behaviour	Balking (refuse to join queue – too long)
		Reneging (leave queue before being served)
		Jockeying (switch from one queue to another)
• Queue	Queue length	Limited or unlimited
• Service facility	Structure	Single- or multi-server
	Speed of service	Constant or random
	Queue discipline	Typically (i) first in-first out (FIFO), (ii) last in-first out (LIFO) or (iii) random

during the initial transient phase does not truly represent its long-term characteristics, most queuing models ignore this transient phase and assume a steady-state situation. Generally, it is assumed that the system has been operating long enough to have settled down into a regular pattern of operation.

CASE STUDY 10.1   *Single-server queuing problem*

MeadowSweet Creameries use their Greenhills subsidiary as a distribution point for their dairy products. Unfortunately, Greenhills has only one loading bay and there have been recent complaints regarding the loading facilities. Thirty-two vans arrive during each eight-hour day with an average of five vans being loaded in one hour. Delivery vans have been delayed due to inadequate resources and it has been suggested that operations could be speeded up if a second forklift truck and driver were available. While such extra resources would indeed reduce, if not eliminate, any delays, they are only required periodically and would be idle when there are no vans to be loaded. MeadowSweet's dilemma is whether the benefits of improved loading facilities outweigh the extra costs of hiring more equipment and personnel.

Queuing, which is a random process, has two main analysis techniques (i) assume that queuing characteristics can be realistically represented by formulae derived from average values, and (ii) use simulation techniques. The contents of the next three sections are outlined below.

Single-server model.   This section looks at the mathematical techniques behind queuing theory. It shows how Excel's statistical functions – POISSON and EXPONDIST – can be used to solve MeadowSweet Creameries problem. If users are not interested in the mathematics behind queuing models, then they should skip to the next section.

Multi-server model.   The next section derives an Excel spreadsheet model using standard mathematical formulae. The model is an extension of the single-server model. It is used to evaluate the three options being considered by MeadowSweet Creameries.

Simulation model.   The third section develops a simulation model for the MeadowSweet Creameries' case study which is used in the two previous sections. Comparisons are then made between the results obtained by simulation and statistical methods.

Single server model: a close look at statistical formulae

A single-server model requires that the following conditions be met before the model can be solved:

- Population   Arrival pattern   : Random, represented by an exponential distribution
  - System capacity : Infinite
  - Queue behaviour : No balking, reneging, or jockeying
- Queue   Queue capacity   : Unlimited
- Service   Structure   : Single-server (i.e., single queue)
  - facility   Speed of service : Random
  - Queue discipline : First in-first out (FIFO)

MeadowSweet Creameries have already collected information on truck arrival and service rates and are confident that a queuing model can be developed. The arrival rate of delivery vans is known to be 32 vans during every eight-hour day while studies have shown that an average of five vans can be loaded during one hour. The standard notation for arrival and service rates in queuing theory is

λ = arrival rate i.e., the average number of arrivals in a specified time interval, T

μ = service rate i.e., the average number of services in a specified time interval, T

Since 32 vans arrive in an eight-hour day, the hourly arrival rate, λ, is therefore four vans. The service rate μ, i.e., the number of vans that can be loaded in an hour, is five. If the vans could be scheduled to arrive at a steady rate of 4 or 5 per hour, MeadowSweet would have no problems. However, since van arrivals are random, this is not the case. The distinction between arrival rates and arrival patterns should be clearly made. While 32 vans on average arrive at Greenhills, their pattern of arrival is random, i.e., they do not arrive at any fixed times. In the context of statistical uncertainty, the terms 'average', 'on average' and 'expected' have the same meaning and are often used interchangeably. When the arrival pattern is random, the expected number of arrivals, x, over a short time period, T, can be represented by the Poisson probability distribution, $P(x)$, as follows

$$P(x) = \lambda^x e^{-\lambda}/x! \text{ for } x = 0, 1, 2, 3, \ldots$$

where $x!$ represents factorial x, i.e., $x(x-1)(x-2)\ldots 3.2.1$, and $e = 2.71828$ (the base of natural logarithms). Note the special case when $x = 0$, i.e., factorial (0) is equal to 1.

Since $\lambda = 4$, the probability that x vans will arrive in any one hour is $P(x) = 4^x e^{-4}/x!$. This expression can then be used to calculate the probability that 0, 1, 2, 3..., vans will arrive at Greenhills during any one hour. The same results can be obtained more easily by using Excel's statistical Poisson function as shown in column two of Table 10.11 below. The parameters of the Poisson(x, mean, cumulative) function are x = number of van arrivals, mean = $\lambda = 4$, and cumulative is a logical value which can be set to 'true' to give the cumulative Poisson probability or 'false' to give the normal Poisson distribution.

The first section of Table 10.11 contains the probability of x vans arriving in any one hour for $x = 0, 1, 2 \ldots 5$. For example, the probability of 0, 1, 2, etc. vans arriving in one hour is 0.0183, 0.0733, 0.1465, etc. The second section in Table 10.11 gives the cumulative probability figures, i.e., the sum of all the probabilities up to and including a particular probability. For example, the cumulative probability of three vans is found by adding the individual probabilities of 0, 1, 2, and 3 vans arriving in an hour. Likewise, the probability that no more than four vans will

Table 10.11   Individual and cumulative Poisson probabilities.

	Individual probability		Cumulative probability	
	POISSON (x, 4, FALSE)		POISSON (x, 4, TRUE)	
$x = 0$	0.0183	(1.8%)	0.0183	(1.8%)
$x = 1$	0.0733	(7.3%)	0.0916	(9.2%)
$x = 2$	0.1465	(14.6%)	0.2381	(23.8%)
$x = 3$	0.1954	(19.5%)	0.4335	(43.4%)
$x = 4$	0.1954	(19.5%)	0.6288	(62.9%)
$x = 5$	0.1563	(15.6%)	0.7851	(78.5%)

arrive in an hour is 62.9%. The probability of more than five vans arriving $= 1 - $ (probability of no more than five vans arriving) $= 1 - 0.7851 = 0.2149 = 21.5\%$.

The time that a customer spends waiting in a queue is called the *queuing time* and the time the customer spends being served is called the *service time*. Both times are distinct and do not overlap. The time spent 'in the system' is defined as the sum of the queuing time and the service time. Service times can be either constant or random. Where service times display a random behaviour, they are best described by the exponential probability distribution.

The exponential distribution is an important element in queuing theory because it gives a very good representation of real-world situations. If service time is denoted by t, then the probability of completing the loading of a van within a specified time-period, T, is given by the cumulative exponential distribution

$$P(t \leq T) = 1 - e^{-\mu T}$$

MeadowSweet Creameries have already observed that five vans can be loaded in any one hour, i.e., $\mu = 5$. Cumulative distribution values can be found using Excel's exponential distribution function EXPONDIST(x, mu, cumulative) where $x =$ specified time T, $mu = \mu$, *cumulative* is a logical value and is set to 'true' to give the cumulative exponential distribution. The service times, t_i, at different specified times, T_i, (1.0, 0.75, 0.5, 0.35 ... hours) are given in Table 10.12.

Table 10.12 shows that vans will almost always (99.3%) be loaded in one hour or less ($t_1 \leq 1.0$). There is a 91.8% probability that vans will be loaded within half an hour ($t_3 \leq 0.5$) and a 52.8% probability that vans will be loaded in nine minutes or less ($t_6 \leq 0.15$), etc. The T_i values have been arbitrarily chosen and can be extended or modified if so required.

At this stage, it is necessary to introduce some more queuing theory definitions (see Wilkes, Chapter 7), all of which are based on the arrival (λ) and service (μ) rates shown in Table 10.13.

Some aspects of the formulae in Table 10.13 need clarification. An important factor in queuing theory is the service utilisation (traffic intensity) ρ, which must always be less than 1. Since $\rho = \lambda/\mu$, this requirement means that the service rate μ must be greater than the arrival rate λ, otherwise the length of the queue will keep increasing indefinitely. In the MeadowSweet example, $\lambda = 4$ and $\mu = 5$, so the service utilisation factor $\rho = 4/5 = 0.8$. The phrase 'number of customers in the queue' refers to the number of vans waiting to be loaded; while 'in the

Table 10.12 Deriving service-time probabilities using the EXPONDIST function.

		Cumulative probability	
T_i (in hours)	Service times t_i	EXPONDIST (T, 5, TRUE)	
$T_1 = 1$ hour	$P\,(t_1 \leq 1.0)$	0.99326	(99.3%)
$T_2 = 0.75$	$P\,(t_2 \leq 0.75)$	0.97648	(97.6%)
$T_3 = 0.5$	$P\,(t_3 \leq 0.5)$	0.91792	(91.8%)
$T_4 = 0.35$	$P\,(t_4 \leq 0.35)$	0.82623	(82.6%)
$T_5 = 0.25$	$P\,(t_5 \leq 0.25)$	0.71350	(71.4%)
$T_6 = 0.15$	$P\,(t_6 \leq 0.15)$	0.52763	(52.8%)
$T_7 = 0.1$	$P\,(t_7 \leq 0.10)$	0.39347	(39.3%)
$T_8 = 0.05$	$P\,(t_8 \leq 0.05)$	0.22120	(22.1%)

Table 10.13

Formula	Description
$\rho = \lambda/\mu$	Utilisation factor or traffic intensity, which is the percentage of time that the service facility is busy
$P_x = \rho^x(1 - \rho)$	Probability that there are x customers in the system
$P_0 = 1 - \rho$	Probability that the system is idle, i.e., there are no customers
ρ^x	Probability that there are at least x customers in the system
$\lambda/(\mu - \lambda)$	Average number of customers in the system (queue + service)
$\lambda^2/\mu(\mu - \lambda)$	Average number of customers in the queue waiting for service
$\mu/(\mu - \lambda)$	Average number of customers in the queue (excluding zero queues)
$\lambda/\mu\,(\mu - \lambda)$	Average queuing time
$1/(\mu - \lambda)$	Average time a customer spends in the system (queuing + service times)
$1/\mu$	Average service time

system' refers to both the number of vans being loaded and those waiting in line to be loaded. MeadowSweet's data can now be calculated.

$$\rho = \lambda/\mu \qquad = 4/5 = 0.8 \qquad\qquad = 80\%$$
$$P_0 = 1 - \rho \qquad = 1 - 0.8 = 0.2 \qquad = 20\%$$
$$\lambda/(\mu - \lambda) \qquad = 4/(5 - 4) \qquad\qquad = 4 \text{ vans}$$
$$\lambda^2/\mu(\mu - \lambda) \qquad = 4^2/5(5 - 4) = 16/5 \qquad = 3.2 \text{ vans}$$
$$1/(\mu - \lambda) \qquad = 1/(5 - 4) \qquad\qquad = 1 \text{ hour}$$
$$\lambda/\mu(\mu - \lambda) \qquad = 4/5(5 - 4) = 0.8 \text{ hours} \qquad = 48 \text{ minutes}$$
$$1/\mu \qquad = 1/5 = 0.2 \text{ hours} \qquad = 12 \text{ minutes}$$

Summarising the above details provides MeadowSweet Creameries with some useful information.

- The service facility (i.e., the single forklift driver and truck) is busy 80% of the time.
- The average number of vans in the system is four.
- There are on average 3.2 vans in the queue waiting to be loaded.
- The average time a van spends in the system is one hour.
- The average waiting time for each van is 48 minutes.
- The average loading time for each van is 12 minutes.

Adding extra resources

The next stage is to see how these figures are affected when extra resources, i.e., a second forklift truck and driver, are available. The arrival rate of vans, $\lambda = 4$, will not alter but the service rate, μ, will be doubled to ten vans per hour. However, from previous experience gained at their other subsidiary Riversdale, MeadowSweet know that it is impractical to simply double the service rate. Because there is only one loading bay (i.e., only one server), both forklifts cannot operate simultaneously. A more realistic figure for μ is 8. Substituting this value of μ in the above relationships, produces the following data:

$$
\begin{aligned}
\rho = \lambda/\mu && = 4/8 = 0.5 && = 50\% \\
P_0 = 1 - \rho && = 1 - 0.5 = 0.5 && = 50\% \\
\lambda/(\mu - \lambda) && = 4/(8 - 4) && = 1 \text{ van} \\
\lambda^2/\mu(\mu - \lambda) && = 4^2/8(8 - 4) = 16/32 && = 0.5 \text{ van} \\
1/(\mu - \lambda) && = 1/(8 - 4) = 0.25 \text{ hour} && = 15 \text{ minutes} \\
\lambda/\mu(\mu - \lambda) && = 4/8(8 - 4) = 1/8 \text{ hours} && = 7.5 \text{ minutes} \\
1/\mu && = 1/8 = 0.\,125 \text{ hours} && = 7.5 \text{ minutes}
\end{aligned}
$$

The two data sets are summarised in Table 10.14 and a final cost-benefit analysis is obtained by adding some cost figures to the extra resources.

MeadowSweet's accountants have provided the following operating costs (including labour): a van costs £30 per hour and a forklift truck costs £15 per hour. From Table 10.14, it is clear that the reduction in the average time that each van spends in the system is $(60 - 15) = 45$ minutes $= 0.75$ hours. When operating costs are applied, there are savings of $0.75 \times £30 = £22.50$ per hour. This amount reduces to a net savings of £7.50 per hour after the extra forklift costs of £15 are included. On the basis of these figures, it would appear to be worthwhile to hire out another forklift truck and employ a second operator. However, it must also be noted that the system's idle time increases from 20% to 50%, i.e., the two forklift drivers would have nothing to do for half the time! Further analysis could also show if there were any benefits to be gained by buying rather than hiring a second forklift.

Multi-server model: building a spreadsheet model

In the single-server model, there is one queue and one service facility, e.g., cars waiting in line to use a single car-wash facility. In a multi-server or multi-channel queuing model there are two or more servers or service facilities available to serve a single waiting line, e.g., cars waiting in line to use two (or more) car-wash facilities. Although several queues could be formed, one for each facility, this arrangement introduces the problem of 'jockeying', i.e., switching from one (long) queue to another (shorter) queue. The model developed here assumes a single queue with multi-service facilities.

Table 10.14

Summary	Current situation	With extra resources
Number of vans loaded per hour, μ	5	8
Service utilisation factor, ρ	0.8	0.5
Probability that the system is idle	0.2	0.5
Average number of vans in the system	4	1
Average number of vans in the queue	3.2	0.5
Average time a van spends in the system	60 min	15 min
Average waiting time for each van	48 min	7.5 min
Average loading time for each van	12 min	7.5 min

	A	B	C	D	E	F	G	H	I
1	Case Study 10.1 - A multi-server queuing model								
2									
3	INPUT			Unit of time =	*hour*				
4				Arrival Rate, λ =	*4*		A Poisson		
5				Service Rate, μ =	*10*		distribution		
6				Number of servers, k =	*2*		is assumed		
7			(up to 9 servers)						
8									
9	OUTPUT			Service utilisation factor, =			20.0%		
10				Probability of system being idle, P_0 =			66.7%		
11				Probability of all servers being busy =			6.7%		
12				Expected* number in the queue =			0.0167		
13				Expected number in the system =			0.4167		
14				Expected waiting time =			0.0042	hour	
15				Expected time in the system =			0.1042	hour	
16				Expected service time =			0.1000	hour	
17									
18	LOOKUP TABLE								
19			k	$(R_A/R_S)^k/k!$	SUM		Table of		
20			0	1.000E+00	1.0000		terms derived		
21			1	4.000E−01	1.4000		from statistical		
22			2	8.000E−02	1.4800		formulae		
23			3	1.067E−02	1.4907				
24			4	1.067E−03	1.4917				
25			5	8.533E−05	1.4918		Single term		
26			6	5.689E−06	1.4918		calculation		
27			7	3.251E−07	1.4918		0.08		
28			8	1.625E−08	1.4918				
29			9	7.224E−10	1.4918				
30									
31			*Note: the terms 'expected' and 'average' have the same meaning						
32									

Figure 10.21 Multi-server queuing model.

The formulae for a multi-server model are extensions of those already used in the single-server model. Although these new formulae may appear rather complicated, they are quite simple to set up in Figure 10.21, as can be seen from the model's formulae template. λ is defined as the arrival rate, μ is the service rate, and k is the number of servers. The new set of formulae (see Wilkes, Chapter 7) for the multi-server model is given in Table 10.15 where ρ is the utilisation factor or traffic intensity, i.e., the percentage of time that the service facility is busy. P_0 is the probability that the system is idle, i.e., there are no customers to be served.

In the single-server section above, MeadowSweet Creameries examined the option of hiring out a second forklift truck and an extra operator in an effort to improve loading facilities at their Greenhills subsidiary. If other alternatives such as a multi-service facility are included, then MeadowSweet should consider the construction of a second loading bay which would double the rate of service from its previous level of five vans to ten vans per hour. In the

Table 10.15 Formulae for a multi-server model.

$$\rho = \frac{\lambda}{k\mu} \qquad\qquad P_0 = 1/((\lambda/\mu)^k/[k!(1-\rho)] + \sum_{n=0}^{k-1}(\lambda/\mu)^n/n!)$$

$P_k = P_0(\lambda/\mu)^k/[k!(1-\rho)]$	P_k is the probability that there are k or more customers in the system.
$\rho P_0(\lambda/\mu)^k/[k!(1-\rho)^2]$	Average number of customers in the queue waiting for service.
$\rho P_0(\lambda/\mu)^k/[k!(1-\rho)^2] + \lambda/\mu$	Average number of customers in the system (queue + service).
$\rho P_0(\lambda/\mu)^k/[k!(1-\rho)^2\lambda]$	Average time a customer is in the queue.
$\rho P_0(\lambda/\mu)^k/[k!(1-\rho)^2\lambda] + 1/\mu$	Average time a customer is in the system (queuing + service times).
$1/\mu$	Average service time.

multi-server model, the service utilisation factor ρ is $\lambda/k\mu$, which must always be less than 1. This requirement means that the maximum service rate $k\mu$ must be greater than the arrival rate λ, where k is the number of servers. A multi-server model is now developed using Table 10.16.

The three user input values for MeadowSweet's multi-server option are: arrival rate $\lambda = 4$ vans per hour, service rate $\mu = 10$ vans loaded per hour, and $k = 2$, the number of loading bays. Entering these values into the multi-server queuing model produces the results (in hours) as shown in Figure 10.21. It should be noted that answers to the previous single-server situations where (i) $\lambda = 4$, $\mu = 5$, $k = 1$, and (ii) $\lambda = 4$, $\mu = 8$, $k = 1$ can also be found by substituting these values into the multi-server model. The final summary for all three options is given in Table 10.17.

It would appear that option 2 offers the best possibility to MeadowSweet's loading difficulties. While option 3 practically eliminates the waiting line (0.02 vans in the queue), there is a low level (20%) of service utilisation as well as a high probability (66.7%) that the operators will have nothing to do! When these figures are combined with the cost of building another loading bay, option 3 appears unsuitable for the current volume of traffic.

Table 10.16 Multi-server queuing model – worksheet formulae.

Cell	Formula	Copied to
E8	IF(E4/(E5*E6) <1,"","Utilisation factor must be less than 1")	
G9	E4/(E5*E6)	
G10	1/(VLOOKUP(E6−1, C20:E29, 3) + G27/(1–G9))	
G11	G27*G10/(1–G9)	
G12	G9*(E4/E5)^E6*G10/(FACT(E6)*(1–G9)^2)	
G13	G12 + E4/E5	
G14	G12/E4	
G15	G14 + G16	
G16	1/E5	
H14	E$3	H15:H16
D20	(E$4/E$5)^C20/FACT(C20)	D21:D29
E20	D20	
E21	E20 + D21	E22:E29
G27	VLOOKUP(E6, C20:E29, 2)	

Table 10.17

Final summary	Option 1 $\lambda = 4, \mu = 5, k = 1$	Option 2 $\lambda = 4, \mu = 8, k = 1$	Option 3 $\lambda = 4, \mu = 10, k = 2$
Service utilisation (%)	80%	50%	20%
Average waiting time for each van	48 min.	7.5 min.	0.25 min.
Average number of vans in the system	4	1	0.42
Average number of vans in the queue	3.2	0.5	0.02
Average time a van spends in the system	60 min.	15 min.	6.25 min.
Average loading time for each van	12 min.	7.5 min.	6 min.
Probability that the system is empty	20%	50%	66.7%

Simulation model for queuing: predicting behaviour patterns

Many real-world situations, including queues, contain so many unknown variables that it is impossible to solve them analytically, e.g., trying to accurately predict when customers will join a queue. In such cases, the best approach is to simulate or mimic the process by developing a model and then studying its behaviour. In a queueing model, random number generation can be used to simulate, say, *interarrival times*, i.e., the time between customers arriving at a service facility.

The queueing approach used in the MeadowSweet example depends upon stringent assumptions being made about the model's characteristics. In practice, these assumptions are often unrealistic. For example, if the patterns of arrivals (λ) and service times (μ) are not properly measured, then the model's conclusions may be invalid. Because simulation models are more representative of the real world, they are very popular among business managers. However, the simulation of many queuing systems is very complex and requires the use of special-purpose simulation software packages such as GPSS, SIMSCRIPT, or SIMFACTORY.

Simulation model for MeadowSweet's queuing problem

Thirty-two delivery vans arrive at Greenhills every day. Because there is one loading bay, an average of only five vans can be loaded during any hour. MeadowSweet has therefore decided to get more accurate information on arrival patterns. It has asked an employee at Greenhills to record the number of vans that arrive during every hour throughout the eight-hour day. Records of arrival patterns for the 32 vans have been kept over a period of ten days. The results are summarised in the table below. The percentages (or probabilities) for each van group can easily be calculated, e.g., probability of zero vans = 0/80 = 0.0, one van 5/80 = 0.06, two vans =15/80 = 0.19, etc.

Number of van arrivals	0	1	2	3	4	5	6
Number of intervals	0	5	15	20	20	15	5
Probability	0.0	0.06	0.19	0.25	0.25	0.19	0.06

The simulation model of Figure 10.22 has found that an average of 3.85 vans arrive every hour. This value is very close to MeadowSweet's average arrival rate of $\lambda = 4$. Because the model has simulated a small number of hourly intervals (only 20), a more realistic answer would be obtained by using a much larger figure, say at least 320 (i.e., 8 weeks). If MeadowSweet had also recorded data of the times taken to load each van, then another probability table for service times could have been added to the simulation model (see Example 2.8 in Chapter 2).

EXCEL FUNCTIONS USED IN MODEL-BUILDING

The models developed in this chapter introduce three Excel functions for the first time, each of which is explained below. The user should remember that a comprehensive on-line help facility is also provided by Excel.

1. EXPONDIST: EXPONDIST (value, lambda, cumulative)

> returns the exponential probability distribution. EXPONDIST is widely used in waiting-line or queuing models to determine the length of time between arrivals at a service facility such as a supermarket check-out.

value = the value for which the exponential probability is required.
lambda = the mean of the exponential distribution.
cumulative = a logical value which can be set equal to TRUE to give the cumulative exponential probability, or set to FALSE to give the individual exponential probability.

Example: Customers arrive at a filling-station at the rate of 25 per hour. If a customer has just arrived, what is the probability that the next customer will arrive within 6 minutes (0.1 hour)? The answer is EXPONDIST(0.1, 25, TRUE) = 0.9179, i.e., 91.8%.

2. FACT: FACT (number)

> returns the factorial of a number. Factorial N is defined as $1.2.3.4.5 \ldots (N-1).N$.

Note the special convention for Factorial $0 = FACT(0) = 1$.
Example: Factorial 4 (usually written as 4!) equals $1.2.3.4 = 24$ and $5! = 1.2.3.4.5 = 120$.

3. POISSON: POISSON (X, mean, cumulative)

> returns the Poisson probability distribution. The Poisson distribution has a wide range of applications. It is particularly useful when the number of successful outcomes is known but not the number of failures. A typical example is predicting the number of arrivals at

	A	B	C	D	E	F	G	H	I	J	K	L
1	Case Study 10.1 - A simulation model for MeadowSweet Creameries											
2												
3		'Van arrivals' table						Random van arrivals				
4		<-- Limits -->		Van				Inter-	RAND	No. of	See	
5		Lower	Upper	Nos.	Freq.	P_i		val	no.	Vans	note A	
6		0	0.00	0	0	0.00		1	0.03	1	0	
7		0.00	0.06	1	5	0.06		2	0.22	2	0	
8		0.06	0.25	2	15	0.19		3	0.05	1	0	
9		0.25	0.50	3	20	0.25		4	0.80	5	0	
10		0.50	0.75	4	20	0.25		5	0.38	3	0	
11		0.75	0.94	5	15	0.19		6	0.28	3	0	
12		0.94	1.00	6	5	0.06		7	0.77	5	0	
13					80	1.00		8	0.38	3	0	
14		*User input cells are shaded*						9	0.84	5	0	
15								10	0.39	3	0	
16								11	0.73	4	0	
17		*Average no. of vans that can be*						12	0.08	2	0	
18		*loaded in one hour is 5*						13	0.94	6	1	
19								14	0.32	3	0	
20								15	0.87	5	0	
21		*Note A : Cells K6:K25 contain the*						16	0.84	5	0	
22		*number of vans waiting to be*						17	0.65	4	0	
23		*loaded each hour*						18	0.94	6	1	
24								19	0.96	6	1	
25								20	0.80	5	0	
26					Average no. of vans arriving each hour =					**3.85**		
27					Average no. of vans waiting to be loaded each hour =						*0.15*	
28												
29		Keep pressing the recalculation F9 key to generate new random numbers										
30												
31		Cell	*Formula*						*Copied to*			
32		E13	SUM(E6:E12)						F13			
33		F6	E6/E$13						F7:F12			
34		C6	F6									
35		B7	C6						B8:B12			
36		C7	C6 + F7						C8:C12			
37		I6	RAND()						I7:I25			
38		J6	VLOOKUP(I6,B$6:D$12,3)						J7:J25			
39		K6	IF(J6<=5,0,J6−5)						K7:K25			
40		J26	SUM(J6:J25)/H25									
41		K27	SUM(K6:K25)/H25									
42												
43		*Note that the model contains data for only TWENTY hourly intervals in lines 6-25.*										
44		*In practice, a much larger number of intervals (320 intervals = 8 weeks) would be simulated.*										
45												

Figure 10.22 Simulation model for MeadowSweet's queuing problem.

a service facility in, say, a 15-minute period, given the average number of arrivals per hour.

X = the number of successes.

mean = the expected or average number of successes.

cumulative = a logical value which can be set equal to TRUE to give the cumulative Poisson probability of X or fewer successes, or set to FALSE to give the probability of exactly X successes.

Example: Customers arrive at a fast-food drive-in facility at an average of 30 per hour. What is the probability that (i) exactly 33 (ii) 33 or fewer customers will arrive in the next hour? The answers are (i) POISSON(33, 30, FALSE) = 0.0599 = 6.0%, and (ii) POISSON(33, 30, TRUE) = 0.7444 = 74.4%.

EXERCISES

10.1 The Bedrock Company has introduced a new addition to its product range. The company will manufacture the new item at its three plants, P1, P2 and P3 which have annual production capacities of 1500, 2000, and 1000 with unit production costs of £4, £3, and £2 respectively. The product will be distributed through the company's two warehouses W1 and W2 which involve unit handling costs of £3 and £4 respectively. Customer demand is concentrated in three main shopping centres located at S1, S2 and S3 with estimated annual requirements of 1000, 1200, and 900 respectively. The unit transportation costs (in £s) from plant to warehouse and unit delivery costs from warehouse to customer are shown in the following table.

	P1	P2	P3	S1	S2	S3
W1	9	7	12	4	5	9
W2	5	6	4	5	3	8

The Bedrock Company wants to determine an optimum production and distribution schedule. (Hint: First set up a table determining the least-costly means of supplying shopping centres S_i from plants P_i.)

(Answer: Plant P1 supplies 1100 units to shopping centre S2, plant P2 supplies 1000 units to S1, and P3 supplies 100 units to S2 and also 900 units to S3.)

10.2 Bloggs Engineering produces an item that requires four different processes in its manufacture. The company recently carried out a work-study exercise to measure the performance of their five employees. It has drawn up Table 10.18 showing how long it takes each worker to perform a particular job (in hours). Bloggs Engineering would now like to determine which employees should be assigned to the various processes in order to minimise total manufacturing time. (Note that this is an unbalanced assignment problem.)

(Answer: Minimum time of 30 hours with employee E1 being assigned to job J2, E2 unassigned, E3, E4, E5 assigned to J1, J3, and J4.)

10.3 The following table gives the map co-ordinates and the amount of goods regularly shipped to Kitchenware Products' six main customers. Kitchenware want to centralise their distribution

Table 10.18

Employee	Job-1	Job-2	Job-3	Job-4
1	10	9	13	10
2	12	10	8	10
3	9	13	16	14
4	11	6	5	11
5	8	13	11	7

operations and would like to know the best location for a new warehouse. Using the facility location model, solve Kitchenware's problem. What is the new location if distance only is considered, i.e., the 'goods shipped' weighting factor is omitted?

Customer	A	B	C	D	E	F
Map co-ordinates	(5, 12)	(1, 6)	(2, 9)	(4, 11)	(1, 2)	(3, 4)
Goods shipped	160	145	220	150	230	180

(Answer 1: (2.2,7.1) Answer 2: (2.4,7.6).)

10.4 The map in Figure 10.23 shows part of the street network for Trendy City, with maximum pedestrian flow values (in 1000s). A new football stadium, with increased capacity, is being planned to replace the old stand. The city architect would like to know if Trendy City's street network will be able to meet the anticipated increase in spectators without causing serious crowding problems. He has asked you to find the maximum number of fans that the system can take from the car park to the new stadium. As this is a network problem, you have decided to use the maximal-flow technique.

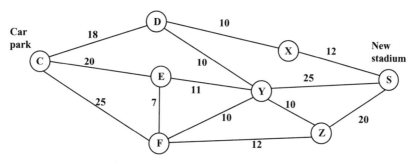

Figure 10.23

(Answer: Max flow = 51via CD(18), CE(11), CF(22), DX(10), DY(8), FE(0), EY(11), FY(10), FZ(12), YZ(8), YS(21), XS(10), ZS(20).)

10.5 MeadowSweet Creameries processes and distributes a variety of dairy products throughout the south-west area. MeadowSweet's most popular product – yogurt – is processed by two smaller creameries at Greenhills and Riversdale and is then transported to the supermarkets via various routes. Weekly figures of yogurt supply and supermarket demand are given in Table 10.19 below, as are transportation costs (per 100 units) for each route. Using the transhipment model, find

Table 10.19

Creamery	Supply	Supermarket requirements					
		1	2	3	4	5	6
Greenhills	3000	1100	650	850	1000	950	1000
Riversdale	4000						
FROM:	TO:	1	2	3	4	5	6
Greenhills (GH)		£20	£25	£20			
Riversdale (RV)					£12	£10	£15
Supermarket 2		£12		£10		£15	
Supermarket 5		£12	£12		£7		£8
Supermarket 6			£10	£4			

the cheapest distribution pattern for transporting yogurt to the six supermarkets. If production at Riversdale is reduced to 3000 units, what is the cheapest distribution pattern?

(Answer 1: £894 via GH-1(1100), GH-3(450), RV-4(1000), RV-5(1600), RV-6(1400), 5-2(650), 6-3(400). Answer 2: £916 via GH-1(1100), GH-2(600), GH-3(850), RV-4(1000), RV-5(1000), RV-6(1000), 5-2(50).)

10.6 Merlene Olonga is a senior sales representative for the KleenUp Company. She has five main customers in her sales area, the distance between each customer's town being shown in Table 10.20. Merlene always starts her itinerary from headquarters at HQ, visits each customer only once and then returns to headquarters, i.e., her itinerary forms a loop or tour. She would like to know the best way to visit customers in order to minimise the total distance travelled. This is the first step in solving the famous 'travelling salesman' problem and should be treated as an assignment problem (assign very large values e.g., 999, to the diagonal cells). Note that d_{ij} need not equal d_{ji} where d_{ij} is the distance between town i and town j.

(Answer: The solution is 178, producing 2 separate sub-tours HQ-A-C-B-HQ and D-E-D. Try to use this initial solution to create a new assignment problem with a view to achieving a single tour!)

Table 10.20

From:	To:	HQ	A	B	C	D	E
HQ		–	27	33	39	35	55
A		35	–	49	26	66	57
B		34	35	–	32	76	99
C		35	33	35	–	79	77
D		36	71	80	83	–	27
E		57	62	99	79	29	–

10.7 The Acme Company manufactures two products, widgets and gadgets. Expected sales for the next three months are: widgets, 3000, 3500, 3000; gadgets, 2500, 2000, 3000. The company has a monthly production capacity of 4000 units which can be extended to 5000 units by utilising overtime. Overtime, however, adds £2.50 to the normal production cost of each item. Monthly unit storage costs are £0.20 and £0.30 for a widget and gadget respectively. The company currently has 2000 widgets and 1500 gadgets in stock. The Acme Company would like to find a production schedule that will minimise total costs (i.e., overtime production and storage costs).

(Hint: Assign any value to normal production costs, say, £1.00 per unit. Then solve as a transportation problem.)

(Answer: Minimum total costs are £17,850; Table 10.21 shows the production schedule.)

Table 10.21

Month	1	2	3
Widgets – on-hand		1000	1000
Normal production	3000	2000	1000
Overtime	–	500	1000
Gadgets – on-hand	1500		
Normal production	1000	2000	3000
Overtime	–	–	–

10.8 LeisureWorld Unlimited manufactures patio furniture. The firm has three products: lounges, chairs, and picnic tables. It takes one hour of labour to produce one lounge, 30 minutes for a chair, and one and a half hours for a table. In addition, it takes 6 units of material for a chair, 8.5 units for a lounge, and 11 units for a table. LeisureWorld has 150 hours of labour and 850 units of material available for the coming production period. Profits on a chair, a lounge, and a table are £20, £30, and £40 respectively. The company has prioritised its three production goals as follows:

1. Achieve a profit of approximately £3,000
2. Produce around 50 lounges
3. Use as much labour hours as possible

Formulate LeisureWorld's requirements as a goal programming (GP) problem and solve using Solver (Hint: Reread the GP example of 6.7. Note that the labour resource constraint is not required since it is already included as goal 3.)

(Answer: LeisureWorld should manufacture 52 lounges and 37 tables to achieve a profit of £3,040. Goals 1 and 2 are achieved while Goal 3 is underachieved by 28.33% using 108 hours of labour.)

10.9 Bill Brown is the owner of Bill's Barbecues, which manufactures barbecues. Because of the prolonged good weather, there has been an unexpected demand for Bill's product. To meet this increase in demand, Bill has decided that he must supplement his normal production rate of 60 units per month with overtime production. Bill has estimated demand for the next four months to be 100, 90, 80, and 70. His unit production costs for each barbecue are £50 for raw materials and £40 labour. Overtime will increase monthly production to 85 barbecues but will also add another £20 to unit labour costs. The company currently has 30 barbecues in stock which incur a monthly holding cost of £3 per unit. Bill wants to plan a feasible production schedule for the next four months that will meet demand on time while minimising product costs. Set up Bill's problem as an aggregate planning model and hence solve using Excel's Solver.

(Answer: Minimum production costs of £29,315 for the next four months, with overtime production of 15, 25, 20, 10 in months 1 to 4.)

10.10 Joe Murphy owns a small firm that specialises in the renovation of houses. Joe has five jobs that must be completed during the month of July, today being 1st July. Joe, however, is doubtful about the order in which the jobs should be carried out. He has decided to use Excel's SORT facility and some sequencing rules (FIFO, SPT, EDD, CR, etc.) to help get a clearer picture of the situation. He will use the following table giving job details about (i) customers' required completion (due) dates, and (ii) duration (in days):

Job	A	B	C	D	E
Due date	10	16	30	5	25
Duration	4	7	10	3	5

(Answer: The EDD (earliest due date) priority rule gives a job sequence of D, A, B, E, C with no late jobs and an average job lateness of zero days.)

10.11   The Acme Company has seven urgent jobs that require the use of two serial facilities. Use Johnson's Rule to find the most efficient way of sequencing the seven jobs. The times (in minutes) for processing each job on each facility are shown in the following table.

Job	A	B	C	D	E	F	G
Facility 1	7	11	4	14	17	20	12
Facility 2	13	16	9	12	8	15	5

(Answer: Correct job sequence is C, A, B, F, D, E, G giving a sequencing time of 90 minutes with total idle time of 17 minutes.)

10.12   Management at the Gizmo Company have noticed that employees seem to be unduly delayed when picking up spare parts from their central stores. A 100-hour study has been carried out and the number of arrivals during each hour was recorded as shown in the following table.

No. of arrivals	0	1	2	3	4	5	6	7	8
No. of hours	1	7	13	20	22	16	11	7	3

1. Calculate the average arrival rate per hour, λ, over the observed 100-hour period.

2. The spare parts store has only one assistant who is able to serve six people in any one hour. Using the multi-server queuing model, help Gizmo to find out if the quality of service could be improved by employing more staff in their central stores. How many (if any) more staff would be acceptable, and why?

(Answers: (1) $\lambda = 4$; (2) One extra assistant. Currently, one server gives a 'waiting time in the system' of 30 minutes with a 33.3% probability of being idle. Two assistants give 'a waiting time in the system' of 11.25 minutes with a 50% probability of being idle. Gizmo should reduce waiting time from 30 to 11.25 minutes, while using idle time to check out stock levels.)

10.13   Fred Bloggs, owner of Fred's Fresh Fish Shop, is planning to open a fish-'n'-chips drive-in facility beside his popular restaurant. Having studied similar drive-in facilities, Fred has estimated that customers will arrive at the following time intervals (i.e., interarrival times):

Time between arrivals (minutes)	1	2	3	4	5
Probability	0.18	0.26	0.23	0.19	0.14

He intends to have one serving-hatch which can service customers (up to a maximum of 4) at the following rates:

Service time (minutes)	1	2	3	4
Probability	0.10	0.30	0.40	0.20

Fred is concerned about the average waiting time for customers. He knows that customers will not wait more than seven minutes to be served and he would like to know how many customers he could lose due to excessive delays. Use the Monte Carlo method to simulate the drive-in facility for 20 cars and find (i) the average waiting time (ii) the number of lost customers.

(Note: If the time that service begins (ends) for customer J is defined as TB_J (TE_J), then $TB_{J+1} = \max (TE_J, TA_{J+1})$ where the time of arrival for customer J, $TA_J = TA_1 + TA_2 + TA_3 + TA_J$ and waiting time $= TB_J - TA_J$).

(Answers: Because of the sensitive nature of Excel's random number generator RAND(), simulation values will differ for each individual model.)

10.14 The Fast CarWash Company has recently purchased a new waxing machine and can now offer its customers two options (i) the standard 4-minute car wash (ii) a new 6-minute 'wash 'n' wax' program. Observations on customer arrival times have produced the following interarrival table:

Time between arrivals (minutes)	1	3	5	7	9
Probability	0.08	0.20	0.27	0.29	0.16

If it is assumed that one quarter of all customers will choose the wash-n' -wax facility, use the Monte Carlo method to simulate the car wash operation over 20 customers. Hence find the average waiting times for each facility.

(Answers: Because of the sensitive nature of Excel's random number generator RAND(), simulation values will differ for each individual model)

REFERENCES AND FURTHER READING

Heizer, J. and Render, B. (2003) *Production & Operations Management* (7th edn), Prentice Hall, New Jersey.

Ragsdale, C. (2004) *Spreadsheet Modeling and Decision Analysis* (4th edn) , Thomson South-Western, USA.

Slack, N., Chambers, S. *et al.* (2004) *Operations Management* (4th edn), Pearson Education, UK.

Urry, S. (1991) *Introduction to Operational Research*, Longman Scientific & Technical, Essex.

Wilkes, F. (1980) *Elements of Operational Research*, McGraw-Hill, UK.

Winston, W. and Albright, S. (2000) *Practical Management Science: Spreadsheet Modeling and Applications* (2nd edn), Duxbury Press, California.

11

Project management

OVERVIEW

Projects are an ongoing aspect of production activities and can range from bringing a new product onto the market to constructing an offshore oil rig. While most projects are unique one-off events, there are some that are cyclical in nature involving periodic activities such as plant maintenance. Large-scale projects consist of numerous jobs that must be completed, some in parallel and others in sequence by various individuals or groups. When there is a large number of interrelated jobs, project control can become very complex. In these circumstances, it is usually advisable to break up the project into smaller, logical components, usually referred to as tasks or activities.

Because considerable expenditure is involved, a project has to be managed carefully to ensure that it is completed on time. Project management comprises the important functions of (i) planning (ii) scheduling and (iii) controlling project activities. The initial phase of project planning involves setting objectives and performance criteria (usually measured in terms of costs and time), identifying resource requirements, and assigning areas of responsibility.

The practical phase of project control is basically a comparison between what has actually been completed against what was planned at the start. Rather than allow a project to be completed without any control checks, management designates certain intermediate activities that are considered particularly relevant, called *milestones*, at which progress will be evaluated. Project control uses milestones periodically to review a project's progress. If a milestone check indicates that a project is running late, then corrective action must be taken to bring the project back on course.

Project scheduling focuses on the activities that make up the project. A schedule shows when each activity starts and ends and how long it will take to complete the activity, i.e., the activity's duration. Scheduling also shows how each activity is related to others in the project. Because projects often have important deadlines to meet, scheduling is a critical aspect of project management. Where there are a large number of interrelated activities, timing and co-ordination become very complex. Nowadays, project managers use computer software to help them identify those activities that must be finished on time in order to avoid delaying the entire project.

PROJECT MANAGEMENT TECHNIQUES

The term 'network analysis' is often used to describe the various mathematical techniques that have been developed for the planning and control of large projects. The primary purpose of such project management methods is to monitor a project's progress, and to identify those critical tasks which can seriously delay the project's completion. Network analysis helps management to answer such questions as

- When will the project finish?
- What are the critical activities, i.e., tasks, which if delayed, will delay the whole project?
- How is the overall project affected if a critical activity is delayed?
- What is the interrelationship between activities?

The two most commonly used techniques are the critical path method (CPM) and the project evaluation and review technique (PERT). The two techniques are very similar, the main difference being their assumptions concerning the accuracy of duration estimates for each task. PERT emphasises the uncertainty in estimating activity times while CPM assumes that task times can be accurately predicted. The CPM method is the scheduling approach used in virtually all project management software today, including Microsoft Project.

CPM and PERT models use a network to portray graphically the project's interrelationships. A network consists of nodes and arcs, also called arrows. Figure 11. 1 shows the main features of a partial network. A node represents a project task (i.e., activity) and is depicted as a circle in the network. Arcs are shown as arrows and define the interrelationships between nodes, indicating what activity must end before another activity can start.

THE PROJECT NETWORK

There are two ways of representing project networks.

1. *Activity-on-arc (AOA) networks*   in which the arcs represent the project's activities and the nodes are the start and finish of those activities. Start and finish nodes are called 'events'. Sometimes a network may contain two activities that have the same start and finish nodes.

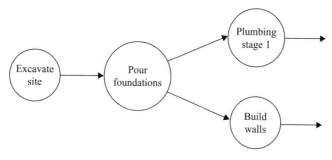

Figure 11.1   Partial network of nodes and arcs.

This problem is overcome by inserting dummy activities which have zero duration times and use zero resources but whose precedence relationships must be met. AOA networks are also referred to as activity-based project networks or arrow diagrams.

2. *Activity-on-node (AON) networks* in which the nodes represent the activities and the arcs (i.e., the arrows) show the precedence relationships between the activities (see Figure 11.1). Because each activity is uniquely defined in an AON network, dummy nodes are required only if the network does not have a unique start (or finish) node. For this reason, it is easier to use the AON notation when developing computer models. AON networks are sometimes called event-based project networks or precedence diagrams. All activity-on-arc (AOA) networks can be converted into AON precedence diagrams as shown in the following example.

EXAMPLE 11.1 *Converting an AOA network into an AON precedence diagram*

Consider the following activity-on-arrow (AOA) table which includes a dummy activity (3, 6):

Activities	(1, 2)	(2, 3)	(2, 4)	(3, 6)	(4, 6)	(3, 5)	(5, 7)	(6, 7)
Times (days)	2	4	3	0	3	1	2	5

Step 1:
Sketch the AOA arrow diagram.

The AOA network contains eight activities, including the dummy activity as shown by the dashed line in Figure 11.2. This dummy activity indicates that activity (2, 3) must be completed before activity (6, 7) can commence.

Step 2:
Construct the AON precedence diagram.

Allocate letters to the AOA arcs, except the dummy activity (3, 6), as shown in the following table. The AON precedence diagram contains eight activities, including a dummy finish node H with zero duration. The AOA dummy activity (3, 6) has been replaced by the AON precedence arrow BG in Figure 11.3.

AON convention	A	B	C		D	E	F	G
Activities	(1, 2)	(2, 3)	(2, 4)	(3, 6)	(4, 6)	(3, 5)	(5, 7)	(6, 7)
Times (days)	2	4	3	0	3	1	2	5

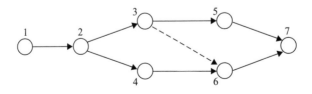

Figure 11.2 An AOA network.

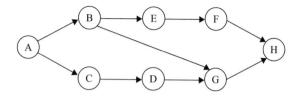

Figure 11.3

CASE STUDY 11.1   *Constructing an AON network*

The MightyBig Corporation has recently won a contract to build a large warehouse. For all projects, the company uses (i) the activity-on-node (AON) convention for drawing its networks, and (ii) the CPM technique for network analysis. The Corporation's first step in developing an AON network is to determine all the specific activities that make up the warehouse project, along with estimated completion times for each activity. Letters or numbers can be used to define activities (i.e., nodes); in this example letters have been used. Figure 11.4 shows how Table 11.1 can be presented as an AON network.

Critical path method (CPM)

A path through a network is a sequence of activities connecting the start node to the finish node, e.g., in Figure 11.4, the nodes A–B–E–F–J–K form a path; likewise the nodes A–C–K form another path. The time required to complete each individual activity in a network must be estimated. An activity is considered to be critical if any delay in its start or completion causes the whole project to be delayed.

The critical path method (CPM) – also called critical path analysis (CPA) – identifies a project's critical path, i.e., the longest path through the network containing the project's critical

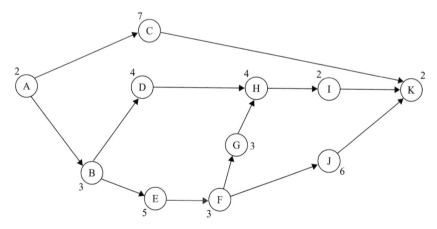

Figure 11.4   AON network with activity times.

Table 11.1

Activity symbol	Activity description	Preceding activity	Completion times (in weeks)
A	Site excavation	–	2
B	Foundations	A	3
C	Underground utilities	A	7
D	Plumbing: stage 1	B	4
E	Framing	B	5
F	Roofing	E	3
G	Electrical work	F	3
H	Interior walls	D, G	4
I	Plumbing: stage 2	H	2
J	Exterior finishing	F	6
K	Landscaping	C, I, J	2

activities. The length of the critical path measures the time taken to complete all activities in the critical path, and gives the shortest time in which the project can be completed. It is possible for a network to have more than one critical path. The CPM technique uses the concepts of forward and backward passes to identify the project's critical path.

Forward Pass

The 'forward pass' is a technique for determining the earliest time that each activity in the network can start and finish. Beginning with the project's start activity or node, the technique moves systematically from node to node in a forward direction towards the project's finish node, hence the name 'forward' pass. Earliest start times (EST) are first determined for each activity, and are then used to find (i) the earliest finish times (EFT), and (ii) the earliest time that the project itself can finish. A forward pass involves the following four rules:

1. The EST for the project's start node is zero.

2. No activity can begin until all its preceding activities are complete.

3. Once an activity's EST value is known, its EFT value is found from the equation $EFT = EST + T$ where T is the activity's duration.

4. The EST for an activity leaving any node equals the largest EFT of all activities entering the same node.

These four rules are now applied to the warehouse network of Figure 11.4.

Node A: Rule 1: Since A is the start node, its $EST_A = 0$
Rule 3: $EFT_A = EST_A + T_A = 0 + 2 = 2$ where T_A is the duration of activity A
i.e., for activity A, (EST, EFT) = (0, 2)

Since rule 2 is satisfied, node B can now be examined.

Node B: Rule 4: $EST_B = EFT_A = 2$
Rule 3: $EFT_B = EST_B + T_B = 2 + 3 = 5$
i.e., for activity B, (EST, EFT) = (2, 5)

Since rule 2 is satisfied, node C can now be examined.

Node C: Rule 4: $EST_C = EFT_A = 2$
Rule 3: $EFT_C = EST_C + T_C = 2 + 7 = 9$
i.e., for activity C, (EST, EFT) = (2, 9)

Since rule 2 is satisfied, node D can now be examined.

Node D: Rule 4: $EST_D = EFT_B = 5$
Rule 3: $EFT_D = EST_D + T_D = 5 + 4 = 9$
i.e., for activity D, (EST, EFT) = (5, 9)

....
.... etc.

Node H has two preceding nodes D and G

Node H: Rule 4: $EST_H = $ maximum of $(EFT_D, EFT_G) = (9, 16) = 16$
Rule 3: $EFT_H = EST_H + T_H = 16 + 4 = 20$
i.e., for activity H, (EST,EFT) = (16, 20)

....
.... etc.

Node K is the finish (end) node and has three preceding nodes C, I and J

Node K: Rule 4: $EST_K = $ maximum of $(EFT_C, EFT_I, EFT_J) = (9, 22, 19) = 22$
Rule 3: $EFT_K = EST_K + T_K = 22 + 2 = 24$
i.e., $EFT_K = $ the earliest finish time for the entire project, namely 24 weeks.

At the end of the forward pass, the earliest start and finish times for each activity have been found. In Figure 11.5, the (EST, EFT) values are shown in square brackets. The complete table of (EST, EFT) values is given in Table 11.2.

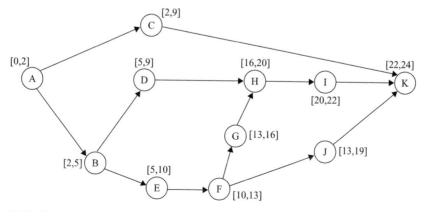

Figure 11.5   Warehouse network with earliest start and finish times (EST, EFT).

Table 11.2 (EST, EFT) values derived from the forward pass.

Activity	A	B	C	D	E	F	G	H	I	J	K
EST	0	2	2	5	5	10	13	16	20	13	22
EFT	2	5	9	9	10	13	16	20	22	19	24

Backward Pass

The 'backward pass' is similar to the forward pass except that it operates in the opposite direction. Beginning with the project's finish activity or node, the technique moves systematically from node to node in a backward direction towards the project's start node. The 'backward pass' technique is used to determine the latest time that each activity in the network can start and finish without delaying the whole project. Latest finish times (LFT) are first determined for each activity, and are then used to find (i) the latest start times (LST), and (ii) the critical activities that must start and finish on time. A backward pass involves the following four rules, which are really the 'forward pass' steps in reverse.

1. The LFT for the project's finish node is equal to its EFT (found by the forward pass).
2. No activity can begin until all its succeeding activities are complete.
3. Once an activity's LFT value is known, its LST value is found from the equation LST $=$ LFT $- T$ where T is the activity's duration.
4. The LFT for an activity entering any node equals the smallest LST of all activities leaving the same node.

The four 'backward pass' rules are now applied to the warehouse network of Figure 11.4.

Node K: Rule 1: Since K is the finish node, its $\text{LFT}_K = \text{EFT}_K = 24$
    Rule 3: $\text{LST}_K = \text{LFT}_K - T_K = 24 - 2 = 22$ where T_K is the duration of activity K
    i.e., for activity K, (LFT, LST) $= (24, 22)$

Since rule 2 is satisfied, node J can now be examined.

Node J: Rule 4: $\text{LFT}_J = \text{LST}_K = 22$
    Rule 3: $\text{LST}_J = \text{LFT}_J - T_J = 22 - 6 = 16$
    i.e., for activity J, (LFT, LST) $= (22, 16)$

Since rule 2 is satisfied, node I can now be examined.

Node I: Rule 4: $\text{LFT}_I = \text{LST}_K = 22$
    Rule 3: $\text{LST}_I = \text{LFT}_I - T_I = 22 - 2 = 20$
    i.e., for activity I, (LFT, LST) $= (22, 20)$

....
.... etc.

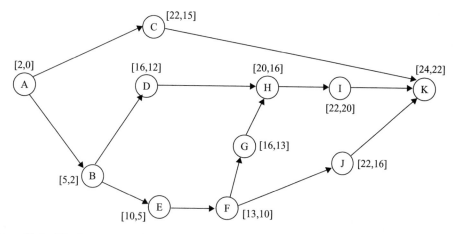

Figure 11.6 Warehouse network with latest finish and start times (LFT, LST).

Node F has two succeeding nodes G and J.

Node F: Rule 4: $LFT_F = $ minimum of $(LST_G, LST_J) = (13, 16) = 13$
Rule 3: $LST_F = LFT_F - T_F = 13 - 3 = 10$
i.e., for activity F, $(LFT, LST) = (13, 10)$

....
.... etc.

Node A is the start node and has two succeeding nodes B and C.

Node A: Rule 4: $LFT_A = $ minimum of $(LST_B, LST_C) = (2, 15) = 2$
Rule 3: $LST_A = LFT_A - T_A = 2 - 2 = 0$
i.e., $LST_A = $ the latest start time for the entire project, namely zero weeks!

At the end of the backward pass, the latest finish and start times for each activity have been found. In Figure 11.6, the (LFT, LST) values are shown in square brackets. The complete table of (LFT, LST) values is given in Table 11.3.

Float and Critical Activities

Float (or slack) is the amount of time by which an activity can be delayed without affecting the project's completion. Activities, which are non-critical, have spare time, i.e., float. However, critical activities have no slack, i.e., their float is zero. The float, F_i, for activity i can be found

Table 11.3 (LFT, LST) values derived from the backward pass.

Activity	A	B	C	D	E	F	G	H	I	J	K
LFT	2	5	22	16	10	13	16	20	22	22	24
LST	0	2	15	12	5	10	13	16	20	16	22

Table 11.4   Slack and critical activities

Activity	A	B	C	D	E	F	G	H	I	J	K
EST	0	2	2	5	5	10	13	16	20	13	22
LST	0	2	15	12	5	10	13	16	20	16	22
Float	0	0	13	7	0	0	0	0	0	3	0

from either of the two formulae

$$F_i = LST_i - EST_i \quad \text{or} \quad F_i = LFT_i - EFT_i.$$

An activity's float is therefore defined as the difference between either (i) its latest and earliest start times or (ii) its latest and earliest finish times. The equation $F_i = LST_i - EST_i$ is used to derive the (LST, EST) values shown in Table 11.4. The EST and LST values are found in Tables 11.2 and 11.3 respectively. Activities C, D and J have slack values of 13, 7, and 3 weeks respectively. Since the rest of the nodes have zero float, they are critical. The critical path is therefore A–B–E–F–G–H–I–K giving a total project time of 24 weeks for completion, i.e., the same value as EFT_K.

Developing a CPM Model

A CPM model is now developed for the MightyBig Corporation's warehouse project using Excel's Solver. The main criterion used is the float formula $F_i = LST_i - EST_i$ discussed in the previous section. The situation requires a relatively simple linear programming (LP) model which uses Excel's Solver twice in order to find two sets of activity times that

- minimise the sum of the EST values subject to the constraint $EST_j - EST_i \geq T_i$ for all (i, j) arcs;

- maximise the sum of the LST values subject to the constraint $LST_j - LST_i \geq T_i$ for all (i, j) arcs. Before running Solver to maximise LST values, an additional constraint must be added because of Rule 1 (Backward Pass), i.e., LST_K must equal EST_K where K is the finish node (cell E15 = D15 in Figure 11.8).

Although the CPM model can be created in a single spreadsheet, it has been divided into two parts for clearer presentation. Figure 11.7 shows how to minimise the EST values, while Figure 11.8 is a slightly modified version where the only changes required are

- in 'Solver Parameters' box, (i) change 'Min' to 'Max' (ii) add an extra constraint, E15 = D15

- copy EST values (cells D5:D15 in Figure 11.7) into cell range E5:E15.

The critical path, ABEFGHIK, is easily found by choosing those activities which have zero values in the 'float' column (F5:F15) in Figure 11.8. Because of rounding errors, calculated values will not be exactly zero, so any float that is less than 0.0001 is be taken to be zero. The duration of the critical path is the shortest time in which the project can be completed, i.e., 24 weeks (cell H19).

	A	B	C	D	E	F	G	H	I	J	K	L
1	Case Study 11.1 - CPM model: finding the activities' earliest start times (ESTs)											
2												
3		User input cells are shaded						From	To	<--- Constraints --->		
4		Activity	Time	EST		Float		Node i	Node j	$EST_j - EST_i$	Time T_i	
5		A	2	0		0		A	C	2	2	
6		B	3	2		2		A	B	2	2	
7		C	7	2		2		B	D	3	3	
8		D	4	5		5		B	E	3	3	
9		E	5	5		5		C	K	20	7	
10		F	3	10		10		D	H	11	4	
11		G	3	13		13		E	F	5	5	
12		H	4	16		16		F	G	3	3	
13		I	2	20		20		F	J	3	3	
14		J	6	13		13		G	H	3	3	
15		K	2	22		22		H	I	4	4	
16								I	K	2	2	
17	Objective: Minimise EST values =					108.0		J	K	9	6	
18												
19					Project Completion Time =							
20												
21												
22		Solver Parameters										
23			Set Target Cell:	F17								
24			Equal to:	Min								
25			By Changing Cells:	D5:D15								
26			Subject to Constraints:	D5:D15 >= 0		= Answers must be positive						
27				J5:J17 >= K5:K17		= $EST_j - EST_i >= T_i$						
28												
29		Cells	Formula								Copied to	
30		F5	D5 - E5								F6:F15	
31		J5	VLOOKUP(I5,B$5:D$15,3,FALSE) -			(cont. on next line)						
32			VLOOKUP(H5,B$5:D$15,3,FALSE)								J6:J17	
33		K5	VLOOKUP(H5,B$5:D$15,2,FALSE)								K6:K17	
34		F17	SUM(D5:D15)									
35		H19	IF(E5="","",SUMIF(F5:F15,"<0.0001",C5:C15))									
36												
37	Switch on the 'Assume Linear Model' parameter in the Solver Options dialog box											

Figure 11.7 CPM model: Step 1 - finding the network's EST values.

Gantt charts

Gantt charts – also called bar charts – were created by Henry Gantt at the beginning of the last century. Until the arrival of network analysis techniques in the 1950s, Gantt charts were the main tools for project planning and control. Because bar charts are easy to construct and interpret, they are still widely used – not least, for their strong visual impact, especially when an overall view of a project's progress is required. The interrelationships between a project's activities can be more easily understood if they are shown on a bar diagram. Excel's Chart

	A	B	C	D	E	F	G	H	I	J	K	L
1	Case Study 11.1 - CPM model: finding the activities' latest start times (LSTs)											
2												
3		*User input cells are shaded*						**From**	**To**	**<--- Constraints --->**		
4		**Activity**	**Time**	**LST**	**EST**	**Float**		Node i	Node j	$LST_j - LST_i$	Time T_i	
5		A	2	0	0	0		A	C	15	2	
6		B	3	2	2	0		A	B	2	2	
7		C	7	15	2	13		B	D	10	3	
8		D	4	12	5	7		B	E	3	3	
9		E	5	5	5	0		C	K	7	7	
10		F	3	10	10	0		D	H	4	4	
11		G	3	13	13	0		E	F	5	5	
12		H	4	16	16	0		F	G	3	3	
13		I	2	20	20	0		F	J	6	3	
14		J	6	16	13	3		G	H	3	3	
15		K	2	22	22	0		H	I	4	4	
16								I	K	2	2	
17		*Objective: Maximise LST values =*				131.0		J	K	6	6	
18												
19					Project Completion Time =			24				
20												
21												
22		**Solver Parameters**										
23			*Set Target Cell:*		F17							
24			*Equal to:*		Max			◀ (Changed!)				
25			*By Changing Cells:*		D5:D15							
26			*Subject to Constraints:*		D5:D15 >= 0			= Answers must be positive				
27					J5:J17 >= K5:K17			$= LST_j - LST_i >= T_i$				
28					E15 = D15			◀ (Added!)				
29												

Figure 11.8   CPM model: Step 2 - finding the network's LST and float values.

Wizard provides a user-friendly way of creating bar charts. Instructions for creating a Gantt diagram for the MightyBig warehouse project are given below.

- Copy the EST cells (E5:E15) and Time cells (C5:C15) from the CPM model of Figure 11.8 into a separate sheet (see Figure 11.9). This step is necessary because there are no activity descriptions in Figure 11.8. Enter activity descriptions into cells B5:B15 in Figure 11.9.

- Select the cell range B5:D15 as input and then click on the Chart Wizard button (with coloured columns) in the standard toolbar.

- From Chart Wizard's Step 1 dialog box, choose chart type 'Bar' and chart sub-type (shown in row 1, column 2). Click the 'next' button twice to proceed to Step 3.

- The dialog box of Step 3 presents chart options. Click on the 'Titles' tab and enter titles for the Chart and the y-axis (note that the y-axis is now horizontal, i.e., the x–y axes have been reversed). Next, click on the 'Gridlines' tab. Click on 'Major Gridlines' in the x-axis panel and, if not already activated, click also on the 'Major Gridlines' in the y-axis panel.

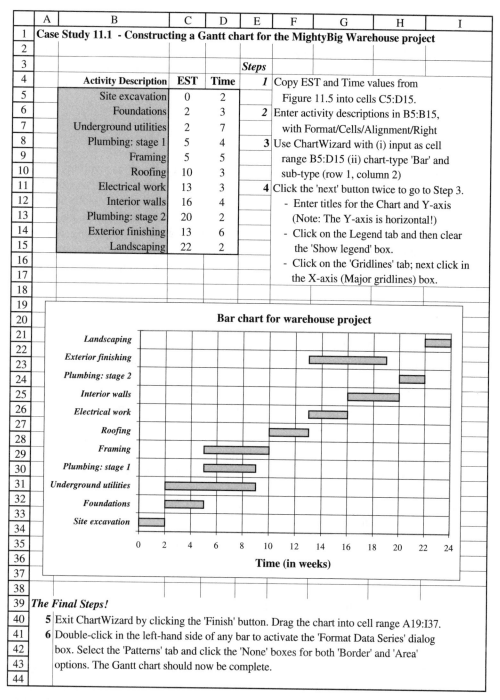

	A	B	C	D	E	F	G	H	I
1		**Case Study 11.1 - Constructing a Gantt chart for the MightyBig Warehouse project**							
2									
3					*Steps*				
4		**Activity Description**	**EST**	**Time**	*1*	Copy EST and Time values from			
5		Site excavation	0	2		Figure 11.5 into cells C5:D15.			
6		Foundations	2	3	*2*	Enter activity descriptions in B5:B15,			
7		Underground utilities	2	7		with Format/Cells/Alignment/Right			
8		Plumbing: stage 1	5	4	*3*	Use ChartWizard with (i) input as cell			
9		Framing	5	5		range B5:D15 (ii) chart-type 'Bar' and			
10		Roofing	10	3		sub-type (row 1, column 2)			
11		Electrical work	13	3	*4*	Click the 'next' button twice to go to Step 3.			
12		Interior walls	16	4		- Enter titles for the Chart and Y-axis			
13		Plumbing: stage 2	20	2		(Note: The Y-axis is horizontal!)			
14		Exterior finishing	13	6		- Click on the Legend tab and then clear			
15		Landscaping	22	2		the 'Show legend' box.			
16						- Click on the 'Gridlines' tab; next click in			
17						the X-axis (Major gridlines) box.			
18									
19									
20									
21									
22									
...									
38									
39		*The Final Steps!*							
40		*5*	Exit ChartWizard by clicking the 'Finish' button. Drag the chart into cell range A19:I37.						
41		*6*	Double-click in the left-hand side of any bar to activate the 'Format Data Series' dialog						
42			box. Select the 'Patterns' tab and click the 'None' boxes for both 'Border' and 'Area'						
43			options. The Gantt chart should now be complete.						
44									

Figure 11.9   Bar chart for the MightyBig Corporation's warehouse project.

- Proceed to Step 4 (the last Chart Wizard step) and ensure that the 'As_object_in:' button is activated. Exit from Chart Wizard by clicking the 'Finish' button.
- Drag the chart into cell range A19:I37 as shown in Figure 11.9. Double-click in the left-hand side of any bar (part nearest to vertical axis) to activate the 'Format Data Series' dialog box. Select the 'Patterns' tab and click 'None' in both 'Border' and 'Area' panels. If necessary, reformat chart text and numbers (see Appendix).

Resources, costs and crash times

An important aspect of project management is concerned with cost analysis involving resource allocation and cost scheduling. The main purpose of project cost analysis is to determine how costs will alter when a project's duration varies. Such analysis is especially important where penalty and/or bonus clauses operate. A project manager must determine whether it is worthwhile using extra resources in order to collect bonus payments by completing the project before the agreed date – or avoiding penalties if the project overruns. Least cost scheduling – also called 'crashing the network' – looks for the cheapest way of reducing the project's overall duration.

The CPM model of Figure 11.8 found the critical path for the MightyBig Corporation's warehouse project, using fixed activity times. It was assumed that it was not possible to reduce activity duration times. In many situations, however, tasks can be speeded up by using extra resources – which in turn will involve extra costs. For example, to say that it takes 2 hours to complete a job is an incomplete statement without specifying that three people were involved! If four people were allocated to the same task instead of three, then the job would be completed in a shorter time, i.e., 1.5 hours. When facing costly penalties, it may be more economical to allocate additional resources to ensure that the job is finished on time.

An activity's normal resource represents the standard or usual amount of time, resources, and costs required to complete the activity. As the task's duration is reduced extra labour, materials, and overheads will be required. Shortening or crashing an activity's completion time will therefore involve additional costs, called 'crash costs'. An activity's crash time is defined as the shortest possible time for the completion of the activity. The two main crash objectives in project management are to:

- minimise project completion time   (find the shortest duration)
- minimise project costs   (find the lowest cost).

Crash model for minimising a project's duration

Project completion times can be reduced only by using more resources which in turn will push up costs. A CPM model is now developed to find the best way of shortening (crashing) the entire project, i.e., to minimise project duration. The first step is to find out what resources are available and at what extra costs. After discussions with the sub-contractors, details of normal time, normal cost, crash time, and crash cost for each activity are entered into the MightyBig Corporation's model (Table 11.5). To allow for greater flexibility, the model's activity duration times have been changed from weeks to days (assume a 5-day week).

Table 11.5

Normal Time (days)

Activity	A	B	C	D	E	F	G	H	I	J	K
Time	10	15	35	20	25	15	15	20	10	30	10
Cost (£'000s)	2	3	10	6	12	9	6	7	3	5	3

Crash Time (days) (i.e. the shortest time in which an activity can finish)

Activity	A	B	C	D	E	F	G	H	I	J	K
Crash time	5	10	25	15	17	10	9	10	5	20	6
Crash cost (£'000s)	3	4	13.5	8	16	10.5	9	11	4.5	7.5	4.5

The crash model (see Figure 11.10) for the warehouse project is set up as a linear programming (LP) exercise to be solved using Solver. The LP objective is to minimise project completion time by minimising the crash EFT for activity K – the last activity in the project. Activity K's normal time is defined as T_K, its crash time as TC_K, and its earliest start time as EST_K. The LP objective function, Z, is then given by $Z = T_K + EST_K - TC_K$. The model's three input areas are highlighted as shaded ranges – all other cells are derived from formulae as shown in Table 11.6. Note that user-input areas in both CPM models (normal and crash) are defined by the number of nodes and arcs in a network.

The crash model of Figure 11.10, which is solved using the details in Figure 11.11, has reduced the project's duration from 24 weeks (i.e., 120 days) to 72 days at a total crash cost of £19,000. The project's completion time of 72 is found by examining details for the last activity K. Cell C16 contains the normal duration for activity K, i.e., $T_K = 10$; cell C32 contains K's earliest start time, $EST_K = 66$; cell D32 contains K's crash time, $TC_K = 4$. Using the objective function's equation, $Z = T_K + EST_K - TC_K$ gives $Z = 10 + 66 - 4 = 72$. The crash costs are found by calculating the cost of each extra crash day. For example, the duration of activity A is reduced from 10 days to 5 days at a crash cost of 5 × £200 (cell D22 × cell I6), i.e., £1000. Similar calculations can be applied to other activities that have utilised available crash days.

Crash model for minimising project costs

The objective of minimising costs for a project involves two 'lowest cost' situations:

- Case 1: Meeting a project deadline by minimising crash costs to avoid overrun penalties

- Case 2: Shortening a project's duration by minimising project costs to avail of bonus payments

These objectives can be achieved by modifying the crash model. Firstly, make a copy of Figure 11.10 and then enter the details in lines 35–44 using the formula template provided in Figure 11.13.

Situation 1: meeting project deadlines As an example, consider the situation whereby the warehouse must now be completed within 22 weeks (i.e., 110 days) rather than the original 24 weeks. Under these new conditions, the MightyBig project is now running behind schedule

	A	B	C	D	E	F	G	H	I	J	K
1		Case Study 11.1 - A crash model for minimising a project's completion time									
2											
3			<-- Normal -->				<-------- Crash Details -------->				
4			Time	Activity		Min.	Activity	Crash days	Cost		
5		Activity	T_i	Cost		Time	Cost	available	per day		
6		A	10	£2,000		5	£3,000	5	£200		
7		B	15	£3,000		10	£4,000	5	£200		
8		C	35	£10,000		25	£13,500	10	£350		
9		D	20	£6,000		15	£8,000	5	£400		
10		E	25	£12,000		17	£16,000	8	£500		
11		F	15	£9,000		10	£10,500	5	£300		
12		G	15	£6,000		9	£9,000	6	£500		
13		H	20	£7,000		10	£11,000	10	£400		
14		I	10	£3,000		5	£4,500	5	£300		
15		J	30	£5,000		20	£7,500	10	£250		
16		K	10	£3,000		6	£4,500	4	£375		
17		Normal project cost =		£66,000							
18											
19			Start	Crash		From	To	<-- Constraints-->			
20			Time	Time		Node i	Node j	$EST_j–EST_i$	$T_i–TC_i$		
21		Activity	EST_i	TC_i		A	C	31	5		
22		A	0	5		A	B	5	5		
23		B	5	5		B	D	26	10		
24		C	31	0		B	E	10	10		
25		D	31	0		C	K	35	35		
26		E	15	8		D	H	20	20		
27		F	32	5		E	F	17	17		
28		G	42	6		F	G	10	10		
29		H	51	10		F	J	10	10		
30		I	61	5		G	H	9	9		
31		J	42	6		H	I	10	10		
32		K	66	4		I	K	5	5		
33						J	K	24	24		
34											
35		Objective 1: Minimise project duration =					72	days			
36				Total Crash Costs =			£19,000				
37				Normal Project Cost =			£66,000				
38				Total Project Cost =			£85,000				
39											
40											
41		Notes: Switch on 'Assume Linear Model' in the Solver Options dialog box.									
42		USER INPUT areas are shown as shaded cell ranges									

Figure 11.10 Crash model for minimising project duration.

Table 11.6   CPM crash model – worksheet formulae.

Cell	Formula	Copied to
H6	C6–F6	H7:H16
I6	IF(H6 = 0, 0, (G6–D6)/H6)	I7:I16
D17	SUM(D6:D16)	
H21	VLOOKUP(G21, B$22:D$32, 2, FALSE) (cont. on next line)	
	–VLOOKUP(F21, B$22:D$32, 2, FALSE)	H22:H33
I21	VLOOKUP(F2l, B$6:C$16, 2, FALSE) (cont. on next line)	
	–VLOOKUP(F21, B$22:D$32, 3, FALSE)	I22:I33
B22	B6	B23:B32
G35	C16 + C32 – D32	
G36	SUMPRODUCT(D$22:D$32, I$6:I$16)	
G37	D17	
G38	G36 + G37	

by two weeks (10 days), and the network must be 'crashed' to avoid overrun penalties. The answer in Figure 11.13 shows that the new deadline of 110 days can be met by crashing activities A and B by five days each at an extra crash cost of £2000 (cell H40), giving a total project cost of £68,000 (cell H43). The results are obtained by making two simple changes (indicated by arrowheads in Figure 11.12) to the Solver Parameters section of Figure 11.11.

Solver parameters		
Set target cell:	G35	
Equal to:	Min	
By changing cells:	C22:D32	
Subject to constraints:	C22:D32 ≥ 0	= Answers must be positive
	C22:D32 = int(eger)	= Answers must be integer
	D22:D32 ≤ H6:H16	= TC_i ≤ No. of crash days
	H21:H33 ≥ I21:I33	= $EST_j – EST_i ≥ T_i – TC_i$

Figure 11.11   Solver parameters for the 'crash' model of Figure 11.10.

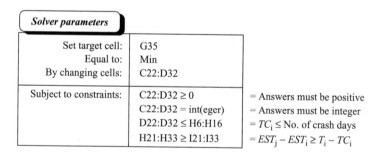

Solver Parameters		
Set Target Cell:	H40	◄── = Objective 2: Minimise crash costs
Equal to:	Min	
By Changing Cells:	C22:D32	
Subject to Constraints:	C22:D32 ≥ 0	= Answers must be positive
	C22:D32 = int(eger)	= Answers must be integer
	D22:D32 ≤ H6:H16	= TC_i ≤ No. of crash days
	H21:H33 ≥ I21:I33	= $EST_j – EST_i ≥ T_i – TC_i$
	H38 <= H41	◄── = Project deadline (extra constraint)

Figure 11.12   Solver parameters for the modified crash model of Figure 11.13.

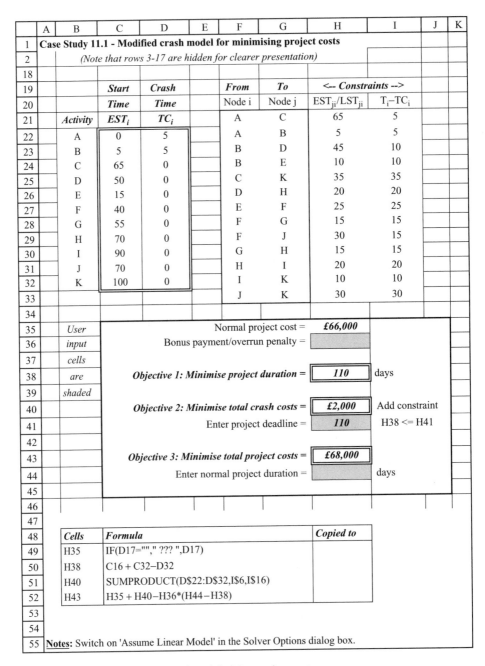

	A	B	C	D	E	F	G	H	I	J	K
1		Case Study 11.1 - Modified crash model for minimising project costs									
2			(Note that rows 3-17 are hidden for clearer presentation)								
18											
19			*Start*	*Crash*		*From*	*To*	*<-- Constraints -->*			
20			*Time*	*Time*		Node i	Node j	EST_{ji}/LST_{ji}	T_i-TC_i		
21		*Activity*	EST_i	TC_i		A	C	65	5		
22		A	0	5		A	B	5	5		
23		B	5	5		B	D	45	10		
24		C	65	0		B	E	10	10		
25		D	50	0		C	K	35	35		
26		E	15	0		D	H	20	20		
27		F	40	0		E	F	25	25		
28		G	55	0		F	G	15	15		
29		H	70	0		F	J	30	15		
30		I	90	0		G	H	15	15		
31		J	70	0		H	I	20	20		
32		K	100	0		I	K	10	10		
33						J	K	30	30		
34											
35		*User*				Normal project cost =		£66,000			
36		*input*				Bonus payment/overrun penalty =					
37		*cells*									
38		*are*				*Objective 1: Minimise project duration =*		110	days		
39		*shaded*									
40						*Objective 2: Minimise total crash costs =*		£2,000	Add constraint		
41						Enter project deadline =		110	H38 <= H41		
42											
43						*Objective 3: Minimise total project costs =*		£68,000			
44						Enter normal project duration =			days		
45											
46											
47											
48		*Cells*	*Formula*					*Copied to*			
49		H35	IF(D17=""," ??? ",D17)								
50		H38	C16 + C32–D32								
51		H40	SUMPRODUCT(D$22:D$32,I$6,I$16)								
52		H43	H35 + H40–H36*(H44–H38)								
53											
54											
55		**Notes:** Switch on 'Assume Linear Model' in the Solver Options dialog box.									

Figure 11.13   Modified crash model for minimising project costs.

Situation 2: availing of bonus payments   The MightyBig Corporation has been recently informed by their client that the warehouse is required earlier than originally agreed. A bonus scheme is now being offered whereby the company can collect £500 for each day that the 'crashed' project is under the normal duration of 120 days. MightyBig must now decide whether these bonus payments outweigh the extra costs of crashing the project. Details of bonus payments (cell H36) and the project's normal duration (cell H44) must be entered into Figure 11.14 by the user.

The answer to this situation is shown in Figure 11.14 in which the target cell is now cell H43, i.e., minimise total project cost. The lowest cost of £59,500, which is under the normal cost of £66,000, is obtained by using the following equation (see formula in cell H43).

$$\text{Project cost} = \text{Normal cost} + \text{Crash costs} - (\text{Bonus payment}) \times (\text{Normal duration} - \text{Crash duration})$$

The project crash duration for the 'lowest cost' model is 86 days. When the crash days in cell range D22:D32 are examined, it can be seen that the 34-day reduction in the project's normal duration was achieved by crashing activities A (5 days), B (5), F (5), H (10), I (5) and K (4 days).

PERT and PERT/Cost

The CPM method assumes that each activity's duration is known and then seeks to optimise resource allocation and job scheduling. On the other hand, PERT emphasises the role of uncertainty in determining activity durations and can therefore be considered as a probabilistic version of CPM (see Wilkes, Chapter 5). In PERT, each activity duration is a random variable described by a probabilistic *beta distribution*. Three estimates of each task's completion time are required. For activity i, they are described as

$$a_i = \text{the optimistic time estimate}$$
$$b_i = \text{the pessimistic time estimate}$$
$$m_i = \text{the most likely time estimate}$$

These three values are combined to produce (i) an expected (i.e., mean) duration for each activity, T_i, and (ii) the standard deviation, σ_i, of each activity's completion time. Noting that σ_i is the square root of the variance, V_i, PERT uses the following two equations:

$$T_i = (a_i + 4m_i + 6b_i)/6 \quad \text{and} \quad V_i = (b_i - a_i)^2/36$$

It should be remembered that PERT does make some improbable assumptions – not least is the requirement that certain (rather unrealistic) conditions must be met before it can be used. For example, it is assumed that task completion times are independent of each other, which is most unlikely. For example, in the warehouse project, the roofing activity time depends upon the framing activity being finished, and electrical work is usually slotted in between interior wall phases.

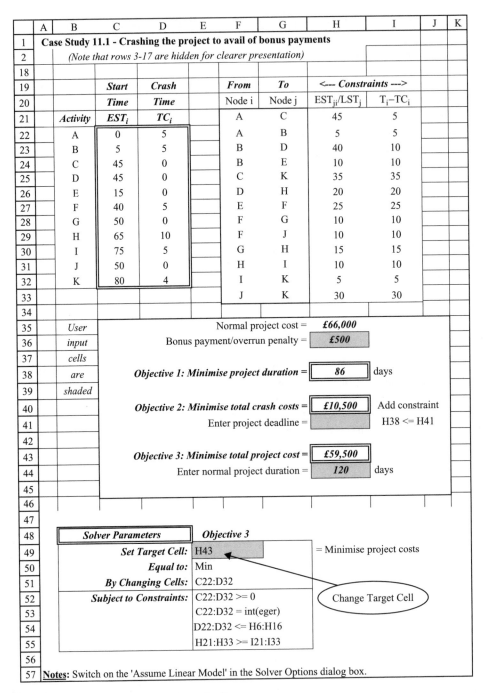

	A	B	C	D	E	F	G	H	I	J	K
1		**Case Study 11.1 - Crashing the project to avail of bonus payments**									
2		*(Note that rows 3-17 are hidden for clearer presentation)*									
18											
19			*Start*	*Crash*		*From*	*To*	*<--- Constraints --->*			
20			*Time*	*Time*		*Node i*	*Node j*	EST_{ji}/LST_j	T_i-TC_i		
21		*Activity*	EST_i	TC_i		A	C	45	5		
22		A	0	5		A	B	5	5		
23		B	5	5		B	D	40	10		
24		C	45	0		B	E	10	10		
25		D	45	0		C	K	35	35		
26		E	15	0		D	H	20	20		
27		F	40	5		E	F	25	25		
28		G	50	0		F	G	10	10		
29		H	65	10		F	J	10	10		
30		I	75	5		G	H	15	15		
31		J	50	0		H	I	10	10		
32		K	80	4		I	K	5	5		
33						J	K	30	30		
34											
35		*User*				Normal project cost =		**£66,000**			
36		*input*				Bonus payment/overrun penalty =		**£500**			
37		*cells*									
38		*are*				*Objective 1: Minimise project duration =*		86	days		
39		*shaded*									
40						*Objective 2: Minimise total crash costs =*		£10,500	Add constraint		
41						Enter project deadline =			H38 <= H41		
42											
43						*Objective 3: Minimise total project cost =*		**£59,500**			
44						Enter normal project duration =		*120*	days		
45											
46											
47											
48			**Solver Parameters**			*Objective 3*					
49			*Set Target Cell:*	H43				= Minimise project costs			
50			*Equal to:*	Min							
51			*By Changing Cells:*	C22:D32							
52			*Subject to Constraints:*	C22:D32 >= 0				Change Target Cell			
53				C22:D32 = int(eger)							
54				D22:D32 <= H6:H16							
55				H21:H33 >= I21:I33							
56											
57		**Notes:** Switch on the 'Assume Linear Model' in the Solver Options dialog box.									

Figure 11.14   Crashing the project to avail of bonus payments.

Table 11.7   PERT time estimates for the MightyBig warehouse project.

Activity symbol	Activity description	Preceding activity	Time estimates (days)		
			a_i	m_i	b_i
A	Site excavation	–	7	10	14
B	Foundations	A	10	15	20
C	Underground utilities	A	30	35	42
D	Plumbing: stage 1	B	16	20	25
E	Framing	B	21	25	30
F	Roofing	E	12	15	24
G	Electrical work	F	12	15	18
H	Interior walls	D, G	15	20	24
I	Plumbing: stage 2	H	7	10	12
J	Exterior finishing	F	27	30	36
K	Landscaping	C, I, J	8	10	12

Another problem is PERT's lack of focus on genuinely critical activities. Non-critical activities, i.e., activities that do not lie on the critical path, can present problems. If such non-critical activities have larger variances than critical activities, they will display a higher degree of uncertainty. Although they are not currently critical they could become so, and possibly cause a delay in the project's completion, i.e., they may become more 'critical' than the critical activities themselves!

PERT analysis for the MightyBig Corporation

The MightyBig Corporation has decided to check out its CPM calculations by using a PERT analysis for its warehouse project. It has therefore gathered (a_i, m_i, b_i) estimates for each activity's duration as shown in Table 11.7.

Developing a PERT model

A PERT model can be constructed from the original CPM model of Figure 11.8. The following instructions show how the PERT model of Figure 11.15 is developed.

- Copy the CPM model of Figure 11.8 and modify it using Table 11.8 to include (a, m, b) time estimates (see cells C27:E37 in Fig. 11.15). Note that Figure 11.8 incorporates the 'Step 1' phase of Figure 11.7.
- Calculate each activity's duration T_i using the formula $T_i = (a_i + 4m_i + 6b_i)/6$.
- Run the CPM model as before using the newly calculated T_i and determine the critical path.
- The expected project completion time, μ_p, is defined as the sum of durations of the critical activities, i.e., $\mu_p = \sum T_i$ for all durations T_i on the critical path.
- The project variance, σ_p^2, is defined as the sum of the variances along the critical path, i.e., $\sigma_p^2 = \sum V_i$ for all variances V_i on the critical path where $V_i = (b_i - a_i)^2/36$.
- The project's duration is assumed to be normally distributed with mean μ_p and variance σ_p^2.

	A	B	C	D	E	F	G	H	I	J	K	L
1	Case Study 11.1 - A PERT model for the MightyBig warehouse project											
2												
3		*User input cells are shaded*						From	To	<--- Constraints --->		
4		Activity	Time	LST	EST	Float		Node i	Node j	$LST_j - LST_i$	Time T_i	
5		A	10.2	0.0	0.0	0.0		A	C	76	10	
6		B	15.0	10.2	10.2	0.0		A	B	10	10	
7		C	35.3	75.7	10.2	65.5		B	D	51	15	
8		D	20.2	61.2	25.2	36.0		B	E	15	15	
9		E	25.2	25.2	25.2	0.0		C	K	35	35	
10		F	16.0	50.3	50.3	0.0		D	H	20	20	
11		G	15.0	66.3	66.3	0.0		E	F	25	25	
12		H	19.8	81.3	81.3	0.0		F	G	16	16	
13		I	9.8	101.2	101.2	0.0		F	J	30	16	
14		J	30.5	80.5	66.3	14.2		G	H	15	15	
15		K	10.0	111.0	111.0	0.0		H	I	20	20	
16		*Objective 1: Minimise EST values*						I	K	10	10	
17		*Objective 2: Maximise LST values*				662.8		J	K	30	31	
18												
19				**Project Completion Time =**				**121.0**				
20												
21		- Use SOLVER twice to (i) Minimise EST values (ii) Minimise LST values										
22		- Copy cell range D5:D15 into E5:E15 before solving for the LST values										
23		- Remember that Solver parameters have to be altered (see Figures 11.7 and 11.8)										
24												
25			< PERT time estimates >									
26		Activity	a_i	m_i	b_i	V_i		Critical path is A-B-E-F-G-H-I-K				
27	*A*	A	7	10	14	1.4						
28	*B*	B	10	15	20	2.8						
29		C	30	35	42	4.0			Project variance =		14.8	
30		D	16	20	25	2.3			Project standard deviation =		3.8	
31	*E*	E	21	25	30	2.3						
32	*F*	F	12	15	24	4.0						
33		G	12	15	18	1.0			*Enter required deadline in cell K34*			
34		H	15	20	24	2.3			Project deadline =		126	
35		I	7	10	12	0.7			Z =		1.3	
36	*J*	J	27	30	36	2.3			Probability of completion =		90.3%	
37	*K*	K	8	10	12	0.4						
38												
39		To obtain the probability of non-critical paths being completed in X days where										
40		X = value in cell K34, enter the path activities in cells A27:A37, e.g. A-B-E-F-J-K										
41												
42				Path variance =		13.1			Path completion time =		106.8	
43			Path standard deviation =			3.62						
44				Z =		5.3			Probability of path completion =		100.0%	
45												

Figure 11.15   PERT model for the MightyBig warehouse project.

Because of rounding errors, float values of critical activities will not be exactly zero. Thus, it is assumed that any float value that is less than 0.0001 can be taken to be zero. The details of Figure 11.15 show a project mean completion time of 121 days (cell H19) with a variance of 14.8 days (cell K29). This result means that there is a 50% chance of the project being completed in 121 days. The probability of the warehouse project finishing on or before 126 days is 90.3% (see cell K36). By repeatedly changing the value of the project deadline (cell K34), a clearer picture can be obtained of maximum and minimum finish times. It is worth noting that project completion times for the CPM and PERT methods differ by only one day, i.e., 120 and 121 days respectively.

One criticism of PERT is that the probability of a project's completion is based upon the standard deviation of the critical path. However, the probability of completion along a non-critical path may be shorter. The PERT model allows for the probability of completion of non-critical paths as shown in lines 39–44. In this example, all non-critical paths have a probability of 100% completion.

The warehouse project contains three non-critical paths: A–C–K, A–B–D–H–I–K, and A–B–E–F–J–K. Because the paths in this example are so short, it is easy to see if a path contains any activities that may become critical and thus alter the path's non-critical status. However, in larger networks, it is advisable to calculate mean finish times and variances for all current non-critical paths in the same way as was done for the critical path. Activity C has a large variance (see cell F29 = 4.0) but cannot affect overall project duration since it appears only once in a very short path, i.e., A–C–K. If there were several such activities in a longer non-critical path, the outcome could be quite different. Table 11.8 contains the additional formulae needed to complete Figure 11.15.

PERT/cost is an extension of PERT that includes cost considerations in its analysis and is almost identical to CPM project crashing. The cost of each activity is assumed to be a linear function of the activity's duration. As with CPM cost scheduling, crash times are introduced, and the objective is to find the minimum-cost solution to meet a specified deadline. PERT/cost focuses on activities that (i) are on the critical path, and (ii) are the least costly of these critical activities. The same linear programming procedure used in the CPM crash model of Figure 11.10 can be applied to crash a PERT model the only difference being activity duration times.

Table 11.8 PERT model – additional worksheet formulae.

Cell	Formula	Copied to
C5	(C27 + 4*D27 + E27)/6	C6:C15
B27	B5	B28:B37
F27	(E27 – C27)^2/36	F28:F37
K29	SUMIF(F5:F15," <0.0001", F27:F37)	
K30	SQRT(K29)	
K35	(K34 – H19)/K30	
K36	NORMSDIST(K35)	
E42	SUMIF(A27:A37,"<>", F27:F37)	
K42	SUMIF(A27:A37,"<>", C5:C15)	
E43	SQRT(E42)	
E44	IF(E43 = 0, "", (K34 – K42)/E43)	
K44	IF(E44 = 0, "", "", NORMSDIST(E44))	

Both CPM and PERT are dynamic processes involving continual updating and readjusting of project input data. As a project progresses, estimated details are replaced with actual figures. The whole project is re-analysed and targets are re-aligned. For example, it may be beneficial to switch resources from non-critical activities to the critical path in an effort to reduce its completion time. Constraint restrictions can also be introduced to ensure that activities (i) start as late/soon as possible (ii) start/finish no earlier/later than a specified time (iii) start no earlier/later than a certain date.

SIMULATION MODEL FOR PROJECT MANAGEMENT

A limitation of the CPM method is its assumption that all activity duration times are known. In real-world situations, external factors such as late delivery of materials, bad weather, and so on can seriously delay the completion of a project. The PERT approach acknowledges the existence of uncertainty and uses a probability distribution to overcome the unpredictability attached to activity times. PERT depends upon the past experiences of a project manager to derive three time estimates for each activity which are then applied to the beta distribution.

In situations where there are many unknown variables, the technique of simulation can be applied. Simulation is very useful for analysing problems that contain elements of uncertainty, especially if some or all of the variables can be represented by probability distributions. The greatest flexibility for activity times is provided by individual distributions which are based on previous events. The following four steps outline a simulation approach for project management.

1. Identify all paths through the network.

2. Establish probability distributions for all project activities.

3. Use Excel's random number generator RAND() to generate activity times.

4. Record simulation details and analyse the results.

Step 1:
By examining the AON network for the MightyBig Corporation's project (Figure 11.16) four paths can be identified:

   (i) A–C–K (ii) A–B–D–H–I–K (iii) A–B–E–F–J–K (iv) A–B–E–F–G–H–I–K

Step 2:
There are eleven probability distributions representing the possible duration times (in days) for each activity in the project. The activity distributions shown in Figure 11.17 have been interpolated from the PERT time estimates of Table 11.7.

Step 3:
In the project simulation model of Figure 11.18, each of the above distributions is named as TaskA, TaskB, TaskC, etc. using Excel's Insert|Name|Define command. For example, the cell range B6:C10 is named as TaskA, cell range E6:F8 is named as TaskB, etc. Random numbers are then generated for each activity on each path, using Excel's RAND() function. The following five steps are used to create the model's 'Simulation details' as shown in cell

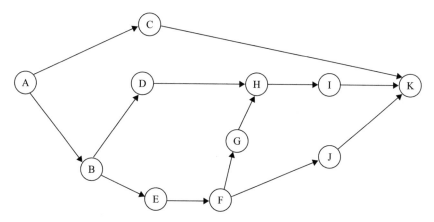

Figure 11.16   AON network for the MightyBig Corporation's warehouse project.

range B34:O41:

1. Enter the formula = IF(D34,"","", VLOOKUP(RAND(), TaskA,2)) into cell D35.
2. Copy this formula into cells E35:N35, changing the letter 'X' in the parameter 'TaskX' as appropriate, e.g., the formula in cells E35, F35, G35, etc. will contain TaskB, TaskC, TaskD, etc. Repeat until cell N35 which will contain the formula =IF(N34,"","", VLOOKUP(RAND(),TaskK,2)).
3. Enter the formula =SUM(D35:N35) into cell O35.
4. Copy the cell range B34:O35 into ranges B36:O37, B38:O39, B40:O41.
5. Enter the appropriate paths into rows 34, 36, 38 and 40. For example row 34, which defines path 1, contains the letters A, C and K in cells D34, F34, and N34 respectively.

Activity A	7	9	10	11	14
Probability	0.1	0.2	0.3	0.3	0.1

Activity B	10	15	20
Probability	0.3	0.4	0.3

Activity C	30	33	35	38	42
Probability	0.1	0.2	0.3	0.3	0.1

Activity D	16	18	20	22	25
Probability	0.2	0.1	0.3	0.2	0.2

Activity E	21	25	27	30
Probability	0.1	0.3	0.3	0.3

Activity F	12	15	20	24
Probability	0.2	0.3	0.3	0.2

Activity G	12	14	15	16	18
Probability	0.1	0.2	0.4	0.2	0.1

Activity H	15	18	20	22	24
Probability	0.2	0.1	0.4	0.1	0.2

Activity I	7	10	12
Probability	0.2	0.6	0.2

Activity H	27	30	33	36
Probability	0.1	0.4	0.3	0.2

Activity K	8	10	12
Probability	0.3	0.4	0.3

Figure 11.17   Probability distribution for each project activity.

	A	B	C	D	E	F	G	H	I	J	K	L	M	N	O	P
1	Case Study 11.1 - A simulation model for the MightyBig warehouse project															
2																
3		Activity A			Activity B			Activity C			Activity D			Activity E		
4		Cum.	Time		Cum.	Time		Cum.	Time		Cum.	Time		Cum.	Time	
5		Prob.	(days)		Prob.	(days)		Prob.	(days)		Prob.	(days)		Prob.	(days)	
6		0.0	7		0.0	7		0.0	30		0.0	16		0.0	21	
7		0.1	9		0.3	9		0.1	33		0.2	18		0.1	25	
8		0.3	10		0.7	10		0.3	35		0.3	20		0.4	27	
9		0.6	11		*User input cells*			0.6	38		0.6	22		0.7	30	
10		0.9	14		*are shaded*			0.9	42		0.8	25				
11																
12		Activity F			Activity G			Activity H			Activity I			Activity J		
13		Cum.	Time		Cum.	Time		Cum.	Time		Cum.	Time		Cum.	Time	
14		Prob.	(days)		Prob.	(days)		Prob.	(days)		Prob.	(days)		Prob.	(days)	
15		0.0	12		0.0	12		0.0	15		0.0	7		0.0	27	
16		0.2	15		0.1	14		0.2	18		0.2	9		0.1	30	
17		0.5	20		0.3	15		0.3	20		0.8	12		0.5	33	
18		0.8	24		0.7	16		0.7	22					0.8	36	
19					0.9	18		0.8	24							
20																
21		Activity K														
22		Cum.	Time													
23		Prob.	(days)		The activity distribution are converted to *cumulative probabilities*											
24		0.0	8		as is the usual practice with all simulation models (see Example 2.8)											
25		0.3	10													
26		0.7	12													
27																
28		*Press the recalculation key F9 repeatedly to generate new sets of random numbers.*														
29		*Store both project completion times and critical paths in the 50 cells below*														
30																
31		*Simulation details*												*Path*		
32														*Length*		
33		*Activities ->*		*A*	*B*	*C*	*D*	*E*	*F*	*G*	*H*	*I*	*J*	*K*		
34		*Path 1*		*A*		*C*								*K*		
35				11		35								10	56	
36		*Path 2*		*A*	*B*		*D*				*H*	*I*		*K*		
37				11	9		22				24	9		10	85	
38		*Path 3*		*A*	*B*			*E*	*F*				*J*	*K*		
39				11	7			27	15				33	8	101	
40		*Path 4*		*A*	*B*			*E*	*F*	*G*	*H*	*I*		*K*		
41				14	9			25	12	16	15	7		10	108	
42																
43		*Critical path length =*		*108*		*i.e.*	*Path 4*							8		
44																

Figure 11.18 Simulation model for the MightyBig warehouse project.

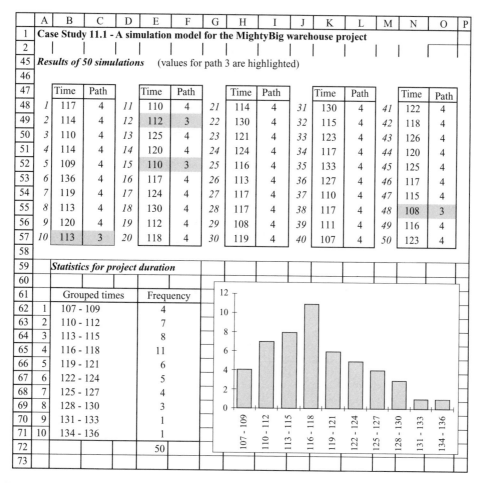

Figure 11.18   (Cont.)

This step is completed by entering the following three formulae into line 43 of Figure 11.18.

Cell F43: = MAX(O34:O41)
Cell N43: = MATCH(F43, O34:O41, 0)
Cell H43: = OFFSET(H40, N43–8, –6)

Step 4:

The recalculation F9 key was used to create 50 simulations as shown in lines 48–57 of Figure 11.18. In practice, a much larger number of simulations (>100) would be generated. The output gives details of the project's duration (in days) and critical path (as defined in step 1) for each simulation. The simulation model shows that path 3 also becomes critical, although on a much smaller scale (8%) than path 4 (92%). Path 4 contains all activities on path 3 except activity J, which has a particularly long duration and may become critical at some stage.

The project's completion times are examined in the statistical section. Duration times span a period of just over five weeks, ranging from 107 to 136 days with the most likely completion time occurring between 116–118 days. These times are shorter than the previous estimates of 120–121 days, reflecting the greater flexibility provided by individual probability distributions for each activity.

EXERCISES ▪▪▪▪▪▪▪▪▪▪▪▪▪▪▪▪▪▪▪▪▪▪▪

11.1 A project which is about to start comprises the activity-on-node (AON) Table 11.9.

Table 11.9

Activity	Preceding activity	Duration (days)	Normal cost per day	Crash cost per day
A	–	3	£180	£60
B	A	2	£100	£20
C	A	5	£280	£30
D	B, C	2	£80	–
E	D	3	£90	£40
F	E	4	£75	–
G	A	10	£300	£70
H	F, G	3	£150	£90

Activities D and F cannot be reduced (crashed). Activities A, B, E and H can be reduced by only one day, while activities C and G can be reduced by 2 and 5 days respectively. Using both CPM (normal and crash) models, find:

- the critical path using normal times, the total time taken, and the total cost of completing the project
- the minimum cost of completing the project in 16 days.

   (Answers: (i) A–C–D–E–F–H, 20 days, £6320 (ii) Minimum crash costs of £160 – by reducing activities A, C and E by 1, 2, and 1 days respectively, giving a total project cost of £6,480)

11.2 The MightyBig Corporation has been awarded a contract to build a new manufacturing plant. The activity-on-arrow (AOA) Table 11.10 gives data of the activities involved in the plant's construction.

   The total cost of completing the project in normal time is £2 million, excluding site overheads which are £8000 per week. The Corporation would like to convert the AOA network as shown below into a precedence (AON) diagram and hence find

- the critical path using normal times, the project's total duration, and the total cost of completing the project
- the shortest time in which the project can be completed and the associated costs
- the lowest cost for which the project can be completed and the corresponding time.

Table 11.10

Activity	Normal time (weeks)	Shortest time (weeks)	Reduction costs (per week)
1–2	6	4	£7000
1–3	8	4	£8000
1–4	5	3	£3000
2–4	6	3	£5000
2–5	5	3	£4000
3–6	10	8	£15,000
4–6	8	5	£6000
5–6	6	6	–

(Hint: Allocate letters to each activity, e.g., A (1–2), B (1–3), etc., and add two dummy activities, X and Y, for the start and finish nodes – see Example 11.1. Treat overhead costs as overrun penalties and, when obtaining the lowest cost (objective 3), leave normal project duration (cell H44) blank)

(Answers: (i) X–A–D–G–Y, 20 weeks, £2.16 million (ii) 13 weeks with crash costs of £96,000 and a total project cost of £2.2 million (iii) lowest crash costs are £10,000 (reducing activity D by two weeks) giving a total project cost of £2.154 million with a project duration of 18 weeks.)

11.3 The Acme Company has decided to produce a new version of its gadget. It has drawn up a list of the various activities required in the design and manufacture of the new gadget. The project will incur ongoing overhead costs of £200 per day. Table 11.11 shows the duration (in days) and associated duration costs for both normal and crash completion times.

Table 11.11

Activity	Preceding activity	←Normal → Duration	Cost	←Crashed → Duration	Cost
A – Calculate cost estimates	–	2	£300	1	£600
B – Agree estimates	A	1	–	–	–
C – Purchase materials	B	4	£150	2	£350
D – Prepare design drawings	B	6	£350	2	£1050
E – Construct new parts	D	3	£600	1	£1100
F – Assemble gadget	C, E	3	£150	1	£450
G – Test gadget	F	4	£400	1	£800
H – Evaluate test results	D	2	£50	1	£150
I – Design new packaging	D	3	£250	2	£450
J – Manufacture packaging	H, I	8	£500	4	£850
K – Final assembly	G, J	2	£400	1	£600
L – Final check	K	2	£100	1	£250

(i) Find the project's normal duration, the total cost of the project, and the network's critical path.

(ii) Find the project's lowest cost and the corresponding duration.

(iii) In order to meet quality assurance requirements, the gadget may have to be tested twice, adding another four days to the duration of activity G. How will the project be affected?

(iv) What is the shortest time in which the project can be completed and the associated costs?

(v) How are completion costs affected if the project has to be finished within 20 days?

(Hint: Treat overhead costs as overrun penalties and, when obtaining the lowest cost (objective 3), leave normal project duration (cell H44) blank.)

> (Answers: (i) 24 days; £8050; A–B–D–I–J–K–L (ii) £7788 with a project duration of 18 days (iii) A 4-day delay to activity G will increase the project's duration to 27 days with a new critical path of A–B–D–E–F–G–K–L (iv) 12 days, with crash costs of £2850 and total project costs of £8500. Because the shortest time can be achieved by crashing the network in a number of different ways, associated costs can vary (v) To finish in 20 days, crash costs = £588 and total project costs = £7838.)

11.4 Murphy Builders have contracted to complete a new building and have developed the following PERT network to help them in analysing the project. The (T_i, V_i) values refer to the mean duration (in weeks), T_i, and variance, V_i, for PERT activities.

Activity	A	B	C	D	E	F	G	H	I
Preceding activities	–	A	A	A	B	B, C	D	G	E, F, H
(T_i, V_i) values	(2, 2)	(4, 3)	(5, 1)	(7, 5)	(6, 2)	(9, 5)	(4, 1)	(8, 3)	(3, 1)

Murphy Builders want to find

(i) the network's critical path and its expected duration

(ii) the probability that the project will be completed by 27 weeks, assuming that the critical path is normally distributed

(iii) the probabilities that the non-critical paths will be completed by 27 weeks. Check if any of these non-critical paths have a probability less than that of the critical path.

(iv) The company has the option of shortening either activity A, B, F or G by one week. It would like to know which of these four activities to crash. (Shortening an activity will reduce T_i by one week but will not affect V_i)

> (Answers: (i) A–D–G–H–I, 24 weeks (ii) 87.2% probability of completion by 27 weeks (iii) Paths A–B–E–I (100%), A–C–F–I (84.1%), A–B–F–I (98.7%), A–D–G–H–I (87.2%). The 'non-critical' path A–C–F–I has a lower probability of completion than the critical path. (iv) There are now two possible critical paths (A–C–F–I and A–D–G–H–I), so activity A should be shortened since it is the only activity on both paths.)

11.5 A project consists of six activities which have their durations represented by the probability distributions as shown in Table 11.12. Using the standard four steps for project simulation, establish the network's four paths and perform fifty simulations. Record details for each path and establish which path(s) are critical. Calculate the percentage of time that each activity was on the longest path. What is the expected duration of the project?

> (Answers: (i) The percentage of time that the four paths appear as critical is shown in brackets: A–B–D–F (16%), A–C–E–F (34%), A–B–E–F (6%), A–C–D–F (44%) (ii) Start and finish activities A,F are on the critical path (100%), activities B (22%), C(78%), D(60%), and E (40%) (iii) The expected duration of the project is 25 weeks.)

Table 11.12

| Activity | ←.....................Time (in weeks)....................→ | | | | | | | Preceding activities |
	3	4	5	6	7	8	9	
A		01	0.3	0.3	0.2	0.1		–
B	0.4	0.3	0.2	0.1				A
C			0.1	0.4	0.3	0.1	0.1	A
D		0.1	0.5	0.3	0.1			B,C
E	0.2	0.3	0.3	0.1	0.1			B,C
F			0.2	0.3	0.4	0.1		D,E

11.6 The Brookside Building Company has recently been offered a contract to build a service station. Details of the project, including activity resource requirements, are shown in Table 11.13. Brookside is already involved in two other construction projects and can only afford to allocate a fixed number of workers to the service-station job which must be completed within fifteen weeks. The company has decided to produce a work schedule based on earliest start dates. Having drawn a Gantt chart, Brookside now want you to see if there is sufficient slack in the network that will allow a minimum number of workers to be assigned to the project.

Table 11.13

Activity	A	B	C	D	E	F	G	H	I
Preceding activities	–	A	A	B	B	C	C	E,F	G,H
Duration (weeks)	1	4	7	3	3	2	2	2	3
Workers (per week)	6	3	4	2	3	7	5	2	5

(Hint: Introduce a dummy finish node J.)

(Answers: Project duration is 15 weeks with a critical path of A–C–F–H–I–J. The Gantt chart shows that the floats for activities D (7 weeks) and G (2 weeks) can be utilised to give a minimum of 7 workers. Weeks 2–15 require 7 workers while the first week needs only 6 workers.)

REFERENCES AND FURTHER READING

Heizer, J. and Render, B. (2003) *Production & Operations Management* (7th edn), Prentice Hall, New Jersey.

Ragsdale, C. (2004) *Spreadsheet Modeling and Decision Analysis* (4th edn), Thomson South-Western, USA.

Wilkes, F. (1980) *Elements of Operational Research*, McGraw-Hill, UK.

Winston, W. and Albright, S. (2000) *Practical Management Science: Spreadsheet Modeling and Applications* (2nd edn), Duxbury Press, California.

Excel refresher notes

BASIC EXCEL COMMANDS

The following brief notes on basic Excel commands, combined with a simple application, should help refresh the memory of those readers who have become a little rusty! The version discussed here applies to Excel 2003 operating under Windows XP. The word 'click' refers to the left-hand button on the mouse unless otherwise stated.

Workbooks and worksheets   Think of a workbook as a binder and a worksheet (or spreadsheet) as a page in the binder (by default, a workbook includes three worksheets, named Sheet1 to Sheet3). Extra worksheets can be added by using the Insert|Worksheet command. Typically, you would store related worksheets in a single workbook to keep them together. A worksheet consists of a grid of cells, with a menu bar and a number of toolbars displayed at the top of the screen. The default values for cell height and width are 12.75 and 8.43 respectively – they are usually referred to as row height and column width. All Excel workbooks end with an .XLS extension.

Entering text into a cell   Activate Microsoft Excel and a new workbook called 'Book1' will automatically appear. Type the phrase 'Fred's Fish Shop' into cell A1 (see Figure A1). Notice that the characters you type into a cell also appear in the FORMULA BAR at the top of the screen. A blinking vertical line (called the insertion point) moves to the right of the characters as you type them. Press the 'Enter' key and the insertion-point disappears, indicating that the formula bar is no longer active. If you have made a mistake, reactivate the formula bar by placing the mouse-pointer (displayed as a white cross or arrow-head) anywhere in cell A1 and then clicking. Move the mouse-pointer – also called the 'cursor' – to the required position in the formula bar. Insert the word 'Fresh' so that cell A1 now contains the text 'Fred's Fresh Fish Shop', and then press the 'Enter' key. Continue entering the rest of the details as shown in Figure A1.

Saving and naming the workbook/worksheet   It is vital that you save the workbook containing your worksheet. It is a good principle to save your workbook several times during a 'hands-on' session by using either the Save button (i.e. the floppy-disk symbol on the Standard toolbar) or the File|Save command. The user will normally save either to the computer's

	A	B	C	D	E	F	G
1	Fred's Fresh Fish Shop						
2							
3		Price/Kg					
4	Cod	4					
5	Halibut	3			Price/Kg		
6	Herring	2.1					
7	Mackerel	2					
8	Salmon	5.5					
9	Trout	2.6					
10							
11	Crab	4					
12	Lobster	3.8					
13	Prawns	3.3			Don't forget to		
14	Shrimps	2.8			SAVE your work!!		
15							

Figure A1   Fred's Fresh Fish Shop: building a simple model.

hard (permanent) drive (C:) or the $3^1/_2$ floppy drive (A:), in which case a diskette is required. When the workbook is first saved, Excel will assign it the default name Book1.XLS unless you enter a more appropriate name, such as FISHSHOP.XLS. Excel will also automatically give the worksheet the title Sheet1. Use the command Format|Sheet|Rename to change Sheet1 to Fred's Fish. If you should delete the worksheet by mistake, you can still retrieve it by using the File|Open command to bring back the latest saved version.

To select a RANGE of cells (A11:B14)   Place the mouse-pointer in cell A11 and, holding the mouse button down, drag the pointer to cell B14. All cells are now surrounded by a black border and, with the exception of the top-left cell, are also shaded. To deselect the range, click a second time. To delete a range of cells, first select the required range, and then press the Del key.

To move/copy a SINGLE cell   Place the cursor in the cell to be moved/copied and then click the mouse's right-hand button. Choose either the Cut (to move) or Copy command from the Edit menu that appears on the screen. A moving dotted line, called the 'marquee', surrounds the selected cell. Move the cursor to the new destination and repeat the previous actions, but now choose the Paste command from the menu. If using the Copy command, press the Esc key to deactivate the command, i.e., to remove the marquee. In Figure A1, copy cell B3 into E5.

To move/copy a RANGE of cells   First select the required range as explained above.

MOVING DATA: Move the pointer towards the border of the selected range and stop when the pointer takes the shape of an arrow. Click and drag the grey outline until it covers the new location and then release the button. In Figure A1, move (i) cell range A11:B14 to D6:E9, and (ii) move range A3:B9 down two rows as shown in Figure A2.

COPYING DATA: Copying a range of cells is exactly the same procedure as moving a range except that the Ctrl key is held down during the activity. A small plus sign appears

	A	B	C	D	E	F	G
1	Fred's Fresh Fish Shop						
2							
3	Today's SPECIALS are highlighted!						
4							
5		Price/Kg			Price/Kg		
6	Cod	4		Crab	4		
7	Halibut	3		Lobster	3.8		
8	Herring	1.8		Prawns	2.2		
9	Mackerel	2		Shrimps	2.8		
10	Salmon	5.5					
11	Trout	2.6					
12							
13					Don't forget to		
14					SAVE your work!!		
15							

Figure A2   Fred's Fresh Fish Shop: a better presentation.

next to the arrow pointer when the Ctrl key is held down. As before, click and drag the grey outline until it covers the new location and then release the button.

COPYING DATA WITH THE FILL HANDLE. Move the cursor towards the bottom-right corner of the selected range and stop when the cursor takes the shape of a black plus sign. This plus sign is called the 'fill handle' and is very useful for copying a range of cells into adjacent columns or consecutive rows. In Figure A2, select the range E6:E9 and then move the cursor to the fill handle. Holding down the Ctrl key, click and drag the fill handle across cells F9 and G9, and then release the mouse button. Cell ranges F6:F9 and G6:G9 should now be filled with the same values as E6:E9, i.e. 4, 3.8, 2.2, and 2.8.

Formatting cells   Formatting is all about enhancing the appearance of the spreadsheet and making it easier to understand. You may want to (a) show numerical data as currency, to one decimal place (b) shade/colour cells (c) change font size/style (d) align text to left, right or centre, etc. To format cells, use the Format|Cells option and then choose the relevant Dialog Tab (i.e., Number, Alignment, Font, Border, Patterns, Protection). First, insert the text 'Today's SPECIALS are highlighted!' into cell A3. Next, select the cell range A3:E3. Using the Format|Cells|Alignment command, choose the 'Center_across_selection' option to align the text. Continue to format the selected range as shown in Figure A2. Finally, place borders around the other cell blocks and highlight cells B8 and E8 by colouring them.

Printing the worksheet   To print out your worksheet, use the File|Print commands. Before printing, it is a good principle to use the File|Print_Preview commands to see what the printed sheet will look like. If it will not fit across the sheet, then change the page orientation from Portrait to Landscape via the File|Page Setup|Page commands. If you want row/column headings, gridlines, etc. to be displayed, then choose the File|Page Setup|Sheet command. To print out formulae, choose the Tools|Options|View command and then click the 'Formulas' box. Remember to de-select this option when finished. When printing formulae, some columns may need to be reduced in width to allow the worksheet to fit on to one page.

Changing the width/height of a column/row   Options exist for changing either (i) a single column or row, or (ii) a selected range.

SINGLE COLUMN/ROW: To adjust a column's width, point to the right edge of the required column's header, say column C. When the pointer is over the border between two columns, it changes to a two-directional arrow. To reduce/increase the width of the column, drag the pointer to the left/right. In Figure A2, reduce the width of column C by half. A similar approach is used for row height.

SELECTED COLUMNS/ROWS: Select the required range by placing the mouse-pointer in the left-most column of the range and, holding the mouse button down, drag the pointer to the right-most column. Then use the Format|Column|Width command. A similar approach is used to change the height of a range of rows. Rows and columns can be automatically adjusted by using the Format|Column|AutoFit_Selection command.

Inserting/deleting rows/columns   To insert a new row, place the cursor on the row above which a new row is to be inserted and select the Insert|Rows commands. To insert a column, place the cursor to the right of where the new column is to be inserted, and then select Insert|Columns. To insert several rows/columns at a time, highlight the required range, and use the previous commands. To delete rows/columns, place the cursor on the row/col to be deleted (or, if deleting more than one, highlight the rows/cols to be deleted), and choose the Edit|Delete|Entire Row (or Entire Column) commands.

Cell Contents   Each cell can contain (i) text (ii) a number, or (iii) a formula, which always starts with an = sign, e.g., =B3*(1-C4). If you want to treat a number as text, put a single quotation mark in front, e.g., '249 . To delete the contents of a cell, place the cursor in the cell and press the 'Del' key. In large worksheets, it may be easier to move to a particular cell by using the F5 key rather than moving the mouse. Simply press the F5 key, type in the cell address, and then press the 'Enter' key.

Functions   To view all available functions, click the Function Wizard button f_x on the standard toolbar at the top of the screen. Some commonly used functions are given below.

=SUM(B4:B8) adds the values in cells B4,B5,B6,B7,B8

=IF(J6="APPROVED", "Go ahead", "Cancel")
   The 'IF' formula reads the text in cell J6 and if contains the word APPROVED, it will print Go Ahead, otherwise it will print Cancel
   The following line contains an example of a NESED IF statement:
=IF(A3<40, "Failed",IF(A3<60, "Grade C",IF(A3>80, "Grade A", "Grade B")))
=INT rounds a number down to the nearest integer, e.g., INT(6.7) = 6, INT(23.3) = 23

The simple model for Fred's Fish Shop does not yet contain any formulae. Firstly, rearrange the existing data in Figure A2 to look like Figure A3. Fred now wants to find his weekly income, which is easily calculated by entering the two formulae as shown in the template. The answer is contained in cell F17. The asterisk (*) in the formula C7*E7 means 'multiplied by'.

	A	B	C	D	E	F	G
1	Fred's Fresh Fish Shop						
2							
3	Today's SPECIALS are highlighted!						
4							
5					WEEKLY SALES		
6			Price/Kg		Sales (Kg)	Income	
7		Cod	£4.00		31.0	£124.00	
8		Halibut	£3.00		16.2	£48.60	
9		Herring	£1.80		27.7	£49.86	
10		Mackerel	£2.00		25.3	£50.60	
11		Salmon	£5.50		15.1	£83.05	
12		Trout	£2.60		27.8	£72.28	
13		Crab	£4.00		9.8	£39.20	
14		Lobster	£3.80		7.2	£27.36	
15		Prawns	£2.20		24.6	£54.12	
16		Shrimps	£2.80		19.2	£53.76	
17					Weekly income =	£602.83	
18							
19		Enter/Copy the following two formulae into the cells as shown:-					
20							
21							
22		Cell	Formula			Copied to	
23		F7	C7*E7			F8:F16	
24		F17	SUM(F7:F16)				
25							
26				Don't forget to SAVE your work!			

Figure A3   Fred's Fresh Fish Shop: entering formulae.

Worksheet commands

(a) NAMING (or RENAMING) a worksheet use either the Format|Sheet|Rename command or simply place the cusor on the sheet tab and click twice.

(b) DELETING a worksheet use the Edit|Delete_Sheet command.

(c) COPYING (OR MOVING) a worksheet

WITHIN A WORKBOOK: Use the Edit|Move_or_CopySheet. Remember, if a COPY is required, then click on the 'Create a Copy' box, otherwise the worksheet will be moved from its original position in the workbook.

FROM ONE WORKBOOK TO ANOTHER WORKBOOK: Firstly, open the two workbooks A and B. Then select Edit|Move_or_CopySheet. The 'To_Book:' drop-down list lets you specify the destination workbook and the position of the copied worksheet. This list contains only already-opened workbooks, as well as a (new book) choice. If a COPY is required, click on the 'Create a Copy' box, otherwise the worksheet will be removed from its original workbook.

Naming a range of cells   You can assign a name (say FRED) to a range of cells. Whenever the name FRED is used, the range of cells is treated as a single unit. This facility is very useful for multiplying two or more matrices, especially when using the mathematical function SUMPRODUCT. To name a range of cells, first select the required range, then use the Insert|Name|Define command.

Relative v. Absolute cell addresses   If a cell containing a formula is copied into another cell, the two formulae will not be the same. In Figure A3, for example, the formula C7*E7 was entered into cell F7 and then copied into cells F8, F9, F10, etc. If you look at the formula in cell F8, the formula has changed relative to cell F7 and now reads C8*E8. Likewise, the contents of F9 have now become C9*E9. If you do not want a formula to change, then make the values absolute (i.e., fixed) by using the "$" sign. If the formula in cell F7 is changed to $C$7*$E$7, then it will always remain the same, regardless of the cell into which it is copied. Greater flexibility can be achieved by placing the dollar ($) sign only in front of cell letters, e.g. $C7*$E7. This formula will remain unaltered when copied across columns but will change when copied down rows. Similarly, the formula C$7*E$7 changes when copied across columns but remains the same for all rows.

Making GLOBAL changes   You may want to change some aspect of the whole worksheet, e.g., text style from Courier to Arial font. First, highlight the entire worksheet by positioning the cursor in the top left-hand blank rectangle at the top of column 1 (to the left of A). When the mouse button is pressed the whole worksheet will shade. Now carry out the required operation and press the 'Enter' key to activate the global change.

ZOOMing a worksheet   When working with a large worksheet, it is often helpful to see all of the worksheet on the screen. The ZOOM command allows you to magnify (or shrink) your worksheet. The ZOOM feature applies only to the spreadsheet's screen appearance and does not affect the print image. Try using the View|Zoom option with a magnification of 75% and 120%.

DRAWING CHARTS WITH CHART WIZARD

The steps necessary to produce charts with Chart Wizard are now demonstrated. The column chart in Figure A4 was created with Excel's Chart Wizard as follows:

1. Make a copy of Figure A3 and rename this new worksheet GRAPH. Clear the contents of cell range A19:G26 using the Edit|Clear|All command. Select the non-contiguous cell ranges B7:C16 and F7:F16. Remember to hold down the Ctrl key before selecting the ranges.

2. Click the Chart Wizard button (with coloured columns) on the standard toolbar. From Chart Wizard's Step 1 'Chart Type' dialog box, choose chart type 'Column' and chart sub-type shown in (row 1, column 1). Click the 'Next' button to proceed to Step 2.

3. Chart Wizard's Step 2 shows the 'Chart Source Data' dialog box. Click on the 'Series' tab and check the 'Series' list box. The only data series that should appear in the list box is the cell range F7:F16, displayed in the 'Values:' field. Delete any other spurious data series by highlighting and then clicking the 'Remove' button.

4. Chart Wizard's Step 3 presents the 'Chart Options' dialog box. Click on the following tabs (i) *Titles* tab and enter the Chart Title: 'Fred's Fresh Fish – weekly sales'; (ii) *Legend* tab

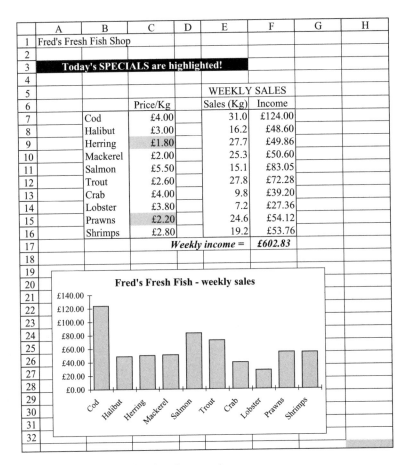

	A	B	C	D	E	F	G	H
1	Fred's Fresh Fish Shop							
2								
3		Today's SPECIALS are highlighted!						
4								
5					WEEKLY SALES			
6			Price/Kg		Sales (Kg)	Income		
7		Cod	£4.00		31.0	£124.00		
8		Halibut	£3.00		16.2	£48.60		
9		Herring	£1.80		27.7	£49.86		
10		Mackerel	£2.00		25.3	£50.60		
11		Salmon	£5.50		15.1	£83.05		
12		Trout	£2.60		27.8	£72.28		
13		Crab	£4.00		9.8	£39.20		
14		Lobster	£3.80		7.2	£27.36		
15		Prawns	£2.20		24.6	£54.12		
16		Shrimps	£2.80		19.2	£53.76		
17					*Weekly income =*	*£602.83*		
18								

Figure A4   Using Excel's Chart Wizard to draw graphs.

and clear the 'Show Legend' box; (iii) *Gridlines* tab and clear the Y-axis (Major gridlines) box. Click the 'Next' button to go to Step 4.

5. The Chart Wizard's Step 4 'Chart Location' dialog box allows the user to place the chart in either a new worksheet or the existing worksheet which is the default option. Keep the default location, i.e., 'As object in: GRAPH'. Step 4 is the last Chart Wizard step, so click on the 'Finish' button to exit from Chart Wizard.

6. Move the chart by placing the cursor anywhere inside the chart close to its perimeter; click and drag the chart so that its top right-hand corner is in cell A19. Next, place the cursor anywhere inside the chart close to its perimeter and click to activate the perimeter. Small black squares, called 'frame handles', will appear on the perimeter. Position the cursor on the lower right-hand handle; then click and drag it into cell G32.

7. There are several problems with the displayed chart. The first problem is that the chart's font type, size and style are incorrect. Place the cursor on the chart's title and the description

'Chart Title' will appear. Click the mouse's right-hand button to activate the shortcut menu and choose the 'Format Chart Title' option. Now click the *Font* tab and change (i) Font to 'Times New Roman', (ii) Style to 'Bold', (iii) Size to '10' and then click the OK button. The user should repeat this step for axes titles and values.

8. The second problem relates to column widths which are too narrow and need to be increased. Click anywhere on a column with the mouse's right-hand button and then click on the 'Format Data Series' option in the displayed menu. Click the *Options* tab, change 'Gap width:' to 50 and finally click the 'OK' button.

9. It should be noted that Excel automatically adjusts the size of chart characters when a chart is resized. If Excel's default chart size is decreased/increased, all text and numbers will also be decreased/increased. This problem can be overcome by reformatting chart features as shown in Step 7 above.

OBJECT LINKING AND EMBEDDING (OLE)

Object linking and embedding (OLE) is a technology that allows different applications to share data with one another. An object can be a workbook, a worksheet, a map, a picture, a button, a text box, a graph, clipart and so on. For example, you may want to include a piece of clipart from Microsoft's ClipArt Gallery in an Excel spreadsheet. Consider Figure A4 which shows Fred's Fresh Fish Shop. Suppose Fred wants to enhance the model's presentation by placing a logo of his business at the top of the worksheet. The following steps will do just that.

1. Position the cursor on the worksheet where you want the clipart to appear, inserting extra rows or columns if necessary to create sufficient space.

2. Use the Insert|Picture|Clip_Art . . . command to bring up the 'Clip Art' dialog box. Type the word 'Animals' into the 'Search for:' edit box and click the 'Go' button. Choose a clipart of a fish and then click on the image to place it on to the worksheet.

	A	B	C	D	E	F	G
1							
2							
3	**Fred's Fresh**					**Fish Shop**	
4							
5							
6	**Today's SPECIALS are highlighted!**						
7							
8					WEEKLY SALES		
9			Price/Kg		Sales (Kg)	Income	
10		Cod	£4.00		31.0	£124.00	
11		Halibut	£3.00		16.2	£48.60	
12		Herriing	£1.80		27.7	£49.86	

Figure A5   Inserting a clipart object into a spreadsheet.

3. To reduce the object's size so that it fits into the allocated space on the worksheet, click anywhere on the object to activate the frame handles. Use the frame's diagonal handle, which is located at any corner, to alter the object's size.

4. To delete the clipart, click the mouse's right-hand button once anywhere inside the object. From the shortcut menu that then appears, click the 'Cut' command and the object is removed.

This procedure is called 'embedding' because the object – in this case, the clipart – is now stored or embedded as an integral part of your spreadsheet. Embedding can be considered as 'application-oriented replication' in the sense that the embedded object is unique to the application in which it is embedded and cannot be accessed by any other applications. Any changes to the embedded object must now be made from its current location. For example, when you embed an Excel worksheet into a Word document, the worksheet is edited using Excel, but the data is stored as part of (embedded in) the Word document. An embedded object maintains a connection to its original location.

There are occasions when you do not want to physically remove the object from its source but you do want to access its contents. In such situations, you can link the object to your current application. For example, you may want to include part of an Excel worksheet in a Word document but you do not want to remove the worksheet from its original location in Excel. Linking can be considered as 'data-oriented replication' in the sense that the linked object can be shared with other applications just like data in a database. Any editing that is made to the linked object is performed via the original source application which in turn updates the linked version to reflect these changes. Linking is the best method if an object is to be used in several applications. Thus when the object is updated, the updated version is immediately available to all other linked applications, similar to updating data in a database.

Index

ABS, 82
absolute cell addresses, 405
acceptable quality level (AQL), 251, 253, 254, 275
acceptance sampling, 10, 243, 249–51
accounts payable and receivable, 55
activity-on-arc (AOA) network, 371, 372, 396
activity-on-node (AON) network, 372, 373, 392, 393, 396
add-ins, 26, 82
aggregate planning, 339, 341, 367
allocated stock, 281
alternative hypothesis, 258
analysis of variance (ANOVA), 258–63
Analysis ToolPak, 26–27, 48, 82, 120, 175
ANOVA, *see* analysis of variance
AOA, *see* activity-on-arc
AON, *see* activity-on-node
AQL, *see* acceptable quality level
arcs, 12, 134, 333, 334, 335, 371, 372, 378, 383
arguments. *see* macro arguments
arithmetic approach to learning curves, 156
arrival pattern in queuing theory, 353
arrival rate, 354, 368
assignable variations in process control, 263
assignment model, 326, 331, 332
attribute control charts, 264, 269–72
average, 168
AVERAGE, 82, 175
average inventory level, 283, 284, 293

back-order policy, 279, 290, 291, 345, 347
backward pass in critical path analysis, 376–77
backward pass in decision trees, 39
balance-of-flow, 333
balance sheet, 55, 56, 146, 150
balking, 353, 354

bar charts, 18, 28, 168, 379–82
batch size, 280, 287
Bayes rule, 27, 35–37
Bernoulli process, 269
beta distribution, 387
between-group variation, 260, 261
bill of materials (BOM), 7, 309, 310–15
BINOMDIST, 31, 46, 247
Black-Scholes option pricing model, 118
BOM, *see* bill of materials
bond valuation, 108–10
bond volatility, 113
break-even analysis, 128
breakdown maintenance, 136
budgeting, 68, 144–50
buffer stock, 281
business model, 3, 4
buttons, 210, 217, 224, 226, 229

c-charts, 269
call options, 117, 118
capability study, 264
capacity planning, 6, 339, 344, 345, 346
capital asset pricing model (CAPM), 106
capital budgeting, 61, 68
capital market line (CML), 106
CAPM, *see* capital asset pricing model
carrying cost, 280, 283, 318, 319, 320, 321
cash flow analysis, 69–70
cell contents, 403
census, 27
central limit theorem, 33, 264
changing cells, 24
ChartWizard, 28, 30, 405–7
class, 28, 245
clipart, 210, 407, 408
CML, *see* capital market line

coefficient of determination, 102, 172
COLUMN, 318
computerised accounting, 55, 56
conditional probability, 35, 36
CONFIDENCE, 273
confidence limits, 255
constraints, 24
consumer's risk, 250, 251
contribution analysis, 128
control charts, 263
control in management, 13
controllable variables, 18
CORREL, 172, 200
correlation analysis, 170
correlation coefficient, 170
cost accounting, 3, 127
cost-volume-profit (CVP) analysis, 128
costs in manufacturing, 3, 127
COUNT, 47
COUNTBLANK, 47
COUNTIF, 161
coupon and coupon rate, 110
COVAR, 83
covariance analysis, 65
CPM, see critical path method
CR, see critical ratio
crash costs, 382
crash times, 382, 391
crashing a project, 382, 387, 391
creditors ledger, 55
critical activities, 12, 371, 377
critical path, 373, 374
critical path analysis, 373
critical path method (CPM), 12, 371, 373, 382,
   387
critical ratio (CR), 348
cumulative probability, 31, 355
current yield, 111
cursor, 400
CVP, see cost-volume-profit
cycle time, 281

damping factor, 178
data normalisation, 206
data redundancy, 206
database
   amending purchase orders, 225
   arguments for macros, 221
   auto_close macro, 224
   auto_open macro, 224
   buttons, 210, 224
   clearing cell contents, 214
   clipart image, 210
   creating a simple macro, 207
   creating a title screen, 210
   creating the database, 219
   creating the purchase order form, 215–219
   dynamic data, 220
   list boxes, 215
   macro listings, 208, 213, 220, 221, 223, 224,
      228, 232, 233–236, 351
   macros for buttons, 224
   protecting data in worksheets, 218, 227, 232
   screen updating, 213
   scroll bar facility, 217
   transposing data, 220
DB, 130
DCF, see discounted cash flow
DDB, 130
debtors ledger, 55
decision analysis, 21, 34–35
decision environment, 20, 21, 34
decision-making, 12–15, 20–21, 27, 91, 293
decision-making characteristics, 14
decision-making stages, 17
decision nodes in decision trees, 38, 39
decision support systems (DSS), 5
decision trees, 37, 68
declining balance, 130, 131
defective inventory, 247, 248
demand, 9, 281, 318
Demming, W. Edwards, 10, 263
dependent demand, 282, 318
depreciation methods, 131
derivative instruments, 117
descriptive statistics, 28
deterministic inventory models, 282
dialog boxes for Solver, 26
direct costs, 127
discount inventory models, 287, 289
discounted cash flow (DCF), 60
discounts, 281
dispatching, 6
diversifiable risk. see unsystematic risk
double-declining balance, 130
DSS, see decision support systems
dummy activities, 372
duration, 113
DURATION, 120
dynamic data, 220

earliest due date (EDD), 348
earliest finish time (EFT), 374
earliest start time (EST), 374
economic order quantity (EOQ), 280, 281,
   282–284

EDD, *see* earliest due date
effectiveness, 324
efficiency, 324
efficient frontier, 95, 97–100
EFT, *see* earliest finish time
enterprise resource planning (ERP), 15–16
EOQ, *see* economic order quantity
equilibrium models, 106
equipment replacement, 132–144
ERP, *see* enterprise resource planning
EST, *see* earliest start time
estimation, 32, 253
event nodes in decision trees, 38
events, 21, 35
Excel add-ins, 26, 27, 82
Excel commands, 400–405
Excel dialog boxes for Solver, 26
Excel functions
  ABS, 82
  AVERAGE, 82
  BINOMDIST, 46
  COLUMN, 318
  CONFIDENCE, 273
  CORREL, 200
  COUNT, 47
  COUNTBLANK, 47
  COUNTIF, 161
  COVAR, 83
  DB, 130
  DDB, 130
  DURATION, 120
  EXP, 161
  EXPONDIST, 362
  FACT, 362
  FORECAST, 200
  GROWTH, 181, 200
  HLOOKUP, 161
  IF, 47
  INDEX, 318
  INT, 201
  INTERCEPT, 121
  IRR, 83
  LN, 162
  MATCH, 162
  MAX, 274
  MDURATION, 121
  MIN, 162
  MMULT, 83
  NORMDIST, 274
  NORMINV, 275
  NORMSDIST, 122
  NORMSINV, 319
  NPV, 84
  OFFSET, 162
  PMT, 84
  POISSON, 362
  PRICE, 122
  PV, 85
  RAND, 48
  ROUNDUP, 162
  ROW, 319
  SLN, 130
  SLOPE, 122
  SQRT, 201
  STDEV, 122
  STEYX, 123
  SUM, 48
  SUMIF, 85
  SUMPRODUCT, 48
  SUMXMY2, 201
  SYD, 130
  TRANSPOSE, 237
  VAR, 85
  VDB, 131
  VLOOKUP, 48
  XIRR, 123
  YIELD, 123
Excel Solver, 23
Excel standard screen, 210
Excel's Analysis ToolPak, 26–27
exception reports, 15
EXP, 161
expected value, 29, 37
EXPONDIST, 356, 362
exponential smoothing, 174, 178
exponential utility function, 94
extrapolation models, 175

facility location planning, 324, 325, 326
FACT, 362
feedback loop, 1
FIFO, *see* first-in first-out
financial engineering, 90
financial management, 3, 4, 64, 89
financial planning, 78
financial risk management, 90
financial statements, 55, 56
first-in first-out, 348, 353
fixed costs, 128
fixed order quantity (FOQ), 315
fixed period inventory system, 5, 7, 280, 301–304
float, 377
FOQ, *see* fixed order quantity
FORECAST, 200
forecasting models, 174–186
forward pass in critical path analysis, 374

forward pass in decision trees, 39
frequency distribution, 28, 244–247
functional organisation, 2
functional subsystems, 2
functions, 403

games theory, 21, 35, 91
Gantt charts, 379–82
goal programming (GP), 23, 167, 190–196
GP, *see* goal programming
gross requirements, 309, 311
grouped data, 33, 255
GROWTH, 181, 200

hedging, 90
hierarchical management levels, 13
histogram, 28, 168
HISTOGRAM function, 245
HLOOKUP, 161
holding cost, 280
Holt-Winters' method, 183
human resources function, 2
hypothesis testing, 32, 257

IF, 47
implied volatility, 119
income statement, 55
independent demand, 9, 282
INDEX, 318
indifference value, 93
indirect costs, 127
inferential statistics, 32, 253–257
INT, 201
integer programming (IP), 23, 26
interarrival time, 361
INTERCEPT, 121
internal rate of return (IRR), 60
inventory control, 9, 279–318
inventory status file (ISF), 309
inventory status report, 4, 7
investment appraisal, 61–64
investment financing, 74
IP, *see* integer programming
IRR, *see* internal rate of return
IRR Excel function, 83
ISF, *see* inventory status file
issue date, 111

JIT, *see* just-in-time inventory
job costing, 150–155
job sequencing, 347
jockeying, 358
Johnson's rule, 349, 352

joint probability, 36
judgemental forecasts, 174
just-in-time inventory, 279, 318

Karmarkar's Algorithm, 22

last-in first-out, 353
latest finish time (LFT), 376
latest start time (LST), 376
lead time, 7, 281, 298–301, 309
learning curves, 155–160
learning rate, 156–160
leasing costs, 133
least squares method, 171
ledgers, 55
LFL, *see* lot-for-lot
LFT, *see* latest finish time
LIFO, *see* last-in first-out
linear programming, 21–26
linear regression, 170–174
list boxes, 215
LN, 162
logarithmic approach in learning curves, 156
logistics, 10, 324, 325
longest processing time (LPT), 348
lot-for-lot (LFL), 310, 311, 316
lot size, 280, 310, 315, 316
lot-sizing methods, 315
lot tolerance percent defective, 251
lower control limit in control charts, 263
LP, *see* linear programming
LP applications, 22
LPT, *see* longest processing time
LST, *see* latest start time
LTPD, *see* lot tolerance percent defective

Macaulay duration, 115, 121
macro, 207
macro arguments, 221
macro recorder, 207, 211
MAD, *see* mean absolute deviation
management accounting, 3, 127
management control, 13
market index, 101, 102, 104
market portfolio, 107
market research, 2
market return, 101, 104, 108
market risk, *see* systematic risk
marketing conditions for a new product, 198
marketing function, 5, 167
marquee, 401
master production schedule (MPS), 6, 7, 308
MATCH, 162

material requirements planning (MRP), 6, 307–318
materials management, 8, 16
matrix multiplication, 65, 67, 83, 328
maturity and maturity date, 110, 111, 120, 123
MAX, 274
maximal-flow problem, 334
maximax decision criterion, 21, 40–42
maximin decision criterion, 21, 40–42
maximum stock, 281
MDURATION, 121
mean, 168, 255
mean absolute deviation (MAD), 180
mean of grouped data, 33, 255
mean of the means, 33
mean squared error (MSE), 180
measures of location and spread, 168
media selection model, 192
milestones, 11, 370
MIN, 162
minimax decision criterion, 21, 40–42
minimum stock, 281
minimum-variance set, 100
MMULT, 83
model-building steps, 18
modelling characteristics, 18
MOLP, *see* multiple objective linear programming
moving average function, 172, 175, 176, 178
MPS, *see* master production schedule
MRP, *see* material requirements planning
MSE, *see* mean squared error
multi-period inventory model, 303, 304
multiple objective linear programming (MOLP), 190
multi-server queuing model, 354, 358

named cell range, 311
natural variations in process control, 10, 244, 263, 264
net present value (NPV), 59–60
net requirements in MRP, 308, 314
network flow problems, 22, 331
networks in project management, 371
Newsboy problem, 295
NLP, *see* non-linear programming
nodes in decision trees, 38, 39
nodes in project networks, 12, 134, 333, 371
non-linear programming (NLP), 23, 64, 66, 98, 181, 186, 188, 189
NORMDIST, 248, 250, 274
NORMINV, 275
NORMSDIST, 122
NORMSINV, 299, 319

NPV, 84
null hypothesis, 258, 261

object linking and embedding (OLE), 407
OC curves, *see* operating characteristic curves
OFFSET, 162
OLE, *see* object linking and embedding
one-tailed test, 258
on-hand inventory, 311
open orders, 309
operating characteristic (OC) curves, 251–253, 254
operational control, 15, 324
operations layout, 11, 325
options, 117
order point, 281, 299
order quantity, 280, 281, 282, 284, 287, 315
ordering cost, 280, 282
organising as a managerial activity, 13, 28, 167
outliers, 160, 172
overdue items, 314

part period balancing (PPB) method, 316–317
payoff table, 35, 40, 41
p-chart, 264, 269
periodic order quantity (POQ) system, 280, 315
periodic review system, 280, 301–304
personnel models. *see* salesforce models
PERT, 12, 371, 387–392
planned order receipts, 309, 314
planned order releases, 309, 311, 314
planned shortages, 279, 282, 290–291
planning in management, 12
PMT, 84
POISSON, 354, 355, 362
Poisson probability distribution, 362
population, 27, 353
POQ, *see* periodic order quantity system
portfolio analysis, 97
portfolio management, 64–67
portfolio selection, 96, 100
PPB, *see* part period balancing
precedence diagrams, 372
present value, 59
preventative maintenance, 136, 140
PRICE, 122
priority rules, *see* job sequencing
probabilistic inventory models, 21, 293–298
probability, 29–31
probability distributions, 244
process-orientated strategy, 5
producer's risk, 251
product costing, 3, 127

product-orientated strategy, 5
product pricing model, 196, 197
product structure tree, 8, 309, 310
production control, 6
production function, 5
production order quantity model, 284
production planning and scheduling, 339–353
production planning with back-orders, 345, 347
profit and loss account, 56–58
project activity, 11, 370
project control, 11, 370
project crash model, 382, 383, 387
project crash times, 382, 391
project deadlines, 383
project management, 11, 370
project milestones, 11, 370
project simulation, 392–396
projected data in budgeting, 5, 127
purchase order processing, 206–39, 209
purchasing subsystem, 8
pure discount bond, 110
put options, 117
PV, 59–60, 85

quality control, 243
quality control subsystem, 9
quality discount inventory models, 287
queue behaviour, 353, 354
queue discipline, 353, 354
queue length, 325
queuing models, 353–362
queuing time, 356

RAND, 42, 48
random number generator (RNG), 42, 48
ratio analysis, 56
R-chart, 264
reducing balance depreciation, 130
regression analysis, 170
regression line equation, 102
regret table, 40, 41
relative cell addresses, 405
reneging, 353, 354
reorder level, 281, 299
reorder quantitiy, 281
required rate of return, 61, 110
residual value. *see* salvage value
revenue, 56, 128
risk and uncertainty in decision-making, 20–21
risk-averse. *see* risk-preference attitudes
risk-neutral. *see* risk-preference attitudes
risk-preference attitudes, 40, 90–92
risk premium, 93

risk-seeking. *see* risk-preference attitudes
risk tolerance, 94
RNG, *see* random number generator
ROUNDUP, 162
route, 333
ROW, 319

safety stock, 281, 299
salesforce models, 186–190
salvage value, 130
sample, 32
sampling error, 32, 255
sampling plan, 249–253
SAP, 16
scattergraph, 102, 160, 172, 173
Scenario Manager, 81
scheduled receipts, 305, 308, 309
screen updating, 221–222, 224, 233, 234, 235
scrolling, 212
seasonal variation, 175
security, 90
security analysis, 95, 96
security market line (SML), 108
semi-structured decisions, 14, 78, 167
sensitivity analysis, 14, 78, 119, 167
service facility in queuing theory, 353
service level, 298
service rate, 355, 357
service time, 356
service utilisation, 356
service-level inventory models, 298
settlement date, 111
setup cost, 280
Shewhart, Walter, 263
shortage cost, 281
shortest processing time (SPT), 348
shortest route model, 132, 133–134
significance levels, 255
SIM, *see* single index model
simulation, 21, 42–46, 74–77, 140–144, 304–307,
        354, 361–362, 392–396
single index model (SIM), 101
single-server queuing model, 354–358
slack, 377
SLN, 130
SLOPE, 122
SML, *see* security market line
smoothing constant, 178
Solver, 23
Solver dialog boxes, 26
SPC, *see* statistical process control
SPT, *see* shortest processing time
SQRT, 201

standard deviation, 85
states of nature, 21, 35
statistical inference, 32, 253, 254
statistical process control (SPC), 10, 243, 249, 263
statistical replacement analysis, 136
STDEV, 122
STEYX, 123
stochastic models, 21, 295
stockout cost, 281
storage and distribution, 10
storeskeeping, 11
straight line depreciation, 130
structured decision, 15
subsystems, 1, 2, 3, 15, 16
SUM, 48
SUMIF, 85
sum-of-the-digits depreciation, 130
SUMPRODUCT, 48, 328
SUMXMY2, 201
SYD, 130
systematic risk, 101, 108
systems view of business, 1

target cell, 24
task. *see* project activity
throughput, 1
time series, 174
time value of money, 59
tolerance limits, 264
ToolPak, 26–27
total quality management (TQM), 10, 243
TQM, *see* total quality management
traffic intensity, 356, 359
transhipment model, 336
transhipment node, 336
transportation model, 327–329
    unbalanced transportation model, 328, 330
TRANSPOSE, 236, 237
travelling salesman problem, 334
trend, 174, 175
trendline function, 102, 141, 171–172, 174, 176–178
two-tailed test, 258
Type I and II statistical errors, 257

uncertainty in decision-making, 20
uncontrollable variables, 18
unstructured decisions, 14
unsystematic risk, 101
updating, *see* screen updating
upper control limit, 263
utility curve, *see* utility theory
utility functions, *see* utility theory
utility theory, 91

VAR, 65, 85
variable control charts, 264, 269
variable costs, 128
variable-declining balance, 131
variables, 18
variance, 5, 65, 85, 96, 98, 102, 168, 255, 258, 260
variance analysis, 65, 127
variances in cost accounting, 5, 15, 127
VBA, *see* Visual Basic for Applications
VDB, 131
Visual Basic for Applications (VBA), 206, 209, 213, 220
VLOOKUP, 48
volatility, 113, 115, 119

waiting lines, *see* queuing models
warehousing, 11
weighting factors in forecasting data, 178
what-if analysis, 70, 167
within-group variation, 260, 261
workbooks and worksheets, 400
work-in-process, *see* work-in-progress
work-in-progress, 9, 127, 279
worksheet commands, 404

$\overline{X}$-chart, 264
XIRR, 123

yield, 83, 110, 111
YIELD, 123
yield-to-maturity, 111

zero-coupon bond, *see* pure discount bond